P9-APB-693

"... an outstanding collection that really does pierce all our myths and suppositions about Latin America with radical interpretations of the reasons for its stagnation and the ineffectuality of the middle classes to clear the way for reform."—*Commonweal*

Which major interest groups in Latin America hold the real power? How do they influence the course of Latin American development?

What is the social base of the military establishment? And what role does the military play in Latin American politics?

How does American control of Latin American economics contribute to political instability?

What aspects of class and economic structures influence the nature of revolutionary movements?

How do unsuccessful revolutions influence those who live through them?

These are some of the questions raised in this volume. The answers are searching and often shocking. Many of the articles have been translated specifically for this volume and are not otherwise available in English.

JAMES PETRAS, Assistant Professor of Political Science and Public Administration at Pennsylvania State University, is the author of numerous articles on Latin American politics and a book entitled *Politics and Social Force in Chilean Development*.

MAURICE ZEITLIN, Associate Professor of Sociology at the University of Wisconsin at Madison, is the author (with Robert Scheer) of *Cuba: Tragedy in Our Hemisphere*, 1963, and *Revolutionary Politics and the Cuban Working Class*, 1967.

Latin America
Reform
or Revolution?

A READER

EDITED BY
James Petras
and Maurice Zeitlin

A FAWCETT PREMIER BOOK
Fawcett Publications, Inc., Greenwich, Conn.
Member of American Book Publishers Council, Inc.

The Political Perspectives Series

Two generations ago historians in the United States were calling for a "New History" that would put the study of the past at the service of the present and future. The demand is now even more urgent.

This series of books is intended to fill this need. Under the overall title "Political Perspectives," a wide variety of books will be issued in inexpensive format. The series will include original works and anthologies, as well as reprints of important older books and monographs. The common theme will be the placing of contemporary political problems in their historical perspective.

Marvin E. Gettleman

Library of Congress Catalog Card Number 68-20770

Third Fawcett Premier printing, November 1969

Published by Fawcett World Library
67 West 44th Street, New York, New York 10036
Printed in the United States of America

FOR A FREE CATALOG OF FAWCETT PAPERBACKS, SEND A POSTCARD TO BOOK DEPARTMENT, FAWCETT PUBLICATIONS, GREENWICH, CONNECTICUT 06830.

TABLE OF CONTENTS

Introduction by James Petras and Maurice Zeitlin

I OVERVIEW

II CLASS AND CLASS CONFLICT

III DEVELOPMENT AND POLITICS

INTRODUCTION

The articles in this volume are about fundamental issues of social structure and politics in Latin America. Analysis of the structural features and tendencies *within* the countries of Latin America, and *between* them and the United States, as the dominant political economic power within the area, links the articles to each other. The authors emphasize the interrelationship between the internal class structures, capitalist economies, and foreign investments in determining the pattern of political and economic development in the countries of Latin America. Generally the authors, either implicitly or explicitly, utilize a "conflict model" of the social system to guide their analyses. Nary an article is premised on the assumption that Latin American social and economic development is in harmony with the prevailing interests of the United States—an assumption that is central to a good deal of influential writing about Latin America.

Among the critical problems dealt with in this volume are the following:

1. The extent and nature of interrelationships between the landholding, banking, and industrial sectors of the dominant economic classes, and between them and private foreign capital. The relative interdependence and autonomy of these respective interest groups, the probability of coalitions and alliances between them, and their responses to movements for social change and national sovereignty are fundamental determinants of historical events in the countries of Latin America.

2. The vulnerability of neocolonial economies to external factors, and how these relate both to economic stagnation and chronic political instability. The control of Latin American economies, and of the terms and conditions of their export markets, resides with foreign, usually American, interests. To what extent does this not only impede development and constrict the economic base of their dominant classes, but also act as a basic source of political instability in the countries of Latin America?

3. The significance of the growth of the industrial sectors, and of "new industrialists," and their relationships of dependence on and integration with foreign capital. The old colonial pattern in which the countries of Latin America provided the raw materials for the capitalist countries that controlled their extraction, while depending for their manufactured goods on imports from them, principally the United States, is changing.

Foreign capital is increasingly important in the manufacturing sector of many countries, and less and less occupies the status of an "economic enclave" alone. Of what importance is this newly emerging pattern for their development?

4. The emergence of the "new" middle classes, their social and economic base, and class polarization occurring in the process of the new industrialization. What political course can be expected of a "new" middle class essentially dependent on increasingly important foreign-controlled, large-scale economic enterprises, as well as the governmental bureaucracy?

5. The meaning of the Alliance for Progress and of United States foreign policy in general for Latin America. Does the Alliance for Progress complement or contradict other aspects of American foreign policy? What consequences do these policies have, and whose interests do they serve?

6. The political, economic, and social significance of so-called feudal institutions, and the feudal heritage, and of the traditional rural "oligarchies." Did Spain, in fact, bequeath Latin America a feudal heritage? What were the economic origins and major activities of the dominant classes, and of what importance was their integration in the world market? What role did they play in the independence movements from Spain, and of what significance are feudal institutions in the present movements for national sovereignty and social revolution?

7. The professionalization of the military, the changing social compositions of its officers, and political democracy and stability. Of what significance is the middle-class social base of the military? Whose interests does it defend, and by what ideologies is it guided? Do the existence of a large middle class and the absence of military intervention in politics go together?

8. The rise and decline of class and polyclass (populist or corporatist) social movements in the underindustrialized urban complexes, and the emergence of peasant-based movements and guerrilla-led units in rural areas, and their relationship to working-class centers of political radicalism. To what extent has a social stalemate or equilibrium of social groups contending for power contributed to the political instability and economic stagnation of the more developed countries in Latin America? What role has this played in the emergence of social movements that cannot be contained within the existing equilibrium? What are the social bases of such movements?

9. The relationship between prerevolutionary social structures, United States interests, and social revolution. What aspects of the prerevolutionary class structures and economic

orders influence the nature and success of revolutionary movements and the emergence of postrevolutionary patterns of development? How do unsuccessful revolutions influence those who live through them?

These problems and the issues involved, while of interest to academics, are hardly academic. They are of profound social relevance, and the answers to them on the theoretical level are scarcely separable from their solutions in reality. What these solutions are will determine the future of Latin America.

J. P.   M. Z.

OVERVIEW

Seven Fallacies About Latin America

RODOLFO STAVENHAGEN

Stavenhagen attacks a number of fallacies about Latin America, the principal one of which is to view Latin American countries as "dual societies" of feudal and capitalist elements in conflict with each other. The relationships established between the colonial power and its colonies repeats itself within the colonies themselves, he argues; and the backward underdeveloped regions are essentially colonies—*internal colonies* as González Casanova has called them—of the developing urban centers and productive agricultural areas, within the framework of an underdeveloped capitalist system. Exploitation of capital, raw materials, foodstuffs, and the labor force in the so-called semifeudal or backward areas actually permits the growth of the "modern" zones; their development is at the expense of the stagnation and underdevelopment of these "traditional" areas. Thus, any supposition that the urban industrialists of the "modern" areas are inevitably in conflict with the large landowners of the backward areas is unfounded.

Rodolfo Stavenhagen received his M.A. in Anthropology from the University of Mexico and his Ph.D. in Sociology from the University of Paris. He teaches at the University of Mexico and is research director at the Centro de Investigaciones Agrarias in Mexico City, Mexico. He is the author of numerous articles on social change in Latin America.

This is a substantially revised and enlarged version of "Siete Teses Erróneas sobre América Latina," which appeared in June 1965 in the Mexican daily, *El Día*. An English version of this article, translation by Otto Feinstein, appeared in *New University Thought*, Vol. IV, No. 4 (Winter 1966/67), pp. 25-37; and the present text is based on this version, with substantial additions and minor revisions by the author. Reprinted by permission.

Note to American readers

THE PURPOSE of this article is to review critically and refute a number of ideas on social development and underdevelopment that are current in Latin America. If the general tone of the article is outspoken and polemical, it is because the "theses" and "antitheses" it develops are directly pertinent to the great political and ideological issues that Latin America is facing today.

In the massive literature dealing with social and economic development and underdevelopment produced in recent years, many doubtful, mistaken, and ambiguous theses have appeared. Many of these are accepted as the working truth, and form a major part of the conceptual framework of Latin American intellectuals, politicians, students, researchers, and professors. Neither facts nor recent research, which contradict these theses, have been able to weaken them. Constant repetition in innumerable books and articles, particularly foreign ones, have given these concepts a growing life of their own, turning some of them, despite evidence to the contrary, into dogmas.

In this article I will deal with the sociological theses, since the debate about similar mistaken economic theses has been quite widespread.

The first thesis:
The Latin American countries are dual societies.

In essence this thesis affirms that two different, and to a certain extent independent—though necessarily connected—societies exist in the Latin American countries: one is an archaic, traditional, agrarian, and stagnant or retrogressive society; the other is a modern, urban, industrialized, dynamic, progressive, developing society. The "archaic society" is characterized by personal and family (kinship) relations; by traditional institutions (ritual coparenthood, certain types of collective labor, certain forms of personalistic political domination, and patron-client relationships); by rigid stratification of ascribed social statuses (i.e., where the individual's status in the social structure is determined by birth, with little likelihood of change during his lifetime); and by norms and values that exalt—or at least accept—the *status quo* and the inherited traditional forms of social life, which are said to constitute an obstacle to economically "rational" thought. The "modern society," on the other hand, supposedly consists of the type of social relations that sociologists call secondary, determined by interpersonal actions that are motivated by rational and utilitarian ends; by functionally-oriented institutions; and by comparatively flexible social stratifications, in which status is attained through personal effort, and is expressed by quantitative indices (like income or level of education) and social function (like occupation). In the so-called "modern society," the norms and values of the people tend to be oriented towards change, progress, innovation, and economic rationality (e.g., maximum benefits at minimum costs).

According to this thesis, each of the two societies facing each other in the Latin American countries has its own characteristic dynamics. The first, the "archaic society," has its origins in the colonial epoch (or perhaps earlier) and preserves many ancient cultural and social elements. It changes little, or does so very slowly. At any rate, changes are not internally generated, but are imposed upon it by the modern society. The other society, the "modern" one, is oriented toward change; it generates within itself its own transformations and is the focal point of economic development, whereas the "archaic" society constitutes an obstacle to such development.

The dual society thesis is expressed on a more sophisticated level by positing an alleged duality between feudalism and capitalism in the Latin American countries. In fact, it is claimed that in a large part of Latin America a feudal type of society and economic structure exists, which constitutes the base for retrogressive and conservative social and economic groups (i.e., the land-owning aristocracy, the oligarchy, local political strongmen, etc.). On the other hand, the theory affirms, there exist nuclei of a capitalist economy, in which we find the entrepreneurial, progressive, urbanized middle classes. Implicit in this description is the idea that "feudalism" is an obstacle to development in Latin American countries and must be eliminated to give way for a progressive capitalism, which will be developed by the entrepreneurial capitalists for the benefit of the country as a whole.

There is no doubt that in all the Latin American countries great social and economic differences exist—between rural and urban areas, between the Indian and non-Indian populations, between the mass of peasants and the urban and rural elites, and between the very backward and the relatively developed regions.

Nevertheless, these differences do not justify the use of the concept of dual society for two principal reasons. First, the relations between the "archaic" or "feudal" regions and groups and the "modern" or "capitalistic" ones represent the functioning of a single unified society of which the two poles are integral parts; and second, these two poles originate in the course of a single historical process.

Let us take the first point. What is important is not the mere existence of two "societies" or a "dual society"—two contrasting poles at the ends of a socioeconomic continuum—but rather the relationships that exist between these two "worlds" and that bind them into a functional whole. To the extent that the localized development of certain areas in Latin America is based on the use of cheap labor (is this not what principally attracts foreign capital to our countries?), the backward regions—those that provide the cheap labor—fulfill a specific function in the national society and are not merely zones in which, for one reason or another, development has not taken place. Moreover, the archaic zones are generally exporters of raw materials to the urban centers of the country and abroad. As we shall see later, the developed areas of the underdeveloped countries operate like a pumping mechanism, drawing from their backward, underdeveloped *hinterland* the very elements that make for their own development. This situation is not new to the underdeveloped countries. It is the result of a long historical process that began with the expansion of mercantilist and colonialist Europe.

Let us turn now to the second point, the single historical process that gave rise to the two poles of Latin American society. The conquest of Latin America was accomplished principally in the context of commercial goals. Essentially, it was accomplished by a series of joint (private and state) mercantile enterprises. In some regions veritable feudal areas were created by means of *encomiendas* and *mercedes* (respectively, grants of Indian labor and land, by which the Spanish Crown rewarded the conquerors). The conquered indigenous populations were subjected to the most brutal oppression and exploitation on the part of the Spaniards. In the same way the slavery of the African Negroes on the Caribbean and Brazilian sugar plantations which satisfied the needs of a mercantilist economy oriented toward the consumer markets of Europe was not characterized by a closed, self-sufficient economy (as was the case in classical European feudalism), but rather satisfied the needs of the export mining industry and of agriculture that supplied these mining centers or the European markets.

During the whole colonial epoch the driving force of the Latin American economy was the mercantilist-capitalist system. The Spanish and Portuguese colonies were large producers of raw materials that supplied various European markets, directly or indirectly, and thus contributed to the later industrial development of Western Europe. The "feudal" economy, if it ever really existed, was subsidiary to the dynamic centers—the mines and export agriculture—which, in turn, responded to the needs of the colonial metropolis.

The one constant factor of the colonial economy was the search for and control of cheap labor for the colonial enterprises. First the colonists tried enslaving the indigenous populations; then the slavery of Africans was introduced. Later they assured themselves of servile Indian labor through a series of arrangements that varied from the encomienda to the forced distribution of Indian workers. The "feudal" living and working conditions of the majority of the Indian peasant population reduced to a minimum the costs of production in mining and in colonial agriculture. Thus, the "feudalism" in labor relations may be considered a function of the development of the colonial economy in its entirety, which, in turn formed an integral part of the world mercantilist system.

The colonial economy was subjected to strong cyclical variations. In Brazil one after another of the major industries grew and then declined. This was true for the primitive extraction of wood, sugar production in the great slave plantations of the Northeast, mining in the central part of the country, the extraction of rubber in the Amazon, and finally, during this century, coffee production in the South and Southeast of Brazil. Each one of these cycles brought an epoch of growth and prosperity to the area in which it occurred. Each corresponded at that moment to a foreign demand. And each one left, in the end, a stagnant, underdeveloped, backward economy and an archaic social structure. In a large part of Brazil, then, *underdevelopment followed upon and did not precede development.* The underdevelopment of these areas is largely the result of a previous period of development that was of short duration and followed by the development of new activities in other parts of the country.

This pattern also can be observed in the rest of Latin America, principally in the mining zones that flourished in one epoch and whose economies decayed thereafter. The economic cycles of colonial Latin America were determined, in large part, by the economic cycles of the Western World. In Middle America, Indian communities that are now closed, isolated, and self-sufficient were not always like that. On the one hand, the colonists displaced the Indian populations who were removed into inhospitable and isolated zones, in which their living standards were reduced to a miserable subsistence level; on the other hand, during the periods of economic depression, those communities that had previously been relatively integrated into the global economy cut themselves off from the world and were depressed through necessity to a subsistence level. We see, then, that in historical terms development and underdevelopment are connected in Latin America, and that frequently the development of one zone implies the underdevelopment of others. We also see that the "feudal" conditions largely respond to the needs of the colonial metropolis and the colonial elite, whom it is hardly possible to define as feudal.

The kinds of relationships that were established between a colonial metropolis and its colonies were repeated within the colonial countries themselves, in the relationships that developed between a few "poles of growth" and the rest of the country. As Spain was to her colonies, so the centers of colonial power in New Spain (and in the rest of Latin America) stood to the outlying, backward areas that surrounded them.

Indeed, the backward, underdeveloped regions of our countries have always played the role of *internal colonies* in relation to the developing urban centers or the productive agricultural areas. And to avoid the mistaken idea that there are two (or more) independent social and economic systems at work in the Latin American countries, we propose to describe the situation in terms of *internal colonialism* rather than in terms of "dual societies." This will become clearer as we discuss the next thesis.

The second thesis:
Progress in Latin America will come about by the spread of industrial products into the backward, archaic, and traditional areas.

The diffusionist thesis is found on many levels. Some speak of an urban—or Western—culture that will spread gradually over the world, and that will little by little absorb all the backward and primitive peoples. Others speak of the effects of modernization as if it were a spot of oil that spreads slowly outward from a central focus. Others affirm that all stimuli for change in the rural areas come of necessity from the urban zones. The fact that transistor radios, bicycles, toothpaste, and Coca-Cola can be found in the most remote parts of the world is cited to support these arguments.

This thesis implies three others, which are not always stated as clearly: (1) the development of the modern sector, which is essentially expansionist, brings with it *ipso facto* the development of the traditional and archaic sector; (2) the "transition" from traditionalism to modernism is a current, permanent, and inescapable process that will eventually involve all traditional societies; and (3) the centers of modernism themselves are nothing but the result of the diffusion of "modernist" traits (technology, know-how, the spirit of capitalism, and, of course, capital) that come from the already developed countries. The thesis can be considered mistaken for the following reasons:

(1) While it is certain that a large number of consumer goods has been distributed to the underdeveloped areas in recent years, this does not automatically imply the development of these areas, if by development we mean an increase in per capita output of goods and services, and in the general social welfare. Often this diffusion of products is nothing but the diffusion of the culture of poverty into the backward, rural areas, for it involves no basic institutional changes.

(2) The spread of manufactured industrial goods into the backward zones often displaces flourishing local industries or manufacturers, and therefore destroys the productive base for a significant part of the population, provoking what is known as rural proletarianization, rural exodus, and economic stagnation in these areas.

(3) The same process of diffusion has contributed to the development of a class of merchants, usurers, middlemen, monopolists, and moneylenders in the backward rural areas, in whose hands is concentrated a growing part of the regional income, and who, far from constituting an element of progress, represent an obstacle to the productive use of capital and to development in general.

(4) The "diffusion" is often nothing more than the extension into the rural areas of monopolies and monopsonies, with negative consequences for a balanced and a harmonious development.

(5) The process of diffusion of *capital* has taken place *from* the backward to the modern areas. Constant decapitalization of the underdeveloped areas in Latin America accompanies the migration of the best-trained part of the population out of the

backward zones: young people with a bit of education who are looking for better opportunities in other areas. It is not the presence or absence of factory-made goods but this unfavorable outward flow from the backward zones that determines the level of development or underdevelopment of these areas.

(6) This process of "diffusion," to which are attributed so many beneficial results, has been going on in Latin America for more than 400 years—and aside from certain dynamic focal points of growth, the continent is still as underdeveloped as ever.

In reality, the correct thesis would be: the progress of the modern, urban, and industrial areas of Latin America has taken place at the expense of backward, archaic, and traditional zones. In other words, the channeling of capital, raw materials, abundant foods, and manual labor coming from the backward zones permits the rapid development of these poles or focal points of growth, and condemns the supplying zones to an increasing stagnation and underdevelopment. The trade relations between the urban and the backward areas is unfavorable to the latter in the same way that the trade relations between underdeveloped and developed countries on a world scale are unfavorable to the underdeveloped countries.

The third thesis:
The existence of backward, traditional, and archaic rural areas is an obstacle to the formation of an internal market and to the development of a progressive and national capitalism.

It is claimed that progressive national capitalism—located in the modern industrial and urban centers—is interested in agrarian reform, the development of the Indian communities, the raising of minimum wages paid to agricultural workers, and other programs of a similar sort. This thesis is mistaken for the following reasons:

(1) With rare exceptions, no progressive or national capitalism exists in Latin America, nor do the international conditions exist that would allow its development. By a "progressive" and "national" capitalism, we mean one which is committed in word and in deed to the independent economic development of the country—i.e., of the masses of the population. This would mean the formulation and acceptance by the capitalist class of economic policies furthering: (a) diversified agriculture for the internal market; (b) transformation of the country's principal raw materials for use in the country itself; (c)

increasing industrialization; (d) a high rate of reinvestment in the country's agriculture; (e) increasing state participation in large economic enterprises; (f) strict control of foreign investments and their subordination to national needs; (g) strict control over exports of capital and profits; (h) preference for nationally owned enterprises over foreign-owned companies; (i) strict limitation of unnecessary imports; (j) strict limitation of the manufacture of nonessential consumer goods; and other such objectives.

These policies are not being pursued in most Latin American countries, and the countries that have tried at one time or another to implement them have suffered tremendous external political and economic pressures. The recent history of Brazil is a case in point. After the U.S.-supported military coup in that country in 1964, the previous economic policies that had furthered a progressive and national capitalism were thrown overboard in favor of the increasing control of the economy by U.S. corporations. The same thing has happened in Argentina, Chile, Bolivia, and other countries. With the exception of Mexico (and at one time, of Brazil), the "national bourgeoisie" in Latin American countries does not have enough power or influence anywhere to make its interests really felt.

(2) Up to this time—and for the foreseeable future—a significant internal market exists among the urban population, a market that is growing continuously and one that is not yet fully supplied. On the other hand, in these same urban areas there is an industrial sector that works at less than full capacity for reasons that have little to do with the internal market, but rather with profits; and for a long time there will be no need for these industries to do more than supply the growing urban zones. That is to say that metropolitan areas like Lima, Callao, São Paulo, Santiago, and Mexico City can grow economically for the indefinite future without necessarily affecting any basic changes in the structure of the backward rural areas, the internal colonies.

The question of the internal market is essentially a question of income distribution. Economists and sociologists speak constantly about the need of incorporating the "backward" subsistence peasants into the money economy in order to strengthen the internal market and further economic development. Yet nowhere in Latin America is the gap between rich and poor greater than in the cities, where the desperately poor "marginal" urban population of the shantytowns is growing rapidly. If the internal market were indeed the driving force of Latin America's bourgeoisie, Mexico's capitalists would not be seeking, as they are, investment opportunities in Central America, or Brazil's in Paraguay and Bolivia; they would not be exporting millions of dollars a year to the security of American and European banks; they would, instead, favor more equitable tax policies, lower profit margins and higher turn-overs, lower prices for their products, and higher levels of production. Generally, however, they favor none of these things.

The fourth thesis:
The national bourgeoisie has an interest in breaking the power and the dominion of the landed oligarchy.

It has often been said that there is a profound conflict of interests between the new elite (or the new upper class) represented by modern commercial and industrial entrepreneurs and the old elite (or the traditional upper class), which derives its prominence from the ownership of the land. Although the latifundist aristocracy was eliminated by revolutionary means in some Latin American countries (however, always by the people, never by the bourgeoisie), there does not seem to be a conflict of interests between the bourgeoisie and the oligarchy in the other countries. On the contrary, the agricultural, financial, and industrial interests are often found in the same economic groups, in the same companies, and even in the same families.

For example, much of the capital coming from the archaic latifundia of Northeast Brazil is invested by their owners in lucrative enterprises in São Paulo. And in Peru the grand families of Lima, associated with progressive foreign capital, are also the owners of the major "feudal" latifundias in the Andes. There is no structural reason why the national bourgeoisie and the latifundista oligarchy should not understand one another; on the contrary, they complement each other very well. And in those cases where there is a possibility of a conflict of interests (as with some legislation that would benefit one group and be prejudicial to the other, for example), there is no lack of bourgeois or military government that will give ample compensation to the group whose interest is prejudiced.

The sorry spectacle of some recent "agrarian reforms" is a case in point. Stung by the Cuban experience and pressured by the U.S., many conservative Latin American governments, at the 1961 Punta del Este economic conference, subscribed to the proposition that it would be safer to bear some sort of land reform than to court peasant revolution. Much publicity has been given to the Colombian and Venezuelan "reforms," and land reform laws or projects in Brazil, Chile, Ecuador, Peru, and other countries have been widely hailed. Where these projects have not been talked to death in parliament (as in Chile), or simply evaded by legal chicanery or specially erected institutional stumbling blocks (as in Brazil, Ecuador, and Peru), the experts agree that what is being done (as in Colombia and Venezuela) is too little, too late, too costly, too badly planned and executed, and these "reforms" are simply insufficient to even keep up with the natural growth of the peasant population, let alone redistribute the land or break the rural power structure. And none of these governments are controlled by the "landed aristocracy" to such an extent that it could be said of them that the local "bourgeoisie" is excluded. Quite the contrary.

The disappearance of the latifundista oligarchy has been exclusively the result of popular movements, not of the bourgeoisie. The bourgeoisie finds a very good ally in the land-owning oligarchy in maintaining internal colonialism, which in the last analysis benefits both of these social classes equally.

The fifth thesis:
Latin American development is the work and creation of a nationalist, progressive, enterprising, and dynamic middle class, and the social and economic policy objectives of the Latin American governments should be to stimulate "social mobility" and the development of that class.

There is probably no other thesis about Latin America more widespread than this one. It is supported by researchers, journalists, and politicians; it is the theme of seminars and conferences, the subject of voluminous books, and one of the implicit but basic assumptions of the Alliance for Progress; it has been transformed into a virtual dogma. But this thesis is false, for the following reasons:

(1) In the first place, the concept "middle class" itself contains ambiguities and equivocations. If it deals, as is often the case, with middle income groups situated between the two extremes of a given economic scale, then it is not a social class but a statistical aggregate. Generally, however, this concept refers to people who have a certain type of occupation, particularly in the tertiary sector of the economy—in commerce or services—and mostly in the urban areas. In this case, it refers to white collar workers, the bureaucracy, businessmen, and

certain professions. At times this concept also refers to certain social groups that have no place in the traditional structural model of Latin America, in which there supposedly exists only a landed aristocracy and peons without land. All other groups, from the small land owners to the urban population as a whole, are then lumped together under the catch-all term of "middle class." As long as there is no clear definition of this term, information concerning the virtues and potentialities of this "middle class" is only a subjective opinion of those who state it.

(2) Very often the term "middle class" is a euphemism for "ruling class." When one speaks of the entrepreneurs, the financiers, and the industrialists in relation to the development of the Latin American countries, reference is made to a class that has the power in the society, that occupies the apex of the social, economic, and political pyramid, and that makes, as such, the overall decisions that affect these countries. In other words, the class in question is in no sense "middle."

When liberal authors (such as John Johnson and Robert J. Alexander, for example) extol the virtues of this "new" class in Latin American politics, it is obviously less embarrassing to use the neutral term "middle class" than to accurately define the nature of this group at the top of the power structure as a new ruling class or power elite.

(3) This thesis of the middle class usually suggests the idea of a potentially majoritarian mass of the population, primarily recruited from the lower strata of society, which will sooner or later totally occupy the social universe. At that time, it is implied, the upper classes will no longer have any economic, nor the lower classes any numerical, importance. There could be nothing more utopian or mistaken. The growth of the tertiary economic sector is no guarantee of development, nor will the growth of the middle social sectors (a statistical fiction) guarantee the disappearance of the economic and social inequalities of society. No matter how accelerated the growth of these middle strata may be in Latin America as a whole, the growth of the lower income groups in both the countryside and the city on the one hand, and that of the miniscule upper income strata on the other, is still greater.

(4) The sectors that compose the middle class in its restricted sense—small- and medium-sized farm owners, small businessmen, public employees, small entrepreneurs, artisans, different types of professionals, etc. (i.e., those who work on their own or who receive a salary for nonmanual labor)—usually do not have the characteristics that are attributed to them.

Instead they are economically and socially dependent upon the upper strata; they are tied politically to the ruling class; they are conservative in their tastes and opinions, defenders of the status quo; and they search only for individual privileges. Far from being nationalists, they like everything foreign—from imported clothing to the *Reader's Digest*. They constitute a true reflection of the ruling class, deriving sizeable benefits from the internal colonial situation. This group constitutes the most important support for military dictatorships in Latin America.

(5) The concept "middle class" is also understood at times in terms of the consumption habits of a certain part of the population. In this way, for example, the fact that the peasants buy bottled beer instead of Chicha or Pulque, or that the urban population buys furniture or electrical appliances on credit, is considered by some as an indisputable sign that we have taken great steps in the march toward a "middle class" civilization. Everyone in Latin America, these authors tell us, has "the aspirations of the middle class." It is only a question of time as to when these aspirations will be realized. This assertion is incorrect for the following reasons:

A social class is not defined by the articles it consumes, nor does the level of aspirations reveal the structure of social institutions and the quality of intergroup relations. The diffusion of manufactured articles is directly related to the overall level of technology as well as to effective demand. The majority of the population—particularly in the urban areas—can enjoy this type of consumption, to some extent, but it requires no basic change in the class structure or in the inequalities of income, social status, political power, or labor relations.

The creation of "aspirations" or "necessities" of a certain type is increasingly the result of an all-powerful advertising industry that has infiltrated all social milieus. Levels of aspiration are rising everywhere, but so is the level of unfulfilled aspirations; and this, as any psychologist would confirm, leads to rising levels of frustration and feelings of deprivation. Thus, the aspirations of the middle class could well be transformed into revolutionary consciousness.

Furthermore, economic studies have demonstrated that in Latin America the proportion of wages in the national income —on which most of the population is dependent—tends to diminish, while the profits and capital returns of a minority tend to increase. This tendency, which has been accelerated in recent years by the process of inflation (especially in countries like Argentina, Brazil, Chile, Bolivia, and Colombia) does not fit with the idea of the slow, harmonious growth of the middle class.

(6) The strengthening of the middle class, as a goal of social policy, is not essentially intended to further economic development in a country, but rather to create a political force capable of supporting the existing ruling class, and of serving as a buffer in the class struggles that endanger the stability of the existing social and economic structure. The ideologues of the middle class have lamented that this class was not sufficiently strong in Cuba to oppose the socialist revolution. On the other hand, they give credit to the "middle class" for the fact that the Mexican and Bolivian revolutions have become "stabilized" and "institutionalized."

The so-called middle classes are closely tied to the existing economic and political structure, and lack an internal dynamic which could transform them into promoters of an independent economic development. Their relative numerical importance is one thing, and their condition and capacity to make decisions as a class that could affect economic structures and processes is altogether another thing. It is noteworthy that the authors who are most attached to the idea of the growth of the middle class give little or no importance to the fact that the lower strata still constitutes the largest part of the Latin American population.

(7) Finally, the thesis of the middle class tends to obscure the fact that there are tensions, oppositions, and conflicts between ethnic groups as well as between classes in Latin America; that the social and economic development of the Latin American countries depend, in the last analysis, upon an adequate solution to these conflicts; and that the growth of the "middle sectors" (as one North American author calls them), though very impressive in certain regions, does not contribute to the solution of these problems. At times, such growth may even postpone a solution and sharpen the conflicts.

The sixth thesis:
National integration in Latin America is the product of miscegenation.

This thesis is frequent in the countries that have major ethnic problems—those that have a large proportion of Indians in the population, and Brazil, with its Negro population. It is argued that the Spanish and Portuguese colonization of America brought two main racial groups, two civilizations, into confrontation, and that the process of national integration represents both a biological and a cultural mixture. In the Indo-American countries it is thought that *ladinoziation* (acculturation of Indians) constitutes a universalizing process in which the major differences between the dominant white minority and the Indian peasant masses will disappear. It is said that out of the traditional bipolar social structure a new, intermediate biological and cultural element is appearing—the *Ladino,* or *Cholo,* or *Mestizo,* or *Mulato,* as the case may be—who bears the "essence of nationality" and who possesses all the virtues necessary for progress in Latin American countries.

The fallacy in this thesis is that biological and cultural mixing (a common process in many parts of Latin America) does not constitute, in itself, a change in the existing social structure.

National integration, as an objective process, and the birth of a national consciousness, as a subjective process, depend on structural factors (i.e., on the nature of the relations between men and between social groups) and not on the biological or cultural attributes of certain individuals. National integration (in the sense of full participation of all citizens in the same cultural values, and the relative equality of social and economic opportunities) will be achieved in the Indian areas, not with the development of a new biocultural category, but with the disappearance of internal colonialism. In the internal colonies of our countries, the Mestizos (or racially mixed population) are, in fact, representatives of the local and regional ruling class who help to maintain the Indian population in a state of oppression. They have not the slightest interest in true national integration. On the other hand, in the increasingly important urban centers, the immigrant rural population, often of Indian stock, is rapidly "integrated" from the national point of view; but this is due more to the positions it occupies in the class structure than to the process of miscegenation.

Furthermore, the thesis of miscegenation very often hides a racist prejudice (which may be unconscious); in the countries where a majority of the population has Indian traits, biological miscegenation signifies "whitening," and in that sense citing the virtues of miscegenation really hides anti-Indian biases. The same prejudice is found in the cultural version of this theory—indeed, it means the disappearance of Indian culture. Thus, making miscegenation the prerequisite for national integration condemns the Indians of America, a group that numbers in the tens of millions, to a slow cultural agony.

The seventh thesis:
Progress in Latin America will only take place by means of an alliance between the workers and the peasants, as a result of the identity of interests of these two classes.

We cannot leave this discussion of Latin America without referring to a thesis that is quite prevalent among the orthodox left. Indeed, on the basis of theories developed by Lenin and Mao Tse-tung, it is said that the success of the democratic revolution in Latin America depends on the ability of the working and peasant classes to forge a common front against the reactionary bourgeoisie and against imperialism.

While this may be correct as a revolutionary ideal or as the desired goal for political organization and action, it must be pointed out that if the analysis of the last six points is correct, particularly if the concept "internal colonialism" is valid, then the existing social structures and their present tendencies in Latin America do not "naturally" favor such an ideal alliance, though I will not offhand deny its possibility. Recent historical experience does not show a single instance of such an alliance having in fact taken place. The Mexican peasant revolution took place when there was hardly an urban working class to speak of. The Bolivian revolution, while greatly beneficial to the peasants, was mainly the work of the tin miners and an intellectual elite. The Cuban revolutionaries finally achieved the support of the organized urban working class only toward the end of the armed uprising when Batista's downfall was assured. The working class of São Paulo (Brazil's largest concentration of industrial workers) has consistently elected the country's most conservative—albeit "populist"—governors and was certainly unable to join forces with the relatively well organized rural workers in the Northeast to save Goulart's democratic regime from military overthrow. In Argentina the organized urban workers (either peronistas or antiperonistas) have not been able or willing to establish an alliance with the peasants and rural workers. In other countries the experience is similar.

In the future, as most of Latin America will become increasingly underdeveloped and will be increasingly controlled by the U.S., through military or pseudodemocratic regimes, the situation may change. Many governments will continue to attempt to carry out some sort of land reform and certainly the political forces of the left will continue to press for it everywhere. In regard to these land reforms (be they the first steps of a democratic revolution or the delaying action of an increasingly frightened bourgeoisie) it is pertinent to emphasize the following points:

(1) One of the indisputable steps in all democratic revolutions is agrarian reform. But the acquisition of land by the peasantry through a noncollectivist agrarian reform transforms them into proprietors whose class interests are those of other landed proprietors.

(2) The objective interests of the peasants and the workers are not identical in the matter of agrarian reform. An agrarian reform usually implies an initial diminution of food deliveries to the cities, the effects of which are first felt by the working class. It also means the channeling of public investments into the rural sectors, with a consequent disfavoring of the urban sector—which, as we have seen, is about the only sector that really benefits from economic development in a situation of internal colonialism.

(3) The struggle of the urban working class (which is politically more powerful than the peasantry) for higher wages, more and better public social services, price controls, etc., finds no seconding in the peasant sector because benefits obtained by the working class in this way are usually obtained at the cost of agriculture—i.e., the peasants.

In Latin America almost half of the economically active population works in agriculture, yet the agricultural sector receives little more than 20 percent of the total income, and its share in the total income has been declining much faster than its share in the total population. Capital formation is much more important in the nonagricultural sector and public and private investment (in public services, education, health, social security, etc.) principally benefits the urban populations.

In other words, the urban working class of our countries is also a beneficiary of internal colonialism. That is one of the reasons why a truly revolutionary labor movement does not exist in Latin America.

(4) In nineteenth-century England the expulsion of peasants from the land and their migration to the industrial sweatshops signified a diminution of their standard of living; in Czarist Russia, rural-urban mobility was strictly limited and the worker-peasant alliance was made in the field of battle; and in People's China the same alliance was forged in the fight against the Japanese invaders. In sharp contrast to all of these examples, rural emigration is not only possible for the discontented of the countryside in Latin America, but in most cases it represents

an improvement in economic and social conditions (even in the favelas, the barriadas, the ranchos, or the colonias proletarias—the shantytowns—of the Latin American cities), as compared with conditions in the countryside. One can theorize that the revolutionary consciousness of the peasants increases in *inverse* proportion to the possibility of their individual upward social mobility, and that this relationship would hold even more strongly if the latter also implies geographic mobility.

(5) We may also suppose that the more severe the internal colonialism in Latin America (i.e., the greater the difference between the metropolis and its internal colonies), the further the possibilities of a true political alliance between workers and peasants will be reduced. The example of recent events in Brazil and Bolivia should illustrate this point.

The preceding picture of Latin America might seem overly pessimistic. If so, it is only because the picture given us by those "experts" who perpetuate these seven fallacies is uncritically optimistic and leads easily to an underestimation of the tremendous tasks that Latin America faces today. Perhaps the greatest single obstacle to economic and social development in Latin America (not localized growth) is the existence of internal colonialism, an organic, structural relationship between a developing pole of growth or metropolis, and its backward, underdeveloped, and underdeveloping internal colony. Quite often not even the best-intentioned policy makers are aware of this relationship, which exists on the economic, political, social, and cultural levels. Whereas several measures of a partial and limited nature can no doubt be taken by progressive governments to remedy this situation, the only way out in the long run seems to be the social and political mobilization of the "colonized" peasantry, which will have to fight its own battles, except for the usual support it can hope to receive from radical segments of the intelligentsia, the students, and the working class. It is noteworthy that not even the governments that have formally acknowledged the need for land reform are willing to tolerate independent peasant organizations.

The myth of the middle class is another false panacea. This does not mean that the diploma-holding sons of the middle-income strata have no role to play in their country's development. Some of them will probably lead the coming peasant revolutions themselves. Others will of course continue to run the petroleum industry, the sugar mills, the hospitals, the universities, and the chain stores. It is rather a question of in whose interest and for whose benefit these organizations will be managed. And in this sense, the "middle class" has hardly ever been able to see further than to their own pocketbooks. The thousands of Latin American technicians and professional people who emigrate yearly to the U. S. and better-paying jobs are a case in point.

In Latin America today there is growing awareness among all sectors of the population of what the real obstacles are to the socioeconomic growth and to democratic political development. Thoughtful people are less and less concerned with single factors such as "lack of resources," "traditionalism of the peasantry," "overpopulation," and "cultural and racial heterogeneity," which are still current among some scholars. They are increasingly conscious of the internal structure and dynamics of the total society and, of course, of the relation of dependence this society has with respect to the industrial metropolis, i.e., the phenomenon of imperialism and neo-colonialism. Such awareness can only lead to deeper and more refined analysis of the Latin American situation and to newer and more correct courses of action.

Latin America: Feudal or Capitalist?

LUIS VITALE

Vitale argues that the old orders never were feudal, and rejects the notion that Spain somehow transplanted feudal relations to the new world of Latin America. Spain itself was in the throes of transition from feudalism to capitalism when its conquests occurred, and its colonization had a capitalist character: exploitation of colonial raw materials for the international market. Within the colonies themselves, the ruling economic classes, while fond of noble titles and feudal pomp, were essentially new capitalist classes made up not only of exporters of agricultural commodities, but also of mine owners, cattle ranchers, and traders. They were unable to go beyond their successful independence movements from Spain and make structural changes in their societies that were necessary for development, precisely because they were dominated by export capitalists with no interest in internal development. With the ascendance of foreign capital in their economies, not only had they no interest in doing so, but they were incapable of it.

Luis Vitale, an Argentinian historian residing in Chile, is the author of *Historia del Movimiento Obrero* (Santiago, Chile: Editorial POR, 1962), and *Esencia y Aparencia de la Democracia Cristiana* (Santiago, Chile: Arancibia Hmnos., 1963).

THE CONTROVERSY over whether Latin America has feudal or capitalist characteristics may appear academic, but for many years the reform movement has based its political strategy on the following propositions:

(1) Spain was a feudal country.
(2) Spain transplanted its medieval system to the New World, and colonization took place under feudal rule.
(3) A feudal aristocracy grew in Latin America and later became independent from Spain.
(4) A feudal aristocracy ruled the Latin American countries during the nineteenth and the twentieth centuries, impeding the development of capitalism and the emergence of a national bourgeoisie.
(5) The Popular parties must support the "progressive bourgeoisie" against the feudal oligarchy to fulfill the democratic-bourgeois aims through a National Liberation Front.

That the question of feudalism vs. capitalism is not merely academic may be seen in the tragic defeat of those who have based their actions on this theory: Frente Popular and González Videla in Chile, Perón and Frondizi in Argentina, Vargas and Goulart in Brazil, Acción Democrática in Venezuela, the APRA and Belaúnde in Peru, and the Guatemalan and Bolivian revolutions, among others.

The primary thesis of the reform movement consists in defining Spain as a feudal country, a characterization that has gained credibility through repeated telling. Liberal historians of the nineteenth century fabricated a false image of Spain, an appraisal serving the immediate politics of the British empire rather than history. The concept of feudal Spain has taken on special significance in the present century. Its standard-bearers are the pseudoleftist sociologists and politicians who confuse *economic backwardness* with feudalism, or *latifundium* with feudalism.

Let us clarify these concepts. What were the general features of feudal systems? Feudalism was an agrarian economic system based on barter, with no salaries, since services were paid for in land, lodging, and food. Its social structure was based on relations of servitude, of vassalage, with punishment for those who left the fief, etc. Politically it was characterized by a weak royalty and an independent nobility. This rule

struck its first roots at the end of the Roman Empire, reaching
its peak between the ninth and the twelfth centuries, and declining during the Low Middle Ages. It was the clash of
Moslem and European culture, through seven centuries, that
undermined the feudal structure. Turks, Arabs, and Jews over-
ran the "Mare Nostrum," creating factories and selling their
merchandise in the fiefs. The middle class grew. A new social
class, the commercial bourgeoisie, emerged on the borders of
the castles, and serfs began to move from the country to the
city. Venetian and Baltic bankers slowly changed the economic
and social life of the Middle Ages. A natural economy was
transformed into a monetary economy. . . .

The Iberian peninsula was in the vanguard of this process.
Portugal, in 1381, witnessed the first bourgeois revolution,
four centuries before that of France. The commercial bourgeoisie of Lisbon, connected through trade with Flanders,
removed the feudal lords from power. The ultimate failure
of the revolution showed that conditions were unripe for the
triumph of the bourgeoisie, but their rise was reflected in the
trade with the North Atlantic, in the plans of Henry the
Navigator, and, above all, in the discoveries of the fifteenth
century.

Spain had less typically feudal characteristics than other
European countries for several reasons:

1) The prolonged Moslem invasion had specific effects
on Spain, interrupting, or rather, changing, the course of the
feudal development that had risen in Visigothic Spain. The
Arabs infiltrated Central and Southern Europe at a rate impressive even to historians accustomed to seeing history from
the European point of view. The Moslem civilization was
absorbed by Spanish society, giving an unusual stimulus to
commerce, especially under Aberranian III in the tenth century. While the rest of Europe lived under a regime of natural
economy, Spain was carrying on a relatively active trade. The
Arabs promoted agricultural and industrial progress. They
introduced sugar, cotton, and the raising of silkworms, the
basis of textile manufacture. "The secret of the industrial
renaissance in Spain and Sicily under the Arabs was the building of canals."[1] The advances in Spanish agriculture were seen
in the irrigation system, in the hydraulic works of Valencia,
Andalucía, and Zaragoza (25,000 acres irrigated), and in
the attention that the Arabic scientists gave it. . . .

[1] Karl Marx, *El Capital*, I, Tr. W. Roces, Ed. FCE (Mexico, 1949),
p. 565.

(2) The Arab invasion forced the Spanish royalty and nobility to revise the socioeconomic system. In the areas most affected by the war, such as León and Castilla, a relatively free peasant population emerged that refused to recognize ancient feudal ties. "For more than a century," says Smith, "the frontier between Christian and Moslem Spain consisted of a wide, uninhabited or sparsely populated zone, which could only be settled by offering lands within it at profitable rates. In this territory the typical settler was, during the ninth and tenth centuries, the free peasant who possessed a small tract of land."[2] . . . The situation of these peasants changed in later centuries when the land holders organized themselves, but it did not fall into the type of servitude that existed in other European countries. Also, the "behetrias" in which the peasants bought the protection of the lord established less rigid ties of vassalage than those of French or German feudalism. Spanish feudalism was of the *sui generis* type. . . .

(3) The war against the Arabs impeded the consolidation of the feudal lords, strengthening the centralizing tendency of the kings. The latter took into their hands the anarchical military command of the nobles. It would be an exaggeration to state that the Spain of the *Reconquista* was a monarchical and centralized state in the modern sense . . . but it cannot be denied that the kings exercised a more or less strict control over the feudal lords. Later attempts at feudal consolidation were checked by means of the Catholic kings, who changed the nobility into courtiers dependent on the throne.

(4) From the fourteenth century onward, a pastoral economy known as *Mesta* developed, a nomadic type of sheep raising that supplied wool to the textile centers of the Low Countries. This sheep-raising system, in spite of its appearance, was not feudalistic, since the wool produced was sent to the international market. Two characteristics of the Mesta—the use of little labor and the use of enormous tracts of land for raising sheep for wool—caused the migration to the cities of the peasants who had been driven out of the country, and weakened the attitudes of servitude. The vast expanses of land themselves were not necessarily feudal, either; the essential feature of feudalism is not the *expanse* of land . . . but the *system* of agrarian production, with a natural barter economy, without markets and without the use of money. . . .

(5) The most conclusive proof that Spain was advancing

[2] R. Smith, *Historia Económica de Europa*, Vol. I (Madrid: Universidad de Cambridge, 1948), p. 416.

toward capitalism lay in the rise of a new social class: the bourgeoisie. Commercial capital, accumulated by the merchants trading with the North Atlantic, Italy, and Provence, began to finance manufacturing enterprises. . . . Kings and nobles, indebted through loans granted by the flourishing bourgeoisie, were obliged to allow it to participate, though to a small extent, in the affairs of the State. Many years before the French and English middle classes were to carry out key political functions, the Spanish bourgeoisie was recognized by the Cortes. Municipalities appeared in the eleventh century. . . . "As far back as the fourteenth century, the cities already constituted the most powerful part of the Spanish Cortes."[3] And the Spanish literature of the period . . . reflects more richly than official documents the cultural influence of the rising middle class.

In brief, Spain during the period of American conquest was a country in transition from feudalism to capitalism, a nation of uneven development combining feudal institutions with a relatively strong bourgeoisie that was dealing with foreign markets. Spanish capitalism of the fifteenth century was not modern industrial capitalism but an incipient capitalism, primitive, essentially commercial, and with remnants of feudalism: feudal institutions and titles of nobility. The sixteenth and seventeenth centuries saw a belated resurgence of feudalism, especially after the defeat of the bourgeoisie in the war of the Comuneros de Castilla and the Hermandades de Valencia in 1550. Under pressure from the feudal lords, the Church, and the Genoese and German capitalists, Charles V expelled the Jews and the Arabs, the bulwarks of the trade and artisanship of the period. But in spite of these temporary feudal victories, Spain developed toward capitalism in . . . an erratic course that culminated during the eighteenth century, under the Bourbons, in the adoption of measures in favor of the bourgeoisie and of national industry. (It *is* necessary to recognize that these setbacks kept Spain from attaining the degree of capitalist development reached by France and England during the industrial revolution.)

The second thesis of the reform movement is that the conquest of America was feudal in character. For us the discovery, conquest, and colonization of America was a natural development for a country that had broken its ties with the rural

[3] Marx-Engels, *La Revolución Española*, (Moscow: Ediciones Lenguas Extranjeras), p. 3.

economy of the Middle Ages. The conquest had a capitalist purpose: the exploitation and commercialization of precious metals. Despite the presence of feudal manors, the colonial economy was not based on a natural economy or the small-scale production of the feudal estate, but on the exploitation of raw materials for the international market on a relatively large scale and through the employment of large numbers of native workers. . . . In three centuries Spain extracted twenty thousand million francs in precious metals from American sources, and the principal colonial cities were created for the purpose of exporting raw materials to Europe. The exploitation of labor during the colonization was not feudal in character; black slavery was not a feudal institution but a capitalist enterprise, organized with large amounts of capital. . . . And the *native* laborers on the encomiendas, while in no way the typical workers of modern industry, did receive a "bastardized salary."[4]

During the first years of the conquest the encomenderos attempted to assert their independence. The Spanish Crown, anxious to avoid the emergence in America of a group of lords who might eventually repudiate its authority, set up a strong administration with the aim of counteracting any feudal outbreak. In 1542 the New Laws of the Indies reasserted royal power: suppression of slavery and repeal of the law of succession for two lifetimes, that is, the end of perpetual concession of encomiendas. The encomendero was not the master of the Indians, nor could he impose justice, because "the Indian was not the encomendero's serf but was the king's subject." The measures of the monarchy "in favor" of the Indians did not come from a sense of respect for the human person, but from a capitalist motive: to preserve exploited labor, to avoid the physical extermination of the labor force, the Indians who were furnishing the Crown with precious metals. Some of these laws were not obeyed and were resisted by the encomenderos through rebellions, such as those of New Granada in 1563 and of Mexico in 1564.

In 1549 the king decreed the abolition of personal servitude in the encomienda, asserting that the Indian was required only to give tribute in kind. In 1569 Viceroy Toledo of Peru stated

---

[4] The writers who have best treated this theme are Jan Bazant, Silvio Zabala of Mexico, Nahuel Moreno y Milciades of Argentina, Marcelo Segall of Chile, and particularly Sergio Bagú, all of whom have contributed to our discussion of colonial economy and society.

that this tribute should be paid in money, a requirement that obliged the Indians to work for a salary. Thus the encomienda of services was replaced by the encomienda of money tribute, a system called *cuatequil* in Mexico and *mita* in Peru and Chile. . . . The salaried worker signified an embryonic capitalist relationship between the classes, and formed a new class of workers. In the seventeenth century, with the explosive increase in the number of mestizos, the landholders and the mine owners were obliged to pay wages to obtain labor. . . .

The third thesis of reformism is that the feudal aristocracy that started in the colony incited the revolt of independence against Spain. We assert that Spain conquered America, not to reproduce the European feudal cycle there, but to incorporate it within the new system of capitalist production. This was to have repercussions not only in the development of social classes but also, in part, in the American revolution. . . . Spanish colonization gave rise to a creole bourgeoisie that, developing and coming into conflict with imperial interests, directed the emancipation of Latin America.

The internal development of Latin America from the beginning had been subordinate to its colonial state. Its economy was created to serve the interests of the mother country. Latin America's role as a producer of raw materials began in the colonial period. The development of local industry—a condition that, together with agrarian reform, is essential for the creation of a domestic market—was restricted by Spain. The colony performed the double function of exporting raw materials and importing manufactured products.

Spain monopolized colonial exports and imports, making it impossible for creoles to obtain better prices in other markets or to buy cheaper manufactured products. To appease those who protested against this monopoly, the kings of the Bourbon House in 1778 allowed the opening of 33 new trade ports with America. The relative upsurge in trade increased the hopes of the creole bourgeoisie. The Bourbon concessions, instead of relieving the discontent of the colonies, stimulated the aspirations of the creole landholders, mine owners, and traders. The reforms initiated by the liberal ministers of Charles III show that Spain had lost her colony long before 1810. . . .

Because the wealthy creoles acquired titles of nobility, established family estates, and performed other acts reminiscent of medieval feudalism, they have sometimes been characterized as a feudal aristocracy . . . but these titles of nobility were acquired with money, not through "blue blood."

. . . Although one can trace a number of causes, essentially the Revolution against Spain was created by this new social class aspiring toward self-government, the creole bourgeoisie. This class controlled the principal sources of wealth throughout the colony, though political power remained in the hands of representatives of the monarchy. The conflict between economic power, largely controlled by the creole bourgeoisie, and political power, monopolized by the Spaniards, precipitated the Revolution of 1810. While the creole bourgeoisie needed new markets, the Spanish Crown restricted production to the bare necessities of peninsular trade. While the bourgeoisie wanted manufactured goods at lower prices, the Empire obliged them to buy merchandise sold by Spanish traders at exorbitant prices. While the natives demanded the lowering of taxes, Spain imposed new tributes.[5] Above all, the bourgeoisie wanted power because it meant controlling the customs house, government monopoly, public revenue, high public positions, the army and state machinery upon which depended the export and import laws.

. . . The Revolution of 1810 was directed by men who adapted to their own interests the liberal ideas of the eighteenth century, of the French Enlightenment and Spanish liberalism. The thinking of creoles like Belgrano and Salas matured under the Bourbon reforms initiated by Masonic ministers such as the Count of Aranda, a friend of Voltaire. However, liberal thinking led in Europe to the democratic-bourgeois revolution; in Latin America the single goal was political independence from Spain. The arguments of the European bourgeoisie against feudalism were turned by the creole bourgeoisie against the oppressive rule of the Spanish Crown. In Europe liberal thought was the banner of the industrial bourgeoisie; in Latin America it was the temporary ideology of the landholders, mine owners, and traders. Political liberalism served to justify economic liberalism, but where liberalism in Europe was a weapon of the industrial bourgeoisie, in Latin America it was used against the Spanish monopoly. There it was used for industrial protection; here for free trade.

The creole bourgeoisie was powerful enough to attempt the seizure of power. It needed only an incident to precipitate revolution, and that incident was the Napoleonic invasion.

. . . The men who led the Revolution were mainly of bourgeois descent—landowners, traders, mine owners, plant-

---

[5] L. Machado Ribas, *Los Movimientos Revolucionarios en las Colonias Españolas* (Buenos Aires, 1940).

ers, cattle raisers, and exporters, often wealthy. . . . The common people were largely indifferent to a Revolution that meant not social emancipation but the consolidation of their immediate exploiters, the creole landlords. This situation was partially modified when the Spaniards began the Reconquest, not because of a change in the creole bourgeoisie, but because of a reaction of the poor classes against the abuses of the Spaniards during the war. The peasant support for Manuel Rodríguez was the key to the success of the guerrilla warfare that contributed to the triumph of the Army of the Andes, led by San Martín. But the participation of the common people became massive only in Mexico and in Alto Peru, where the Indians connected the struggle for independence with the agrarian revolution. In the Spanish colonies there were few men like Hidalgo and Morelos, who fought with the Spaniards and dispossessed the creole landholders as well.

In short, the Revolution of 1810 was not a democratic-bourgeois revolution because it neither accomplished agrarian reform nor developed industry and the domestic market. It was a political, not a social, revolution, in which the creole bourgeoisie fulfilled only one democratic aim—political independence—which it was later unable to protect against imperialism. The history of Latin America is the history of a frustrated democratic-bourgeois revolution.

The fourth thesis of reformism is that the feudal aristocracy governed the Latin American countries during the nineteenth and twentieth centuries, delaying capitalist development and the emergence of a national bourgeoisie. The conclusion of this thesis is that Latin America failed to reach a phase of capitalist development, a duty that must be undertaken by the "progressive bourgeoisie."

But we have seen that the Latin American countries were ruled *not* by feudal lords but by a bourgeoisie that had no desire to develop the domestic market and national industry because its basic source of income lay in the export trade. After foiling the first plans for industrial development drawn up by the *avant garde* of the first generation of rebels in 1810, the landholders and traders—who had compromised with England and France to allow the introduction of foreign merchandise into Latin America in exchange for a good market for their raw materials—destroyed the incipient artisan industries in each country.[6] Free trade was advantageous to the

[6] Juan Álvarez, *Las Guerras Civiles Argentinas* (Buenos Aires).

exporting creole bourgeoisie that retained power, but it meant the destruction of the small regional factories that had reached a small peak during the War of Independence by supplying the necessities to the patriotic armies. . . .

A few decades after the War of Independence the process of primitive accumulation of land through violent conquest was accelerated, accounting for the great latifundia. The foundations of the modern estate were laid during the second half of the nineteenth century as a result of the development of agrarian capitalism, conditioned by the ever-increasing demand of highly industrialized nations for raw materials.

To some economists capitalist development and bourgeois social power can mean only productive mechanization or advanced industry. That is, neither capitalism nor a bourgeoisie could exist where there was no industry. This belief serves to measure whether one country is more advanced than another, but it is confusing if applied to colonial or semicolonial countries, for in these countries there is no advanced industry, but a system of capitalist exploitation of agriculture, livestock, etc., and a social class ruled by laws of price, credit, and profit. In the middle of the past century this class introduced the railroad to Latin America and inaugurated the banking system, which began to finance agricultural enterprises, refrigeration firms, sugar mills, and foundries. The Chilean miners attained high productivity rates in their copper and saltpeter mines. The Argentinian landholders increased livestock export by introducing new techniques and initiated agrarian capitalism. The landholding bourgeoisie of Cuba was converted into the world's principal supplier of sugar, just as the tin-mine owners of Bolivia became the leading suppliers of tin.

The exporting class of Latin America has been riding for more than a century on a horse that resisted, not a feudal bridle, but a bourgeois one. Backwardness was caused, not by feudalism, but by Latin America's limited role as producer of raw materials and its dependence on the world market. Backwardness coexists with the most modern technical advances. Side by side with small domestic production and the miserable artisan workshops are large capitalist enterprises, the distinctive signs of uneven development that characterize backward nations. . . .

The beginning of imperialism—a new phase of capitalism— at the end of the nineteenth century determined the next phase of Latin America's development. The investment of foreign finance capital transformed the Latin American countries from dependent to semicolonial. Raw materials, in the hands of the national bourgeoisie in the past, began largely supplying European and then United States imperialism, which took over control of Chilean copper, Bolivian tin, the Central American plantations, etc. . . .

Unlike the European industrial bourgeoisie, which arose in the struggle against the landed nobility in a period characterized by free trade and competitive capitalism, the Latin American bourgeoisie was associated from the beginning with landholders and foreign investors. Toward the end of the last century the industrial capitalist countries not only flooded the markets with manufactured products but also controlled the majority of stocks in the principal industries that had been established in Latin America. Light industry (e.g., textiles, footwear) did develop somewhat during the two world wars because of the difficulties of importing manufactured consumer goods, but there is *not,* as reformists would have us believe, a conflict between imperialism and this development of light industry in the backward countries. Native light industry is advantageous to foreign imperialism, especially American monopolies, because it creates new markets for heavy industry. It is one hope of the Alliance for Progress, when it praises "agrarian reform," that as a result of the increased purchasing power of the peasant there will be an expansion of Latin American light industry and a subsequent increase in the demand for heavy machinery manufactured by U.S. firms. . . . Reformists tend to overlook the fact that the basis for great monopoly profit today is not the exportation of consumer articles (clothing, footwear, foodstuffs, washing machines, etc.) but the sale of machinery produced by heavy industry and necessary to light industry. The old capitalism, as Lenin said, was interested in the export of merchandise, modern imperialism in the export of capital goods. And the Latin American bourgeoisie depends more than ever on capital goods produced by foreign monopolies. . . .

In other words, the bourgeoisie, concentrating on the export of raw materials, has contributed to the backwardness of Latin America. Dependent from the beginning on imperialism because of its own inability to develop heavy industry, it has exhausted all the possibilities for the development of a semicolonial society in an imperialist period. It is a mistake to claim, as the reformers do, that the phase of capitalist development has not yet been reached and that this phase can be attained through the "progressive bourgeoisie."

We come now to the political strategy that forms the final thesis of reformism: "The popular parties must support the progressive bourgeoisie against the feudal oligarchy to fulfill the democratic-bourgeois aims through a National Liberation Front."

. . . Latin America is not a copy of nineteenth-century Europe, in which the new rising middle class had to overthrow feudalism to initiate the cycle of democratic-bourgeois revolutions. As we have shown, Latin America has not gone through the classic stages of the Old World, but has passed directly from primitive indigenous communities to the incipient capitalism introduced by Spanish colonization. The Latin America that gained its independence from Spain was governed, not by a feudal oligarchy, but by a bourgeoisie that, through its dependence on the world market has contributed to the backwardness of the continent. This bourgeoisie is incapable of fulfilling the aims of democracy. . . . It is neither able, nor desirous of achieving agrarian reform because all of the dominant classes are committed to the holding of land. . . . It is incapable of breaking away from imperialism because of its dependence on foreign finance capital. This bourgeois class may have certain disagreements with foreign enterprises that introduce products in competition with its own light industry, but its solution does not go beyond the imposition of feeble customs restrictions. A class whose very existence depends upon imperialism cannot break away from it without committing suicide. . . . Agrarian reform and the expulsion of imperialism is, and will always be, against the bourgeoisie rather than in its favor. . . .

Growth and Crisis in the Latin American Economy*

MAURICE HALPERIN

The excessive vulnerability of Latin American societies to external factors as a basic source of their economic stagnation and their dependence on the export of raw materials and the importation of manufactured goods is analyzed in detail by Halperin. He also emphasizes the interlocking of the factors responsible for stagnation; land tenure and utilization, basic industrialization, and external vulnerability are, he argues, aspects of the fundamental problem: the control of the Latin American economies themselves, as well as control of the terms and conditions of the export markets, resides with foreign economic interests.

Maurice Halperin is an economist residing in Moscow.

LATIN AMERICA is currently undergoing its third major economic crisis of the twentieth century. In general terms the present disturbance can be attributed to the excessive vulnerability to external factors of an economy dependent on the export of raw materials and the import of manufactured goods. In this sense it is the classic crisis of neocolonial underdevelopment such as occurred with the breakdown of international trade during the World War of 1914-18 (the first crisis) and the worldwide depression of the early 1930's (second crisis).

The present downturn assumed unmistakable crisis proportions at the beginning of 1958. Although in some respects it has

* Reprinted from *Science and Society*, Vol. XXV, No. 3 (Summer 1961), pp. 192-228, by permission.

thus far not attained the intensity of the second crisis, it has shown a stubborn persistency and a tendency to deepen as it drags on into its fourth year. At the same time, several aspects of the current crisis distinguish it from its predecessors and give it special significance.

In the first place, although like the previous crisis it was set in motion by external factors, it has been more sensitive to the downward swing and less sensitive to the upward swing in the cyclical movements of the industrialized capitalist economies. The decline in the price structure of Latin American exports preceded the 1957-58 recession in the United States, and the latter in turn led to a serious fall in Latin American export earnings. However, the downward trend continued after the recovery of the United States (prior to the new recession beginning in the latter part of 1960) and despite the continuing high level of economic activity in the principal industrial countries of Western Europe.

In the second place, there is little prospect that Latin America's normal markets can provide sufficient export earnings in the foreseeable future to restore the economy to previous levels. As the United Nations Economic Commission for Latin America (ECLA) states the matter after exhaustive long-range analysis (and excluding the factor of a major depression in the United States or Western Europe): "The perspective of export growth . . . is so limited that it barely exceeds probable demographic growth."[1] This envisages at best a rate that would be little more than half the rate registered prior to the present crisis, and consequently extraordinary pressures on the structural viability and growth mechanism of the economy.

In the third place, the general weakening of the world colonial and neocolonial system, coupled with the expanding economy of the world socialist system, provide new opportunities for coping with the habitual political and economic change-resisting pressure exerted on Latin America from abroad. Of particular importance is the availability of markets and other economic resources of the socialist countries that can be utilized in undertaking an effective solution of the region's economic crisis.

Hence, whereas the first and second Latin American crises

[1] *El Mercado Común Latinoamericano* (United Nations, 1959), p. 51. Apart from the ending of the postwar boom, other factors are production shifts, technological changes affecting consumption of natural raw materials, and various kinds of discrimination and competition by importers of Latin American products, the European Common Market, African competition, etc.

created the necessity and the conditions for limited economic and sociopolitical structural changes, *but within the framework of existing neocolonial dependency,* the present crisis appears to be developing under conditions that will both require and permit *the elimination of the dependency itself* in a relatively short period of time. The recent Cuban developments support this outlook, and we believe that the underlying factors responsible for the Cuban breakaway are not exceptional. The evidence can be found by examining the antecedents of the present crisis, i.e., the overall performance of the Latin American economy in the recent past.

For more than a decade after the end of the Second World War—broadly speaking from 1945-57—economic activity in Latin America taken as a whole sustained a greater rate of expansion over a longer period of time than the region had previously known.

To place this period in a proper frame of reference, two preliminary observations should be made. The first is that the base from which the upward movement began was relatively high for the region and significantly higher than the existing level of development in the dependent areas of Asia and Africa. Not only had a substantial recovery from the debacle of the early 1930's taken place, but also in the more advanced republics containing the bulk of the Latin American population and productive capacity, a large amount of import substitution had taken place. Thus by the end of 1945 the manufacturing industries, which prior to 1930 represented a small proportion of Latin American output, contributed almost 65 percent as much as agriculture to the gross product, and considerably more than the mining industries.

The second point to be noted is that exceptionally favorable external conditions prevailed during the period under consideration. The initial impetus for economic expansion was supplied by Latin America's accumulation of foreign exchange during World War II.[2] Rising trends, however, were primarily stimulated by the postwar expenditures for reconstruction, armaments, and the satisfaction of delayed demand in the leading capitalist countries. The termination of these special postwar adjustments in turn sharply restricted the external means by which Latin America could maintain its expansion, thereby setting the current crisis in motion.

[2] Between 1939 and 1945, holdings of gold and foreign assets increased five-fold, according to *Post-War Price Relations in Trade between Underdeveloped and Industrialized Countries* (United Nations, February 23, 1949), p. 114.

Viewed in this light, it becomes particularly interesting to evaluate the economic experience of this period. Given the relatively high takeoff level and the exceptional opportunities available, the growth achieved might well represent something close to the maximum performance that the Latin American economy, as it has traditionally functioned, could generate. Hence the extent to which this performance failed to satisfy the growth requirements of the region will permit us to estimate the true dimensions of the present crisis.

According to data compiled by ECLA (see table below), the cumulative annual average real increase of the region's gross product was 5 percent for the twelve-year period. If we exclude 1956 and 1957, during which the postwar boom began to taper off, the rate was 5.2 percent. For our purposes the difference is not significant: even the lesser rate matches or exceeds that of a number of industrialized countries of Western Europe, and exceeds that of the United States for the same period.

LATIN AMERICA:
GROSS PRODUCT AND OTHER DATA, 1945-57[3]
(billions of 1950 dollars)

Year	Gross Product	Consumption	Gross Fixed Investment	Export Goods Services	Import Goods Services	Population (millions)
1945	30.2	23.2	4.0	6.7	3.6	138.5
1946	32.8	25.1	5.0	7.4	4.8	141.6
1947	31.4	27.5	6.8	7.2	7.1	144.9
1948	36.4	28.7	6.8	7.5	6.6	148.2
1949	37.6	30.1	6.4	6.9	5.9	151.8
1950	39.8	32.1	6.6	7.2	6.1	155.4
1951	42.1	35.1	7.4	7.1	7.5	159.2
1952	43.0	35.5	7.6	6.7	7.0	163.0
1953	41.7	36.1	7.6	7.8	6.9	166.9
1954	47.3	39.1	8.2	7.7	7.8	170.9
1955	50.0	41.0	8.6	8.4	8.0	175.1
1956	51.4	41.4	9.1	9.2	8.2	179.4
1957	53.8	43.8	10.3	9.3	9.6	183.8

It is true that because the population of Latin America grew at an average annual rate of 2.5 percent the yearly per capita rate of increase was only 2.7 percent for the "golden decade," or 2.5 percent for the longer period. Nevertheless, even the latter figure is one-fifth greater than the "historic" per capita yearly rate of growth of 2 percent in the United States, though

[3] From *El Mercado Común Latinoamericano*, p. 46.

of course several times lower than that of the socialist countries.[4]

In addition, and more relevant, is the probability that 2.5 percent represents more than double the "historic" rate of increase in Latin America. Although there are insufficient data to establish the latter for the entire region, it is a fair assumption that from 1900 to 1929 no Latin American country exceeded the Argentine rate of increase, which has been estimated as averaging 1.2 percent per capita per year.[5] In the case of Mexico, for example, it is believed that between 1803 and 1934 there was practically no increase in per capita income.[6]

From the above evidence, the conclusion seems to be justified that, for the region considered as a single unit, the period we are dealing with was one of unusual expansion of economic activity, or more precisely, of the gross national product (GNP), a concept that in the official Latin American and United Nations usage includes both goods and services, and whose rate of increase is commonly defined as "growth."[7]

[4] Beginning with 1955 the annual per capita rate of growth in the United States has averaged about 1 percent. For further perspective on the Latin American rate, it is interesting to note that for the period under consideration it has been higher than in underdeveloped South Asia as a whole, but much lower than in the socialist countries of Eastern Europe where by the most conservative estimates per capita growth (material goods) has most certainly averaged over 7 percent annually in all countries and probably up to 10 percent in some: *Economic Survey of Europe 1956* (United Nations, 1957), Chapter II, p. 2. From 1957 to 1959, when growth in Latin America came to a standstill, "the average annual rate of growth amounted to 17 percent [15 percent per capita] for all the socialist countries. Soviet Union . . . 10.9 percent [over 9 percent per capita]," according to a report by N. S. Khrushchev, *Kommunist*, No. 1, January 1961, p. 10.

[5] *Análisis y Proyecciones del Desarrollo Económico*, V. *El Desarrollo Económico de la Argentina* (United Nations, 1959), Vol. I, p. 15. The rate of global expansion was 4.5 percent per annum, but immigration pushed up population increase to 3.2 percent yearly. High expansion rates, of course, occurred in various countries from time to time, but only for brief periods.

[6] Ifigenia M. de Navarrete, *La Distribución del Ingreso y el Desarrollo Económico de México* (Mexico, D. F., 1960), p. 11.

[7] The GNP at market prices is one of two most comprehensive measures of economic activity, the other being *national income*, which measures output expressed in terms of earnings derived from the GNP. ECLA, to which we are indebted for the bulk of our data, considers that for Latin America "the changes in the per capita gross product, expressed in a specific year's constant prices, is the most satisfactory and practical means of assessing the rate of economic growth." It defines "gross income" for the region as "equivalent to gross product . . . plus or minus the net gain or loss resulting from changes in the terms of trade," and hence less indicative of the "success of the productive effort": *Economic Bulletin for Latin America*, Vol. I, No. 2 (United Nations, September 1956), pp. 30-32. From 1945 to 1955 the average annual per capita increase of income was about 22 percent higher than that of the GNP; from 1955 to 1958 it was 50 percent lower.

Later we shall examine the reliability of this concept as a device for measuring economic growth in Latin America. For the moment, let us turn to the external factors that stimulated the high output of goods and services.

Foreign trade has invariably had a predominating influence upon the cyclical fluctuations of the Latin American economy. Thus in 1932, at the depth of the great depression, Latin American exports were reduced by 65 percent in comparison with 1929, while imports diminished by 75 percent.[8] However, a comparison between the level of foreign trade during this crisis year and the period with which we are dealing would provide a distorted picture of the foreign trade factor in the economic expansion of 1945-57. Hence the figures for 1934-38, when a fair amount of recovery had occurred, would provide a better base for comparison. During the latter period, average annual exports and imports combined amounted to 3,500 million dollars in round figures, or 5,250 million dollars in terms of 1950 dollars.[9]

If we turn back to our table, we can see that by 1947, when the postwar foreign trade upswing was in full momentum, total exports and imports were something over 14,000 million dollars (1950 dollars), or more than 170 percent above the annual average of 1934-38. In addition, from 1945-55 the purchasing power of Latin American exports had increased at an average annual rate of 5.4 percent, or slightly more than the rate of increase of the GNP.[10] Clearly better times had come to Latin America.

However, further analysis is necessary in assessing the role of foreign trade in the region's post-World War II economic experience. If we go back to the predepression and relatively preindustrial period of 1925-29, we find that the importer coefficient, i.e., the value of imports calculated as a percentage of the GNP, stood at 30.2. In the corresponding four-year period of the following decade, when Latin America's foreign trade had pulled out of the depression, the import coefficient failed to regain its previous magnitude, registering only 16.6. This new and, from the point of view of economic develop-

[8] *Economic Survey of Latin America 1948* (United Nations, 1949), p. 190.

[9] *Study of Inter-American Trade* (United Nations, 1957), pp. 19, 22; dollar adjustments according to *Statistical Abstracts of the United States*, (Washington, 1959), p. 329.

[10] *El Mercado Común Latinoamericano*, p. 47.

ment, improved relationship between the GNP and foreign trade reflected the progress achieved in the domestic production of current consumer goods, especially in the more advanced countries such as Argentina, Brazil, Mexico, and Chile.

When imports were again drastically cut during World War II, a further impetus was provided for the expansion of industry. As a result, when the postwar period opened, the structure of the economy was such that despite the extraordinary improvement in foreign trade compared with the postdepression recovery of the 1930's, the relationship between the GNP and imports did not return to the level of 1925-29. Instead, as the figures in our table indicate, imports fluctuated around 16 percent of the GNP thereby maintaining the same relative level as in 1935-39.

At first glance, this would seem to indicate a diminished role for foreign trade in providing the means for the recent expansion of economic activity in Latin America. However, further examination of this matter shows that just the opposite is true .The most striking evidence relates to the acquisition of machinery and equipment with which to produce expanding raw material exports as well as the growing output of the manufacturing industries. In this obviously strategic sector of investment (about 25 percent of the total), domestic production provided less than 10 percent of the goods obtained. The rest was purchased abroad and consumed close to 33 percent of the value of total imports.

It thus becomes clear that the change in the composition of Latin American imports became a new and crucial factor perpetuating the region's dependency on foreign trade. Before 1914, for example, textiles alone accounted for more than half of its imports.[11] During the 1930's, although a notable increase took place in the proportion of durable and capital goods, the bulk of goods was still composed of consumer and construction materials. However, after 1945 the balance definitely shifted. If to machinery and equipment we add intermediary goods and industrial raw materials—such as various types of steel, chemical, rubber, etc.—and fuel, we find that by 1955 about two-thirds of the region's total imports consisted of the means of production and supplies for production.[12] In short, Latin America's exports, which basically determined its ca-

[11] *Economic Survey of Latin America 1948*, p. 45.
[12] *Ibid.*, p. 58.

pacity to import, were unquestionably the decisive element promoting the economic expansion of 1945-57.[13]

The uniqueness of the favorable external situation affecting economic activity during this period requires some additional comments if it is to be fully understood. Latin America's vastly increased capacity to import was not only due to the exceptional postwar demand for its exports, but also to another and even rarer (though associated) phenomenon.

In common with all other dependent regions, Latin America's international trade has been adversely affected by the historic trend of an ever-increasing gap between the slowly rising prices of its raw material exports and the more rapidly increasing costs of the manufactured goods that it imports. As a result, although with considerable fluctuations from year to year and country to country depending on the types of commodities exported and the changing structure of imports, for the region as a whole its terms of trade over the long run have been deteriorating.[14]

However, an extraordinary reversal of this trend took place for Latin America as a whole, and for all but two of the republics considered separately (Argentina and Cuba) in the decade following World War II. In eight of the republics, including Brazil, Colombia, and Chile, terms of trade between 1947-49 and 1954-56 improved from 45 to more than 100 percent.[15] As a result, more than half of the increased purchasing power of Latin American exports previously mentioned was due to the terms of trade effect, with the rest accounted for by an increase in export volume.[16]

[13] Imports are also financed by foreign investments and loans, but even during a given period when the inflow of foreign capital may temporarily exceed outflow (in the form of profits, interest, and amortization), the resulting foreign exchange assets represent only a fraction of foreign exchange accumulated through export earnings. Thus in the three-year period 1954-56, when the postwar inflow of foreign capital into Latin America reached its highest level, the net inflow (approximately 2,000 million dollars) was 8 percent of the value of total exports (24,000 million dollars in round figures).

[14] ". . . from the latter part of the 19th century to the eve of the Second World War . . . on the average, a given quantity of primary goods exported would pay, at the end of this period, for only 60 percent of the quantity of manufactured goods that it could bring at the beginning of the period" (*Post-War Price Relations*, etc., p. 6).

[15] *Economic Survey of Latin America 1957* (United Nations, 1959), p. 72 (table 69).

[16] *El Mercado Común Latinoamericano*, p. 47. In the primary exporting countries of South East Asia taken as a whole, average terms of trade improved only slightly from 1948 to 1954, after which a deteriorating trend set in: *Economic Survey of Asia and the Far East 1959* (United Nations, 1960), p. 63.

It would take us beyond the scope of the present discussion to examine in detail the fluctuations and the complexity of the factors that affected the evolution of prices of the main exports and imports of the region. In the case of coffee, for example, a leading export item for more than a third of the republics, a temporary but sharp decline of Brazilian production due to adverse weather conditions boosted prices and stimulated a wave of speculative buying. With respect to imports, the shift from consumer to capital goods played a role since prices of the latter tended to rise more slowly than the former.[17] In addition, prices of West European manufacturers tended to decline for a period because of the devaluation of the pound sterling and other currencies, and a certain shift to European sources of supply took place in some countries.

However, the main factor in the terms of trade improvement was the upward price movement of Latin American exports, for which the underlying reason was the unusual demand created by the postwar situation to which we have already referred. Thus special circumstances, rather than basic economic forces, were responsible for the shift in the terms of trade and for sustaining the trend for so long a period of time. When these circumstances vanished, the historic downward trend reasserted itself[18] and the period of maximum perform-

[17] The price level of capital goods very likely reflects the fact that a considerable quantity of these imports took place on behalf of foreign enterprises operating in Latin America. "Prices in intracompany dealings are not genuine market prices; consigner and receiver have no opposing interests. The only effect of the charges made to subsidiaries operating abroad for equipment . . . shipped to them is of an accounting nature; profits are shifted between the home company and its subsidiary abroad. . . . Where the balance of advantage lies depends on . . . relative rates of profit, taxation," import duties, etc. (*Post-War Price Relations*, etc., p. 126). Since the operations of foreign subsidiaries or branches in Latin America are statistically integrated in the overall economic performance of the region, in this sense their manipulations of import prices do not alter the significance of the changing terms of trade. On the other hand, it cannot be excluded that in some of the republics the improvement in the terms of trade benefited foreign investors rather than national enterprises. Cf. *ibid.*, p. 111.

[18] The following indices, weighted for the region as a whole, show the evolution of export and import prices and the terms of trade (obtained by dividing export by import price indices) from 1955 to 1959:

| | 1953 = 100 | | | | |
	1955	1956	1957	1958	1959
Export	101	102	101	95	90 (Oct.)
Import	100	104	107	106	107 (Sept.)
Terms of trade	101	98	94	90	84

Source: *International Financial Statistics*, International Monetary Fund, March 1960, pp. 38-39.

ance came to an end. In 1958 the per capita increase of the GNP was only 0.5 percent, declining to 0.3 percent in 1959 and probably to a somewhat lower level in 1960.[19]

Returning now to the performance itself, we recall that for Latin America as a whole the average annual per capita rate of growth of the GNP was 2.7 percent for the decade following the war and 2.5 percent for the twelve-year period. As for the individual republics, the great majority shared in this expansion to a greater or lesser degree and relatively little change in the comparative levels of their respective per capita GNP's took place. Trends in some of the more important countries, however, should be examined.

Mexico's rate of growth, although it slowed down after 1950, over the twelve-year period was approximately that of the region taken as a whole. By 1957 Mexico's per capita GNP reached 280 dollars, which was still less than the 335-dollar level registered in that year by Latin America taken as a whole.[20]

The Brazilian performance was distinctly better than average, with a yearly per capita increase of close to 3.5 percent. As a result, during the twelve years the relatively low Brazilian per capita GNP improved sufficiently, so that by 1957 it was roughly equal to that of Mexico. The Brazilian phenomenon in part reflects the especially favorable situation of the coffee exporters. Thus the per capita growth of the Central American coffee producers and of Colombia was higher than the average for Latin America. The latter republic, for example, showed an annual per capita increase of approximately 3 percent from 1945-57.

In the case of Argentina, there was a considerable deviation from the average regional growth record. Although from 1945-48 an extraordinary annual per capita increase of 6.4 percent took place, for the twelve-year period per capita growth averaged only 1 percent. A significant factor in the post-1948 decline was the unfavorable situation of Argentine meat and grain exports. As a result, a steady deterioration in the terms

[19] For 1958, *Economic Survey of Latin America 1958* (United Nations, 1959), p. 71; for 1959, ECLA calculation reported in *Excelsior*, Mexico, D. F., July 5, 1960; for 1960, preliminary estimates from the "South America Economic Review" and "Caribbean Area Economic Review," *New York Times*, January 1961.

[20] Unless otherwise indicated, individual country data are taken or computed from the annual editions of the United Nations *Economic Survey of Latin America*. GNP figures converted by the latter into 1950 dollars have been reconverted into 1957 dollars (an increase of 14 percent). All percentage increase or decline of the GNP is calculated on the basis of dollars of constant value.

of trade took place—an exceptional trend for Latin America (shared only by Cuba) as we have already indicated. Nevertheless, with a per capita GNP of 525 dollars in 1957, the Argentine level remained well above the Latin American average and second in magnitude only to that of Venezuela, a country to be dealt with at a later stage of our discussion.[21]

The Chilean deviation from the regional norm was even greater than that of Argentina. From 1945-55 the per capita GNP remained practically stationary, while in the following two years it dropped by about 8 percent. Actually, beginning with 1953 the rate of growth failed to keep up with the increase of population. Thus the Chilean per capita GNP, which stood well above the Latin American average in 1945, fell below 300 dollars in 1957.

The Chilean experience is also exceptional from another point of view; the country's economy stagnated even though it enjoyed a substantial improvement in the terms of trade. This phenomenon partly reflects the failure of the post-World War II gains to recover the ground lost after the copper debacle of the depression of the 1930's, but even more the unproductive dissipation of resources acquired during the postwar boom.[22]

Finally, Cuba—hard hit by the sugar slump following the end of the Korean war and despite the recovery in 1956-57—also failed over the twelve-year period to increase its per capita GNP. The latter, at 485 dollars in 1957, still remained considerably above the Latin American average.

Thus the exceedingly slow growth of Argentina and the stagnation of Chile and Cuba (together accounting for about 17 percent of the Latin American population) clearly represent uncommon trends, and their exceptional status must be noted.[23] Nevertheless, for purposes of global generalization this should not seriously detract from whatever meaning may be attributed to the official calculations of growth in Latin America as a whole.

[21] In addition to Argentina and Venezuela, 1957 per capita GNP's above the regional mean are attributed to Uruguay, Cuba, Costa Rica, and Panama.

[22] See also footnote 17, above.

[23] For the most backward countries, like Haiti, Bolivia, and Paraguay (aggregate population less than 5 percent of the Latin American total) statistical gaps and irregularities make it extremely difficult even to guess the size of the per capita GNP. In Bolivia, e. g., there was no census between 1900 and 1950. According to the latter, Bolivia's per capita GNP was estimated at slightly over 80 dollars. It probably declined somewhat during the next seven years. Cf. *Análisis y Proyecciones del Desarrollo Económico*, IV. *El Desarrollo Económico de Bolivia* (United Nations, 1956), p. 17.

The question now arises: what *is* the meaning of these calculations? How much and what kind of growth was achieved by this historically maximum performance of the Latin American economy? Let us begin by accepting at its face value the 2.5 percent average yearly per capita increase of the region's collective GNP. In 1957, as we have seen, the GNP reached an all-time high of 335 dollars. If and when Latin America could recover and maintain uninterruptedly its 1945-57 rate of growth, from the moment of recovery it would take it about 55 years to reach the 1957 French or United Kingdom per capita GNP of 1,300 dollars. To attain the 2,600 dollars per capita GNP of the United States in 1957, would require close to 85 years.

If we consider the hypothetical prospects of some of the Latin American republics separately, the outlook would be scarcely more encouraging. Although Brazil with its 3.5 percent rate of per capita increase would do better than the average, pulling up to 1957 levels in 45 and 65 years respectively, Argentina—with its lower than average growth rate and despite its much higher base—would require over 90 years to approximate the 1957 British and French GNP and 160 to equal that of the United States. For about half of the republics, with a GNP under 200 dollars and moving at the 2.5 percent rate, the lapse of time on the average would be 80 and 110 years respectively.

Meanwhile, another aspect of the "catching up" process must be kept in mind. While in 1940 the Latin American per capita GNP was one sixth of that of the United States, in 1957 the proportion had dropped to one-eighth. In the case of Argentina, the decline was from approximately one-half to one-fifth of the United States level.

Thus, from the point of view of meeting Latin American growth requirements, it would appear that the acceleration of economic activity that the region as a whole experienced from 1945-57 leaves something to be desired. Even if the rate of increase of this period could be revived—which is the maximum goal proposed by the economic specialists of ECLA[24]—

[24] In proposing the Latin American Common Market as an urgent solution to the post-1957 development problems of the region, growth is projected to 1975 on the basis of two alternative rates of annual per capita GNP increase: 2 percent and 2.75 percent. These rates, as well as the role assigned to the Common Market (if and when it materializes), in promoting growth seem to be thoroughly unrealistic. *Cf. El Mercado Común Latinoamericano, passim.*

for a people of whom the vast majority cannot satisfy the minimum necessities of food, clothing, and shelter, to say nothing of the elementary necessities of civilized living, the hypothetical prospect in even the most favorable instance of delaying for nearly half a century the achievement of a standard of living implied by a GNP only 50 percent of the current United States GNP could hardly be accepted with equanimity.

So much for the face value of the growth achievement registered during this twelve-year period. However, the real implications to be drawn from this maximum performance are far more discouraging. The reason is that the conventional device for measuring the overall Latin American economic performance is extremely deceptive. It greatly exaggerates both the operative level of development vis-à-vis the highly industrialized countries and the real growth achievement in purely regional terms. Let us now consider the two aspects of the deception in that order.

Many economists concerned with the problems of underdevelopment readily admit that a comparison of the magnitudes of the GNP of a backward and an industrialized country is a rough measurement of the relative levels of their respective economies. However, they rarely take the trouble to examine how rough this measurement is. Consequently, they fail to see that the real gap that separates them is significantly greater than the GNP statistics would indicate.

For example, in 1955 the United States per capita GNP was eight times greater than that of Latin America, but the per capita consumption of steel in the United States—a basic indicator of the level of economic development—was sixteen times greater.[25] A similar discrepancy is revealed comparing Latin America with other developed countries: the per capita GNP of the United Kingdom was four times higher while per capita consumption of steel was nine times higher. In France the respective amounts were four and seven, and in Austria two and five.[26] Other significant criteria of economic development, such as per capita consumption of energy or copper,

[25] The gap would be considerably greater if per capita production figures were compared. In 1955-56 Latin American output of steel was less than 40 percent of consumption. Since 1950 consumption has steadily increased at a faster rate than production: *Economic Survey of Latin America 1958* (United Nations, 1959), p. 81.

[26] *El Mercado Común Latinoamericano*, p. 62. Per capita GNP of all countries adjusted to 1955 dollars where necessary.

more or less coincide with that of steel consumption.[27]

Certain economists who overlook this aspect of comparability prefer another approach to the question. They maintain that the conversion of monetary units of underdeveloped countries into dollars exaggerates the real gap between the levels of the backward and advanced economies. "The per capita income [product] figures of the poor countries, when stated in dollars, are too low; this helps explain why people remain alive with a 50-dollar per capita income per year. . . ."[28] It is undoubtedly true that the 50-dollars per year individual has lower rent, food, and clothing costs, but the reason is that he is probably a squatter in a homemade shack without sanitation, is undernourished, goes barefoot and his only clothing are the tatters on his back. As a matter of fact, he "remains alive" for a relatively short period of time, since his life expectancy would be less than half that of the average inhabitant of the United States.

Comparability of the Latin American GNP data and those of the developed countries is also materially affected by the foreign investment factor. Venezuelan statistics illustrate this point rather well. As W. W. Rostow puts it dryly: "Venezuela has been for some time an 'enclave economy,' with a high investment-rate concentrated in a modern export sector whose growth did not generate economic momentum in the Venezuelan economy."[29] Let us examine this situation a little more closely.

According to the available published data, in 1957 the mining sector—which for practical purposes is synonymous with foreign owned and extracted petroleum—accounted for 34 percent of the Venezuelan GNP. The real proportion is probably even greater, but it is difficult to establish how much of what is included under construction, transportation, communications, and "all others" is a part of petroleum operations. A further indication of the significance of petroleum is the fact that agriculture and manufacturing represent 7 and 11 percent

[27] During 1955-57 average annual per capita consumption of copper in Latin America was 0.4 kilograms; the comparative figure for the United States was 7.0; for the United Kingdom, 9.0; for France, 4.3 and Austria, 3.5 (*ibid.*). Per capita consumption of energy (million metric tons of coal equivalent, rounded) was as follows: Latin America, 600; Austria, 1,900; France, 2,400; United Kingdom, 4,700; and the United States, 7,600 (*United Nations Statistical Yearbook 1959*, pp. 306 ff).

[28] *Worldwide and Domestic Economic Problems and Their Impact on the Foreign Policy of the United States*, Committee on Foreign Relations, United States Senate, August 1959, p. 24.

[29] *The Stages of Economic Growth: A Non-Communist Manifesto* (Cambridge, 1960), p. 44.

respectively in the Venezuelan GNP.[30] At the same time, the petroleum companies employ less than 2 percent of the country's active labor force.

Venezuelan statistics of economic growth are most impressive. From 1945-57 the per capita rate of increase of the GNP was 4.5 percent, by far the highest in Latin America. In 1957 the per capita GNP in Venezuela was approximately 1,000 dollars—three times that of Latin America as a whole (including Venezuela), twice that of Argentina with by far the most developed economy in the region, and substantially higher than that of Italy. Venezuela's per capita consumption of steel was more than six times greater than the average for Latin America as a whole, and approximately equal to that of Switzerland. In 1958 its per capita consumption of energy was somewhat greater than that of France.[31]

These figures, of course, reflect the activities of the United States and Anglo-Dutch petroleum companies operating in Venezuela, but they tell us next to nothing about the national economy properly speaking. Harvey O'Connor describes some of the realities of this economy:

Before oil, Venezuela fed itself, somehow. Today it produces only half the corn, half the meat, one-third of the green vegetables and grains, and half the milk it consumes. There are fewer cattle than at the time of the Revolution of 1812. . . . As unreal as anything out of Hollywood is the fantastic prosperity that has descended upon Caracas. . . . All this, of course, is merely a matter of wonderment for nine-tenths of the people, who live outside the charmed world of oil. Disease-ridden and hunger-wracked . . . at least 200,000 have fled the countryside for gilded Caracas, where they live under the bridges, along the gullies, or far up the mountainside in ironically named "ranchos" built of the city's refuse.[32]

As a matter of fact, the Venezuelan "enclave economy" seriously distorts the meaning of a number of growth statistics for Latin America as a whole. For example, during the five-year period 1953-57 the foreign companies operating in Venezuela were responsible for approximately 23 percent of total Latin American exports. For the year 1957 the figure was close to 28 percent.[33] With respect to GNP calculations, if Venezuela, with a little over 3 percent of the total Latin American

[30] *United Nations Statistical Yearbook 1959*, pp. 450 ff.
[31] Figures from the annual editions of the United Nations *Economic Survey of Latin America*, and sources in footnotes 26, 27 above.
[32] *The Empire of Oil* (New York, 1955), pp. 266-67.
[33] *Economic Survey of Latin America 1957*, p. 48.

population, is removed from the picture during the seven-year period of 1950-57, the annual average per capita rate of growth of the Latin American GNP is reduced by nearly a quarter.[34]

Venezuela is not the only "enclave economy" in Latin America, although it is the most spectacular. Banana-dominated Honduras, where two foreign corporations, as Robert Alexander describes it, "command what are virtually states within a state,"[35] is another and, to a significant degree, so was prerevolutionary Cuba, where, according to a public statement by a recent United States Ambassador to Cuba, ". . . until the advent of Castro . . . the American Ambassador was the second most important man in Cuba; sometimes even more important than the President."[35a] In fact, there are practically no Latin American republics lacking a foreign-owned "modern export sector," some of which constitute smaller and others larger "economic enclaves" whose contributions to economic income and growth "more properly belong to the economies of the countries in which the companies are domiciled" than to those of the countries in which they operate.[36]

A few facts and figures will indicate to some extent the padding with which these "enclave economies" inflate the real performance of the Latin American national economies. In 1957, for example, United States direct investment enterprises (probably representing about 85 percent of total foreign direct investments) accounted for approximately 8 billion dollars of Latin America's gross production,[37] or more than 13 percent of its 1957 GNP and undoubtedly considerably more of its material output. These enterprises shipped goods out of Latin America valued at close to 3 billion dollars,[38] or nearly half of all goods exported from Latin America (excluding intraregional trade), and about 80 percent of the region's exports to the United States.[39]

These figures in turn point to a serious distortion of the real earnings of the national economies as a result of the various kinds of profits extracted by the foreign investment operations. Many of these are difficult to track down, but we can

[34] *Ibid.*, p. 3.
[35] Cited by Preston James, *Latin America* (New York, 1959), p. 690.
[35a] Earl E. T. Smith, cited in *Monthly Review*, December 1960, p. 432.
[36] Cited from a 1951 ECLA publication on Venezuela by Paul Baran, *The Political Economy of Growth* (New York, 1957), p. 193.
[37] *Survey of Current Business*, United States Department of Commerce, September 1960, p. 22.
[38] *Ibid.*
[39] Total exports of goods in 1957 were 7,918 million dollars (*Economic Survey of Latin America 1958*, p. 37); total exports to the United States were 3,765 dollars (*ibid.*, p. 15).

form some idea of their importance if we consider only published remittances of profits and interest. For example, this outflow (excluding amortization) amounted to 3,625 million dollars during 1955-57, a seemingly negligible proportion of the GNP. However, since it was an outflow of foreign exchange, it absorbed 14 percent of total export earnings during this three-year period. Furthermore, the rate of absorption steadily increased after the early postwar years, when it averaged about 10 percent. In absolute terms, the outflow nearly doubled from 1947 to 1957.[40]

In view of the decisive role that the capacity to import plays in the Latin American economy, and especially in acquiring the means of production, this shrinkage of economic assets is not as small as it appears to be. In 1957 it was the equivalent of approximately 70 percent of the cost of all industrial machinery imported during the year, hence only a little under 70 percent of the year's total investment in this key sector.[41]

Turning now to the second aspect of the disparity between the apparent and real growth achievement of what we have described as the maximum performance of the Latin American economy, we recall that the concept of the GNP officially employed to measure growth combined both goods and services. Whether or not it is a valid concept in the case of a highly industrialized country like the United States, it is unquestionably and grossly misleading when applied to an underdeveloped economy.

By very definition, such an economy is primarily and basically deficient in production, that is, both in productive capacity and the actual output of industrial and agricultural goods that in the aggregate determine the physical capability of a country to maintain a given standard of living. For an underdeveloped economy, only the production of material goods can have any relevance to growth. Certainly, for a region such as Latin America, an increase in the number of beauty parlors or nightclubs or the size of the police force or other activities that come under the heading of services, whatever their contribution to the joy or sorrow of one or another segment of the population

---

[40] *Economic Survey of Latin America 1957*, p. 66. For a given country in a given year, the loss could be proportionately much greater, as in the case of Ecuador, e. g., where in 1957 the outflow was more than 20 percent of export earnings (*ibid.*, p. 76).

[41] Gross remittances of profits and interest were 1,345 million dollars (*ibid.*, p. 66); imports of industrial machinery estimated at 1,940 million dollars (*Economic Survey of Latin America 1958*, p. 52); investment percentage assumed to be approximately that of 1954-56, as calculated in *El Mercado Común Latinoamericano*, p. 60.

may be, cannot represent economic growth. Indeed, as Paul Baran suggests with respect to "most countries," and we include Latin America under that heading, the reverse is undoubtedly true. Services absorb capital and other resources desperately needed for production and hence retard economic growth.[42]

The extent to which services inflate Latin America's GNP is revealed by an examination of its components. In 1956-57 their respective proportions of the total (in rounded percentages) were as follows:[43]

Agriculture	23.5	
Industry	20.0	
Construction	3.5	
Mining	5.0	
(*subtotal for production*)		52.0
Trade and Finance	17.0	
Other Services	15.0	
Government	7.5	
(*subtotal for services*)		39.5
Transportation and Communications	8.5	8.5
	100.0	100.0

Thus, in round figures, slightly over 50 percent of the Latin American GNP is clearly accounted for by the production of material goods, and roughly 40 percent by services. The remainder, "Transportation and Communications," is composed of both and cannot be classified without a further breakdown. However, for our purpose a more precise estimate is not required. It is sufficient to note that services very likely comprise not far from one-half of the region's GNP. Furthermore, for the region as a whole and most of the republics taken separately, during 1945-57 little change took place in the ratio of services to production in the GNP.[44] Per capita services in-

[42] *The Political Economy of Growth, op. cit.*, p. 19. Baran also cites the following useful remark from the United Nations *Economic Survey of Europe Since the War, 1953*, p. 25: "In the eastern European countries services not directly connected with the production and transport of goods are not regarded as productive and their value is thus excluded from national income [product]. For a poor country that is trying to develop its industry and to reduce the underemployment common in service trades, the Marxist definition of national income [product] has some obvious advantages over the more inclusive concept suited to wealthy industrialized economies and now commonly adopted in underdeveloped countries."

[43] *Economic Survey of Latin America 1957*, p. 85.

[44] *Ibid.*, and *Economic Survey of Latin America 1955* (United Nations, 1956), p. 9.

creased at an average annual rate practically identical with that of the GNP. Consequently nearly one-half of the economic expansion of 1945-47 contributed neither to Latin American growth nor to capacity for growth.

Turning now to the output of material goods, it follows that in the aggregate they also increased at approximately the same rate as the GNP. Hence it may be argued that even though the latter greatly exaggerates the extent of real growth in *absolute* terms, in this instance it accurately indicates the *relative* gains in material production and hence is a reasonable measurement of the *rate of real growth*. Nevertheless, not only does it remain a thoroughly unsatisfactory rate, as we have already seen, but the dimensions of its inadequacy are considerably greater than they appear to be at first glance.

The reason is that the evaluation of the GNP in Latin America, and in underdeveloped regions in general, is further complicated by the uneven behavior of the main sectors of production and by special *qualitative* considerations. Not only *how much* but also *what kind* of production is a basic question in dealing with the growth process of a weak and distorted economy. For example, an increase in output that reflects the expansion of monoculture or foreign exploitation of natural resources or the manufacture of luxury goods for domestic consumption would invariably be counted as a contribution to economic growth in the statistical compilations. However, in terms of the only kind of growth that makes sense for an underdeveloped country, the principal connotations of such an increase would very likely be unfavorable. For this reason, we must examine a few salient aspects of growth in the main production sectors of the GNP.

The average yearly per capita increase of agricultural production in Latin America from 1945-57 was only 1.5 percent. The key indicator of growth in this sector would be the output of foodstuffs for domestic consumption, but the latter increased at an even lower rate than export crops. In any case, the overall rate of 1.5 percent was not sufficient to maintain the pre-World War II per capita level of output, either for agriculture as a whole or foodstuffs considered separately. The per capita decline in production was substantial during most of the period. Only in 1956/57, the best year of the period, did the level approach that of 1933/34 to 1937/38.[45]

[45] *Economic Survey of Latin America 1957, op. cit.,* p. 85. Since 1957 per capita production has again fallen.

For a region where, as Preston James puts it bluntly, "we can report that a very large proportion of the people are suffering from hunger,"[46] this record obviously does not represent growth in any sense of the term. It is rather a statement of the aggravation of a permanent crisis rooted in the familiar and deeply entrenched system of feudal and neofeudal land monopoly. All available data point to the continued, and probably increasing, concentration of land ownership in recent decades. A study by Moacyr Paixao shows that in Brazil slightly over 3 percent of landowners are in possession of 62 percent of the arable land, while 85 percent of the peasantry owns less than 17 percent of the land.[47] The situation in Cuba prior to 1959 was comparable: less than 1.5 percent of agricultural enterprises owned 47 percent of the farmlands, while nearly 70 percent of the farms occupied a little over 11 percent of the land.[48]

Even in Mexico, where an extensive but only partially effective agrarian reform had taken place prior to 1940, after this year a new process of land concentration began. According to Luis Yáñez-Pérez, by 1960 some 50 percent of farm lands were in the possession of 13 percent of the farmers, while 708 large operators accounted for 35 percent of the total farm income of the republic.[49] By 1955, according to a semiofficial Mexican estimate, the private farm sector, as contrasted to the communal sector created by the agrarian reform, had expanded to such an extent that it "very likely was larger than that of the private holdings in 1930,"[50] that is, before the bulk of land redistribution under the agrarian reform had taken place. The fact that many of the new large holdings are relatively efficient capitalist enterprises does not alter the significance of the "counterreform," since they are almost exclusively engaged in producing export crops, employ far less workers than could otherwise secure a living from the land and hence retard desperately needed food production for domestic consumption and aggravate the increasingly serious agricultural unemployment.

For Latin America as a whole, Otto Feinstein conservatively

[46] *Op. cit.*, p. 870.
[47] "Elementos da Questão Agrária," *Revista Brasiliense*, No. 24, 1959, pp. 38 ff.
[48] *Report on Cuba*, International Bank for Reconstruction and Development (Baltimore, 1951), p. 88.
[49] *Mecanización de la Agricultura Mexicana* (Mexico, D. F., 1957), pp. 108, 375.
[50] *La Agricultura* (Mexico-Buenos Aires, 1957), p. 77.

sums up the current status of land tenure and utilization as follows:

"The distribution of land is such that an infinitesimal proportion of those classified as legal owners of land own the vast majority of land. Less than 5 percent of the landowners usually own more than 50 percent of the land. This not only means concentration of land into large estates, usually incapable of financing modernization, but that nearly all other landowners really own small holdings usually too small for rational production."[51]

To this we need only add that without an agrarian revolution, not merely reform, that would make possible the assimilation of twentieth-century technology in agricultural production, any performance of the Latin American economy, maximum or otherwise, is inherently incapable of meeting the growth problems of the region.

Although the stagnation of agriculture, and in particular that of food staples, considerably reduces the significance of the over-all increase in output of material goods, the fact that industrial (manufacturing) production rose at an average annual rate of 3.2 percent per capita, or more than double that of agriculture, provides some substance, both quantitatively and qualitatively, to the achievement of material growth during this period.[52] One result is the shift that took place in the sectoral distribution of the Latin American GNP. In 1945 manufacturing and construction accounted for 17 percent and agriculture 26 percent of the GNP, whereas by 1957, as we have noted, the share of manufacturing and construction jointly equaled that of agriculture, each representing 23.5 percent.[53]

[51] "A Changing Latin America and U. S. Foreign Policy," *New University Thought*, Spring 1960, p. 56.
[52] The mining sector (almost exclusively a foreign operation) registered an even greater increase than manufacturing, but this was due almost entirely to the extraction of crude petroleum in Venezuela. Excluding petroleum, average per capita increase would be less than the increase for the GNP as a whole (*Economic Bulletin for Latin America*, ECLA, Santiago, Chile, Vol. IV, No. 1, March 1959, p. 49). Including petroleum, the share of mining in the Latin American GNP rose from approximately 3.5 percent in 1945 to 5 percent in 1957.
[53] For purposes of comparison it is interesting to note that during roughly the same period in the less developed countries of the socialist bloc the proportion of the GNP (material goods) represented by industrial output generally increased more rapidly and reached higher levels. By 1958-59, it rose from 40.5 to 66.6 percent in Rumania; 24.8 to 70.6 percent in Bulgaria; 9.8 to 55.7 percent in Albania; 28 to 71 percent in the Korean People's Democratic Republic; 10 to 37.1 percent in the Democratic Republic of Vietnam (*New York Times*, English edition, No. 51, 1960, p. 6).

If we consider the countries separately, we find that the relative increase in the manufacturing sector was generally more pronounced in the less industrialized republics, though at the same time, at the end of the period, agriculture in these countries still retained its dominant position. Thus in Colombia, for example, where the agricultural sector dropped from 45 to 31 percent of the GNP, this proportion still outweighed manufacturing by a large margin. The pattern in Brazil, an exception in this respect among the four leading industrial producers, was similar to that of Colombia, with the agricultural sector still in the lead in 1957. As for Argentina, Chile, and Mexico, where manufacturing had already surpassed agriculture by a small margin in 1945, actually very little subsequent change in the respective weight of these sectors took place.[54]

While for the underdeveloped economies of Latin America considered in the aggregate, the relative industrialization indicated by the shift in these two sectors of the GNP has some positive growth implications, the degree of industrial growth achieved is overstated by many of the statistical generalizations. For example, we find that a significant proportion of what is classified as industrial activity—even in the most developed republics—remains technically on the level of the operations of a village blacksmith shop.

The situation in Peru, for which recent and fairly extensive data are available, can be considered quite typical for most of Latin America. From the point of view of the general level of industrial development, Peru ranks somewhat above the middle among the twenty republics, and its GNP and industrial growth record conforms fairly closely to the average for the region. Peru, in addition, boasts of a modern integrated iron and steel mill. In 1955 slightly over 80 percent of the employed manufacturing (including artisan) labor force worked in shóps that it can be safely assumed averaged less than 14 operatives each, and probably as little as half that number, and produced 40 percent of the country's manufactured goods. For Peru it is difficult to speak of serious industrial achievement for still another reason: from 1945-55 there was a *decline* of the relative share of domestic industry in the total supplies of manufactured goods.[55]

If we turn now to Latin America's increase in the output of

[54] *Economic Bulletin for Latin America*, Vol. III, No. 2, October 1958, pp. 46-47.
[55] *Analyses and Projections of Economic Development:* VI. *The Industrial Development of Peru* (United Nations, 1959), pp. 9, 41, 53.

capital goods,[56] it appears to have been more substantial than it actually was, partly because of the low base from which it is measured. In view of the complexity of industrial production and differences in terminology and other statistical criteria used by the various republics, it is difficult to determine the relationship between capital and consumer goods production, a matter of some interest in evaluating the level of industrial maturity. However, we can get some approximation from a United Nations estimate of 1954. According to this estimate based on data from six countries—Argentina, Brazil, Colombia, Chile, Mexico, and Venezuela—representing the bulk of Latin American industrial activity, "capital goods industries . . . represent no more than 15 percent of the total Latin American manufacturing industry."[57] This percentage was probably higher in 1957 but not appreciably so.

At the same time, a considerable nonproductive dissipation of capital goods output limits its significance as an indicator of basic economic development. From 1945 to 1957—for the region as a whole and practically all countries separately— more than half of the fixed capital investments consistently went into "building and construction," the major portion of which was concentrated in "dwellings," which in Latin America is overwhelmingly luxury housing, an important commodity in the highly lucrative urban real estate speculations.[58]

Among the industrially most active republics much attention has been focused on Brazil, and with a certain amount of justification. In Brazil the quantum of output of steel ingots quintupled in ten years and the value of production of capital goods rose nearly three times faster than that of consumer goods. However, viewing the industrial economy as a whole, we find that the resulting structural changes have not been as spectacular as these developments appear to indicate.

Although the value of capital goods production rose from about one-quarter to one-third of total manufacturing output in less than a decade, this achievement is seriously undermined by the fact that by 1957 output of machinery accounted for

[56] From 1948 to 1959, textiles and foodstuffs-beverages-tobacco jointly increased about 45 percent, while basic metals and chemicals each advanced more than 80 percent. Production of steel ingots, sulphuric acid, sodium alkalis, and cement each more than doubled between 1950 and 1957. (*Economic Bulletin for Latin America*, Vol. IV, No. 1, March 1959, pp. 51, 54.)

[57] *Estudio Económico de América Latina 1954* (United Nations, 1955), p. 99.

[58] *Economic Bulletin for Latin America*, Vol. III, No. 2, October 1958, pp. 48-49.

less than 3 percent of the total value of manufacturing.[59] Operating in an economy plagued by long-standing and acute power and transport deficiencies (a characteristic of practically all Latin America), lacking reproductive capacity, producing exclusively for the domestic market, and depending on earnings of coffee exports and on direct foreign investments for capital equipment and various industrial raw materials, Brazilian industry has increased the vulnerability of the economy to external factors without providing the means for basic industrialization.

Argentine industry, traditionally the strongest in Latin America in terms of per capita production, exhibits structural characteristics similar to those of Brazil. Output of machinery and equipment increased by more than 300 percent between 1937-38 and 1955, while their relative share of industrial production rose from 3.7 to 6.1 percent. However, repairs and replacement of parts accounted for 40 percent of this amount, as a result of which only 60 percent of production in this sector represented an addition to the stock of machinery and equipment, of which 60 percent in turn was concentrated in transport facilities.[60]

This fundamental deficiency of industrial growth in Argentina and Brazil is prevalent without exception throughout the region. It is summed up by the fact previously mentioned that at the end of a twelve-year period of intensified industrial activity, culminating the modern phase of a process that began at the time of the First World War, Latin America was still dependent on imports for over 90 percent of its machinery and equipment.

Mention must also be made of an additional factor, related to the "enclave" problem already discussed, that further complicates the evaluation of Latin American growth. A large majority of up-to-date manufacturing enterprises in the region is foreign-owned. United States private direct investments in this sector more than doubled during 1945-57 and by 1959 had a book value of approximately 1.4 billion dollars, or greater than that of any other sector except petroleum, and represented about one-sixth of the total United States private investment in Latin America.

By far the greater part of this investment has gone into heavy industry and food-processing, while 70 percent is con-

[59] *Estudio Económico de América Latina 1956* (United Nations, 1957), p. 86 and *Anuário Estatístico do Brasil 1958*, pp. 82, 94-95, 101.
[60] *El Desarrollo Económico de la Argentina*, Vol. II, pp. 165, 191, 225.

centrated in Brazil, Mexico, and Argentina. Brazil alone received over 30 percent of the total.[61] It is estimated that in the course of a steadily rising trend, by 1957 private foreign (United States and European) participation in manufacturing investments in Brazil represented 37 percent of the total.[62]

The impact of this situation on Latin American industrial and economic development, broadly speaking, is contradictory, to say the least. On the one hand, there is new production with its multiplier effects. At the same time, this is not an unmixed blessing, since much of this production is actually an assembly operation of imported components and otherwise depends on imported raw materials.

On the other hand, the capacity of expansion of foreign enterprises through reinvestment of profits is limited in the long run by the possibility of remitting profits. Hence, the greater the expansion, the greater the eventual export of capital and *ipso facto* the increasing decapitalization of the seriously undercapitalized Latin American economies. As the Brazilian economist Caio Prado Júnior aptly puts it, whatever the initial stimulus to development provided by foreign-owned factories, "in time it is transformed into an obstruction."[63]

A final observation may be made confirming the limitations of industrial growth in Latin America. It is well known that in any underdeveloped region, the role of industry in the absorption of manpower is of decisive importance both in the acceleration of industrialization and economic growth in general. In this connection we note that between 1945 and 1955 the proportion of the Latin American labor force engaged in agriculture dropped from 57.4 to 51.6 percent.[64] This represents a sizable decrease in absolute numbers and a phenomenon theoretically associated with economic growth.

In Latin America the contrary is true. As an official of the Organization of the American States has recently described the vicious circle, the intensification of the poverty in the countryside has stimulated an ever-increasing exodus of the rural population to the cities, the level of agricultural technology has been too low to compensate for the loss of farm labor, and industrial development has been too slow to provide employ-

[61] *Survey of Current Business,* United States Department of Commerce, September 1960, pp. 20, 22.

[62] *Economic Survey of Latin America 1957,* p. 142.

[63] "Nacionalismo e Desenvolvimento," *Revista Brasiliense,* No. 24, 1959, p. 15.

[64] *Report on World Social Situation* (United Nations, 1957), p. 179.

ment for the rural refugees.[65] Thus, the proportion of the labor force engaged in manufacturing and construction increased only from 17 to 18.5 percent of the total. At the same time, the service sector increased its share from 23 to 27.4 percent, or at more than double the rate of manufacturing and construction.[66]

In other words, the bulk of the labor force released (or in flight) from agriculture swelled the ranks of clerks, bootblacks, newspaper vendors, domestic servants, and the like, not to mention the unemployed. This phenomenon at the same time explains the discrepancy between the unprecedented increase of Latin America's urban population and the region's much more modest tempo of industrialization.

In evaluating the over-all performance of the Latin American economy, a final question must be answered: how did it affect the living standards of the great mass of people? The first point to be noted is that from 1945 to 1957 per capita consumption for the region as a whole increased by 40 percent as compared with 31 percent for the per capita GNP. This phenomenon has been described as "gratifying" by the ECLA economists.[67]

However, an examination of the distribution of income generated by the GNP reveals that the increase in private consumption (roughly 80 percent of the total consumption) was strictly limited to an affluent minority and hence, apart from its social implications, might be better characterized as a deplorable squandering of surplus value. Assuming that even in the case of Latin America there can be some justifiable debate among theoreticians as to how much could or should be "squeezed out from the population . . . through a delayed rise in consumption standards . . . and used for heavy investment, with a view to the . . . rapid growth of production,"

[65] Armando Samper, as reported in *Política* (Mexico, D. F.), September 1, 1960, p. 45.

[66] "At first glance it might seem that this increase in personal services is the same phenomenon as occurs in more developed countries where, as per capita income rises, the demand for highly-paid specialized services is very elastic. However, this does not appear to be the case in . . . [Latin America] where poorly remunerative personal services prevail and the surplus of labor that cannot be absorbed in other occupations . . . is thus concealed. . . . In the second place, . . . the middle class, which cannot find productive occupation in private economic activities, exerts a constant pressure on the public sector, which, therefore . . . must fulfill a role of absorption of no minor social significance" (*Economic Survey of Latin America 1954*, United Nations, 1955, pp. 26-27).

[67] *El Mercado Común Latinoamericano*, p. 45.

as Gunnar Myrdal puts it in another context,[68] there can be little justification for the kind of "squeezing" that results in superconsumption and subinvestment by profit takers, and consequently provides no prospect for the rapid growth of production.

While the data on personal income are scattered and of different degrees of reliability, all evidence points to the fact that the notorious disparity of income between the propertied and working classes in Latin America increased and that, in effect, for the great majority of Latin Americans the material and social problems of poverty were as great if not greater during the postwar boom period than before.[69]

Some confirmation of this situation is furnished by the steady migration of destitute peasants and the prevalence of hunger, to which we have previously referred. Other symptoms have been the widespread social struggles and the savage political repressions that attained a degree of intensity and a geographic scope probably unequaled in Latin America in any other period of high economic indices.

Another general clue is provided by the steep rise in costs of living in most countries, which, even according to official figures, reached phenomenal proportions in some republics—

[68] *An International Economy* (New York, 1956), p. 62. As indicated in our table, from 1945 to 1957 the gross fixed investment coefficient for Latin America as a whole fluctuated around an average of 17 percent of the GNP. In some quarters this is considered to be a respectable figure, especially when compared with the great majority of underdeveloped countries of South East Asia where the coefficient usually runs under 10 percent. This comparison, however, emphasizes the extremely low rate of capital formation in South East Asia rather than an adequate rate for Latin America. In 1955, e.g., the coefficient for both the United States and Latin America was approximately 17 percent. This meant a per capita gross investment rate of 370 dollars for the United States as compared with 55 dollars for Latin America, i.e., in inverse proportion to the relative growth needs of the two areas. It should also be pointed out that the *net* investment coefficient in Latin America has been about 12 percent. As Simon Kuznets suggests (*Economic Growth: Brazil, India, Japan,* Durham, N. C., 1955, p. 23), in developed countries obsolescence plays a large role in capital consumption, while physical deterioration is the main factor in underdeveloped countries. Hence ". . . the proper comparison, from the standpoint of economic growth, may be between *gross* capital formation in an industrially developed country and *net* capital formation in an underdeveloped one." If we also consider the questionable growth function in Latin America of investment in extractive activities and luxury residential construction, it becomes quite clear that the problem of capital formation in this region is indeed a formidable one.

[69] For a scientifically controlled and at the same time vivid portrayal of the material and human aspects of these problems, consult a recent study by Oscar Lewis: *Five Families, Mexican Case Studies in the Culture of Poverty* (New York, 1959).

this despite the habitual and notorious underestimation practiced by the various government statistical agencies involved.[70] Wages normally lagged and even in those cases where strike action would force more or less equitable temporary adjustments, the upward movement of prices was so rapid that there was always a time gap during which the real income of wage earners fell.

Trends, of course, fluctuated depending on the country and the years. Argentine data indicate a rise in real industrial wages and salaries during the early postwar years followed by a declining trend after 1949.[71] The record is not so clear in Brazil and Colombia where in any case "per capita real wages in industry have actually declined to some extent in recent years, in spite of increasing per capita production."[72] By and large and over the longer run, the classical "redistribution of wealth" characteristic of rapid and prolonged inflation took its toll among Latin American wage earners.

Chilean statistics in this connection are worth noting because they are more complete and more reliable than most in Latin America. From 1945 to 1957 the relative share of total national consumer expenditure represented by wages and white collar salaries fell by 10 percent, while that derived from profits, interest, and rent increased by nearly 15 percent. At the same time, the fact that per capita consumption of such staples as meat, potatoes, and especially wheat declined significantly during this period suggests that the majority of Chileans underwent absolute as well as relative impoverishment.[73]

Apparently in Peru, where a good deal of income is not measured in wages, the "general characteristics of income

[70] Indices (1950 = 100) from 1948 to 1957: Argentina—61 to 326; Brazil—90 to 329; Colombia—78 to 152; Chile—73 to 1,173; Bolivia—66 to 6,937. From Table 35, *Cost of Living in Selected Countries, Economic Bulletin for Latin America*, Vol. III, No. 2, October 1958, p. 81. In most countries indices have continued to rise. In Brazil the level in December 1960 was more than double that of 1957 (*Monde*, February 2, 1961).

[71] *Economic Survey of Latin America 1957*, Table 115, p. 115.

[72] *Report on the World Social Situation* (1957), p. 182. According to Cleantho da Paiva Leite, in the state of Piauí, typical of chronically depressed Northeast Brazil, annual per capita income has averaged about 45 dollars or less than 13 percent of the average for the state of São Paulo, most important coffee-growing and industrial center of the country. About one third of the Brazilian population lives in the Northeast ("Brazilian Development: One Problem and Two Banks" *Inter-American Economic Affairs*, Vol. XIV, No. 1, Summer 1960, p. 4).

[73] *Economic Survey of Latin America 1957*, pp. 199, 206.

distribution do not seem to have undergone any significant change between 1945 and 1955." During this decade about 45 percent of the total Peruvian population could satisfy only the "barest subsistence requirements," which translated into monetary terms would mean an annual per capita consumption equivalent to no more than 50 dollars, less than one-third the national per capita average.[74]

In Venezuela most of the evidence points to a widening income gap between the upper brackets and the majority. According to one analysis, roughly three-quarters of the Venezuelan population receive less that one-third of the highly inflated per capita national income.[75] In Cuba one statistic alone tells us a good deal about income distribution: prior to the revolution of 1959, the *normal* rate of unemployment, year in and year out, was 25 percent.[76]

It may be argued that Cuban, Chilean, and even Argentine data are not entirely relevant, since these republics registered little or no growth from 1945 to 1957. The same cannot be said about Mexico, for which, moreover, considerable information concerning income distribution has recently been made available.

According to a detailed and, on the whole, conservatively oriented analysis by the Mexican economist Ifigenia de Navarrete, the following pertinent facts emerge:[77]

1. From 1940 to 1950 personal income of entrepreneurs rose from 60 to 66 percent of total personal income in the republic, while that of wage earners declined correspondingly from 40 to 34 percent of the total.

2. From 1950 to 1957, calculating in terms of family income (*a*) the average monthly income of families in the lowest bracket, comprising 20 percent of the Mexican population, was 22.3 dollars in 1950 and 19.8 dollars in 1957 (computed in 1957 pesos and converted into 1957 dollars) representing a relative decline from 6 percent of total income to 4.5 percent, and an absolute decline of 11 percent; (*b*) for half of the population (including the 20 percent in the lowest bracket)

[74] *The Industrial Development of Peru*, pp. 10, 11.

[75] Cited by Otto Feinstein from Carl S. Shoup (director), *The Fiscal System of Venezuela* (Baltimore, 1959), pp. 29-34.

[76] Leo Huberman and Paul M. Sweezy, *Cuba, Anatomy of a Revolution* (New York, 1960), pp. 6-7. The authors note that this rate was the same as that "in the worst year of the worst depression in United States history" and reflected the fact that the Cuban economy "was in a permanent state of crisis."

[77] *La Distribución del Ingreso y el Desarrollo Económico en México* (Mexico, D. F., 1960), pp. 65, 85.

average family real income in 1950 and 1957 was approximately the same, or about 28 dollars per month (1957 dollars), but representing nonetheless a relative decline from 19 to 11.5 percent of total family income; (c) whereas in 1950, 70 percent of families received 31.5 percent of total family income, in 1957 they received only 28.5 percent.

There is probably little, if any, exaggeration in this study of the stationary or declining real income trend of most Mexicans, and there may be some underestimation. For example, according to the Soviet scholar M. D. Danilyevich, the real income of manufacturing workers in Mexico from 1939 to 1958 showed a declining trend after 1940,[78] thereby leading to the suspicion that absolute impoverishment was more widespread than indicated by the Mexican analysis. This suspicion is supported by trends in per capita food consumption. From 1934-36 to 1952-56, according to a United Nations survey, an examination of available information "has revealed the existence of several important tendencies that have been reflected in a lowering of nutritional standards."[79]

In any case, there is probably no overstatement in the general conclusion proposed by Señora de Navarrete as a result of her study, namely, that from 65 to 70 percent of the Mexican population has had no share in the "benefits of economic development."[80] Nor would there be any danger of stretching the point to surmise that the privations endured during the period of maximum economic performance by the bulk of the Mexican population—under the relatively favorable conditions of the Mexican economy—were more intense in the great majority of the Latin American republics.

There has been no lack of awareness in many quarters of the gravity of the current crisis in Latin America, both as an economic disaster and a sharpening of political and social conflicts. Nor has there been a lack of factors, real or imaginary, that have been brought forward in explanation of this state of affairs. However, all too often there is a tendency—even among specialists of some competence—to give credence to the notion that economic development has been "rapid" in Latin America, or that "Latin American growth has been impressive" or that Latin America "has reached the age of

[78] *The Working Class in the National Liberation Movement of Latin America* (in Russian), typewritten doctoral dissertation, USSR Academy of Sciences, 1960, Vol. I, p. 233. Publication date not announced.
[79] *Economic Survey of Latin America 1957*, p. 292.
[80] *Ibid.*, p. 90.

vigorous economic development."[81] This, we have tried to show, is far from being the case, according to the available evidence. What we have called the maximum performance of the Latin American economy has been confused with an adequate performance.

How shall we sum up the evidence? If there is a mathematical device that can weigh and measure the nongrowth and antigrowth content of the economic activities we have examined and thereby define with precision the real Latin American GNP, its relative magnitude on a world scale, and its rate of change in time, this writer does not know of such a device nor does he have the capacity to invent one. But perhaps, to borrow a phrase from Joan Robinson, "it is of no use framing definitions more precise than the subject matter to which they apply,"[82] and, we might add, than the very scanty and imperfect statistical materials with which we have to work.

Hence we need attempt no formulation beyond a general conclusion that such growth as has occurred has been vastly exaggerated and has failed to meet by almost any standard—social or economic—the growth requirements of the region. Or to put it more concretely, the decisive characteristic of this growth is that it failed to provide, or establish the basis for, an increase of sufficient tempo and magnitude in the productive and reproductive capacity of those branches of the economy whose fundamental deficiencies are chiefly responsible for the perpetuation of underdevelopment. Consequently, the current Latin American crisis does not mark a turning point after an era of progress, but the culmination of a process that in essential respects aggravated the chronic internal ailments and the external vulnerability of the region's underdeveloped and dependent economy.

The factors that distort the Latin American economy and impede its growth are so tightly interlocked that they can no longer be acted upon separately. The problems of land tenure and utilization, of basic industrialization and external vulnerability are facets of the larger problem: the economic and political ramifications of the region's controlling function, which is the export of raw materials under terms and conditions determined outside the region.

The maximum performance that we have scrutinized and

---

[81] In the order quoted: James (*op. cit.*, p. 880); Feinstein (*op. cit.*, p. 52); Navarrete (*op. cit.*, p. 11).

[82] *The Accumulation of Capital* (London, 1956), p. viii.

its crisis offspring seem to indicate clearly enough that the Latin American economy has reached the stage where the elimination of its neocolonial dependency must be placed on the agenda, and with it the abandonment of a spontaneous approach to development.[83] Only on this basis will it be possible to adopt the social objectives and the rational economic methods that a successful attack on underdevelopment requires.

[83] Otto Feinstein (*op. cit.*, p. 76) maintains that Latin America "is the underdeveloped area in which the chances for capitalism are the best." Quite apart from long-range world perspectives, the chances are not bright in any underdeveloped area, and particularly slim in Latin America. In regions emerging from direct colonial domination, the colonial powers frequently adjust to the change by retaining their principal economic positions under a neocolonial arrangement; this factor discourages noncapitalist experimentation. In addition, given the extremely low economic base, some initial, although slow, growth can take place through combined private and state capitalism. In Latin America (taken as a whole) direct colonialism lies in the distant past and a fair amount of native (including state) capitalist development has already taken place under neocolonial conditions. Decisive native private capitalist sectors such as banking and the larger industrial, commercial, and transport enterprises are to a significant degree dependent on foreign financing and imports. They also depend on the neocolonial state apparatus to defend their class interests vis-à-vis the wage earners. Their economic, political, and social prerogatives, however limited by neocolonialism, are anchored in it. The crisis of neocolonialism in Latin America is thus also the crisis of native capitalism, and consequently the elimination of the former (especially if stubbornly resisted as the Cuban experience forecasts) is apt to spell the rapid elimination of the latter (at least in basic spheres of production). Such a prospect, of course, is not impaired by the fact that in the sixth decade of the twentieth century too many people in Latin America know that there is a much more speedy and efficient alternative to capitalist development.

Toward a Theory of Power and Political Instability in Latin America

MERLE KLING

The fundamentally colonial nature of many Latin American countries' economies not only constricts the economic bases of their dominant classes, but also, Kling argues, is a basic source of political instability. A close relationship exists between the economic dominance of American corporations and the patterns of politics; among other reasons this is because control of the governmental apparatus is a means of social ascent and of securing an economic base, a route to wealth and power, not otherwise available in a colonial economy. Chronic political instability results, in Kling's view, from "the contradiction between the realities of a colonial economy and the political requirements of legal sovereignty" in many Latin American countries.

Merle Kling is Professor of Political Science and Dean of the Faculty of Arts and Sciences at Washington University at St. Louis, and the author of, among other works, *A Mexican Interest Group in Action* (Princeton, N.J.: Prentice-Hall, 1961).

Reprinted from *Western Political Quarterly*, Vol. IX, No. 7 (March 1956), pp. 21-35, by permission of the University of Utah and the author.

76

I

"ONE MAY consider science," James B. Conant has observed, "as an attempt . . . to lower the degree of empiricism or to extend the range of theory. . . . Almost all significant work of scientists today, I believe, comes under the heading of attempts to reduce the degree of empiricism."[1]

Despite the conception of science and theory prevalent in the natural sciences and reflected in the formulation of Conant, the discipline of political science has yet to reject decisively the notion of theory as an aggregation of metaphysical speculations unrelated to experience and practice. Academically, in fact, the field of political theory, within the discipline of political science, traditionally has defined its role as recording, with varied degrees of interpretation, the history of metaphysical speculations in the area of politics and the state.[2] But "theorizing, even about politics," as Lasswell and Kaplan correctly assert, "is not to be confused with metaphysical speculation in terms of abstractions hopelessly removed from empirical observation and control."[3]

Within a scientific framework, consequently, a theory of power and instability in Latin America must attempt to discharge at least four functions. (1) An adequate theory must serve "to reduce the degree of empiricism"; that is, it must place in a broad and meaningful context the apparently disconnected manifestations of instability in Latin America. (2) It must offer generalizations regarding the exercise of power and the prevalence of instability in Latin America that are compatible with the available evidence. (3) It must offer a guide and provide a framework for relevant research. A scientific theory neither anticipates every future event nor solves every practical problem. A theory with scientific pretensions, however, does provide directions for the investigation and solu-

[1] James B. Conant, *Science and Common Sense* (New Haven: Yale University Press, 1951), pp. 58-59. "Only by the introduction of a theoretical element can the degree of empiricism be reduced." James B. Conant, *Modern Science and Modern Man* (New York: Columbia University Press, 1952), p. 28.

[2] For a systematic expression of dissatisfaction with the contemporary state of theory in American political science, particularly its "decline into historicism," see David Easton, *The Political System: An Inquiry Into the State of Political Science* (New York: Knopf, 1953).

[3] Harold D. Lasswell and Abraham Kaplan, *Power and Society: A Framework For Political Inquiry* (New Haven: Yale University Press, 1950), p. x.

tion of subsequent problems. (4) A theory of Latin American instability, if it is to endure, must not be rooted in relatively static elements in the Latin American environment; it must take account of dynamic forces that are subject to change. For example, a "theory" that "explains" instability in Latin America on the basis of the "hot blood" of the "Spanish temperament" is vulnerable on at least two grounds: the biological laboratory cannot sustain the assumption of peculiar heat in the blood of persons of Spanish descent; and the ultimate development of political stability in Latin America can be rationalized only by the projection of fantastic concepts of biological mutation.[4] Similarly, a "theory" of Latin American instability rooted in geographical factors is not reconcilable with probable changes of a significant order; for the Andes mountains are not likely to lose important elevation and the Amazon River is not likely to contract in length appreciably in the relevant future. By ignoring the dynamic aspects of Latin American society, however, such a "theory" postulates major geographical transformations if political stability is achieved.[5] To attribute political instability in Latin America, finally, to "history" and the heterogenous cultures of Spaniards and Indians buries any viable theory in an inextricable maze of historical and cultural determinism. This arbitrarily excludes the possibility of rapid developments in the direction of political stability.

A theory of power and political instability in Latin America, therefore, is not a substitute for empirical research. But, while subject to verification by experience, the theory must reach beyond the scope of analysis of isolated and superficially hap-

[4] Reflecting a "racist" emphasis, William Lytle Schurz—two years before the *coup d'état* that brought Perón's group to power in Argentina —wrote: "Conditions in Argentina are unusually favorable to the development of political democracy. It is peopled by a predominantly white race. It is free from the dead weight of a heavy Indian population, the too mercurial influence of the Negro, and the disturbing leaven of mixed peoples, who move in an uncertain world between the fixed status of the pure bloods." *Latin America: A Descriptive Survey* (New York: Dutton, 1941), p. 140. In a new and revised edition (1949), Schurz, while retaining his descriptive comments on the "races" of Argentina, rephrases his opening conclusion in a more cautious vocabulary: "Basic conditions in Argentina would appear to be unusually favorable to the development of political democracy," p. 135.

[5] " . . . policy consists of decisions about the future. The scientist who wishes to contribute to such decisions therefore focuses his research on problems that bear upon the relevant future. . . ." Ernest R. Hilgard and Daniel Lerner, "The Person: Subject and Object of Science and Policy," in Daniel Lerner and Harold D. Lasswell, *The Policy Sciences: Recent Developments in Scope and Method* (Stanford: Stanford University Press, 1951), pp. 42-43.

hazard political episodes; and the theory should provide a guide for fruitful and detailed investigations.

II

Political instability in Latin America is distinguished by three characteristics: (1) it is chronic; (2) it frequently is accompanied by limited violence; (3) it produces no basic shifts in economic, social, or political policies.

Political instability in a Latin American country cannot be evaluated as a temporary deviation in a pattern of peaceful rotation in office. In many Latin American republics, despite prescriptions of written constitutions, an abrupt change of governmental personnel through violence is a regular and recurrent phenomenon. In Honduras, "from 1824 to 1950, a period of 126 years, the executive office changed hands 116 times."[6] "During the nine-year interval ending in 1940, Ecuador had no less than fourteen presidents, [and had] four of them during the single month that ended on September 17, 1947. Instability is likewise dramatized on the cabinet level: twenty-seven different ministers occupying eight cabinet posts between May 29, 1944, and August 23, 1947. Twelve foreign ministers attempted to administer Ecuadoran foreign policy in the two-month period between August and October, 1933."[7] And the observations of a member of a United Nations mission to Bolivia in 1951 would not be inapplicable in substance to many Latin American states: "In the past ten years Bolivia has had nine major revolutions. None of its Presidents has served out his constitutional term of office during the last twenty-five years. There have been eighteen Ministers of Labor in four years; eight Ministers of Finance in eighteen months."[8]

Reflecting the persistence of political instability since World War II, governing personnel, including presidents, have been displaced by "irregular" methods on at least the following occasions:

October 1945. Venezuela	July 1946. Bolivia
October 1945. Haiti	January 1947. Paraguay
January 1946. Haiti	May 1947. Nicaragua

[6] William S. Stokes, *Honduras: An Area Study in Government* (Madison: University of Wisconsin Press, 1950), p. 181.

[7] George I. Blanksten, *Ecuador: Constitutions and Caudillos* (Berkeley: University of California Press, 1951), p. 181.

[8] Albert Lepawsky, "The Bolivian Operation," *International Conciliation*, No. 479 (March 1952), p. 106.

August 1947. Ecuador
September 1947. Ecuador
March 1948. Costa Rica
June 1948. Paraguay
October 1948. Peru
November 1948. Venezuela
December 1948. El Salvador
January 1949. Paraguay
November 1949. Panama
May 1950. Haiti
June 1950. Peru
May 1951. Bolivia
May 1951. Panama

March 1952. Cuba
April 1952. Bolivia
December 1952. Venezuela
June 1953. Colombia
May 1954. Paraguay
July 1954. Guatemala
August 1954. Brazil
December 1954. Honduras
January 1955. Panama
September 1955. Argentina
November 1955. Argentina
November 1955. Brazil

Occupancy of key governmental positions, consequently, has been secured at least 31 times in disregard of formal procedures since the Second World War. Nor does the above list take into account the numerous "unsuccessful" plots, suppressed uprisings, arrests, deportations, declarations of state of siege, boycotts, riots, and fraudulent "elections" that have punctuated Latin American politics in the last decade.[9] And the list, of course, does not include references to political irregularities in nonsovereign areas such as British Guiana.

Revolts, uprisings, and *coups d'état,* moreover, constitute incomplete evidence of the range of political instability in Latin America. For obscured by data of these kinds is the presence of "concealed" instability. The protracted tenure of a Vargas in Brazil (1930-1945), of an Ubico in Guatemala (1930-1944), the single candidate (*candidato único*) "elections" of Paraguay, Honduras, the Dominican Republic, Nicaragua, and Colombia, and the abortive "elections" of 1952 in Venezuela are not to be construed, of course, as symptomatic of political stability. For these also constitute instances in which governmental authority has been retained by the exercise of force in disregard of formal requirements. *Continuismo,* prolonged office-holding by a strong caudillo, in its essence represents the reverse side of the shield of political instability. *Continuismo* signifies not the absence of political instability, but the effective suppression of potential and incipient rebellions by competing caudillos. *Continuismo,* in fact, may be regarded as perpetuation in office by means of a series of successful *anticipatory* revolts.

Unlike cabinet instability in France, political instability in the Latin American states is neither sanctioned by the written

---

[9] Evidence of recent political instability, particularly for the year 1952, is summarized in a pamphlet by Miguel Jorrín, *Political Instability in Latin America* (Albuquerque: University of New Mexico, 1953).

constitution nor dictated by the rigidity of domestic party alignments. Latin American instability, in contrast with the French version, occurs in an environment of amorphous political parties and involves the limited employment of violence. It is not the withdrawal of votes by a doctrinaire bloc of deputies that precipitates the collapse of a Latin American regime; rather, it is the personal military following of an opportunistic caudillo that impresses a Latin American president with the timeliness of seeking asylum in a foreign embassy. The pervasiveness of violence justifies the conclusion of Stokes: "Violence seems to be institutionalized in the organization, maintenance, and changing of governments in Latin America."[10]

Although violence provides a continuing strand in the fabric of Latin American politics, revolution, in the sense of a fundamental transformation of society, "is rare in Latin America, and even mass participation in violence is only occasionally found."[11] A leader may be assassinated or exiled, a new junta may assume the posts of political authority, but control of the economic bases of power is not shifted and the hierarchy of social classes is not affected; in short, there is no restructuring of society. The label "palace revolution," as defined by Lasswell and Kaplan, can be appropriately applied to the pattern of political change in Latin America; for political instability in Latin America, like a palace revolution, involves "a change in governors contrary to the political formula but retaining it." Again violence in Latin America, in conformity with the characteristics of a palace revolution, produces a "change in government without corresponding changes in governmental policy."[12] General Gustavo Rojas Pinilla may be a party to a successful revolt in Colombia, and General Zenón Noriega may

[10] William S. Stokes, "Violence as a Power Factor in Latin-American Politics," *Western Political Quarterly*, V (1952), p. 445.
"One of the most typical aspects of Latin American life is the tendency to settle political issues by force. Government by revolution might almost be said to be the rule. Since the turn of the present century the governments of the nations to the south have been overthrown by revolt seventy-six times—an average of nearly four successful uprisings per country. No one knows how many unsuccessful rebellions have occurred during these years because no one has ever taken the trouble to count them, but they certainly run into the hundreds."
Austin F. Macdonald, *Latin American Politics and Government* (2d ed.; New York: Crowell, 1954), pp. 11-12.
[11] Stokes, *op. cit.*, p. 461.
[12] Lasswell and Kaplan, *op. cit.*, p. 270. For striking evidence of the equanimity with which economically dominant groups view rivalries among military cliques in El Salvador, see *New York Times*, February 6, 1955, p. 12.

be a party to an unsuccessful revolt in Peru; but the basic economic, social and political policies of Colombia and Peru are not altered by either the successful or the unsuccessful general. Violence is virtually always present; fundamental change is virtually always absent.

III

"In the general course of human nature," wrote Alexander Hamilton in *The Federalist* (No. 79), "a power over a man's subsistence amounts to a power over his will." And research in Latin American studies suggests that the distinguishing characteristics of the Latin American economy, despite the influence exerted by the Church and other institutions, are of primary importance in determining conditions for the retention and transfer of power.

Traditionally, ownership of land has been regarded as a major economic base for the exercise of power in Latin America. Despite the continued dependence today of more than two-thirds of the Latin American population on agriculture as a chief source of income, the system of land tenure operates to prevent the widespread diffusion of economic power. Concentration of land ownership in the hands of a tiny minority—whether symbolized by the *latifundio, hacienda, estancia, fazenda,* or *finca*—represents the prevailing, as well as historic, agrarian pattern of Latin America. "In many countries in Latin America," concludes a recent analysis by the United Nations Department of Economic Affairs, "the main feature of the agrarian structure is the high degree of inequality in land ownership."[13]

Although they can be introduced only with qualifications as to reliability, statistical estimates offer striking evidence of the narrow agrarian base of power. In Chile, whereas 43.4 percent of all land holdings are under five hectares, they account for only 0.5 percent of the farm area; large holdings (1000 hectares and over), on the other hand, constitute only 1.4 percent of all holdings, but they incorporate 68.2 percent of the farm area. Acknowledging that "the agrarian structure of Chile is characterized in the main by an abundance of very small holdings and a large concentration of large estates in the hands of a small number of proprietors," the government of Chile, in reply to a United Nations questionnaire, empha-

[13] United Nations, Department of Economic Affairs, *Progress in Land Reform* (New York, 1954), p. 37.

sized the difficulty of modifying the pattern of land ownership:

> Owing to the economic and political structure of the country, land reform in Chile is difficult to carry out. Landholders who would be affected by any action of an economic, political, administrative, legal, or social nature will vigorously oppose its implementation, and their political and economic influence is very powerful.[14]

In Brazil 1.5 percent of all land holdings account for 48.4 percent of the farm area.[15] According to the 1950 census of Bolivia, 4.5 percent of the rural landowners possess 70 percent of the private landed property.[16] In the provence of Pichincha in Ecuador 1.5 percent of all holdings incorporate 65.3 percent of the farm area, and the government reports that "Ecuador has not developed a policy of land reform."[17] In Cuba 1.4 percent of all holdings comprise 47 percent of the farm area.[18] Even in Mexico, where the government claims that about 23 percent of the total area in holdings was distributed to *éjido* farmers between 1916 and 1940, in lands not under the *éjido* system 0.8 percent of all holdings constitute 79.5 percent of the farm area.[19] And patterns of highly concentrated land ownership persist in Argentina, Peru, and Venezuela.

This monopolization of agrarian wealth injects an element of rigidity into the power relations of Latin American groups; for the effect of the land tenure system is to establish relatively fixed economic boundaries between the landowners and the peon, since "the relationships growing out of the large estates have matured into deep inflexibility."[20] Indeed, the authors

[14] *Ibid.*, pp. 42-43.

[15] *Ibid.*, p. 41.

[16] *Ibid.*, p. 40. In Bolivia "the most usual model, surviving with little change from colonial times, is the large estate with absentee owner and cultivated by native labor." Harold Osborne, *Bolivia: A Land Divided* (London: Royal Institute of International Affairs, 1954), p. 111.

[17] United Nations, Department of Economic Affairs, *op. cit.*, pp. 43-44. "An Ecuadorian economist recently called attention to the fact that, according to the register on real-estate tax paid in the greater part of the Sierra between 1943-8, 486 landowners, i.e., less than 2 percent of the persons subject to the tax, owned three-quarters of the land, while the remaining quarter was distributed among over 23,000 small owners. Many properties were no larger than one-tenth of an acre, while others extended over more than 15,000 acres." Lilo Lanke, *Ecuador, Country of Contrasts* (London: Royal Institute of International Affairs, 1954), p. 118.

[18] United Nations, Department of Economic Affairs, *op. cit.*, p. 46.

[19] *Ibid.*, p. 39.

[20] Simon G. Hanson, *Economic Development in Latin America* (Washington: Inter-American Affairs Press, 1951), p. 67.

of a very carefully documented study of Latin America have concluded: "Monopolization of land has been and still is both the source and the technique of political power in Latin America."[21]

Yet it is possible to exaggerate the independence, the freedom from restraint, of the landowner in Latin American society. Viewed solely in terms of domestic Latin American patterns of land tenure, the landowner appears almost to personify the classical definition of sovereignty. He seems to possess virtually absolute power. But an analysis of the nature of agricultural production reveals important inhibitions on the discretionary power of the landowner, and he fails to qualify as an economic sovereign. For as a producer of crops peculiarly dependent on foreign markets, in an agrarian economy characterized by monoculture, the landowner finds his economic base of independence subject to severe limitations. When 50 percent to 60 percent of Brazilian exports consists of coffee,[22] when normally 80 percent of the total value of exports of El Salvador consists of coffee,[23] when "coffee cultivation . . . contributes more than 70 percent of total exports and is the basic cash crop on which nearly everything else depends" in Guatemala (according to a Mission sponsored by the International Bank for Reconstruction and Development),[24] when coffee represents 73.2 percent of the value of all exports in Colombia for 1953,[25] when coffee is the predominant export of the Central American Republics (representing 56.4 percent of all exports in 1953)[26]—when the Western Hemisphere produces about 85 percent of the world's exportable coffee and the United States consumes 65 percent to 75 percent of all the coffee shipped[27]—the domestic proprietors of coffee plantations cannot be immune to the pressures (regardless of the indirection, diplomacy, and circumspection with which they may be exerted) that emanate from their principal export

[21] George Soule, David Efron, and Norman T. Ness, *Latin America in the Future World* (New York: Farrar and Rinehart, 1945), p. 63.

[22] United Nations, Department of Economic Affairs, *Economic Survey of Latin America 1953* (New York, 1954), p. 54; Pan American Union, Division of Economic Research, *Economic Developments in Brazil 1949-50* (Washington, D.C., 1950), p. 37.

[23] United States, Department of Commerce, *Foreign Commerce Yearbook 1949* (Washington, 1951), p. 402.

[24] International Bank for Reconstruction and Development, *The Economic Development of Guatemala* (Washington, D.C., 1951), p. 24.

[25] United Nations, Department of Economic Affairs, *Economic Survey of Latin America 1953* (New York, 1954), p. 56.

[26] *Ibid.*, p. 64.

[27] *Americas*, II (January 1950), 2.

market. When over half of the total value of exports of the Dominican Republic[28] and about three-fourths of the total value of Cuban exports[29] consists of sugar, the domestic owner of sugar plantations cannot be indifferent to the influence of international markets. "Sugar," reported an Economic and Technical Mission organized by the International Bank of Reconstruction and Development, "is not only Cuba's principal source of livelihood. It dominates the economy—and the outlook of the people—in various ways. Sugar plays an even greater part in the exports of Cuba today than it did in the past."[30] Hence the fundamentally colonial and monocultural nature of the Latin American economies, as evidenced by the role of coffee and sugar exports, constricts the economic base even of the apparently omnipotent landowner.[31]

The main characteristics of the ownership of mineral wealth and the conduct of the mining industries in Latin America further accentuate the colonial nature of the economies and add to the obstacles in the path of discovering native, local command over decisive economic elements of power. Foreign ownership of mineral resources and foreign utilization of mineral products imply that an important economic base of power in Latin America is not indigenously controlled. Thus, over 90 percent of Chilean copper is regularly produced by United States-owned enterprises; of 351,000 tons of copper mined in 1953, in excess of 325,000 tons were produced by large mining companies financed by United States capital.[32] The United States-owned Cerro de Pasco Corporation of Peru accounts for about two-thirds of the Peruvian copper output.[33] In the case

[28] Pan American Union, *Foreign Commerce of Dominican Republic 1941-1947* (Washington, D.C., June 1950), p. 17.

[29] United Nations, Department of Economic Affairs, *Economic Survey of Latin America 1953* (New York, 1954), p. 57.

[30] International Bank for Reconstruction and Development, *Report on Cuba* (Washington, D.C., 1951), p. 7. In 1954 the United States absorbed 60.1 percent of Cuban sugar exports. United Nations, Department of Economic and Social Affairs, *Economic Survey of Latin America 1954* (New York, 1955), p. 59.

[31] In certain conspicuous instances, of course, the landowner is not a native of a Latin American state. The United Fruit Company, for example, is reported to own about 3,000,000 acres, mainly in Colombia, Costa Rica, Cuba, the Dominican Republic, Ecuador, Guatemala, Honduras, and Panama. *New York Times,* July 4, 1954, p. 4E.

[32] United Nations, Department of Economic Affairs, *Economic Survey of Latin America 1953* (New York, 1954), p. 185.

[33] *Ibid.,* p. 187. The Cerro de Pasco Corporation "accounted for 84 percent of the copper, 36 percent of the gold, and 55 percent of the silver produced in Peru between 1906 and 1938." Division of Economic Research, Pan American Union, *The Peruvian Economy* (Washington, D.C., 1950), p. 104.

of Bolivia, despite the nationalization of the principal tin mines, the virtually complete reliance on exports of the mining industry as a source of indispensable foreign exchange perpetuates a political climate that is subject to foreign pressures. For "the products of the mining industry account for some 98 percent of the country's total exports. And tin concentrates account for some 75 percent of the total mineral exports." Consequently, "the financial position of Bolivia is always peculiarly sensitive to—is indeed dangerously dependent upon—fluctuations of price and demand in the world markets for nonferrous metals."[34] Control of petroleum production in Latin America resides almost exclusively in the hands of foreign-owned corporations. A United States company produces more than 70 percent of Peru's crude petroleum; in Venezuela, which accounts for almost 80 percent of the crude petroleum output of Latin America, a subsidiary of a United States company ranks as the largest oil company in the country.[35]

Venezuela and its oil industry perhaps may be cited as a case study in the predominant role of foreign capital with respect to the control of the mineral bases of power in Latin America. Petroleum, which is exploited almost exclusively by foreign-owned companies, operating under government concession, occupies a crucial position in Venezuelan exports.[36] In one fashion or another, more than 60 percent of the revenue of the Treasury in Venezuela is contributed by the oil companies; during the budget year 1949-1950 about one-third of the total budget receipts consisted of petroleum *royalties* alone.[37] Unlike other mineral industries, moreover, petroleum has continued to attract new capital investment from the United States. Since 74 percent of United States private direct investment in the period following the Second World War (1947-1949) was channeled to the petroleum industry, a considerable share has been invested in Venezuela as a country with exploitable petroleum resources.[38] Clearly the foreign-owned oil companies constitute factors that cannot be ignored in the power structure of Venezuela. But a precise description of the manner in which power is exercised by the petroleum in-

[34] Osborne, *op. cit.*, p. 107.

[35] United Nations, Department of Economic Affairs, *Economic Survey of Latin America 1953* (New York, 1954), pp. 233-238.

[36] *Ibid.*, p. 62; United States Tariff Commission, *Mining and Manufacturing Industries in Venezuela* (Washington, 1945), p. 47.

[37] United Nations, Department of Economic Affairs, *Public Finance Surveys: Venezuela* (New York, January 1951), p. 47.

[38] Gordon Gray, *Report to the President on Foreign Economic Policies* (Washington, November 10, 1950), pp. 61, 121.

dustry cannot be documented. It would be valuable, for purposes of a study of power, to have accessible a public record of the specific reactions of the oil companies to the seizure of governmental authority by a revolutionary junta led by Romulo Betancourt in 1945. It would be valuable, for purposes of a study of power, to have available an accurate record of the policies and decisions of the oil companies insofar as they affected the deposition of President Romulo Gallegos and his supporters, including Betancourt, in 1948. But details of this type are unavailable not only to academic investigators of power in Latin America; they elude public detection and identification in most systems of power. The obscure nature of certain details, however, cannot serve to justify the rejection of an inference that a correlation exists between the economic dominance of the oil companies and the pattern of political behavior in Venezuela. While the exact techniques of the exercise of power are not easily demonstrated, obviously a substantial economic base of power in Venezuela is controlled by economic institutions beyond the geographical boundaries of the country. The control of mineral wealth, consequently, within the framework of colonial economies, introduces an external element of restraint on the exercise of power by domestic forces and movements within Latin America.

Industrialization would appear to represent a significant challenge to the economic forces of colonialism in Latin America. Undoubtedly a successful program of industrialization could alter radically the distribution of power in the Latin American area. Tangible fragments of evidence, in fact, suggest that the present level of industrialization has stimulated modifications in the established patterns of economic power. Consumer goods industries, particularly textiles, have expanded rapidly. Reflecting the influence of domestic manufacturing interests, Latin American governments have been anxious to maintain protective tariff policies. With industrialization, labor organizations have evolved and have made it possible for new leaders, drawing upon fresh sources of support, to compete for the possession of power. The well-publicized role of Lombardo Toledano in Mexican politics, the prolix constitutional and statutory provisions for social security, the turbulent strikes in some of the Latin American states, the ostentatious, if demagogic, manifestations of solicitude for labor on the part of Juan Domingo Perón testify to the enhanced prestige of labor and labor unions in a society experiencing the initial tensions and strains of industrialization in the twentieth century.

But the position of manufacturing as an economic base of power in Latin America can be overstated. Hitherto a level of industrialization has not been achieved that would make possible the displacement of the conventional economic bases of power. By United States standards the Latin American consumer continues to absorb only a small amount of manufactured goods. The Latin American countries continue to be dependent on imports for many items utilized in manufacturing, as well as for much of their machinery, transportation facilities, and factory equipment. And "the most significant economic trend in 1953," according to the Secretariat of the Economic Commission for Latin America, "was, without doubt, the clear indication of a slackening in the rate of industrialization. . . . As a consequence, the industrial share of the gross product in 1953 was only 25.6 percent, no greater than in 1945." The fact, moreover, that the industrial labor force, compared with total manpower, has not increased since 1950 constitutes evidence of a "fundamental decline in industrialization" in Latin America.[39] A decline of 21 percent in total Latin American imports of capital goods in 1953, in relation to 1952, also emphasizes the limited potentialities of industrialization in the immediate future.[40]

Notwithstanding the somewhat spectacular construction of the Volta Redonda steel plant in Brazil and the opening of the earthquake-proof Huachipato steel works in Chile, heavy industries remain in an embryonic stage of evolution. By 1954, for example, Brazilian industry produced only 1,100,000 tons of steel ingots annually, and total Chilean production of steel ingots in 1954 amounted to 320,000 tons.[41] "Such industrialization as exists," Gordon concludes with ample evidence, "is either an undernourished image of the Great Society or else a highly specialized form, such as in mining, that exists by grace of foreign ownership and foreign markets."[42]

[39] United Nations, Department of Economic Affairs, *Economic Survey of Latin America 1953* (New York, 1954), pp. 10-11.

[40] *Ibid.*, p. 68.

[41] United Nations, Department of Economic and Social Affairs, *Economic Survey of Latin America 1954* (New York, 1955), p. 96. For data regarding the share of manufacturing in Latin American national incomes, see: George Wythe, *Industry in Latin America* (2d ed.; New York: Columbia University Press, 1949), p. 13; and the United Nations, Secretariat of the Economic Commission for Latin America, *Economic Survey of Latin America 1948* (New York, 1949), p. 2.

[42] Wendell C. Gordon, *The Economy of Latin America* (New York: Columbia University Press, 1950), p. 20.

From the point of view of locating the economic sites of power, the current program of industrialization in Latin America presents an apparent paradox. The desire for industrialization evidently originates with leaders who seek to transfer economic bases of power from foreign to domestic jurisdiction; and the economic nationalism that normally has accompanied the drive for industrialization would seem to substantiate this assumption. But the financial techniques utilized have not hastened the transfer of power, based on control of industry, to native groups in Latin America. For, lacking huge reservoirs of local capital to finance heavy industry, unwilling (and perhaps unable) to compel modifications in the investment practices of landowners, the Latin Americans, in their attempt to move toward the goal of industrialization, once again have sought foreign capital. Prominent among the suppliers of new capital to Latin America has been the Export-Import Bank of Washington. Every sovereign state in Latin America except Guatemala has received funds from this Bank. By 1954 the Export-Import Bank, which supplied more than half of the investment capital required by the Volta Redonda and Huachipato steel plants,[43] had authorized credits of $2,152,023,000 to the Latin American countries.[44] In addition, half of the states in the Latin American region have received loans from the International Bank for Reconstruction and Development. By 1954 this specialized agency of the United Nations had authorized loans of $426,000,000 to Latin American countries.[45] Since voting power in the International Bank for Reconstruction and Development is based on the proportion of

[43] *New York Times*, November 26, 1950.

[44] Export-Import Bank of Washington, *Seventeenth Semiannual Report to Congress for the period July-December 1953*, p. 22.

At least one member of the Chilean Senate has argued that President Gabriel Gonzalez Videla was forced to revise his internal policies in order to qualify for an Export-Import Bank loan designed to encourage industrialization. Salvadore Ocampo, "You Have Invaded My Country," *New Republic*, CXVII (December 1, 1947), 10-12. Also see Roger S. Abbott, "The Role of Contemporary Political Parties in Chile," *American Political Science Review*, XLV (1951), 454, 457.

[45] United Nations, Department of Economic and Social Affairs, *Foreign Capital in Latin America* (New York, 1955), p. 13.

". . . one of the most noteworthy developments in the field of foreign investment during 1954 was the marked increase in the loan activity of the International Bank for Reconstruction and Development and of the Export-Import Bank. After authorizing development-type credits to Latin America to a value of 90 million and 57 million dollars in 1953 and in the first half of 1954, respectively, they approved total credits for 196 million dollars during the second half of the year and over 100 millions in the first quarter of 1955." United Nations, Department of Economic and Social Affairs, *Economic Survey of Latin America 1954* (New York, 1955), p. 51.

capital subscribed by each member, the United States speaks
with a dominant voice in the affairs of the Bank.

Potentially, then, industrialization may prove of large consequence in creating new economic bases of power in Latin
America. At some future date, it may modify drastically the
position of the conventional economic bases of power. But industrialization on such a scale has yet failed to materialize.
Promise, hope, and aspiration must be distinguished from performance and accomplishment. Accordingly, at the present
time, industrialization in Latin America, realistically appraised,
is taking place within the context of an environment that in
its economic content remains basically colonial.[46]

IV

An analysis of the distinguishing characteristics of the economic bases of power in Latin America suggests that the conventional economic sources of power constitute relatively static
elements of power. Since ownership of land or mines does not
pass readily from the hands of one group to another, control
of conventional bases of power cannot be secured by the ambitious mestizo, mulatto, or Indian without a major social upheaval. The system of land tenure dooms to frustration ambitious individuals in search of a new agrarian base of power.
Foreign exploitation of mineral resources effectively blocks
the possibilities of shifts in the possession of mineral bases
of power. And at its current pace of development, industrialization has failed to expand into a broad, substantial base of
power.

But while the conventional economic bases of power, land
ownership, and control of mineral resources represent essentially economic constants in the contemporary equation of
power in Latin America, government and the army—often indistinguishable in Latin American society—represent notable
variables. For in Latin America government does not merely
constitute the stakes of a struggle among rival economic interests; in Latin America government itself is a unique base of
economic power that, unlike the conventional economic bases
of power, is subject to fluctuations in possession. Whereas
direct profits from oil fields or copper mines may not be within
the grasp of the Latin American, the legal sovereignty of the

[46] Fourteen Latin American states are classified as "underdeveloped"
and none as "highly developed" by Eugene Staley, *The Future of Underdeveloped Countries: Political Implications of Economic Development*
(New York: Harper, 1954), pp. 16-17.

Latin American states demands that the governmental personnel who serve as intermediaries between the foreign-owned company and the domestic concession shall be of native origin. Thus the discrepancy between the political independence and the economic colonialism of the Latin American states permits government, in the power system of Latin America, to occupy an unusual position as a shifting base of economic power. With the number of lucrative governmental and army posts necessarily limited, the competition understandably is keen. As political office provides a uniquely dynamic opportunity to acquire an economic base of power, however, sufficiently large segments of the population are prepared to take the ultimate risk, the risk of life, in a revolt, in a *coup d'état,* to perpetuate a characteristic feature of Latin American politics—chronic political instability. In the distinctive power structure of Latin America, government serves as a special transformer through which pass the currents of economic ambition.

The pattern of political instability, significantly, has not evolved as a challenge to the conventional economic bases of power, for irregular shifts in control of government take place without disturbing the established economic bases of power. Although widespread industrialization, accompanied by an intensification of economic nationalism, could alter the existing pattern of power, although an extensive program of land reform could not help but affect the distribution of power, seizure of government by a new *caudillo,* on the contrary, does not provoke profound social and economic repercussions in Latin America. Thus chronic political instability serves as an avenue of socioeconomic mobility, but it does not pose a genuine danger to the control of the conventional economic bases of power. When a "revolutionary" junta replaced Federico Chaves as President of Paraguay in May 1954 with Tómas Romero Pereira and subsequently, in July, arranged for the election of General Alfredo Stroessner without opposition, the pattern was a familiar one: the cast of political characters was shuffled, and the colonial economy of Paraguay remained intact. Indeed, such events can be evaluated adequately only in terms of the French aphorism, "Plus ça change, plus c'est la même chose."

The interpretation of power and political instability in Latin America developed by this study may be summarized in a series of generalized propositions. A decisive correlation exists between the control of the economic bases of power and the real exercise of political power in Latin America. Control of the conventional economic bases of power remains relatively static. Because of the colonial nature of the Latin American economies, an exceptional economic premium attaches to control of the apparatus of government as a dynamic base of power. Whereas the conventional bases of power effectively restrict mobility in economic status, control of government provides an unusually dynamic route to wealth and power. Thus the contrast between the stable character of the conventional economic bases of power and the shifting, unconventional position of government provokes intense and violent competition for control of government as a means of acquiring and expanding a base of wealth and power. In the vocabulary of mathematics, *chronic political instability is a function of the contradiction between the realities of a colonial economy and the political requirements of legal sovereignty among the Latin American states.*

V

Significant implications for both public policy and research appear inherent in the interpretation of Latin American politics here formulated. In the field of public policy, this interpretation implies that it is not possible for the United States to have powerful allies in Latin America so long as present economic patterns persist. Contemporary economic patterns of colonialism are conducive to the maintenance of reliable *diplomatic* allies for the United States in Latin America; and the *diplomatic* reliability of the Latin American states is faithfully registered, on many issues, in the voting records of the General Assembly of the United Nations. But the same economic conditions that ensure diplomatic reliability weaken the *power* position of the Latin American states. For, as Hans Morgenthau recognizes in the second (and not the first) edition of his *Politics Among Nations,* the quality of government itself is a factor of power in international politics.[47] Hence economic colonialism promotes political instability, which detracts from the power of reliable diplomatic allies of the United States; but, while the achievement of political stability would augment the power of the Latin American states, the elimination of a status of economic colonialism may diminish the diplomatic reliability of their governments! And the dilemma thus brought to the surface by the interpretation of Latin American politics

[47] Hans J. Morgenthau, *Politics Among Nations* (New York: Knopf, 1954), p. viii.

offered in this study has never been publicly acknowledged by the United States Department of State.

For research, the implications of this interpretation of Latin American politics are rather obvious. If political studies of the Latin American area are to rest on more than superficial foundations, they can rest neither on formal analyses of constitutions nor on the diplomatic exchanges between the United States and various Latin American countries. Nor, in the light of this interpretation, can a study nourish the illusion that it has penetrated to the realities of Latin American politics when it has applied the label "dictator" to a particular holder of governmental office in Latin America. The Latin American caudillo, according to the implications of the interpretation presented here, operates within a narrowly circumscribed range of power, since he may not tamper with the traditional economic bases of power. Serious attempts to analyze the nature of politics in Latin America, therefore, must seek to identify the ambits of political maneuverability within which power may be exercised by those who occupy posts of governmental authority in sovereign states with colonial economies. The successful conclusion of such attempts should result in a new awareness of the limitations on the nature of the power actually exercised by presidents and junta members in the politically unstable environment of Latin America.

The Changing Structure of Foreign Investment in Latin America

TEOTONIO DOS SANTOS

Dos Santos shows how the classical pattern of the colonial economy is changing in Latin America, and a new type of vulnerability and control is emerging. Foreign investment has increasingly been flowing into the industrial manufacturing sectors of the more advanced Latin American economies rather than the mining and agricultural sectors. In place of the foreign investment "enclaves" that were merely part of their countries in a geographical sense, foreign capital has now become substantially integrated with the basic sectors of the economy as a whole and is determining their patterns of development in even more fundamental ways than was true in the past and is still true of the least-developed Latin American countries. He, Quijano, and Polit deal with this question later in some detail for Brazil, Peru, and Argentina.

Teotonio dos Santos, a Brazilian economist currently teaching at the University of Chile, is carrying out research on the impact of United States investment on Brazilian development.

THE IMAGE OF Latin America among most social scientists is outdated historically.

The increasing industrialization and urbanization of Latin America, particularly in the last decade, has not been sufficiently well recognized. The importance of the new classes that have emerged in this period—especially the industrialists and urban workers—has not been well understood. The image that has persisted is that of an agrarian-exporting, nonindustrial Latin America, dominated by a rural oligarchy in league with foreign interests.

Even more crude is an image in which foreign interests are linked solely with the agrarian-exporting sector, in opposition to industrial development. This model may still apply in some countries, but it is completely outdated for the developing countries, where industrialization and foreign capital are being combined and increasingly unified.

Foremost among the characteristics that essentially alter the meaning of industrialization in Latin America, and perhaps in developing countries in general, are the specific conditions of world economy under which industrialization takes place. In these countries it takes place within the boundaries of international capitalist integration, dominated by large corporations in an oligopolistic economy.

Since the end of the Second World War the world economy has undergone an intense process of economic integration. On the one hand, the socialist bloc was established; on the other, in the capitalist world, U.S. capital was the source of European economic reorganization and extended itself throughout the world. The process of capitalist international economic integration took place under American hegemony.

We can understand this process in Latin America if we consider the value, in millions of dollars, of American investments in our countries (Table 1). If we compare the value of these investments before the Second World War with that during and after the war, we can draw significant conclusions. We see that the value of these investments dropped in the period midway between the crisis of 1929 and the end of the Second World War. This drop in value was a result of the disorganization of the U.S. economy, caused by the crisis, and by the increased domestic investment demanded by the wartime economy. When the war no longer necessitated domestic investments in a depressed economy, capital was redirected to the backward economies. Now, though, foreign capital found these economies in the process of industrialization, ruled by nationalist and industrialist ideologies. This factor was decisive for the new investments. Set against a growing domestic market and the first fruits of a highly lucrative mercantile economy, the inducements to foreign investment were very great. The data show that from 1950 to 1961 the value of North American investments in Latin America practically doubled.

TABLE 1

YEAR	1929	1936	1940	1943	1950	1961
Millions of Dollars	3.462	2.803	2.696	2.721	4.445	8.200

Data from *El Financiamiento Externo de América Latina*, CEPAL, United Nations, December 1964.

Breaking down the capital by economic sectors, we note a significant change. Before the 1940's the greatest activity was in the primary sector (agriculture and mining) and in railroads. This indicates the integration of foreign capital with the colonial-exporting character of the Latin American economy. Foreign capital was invested in an economy that turned out raw materials and agricultural products, complemented by the means of transportation for their export.

The data on American investments in Latin America for this period clearly show this (Table 2): Manufacturing represented only 6.3 percent of the direct American investments in Latin America in 1929. The primary sector (agriculture and mining), railroads, and trade represented, in 1897, 91.6 percent, and in 1929, 55.7 percent of these investments. Within this period we note a growth in the oil and public utilities sectors. Oil, which had 3.5 percent of the investments in 1897, already had 20.1 percent in 1929. At the same time, public utilities rose from 3.3 percent to 15.8 percent. During this same period investments in manufacturing rose from 3 percent to 6.3 percent of the total.

TABLE 2

DIRECT AMERICAN INVESTMENTS IN LATIN AMERICA, BY SECTORS, 1897-1929, IN MILLIONS OF U.S. DOLLARS

Economic Sector	1897 Total	%	1908 Total	%	1919 Total	%	1929 Total	%	1950 Total	%
Agriculture	56.5	18.6	158.2	21.1	500.1	25.3	877.3	14.1	a	a
Mining	79.0	26.0	302.6	40.4	660.8	33.4	801.4	22.0	628	14.1
Oil	10.5	3.5	68.0	9.1	326.0	16.5	731.5	20.1	1233	27.7
Railroads	129.7	42.6	110.0	14.7	211.2	10.7	230.1	6.3 }	927	20.8
Utilities	10.1	3.3	57.5	6.9	101.0	5.1	575.9	15.8 }		
Mfg.	3.0	1.0	30.0	4.0	84.0	4.2	231.0	6.3	780	17.5
Trade	13.5	4.4	23.5	3.1	71.0	3.6	119.2	3.3 }	877	19.9
Others	2.0	0.6	5.0	0.7	23.5	1.2	79.4	2.2 }		

Source: *El Financiamiento Externo de América Latina*, Table 15.

a Included in Trade and Other Industries.

By 1950 investments in manufacturing increased to 17.5 percent of the total, and agriculture and mining decreased in relation to the other sectors. Oil took the lead among the products. These changes were underscored in later years, as the data in Table 3 show. Between 1951 and 1962 investments in oil rose to 33 percent of the total, and those in manufacturing to 31 percent. Mining represents 12 percent, and trade and other industries, 24 percent of the total investments. As Table 3 shows, manufacturing held 60 percent in 1961-62, partly because of a problem in the consolidation of investments in oil.

TABLE 3

PRIVATE INVESTMENTS FROM THE UNITED STATES IN LATIN AMERICA, BY PRINCIPAL SECTORS, 1951-1962 [a]

Industrial Sector	1951-55 Millions of Dollars	%	1956-60 Millions of Dollars	%	1961-62 Millions of Dollars	%	1951-62 Millions of Dollars	%
Total	1,751	100	3,398	100	616	100	5,765	100
Oil	348	20	1,571	46	−7	−1	1,912	33
Mining	339	19	301	9	46	7	686	12
Mfg.	613	35	791	23	370	60	1,774	31
Trade & Others	451	26	735	22	207	34	1,393	24

Source: United States Department of Commerce, *Balance of Payments, Statistical Supplement to Survey of Current Business* (1963), and *Survey of Current Business* (several numbers from 1963 and 1964).

[a] Reinvested profits from affiliates included. Taken from *El Financiamiento Externo de América Latina,* Table 179.

The data presented here show that American investments (and foreign capital in general) not only have tended to penetrate more deeply into Latin America, but also have become more and more thoroughly integrated in the industrial sectors. Distribution of these data by countries would unquestionably show that the still-important investments in the primary and trade sectors, representing 36 percent of the total in 1951-62, are in the less developed countries. On the other hand, the oil investments are mainly in Venezuela. In the developing countries, manufacturing is the principal recipient of investments.

Our data reveal the process of economic integration mentioned earlier in this paper. Foreign investment is gradually ceasing to be a colonial-exporting enclave and is changing the old international division of labor: the production of raw materials by underdeveloped countries and the production of manufactured goods by developed countries. Faced with the industrial growth of Latin America in the 1930's and the protectionist measures taken by the governments of that period, foreign capital is turning toward the manufacturing sector, is being integrated with the present economies, and is proceeding to dominate their industrial capitalist sectors. This is what is now happening in Latin America. What effects has this process on the economic structure of Latin America?

In the first place, there are qualitative changes in the size of the enterprises. Corporations are being formed, generally affiliated with North American or European corporations. The possibility of monopolizing the existing market allows them to increase their profits without opening up new markets. This diminishes the stimulus to development that the enterprises might have given these economies.

In the second place, an intensive integration of the economy of these countries with foreign capital is taking place. Contrary to what is believed by many social scientists, this integration increases the economic dependence of these countries on other countries. There is, however, an internal contradiction in this dependence: *as it increases, the need for it diminishes.* This may be explained in the following manner:

During their agrarian-exporting stage based on the international division of labor between the producers of raw materials and the producers of manufactured goods, the underdeveloped economies essentially depended on the importation of manufactured products. Financial dependence implied as well a dependence on the level of production.

With the industrial growth of the underdeveloped countries, production has been increasingly directed toward the domestic market. However, while the foreign capital on which this industrialization has been based takes over the more advanced economic sectors and tightens its hold on these economies, causing them to be even more dependent, this capital is no longer necessary, precisely because the economy, now industrially integrated, is less dependent on foreign capital. This process is completed by the establishment of heavy industries, of machine-producing machinery—a step that has not yet been completed in the countries of Latin America. There remains, however, a division of labor between countries producing manufactured goods and light machinery, and countries producing heavy machinery. This should not obscure the general tendencies that we are tracing. The conclusion remains that there is a growing contradiction between the control exercised by foreign capital over the economy and the technical capacity of this economy to support itself.

The result is the increasing historical uselessness of foreign control and consequently of the socioeconomic system that maintains it.

The United States and Latin America

J. P. MORRAY

Morray argues that the United States has tried, since
frightened by the Cuban revolution, to devise new policies
to fulfill old and consistent purposes—the protection of
the interests of what he terms the "investor classes" of the
United States, and of the Latin American countries themselves. The Alliance for Progress, he believes, is one such
device, an attempt to make the dominant classes of Latin
America make just such reforms as are necessary to perpetuate the reign of capitalism. Thus, while talking of
reform and development, the Alliance itself imposes conditions on countries recipient of "aid" that makes it well
nigh impossible for these countries to realize rational
development programs.

Joseph Parker Morray graduated from the United States
Naval Academy at Annapolis and from Harvard Law
School, served as Assistant Naval Attaché of the United
States in Spain and Paraguay, has been Visiting Professor
of Law at the University of California at Berkeley, and
presently is Professor of Sociology at the University of
Chile. He is the author of *From Yalta to Disarmament* and
The Second Revolution in Cuba, both Monthly Review Press.

THE LATIN AMERICANS have a peculiar ability to exasperate
the United States Government. Their comportment generally
does not conform to Washington's model of civilized and rational behavior. In earlier times this exasperation was frequent-

ly and openly proclaimed by United States officials, even by Presidents and Secretaries of State and War. During a crisis in Santo Domingo in 1904 President Theodore Roosevelt announced that "chronic wrongdoing or an impotence that results in a general loosening of the ties of civilized society may . . . require intervention by some civilized nation." The United States would be forced, he said, "in flagrant cases of such wrongdoing or impotence, to the exercise of an international police power." Elihu Root proposed the imposition of the Platt Amendment on the Cubans as a necessary safeguard against the inability of the Cuban leaders to maintain order and secure the safety of life and property. Roosevelt concurred and solemnly warned the Cubans that "if elections become . . . a farce and if the insurrectionary habit becomes confirmed . . . it is absolutely out of the question that the Island should remain independent."

Republicans and Democrats, Northerners and Southerners have shared the exasperation. The image of Latin America that has prevailed in Washington and still prevails is filled with turmoil and chaos, with *coups d'état* and insurrection, with inflation, bankruptcy, and defaulting debtors. It is an understatement to say that Washington has lacked confidence in the competence of the Latin Americans to run their own affairs. A question arises over whether the ruling image is an accurate one and whether this lack of confidence is truly deserved. Undoubtedly there is some inaccuracy in the stereotype. It does not discriminate sufficiently among more than 20 different countries, each with its own history and its own record of successes and failures. It is unfair to lump all together and hold all responsible for their separate defaults. Nevertheless, some very unfavorable generalizations about the states of Latin America are surely justified by the facts. Statistics on per capita income, living standards, productivity, literacy, disease, food consumption, sanitation, and life expectancy speak for themselves. The ruling classes in Latin America can hardly expect vindication on this record.

A major factor in the present chapter of relations between the United States and Latin America is the mixture of condescension and thinly veiled contempt in Washington toward its Latin allies. The style of public language has become more diplomatic in recent decades, but the level of vexation is hardly any lower. Congressmen frequently give it vent. Any hearing on Capitol Hill that treats of the Alliance for Progress is apt to reveal the typical sentiments of the undisciplined and outspoken Senators and Representatives. Senator Dirksen frequently expresses his disdain with such questions as "Where is the Alliance?" and "Where is the Progress?" Senator Ernest Gruening, generally a supporter of foreign aid, warned Congress and the Administration through his case study of the Alliance for Progress in Chile that "Chilean agencies cannot be depended upon to exercise adequate control over the end use of investments."[1] His report is full of annoyance with the Chileans and also with American aid officials who have failed to give the Chileans detailed and continuous supervision. Such supervision is indispensable, in his view, to making the Alliance effective as "an alternative to Communist blandishments and revolutionary chaos." His premise is:

> Latin American people, accustomed to high-sounding rhetoric and campaign promises that do not materialize, are understandably cynical. To gain their support, the Alliance for Progress must demonstrate its serious intentions with visible achievements.[2]

Though Chile during the first five years of the Alliance had received the highest per capita aid in Latin America and was one of the eight nations in which United States aid was concentrated, Gruening concludes:

> Disappointingly, there is little to indicate that U.S. assistance is having a meaningful impact upon Chilean economic and social development.[3]

It is a part of the role of the executive departments of the government to speak kind and flattering words to their proud and sensitive Latin American allies. But occasionally flashes of impatient disgust show through the diplomatic mask. This was the case in the attitude of "no-confidence" toward the Cuban emigré leaders, whose humiliation during and after the Bay of Pigs fiasco brought a public resignation by José Miro Cardona from the emigré Council and an exchange of recriminations between him and President Kennedy. The blunt words of the President addressed to Latin American leaders on April 20, 1961, were hardly less insulting than the warning of Theodore Roosevelt in 1904. Mr. Kennedy dropped diplomatic tact to show his anger:

[1] *United States Foreign Aid in Action: A Case Study*, submitted by Senator Ernest Gruening to the Subcommittee on Foreign Aid Expenditures of the Senate Committee on Government Operations. (June 28, 1966) (Washington: U.S. Government Printing Office), p. 68.
[2] *Ibid.*, p. 69.
[3] *Ibid.*, p. 121.

But let the record show that our restraint is not inexhaustible. Should it ever appear that the inter-American doctrine of non-interference merely conceals or excuses a policy of nonaction—if the nations of this hemisphere should fail to meet their commitments against outside Communist penetration—then I want it clearly understood that this Government will not hesitate in meeting its primary obligations, which are to the security of our nation.[4]

In an authoritative study prepared for the Council on Foreign Relations the former United States Representative in the Organization of American States, Ambassador John C. Dreier, expressed a similar warning:

If they [the leaders of the Latin American states] attempt irresponsible use of their numerical strength in the Organization of American States, if they carry to extremes the doctrine of non-intervention, if they leave the United States no alternative but to act unilaterally to protect itself, they will have destroyed not only the basis of hemispheric cooperation for progress but all hope of a secure future for themselves.[5]

In 1965 the executive branch sharply amplified these previous expressions of doubt concerning the reliability of Latin American leaders to do their duty. President Johnson's hasty intervention with United States armed forces in the Dominican Republic was an index of his confidence in the Dominicans to manage their own affairs. This precipitate and presumptuous action spoke louder than words; and the message it conveyed caused resentment throughout Latin America.

Yet, despite these demonstrated feelings of impatience, condescension and exasperation on one side and feelings of humiliation, resentment, and indignation on the other, we have what is called the Alliance for Progress. Why? The answer requires us to examine briefly the state of affairs in Latin America and the nature of the Alliance.

Concrete analysis of one country will give us suggestive clues to what has been happening in all. Let us take the largest of the Latin American countries, Brazil, with a population of 80 million people and a territory roughly equal to that of the United States. Before approximately 1930 Brazil's economy had developed as a colonial appendix to that of the United

[4] Address by President John F. Kennedy before the American Society of Newspaper Editors, Washington, D. C., April 20, 1961. Department of State, *American Foreign Policy: Current Documents, 1961* (Washington, U.S. Government Printing Office, 1965), p. 300.
[5] John C. Dreier. *The Organization of the American States and the Hemisphere Crisis* (Published for the Council on Foreign Relations by Harper and Row, New York and Evanston, 1962), p. 114.

States and Europe. Agricultural products, especially coffee, sugar, cacao, and cotton, were cultivated and harvested for export to the European and North American markets. Capital for these enterprises came mainly from the fazendeiros, Brazilian owners of great rural estates, and from absentee investors who were nationals of the purchasing countries. Heavy industry did not exist in Brazil, and even light industry was insignificant. Most manufactured goods had to be imported from abroad at high prices, another source of profits and additional capital accumulation for the metropolitan countries. Brazil hardly existed as a unified nation. It was a group of agricultural regions isolated from each other, some serving the needs of foreign buyers and investors, some producing with primitive techniques for local and regional consumption. Government was dominated by the fazendeiros and especially by the great coffee planters of São Paulo and Minas Gerais, who were closely affiliated with foreign capital. Both federal and state governments depended on loans from foreign banks and investors. Commerce in imports and exports, electric power, the telephone monopolies, railways, shipping, urban transport, insurance, and the larger banks were in the hands of foreigners. Brazil was integrated financially and economically into the world capitalist economy as a semicolony.[6]

The world-wide crisis of the European and United States economies in 1929 and the 1930's inflicted such prolonged hardships on the Brazilians that new initiatives were begun, both economic and political, to repair the damage and give Brazil a new independence. The coffee and sugar barons, principal Brazilian beneficiaries of the colonial system, were driven from power in the federal government by a liberal Revolution headed by Getulio Vargas. A "Liberal Alliance" led by landowners and ranchers of Río Grande del Sur as well as landowners and bourgeoisie of other less important states took over the direction of affairs. The petty bourgeoisie of the cities gave support. For the first time in Brazilian history the masses, including industrial workers in the cities and in some of the rural areas, began to take part in political life. Young officers took over the direction of the army and converted it into an instrument of revolution in support of the Liberal Alliance led by the national bourgeoisie. Economic policy of the new lead-

[6] See the essay by Luis V. Sommi, which appears as a prologue to Franklin de Oliveira, *Revolución y Contrarevolución en el Brasil* (Buenos Aires: Ediciones Iguazu, 1965). (Translation from Portuguese into Spanish by Luis V. Sommi.)

ership accorded with its class interests. It was capitalist, protectionist, and antiimperialist.

In the decades since 1930 Brazilian society has developed within the context of this struggle of a renovating alliance led by the national bourgeoisie against the coffee-sugar plantation owners, traditional Brazilian allies of foreign capitalists. Population has grown rapidly, and this growth has been accompanied by a great migration of persons born in the rural areas to the mushrooming cities. By 1965 one-half the population lived in cities, compared with 20 percent in 1930. Some heavy industry has been created, and light industry has grown within a protected market. The industrial working class, which has grown into a force of 2.5 million persons concentrated in a few cities, is now a political factor of major weight, as are the other five million Brazilians who work for wages. This is a change of historic importance. The petty bourgeoisie of the cities has also increased greatly in numbers.

The rural population, despite the migration to the cities, has grown in absolute numbers from 25 million in 1930 to 42 million in 1965. The continuing supply of surplus labor in the countryside has retarded modernization in agriculture, since manpower is still cheaper than machinery. Conditions of poverty and privation in the rural areas are the principal determining factors in the migration to the cities. In the latter, unemployment and underemployment are high, and life in the slum areas wretched but nevertheless not so hopeless as life in the countryside. This lesser evil of escape to the cities has also served as a kind of protection to the archaic and stagnated system of land tenure, since it removes some of the most desperate from the struggle between landlord and landless campesino.

Throughout this period the national bourgeoisie has continued to lead the major political parties, who compete with each other to enlist the support of the petty bourgeoisie and wage workers. As a stimulus to development some of these leaders advocated a resort to state capitalism, with the government playing a leading role in accumulating capital for investment in basic industries through taxation and borrowing on government credit. Others favored reliance on private enterprise, assisted by government policies favoring the private investor. Economists argued the convenience of agrarian reform to capitalist development to widen the internal market for manufactured products. Almost all political leaders gave this at least verbal support; those with social democratic tendencies, such as

João Goulart, actually tried to persuade Congress to enact an agrarian reform. But the leadership of the parties includes many landowners and ranchers who would be hurt by land redistribution. They are able to weaken worker support for the reform with predictions of food scarcities and higher prices in the cities. The issue became more urgent and ominous in 1958 with the appearance of armed peasant leagues in northeastern Brazil, led by the lawyer Francisco Julião. These spread south into Minas Gerais, stronghold of an oligarchy of great landowners, hitherto impregnable. A national congress of more than 1,000 peasant leaders in Belo Horizonte in 1961 showed the impressive political strength of the new movement. Agrarian reform had passed from the realm of abstract discussion by experts to become an important factor in the struggles of the Brazilian masses.[7]

The rise of social tensions in the countryside was matched by growing strife in the cities and widespread discontent with the slow pace of development in the industrial sector. Brazil's bourgeoisie blend of free enterprise and state capitalism has not been meeting the needs of a rapidly growing population with rising aspirations and consciousness of revolutionary examples in other countries. This generalized and deepening impatience among the poor Brazilian masses, added to the antagonism between the growing working class and the owners of industry, threatens to bring on a struggle for a social revolution that would liquidate the bourgeois order and establish a working class dictatorship committed to the building of socialism. This is the goal of many leaders of the powerful labor organization, Workers' General Command (CGT). The Communist Party thinks that this is premature and has advocated instead a longer period of capitalist development under the leadership of the nationalist and antiimperialist bourgeoisie. But the Communist Party finds itself pressed forward by excited masses, who are constantly inflamed by non-Party Marxists, Fidelistas, Pekinistas, Trotskyists, and petty bourgeois radicals. The objective situation, a "hidden civil war," as Franklin de Oliveira calls it, in which poverty kills millions before they reach the age of thirty, cries out for drastic remedy, and any vanguard party that counsels caution and delay finds itself on the defensive.

The bourgeois directorate of the faltering state was and is divided on what to do to save the social order from the threat-

[7] Ruy Mauro Marini, "Contradicciones y Conflictos en el Brasil Contemporáneo," *Arauco*, Santiago de Chile, October 1966, p. 20.

ening storm. Juscelino Kubitshek, President from 1956 to 1960, arrived at the conclusion that Brazil must have outside help if disaster was to be averted. His *Operation Pan America* proposals, in which United States aid was entreated, set the stage for the new and noisy entry of the United States Government into Latin America with the Alliance for Progress. The plight of the Brazilian bourgeoisie is repeated in the other Latin American countries. It is unable with its own resources and techniques to produce a rate of development satisfying to the awakened masses. It cannot force this rate under capitalist relations without exacerbating its difficult contradiction with the working class. And to seek help from the wealthy capitalist countries means a loss of economic independence to imperialism. No wonder spokesmen for the national bourgeoisie of these countries are divided and vacillating. Some, like Victor Haya de la Torre in Peru, have concluded that imperialism is the best form of development in the underdeveloped countries. He proclaims that "imperialism is necessary for Latin America's development."[8] President José María Velasco Ibarra of Ecuador came to a similar conclusion for his country. "Ecuador has no native capital," he said. "Only foreign investments will bring in such capital, needed to develop the country."[9] President Frei in Chile, though he does not state his position so plainly, expresses a similar opinion through his policies. So did Rómulo Betancourt in Venezuela.

But other representatives of the national bourgeoisie resist this turning to an old enemy for a dangerous kind of help. In Brazil Janio Quadros and João Goulart shrugged off United States aid and tried to strengthen the state sector in the Brazilian economy. They were willing to accept help from the socialist countries in the fight to strengthen independence from imperialist domination. But they encountered powerful opposition from their own class in Brazil, as well as from a United States Government embarked on a vigorous new offensive, which we are about to examine; and they were handicapped by their own vacillations. Goulart won a great popular victory in a plebiscite in 1963, but this only fed the flames of social conflict. During the following months he lost support among the bourgeoisie and the petty bourgeoisie as his ability to contain the radical masses of workers and peasants became more doubtful.

The overthrow of Goulart in 1964 by the high command of

[8] John Gerassi, *The Great Fear* (New York: Macmillan, 1963), p. 122.
[9] *Ibid.*, p. 127.

the Army and a section of Congress was carried out with United States support as a necessary clearing of the ground for implementing the Alliance for Progress. Washington quickly recognized the new regime and the United States Ambassador in Brazil, Lincoln Gordon, publicized his satisfaction with the change of direction and command. Evidently the "Alliance" is open only to certain kinds of leaders and aims to promote only certain kinds of "Progress." The Alliance is discriminating and selective; it is not indifferent to the contests for power inside each Latin American country, not even the contests between competing bourgeois factions. The era of the Good Neighbor, during which the United States Government formally renounced the practice of intervention, is dead. Why this is a necessary corollary to the Alliance becomes evident from its character and content.

Getting to the heart of the Alliance is made somewhat difficult by the fanfare of verbiage that announced its birth. Speeches of the Latin American delegates to the Conference at Bogotá, Colombia, in 1960, and at Punta del Este, Uruguay, in 1961, reflected the reformist position, more or less demagogic, of many of these leaders in their internal struggles with an oligarchy that had always enjoyed imperialist support. There was repeated insistence on the need for land reform, for social progress, for raising rapidly the income and standard of living of the needier sections of the population, for a more equitable distribution of national income, and for industrialization. Special emphasis was placed on the development of capital-goods industries to liberate the Latin American countries from their colonialist dependence on export of a limited number of primary products and importation of capital goods from the United States and Western Europe. The United States consented to the inclusion of these goals in the Charters of verbal commitments prepared at the conferences. The Punta del Este Charter even speaks of "taking full advantage of both private and public sectors . . . in the development of capital-goods industries."[10]

But the United States delegates insisted on the inclusion of other phrases as well, for example, a clause in the Punta del Este Charter that commits the signatories to the promotion "of

[10] The Charter of Punta del Este Establishing an Alliance for Progress Within the Framework of Operation Pan America, Title I, Paragraph 4 (August 17, 1961). The Charter as well as other important reference material are reprinted in *Regional and Other Documents Concerning United States Relations With Latin America,* compiled by the House Committee on Foreign Affairs (Washington: U.S. Government Printing Office, 1966).

conditions that will encourage the flow of foreign investments."[11] Though these brief words are inconspicuous in the
Charter as a whole, they are, from the point of view of Washington, the main purpose of the Alliance. To this must be
added, as we shall see in the implementation of the Alliance by
Congress, another purpose nowhere explicitly stated: the promotion of United States exports to Latin America by means of
loans to purchasers and insurance against credit risks. Many
have thought the Alliance represents an undertaking by the
United States to finance the economic development plans of
independent Latin American countries. In truth, it represents
something quite different—the use of United States public
funds in the battle to reopen Latin America to United States
investors.

The task of checking the development of independent economies and reintegrating Latin America into the international
capitalist system has many facets. Some of these lend themselves to ambiguous interpretations. For example, the initial
emphasis on public health projects, on the elimination of ma-
laria and the provision of potable water, on the construction of
schools and on the reduction of illiteracy draw favorable attention. Such laudable projects were not unrelated to a veiled
strategic purpose. They were felt to be indispensable to the
generation of a measure of hope in the restive masses, to the
immediate reduction of explosive social tensions in the years of
the portentous Cuban Revolution, which Washington read as a
warning of what might occur throughout Latin America. They
were measures designed to buy time and to revive faith in the
potential of the existing bourgeois social order to meet the
problems of the hemisphere. It was not necessary to agree on
the role of imperialism in future development in order to agree
on the necessity for such emergency steps. Likewise, all could
agree on the importance of promoting the development of such
infrastructure projects as road and bridge building, electrifica-
tion and improvement of ports, harbors, and docks. In the
eyes of the national bourgeoisie these improvements facilitate
the development of an independent economy. In the eyes of
U.S. officials they also enhance the projects of profitable investments for themselves. The specification of who is to benefit
most from these infrastructure expenditures depends on
whether the other conditions of security and confidence are
created for the foreign investor.

These other conditions are all related to the possibility of

[11] *Ibid.* Title II, Chapter II, Paragraph 2 (f).

receiving high profits and remitting them more or less freely to the United States. And it is in the disputes between Washington and Latin America over the creation of these conditions that the true character of the Alliance begins to appear. One of these conditions is security against expropriation. The right of a poor country to expropriate does not exist if it is conditioned on an obligation to pay full compensation promptly. Congress is using the offer of Alliance funds to purchase a renunciation by the Latin American countries of an effective right to expropriate the property of United States citizens. The Foreign Assistance Act, which fixes the conditions on the expenditure of Congressional appropriations of aid funds, prohibits their use to benefit a state that fails to make "speedy compensation ... in convertible foreign exchange ... to the full value" of any property expropriated from United States citizens.[12] U.S. aid funds may not be used to make the compensation.[13] This 1963 amendment to the original act proved to be an effective weapon in the hands of the United States Ambassador in Brazil. When the governor of Rio Grande del Sur, Leonel Brizola, carried out an expropriation of properties belonging to a United States telephone company, he received the support of President Goulart. But this blow at U.S. private investment divided the Brazilian bourgeoisie and the Brazilian Army, because it raised the threat of an end to all aid—economic, social, and military —from the United States. Ambassador Gordon, by bringing this clause to the attention of Brazilian generals and politicians, contributed to the plotting that forged the 1964 coup. It was an argument that united the oligarchy and the free enterprise bourgeoisie against the more radical champions of development along state-capitalist lines. The latter were prepared to accept the loss of U.S. aid and to turn to the Soviet Union for credits. This would be accompanied by a change in foreign policy toward independence and neutrality in the cold war between the United States and the U.S.S.R. To foreclose such a line of development is one of the purposes of the Alliance.

The investment-guarantee program also indicates Washington's intentions concerning the hemisphere. It insures United States investors in Latin America against loss of their investment due to war, revolution, insurrection, or expropriation. It also insures them against the inability to convert their profits

---

[12] The Foreign Assistance Act of 1961, as amended, Section 620 (e) (1), *Regional and Other Documents Concerning United States Relations with Latin America*, House Committee on Foreign Affairs (Washington: U.S. Government Printing Office, 1966), p. 143.

[13] *Ibid.* Section 620 (g).

into United States dollars.[14] The political climate in Latin America has been changing over the past few decades in a direction unfavorable to U.S. economic and political domination. Many parties are openly hostile to it and others have become indifferent to the effects of their policies on the foreign investor. Inflation, exchange controls, discriminatory taxation, expropriations, and insurrections are some of the realities that investors see in Latin America, and they are naturally disheartened. The level of United States investment in Latin America has risen slowly compared to its rise in such safer regions as Canada and Western Europe.[15] The Cuban Revolution dealt another blow to the confidence of investors in Latin America.[16] It was a situation that no single investor or investor group could resolve with its own resources. Yet the reluctance of investors to go into Latin America threatened the U.S. with the loss of the whole area by default. The Latin American governments seemed unable to prevent it.

But there was one government to which the investors could turn for help. Through the investment guarantee program the extraordinary risks in the area are shifted to the U.S. Government, and investors can discount them in weighing their deci-

---

[14] *Ibid.* Section 221 (b) (1), Department of State, *American Foreign Policy: Current Documents 1961* (Washington: U.S. Government Printing Office, 1965), p. 1273.

[15] Between 1950 and 1960 the value of United States direct investments in the Latin American Republics doubled (from $4.4 billion to $8.4 billion). During the same period their value in Canada tripled (from $3.6 billion to $11.2 billion); and their value in Europe quadrupled (from $1.7 billion to $6.6 billion). U.S. Department of Commerce, *Balance of Payments: Statistical Supplement, Revised Edition* (Washington, U.S. Government Printing Office, 1963), Table 57, pp. 208-9. The lagging rate of private investment in Latin America was the subject of Hearings held by a Subcommittee of the Joint Economic Committee of Congress on January 14, 15, and 16, 1964. The Subcommittee opened its report on the Hearings with the following statement: "North Americans (and Western Europeans, as well) who live under and enjoy the benefits of a predominantly free-enterprise, private-investment market system of economic organization are increasingly concerned about the lagging rate of private investment in the Latin American development program. They are concerned also with the attitude of seeming indifference in many parts of Latin America itself to the potential contributions of the private sector. This local apathy is manifest in a concentration of energies on governmental development programs, the reported exodus of domestic capital, the flight from local currencies, and the persistent discouragements which private, and especially foreign private, capital seemingly must face." *Private Investment in Latin America*, a Report of the Subcommittee on Inter-American Economic Relationships of the Joint Economic Committee (Washington: U.S. Government Printing Office, 1964), p. 1.

[16] This factor is analyzed in Leland L. Johnson, *The Course of U.S. Private Investment in Latin America Since the Rise of Castro* (Santa Monica, California, The Rand Corporation RM-4091-ISA, 1964).

sions. Furthermore, the insured investor and the Latin American governments both know that the relationship between them is altered by the investment guarantee of the United States Government. The investor enjoys the engaged solicitude of a powerful champion in any dispute that arises with the local government. Like other insurers, the United States Government, after making good the losses of its aggrieved investors, takes over their claims against the Latin American governments. The United States increases the pressure on the host country by insisting in advance on a recognition of this "subrogation," or substitution of government for investor in case of loss through expropriation or inconvertibility.[17] When Congress was informed of the resistance of Latin American governments to this substitution, it added an amendment cutting off aid to any country that had not given its formal consent prior to December 31, 1966.[18] This was an effective threat, and investment guarantee agreements have now been signed by nearly all.[19] Having improved the climate to this extent, the investors are now asking that the coverage be broadened to include the risks of damage by rioting and demonstrations of the kind that destroyed Sears Roebuck stores in Caracas, Venezuela, and Cali, Colombia, and seriously damaged properties of Pan-American Airways, Braniff-International, and the Goodyear Tire and Rubber Company, in Panama.[20]

Washington has other levers for use in the effort to accelerate the rate of private American investment. A major factor in the investment climate is the ease of converting profits into dollars, and this is affected by the amount of foreign exchange a government commands. Hence, it is an important Alliance goal in the view of the United States Government to press the Latin Americans into measures that will permanently improve

[17] "Since these guarantees involve commitments on the part of the capital-importing as well as the capital-exporting government, an important part of their function goes beyond that of mere indemnification. They are intended also to prevent or discourage changes in the legal conditions under which an enterprise must operate in the host, capital-importing country." *Private Investment in Latin America,* A Report of the Subcommittee on Inter-American Economic Relationships of the Joint Economic Committee (Washington, U.S. Government Printing Office, 1964), p. 15.
[18] The Foreign Assistance Act of 1961, as amended, Section 620 (1).
[19] *Regional and Other Documents Concerning United States Relations with Latin America* (1966), pp. 259-330.
[20] Testimony of N. R. Danielian, President, International Economic Policy Association, in Hearings on *Foreign Assistance Act of 1966* before the House Committee on Foreign Affairs, March 16 to May 17, 1966 (Washington: U.S. Government Printing Office, 1966), p. 861.

their ability to accumulate reserves of foreign exchange. Pressure is applied through the device of the "program loan." The loan is not credited all at once but in periodic increments; it will be suspended if the local government is not acting to improve its foreign exchange position as required.[21] The United States can also apply pressure in the same direction through the International Monetary Fund, which was created to promote the freer convertibility required by international capitalism.

In some countries, such as Chile, governments are advised to reduce food imports by raising the selling price to consumers. This is supposed to stimulate the local farmers into increasing production as imports are reduced step by step. In all countries the United States presses for changes that would help raise the level of exports. This involves essentially an effort to lower costs of production through fiscal, credit, and monetary policies that will increase unemployment and keep wages down. There are also efforts to persuade the Latin Americans to devalue their currencies on the ground that they can then sell their products at lower prices in foreign markets with a net increase in foreign exchange earnings due to increased volume of sales. But one consequence of devaluing a currency is an increase in the cost of living, since the cost in local currency of imports increases. Therefore, U.S. policies for Latin America imply lower real wages for working people and higher living costs. These are bitter issues in the daily struggle between workers and employers. Development policies designed to secure foreign investment exacerbate social tensions.* This contradiction between the proclaimed goals of social progress and economic development is one of the principal reasons for the failure of the Alliance to achieve the results hoped for. It also explains why implementation of the Alliance has been accompanied by a decline in democratic liberties and a turn to dictatorship and repression in so many countries. Force is

[21] *United States Foreign Aid in Action: A Case Study*, submitted by Senator Ernest Gruening to the Subcommittee on Foreign Aid Expenditures of the Senate Committee on Government Operations (June 28, 1966), p. 30.

* Arthur Schlesinger, Jr., blamed these policies for the crisis in the Dominican Republic that led to United States intervention in 1965. He wrote in *A Thousand Days* (Boston: Houghton Mifflin Company, 1965; Fawcett Crest paperback, 1967): "Undeterred by past error, the International Monetary Fund in 1964-65 persuaded a complaisant government in the Dominican Republic to accept a fiscal program that reduced per capita income, increased unemployment, and led in the spring of 1965 to political convulsion and United States intervention," p. 174.

needed to create an appearance of the peace and stability important to investors. They must feel that the local authorities have the situation securely in hand.

There is one exception to United States interest in helping the Latin American countries increase their exports: aid is not to be furnished to any enterprise that will compete with a United States business, unless the country concerned agrees to limit the export of the products to the United States to 20 percent of output. Congress has made this exception part of the Foreign Assistance Act, allowing the President to waive the restriction "in the national security interest."[22] The conflict here is between different groups of United States investors, some concentrating on production in the United States, others looking for investment opportunities abroad. In Alliance doctrine it is a good thing for the underdeveloped countries to be enabled to earn more foreign exchange through new and increased exports; this is one way of attracting investment, both with the prospect of good profits and with the prospect of unrestricted convertibility. But against this advantage to foreign investors must be weighed the interest of other investors in continuing to dominate an established market without intrusion from new and competitive producers. The 20-percent figure represents the compromise between these two interests, both of which Washington must take into account.

When Congress and Administration ponder the question of Latin American development, they not only express a preference for free enterprise development as against state capitalism and socialism, but also insist that U.S. aid be used to favor the U.S. investor. For example, benefits under the investment guarantee program may be paid only to U.S. citizens or to corporations "substantially beneficially owned" by U.S. citizens.[23] Similarly, only that select group is entitled to draw upon a fund established to encourage the survey of investment opportunities by sharing their cost with the private investor.[24] The true Alliance is between U.S. investors and Washington, with the Latin Americans expected to rest content with what the growing prosperity of U.S. investors would pay to them in taxes, dividends, wages, and protection from revolution. We will not understand the present moment nor foresee the future unless we put ourselves into the shoes of the officials in Wash-

[22] The Foreign Assistance Act of 1961, as amended, Section 620 (d).
[23] Ibid. Section 223 (e).
[24] Ibid. Sections 231-233.

ington who make the decisions. Whether they believe the rights of investors to be divine or not, they do look upon them as sanctified by the Constitution, the legal system, and public convenience. There is a note of desperate determination in the Administration's reiterated proclamation that there are to be "no more Cubas" in Latin America. President Johnson has said that "the American nations cannot, must not, and will not permit the establishment of another Communist government in the Western Hemisphere."[25] Walt W. Rostow, the Chairman of the State Department Policy Planning Council under Kennedy and presently Special Assistant to President Johnson, speaks of the necessity "to maintain an environment on the world scene which will permit our open society to survive and flourish."[26] "Our open society" is Rostow's euphemism for a society that enforces respect for the peculiar rights of an investor class. It is not enough that these rights be respected within the borders of the United States. The destruction of investor rights in Latin America would undermine them in the United States. It would be one more large chink in the armor of obscurantism, which has so far shielded the investors from serious challenge from within.

The United States therefore complements its aid program with actions and threats designed to intimidate any Latin Americans who might feel inclined to put an end to capitalism in their countries. The hardships inflicted on Cuba are lessons in morality for the rest of the hemisphere. They include an embargo on trade and a virtual economic blockade through pressure on other countries. The Alliance is an alliance against Cuba, even though some of the "allies" do not put their hearts into it. Washington has told them that there will be no aid for any country that allows its ships or aircraft to carry any equipment, materials, or commodities to Cuba so long as it is governed by the Castro regime.[27] The refuge given the Cuban emigrés in the United States, the public and private assurances that they will be enabled to return to a liberated island on some uncertain date, the provision of arms to the underground, the diplomatic isolation of the Cuban government, and the attitude of unrelenting hostility in Washington—these harassments are

[25] Speech on television on May 2, 1965 (during crisis leading to United States intervention in the Dominican Republic). Tad Szulc, *Dominican Diary* (New York: Delacorte Press, 1965), p. 107.
[26] Walt W. Rostow, *View From the Seventh Floor* (New York: Harper and Row, 1964), p. 116.
[27] The Foreign Assistance Act of 1961, as amended, Section 620 a (3) (A) (iii).

an attempt to inspire the embattled and demoralized Latin American bourgeoisie to pluck up its courage and fight against popular revolutionary forces.

The United States began to lay the foundation for intervention with its own armed forces in the name of the Organization of American States by negotiating the Treaty of Rio de Janeiro in 1947. That treaty provides for an immediate meeting of the Ministers of Foreign Affairs whenever "the political independence of any American State should be affected by . . . any . . . fact or situation that might endanger the peace of America."[28] At Caracas, Venezuela, in 1954, the United States proposed and successfully pressed on the Tenth Inter-American Conference a resolution declaring that "the domination or control of the political institutions of any American State by the international communist movement" would "endanger the peace of America" and would therefore set the procedures of the Rio Treaty in motion.[29] The foundation was also laid at this conference for a working collaboration between the Federal Bureau of Investigation, the Central Intelligence Agency, and the secret police of Latin American governments. This collaboration has since been extended from exchanges of information and collective committees to material aid and FBI training schools for the secret police of the hemisphere.[30] The Adminis-

[28] Inter-American Treaty of Reciprocal Assistance, adopted by the Inter-American Conference for the Maintenance of Continental Peace and Security at Rio de Janeiro, Brazil, September 2, 1947, Department of State *Bulletin*, Vol. XVII (1947), pp. 565-567, Article 6.

[29] Pan-American Union, Tenth Inter-American Conference, Caracas, Venezuela, March 1-28, 1954, *Final Act* (Washington, 1954), Resolution xciii approved by the Conference on March 13 by a vote of 17 to 1 (Guatemala) with 2 abstentions (Mexico and Argentina).

[30] The Assistant Secretary of State for Inter-American Affairs, Lincoln Gordon, stated on April 5, 1966, that "police assistance programs" were increasing "the internal security capabilities of the Latin American countries. . . . Continued vigilance on this front, however, is essential." *Foreign Assistance Act of 1966*, Hearings before the House Committee on Foreign Affairs (Washington: U.S. Government Printing Office, 1966), p. 372. A Special Consultative Committee on Security Against the Subversive Action of International Communism was established in 1962 by the Organization of American States. It is the OAS counterpart of the House Un-American Activities Committee and the Senate Internal Security Subcommittee. Like its predecessors, the OAS Committee gives the terms "communist" and "subversive" broad definitions and uses them loosely. The reports of the OAS Committee are published and distributed by the Senate Subcommittee. See *Organization of American States Combined Reports on Communist Subversion*, published by the Subcommittee to Investigate the Administration of the Internal Security Act and other Internal Security Laws of the Senate Committee on the Judiciary (Washington: U.S. Government Printing Office, 1965), with an introduction by Senator Thomas J. Dodd.

trator of the U.S. Agency for International Development, David Bell, assured the House Committee on Foreign Affairs in 1966 that "the Rio Treaty machinery is available to generate collective action to help a country check Communist subversion."[31]

But the United States wants this machinery improved. The Alliance cannot succeed unless this critical condition of investor security is satisfied. At the same time that President Kennedy was proposing the Alliance, he was also proposing a military aid program focused for the first time on internal security. Under this program the United States has trained and equipped Latin American armed forces for civil war, hot and cold, and for service as permanent occupation forces in their respective countries. This training is provided mainly at Fort Gulick, in Panama, under the supervision of the United States Army Forces Southern Command.[32] Civic action roles, such as road and irrigation construction, are added to training in counterinsurgency. The aim is to improve the image of the Latin American armies in the eyes of their own people while teaching them the latest techniques of suppression in case trouble breaks out. These contacts are also supposed to improve the prospects of gaining another U.S. objective: the creation of an Inter-American Peace Force. Since there is so much resentment against unilateral U.S. intervention like that in the Dominican Republic in 1965, the hope is that an OAS insignia on the uniform and the name "Inter-American" in the mass media will prove to be diplomatic and psychological assets, even if most of the troops speak nothing but English. Since 1961 Congress has been telling the Latin Americans that such a force should be created and that money is available for the purpose.[33]

But the Latin Americans continue to be exasperating. A majority of their governments still oppose the creation of the Inter-American Peace Force. And they still resist taking the steps required to make the Alliance succeed, that is, they are

[31] *Foreign Assistance Act of 1966,* Hearings before House Committee on Foreign Affairs, March-May 1966, p. 39.

[32] See Richard R. Clark, "U.S. Military Assistance in Latin America," *Army Digest,* September 1966, pp. 18-19. Clark is Command Information Officer, Headquarters U.S. Army Forces Southern Command.

[33] The Foreign Assistance Act of 1961, Public Law, 87-195, Section 502. In later years a section was added providing that "$25,000,000 may be used for assistance on a cost-sharing basis to an inter-American military force under the control of the Organization of American States." Section 511.

backward at wooing and winning United States investors.* The rate of foreign investment in Latin America continues to be low.[34] The Assistant Secretary for Inter-American Affairs, Lincoln Gordon, had to report to Congress in April, 1966:

> One signal disappointment in our progress thus far, compared with the targets of Punta del Este, is the small volume of new private foreign investment participating in expanded Latin American development.[35]

He cited political instability and unrestrained inflation as the principal reasons. David Rockefeller, President of the Chase Manhattan Bank and Chairman of the Council for Latin America, stated the investors' complaints in an article in *Foreign Affairs*. He deplored the fact that so many Latin Americans equate foreign investment with colonialism and condemn the profit motive. He cautioned against "overly ambitious concepts of revolutionary social change" such as those endorsed in the Punta del Este Charter. "Revolutionary change that shakes confidence in the fair treatment of private property," he warned, "is incompatible with rapid economic expansion."[36]

Guerrillas in Venezuela, Colombia, Peru, and Guatemala, strikes in Chile and Uruguay, inflation still out of control, the resistance of governments to advice from Washington, their nationalism, their vacillation in their dealing with imperialism, their skepticism about the Alliance, their inability to arouse and stimulate and exalt the masses, the heavy inertia of the bureaucracies—the picture is dark and the sense of frustration strong in the councils of review. Six Assistant Secretaries of State for Inter-American Affairs have come and gone since the Alliance was born. The burdens of the Alliance on the Latin Americans are feeding resentment. Their accumulated debts to the United States Government and the international lending

---

* ". . . investment must be attracted and experience teaches us that it will be attracted to those fields where the return is most promising, and where the safety of its capital is most assured." *Private Investment in Latin America*, Report of the Subcommittee on Inter-American Economic Relationships of the Joint Economic Committee of Congress (Washington: U.S. Government Printing Office, 1964) p. 8. This statement by a committee of bankers and businessmen is commended by the Subcommittee as basic to an understanding of the problem.

[34] United Nations, Economic and Social Council, Economic Commission for Latin America, *Economic Survey of Latin America, 1965*, Part I, p. 12 (E/CN. 12/752, 27 May 1966).

[35] *Foreign Assistance Act of 1966*, Hearings before House Committee on Foreign Affairs, March-May 1966, p. 396.

[36] *Foreign Affairs*, April 1966, p. 408.

agencies must be serviced with payments of foreign exchange for interest and amortization. They are being scolded for failing to exert more effort in "self-help." Yet they are losing control over their own economies. As United States policy has hardened under the pressure of its own balance of payments difficulties, it has restricted the freedom of the Latin Americans to shop in other markets. Virtually all loans from the United States are now tied to purchases of goods and services in the United States.[37] U.S. ships must be used to haul at least 50 percent of the cargo, despite their higher charges. In practice, the Inter-American Development Bank is required by its richest patron to give similar preference to United States suppliers. These restrictions gall the Latin Americans and arm opposition movements with potent arguments.

The Alliance was born one hundred years too late. The industrialization of Latin America will require heroism, asceticism, perseverance, and sacrifice, but these virtues, possessed in full by the Latin peoples, can no longer be enlisted in the service of imperialism nor even in the service of the national bourgeoisie. Senator Gruening gave voice to a widespread pessimism in Washington regarding the quality of leadership in Latin America. He describes the area as "impoverished in leadership," in the abilities "to galvanize public support."[38] He might have added the one significant exception, Cuba, where leaders emerged who were equal to the tasks they set themselves. This contrast is the best index of the prospects for the Alliance. For Castro's achievement is not due only to his personal qualities. As Lenin said, there are many men with splendid moral qualities whom history treats none too politely. Castro differs from other Latin American leaders in his assessment of the class struggle. His Marxist attitude toward it, in fact, put him at odds with the Alliance and led to Cuba's expulsion from the Organization of American States. The Alliance selects only those leaders who profess to believe in class harmony; in Washington the class struggle does not exist. Castro, on the other hand, came to acknowledge the reality and the overriding importance of an elemental class

[37] "Funds made available under this Act may be used for procurement outside the United States only if the President determines that such procurement will not result in adverse effects upon the economy of the United States or the industrial mobilization base . . ." The Foreign Assistance Act of 1961, as amended, Section 604 (a).

[38] *United States Foreign Aid in Action: A Case Study*, submitted by Senator Ernest Gruening to the Subcommittee on Foreign Aid Expenditures of the Senate Committee on Government Operations (June 28, 1966), p. 117.

struggle that exists independently of the will of all leaders. He put himself at the head of the oppressed working people of Cuba and confronted the consequences. He has since been carried to the heights by the exceptional exaltation and exertion of all the human faculties—consciousness, will, passion, fantasy—of millions of Cubans and Latin Americans, spurred on by the bitterest class war. No friend of Washington can tap such a source. It might make him a great leader, but it would also remove him from the Alliance.

The Failure of Latin America's Economic Integration

MICHEL TEUBAL

Along with the Alliance for Progress, and military programs, the U.S. has also been urging the establishment of a Common Market in Latin America. Given the appropriate measures suggested by the UN Economic Committee for Latin America, Teubal suggests, economic integration could possibly facilitate the development programs of individual countries. However, as visualized by the U.S., and as presently proceeding, profound internal structural changes in the distribution of power, property, and income, and central planning for coordinated development programs, are certainly not contemplated. Economic integration, under such circumstances, essentially means indiscriminate tariff liberalization—a policy that will most benefit the firms best suited to take advantage of the removal of such remaining barriers to their economic penetration— the large multinational corporations of the U.S.

Michel Teubal, an Argentinian, is a doctoral candidate in economics at the University of California at Berkeley.

THE FORMATION of a Latin American Common Market (LACM) has often been cited as a principal objective of policy makers coping with Latin America's economic development. Observers of the European Common Market often believe that similar measures taken in Latin America would have similar results. Also, the United Nation's Economic Commission for Latin America (hereafter referred to by the Spanish initials

CEPAL) has persistently prepared basic documents and research explaining the need for a LACM and has organized the principal international meetings at which steps toward its institution were taken. The Treaty of Montevideo, signed in 1960, was instrumental in creating the Latin American Free Trade Area (LAFTA),[1] which CEPAL considered a step toward a full-fledged LACM.

But LAFTA has not fulfilled expectations. It was only a Free Trade Area[2] and it performed only modestly during the first years of existence. Stipulated tariff reductions on behalf of the member countries were fulfilled, and there was a slight increase in trade, but in no way did LAFTA exert a real influence on the industrialization of the member countries. As time passed, it was felt that the process of economic integration begun with the formation of LAFTA was stagnating. The rhythm of tariff concessions began decreasing, and interregional trade did not increase significantly. Realizing this, CEPAL pointed out the need for a more positive approach and the adoption of more "radical" measures to implement economic integration.[3]

[1] The signatory nations of the Montevideo Treaty that created the LAFTA were Argentina, Brazil, Chile, Paraguay, Peru, Uruguay, and Mexico. Later on, Colombia and Ecuador became members, and more recently, Venezuela and Bolivia.

[2] There are several types of Economic Unions between countries: Free Trade Areas, Custom's Unions, Common Markets, etc. The members of a Free Trade Area agree to reduce the tariffs and trade restrictions to their mutual trade while maintaining their own commercial policies with respect to the "rest of the world." The formation of a Custom's Union implies, in addition, the adoption of a uniform tariff level vis à vis the "rest of the world." A still more advanced degree of economic integration is acquired in a Common Market wherein not only all restrictions to interregional trade are eliminated, but also those that affect the free mobility of factors of production. Its efficient operation usually requires a coordination of the monetary, fiscal, and, in many cases, investment policies of the member countries.

When we refer to the process of economic integration, we are considering the adoption of different measures tending toward higher forms of international economic cooperation. Among the more recent measures proposed by CEPAL but not accepted by member countries are found the following: (a) that all types of restrictions to the reciprocal trade of the members of LAFTA be eliminated within 10 years; (b) that in a period no longer than 5 years a common tariff vis-à-vis third countries be elaborated and put into effect; (c) that in the cases when tariff reductions are insufficient to promote interregional trade, other measures be devised; (d) that a common regional investments policy be established, which could also be instrumental in encouraging the increase of exports to third countries, in particular the exports of manufactured goods; (e) that an interregional payments' system be established so that commercial transactions between firms of different member countries would be more viable.

[3] See UN-ECLA, *Toward a Dynamic Development Policy for Latin America*, E/Ch. 12/680 (unbound), Chapter 2.

Several international meetings took place, among which the most important were those of the Ministers of Foreign Affairs of the member countries of LAFTA and the recent meeting of the presidents of countries forming the Organization of American States (OAS), in which support for the formation of a LACM was being voiced. Opinions differ about the results and probable consequences of the meetings, many regarding an LACM as a panacea for the economic problems of Latin America. A critical evaluation of CEPAL's "doctrine" of economic integration is necessary.

We shall analyze several aspects of the "CEPAL vision" and theory of economic integration, considering CEPAL's description of Latin America's industrialization process and some of the obstacles hampering it; CEPAL'S economic integration model; and some of the basic assumptions underlying CEPAL'S doctrine,[4] to determine how realistic they are, given the present social and political context of Latin America. Finally, we shall consider some perspectives on Latin America's future economic integration process.

The CEPAL economists have for many years analyzed and encouraged the industrial development of Latin America. And they feel that an LACM will be instrumental in overcoming some of the principal obstacles to the industrial development of the continent, and is the logical answer to some of the major problems of the industrialization process.[5]

Almost all of the Latin American countries face a series of chronic deficits in their balance of payments. Although special circumstances affect each country, in general Latin America's exports have not kept pace with her demand for imports. Demand for these exports—almost all primary products—has

[4] The CEPAL "doctrine" has been presented in numerous documents published by this organization. Raul Prebisch is maybe the best-known economist who could be considered the spokesman of the CEPAL economists. See the document mentioned in the previous footnote. Other "Cepalist" economists who, in spite of differing opinions, sustain similar theses are O. Sunkel, A. Pinto, J. A. Mayobre. We could also include C. Furtado and A. Ferrer as presenting theories very akin to those of CEPAL. Dudley Seers and Sydney Dell are two of the "extraregional" economists who are very sympathetic to the CEPAL position.

[5] Cf. UN-ECLA, *The Latin American Common Market* (United Nations, 1959); UN-ECLA, *Toward a Dynamic Development Policy for Latin America;* J. A. Mayobre, and others, *Hacia una dinámica acelerada de América Latina* (Mexico, 1965), (parts of this work were published as "Document: Proposals for the Creation of the Latin American Common Market," Journal of Common Market Studies, Vol. V (1) (September 1966), pp. 83-110; S. Dell, *A Latin-American Common Market* (Oxford University Press, 1966).

not always been satisfactorily sustained in the world markets. In some cases, their relative prices have tended to diminish; in others they have brought low income because demand varies. Sometimes the rigidities inherent in the structure of production in the primary sectors have caused limited production. And we must not underestimate the impact protectionist measures applied by the advanced foreign industrial nations have had in limiting Latin American exports.[6] Meanwhile, imports into the Latin American countries have risen rapidly, more rapidly than their exports, partially because the industrialization process has created new demands for intermediary and capital goods as well as fuel—all of which are essential to maintain a satisfactory rate of industrial growth.

Industrialization in Latin America has been associated with the process of "import substitution": in the initial stages of industrial development, national products are used in place of imported consumer goods. In some Latin American countries these "easy" substitutes have increased considerably, partially because protective measures have generated an internal demand for local manufactured goods as opposed to equivalent imports. Thus, local light industry in Argentina and Brazil supplies practically all of the consumer goods demands of the domestic markets. There is room for more expansion of these "easy" substitutions in countries like Colombia, Peru, and even Venezuela. In Chile and Uruguay the extent of the internal market is more limited and constitutes a serious obstacle for the establishment of a series of light industries sufficiently diversified and consolidated.[7] Theoretically, these countries would be able to develop more, and a more diversified, light industry if they formed part of a wider regional market.

With stagnating exports, and with industrialization bringing about a change not only in the structure of imports, but also by way of an increase in import needs, the industrializing Latin American countries experience increasing "external vulnerability." CEPAL feels that these problems will not be solved without a substantial change in the structure of imports and

---

[6] These propositions are frequently discussed in the CEPAL literature; see, for example, *Toward a Dynamic . . . op. cit.*; see also United Nations, *Toward a New Trade Policy for Development*, Report by the Secretary-General of the United Nations Conference on Trade and Development (United Nations, 1964), and *World Economic Survey, 1961* (United Nations, 1962).

[7] Chile's situation is worsened by the existence of an important iron and steel complex that cannot sell all of its production in the domestic market. The important support Chile gives to Latin America's economic integration is due, to a large measure, to this factor.

exports, and that these changes—new import substitutions as well as new nontraditional exports—are contingent upon changes in the structure of domestic production.

By the 1950's the situation had become critical. During the period 1946-1950 the overall balance of payments deficit of Latin America amounted to some 129.3 million dollars, increasing to 665.5 million in 1951-1955 and reaching 1,148.3 million by 1956-1960. (See Table 1.) This enormous rate of increase continued in 1961, when a deficit of 1516.6 million dollars was registered (Cuba and Venezuela are excluded). This substantial deficit was largely due to Argentina (584.4 million as against an average of 177.5 million for the period 1956-1960), but the balance of payments deficit of Chile (273.6 million) and Brazil (292.0 million) were also substantial in that period. Only Peru and Venezuela managed to overcome their previous deficits and acquire a surplus of 18.2 and 447.4 million respectively in the year 1961. (See again Table 1.)

TABLE 1

LATIN AMERICA: EVOLUTION OF BALANCE-OF-PAYMENTS POSITION
ON CURRENT ACCOUNTS, SELECTED COUNTRIES

(*Annual averages in millions of dollars*)

Groups of countries	1946-50	1951-55	1956-60	1961
Argentina	+84.9	−140.4	−177.5	−584.4
Bolivia	−9.2	−13.9	−27.4	−32.1
Chile	−36.9	−14.0	−84.3	−273.6
Paraguay	−1.8	−2.2	−10.2	−10.7
Uruguay	+3.1	−27.3	−53.3	−16.5
Colombia	−45.3	−24.5	−21.0	−141.8
Ecuador	−5.1	−4.3	−12.3	−23.4
Peru	−10.4	−41.8	−72.4	+18.2
Brazil	+9.4	−288.8	−297.6	−292.0
Mexico	−82.9	−46.5	−142.3	−91.4
Venezuela	−101.2	+7.5	−105.9	+447.3
Total Latin America, excluding Cuba and Venezuela	−111.1	−625.2	−955.5	−1,516.6
Total Latin America, excluding Cuba	−212.3	−617.7	−1,061.4	−1,069.3
Total Latin America	−129.3	−665.5	−1,148.3*	

Source: International Monetary Fund, *Balance of Payments Yearbook,* Vols. 8, 12, 13 and 14; E.C.L.A.

* Net including Cuba in 1960.

According to CEPAL, there are several broad alternatives to the industrialization problem. On the one hand, to avoid industrial stagnation in some of the countries it is necessary to pass on to the stage of "difficult" substitutions, with the establishment of a heavy industry capable of producing equipment, machinery, basic chemicals, and all types of intermediary goods. This means substitution of national goods requiring a more complex technology than required by light industry. And it also requires greater initial investments and a rate of return of slower maturity. All of this cannot be easily realized without correspondingly significant State help.

Not all of the Latin American countries—not even the larger, more industrialized ones—can individually promote the establishment of a wide range of heavy industries. Mexico and Brazil, and to a lesser degree Argentina, have developed considerable iron and steel complexes, and can efficiently produce certain types of fairly complex machinery and chemicals. But not all Latin American countries have sufficient raw materials; not all have sufficiently large internal markets to support the efficient operation of large-scale heavy industry or to generate the corresponding economies of large-scale production.

This difficult import substitution process that the more industrialized countries could carry out contains contradictions similar to those created by the establishment of light industry: the establishment of heavy industry generates not only a change in the composition of imports and import substitutes, but also an *increase* in the demand for new imports. And the increased demand for intermediary and capital goods can increase the "external vulnerability" of the Latin American economy. True, once these industries have been established and are producing, the imports would be reduced, and consequently the external vulnerability would be reduced. But until then the developing economies would pass through critical stages, and industrial growth could stagnate because of difficulties arising from increasing balance of payments deficits.

CEPAL points out another approach to the problem of industrial development—the massive promotion of exports. Where traditional exports cannot be increased because of unfavorable world market conditions, "nontraditional" exports could make up the deficit. It is felt that many manufactured goods, particularly those of light industry, could be exported either to the world market or to other Latin American countries. Of course, it would be necessary to reduce manufacturing costs so that the goods could compete with prices of similar products from the highly developed countries, but industrial development has advanced sufficiently in several Latin American countries so that new items of good quality could be exported if the commercial policies of the advanced industrial countries would permit.[8]

In short, according to CEPAL, industrial stagnation in Latin America can be traced to a disequilibrium in the economies, with exports not increasing sufficiently to counterbalance new import demands. The situation is not due to "errors" of substitution nor to an "artificial" industrial development, but rather to the fact that the import substitution process has not intensified enough in many lines of production and has not been sufficiently coordinated and planned to take into account the new imports that established industry requires for its proper functioning. And, according to CEPAL, these problems can be solved only by an attack on the "structural deficiencies" of the Latin American economies, of which the foreign trade situation is a clear reflection. What is needed is (1) an intensification of the import substitution process to the stage of "difficult" substitutions, with their corresponding problems, and (2) an increase in the level of exports, particularly non-traditional exports. These are somewhat complementary alternatives and lead us to the central topic of this article: the reasons for the economic integration of Latin America.

Economic integration through the formation of LAFTA, and, as an ultimate objective, an LACM,[9] is justified partially by the need to implement the different alternatives for industrialization of the region. Among the measures proposed is that of forming "integration industries," coordinating expansion of certain strategic industries so that the establishment of heavy industry in Latin America becomes viable. These industries would be developed regionally, avoiding unnecessary duplication of a particular industry in several countries. It is felt that a limited number of industries, strategically located, would, in addition to being import-substitute industries, strengthen the economic structure and accelerate the pace of overall develop-

[8] The President of Ecuador at the recent Punta del Este Conference asked of the U.S. a more favorable treatment of Latin America's primary product and manufactured goods exports, as well as more favorable payments conditions for the Latin American countries. Nevertheless, none of these proposals was considered seriously. The need to increase Latin America's manufactured exports to the industrialized countries has been expounded vigorously by Prebisch; see his report to the Conference on Trade and Development mentioned in footnote number 6.

[9] The professed idea is to incorporate into a large Latin American Common Market the present members of the LAFTA, those of the Central American Common Market, and the remaining Caribbean countries. At present Cuba seems to be excluded.

ment. And in this way the Latin American countries would be able to operate under large-scale production, utilizing productive capacity more efficiently.

Also, the possibility of increasing exports of nontraditional products to the world and to other Latin American countries must not be underestimated.[10] Although at present interregional trade is not very significant, CEPAL recognizes the need for its drastic increase. Competition in world markets is difficult because of the advanced technology and enormous financial resources of the industrially advanced countries. The application of common customs duties for all of the member countries of an LACM is seen as necessary to protect Latin American exports from world competition. In the present "infant stages" of Latin America's industrial development the transformation of LAFTA into a Customs Union with a common external tariff for member countries seems a necessary step.

Both the coordination of interregional heavy industrial development and the promotion of nontraditional exports are compatible with the import substitution processes the individual countries have been developing in recent years. In the case of heavy industry, the Latin American countries would substitute imports from the "rest of the world" on a regional basis, thus using the regional resources more efficiently, as well as taking advantage of large-scale-production economy. Not only would unnecessary duplication in industry be decreased, but so also would unnecessary independent imports. Also, in light industry member countries could import from other mem-

---

[10] The opportunities for increased interregional trade seem to be great. The "suspension or contraction of the normal supplies of manufactured goods from the industrialized countries (for example, during World War II) permitted the Latin American established industries to considerably expand their production to a maximum of capacity so as to satisfy internal demand and—in countries with a greater degree of industrialization, such as Argentina, Brazil, Chile, and Mexico—to supply the markets of other Latin American countries.

"Thus in 1943 Argentina exported 19,000 tons of textiles, 70,000 dozen pairs of shoes for women and children, 510 tons of other leather manufactured goods, etc. Brazil exported 26,400 tons of cotton textiles, as well as large quantities of wool yarn and textiles, medicine products, glass products, etc. . . . All these exports were strongly reduced in the post-World War II years, especially after 1948. At the beginning of the 1950's they practically disappeared." Santiago Macario, "Proteccionismo e Industrialización en América Latina," *Boletín Económico de América Latina*, Vol. IX, No. 1 (March 1964), p. 64. At present, given the greater industrial advancement of many of Latin America's countries, the new exports could probably include other products of greater technological complexity.

ber countries, where in the past they had imported from "the rest of the world."

That is, a series of economic integration measures—the liberalization of interregional trade, the adoption of a common tariff for the members of the LAFTA, and the coordination of their investment policies—could make the regionalization of the import-substitution policies more viable. It would mean that the Latin American countries would not continue developing their industry in "tight compartments," but would embark upon an "open" industrialization directed principally to the member countries of an LACM. More liberal in their interregional trade, they would also be protected from the vast resources of international competition with which they are now incapable of coping.

The targets and projections set forth in the now-famous report *The Latin American Common Market*[11] illustrate the importance CEPAL assigns to the proposed new arrangements. According to this study, if the per capita Gross Domestic Product of Latin America as a whole were to increase at an average of 2.7 percent per year in the period 1954-56—1975, interregional exports would have to increase from roughly 756 million dollars in 1954-56 to 8,600 million in 1965 (constant dollars of 1950)—in other words, increase by 11 times. Import substitution on a regional basis would hence appear an absolute necessity. The value of production of capital goods would have to increase 27 times, from 200 million produced in the initial period to 5400 million in the target year. CEPAL considered that these capital goods must constitute 32 percent of total Latin American exports in 1975, and that the interregional trade in capital goods would have to increase from negligible levels in 1955 to 2,671 million in 1975.

Evidently, to effect CEPAL's "vision" of Latin America's future industrialization would require a series of significant changes and structural reforms.

The CEPAL integration model provides not only an interpretation of Latin American economic reality, but also the theoretical foundations for an overall Latin American policy to further industrialization. At the base of CEPAL's analysis is the assumption that industrial and economic integration can be realized only through efficient planning. This is obvious in the case of the regional development of heavy industry, but

[11] *Op. cit.*

what is implied is a broader problem than the mere quantitative projection of a series of tendencies, the mere technical problems. Nor is the broader problem merely the need for "government intervention," although rational government supervision and intervention is assumed: "Although the State has played an important role in Latin America's industrialization, this did not come about as a consequence of the deliberate resolution of a bureaucratic or political 'elite'; rather, its decisions were usually imposed by 'exogenous' circumstances, although in recent years the situation has tended to change."[12] In other words, apparently certain social groups or classes initiate social and economic changes or else induce the government to create conditions conducive to the changes.

It is necessary to analyze the nature of planning within the context of the CEPAL model for industrialization, and to examine the role of the so-called national bourgeoisie and the characteristics of the "developmentalist" or "reformist" governments that CEPAL seems to have in mind when describing the need for economic integration.

Latin America's industrialization has not followed deliberate or coherent planning or policy making. On the contrary, external circumstances have been more important in stimulating industrial growth than local social groups have been. Not theories about the advantages of free trade or protectionism, nor theories about the advantages of agricultural production versus manufacturing, but external circumstances related to the world situation gave Latin American industrialization its first big push—particularly the two World Wars and the Great Depression of the thirties, together with the breakdown of the gold standard system. Many Latin American countries then developed commercial policies that affected industrial development: with the breakdown of foreign trade, and because of the balance of payments problem, they needed to acquire new government income; and during this period it was impossible to import manufactured goods from Europe and the U.S. The customs duties and restrictions imposed in the thirties were necessary steps to meet a world crisis; only later, with pressures from an emerging industrial class, were clearly "protectionist" measures applied with a long-range economic plan in mind. Imports considered superfluous were restricted or prohibited, while new substitution activities were encouraged and

[12] A. Pinto, "Aspectos políticos del desarrollo económico latinoamericano," *Revista de Economía Latinoamericana* (Caracas, Autumn 1965), p. 70.

scarce economic resources oriented toward them. And because of the restriction of imports there was an effort to produce domestically all sorts of items—"choice . . . was based not on considerations of economic viability, but on immediate feasibility, whatever the cost of production."[13] Only later did CEPAL rationalize the process and set forth the concept of an "import substitution policy" such as we have already described. Thus CEPAL began to construct the theoretical scheme that justifies the industrialization that has been carried out to the present, while pointing out its deficiencies and imbalances. "Protection has, of course, been essential in the Latin American countries. But it has not been applied with moderation, nor has there generally been a policy laid down rationally and with that sense of foresight that is essential to the alleviation, if not the prevention, of balance of payments crises."[14]

Also, while there remained considerable margin for additional "easy" import substitutions and favorable conditions for an increase in the value of exports, the need for rational planning was not self-evident. But as the Latin American countries were faced with a succession of balance of payments crises and the consequent stagnation of their economic growth, planning was recognized as a necessary condition for industrial growth, as a means of rationalizing economic activity, especially for those semideveloped countries faced with acute external imbalance problems.

The CEPAL economists have either outlined or implied a number of reasons to justify a certain degree of planning, most of them concerned not only with the rigidities inherent in the underdeveloped economies, but also with the essentially capitalistic nature of the economies. As we shall see, they are essential to the practical application of any sort of economic integration policy:

(1) One is the need to realize investments in strategic sectors of the economy, because of structural limitations and imperfections in the Latin American economies. We have already mentioned, for example, that without a regional approach to the problem of establishing heavy, or "dynamic," industries, with the multinational coordination of heavy industry investments, unnecessary duplications are likely to occur, and the maximum economy of large-scale production will not be realized. CEPAL feels that this type of investment

[13] *Toward . . . op. cit.*, p. 88.
[14] *Ibid.*, p. 88.

requires state promotion to the same extent that the traditional investments in the infrastructure (i.e., in roads, electricity, etc.) require it. The private sector avoids these investments because (a) many of them require large financial resources, which are not always available, or else are highly risky for the individual entrepreneur, given the imperfections inherent in the capital markets; (b) the entrepreneurs tend to look for short-term gains; and (c), related to (b), the "opportunity costs" of these investments are very high compared to those for the more traditional investments. For example, it is usually more convenient to invest in other countries with greater economic and political stability, or to invest in land or real estate, which act as a security against intense inflation. In other words, private investments, without state support and adequate economic planning, tend to be in areas of high immediate returns but low social and long-run returns. They don't help solve structural difficulties that affect the balance of payments difficulties. CEPAL feels adequate integrated planning is necessary so that investments in "dynamic" industries— which will get to the root of the balance of payments problem —can become viable.

According to CEPAL, planning can also encourage the increase of nontraditional exports in various ways, including fiscal and monetary incentives, subsidies, and the diffusion of information and technical assistance to producers and exporters, for example. On a regional level, CEPAL considers it necessary to enforce rational tariffs, reducing those that are excessive to promote competition between countries; and this requires a broad view of overall regional requirements so that competitive "excesses" are set aside.[15]

(2) Rational economic planning would also involve the regional distribution of investments to the less-developed regions of the LAFTA, particularly to those countries considered to be "of lower relative degree of development." Justification for this type of planning is similar to justification for the kind of planning discussed above, but here reference is made particularly to the *location* of an investment.

It is generally agreed that tariff reduction in itself will not favor the less industrialized countries (this is one of the reasons why these countries are permitted to reduce their tariff levels at a slower rate). Investments must also be consciously oriented toward the less-favored regions. The market situation

[15] *Ibid.*, p. 113.

itself won't efficiently allocate regional resources; new forms are required to coordinate them on a regional level.

The disadvantages in these countries would increase once a common tariff was established for all the member countries of a Custom's Union (or LAFTA), because they would permanently lose any chance to attract new industries. Also, they would be hurt to the extent that they would be induced to purchase higher-cost regional products rather than less expensive similar products on the world market. The situation for these countries could worsen as the industrialization of neighboring countries proceeds. The temporary advantages presently enjoyed by them under LAFTA could be completely wiped out once a full-fledged common market was established. There is a need for adequate mechanisms to guarantee a more equitable distribution of regional resources and income.

(3) Finally, there are political reasons for national economic planning and its coordination on the multinational level. The Cepalists point out the need to promote cooperation between Latin American national businesses and foreign businesses, but they emphasize the need to favor particularly the enterprises of the member countries. The Latin American experts consulted by President Frei present this problem in the following way:

> The signatories to this document share a concern that is extremely widespread in Latin America: that in the most complex and investment-attracting sectors of the common market—i.e., in basic industry—private initiative in the great industrial centers enjoys so great a technical and financial superiority that it may well acquire a predominant position to the decided detriment of Latin American entrepreneurs. . . . If the Latin American entrepreneur is to be enabled to take an efficient and equitable part in this type of association (a common market), the rules for foreign investment will have to be based on the principle that the regional market must be an instrument to strengthen the position of our entrepreneurs and confirm their paramount role in the development of Latin America.[16]

Prebisch has also pointed out that

> The fundamental solution is to support Latin American enterprise so that it can achieve its full vigor in the formation of a common market, and stand up to foreign enterprise, either by making common cause with it or by competing on an equal footing, since competition on an unequal basis usually boils down to the alternative of liquidation of the weaker part by the stronger.[17]

[16] *Document: Proposals* . . . pp. 104-5.
[17] *Toward . . . op. cit.,* p. 121.

In other words, national economic planning projected on a regional scale is necessary for the establishment of an LACM in order to break certain "bottlenecks" inherent in the economic structure of the Latin American areas, bottlenecks related to the external sector being important in this respect. Planning is necessary to guarantee a more equitable distribution of economic resources among countries of unequal development and also to favor "national enterprise" in the context of the world market.

However, the type of economic planning proposed by CEPAL is to be developed within the context of an essentially capitalist economy, and the deficiencies of the market that warrant planning are due not only to imperfections in the economic structure of semideveloped and underdeveloped economies, but also to imbalances deriving from the capitalist nature of the system itself. What is envisioned is a sort of State Capitalism by which the state exerts an important influence on economic development and investments while maintaining the essential nature of the capitalist society. To what extent this is viable in the present social and political structure of Latin America we shall comment on later.

Although CEPAL points out the need for structural reform, it is careful not to antagonize the bourgeoisie by presenting too strong an "interventionist" approach to the economic planning process. There is a certain caution in the statement: "planning is not incompatible with competition. It is an indispensable requisite for the efficacious operation of the economic system under which we live," or that impersonal intervention on the part of the State is "designed to guide, safeguard and encourage, but not interfere with the conduct of individuals in economic life or subject them to arbitrary restrictions."[18]

CEPAL envisions economic planning in an essentially capitalist context, with the purpose of making the system more efficient, not to promote social reform. But a summary of the essential characteristics of CEPAL's vision provokes this question: what social groups or classes are interested in carrying out the industrialization and economic integration process? To what extent are they capable of embarking on rational and deliberate economic planning? CEPAL doesn't always answer these questions directly, but to the extent that CEPAL's proposals are not sustainable in the social reality of Latin America, they become ideal concepts only, prophetic cries in the wilder-

[18] *Ibid.*, p. 113.

ness that evoke no response from the more dynamic sectors of Latin American society.

CEPAL's basic ideas are accepted by many Latin American economists, government functionaries, and officials. But if they are to be realized, the "modernizing" sectors in Latin America must be interested in carrying them out. Since we are considering essentially "free enterprise" economics, it would seem that the agents of industrial and economic integration would have to be those sectors of society associated with modern industry, especially certain "middle-class" groups or members of the so-called "national bourgeoisie." And at least three conditions must exist for the national bourgeoisie of Latin American countries to become such agents: (a) an "industrialist conscience," which would encourage them to turn from the more traditional sectors of industrialization; (b) an "integrationist conscience," which would make them accept certain "rules of the game" for the region as a whole as opposed to "extraregional" interests; and (c) a certain minimum political power, which would permit them to carry out these objectives: But for several reasons there is insufficient indication that the national bourgeoisie is capable of assuming the role that has been assigned to it, explicitly or implicitly, by CEPAL.

In the first place, these industrialists and entrepreneurs have appeared only recently. In some of the Latin American countries they constitute a class without much political force nor a clear ideology of their own upon which to act. Secondly, their interests are difficult to reconcile with the interests of the national bourgeoisie of other countries, so that it is difficult to visualize their acceptance of a set of rules of the game applicable to the region as a whole. And, finally, it would seem that the national bourgeoisie, rather than strongly oppose the more traditional and extraregional interests, would probably be more willing to cooperate with them. Essentially, all of this means that the Latin American bourgeoisie is weak, a hypothesis that is reinforced by the general characteristics suggested below.

Compared to European industrialization, Latin America's is still in its infant stage, being very little diversified and heavily concentrated in certain regions. Table 2 shows that the per capita manufacturing product, the proportion of the manufacturing product to the Gross Domestic Product, and the proportion of the work force used by the manufacturing sector are all generally lower in the Latin American countries than in

Europe. The per capita manufacturing product reached a maximum of 485 dollars in Belgium-Luxembourg and a minimum of 170 dollars in Italy—these countries being part of the European Economic Community (European Common Market). The member countries of LAFTA produced a much lower value of manufactured goods: only Argentina produced 140 dollars per capita of manufactured goods while all the other countries represented in Table 2 produced less than 100 dollars per capita. The manufactured product represented more than 30 percent of the GDP in all of the member countries of the European Common Market but represented only between 20 and 27.1 percent of the GDP in all of the LAFTA countries except Argentina, where it represented 32.1 percent. And similar contrasts are revealed in the ranking of the participation of the total work force in the manufacturing sector.

TABLE 2
COMPARATIVE INDUSTRIAL DEVELOPMENT, SEVERAL COUNTRIES

Groups of Countries	(1) Gross Domestic Product/Capita, 1957 (Constant Dollars at 1955 Prices)	(2) Total Manufacturing Product, 1957 (Billions of Dollars)	(3) Manufacturing, Product/Capita 1957	(4) Share of Manufactured Product in G.D.P. %	(5) Share of Manuf. Labor Force in Total Labor Force %	(6) Share of Consumer Goods in Total Manuf. Product %	(7) Share of Manufactured Goods in Total Exports %
Belgium-Lux.	1375	4.49	485	(1957) 35.2	37	(1953) 34.3	35
France	1075	14.40	325	(1957) 32.0	24	(1950) 34.2	38
West Germany	1070	23.20	450	(1957) 42.0	31	(1953) 38.8	65
Italy	520	8.30	170	(1957) 32.7	22	(1953) 38.8	47
Netherlands	920	3.10	280	(1957) 30.7	24	(1953) 43.0	31
U.K.	1280	23.50	455	(1957) 35.5	37	(1954) 27.4	62
U.S.A.	2185	119.30	695	(1957) 31.8	27	(1954) 26.0	48
Argentina	605	2.80	140	(1960) 32.1	22	(1954) 51.0	.4
Brazil	245	3.15	50	(1960) 25.8	13	(1953) 51.5	.4
Chile	315	0.53	75	(1961) 22.9	19	(1953) 56.6	1.4
Colombia	265	0.57	45	(1963) 21.9	12	(1953) 71.6	0.6
Mexico	255	2.05	65	(1964) 25.8	12	(1950) 51.8	3
Peru	145	0.38	39	(1963) 27.2	..	(1954) 63.9	....

Sources: Col. (1), (2), (3), (4), (5), and (7), Maizels, *Industrial Growth and World Trade*, N.I.E.S.R. (London, 1963); U.N.-E.C.L.A. *Statistical Bulletin for Latin America*, Vol. III, No. 1 and 2, 1966, S. Kuznets, *Modern Economic Growth* (Yale, 1966), Col. (6) U.N., *Patterns of Industrial Growth, 1938-61* (New York, 1963).

It should also be pointed out that Argentina, Brazil, Chile, and Mexico produce more than 70 percent of the manufactured products of Latin America and that industry is concentrated primarily in regions such as Greater Buenos Aires, the São Paulo area, Santiago de Chile, and Mexico City.

These data suggest the small influence exerted by the manufacturing sector upon the economic development of the Latin American countries. Similarly, an analysis of exports reflects a continued dependence in these economies on the fluctuation of the export markets for primary products. Manufactured goods represent a small proportion of total exports—a negligible proportion compared to European export of manufactured goods. As Table 2 reveals, they never represent more than 3 percent of the total exports of the individual Latin American countries we are considering.

These comparative data reflect the weakness of Latin America's national bourgeoisie; and, as we point out later, any trade liberalization—even of interregional trade—might be considered an "external menace" that would be reconciled only with difficulty with the interests of the established industry in the countries of LAFTA.

It is to the point here to compare the manufacturing structure of the LAFTA countries with that of the European Common Market. Most Latin American industry is the traditional light industry: textiles, foodstuffs, wood products, etc. These products represent a greater proportion of total manufactured output than they do in Europe or in the U.S. In Table 3 the structure of manufactured output for several regions is compared. Whereas foodstuffs, textiles, clothing, footwear, and wood products constituted about 55.4 percent of total manufactured production in Latin America in 1953, these products represented only 33.4 percent of regional manufacturing production in Europe.

TABLE 3
COMPOSITION OF MANUFACTURED PRODUCT, 1953

I.S.I.C. Code	Product	North America %	Western Europe %	Latin America %	Asia %
20-22	Food, Beverages, Tobacco	11	13.6	32.1	15.3
34	Basic Metals	8.9	8.3	5.7	7.1
35-38	Metal Products	26.3	32.2	11.6	17.1
31	Chemicals	9.8	10.1	13.8	11.2
23	Textiles	4.3	10.2	13.0	17.7
24	Clothing & Footwear	5.5	5.2	5.9	6.0
25-26	Wood Products	4.5	4.4	4.4	7.4
27	Paper & Printing	8.7	6.4	4.0	5.0
29-30	Leather & Rubber	2.2	2.2	2.8	3.2
	Miscellaneous	8.9	7.4	7.1	9.0
	G.D.P. (billions of dollars)	287	257	57	76
	G.D.P./Capita (dollars)	2,130	820	310	90
	Manuf. Prod./G.D.P.	32	34	18	15

Source: Maizels, op. cit., Table 24, p. 19.

There seems to be an inverse correlation between the degree of industrial development and the proportion of consumer goods production to the total output, or so we deduce from Table 2. While the proportion of consumer goods production was never greater than 43 percent in the European countries, this proportion never fell below 51.2 percent in the Latin American countries. And while these proportions were 51.5, 51.2, 51.8, and 56.6 percents in the cases of Brazil, Argentina, Mexico, and Chile respectively, they increased notably in the cases of Colombia and Peru (71.6 and 63.9 percents respectively).

It is evident that industrial development in Latin America follows a traditional pattern, light industry being established in the initial stages, producing for the domestic market, and "dynamic" industries of greater technological complexity appearing later. At the present stage of Latin America's industrial development the national bourgeoisie is involved basically in the traditional light industry of the type that typically depends upon state paternalism for the application of a series of protective measures favoring it. Although very large firms may exist, the majority of these are either wholly or partially state-controlled or else belong to foreign companies that do not form part of the national bourgeoisie.

Other factors work against the emergence of an "integrationist conscience." Since the overall markets are smaller in Latin America than in Europe, within each of the traditional industrial branches we have considered there is a smaller number of firms operating than operate in Europe. This means that each enterprise represents a greater part of the industry as a whole, so that if one enterprise must close because of foreign competition, it leaves a considerable proportion of the industry's work force unemployed. The situation seems considerably different in Europe. European economic integration has evolved within a highly industrialized region that contains great diversity of industries and even productive processes within each industrial branch, as well as a greater flexibility in the adoption of technological innovations. Even before the movement toward European economic integration there was a greater degree of vertical and horizontal integration among the industries of the different countries. European prosperity during the post-World War II years brought about a shortage of labor that facilitated greatly the adaptability of the different firms to changing competitive situations.[19]

[19] There are innumerable books and articles on the evolution of the European Economic Community (The Common Market). See for example, H. H. Leisner, J. E. Meade, and S. J. Wells, *Case Studies in European Economic Union* (Oxford University Press, 1962).

Latin America's economic situation was very different, and the difficulties of adapting the national industries to the postwar situation were greater, so that one could expect greater resistance to the total liberalization of foreign trade. This resistance would not, evidently, be so intense if the Latin American economies were more capable of adjusting to foreign competition, but several factors militate against this adaptability: the low rates of industrial growth in some countries; the low capacity to absorb technological innovations; and the rigidity of institutional organization in the countries. Apparently only the large international companies would not fear the possible impact of external competition. . . .

Finally, if Latin America's economic integration is to be successful, there would have to be greater reciprocity of interregional trade . . . and this is possible only to the extent that countries increasing their exports to another Latin American region also increase their imports from it. Regionalization of the import-substitution process could be effective in promoting the industrialization of the region as a whole only if it is complemented by a process of "export substitution."

This process would function well for the better-developed countries, in which industry is more capable of producing articles of greater technological complexity, precision, etc. If their costs were on a competitive level, their exports to other regions of Latin America could substitute for extraregional imports. The less-developed Latin American countries could increase the range of territory to which they could export, particularly if those countries did not yet produce certain of the consumer goods or consumer durables of a certain complexity and precision. . . . But effective reciprocity would be more difficult, for the more industrialized countries would have to increase their imports from the less industrialized ones. They could import primary products or the simpler manufactured goods, but their capacity for absorbing the primary products would be limited, and the manufactured goods would constitute a menace to their own established industry.

The conclusions are evident. It is doubtful that Latin America's economic integration would be given great impulse by the national bourgeoisie of each country, which is not necessarily capable of seeing beyond its immediate interests, which, given its weak position in the economic structure, tends to operate with a short-run view. Its interests tend to conflict with the interests of the national bourgeoisie of other Latin

American countries and it is not willing—probably because of the low adaptability of the Latin American economic structure to changing competitive situations—to devise a consistent set of "ground rules" that would be applied to all regions. Given Latin America's present capitalist structure and degree of industrialization, it would be utopian to think that Latin American businessmen would become the prime movers of economic integration or even approach it enthusiastically.

If the so-called national bourgeoisie is incapable, in the present context of capitalist Latin America, of carrying out by itself the economic integration process as part of an "autonomous industrialist" ideal, what types of government does CEPAL have in mind when proposing the formation of an LACM?

It would seem that the governments favorably disposed to the objectives set forth by CEPAL are those based on the "rise to power of new social groups with an ideology favorable to change and with developmental (*desarrollista*) attitudes." These reformist, or *desarrollista*, governments are interested in promoting national industry and base their policies on a sort of economic planning fundamentally sustained by national sectors. They are the governments most willing to coordinate their domestic policies in accord with regional integration aims.

But for these governments to subsist in the present capitalist structure, three things must coexist: (a) a significant "public sector" or a sector of state enterprises with a stratum of functionaries and technocrats interested in maintaining them; (b) "populist" type governments, or governments sustained by wide consensus or popular support; and (c) favorable international circumstances, whether these be favorable prices for their exports, large gold or foreign exchange reserves, or a large amount of foreign aid without strings attached.

Governments approaching the *desarrollista* ideal have existed for limited times in limited historical circumstances in Latin America. They seem to have been sustained by a combination of favorable international circumstances, an "unlimited supply of labor," and protectionist measures favoring the beginnings of a national industrialization process.

Probably the Mexican case is the most characteristic in Latin America. Mexico's *desarrollista* government is basically the product of profound revolution at the beginning of this

century, which permitted the rise to power of progressive
new middle-class groups and of an important State Enterprise
sector with an important class of functionaries interested in
maintaining and expanding it.[20] Under these favorable circumstances policies were adopted favoring a series of investments in
strategic sectors of the economy as well as the early promotion
of some heavy industries, such as the iron, steel, and petrochemical complexes. At the present time the Mexican Government visualizes Latin America's economic integration as a boost
to domestic industrialization, given Mexico's limited internal
market.

Some consider the Vargas period (and even later) in Brazil,
the "Perón Era" in Argentina,[21] and the present Frei government of Chile as reformist, or *desarrollista*, governments interested in carrying out national industrial policies. All of these
governments were based on a popular consensus that permitted an industrial development sustained by a national bourgeoisie within the context of a *sui generis* local capitalism.
Evidently these governments can maintain power to the extent
that the industrial and landowning bourgeoisie does not fear
the advance of the working classes and there exists (or existed)
a large supply of cheap labor—provided either by immigration, or of internal migration from rural to urban areas—
which limited the possibilities of the unionization of the working classes. And we must not underestimate the significance
of international circumstances favorable to the stability of
these governments. The large amounts of foreign exchange
reserves accumulated during the Second World War permitted
Perón to intensify the country's industrialization while at the
same time bettering the conditions of the working classes;
the rise of the price of coffee in world markets after the war

[20] "In Mexico State participation covers all sorts of industries from
iron and steel complexes to theatre chains. Eighty-two percent of the
30 most important enterprises of the country belong to the State. The
Government owns a very important petroleum and petrochemical complex with a strata of advanced middle managers, engineers, and specialists in labor relations, using the most advanced techniques of private
enterprise." J. D. Harbron, "The Dilemma of an Elite Group: The
Industrialist in Latin America," *Inter-American Economic Affairs*, Vol.
XIX, (Autumn 1965). This is a case where the national bourgeoisie has
been able to affirm itself behind an important state-controlled sector,
even though in recent years the situation may have changed somewhat.

[21] We are not including the Frondizi administration among the
desarrollista governments, although his followers have continuously used
this term to describe his policies. His 1958 presidential campaign program may have been "desarrollista" in the sense in which we are using
the term here; but his actual policies were not.

had much to do with the Brazilian "boom" of this period; the increase by 26 percent of the price of copper in the last year (related to the war in Vietnam) has been a determining factor in the recent rise by 7 percent in Chile's GDP; and even Mexico's "everlasting stability" is at least partially sustained by the diversification of her exports and by "tourism," which constitutes a significant factor in her earnings.

These governments do not last for a very long time. They subsist, as we have said, only to the extent that the traditional classes and the rising bourgeoisie do not feel threatened by the working classes, and to the extent that external factors favor an economic growth the benefits of which are distributed among the different sectors of the economy. And historically these favorable external circumstances are temporary. Hence, even if they remain popular, the governments concerned begin "stabilization programs" with all their ill consequences for the autonomous industrial growth of the countries involved. In many respects the present military governments of Argentina and Brazil demonstrate this fear of the advance of the popular classes, and the burial of the "alliance," whether it be manifest or implicit, of the working classes with the national bourgeoisie under the banner of a national industrialization ideology. The recent tendencies in both countries toward greater overall economic liberalization represents, also, the rejection of the "CEPAL vision" and the beginnings of a new "open door policy" with respect to international capitalism.

The process of Latin American economic integration that began with LAFTA is running into ever-greater difficulties. No very significant cooperative industrial agreements have taken place. Tariff negotiations between member countries have virtually stagnated, with the possibilities for new tariff reductions slowing down once reductions were made on "noncompetitive" articles. Interregional trade has not increased sufficiently to affirm that the Treaty of Montevideo is exerting a noticeable impact on LAFTA's industrial growth. As shown in Table 4, interregional imports and exports of the LAFTA have increased by only 35 percent in the first four years of LAFTA's operation. This foreign trade is insignificant when compared to the projections CEPAL made originally. Furthermore, interregional trade continues representing less than 10 percent of the total foreign trade of LAFTA's member countries. Needless to say, the exchange of manufactured goods is minimal.

TABLE 4

L.A.F.T.A.: FOREIGN TRADE

YEARS	EXPORTS		%	IMPORTS		%
	INTER-REGIONAL (millions of dollars)	TOTAL (millions of dollars)		INTER-REGIONAL (millions of US$)	TOTAL (millions of US$)	
1960	339.1	4,762.2	7.1	373.6	5,658.3	6.6
1961	297.2	4,932.4	6.0	355.1	5,998.2	5.9
1962	272.0	4,710.5	7.9	421.8	5,916.9	7.1
1963	424.4	5,608.9	7.6	524.5	5,743.2	9.1
1964	553.5	6,096.2	9.1	...	...	...

Source: J. M. Daguino Pastore, "Antecedentes y Perspectivas de la ALALC," *Desarrollo Económico*, Vol. IV, No. 14/15 (July-December 1964).

Despite international meetings and flowery public statements declaring unlimited support for the establishment of a Latin American Common Market, it is evident that the vision of CEPAL is not being fulfilled. Very little is left of the idea of an autonomous development, supported by local groups, independent of the highly industrialized nations. The LAFTA signatory nations have not created a workable mechanism to insure equal distribution of the benefits of integration. No provision has been made for planning industrial development on a regional basis. No adequate system of regional payments has been devised. The failure to coordinate transportation has allowed shipping monopolies to continue exploiting the area. As one observer has commented, "LAFTA is dying with hardly a whimper."[22]

Essentially, conditions in Latin America are not favorable to the implementation of the CEPAL vision. The basic weakness of the doctrine has been a lack of realism about the social groups that were to be instrumental in beginning and sustaining the economic plans. The CEPAL vision seems to have been devised in a "socioeconomic vacuum." Besides this, the U.S. and some of the major international organizations have been reluctant to accept this kind of economic integration program. The International Monetary Fund, for example, has systematically blocked all attempts to establish an urgently needed method of financing interregional trade; the World Bank has refused to support industrial planning or to finance integration industries; although the Inter-American Development Bank has taken up some of these projects, its program has not been extensive; and the "U.S. has been unflagging in its efforts

[22] Keith B. Griffin, review of S. Dell, *A Latin American Common Market?*, in *Journal of Common Market Studies*, Vol. V, No. 74.

to make the region safe at any cost for foreign business." In short, external economic and political pressures have hampered moves toward industrial coordination and have strengthened those Latin American groups that favor maintenance of the *status quo*.[23]

Also, the overall policies of the Latin American countries have tended to shift away from pro-CEPAL positions to an emphasis on tariff liberalization as an end in itself, without consideration of CEPAL's recommendation to apply a common external tariff to the region as a whole. "Free enterprise at any cost" has superseded CEPAL's idea that planning, in the sense we have described, and interregional coordination are essential for attaining certain structural changes in the Latin American economies. Finally, the contribution of foreign investment is constantly emphasized, with no specific consideration of the interests of Latin American enterprises.

The integrationist camp has become somewhat reduced. Only Chile, Colombia, and Venezuela[24] are vocal about the need for economic integration as an instrument for their economic development. And Argentina and Brazil have taken a "hard" line concerning the implications of an integrationist policy. Brazil has reduced many of her tariffs, not only for the LAFTA member countries but also for international competition. Also, she has introduced laws highly favorable to foreign capital. Argentina has declared interest in "integrating the country inward, first," of acquiring some kind of national autonomy before considering the possibility of increasing trade with the LAFTA countries. However, it is probable that she will eventually follow Brazil in a liberalization policy.[25]

Evidently economic integration has different meanings for

[23] For an evaluation of these policies, see S. Dell, *A Latin American Common Market*.

[24] At least this is what we have gathered from the declarations of the Presidents and the Foreign Ministers after their respective international conferences.

[25] The Argentine Government has recently tended to a liberalization of the foreign exchange market and the tariff structure, measures that give some idea of the ever-greater liberalization tendencies. Furthermore, Economic Integration does not seem to be an important objective for this government. At the recent Punta del Este Conference, General Onganía declared: "The present reality of America has also other important matters to resolve, matters that, because of their extreme urgency, are prior to those we are now considering. The principal evil of our times is revolutionary violence, a tragic fact of our days. . . . The continental security is a prior condition of economic development. We require security to be able to reach development." Quoted in *Marcha* (Uruguay, April 17, 1967), p. 17.

different people.[26] The present institutional arrangements as well as a liberalization *à outrance* favor large international companies. LACM can become a convenient instrument through which these companies can control wider markets and exert a greater sphere of influence with each investment. It is basically in the more industrially advanced countries of Latin America, which can develop large-scale heavy industry, that foreign capital can achieve a new influence. In a world of great international monopolies and oligopolies, an increased indiscriminate liberalization, even though disguised as a Common Market,[27] favors only these interests.

Latin America has tried to embark on an autonomous industrialization process within the context of a highly developed international capitalist system. This experience seems to be nearing an end. Capitalist industrial development was due, to a large extent, to the disintegration of the international economic system beginning with World War I. Today Latin America once again confronts a reconstructed international capitalist system. But by now Latin America is not merely a source of raw materials and primary products. She is to a large extent a semiindustrialized area that can become a favorable area for new foreign investments. The Latin American Common Market is now seen as an efficient method of promoting these new objectives.

[26] One of the most interesting definitions of this was made by an important Argentinian public official: "The growth of nations, well or badly endowed, is, prior to being a product of economics, a political fact, and prior to being a political fact, a mystery of the soul, because it is faith in a sacrifice, sometimes without benefit for generations. . . . Thus economic integration must be accompanied or even preceded by a real integration, a wide cultural dialogue, and a complete and profound spiritual and physical communication." *La Nación* (Buenos Aires, September 30, 1967).

[27] "Modesty must not stop Brazilians from recognizing that Brazil's action was a decisive factor for the success of the Conference (of Presidents at Punta del Este), and in particular concerning the thesis of the continent's Economic Integration. . . . The most important thing that came out of the Conference is that the U.S. will integrate into the Latin American Common Market." Quoted by *Marcha* (April 21, 1967), p. 20.

CLASS AND CLASS CONFLICT

A Latin American Phenomenon: The Middle-Class Military Coup

JOSÉ NUN

In contrast to the standard assumptions that the middle class is an inherently democratic force, and the size of the middle class and political stability go together, Nun argues that the middle classes are destabilizing and antidemocratic. Their instrument for protection against political parties and movements based on the "popular classes" is the army, which acts to defend their interests against what Nun politely calls "premature democratization." He also attacks the myth that "professionalism" in the military leads to its withdrawal from politics. On the contrary, the more developed countries in which the military has taken direct control of the government, as in Brazil and Argentina, have highly professional armed forces. The armed forces are based on and representative of the middle classes; divergences and differences in the armed forces reflect conflicting ideological orientations and interests in the relatively unorganized middle classes. These strata, unable to rule by themselves, require military rule.

Reprinted from *Trends in Social Science Research in Latin American Studies: A Conference Report* (Berkeley: Institute of International Studies, University of California, March 1965), pp. 55-99, by permission.

José Nun, an Argentinian, was Visiting Professor of Political Science at the University of California, Berkeley, from 1964 to 1966, and is currently employed by the UN Economic Commission for Latin America, where he is engaged in a study of comparative urban politics in Latin America.

WHAT FOLLOWS is a commentary suggested by the reading of different American sociopolitical works about Latin America and not an attempt at systematic investigation of primary sources. Therefore, it seems fair to anticipate briefly my conclusions so the reader can decide whether or not to go on to the main body of my discussion.

A good deal of the American sociopolitical literature about Latin America is based on a three-legged conceptual system: political instability, size of the middle classes, and militarism.[1] The scheme has two alternatives, which I will call *traditional* and *modern*. According to the *traditional* analysis, militarism —conceived as a typical Latin American phenomenon—is the principal cause of political instability, which in turn victimizes the recently emerging middle classes. Only through the consolidation of these middle classes will the army men go back to their headquarters and a stable democracy be established south of the Rio Grande. From the *modern* point of view, even though militarism—conceived as a typical phenomenon of developing countries—is a factor in political instability, it can promote economic development, which in turn will foster the growth of middle classes and allow in this way the democratization of Latin America. In both perspectives value connotations go beyond the cognitive meaning of the concepts in use: democratic stability and growth of middle classes are a priori positive and interdependent phenomena, while militarism has an ambiguous conceptual status: from being a total misfortune to being a partial misfortune and even a commendable inconvenience.

In my judgment the simple reading of those works and of the sparse empirical data they present authorizes a completely different ordering of the above-mentioned conceptual system. I leave aside the doubtful convenience of taking Latin America as a unit of analysis, and I accept provisionally the

[1] Blanksten [:325] points out another possible trilogy: "Westernization," "political modernization," and "middle sectors." But I understand that he refers to underdeveloped countries in general, while I am considering specific studies about Latin America.

narrow definition of democratic stability as a periodic renewal
of authorities through constitutional elections. But, inverting
the equation, I consider that, in many cases, Latin American
middle classes are threatened by the oligarchy or by the working classes, and *voting is one of the principal instruments of
this threat.* Therefore, the army—that in the majority of the
countries represents the middle classes with all their contradictions—comes to the defense of the threatened sectors and
*allows for political instability in the defense of a premature
process of democratization.* Middle classes are, then, confronted with a dilemma, which, according to Costa Pinto, constitutes a double fear: fear of the problem and fear of the solutions. In other words, I suggest that there are enough reasons
to see the Latin American middle classes as factors of political
instability, whose instrument is the army, and whose detonator
is precisely the democratic institutions that those sectors appear
to support. This is a peculiar Latin American phenomenon that
may be called the *middle class military coup.*

Attention has been called to the impressionistic and journal-
istic character of the American works about Latin American
politics. I believe that this is the superficial aspect of a deeper
problem: the defective structuring of the object of analysis.

Latin American militarism is a good example. It is true that
the army—or some of its members—plays politics; and it is
also true that the army, as an institution, experiments, changes
in time, and in each concrete instance is represented by real
people. The *realistic* analyst tends to choose between two
ways of observing: one is the psychological; the other is the
institutional. If he chooses the first, he will tend to analyze
the frequent seizure of political power by the army in terms of
the personal ambitions of its leaders. This point of view is
represented by Lieuwen [:20] in his analysis of nineteenth-
century Latin America. He views it as a potpourri of "ambitious, opportunistic men" who use their armaments to keep
themselves in power one after the other.[2] The second way is

* See Bibliography; this citation refers to author and page number.
[2] More than fifty years ago the Argentine historian, Juan Agustín
Álvarez [:26], made the following observation: "A great part of the
mistake is to attribute more importance to the external appearance of
facts than to the investigation of causes. It is as though the detonating
system were confused with the explosive charge. Almost always the military chief or caudillo was the detonator. . . . That is why the revolution
appears as the result of the will of the caudillo. This would be like
believing that the evolution of prices is due to the skill of the auctioneer."

more sophisticated. It tries to understand the characteristics of the military organization itself. Professionalization of the army seems to offer a field of speculation [Lieuwen:151-53; Johnson:69-78]:[3] the increasing dedication of the army men to their specific tasks will remove them from political interests and isolate them from the struggles of society. But it is clear that an overwhelming number of examples (Argentina and Brazil being the most recent) have led to the melancholic verification of Whitaker [:99]: "On the contrary, in those countries in which they (the Latin American armed forces) have been most highly professionalized, they seem to have become even more closely linked with the rest of society than formerly. But there is even more: allowing themselves to be confused by the changing but still similar appearances of the phenomena, observers try to appraise their diversity by applying labels whose uniform character, as we will see, is highly unlikely. In this way the painful task of structuring the object of knowledge is avoided: one gains the illusion of touching reality at the cost of using the same significance for different events, and a solid base for explanation is thus denied."[4]

Generalization in History

Before considering more closely the conceptual scheme mentioned above, I want to make another general observation that can provide a clue to the understanding of the recurrence of the epistemological problem sketched in the previous paragraphs.

In the United States, in addition to geographers and anthropologists, historians have been more occupied than others with Latin American problems. The scientific status of the historian

[3] In a broader theoretical context, professionalism of the army is the central concept of Huntington's excellent study of military intervention. Nevertheless, Finer [:26-30] has shown how the same process may stimulate military intervention, pointing out some specific features related to it, such as a private notion of the national interest, the development of military syndicalism and an increasing reluctance to be used to coerce the government's domestic opponents. But Finer himself, trying to find an explanation at the level of the phenomenon, ends that part of his analysis with a tautology: "The most important factor, however, [inhibiting the desire of the military to intervene in politics] is the armed forces' acceptance of the principle of civil supremacy." [:32]

[4] This problem is made more acute by a kind of pragmatic subordination of the social scientist [Cf. Blanksten: 324]. The American Government, for example, may be interested in discovering the best ways to deal with armies south of the border. But this does not mean that in order to give an answer about the military, first priority should be given to a study of the military by themselves. It would be a poor doctor who diagnosed only on the basis of what the patient told him.

is particularly ambiguous. We may say that one could draw a continuum between mathematical knowledge at one end and historical knowledge at the other—that is to say, on the one hand a kind of investigation that gets rid of reality to work with models, and on the other hand a type of investigation that sacrifices models in order to work with reality. [Granger: 207] But the contraposition is only relative. What characterizes the task of the historian is a constant tension between the immediate appraisal of an experience and the attempt to reach scientific objectivity through valid generalizations. In other words, a tension between art and science. Historical explanation attempts to show that the event was not simply "a matter of chance" that "was to be expected in view of certain conditions" [Hempel:463]—that is to say, that the singular episode can be registered in the frame of a general law that should be *provided by the social scientist*.[5] In the absence of a good theory of change (at least up to now) the social scientist is not able to provide the historian with the general laws that he needs and therefore he resorts very frequently to propositions abstracted, in a noncritical way, from other explanatory contexts. A process of circular causation is thus produced: the social scientist receives distorted historical information that disrupts his elaboration of fruitful models without which that kind of information has a high probability of remaining partially or totally erroneous.

Let us go back to the initial topic of these notes. What do American authors mean when they write about Latin American militarism? I do not want to be guilty of what has been called "the semantic myth of the social sciences." [Kaplan:71] I agree that the process of specification of meaning is a part of the research process itself. But a system of progressive definitions is not to be equated with those erratic conceptual marches and countermarches that prevent the delimitation of an acceptable context of verification. To avoid a long methodological exercise I will attempt to reconceptualize in a simple way the current meanings of Latin American militarism found in the literature. I will confine myself to the use of the following three dichotomous variables:

(a) *Military-nonmilitary:* defined by membership or not in the organization to which the government of a nation trusts

---

[5] This problem is frequently obscured by the fact that many historians are social scientists who, instead of working with data of the present, are working with material of the past.

the partial or total monopoly[6] of the public force, according
to an institutionalized system of norms.

(b) *Accession to power: constitutional-nonconstitutional:*
the perspective of liberal democracy—that orients the majority
of the American sociopolitical literature—definies democracy
as accentuating the mode by which the authority is appointed.[7]
The best example is given by Lipset with his definition: "Democracy in a complex society may be defined as a political
system that supplies regular constitutional opportunities for
changing the governing officials, and a social mechanism that
permits the largest possible part of the population to influence
major decisions by choosing among contenders for political
office." [Lipset:45] Therefore, this dimension occupies a central place in the analysis of democratic stability in Latin America and comes to be the only indicator that Lipset himself
utilizes to distinguish between the political systems of this area
[Lipset, 1960:45-50].

(c) *Economic and social development: positive orientation-
negative orientation:* although development is the typical postwar period subject, only at the end of the fifties did Americans
focus their attention on Latin American development. To avoid
a detailed elaboration of this topic, which does not relate to
my purposes, I will take as a criterion of reference the *status
quo ante* and I will consider negative the orientation that tries
to keep it or restore it, and positive the one that attempts to
bring about changes of a certain magnitude.

The cross-classification of these variables allows the construction of the table on page 151.

It seems unnecessary to point out that this schema is very
simple and serves no purpose other than to facilitate the understanding of what follows. The adjectives used in each box of
the cross-classification are only examples of certain outstanding
features of the instances that could enter in each category.
This does not imply, for example, that a conservative government, or a reformist one, could not be as *personalista* as the
one classified in box (g). I will leave aside column 1 (types

[6] I make this distinction in order to differentiate other agencies legally
armed to defend order: police, gendarmerie, etc. This seems to be relevant for an analysis of the nineteenth century, insofar as the weakness
of the national army gave preponderance to the urban guards. An additional proof of the relevance of the distinction is given by the role played
by the Argentine Federal Police during the decisive events of October
1945.

[7] For an excellent elaboration of this point, see Burdeau [:V:408 and
VI: *passim*]. The different types of representation are sharply analyzed
by Cerroni [:45-74].

	Nonmilitary		Military	
	Constitu-tional (1)	Nonconsti-tutional (2)	Constitu-tional (3)	Nonconsti-tutional (4)
Negative orientation toward development	Conserva-tive government (a)	Fraudulent government (c)	Conserva-tive government (e)	Reactionary government or *personalista* (g)
Positive orientation toward development	Reformist government (b)	Revolution-ary government (d)	Reformist government (f)	Government of the Nasserite type (h)

a and b) because they are irrelevant to my present objective. I will then maintain that the current literature about Latin American militarism does not distinguish among the other categories, and that this fact leads to a great deal of contradictions.

Type c: In this case the error is by omission because this type is not included in the analysis. As it has been pointed out recently: "to the extent that a person or group—consciously or unconsciously—creates or reinforces barriers to the public airing of public conflicts, *that person or group has power.*" [Bachrach-Baratz:949] If we think that the army's specific mission is to guard the enforcement of constitutional norms, when these norms are violated and the army does not intervene, would we accept the apolitical stand that the observed ones attribute to themselves, or would our obligation be to examine all the components of that restrictive phase of power?[8]

[8] Cf. Finer [:23] Contemporary Argentine history offers good examples of the problem. Maybe the best one is given by Gral. Manuel A. Rodríguez, minister of war of the government of Gral. Justo, "member of the Lodge [San Martín], and called by some apologists 'man of duty' [who] kept the army out of the discussion and consideration of national problems. This will be called not playing 'politics.'" [Ramos: 63] But one of the principal missions of that Lodge was to purify *politically* the army by separating those officials with sympathies toward radicalism. On the other hand, Gral. Rodríguez was minister of a government that acceded to power through the fraudulent elections of 1932. Also, the regime of Gral. Justo constituted the central stage in what has been called "the infamous decade," characterized by the violation of constitutional norms, by the reappearance of the traditional oligarchy in all the posts of command, and by the opening of the country to the entrance and subsequent domination of foreign capital. See *Revista de Historia* (Buenos Aires), n. 3, with its bibliography. Also Imaz [:39]. This author points out an important fact: "The Secretary of Information [of Argentina]—with its implicit right of veto to the election of high and median governmental officials—has always been in the hands of the army." [Imaz: 56]

Type d: It is trivial to remember that even the cunning David needed a sling and a stone to defeat Goliath. It is not so trivial if one thinks of the difficulties in which many authors find themselves when they include all types of armed movement in the military phenomenon. Do the unorganized groups of armed *peones* following their *patrón* and/or *caudillo* in the nineteenth century constitute an army? Can the Cuban guerrillas be included in a universe of discourse filled with considerations about the attributes of a military career?[9] Lieuwen, however, includes both in his study. Contrary to Johnson [:17], he considers as armies those informal and temporary crews of the nineteenth century; moreover, he devotes a chapter to the Cuban Revolution, in which Fidel Castro is never qualified as a university educated man but never fails to be qualified as a major. [Lieuwen:17-28 and 263-98]

Types e and f: I assume that the interest in Latin American militarism has sprung from a historical fact: the frequency with which army men have seized power through illegal means. Because of this, it is hard for me to understand the systematic inclusion in the analysis of the categories of column 3. I can judge positively or negatively the governments of Carlos Ibáñez, Jorge Ubico, Juan Domingo Perón, or Jacobo Arbenz: what I cannot argue against is that they attained power legitimately, elected in a regular way and according to the established constitutional procedures of their countries. It is clear that the military condition of the head of state is a necessary aspect of analysis of a regime within the phenomenon of militarism, but, besides being necessary, is this a sufficient condition? If so, I would be sorry for Washington and even for Eisenhower.[10]

[9] Lyle McAlister [:148-52] includes among those attributes: order, hierarchy, discipline, sense of mission, esprit de corps, honor, loyalty to the state and the institution—which can be in conflict—and authoritarianism.

[10] According to Lieuwen [:70ff.] himself, "curiously enough," Perón gave a strong stimulus to professionalism "advising young officers to stick to their military business and stay out of politics." The same author has characterized professionalism as "a strong counterforce that reacted against militarism." [:151-53] The logical inference is that Perón was not prone to militarism. With respect to Perón, Lieuwen makes a very serious mistake in maintaining that "he armed and equipped and organized a workers' militia that was numerically stronger than the regular army. . . ." [:69] The datum is erroneous, and it is surprising that this author included it without elaboration. To arm a workers' militia "numerically stronger" than the strongest army in Latin America would have been something more than an administrative decision, and if it had happened it would have led observers to a completely different interpretation of Peronist ideology.

Types g and h: Column 4 delimits what to my judgment constitutes the typical militarist phenomenon, taking into account that all the authors consider the *government* as the central unit of their analytical system.[11]

From the interpretative point of view, I think that one can distinguish two stages in the works about the subject: one culminates with Lieuwen's book and the other begins with Johnson's work. In terms of the previous scheme, the first one favors the vertical axis (forms of accession to power), while the second is more concerned with the horizontal dimension (orientation toward development).

Going back to my initial observations about a defective structuring of the object of analysis, I want to explain why both perspectives, even though they aim to remain themselves at the phenomenon level, are based on implicit models uncritically transferred to the Latin American context. The first perspective is connected with the European antimilitarism of the nineteenth century. This tendency takes form in the Comtean contraposition between military and theological societies on the one hand, and industrial and scientific societies on the other, and it strengthens itself in Spencer's work.[12] American thought was fed by the antimilitarist tradition; this tradition offered an appropriate frame for a "business pacifism" that managed to conceive military landings in Cuba, Nicaragua, or Santo Domingo as outposts of progress. The

[11] I make this qualification because the consideration of the phenomenon can be centered on other units of analysis—thus, the "military participation ratio" that Andreski [:54] defines as "the ratio of utilized individuals to the total adult male population." Finer's [:23] definition of the military intervention in politics is broader: "The armed forces' constrained substitution of their own policies and/or their reasons for those of the recognized civilian authorities."

[12] "Although he was an Englishman, his doctrines had greater vogue in the United States than in his home country. He became an intellectual fad that persisted for two generations and that penetrated into the most unintellectual strata of society." [Huntington: 222] See the excellent analysis that Huntington [:222-26] devotes to what he calls "business pacifism" and that he labels "industrialism versus militarism." For a general perspective of the problem, consult Vagts [:293-406]. About the United States, see the critical note of Oeconomo [:119-131]. It is interesting to underline an important difference between Comte and Spencer: while for the first one progress of industrial civilization will cause the disappearance of wars, for the Englishman—less optimistic—the abolition of wars is a necessary condition for the transition of the military type to the industrial type of society. It is clear that it is according to this line of thought that assertions such as the following are written: "Fortunately [Mexico] has solved the problem of militarism. *That is a major reason why it has become one of Latin America's most progressive nations.*" [Lieuwen: 121].

explanation was relatively coherent: Latin America did not develop, and in Latin America military interventions in politics were a daily phenomenon. Therefore it was a repetition of the European problem: backwardness and militarism were synonymous.[13] The weak points of the scheme are evident— from the simple fact that Latin America is *not* Europe to the more or less explicit assumption that progress and civilian rule are in turn synonymous.[14]

This scheme—not even valid for the European context (remember the revolutionary role of the Napoleonic armies)— was not only partially disproved by a reiterated experience of more or less progressive military governments and of overtly reactionary civilian governments, but received the theoretical impact of a system of interpretation that was elaborated for African and Asian countries. The emphasis has been displaced from liberal antimilitarism[15] to a kind of protechnical militarism. [Kautsky:436-43] According to the happy phrase of Seton-Watson [:176], when one talks about a military dictatorship, it is necessary to distinguish between "the order restorers" and "the intelligentsia-in-uniform." In this respect the analysis of Lucian Pye of Afro-Asian militarism[16] is a meaningful starting point: in the context of underdevelopment the army can be conceived as a modern organization and as a modernizing agent at the same time.

This approach finds an echo in the work of John Johnson about the military problem in Latin America. He adopts an apparent *realistic* position: if military intervention is an undeniable fact in Latin American political life, and if it is a "deterrent" to the violence that extremism can cause, it is necessary to try to transform the army forces "into more

[13] The point is explicitly made by T. V. Smith [:*passim*] who suggests that the supremacy of the civilian over the military, along with the separation of church and state, and with judicial supremacy, are particularly exportable elements of American democracy.

[14] In a period of acute transition the European armies of the eighteenth and nineteenth centuries tended to become the trustees of aristocratic traditions through a body of officers that, as Mosca [:232] stated melancholically, "more and more became a sort of bureaucratized nobility."

[15] The equation is not only disproved by examples like Costa Rica, which, even without an army since 1948, is still a "banana republic" with a per capita income of less than two hundred dollars, but by the phenomenon that Johnson [:120] calls "civil militarism."

[16] Antimilitarism and anticlericalism are typical ingredients of the liberal syndrome. A clownish example is offered by the "Dolores strike," a yearly celebration of the students of Guatemala to make fun of the church and the army.

socially constructive institutions." [Johnson:262] In this way, through what the Department of State has called "civic action," the army would be transformed into an effective agent of modernization.[17] Here again the attempt is made to analyze an aspect of Latin American reality making use of implicit models elaborated for other contexts.

The European antimilitarist conception of the nineteenth century had in sight an army that represented the last shelter of a displaced traditional aristocracy[18] and was, therefore, a potential threat for the industrial bourgeoisie. The analysis of Africa and Asia deals with *new* countries, characterized by "the introduction of institutions from outside, with a minimum concession to the values and behavior of the people," the army being a modern organization "that has been somewhat artificially introduced into disorganized transitional societies." [Pye:82-3]

According to these points of view, Latin American armies are conceived more as external forces that interfere with "normal" historical processes than as integrative elements of those processes. [McAlister, 1963:342] What eventually changes in both perspectives is the direction of that interference: negative in the first case, when they appear as obstacles to progress, and positive in the second case, when they are introduced as agents of change. But in none of these assumptions is there an answer to the key questions: Why do army men intervene in Latin American politics? What will be the orientation of this intervention? [Cf. Raway:*passim*] I believe that the answer can be sought at the level of the armed forces as institutions or in terms of the society as a whole.

The first approach (implicit in almost all the existent works), which in my judgment remains at the phenomenon level, tries to define the attributes of the military subculture as the principal explanatory element. Up to now the results

[17] A distinguished predecessor of these works is "L'Arte della Guerra" by Machiavelli. For this author the creation of national militias is useful to transform the apolitical people into citizens of the new State founded in *"buoni ordini";* the collective idea of Fatherland will emerge from the unifying contact between the people's infantry and a bourgeois cavalry. See also Janowitz [:473-93] and Braibanti [:173-75].

[18] The viability of the propositions—and the attraction that they can have for the Latin American army men—can be judged through this well-disposed sample: "Republics such as Ecuador and Peru could quarter troops at elevations ranging from sea level upwards to 16,000 feet and *use them as human guinea pigs."* [Johnson: 266, emphasis mine]

are quite unsatisfactory, and the support of systematic empirical data is inadequate.[19]

In spite of the shortcomings of these notes—their impressionistic character and the impossibility of generalizing about Latin America—it seems, however, worthwhile to analyze the phenomenon more deeply to reveal its internal features in relation to the total society. The rationale of this attempt is given by what seems to be a simple fact about which all the authors agree: the majority of Latin American army officials are of middle class origin.

The analysis of the first dimension of the system leads us to examine the second one, because if I want to explain militarism in terms of the middle classes, I have to state two propositions: (a) that given certain circumstances, in certain

[19] There are no empirical studies that try to measure the impact of military training on the Latin American career official. This fact helps to increase the interest in attempts such as Mario Monteforte Toledo's study, in which he analyzes two samples: one (which I will call A) of thirty students registered in the *Escuela Politécnica* (Military Academy) of Guatemala, 1950 and 1951 classes; and the other (which I will call B) of thirty Guatemalan graduated officials in service in 1950 whose age *ranged* between 29 and 30 years. The author considers that "the data from this last group are related to the data of the students who just began their career, because the conditions of the candidates, the education methods and circumstances of the Academy, and the type of regime of the graduates have not varied for at least two decades (with the exception of the political changes occurring since 1944)." [:367] I have selected certain questions that seem to be especially relevant.

		Sample A	Sample B
1. Ethical values that deal with:	Religion	8	4
	Social justice	9	12
	Order and discipline	11	12
	Other	2	2
2. Communism:	For	3	4
	Against	24	25
	Indifferent	3	1
3. The best government of the country would be:	Civilian	13	14
	Military	17	12
	Mixed		4

Neither the technique nor the questionnaire used in the survey allow definitive conclusions. However, it should be noted that in question 1 there is equal support for values dealing with order and discipline, which are considered typical of the military education. (The most significant variations with respect to religion and social justice should possibly be connected with the revolutionary period of that decade.) With respect to Communism there are no important variations, even though here again the same can be said with respect to the "pro-Communism" group.

Latin American countries, sectors of the middle classes induce and/or favor military interventionism; and (b) that the contradictory orientation of those military interventions are reflections of the ideological contradictions of the middle classes.

Before going on, I want to make clear that: *I neither postulate a monistic explanation nor believe that the military phenomenon is only apparent and that its only true explanation lies in the problems of the middle classes.* I hope that this statement will exempt me from further partial explanatory notes.

From my point of view, this is a typical superstructural problem, with a certain consistency of its own. In this case, as in others, the *ultimate* determination by the class structure appears to be mediated and determined in turn by national traditions, by values that are acknowledged as theirs by the particular group, by international contingencies, etc. [Cf. Sartre:35ff; Althusser:*passim*] But I firmly believe that to pose the problem in this way—in its relation to the middle classes— will help to throw some light on the specific features of the phenomenon, and that to conceive these features as particular instances of a more general contradiction can pave the way for some valid predictions.[20]

It is possible to establish a dichotomous classification of Latin American countries taking into account the proportion of the middle classes over the total population as an indicator of their political importance. (See Table 1)

Sources for Table 1

(a) & (c): Centro Latinoamericano de Pesquisas em Ciencias Sociais, *Situacão social da América Latina* (Rio, 1965).

(b): UNESCO, *Freedom of Information* (New York, 1961). For Peru and Uruguay, UNESCO, *World Illiteracy at Mid Century* (Paris, 1957).

(d): Gino Germani, *Política y sociedad en una época de transición* (Buenos Aires, 1962). * Figures for Uruguay are of 1958, taken from Carlos M. Rama, *Las clases sociales en el Uruguay* (Montevideo, 1960).

(e): Data estimated by Torcuato S. Di Tella, *El sistema político argentino y la clase obrera* (Buenos Aires, 1964), based on figures of Gino Germani.

[20] "The most facile of all the theories of military intervention seeks to explain everything in terms of class interest. According to this theory, the military support the civil power when this is drawn from a similar social class and overthrow it when it is drawn from a different and hostile class." [Finer: 40] I quote this paragraph to underscore what I do *not* intend to do. Anyhow, it seems to me that Finer's statement is somewhat unfair insofar as he builds up an adversary that is very easy to defeat. Such a simplistic "class interest interpretation" has already entered the museum of vulgar interpretations of Marx. A few pages later [:esp. 42-3], Finer himself tries to apply a similar interpretation that "[In] certain instances, however, [it] is of great and sometimes decisive importance." [:40]

TABLE 1

	(a) % Urban (1960)	(b) % Illiteracy (1961)	(c) % Economically active pop. in mfg. & const. (1960)	(d) % pop. in middle and upper classes (circa 1950)	(e) % of urban pop. in middle and upper class (circa 1950)	(f) % GNP per capita ($US, 1960)	(g) Total in Regular Armed Forces	(h) Ratio of "(g)" to Total Population	(i) Military Budget as percent of total National Budget	(j) Successful Military Coups (1930-1965)
GROUP A										
ARGENTINA	68	14	29	36	38	466	108,500 (1963)	0.51	13.2	7
URUGUAY	82	15	28	(33)*	..	..	13,110 (1963)	0.49	1.0	..
CHILE	63	20	24	22	30	439	45,710 (1965)	0.62	18.0	2
CUBA	55	22	18	22	36	..	79,000 (1963)	1.21	..	4
VENEZUELA	62	48	15	18	27	885	22,240 (1962)	0.33	8.0	4
COSTA RICA	38	21	15	22	31	310	1,230 (1964)*	0.09	1.0	1
MEXICO	54	43	15	17	37	272	52,850 (1964)	0.15	1.0	5
BRAZIL	39	51	17	15	35	168	263,100 (1950)	0.37	11.4	2
COLOMBIA	46	38	17	22	28	250	22,900 (1964)	0.15	..	9
GROUP B										
ECUADOR	35	44	25	10	21	161	13,280 (1963)	0.30	..	3
PANAMA	41	30	10	15	32	363	3,439 (1964)**	0.32	..	..
PERU	36	53	18	..8	..	190	44,940 (1963)	0.41	18.0	4
BOLIVIA	30	68	13	14	26	86	11,010 (1960)	0.31	11.0	9
PARAGUAY	34	34	17	10	27	129	9,100 (1962)	0.50	..	7
EL SALVADOR	33	61	14	..	25	200	6,650 (1961)	0.25	12.0	6
NICARAGUA	34	62	13	..	23	229	4,100 (1963)	0.25	..	1
DOMINICAN REP.	29	57	11	..	..	207	17,200 (1963)	0.57	26.0	4
HONDURAS	22	65	9	4	25	186	4,200 (1965)	0.21	7.0	2
GUATEMALA	31	71	10	8	16	156	8,500 (1965)	0.22	..	6
HAITI	13	89	7	3	14	98	....	..	23.0	5

(f): Annual averages for period 1950-1960. Charles Wolf, Jr., The Political Effects of Economic Programs: Some Indications from Latin America (*Economic Development and Cultural Change*, XIV, 1, October, 1965).

(g) & (i): Irving L. Horowitz, *The Military of Latin America*, *loc. cit.*, pp. 11 & 13. * Guardia Civil. ** Officially, the armed forces are under the control of the police.

(h): I calculated these figures as merely one crude index of the differences in magnitude. Data are unavailable on the male economically active population of the type necessary to make estimates like Andreski's "military participation ratio."

(j): This column should be understood as *illustrative* because of the difficulties in operationally defining a "successful coup." I limit myself to registering those occurrences between 1930 and 1965 that resulted in the dismissal from authority of the chief of state. Obviously, this method excludes from consideration military intervention that, without toppling a government, modifies its course of action—this occurred, for example, in Uruguay in 1933, under the presidency of Gabriel Terra. See above for a discussion of the conceptual problems involved.

Note: For quantitative illustration, I computed Spearman's rank-order correlation between columns (e) and (j), and (h) and (j). The principal limitation is that while (j) quantifies occurrences over a 35-year period, (e) and (h) are measures of their respective variables in a given year. Whatever the case, the correlation between (e) and (j) is 0.02 and between (h) and (j) is 0.39. Therefore, neither supposition gives a significant correlation.

Chronologically, the events registered by country are the following:

Argentina: September 1930; June 1943; February 1944; September 1955; November 1955; March 1962; June 1966;

Chile: June 1932; September 1932;

Cuba: August 1933; September 1933; March 1952; January 1959;

Venezuela: October 1945; November 1948; December 1952; January 1958;

Costa Rica: May 1948;

Panama: October 1941; November 1949; May 1951;

Brazil: October 1930; October 1945; August 1954; August 1961; April 1964;

Colombia: June 1953; May 1957;

Ecuador: August 1931; October 1931; August 1932; August 1935; October 1937; May 1944; August 1947; November 1961; July 1963;

Peru: August 1930; February/March 1931; October 1948; June 1962;

Bolivia: June 1930; November 1934; May 1936; July 1937; December 1943; July 1946; May 1951; April 1952; November 1964;

Paraguay: February 1936; August 1937; June 1948; January 1949; February 1949; September 1949; May 1954;

El Salvador: May 1944; October 1944; December 1948; January 1949; October 1960; January 1961;

Nicaragua: June 1936;

Dominican Republic: February 1930; January 1962; September 1963; April 1965;

Honduras: October 1956; October 1963;

Guatemala: December 1930; July 1944; October 1944; June 1954; October 1957; March 1963;

Haiti: January 1946; May 1950; December 1956; May 1957; June 1957.

I want to emphasize the purely tentative nature of these data: unless an automatic correlation between occupational structure and political orientation is assumed, occupational structure simply serves to show the area to be explored. There are other sources of arbitrariness in the use of this indicator. For example, in the case of Bolivia in 1952 (and probably now), the contextual conditions can give to the middle classes a political weight that is unrelated to their numerical proportion. The same can be guessed in the case of Peru. On the other hand, the lack of congruence between occupational structure and other indicators of economic development can minimize to a certain point the relevance of the proportion of middle classes in Panama, which is the same as in Brazil. [Lambert: 37] By comparing the above table with Lambert's list [:291-94] of the military coups in Latin America, *it is possible to disprove hopeful hypotheses about an inverse relationship between the size of the middle classes and the recurrence of military coups*.[21]

On the other hand, I think that the proposed dichotomy permits the discrimination of the relevance of certain hypothesis. I am referring here to the excellent work by Merle Kling, one of the few efforts to inquire deeply into the phenomenon of Latin American political instability. That phenomenon would be, according to Kling, "a function of the contradiction between the realities of a colonial economy and the political requirements of legal sovereignty among the Latin American States." [:138] In my judgment this conclusion is valid, in general, for countries of group B but not for countries of group A. The degree of development of these "A" countries makes it difficult to accept the idea that the government is "a unique base of economic power that, unlike the conventional economic bases of power, is subject to fluctuations in possession." [:136] Accepting, then, the validity of Kling's hypothesis for countries of group B, I am going to focus my comments on the countries of group A. Unfortunately it is commonplace to make reference to the middle

[21] Lambert's table has some omissions that I have tried to correct. It covers up to the beginning of 1963, and I have completed it with the principal military events from 1963 to 1964. The data are, in any case, approximate ones, given the difficulties of definition that I suggest in the text. On the other hand, the comparison has a relative value because the percentage of middle classes has been calculated for one point in time, and the coups have been enumerated for a period of 35 years. In any case, the Spearman coefficient is .02, which supports the lack of an inverse correlation between the proportion of the middle classes and the frequency of military coups. Moreover, if one takes 1945 as the base —given the growth of the middle classes during the war period—the coefficient is equal to .39, showing the existence of a very weak and not significant negative correlation. In any case I do not pretend the existence of any type of statistical regularity between the proportion of the middle classes in the total population and the frequency of military coups. And this, at least, seems to be verified by those calculations.

classes by saying that we lack systematic studies about their political behavior.[22] In general, American literature has considered them with an Aristotelian criterion as being the defenders of democracy and the carriers of progress, to the extent that one author has inverted the terms and has considered the supporters of progress as members of the middle classes.[23]

I will leave aside the unsolved semantic problem of the mere use of the concept "middle class" and limit myself to pointing out that, in general, middle class is defined by opposition with the other two classes—working and upper classes—or by enumeration of the groups forming it. The last type of definition allows the subcategories of *old* and *new* middle classes. In any case, *what is meant by the definition are groups of individuals of different characteristics but with assumed homogeneous political orientations.*[24] John Johnson, for example, includes in what he prefers to call "middle sectors" a group that "ranges upward from the poorly paid white-collar employees in government, with a limited education and often a lack of helpful family connections, to the wealthy proprietors of commercial and industrial enterprises on the one hand and

[22] A quarter of a century ago, Bouglé [:5] already stated that without large national surveys and comparative works it was impossible to decide whether the heterogeneity of the middle classes is essential or superficial. And recently Lane [:322] has written: "We know of no systematic studies of the political behavior of the 'old' as contrasted to the 'new' middle classes in the United States." In this respect, Mill's work is still the most important one.

[23] "A member of the middle class, as understood in this study, is an individualist who may be anywhere in the social scale from the bottom to the top. The fundamental characteristic that marks him out as a member of the middle class is not his position in the social hierarchy, but rather his attitude toward the society in which he lives. If he is determined to move into a preferred position in the social scale, he is middle class. He is an energizer, a changer, a rearranger, whose fundamental purpose is not to tear down the society but to alter the structure in such a manner that he as an individual will attain a preferred position. When he ceases to seek a higher standing and concentrates upon maintaining the position he now has, then he is no longer a member of the middle class. He has become more interested in privilege and restriction than in change." [Grayson: ix]

The following paragraph—written by the Archbishop of Tarragona—may be a sample of some literature about the middle classes: "If Marxism attacks private property . . . and if in that attack it also includes the middle classes, because it finds in them the strongest resistance to its subversive plans, it is logically clear, a priori, what the position of the Church must be in judging, esteeming, and defending the middle classes in this respect." [Benjamin y Castro: 192]

[24] Although it does not seem to be supported by the available data, Hoselitz's hypothesis about the different orientations of the "old" and the "new" middle classes constitutes a highly stimulating exception. For a discussion of its validity, see Germani. [:175-76]

to the educated professional men, teachers, and high level government bureaucrats, usually from old established families, on the other." [Johnson, 1958:xx] These sectors that according to the same author "do not fulfill the central condition of a class" because "their members have no common grounds of experience" appear, however, in the book as a relatively homogeneous factor. Moreover, in the last chapter, the book culminates with a prediction about "the middle sectors' political role in the foreseeable future." [:181] The only argument that Johnson gives to support the "cohesiveness and continuity" of his "middle sectors" is that they seem to have six common characteristics: urban, education, support to industrialization, nationalism, pro-state interventionism, and adherence to political parties.[25]

Before questioning the validity of these assumptions I want to call attention to two circumstances:

(a) *The myth of the "invisible hand":* This type of interpretation of the subjective attributes of a social class is based implicitly on the idea (very much to the liking of the classical economists) of an automatic adjustment of the orientations. Almost in a magic way, and through certain "market mechanisms," different social groups without common grounds of experience would converge around certain principles as if the individual dispersion of perspectives were the best guarantee for their final cohesion. The "invisible hand" acts here through voting, the act that integrates isolated orientations. The electoral market will perform its crucial role, and harmony will stem from dispersion. Different people, with different incomes and occupations and statuses, although all more or less urban and educated, will naturally perceive the same enemies and find convenient the same solutions for different problems. The only requisite seems to be a voting system of perfect competition, giving after all reason to Proudhon's pessimistic view of suffrage as "a device to make the people lie."

(b) *The fallacy of isolation:* The previous observation leads to this one, which seems to me of decisive importance. The bridge between them is the following elementary question:

[25] In the way of "discovering" characteristics of the Latin American middle classes, Alba [:468-69] surpasses Johnson: he finds fifteen. As a matter of fact, they look more like the author's own political program for the middle classes than like a description of the actual orientations of these groups. This assumption is further sustained by statements like this: "In Latin America today, the interests of the middle classes coincide with the interests of the Latin American society as a whole (and, in the present conjuncture, with those of mankind)." [:470]

assuming that the middle classes share certain values, where do these values come from and why are they shared? In my opinion, if the observer isolates the particular class he wants to analyze, he does not have any way to solve the problem except if, here again, he works by analogy, transferring attributes from other contexts, because by attempting that isolation, he forgets that by definition a class is only conceivable as an element of a certain system of relations. "This means that the definition of any class must take into account the relation of this class to the other groups in this system. To explain who is a proletarian in the Marxian sense we must bring in the concept of a capitalist. When we speak of a middle class, we assume the existence of a lower class and an upper class. This constitutes a fundamental distinction between a social class and an occupational group irrespective of size. In this respect occupational groups can be compared with ethnic or religious groups; they can be described without reference to their relation with each other." [Ossowski:133] In other words: it is impossible to conceive of the middle classes in a vacuum, and if this is so, *only an examination of the relationship of these classes with other social groups will allow us to formulate valid propositions about the homogeneity of the political orientations of their components and about the form and mode of appearance of these orientations.*

Lipset says: "The growing middle class in these countries [Latin American countries], *like its nineteenth-century European counterpart,* supports a democratic society by attempting to reduce the influence of the anticapitalist traditionalists and the arbitrary power of the military." [1960:138] This assertion, representative of a majority tendency in the American literature about Latin America,[26] does not take into account several factors of radical importance. In the first place, while during the nineteenth century a considerable proportion of the European (and also the American) middle classes were of rural origin, Latin American middle classes are mainly urban.[27] On the other hand, European middle classes consolidated their positions during a period in which working class pressure

[26] Nevertheless, a new trend appears in some very interesting recent contributions, such as those of Wagley [:*passim*] and Whitaker [:*passim*].

[27] For an excellent analysis of the connections between social classes and the process of urbanization, see Pizzorno, A., "Sviluppo Económico e Urbanizzazione," *Quaderni di Sociologia*, XI, 1962, pp. 23-51. I consider that some of his findings may be rephrased precisely in terms of the dialectical model implicit in my explanation.

was relatively low. Disraeli could refer to "two nations between whom there is no intercourse and no sympathy; who are as ignorant of each other's habits, thoughts, and feelings as if they were dwellers in different zones or inhabitants of different planets, who are formed by a different breeding, are fed by a different food, are ordered by different manners, and are not governed by the same laws." [quoted from Bendix:66] In Latin American countries of our group A, and especially since the 1930's, the same process of industrialization that strengthens the middle classes places them before a mobilized working class. This working class enters the industrial society through consumption rather than through production patterns. [Touraine, 1961:85ff.] In other words, its presence in the political stage and its claim for gratification are not the result of development, as in the European case, but are present from the very beginning of the process.

From another point of view the European cycle can be thought of in terms of the Marxian law of industrial concentration; that is to say, small and middle-sized enterprises are gradually absorbed by the big economic units that characterized the stage of monopolistic capitalism. On the other hand, in Latin America there occurs a sort of inverse law of concentration: in the first stage, big industrial enterprises, mainly of foreign origin, are settled, and second, as a consequence, smaller units appear in charge of tasks that are subordinated to the production plans of the big industries (production of parts, repairs, services, etc.). This process is extended to other fields of activities. A typical example is the native lawyer of foreign enterprises. Why would these groups of the middle classes, developed under the protection of foreign capital, be especially nationalistic?

Of the same complexity are the relations between middle and upper classes. In the sphere of rural production, and in the same way as the small businessmen and artisans are threatened by the establishment of big enterprises, the small producers are in constant conflict with the landowners who rent them the land and/or with the big enterprises that constitute the necessary market for their production. Referring to the industrial sector, Brazil and Argentina are typical examples of unplanned industrial development that has emerged in the shade of regulations basically enacted for the benefit of traditional rural groups and of the automatic protection offered by World War II. In this case, some sectors of the middle classes have perceived the return of the oligarchy to effective political power as a direct threat to their interests.

The purpose of this enumeration is not to make a complete list of differential factors but to indicate the serious risks of assimilating the growth of Latin American middle classes to their European counterpart. Of the same importance would be to deal with the analysis of the political consequences of the foreign origin of important groups of the middle classes, especially in Argentina, Uruguay, Chile, the south of Brazil, and Cuba [Germani:179-217]; the effects of the scarcity of middle class occupational possibilities for individuals with higher education and therefore with high expectations [cf. Di Tella, 1961:*passim;* Lipset, 1964:28]; and the differences and similarities of orientation between the members of the old and the new middle classes, etc.

I think that what has been said in the previous paragraphs is enough to support my argument against the a priori assumption of political homogeneity of the middle classes: different groups perceive different foes, and the dialectic of the political conflict defines different conceptions of the total society that are not necessarily in agreement.[28] Touraine [1963:165ff.] analyzes another meaningful factor: the advanced or delayed position that a group occupies in relation to its potential or real foe, taking as criterion of reference a certain project of development. Such groups will explicitly or implicitly elaborate their strategies and counterstrategies according to their relative positions.

With this frame of reference it is possible to understand phenomena that generalizations of the Johnson type leave aside. For example, the ambivalent attitude of middle class groups with respect to State intervention in the economy. In Argentina it was not the middle classes but the oligarchy who, confronted with the 1929 crisis, fostered the active participation of the State. It is true that at the end of the war upwardly mobile entrepreneurial groups asked for official protection as they needed it. But once their interests were consolidated, some

[28] Partisans of formal logic that reject dialectics may reshape my statement in terms of what Boulding [:25] calls *reaction processes,* "in which a movement on the part of one party so changes the field of the other that it forces a movement of this party, which in turn changes the field of the first, forcing another move of the second, and so on." Although it does not alter the core of my argument, it would be perhaps convenient to underscore once more that *dialectical* and *reaction processes* are not the same thing.

of them would turn against the attempts of the State to promote new industries.[29]

As a recent study on Brazil points out: "The principle of noncontradiction seems to lose its validity insofar as the modern fabrications of the Brazilian industrialists are concerned. The State that helps 'my industry' has nothing to do with the more abstract State that, legislating and acting, participates in the economic life and becomes the eternal symbol of the anti-enterprise." [Cardoso:164]

The proindustrialist character of the middle classes, in general, seems to be disproved by notorious examples, such as the Unión Cívica Radical of Argentina, which Johnson correctly considers as a typical middle-class party, even though he exaggerates the "xenophobic nationalism" of Yrigoyen. This does not mean that in the 1940's, as a result of spontaneous industrial growth that I have mentioned before, there were not proindustrial groups. But in that moment, as in the present, "to be in favor of industry" was a general formula that did not indicate very much concerning the concrete terms of the conflict: priority of light or heavy industry; planned economy or free enterprise; financing of industry through foreign or national investments; preference for monetary stability at the cost of industrial development, or vice versa; etc.

Again, with respect to the middle classes' "nationalism," in the century of slogans, should one favor the analysis of the "language of words" or of the "language of facts"? Lipset describes Perón as an "anticapitalist." It seems too much to say of a government that did not change the structure of Argentine rural property, that fostered by all means the growth of private light industry, that tried to solve the rural crises of 1951 through price mechanisms that permanently subsidized the big meat-packing industries and the big producers of wool, that inaugurated in Argentina a new cycle of oil concessions to foreign enterprises, etc. It is true that it also enacted an advanced

[29] Some sectors of the Argentine light industries provide good examples of this point. Of course, they were all deeply protectionist in 1945, when the end of the war posed the problem of competitive imports. But ten years later, when it was strong enough, the Argentine Federation of Metallurgical Industries was already complaining about protection of "those industries that pretend to produce delicate elements of high precision that other industrialists must employ in machines or equipments of their own production." (Federación Argentina de Industrias Metalúrgicas, *Memoria 1955*.) In the same way, the Cámara Gremial de Fabricantes de Caños y Tubos de Acero was asking for free importation of iron hoops, provoking the indignation of the Centro de Industriales Siderúrgicos. (*La Nación*, 4/30/1957. I take the preceding one and this quotation from Polit:66). Protectionism becomes a matter of personal convenience and, finally, a mere problem of costs.

social legislation and gave the popular masses a real sense of participation. *But the fact is that neither Perón nor Vargas, nor any other representative of the middle classes placed in their position, can be a capitalist if, as such, one understands a leader of state to be purely engaged in the values of free enterprise and liberal democracy.*

These types of governments are precisely a reflection of the deep contradictions of the middle classes, with their ambiguities, their attempts to use the working class as a maneuvering tool against the oligarchy, and their need of the protection of this oligarchy when the masses seem to be out of control. Therefore Whitaker is right when he postulates as "law" that "the only sure thing about the more enterprising members of the Latin American middle class is that they will not stay in the middle." [Whitaker:97] The contradiction can be solved with a half-turn, as in the cases of Perón or Quadros, or with a shot, as in the Vargas case.[30]

This line of analysis helps us to understand the cleavages that divide the middle classes of the countries of our group A. At the same time, it departs from mechanistic and a priori interpretations, some of which try to accommodate the contradictory reality of these groups to a preconceived harmony; others are characteristic of vulgar Marxism forcing distinctions between the "good ones" and the "bad ones," between a sector of the middle classes that, by definition, is inclined to form an alliance with the oligarchy and to deal with the foreign investor, and another sector that, also by definition, is the natural friend of the proletariat and advocate of progress.

Several hypotheses emerge from the point of view that I have adopted. Here I cite only some of them as examples:[31]

(a) It is possible that traditional sectors of the rural middle classes (especially artisans and small businessmen), threatened by technical and industrial progress, will find refuge in vernacular values, retreating in the ideological defense of the

[30] The lack of understanding of this contradictory character of the middle classes leads Johnson [:1958:138ff.] to a blind alley: he finds in Peronism most of the attributes of his middle sectors but still he does not consider Perón as a representative of those groups. It is perhaps worthwhile listening to Perón himself: "The historical development of the modern peoples of the world shows, in an absolutely indisputable way, that the better its middle class, the greater the modern State." [Perón:115] A few paragraphs later he considers the middle class "undoubtedly the source of the most important values of the Argentine people." [:130] For an "anticapitalist" who does not represent the interests of important groups of the middle classes, he behaved very politely.

[31] Given their mere illustrative character, I chose these propositions at random, without any attempt at systematization along one or more dimensions.

past. [Cf. Kautsky:40-1] In this way they can become a good clientele for conservative movements, or, given their lack of identification with the big proprietors who constitute the elite of such movements, they can become supporters of "populist" tendencies, attracted by the attack on foreign investments that those populist movements generally imply. That is to say, in this last assumption, the nationalism of the group can be positive as far as it opposes the obstacles of an independent development but can also be transformed into a hindrance if the movement accedes to power and cannot put this nationalism at the service of industrial development.

(b) On the other hand, new sectors of the rural middle classes that find an upwardly mobile way through education—that usually develops faster than industrialization—can become radical and potential nuclei of revolutionary movements when they find that the expected occupational possibilities are blocked by lack of demand or by the preponderance of arbitrary selections.

(c) Urban sectors of the middle classes connected directly or indirectly with public administration can adopt a *pro-status quo* orientation pervaded only by claims toward a better income distribution. [Cf. Hoselitz:60-65] In countries in which the "spoil-system" plays a dominant role the orientation of these sectors can be related to their position in the hierarchy of power, as Dahrendorf [:55-6] suggests, and/or with the threat that a new regime always implies with respect to a new distribution of public employment. The size of the tertiary sector in Uruguay—out of proportion with the other sectors of activity—could thus explain, at least partially, the traditional stability of this country.

(d) The suggestion of propositions about the industrial sector itself—especially if one includes the managerial group—is far more complex. Besides the problem of analyzing the political orientations of the managerial group, one has to add the classic question about the behavior of white collar workers and of the upper strata of the working class. In my judgment, one should look for the clues in the way these sectors tend to define: (1) their membership group; (2) their reference group; and (3) their adversaries. These definitions are of decisive importance in making inferences about their perspectives on the total society and, therefore, about their political orientations. Moreover, these definitions should be considered as interacting with each other and determining the one to the other, their separation serving only analytical purposes. Do the nonmanual workers tend to identify themselves with the manual workers or with the independent sectors of the middle classes? Do they plan their mobility in traditional terms (transients in a job that, through savings, will lead them to their own business), or in modern terms ("making a career" within the enterprise through specialization; identification of their personal progress with the growth of the enterprise)? Do the entrepreneurs recognize themselves as members of a closed migrant community, as promoters of an upwardly mobile sector of technicians and specialists, as inhabitants of the borders of an upper class that is the depository of social prestige, etc?

What is the form of the manifest or latent conflict between employer and employee according to their respective initial orientations? Between a white collar worker who perceives the industrial entrepreneur as his ally in the development of the country and another who identifies him with the defenders of the status quo? Or between an entrepreneur that favors family traditions in his company and one that tries to impose rational patterns in his organization? There is no doubt that there are deep differences and that according to these differences the terms of the struggle or the contract will vary. The reciprocal actions of all these factors are manifest when one thinks how a paternalistic relation—and even a less traditional system of personal gratifications—can separate white collar workers from other workers besides separating the workers themselves.

These relations, of course, are included in a wider field of action that is bounded by the State. The ambiguities of the State behavior emerge and act over them. For example, in Brazil, Varguismo created labor legislation in favor of the workers but at the same time closed the legal means for their independent organization. Peronism, confronted with a preexistent syndical structure, not only took it over (which was not enough to control it), but tended to an increasing bureaucratization of the conflicts, the explosive potentiality of which then usually became diluted in the corridors of the Ministry of Labor.

The validity of any generalization about the middle class seems to be doubtful without at least a rough knowledge of these matters, except if one starts from a philosophical idealism *à outrance*, recognizing that concepts have a Kantian power to constitute reality.

At this point, I should make clear that the sociopolitical literature has plenty of prescriptive works that limit themselves to verifying what we already know: that is, how much we do not know. It is not my purpose to add to such literature. I welcome, of course, the kind of research I have suggested, in which, fortunately, many specialists are by now engaged. What I am saying is that in the meantime, based only on sparse data and even on impressionistic studies, the *only thing that can be postulated is the basic lack of cohesion and homogeneity of the Latin American middle classes*. This lack of homogeneity underlies an immediate political problem: the struggle for power within the framework of a representative democracy.

Here again the observer can remain at the level of the phenomenon or go further, not to look for its essence *behind* it but *in* the phenomenon itself, because the harmonious appearance of the electoral act can disguise—and, in fact, does disguise—the truth of that harmony, which is *compromise*. In elaborating this topic we reach the third dimension of the conceptual scheme under analysis.

It is necessary to insist on the importance of the well-known process of extension of voting. [Cf. Marshall: *passim*; Bendix: 74-100] In the European case, those middle classes "that never are in the middle" find in voting the necessary instrument to break the political control of the upper class. It is a necessary instrument, but it is not a sufficient one because the upper class, confronted with an adversary that articulates a more rational project, can accept the challenge and respond with a strategy placed at the same level. This is what happened, for example, in the famous German National Assembly, Frankfurt, in 1848, when the liberals defended qualified voting and conservatives (encouraged by the possibility of a paternalistic handling of the rural masses) advocated universal suffrage. [Bendix:97] In the same way, today rural voting can be difficult to handle for the more progressive sectors of the Latin American middle classes.

In 1957 Emilio Willems [:552] wrote with reference to Brazil: "The main social function of suffrage was that of *preserving the existing power structure*. Within the traditional patterns, suffrage added opportunities for displaying and reinforcing feudal loyalty. At the same time, it reinforced and legalized the political status of the landowner. Despite all changes that have taken place, this is still the prevalent situation in most rural areas of Brazil." This observation was verified by the elections of 1962 when the tendencies *conservadora-señorial* and *clientelista* received 41.2 percent of the votes against 27.8 percent of the *nacional-progresismo*, and 31.0 percent of the *conservadorismo-liberal*. (I use the categories and data elaborated by Helio Jaguaribe [:*passim*].) As one could expect, 63.5 percent of the votes received by the two first tendencies came from the northern and northeastern backward rural areas, with the exception of Pernambuco. The intensity of the phenomenon is, however, decreasing in direct relation with the mobilization of the Brazilian rural masses, as a result of the political action of laborism, of Christian Democracy, of Communism, and of the *Ligas Campesinas* of Francisco Julião. One of the means of that political action has been the literacy campaigns that tried to qualify rural workers for voting. The motivations of the coup of 1964 were not alien to the fear the traditional elites felt of that important process.

But to this problem of the middle classes—that in simple terms we can label the *threat from the right wing*—one has to add another of the same, if not greater, complexity. The countries of our group A have a high rate of urbanization, and there is enough evidence to state that urbanization and industrialization are independent phenomena [cf. Germani:*passim*], and to hypothesize that radical political ideologies are urban products more than industrial ones. [Soares, 1964:*passim*]

The processes of collective mobility and of mass mobilization brought about by urbanization pose the problem of an electorate increasingly conscious of the value of its vote, at least as an instrument of negotiation; and by the same token, they affect the structure of urban areas in such a way that it is impossible to study these movements only in terms of a context that is changed *by the mere presence of those migrants*. [Cf. Costa Pinto:41ff; Touraine, 1961:83ff.]

Some writers have conceptualized the problem by differentiating between two stages of the process. The first one corresponds to the growth of the middle classes; and the second to their consolidation. [ECLA:94ff.] In the first stage the middle classes would look for the backing of the popular classes as support for their social promotion; in the second stage, once settled in the established social order, they would become "domesticated middle classes," guardians of that order. In both cases the liberalism of these classes would be a function of their pragmatism.

Even though this is a useful approach, its exaggerated schematism makes it vulnerable and contradicts what the same authors have stated about the heterogeneity of these middle classes ("middle classes without physiognomy" in the Latin American context [ECLA:108]). I believe that the middle class tendency to compromise exists in both stages and that its intensity and form will vary with the sectors of the middle classes under consideration.

At this point it is necessary for me to make a quasi-Rousseaunian digression. For Rousseau, the idea of representation destroys the idea of democracy in that he conceives democracy as a system where the interested individuals themselves, and only they, can find solutions to their problems. The implicit notion is that *the majority can be constituted as a general will* through the majority procedure. In other words: *it is necessary that the sovereign know what he wants* (that the program for which he votes will be the potential law that the elected will translate into action) for the mandate to be imperative and not merely representative, and for the mandatory to be strictly dependent on the popular will. What is paradoxical is that to make this possible a high degree of previous consensus is needed; otherwise the majority procedure imagined for the solution of conflict is only efficient when individuals are in agreement or separated by very narrow margins of disagreement. [Bourri-caud:780]

Present societies are far from meeting this requirement of cultural integration and social homogeneity. They can be better characterized as kingdoms of negotiations. To accommodate themselves to the majority procedure, the heterogeneity of opinions has been obliged to compromise to the point that it has been said—with respect to Western industrial countries—that typical political phenomena are precisely party coalitions. This allowed Robert Dahl to elaborate his theory of polyarchy based "not on the constitutional prerequisites but on the social prerequisites for a democratic order." [:82]

A polyarchy is a special combination of two opposite tendencies: one, toward inequality in the control of the decision-making process, as formulated in the "iron law of oligarchy" of Michels; the other reciprocal, toward increased control of the nonleaders over the leaders. The exclusive domination of the first tendency produces a pure unilateral dictatorship, just as the absolute maximization of the second leads to the kind of pure democracy imagined by Rousseau. Polyarchy falls between the two extremes as far as nonleaders exercise control over leaders but "leaders by no means share equal control over policy with nonleaders." [Dahl-Lindblom:284]

The ambiguity of the majority will is what transforms the function of the leaders: the mandatory has not only to carry out a collective decision but to interpret its incoherences, decide between incompatible options, and balance dissenting requirements. In other words: the sovereign presents, instead of a coherent will, expressions of desire that leave a wide area for the decision of the mandatory. A condition of polyarchy is an irreducible multiplicity of the centers of decision. "Polyarchy requires a considerable degree of social pluralism—that is, a diversity of social organizations *with a large measure of autonomy with respect to one another.*" [Dahl-Lindblom:302; emphasis added] Thus, the existence of different organized influential nuclei limits, "the capacity of officeholders to extend their control over ordinary citizens," [:97] this last being the danger implicit in the contradictory structure of the majority rule.

Since the 1930's and even before in countries like Argentina and Uruguay, the middle classes have played an important role in the politics of the countries of group A. In these nations the majority procedure is constitutional datum to which the struggling sectors must adjust in one way or another. All the ambiguities and contradictions of the middle classes are therefore reflected in the inconsistencies of their party programs and in the singular alliances that they try to establish.

"In a rough sense, the essence of all competitive politics is bribery of the electorate by politicians." [Dahl:68] But here I have in mind something more: I refer to structural tension of the orientations of middle-class sectors that want such conditions as: economic development *and* monetary stability; State protection *and* nonintervention; betterment of the public services *and* tax reduction; increase of rural productivity *and* respect for rural property; freedom of opinion *and* repression of the manifestations of *anti-status quo* opinions; abolition of privileges *and* access to aristocratic drawing rooms, etc. All this must be encompassed in a phraseology able to attract the feared popular masses without alienating the protecting oligarchy.

As Wagley states: "The middle class of Latin America helps create the preconditions for revolution, but it really does not want to live it through." [:7] One should not be surprised, then, if among the sectors of the middle classes one finds the more frustrated groups of today's Latin American society. "Of course the basic trouble with people like us," says a character of Orwell speaking for all the white collar workers, "is that we all imagine we've got something to lose." [quoted by

Mills:xi] This thought can be extended to the entrepreneurial sectors that are always imagining that they have something to gain.

As in the Western countries where liberal norms are enforced, the electoral act becomes the synthesis of compromises among the internal and external contradictions of the middle classes. *The basic problems of the polyarchy are thus posed, but the necessary means for their solution are lacking,* because their divisions, their difficulty in articulating a coherent ideology, and, in the majority of cases, their individual resistance to organizing themselves in guilds or unions,[32] together with their recent origins, do not help to provide the middle classes with autonomous organizations of their own. In this organizational vacuum these classes are at the mercy of circumstances.

If a government has enough economic resources—like the Perón government until 1949—it is possible that it could maintain for a while the ambiguous situation favoring at the same time the working and the middle classes without actually harming the oligarchy very much.[33] But if those resources are lacking and the government still wants to be supported by the landowners, then it will very often resort to monetary devaluation. The effects of this measure on the middle classes will be different according to the stage of development of the country.

[32] To put it in Perón's own words: "You must have noticed that a worker never asks for an increase in salary for himself but for all the members of his union. A man of the middle class never asks on behalf of the people of his same position. He asks only for himself. This is the source of the weakness of the middle class." [:131]

[33] It is necessary to distinguish generally at least two moments in the development of Peronism: the more populist one, supported by the financial reserves accumulated during the war, and a second one, a consequence of the exhaustion of those reserves and of the crisis of 1951. While in the first phase, the regime was able to cope with the demands of a mobilized mass by increasing its gratifications without actually introducing deep structural reforms in the Argentine socioeconomic regime, the critical situation of the early 1950's confronted it with a narrower range of choice in order to foster the economic development of the country. That was the "moment of truth" for Peronism, and its choices were relatively clear: to slow down popular claims, to place emphasis on the development of free enterprise, to attempt to increase rural production through better prices for traditional agrarian sectors, and even to try an explicit return to an effective liberal democracy. Without further elaboration at this time, I want to stress the fact that Peronism was by no means an *alternative* to capitalism but one of the peculiar forms that capitalism itself may assume in an underindustrialized but modern country with a highly mobilized urban mass. This approach shares some aspects of Jaguaribe's characterization of "neo-Bismarckism" but at the same time tries to show the shortcomings of that solution, my view being less optimistic than the one stated by the Brazilian scholar.

In Brazil in the 1930's the resulting redistribution of income that favored the traditional groups favored at the same time the middle classes because industry received indirect protection [Furtado, 1962:183ff.]; but in Argentina the same measure, during Frondizi's government, led to a radical deterioration of the position of the middle classes. [Ferrer:b:*passim*] It is necessary to emphasize not only the serious effects that high rates of inflation have on the income of the middle classes, but the lack of ability of these sectors for an efficient and immediate reaction due to the lack of adequate representative organizations.

To these examples taken from the economy can be added other examples at the institutional level, such as the consequences of the coexistence of federalism and qualified voting in Brazil, that pose to the executive power a choice between two sources of legitimacy: one stemming from the constitution, the other from the will of the electorate.[34] The variety of situations that I give as examples tend to diminish any mechanically conclusive character of these comments. My summary observations thus will refer to a *tendency* in Latin American political development.

What is seen as exceptional is that a government (*a constitutional government chosen through normal elections*) could maintain itself for a long period in an ambiguous situation. To

[34] Relating the problem of federalism and the restriction of voting only to literates, Furtado says [1964]: "The present federal system, by giving great power to a senate controlled by the small agrarian states and by the most backward areas, places in fact the legislative power in the hands of a minority of the population, who live in regions where the interests of the landowners exert an absolute power. In the house of representatives the number of deputies is proportional to the population of each state. Therefore, the more the number of illiterates in a state, the greater the value of the voting minority. . . . Given the fact that the oligarchy is more powerful in the areas of a higher proportion of illiterates, the electoral system helps to preserve its predominance." [:13] "In the peculiar characteristics of the recent Brazilian political process, the principle of legitimacy of power itself poses a contradiction. To be legitimate the government must operate within the constitutional framework. But, on the other hand, to respond to the expectations of the large majority that elected him—especially the urban population politically conscientious—the president would have to fulfill aims that are incompatible with the limitations created by the congress within the rules of the constitutional game. Therefore, the two principles of legitimacy of the authority—its subordination to the constitutional framework and its obedience to the substantive mandate that stems directly from the popular will—become conflicting principles, confronting the president with the alternative of betraying his program or of forcing a nonconventional outcome, that may even be his resignation." [:16] For a similar analysis, see Soares. [1964:1-19]

come out of that situation *it has to make a choice, and in making a choice, it will unavoidably alienate some of its supporters*. This is exemplified by the famous "historical half-turns" of a Frondizi or of a González Videla. On the other hand, what also surprises the observer is the obstinacy by which the government of Illia maintains itself in an ambiguity without apparently realizing that, in the long run, this will also polarize the electorate.

When the moment of decision finally arrives, the working and upper classes *may or may not* be affected by the decisions adopted by the government. It depends on whether the solution is an overt labor policy or an oligarchic one. But, owing to their position in the sociopolitical space, certain sectors of the middle classes will always be affected, whatever the decision may be. And, as I have noted before, the capacity for defense of these sectors is reduced by their lack of such organizations as the unions of the working class, and their lack of traditional representative instruments like the ones efficiently used by the oligarchy.

It is here that the army intervenes.[35] Bourricaud says with reference to developed countries with a socially organized pluralism: "The 'appel au soldat' has no possibility of being heard *in normal times;* even though many sectors of public opinion are always ready, they will succeed only in mobilizing the rest of the population in those circumstances in which the resource of the sword appears to the majority as a kind of *ultima ratio*." [Bourricaud:788; emphasis added] But, what are *normal times* for the middle classes in the countries we are concerned with? In the best case, for the more middle-of-the-road groups, they are times of exhausting activity, an activity of Sisyphus, for they are trying in vain to conciliate and unite the extremes. The typical representation of these groups in the political arena is the Latin American Social-Democrats, revolutionaries, and pacifists, supporters of adjustments more than of changes of structure, leaders of an imaginary working class "in the European way," in frequent alliances with traditional

---

[35] As I did in the case of the comparison between the size of the middle classes and the frequency of military coups—and keeping in mind the same methodological shortcomings—I have tried to correlate the latter with voting participation in general elections. (I have used as my source for the data on voting participation those supplied by the Statistical Abstract of Latin America, 1960 [Los Angeles: University of California, 1960, p. 14]. Again, the application of Spearman's index showed no correlation between both variables: 0.035 (1930-64) and 0.03 (1945-64).

groups, and attempting to become the "loyal opposition." A socialism, defender of private property and free enterprise, that, confronted with the threat of social revolution (not shaped precisely in Fabian terms), becomes supporter of coups and angrily asks—as in Argentina—for the intervention of the army.[36] The answers of the army can vary within certain limits. If my reasoning thus far is correct, *the army being today an institution representative of the middle classes in the countries I am considering* [cf. Lambert:266ff.], the contradictions of these classes will be reflected in their internal cleavages mediated by some peculiar traits of the institution itself. This topic has been considered very lightly in American literature, which, certain caution notwithstanding, tends to consider the army as a unity.[37]

One of the pillars of the antimilitarist logic—exemplified by the French republican constitutions of 1791 and 1875—is the effort to avoid the politicization of the army because this presupposes deliberation, and deliberation, in turn, brings divisions that could weaken the army forces and therefore the

[36] Even in a country like Ecuador, where the small size of the middle classes would allow predictions about their radicalization, confronted with a traditional aristocracy, the observers have been puzzled by their tendency to compromise with the upper class. Diaz [:109] stresses the fact that the *Partido Socialista Ecuatoriano*—typical representative of the middle classes if one leaves aside the bourgeoisie, represented by the liberals—has had many opportunities since its creation in 1926 to seize power and to transform the country. Not only has it failed to do that, but on several occasions (e.g. 1931, 1933, 1938, 1945), notwithstanding its majority position, the Party supported candidates from the Right. This was the case of the conservative Velasco Ibarra, elected in 1945 with the contribution of socialist votes. Immediately after, Velasco Ibarra nullified the Constitution of 1945—elaborated by the majority Partido Socialista—and persecuted systematically the socialist leaders. Diaz [:110] points out that one of the main reasons for the Socialist failure in Ecuador is its tendency to collaborate with the landowners and with the bourgeoisie.

[37] See, for instance, Alba's distinction among *militares de cuartel, militares de escuela* and *militares de laboratorio*. [:56-72]

[38] See Domenach's "petit catéchisme de l'armée en république." [634-35] The constitutions of Bolivia (1945) and Colombia prohibit explicitly military deliberations, as did Alberdi's constitutional project: "The armed forces cannot deliberate; its role is only passive." [art. 25] The constitutions of El Salvador, Venezuela, and Guatemala state the apolitical aspects of the army, while the constitutions of Nicaragua and Panama prohibit the military from addressing petitions to the authorities if these petitions are not strictly related to their specific tasks. [Cf. Bidart Campos:74-5] It would be worthwhile revisiting the liberal principle of military apoliticism. On one hand, the attempt at reducing the mission of the armed forces to a pure and narrow technique precludes "the comprehension of the very meaning of the profession." [Lacroix: quoted by Domenach: 637] On the other hand, the passivity and the indifference of the army contradict the same democratic tenets from

law.[38] The evidence of military politicization in Latin America would then have had to lead the observers to the analysis of the evident factionalism of the Latin American armies that can crystallize in *lodges*,[39] which in turn reveal clearly the variety of nuances in the "sense of mission" that the army men usually attribute to themselves.

Given the present state of research about Latin American militarism, it would be naive and premature to agree that divisions in the army are mere replicas on a smaller scale of the differences that separate the diverse sectors of the middle classes, especially because I insist on recognizing that the military phenomenon has a relative consistency of its own. But I understand that it is most important to analyze the relationships between both group levels. This will also reveal the eventually characteristic features of the military subculture itself.

One should not be content only with analyzing the frequent cases of civilians explicitly inviting army men to intervene in politics.[40] This would be simple, but it would mean again that analysis was remaining at the level of the event, *because it is not necessary for two persons or two groups to know each other in order to share similar ideologies*. Moreover, in many cases, the organizational structure that the army presupposes can lead some of its groups to shape scattered claims in a more

which they stem. "When the aim is to educate each individual to shape a responsible citizen, how can a national body be reduced to a blind obedience, to a stupid servility?" [Domenach:637] See also García Lupo [:1962 (b): 9-29].

[39] There are very few studies of the Latin American military *logias*. For the Argentine case, see García Lupo. [:1962 (a): 53-66] It is also important to stress the fact of the very *limited* participation of the military in these kinds of concrete political activities. The global phenomenon hides the fact of the very small size of the groups actually engaged in politics. Under Perón, from about one hundred generals— "according to reliable sources—hardly fifteen were 'personally and institutionally' identified with the political conduction." [Imaz:38] For a highly interesting "case study," see Perón [1931:10-86].

[40] Colombia provides a very good example. Traditionally the civilians were in power, the number of officers and their salaries were very low, and, even the minister of war was usually a civilian. Up to 1950 there was only one military attempt to seize power, in 1944, during the government of Alfonso López, and it was a total and immediate failure. But it was Laureano Gómez, a civilian president, who from 1950 started strengthening the armed forces to oppose the liberals. During that decade the deterioration of the Colombian political context reached such a critical point that "The army became the rock upon which the state clung for survival" [Helguera:355], and finally a well-known professional, General Rojas Pinilla, took power.

or less coherent way *before* these claims reach a certain degree of consistency among civilians.

On the other hand, neither the middle classes nor the army are acting in a vacuum but within the frame of a dominant culture *that is still controlled by the traditional upper class*. This upper class largely controls the press and the coveted attributes of prestige.

This fact may lead sometimes to erroneous assumptions: that is, the oligarchical propaganda may be a clever façade to cover the unrest of the middle classes, that the aristocracy tries to accommodate to its own purposes. Therefore, that propaganda becomes as revealing of the fears of the upper class as it is a symptom of the unrest and the vulnerability of its middle-class consumers. Here again it is a mistake to believe that the skills of the auctioneer are the main determinants of the system of prices. The oligarchical paraphernalia may conceal the middle-class components of the process, leading once more to a false interpretation that leaves the middle classes in the middle.

Brazil is, perhaps, a good example. The Brazilian aristocracy was threatened more by a social process than by measures taken by the Goulart government. As one would expect, the attacks against Goulart were concentrated in the superstructural aspect of the regime: administrative corruption, inflation, danger of Communism, threat to religious values, etc.[41] After the coup a possible and comfortable interpretation would lead one to expect the mere accession to power of the traditional right wing. In this way any "lukewarm" reformist policy of the *de facto* government must be taken as nonexistent because it does not fit with the preconceived model. But this interpretation does not take into account at least two factors: (a) the *moralist* tendencies of the different sectors of the middle classes themselves (classes that not only were passive recipients of that rightist preaching, but also were suffering the consequences of an unplanned development, "lack of public facilities, crowded

[41] The Right defends [also] a superstructural view of underdevelopment, trying to support the thesis that Brazil owes its poverty to a crisis of men and to a lack of consolidation of the elites; other spokesmen of the Right stress the problem of education, which they consider to be a cause and not a result of underdevelopment; others assign priority to hygiene problems, but all, without exception, typically neglect the consideration of the structural problems of the country and defend nervously the traditional lines of semimonopoly of our foreign trade, subordination of our foreign policy, and unconditional adhesion to the Western block (under the political and economic leadership of the United States), arguing that this is the only way to cope with the communist danger." [Josué de Castro:211-12]

schools, and rampant inflation."[42] [Wagley:7] This pushed
them to the opposition of a regime that allowed the growth
of a leftist—or, at least, populist—threat.) (b) An equal
moralist emphasis of the army forces increased when they were
confronted with the subversion of its hierarchy on the part of
the government, which stimulated the political action of the
noncommissioned officials, and increased also because of the
identification of different groups of the army with the problems
of the upper class and, mainly, with the problems of some
sectors of the middle classes. What happened after, says Wagley, occurred "with the acquiescence of the Brazilian middle
class. Even more, it would seem . . . that the middle class
feels relieved that the military forces have taken over." [Wag-
ley:8]

This is precisely the Latin American phenomenon that I
want to point out and to which, as far as I know, no attention
has been given.

This would not be the simple schema of the coup from the
Right or the coup of the ambitious army official. *Golpistas
duros* and *golpistas blandos*[43] represent contradictions existent
among the sectors of the middle classes and the upper class.
The reformist measures might be impracticable or inconsistent,
but they are *true* measures, as true as the impracticable and
inconsistent programs of the middle classes.

An equation in which the army was always a threat to those
lovers of democratic stability, the middle classes, has prevented
us from seeing, up to now, the phenomenon, a phenomenon
that cannot be understood in terms of either the European
context of the nineteenth century or the Afro-Asian context
of the twentieth century.

The "premature" extension of suffrage to the masses confronts the different sectors of the middle classes with the
problem of competing for power both with the upper and with
the lower classes, before they have consolidated their own

[42] Linked as it is with bureaucratization, the Brazilian middle class is
an urban category par excellence and chronologically recent in the
system of social stratification. Their problems seem to stem from the
simultaneous and contradictory action of two types of factors: (a)
structural factors, related to development, that stimulate its growth;
(b) economic factors, related to inflation, that contribute to deteriorating its status, based on fixed incomes. *The result is that among the salaried groups that coexist in the Brazilian society, those groups of the
middle class are the most unstable ones. This characteristic, if not
unique, is undoubtedly a recent feature of the social stratification of
Brazil.* [Costa Pinto:83. Emphasis added.]

[43] Literally, these would mean "hard coup partisans" and "soft coup
partisans."

position through an articulated organizational system. The electoral period becomes, then, the arena of negotiation par excellence. As in any compromise, afterward each partner tries to solve the resulting ambiguity by getting the best part. Through increasingly powerful trade unions, the labor movement (usually reformist) pressures *against privileges*. Through their experienced channels of influence, the traditional elite pressures *to preserve privileges*. The threat of socialism or populism on one hand; the threat of an oligarchical rule on the other hand, and, at the center, these middle classes that cannot just stay in the middle. When these precarious alliances reach the point of rupture—i.e., when critical decisions have to be made—there is then a high probability that members of the army will be called for help and/or will come to the rescue of those middle class sectors with whom it tends to become increasingly identified. The reason for this, in the final analysis, in most of the countries I have considered, is that the armed forces seem to be today one of the better, if not the best, structured institutions of the middle classes.

Final Note

This article was prepared on the basis of notes utilized in my paper delivered at a Conference on "Trends in Social Science Research in Latin American Studies," Palo Alto, California, October 9-11, 1964. I have authorized the editors of this *reader* to republish it here, but I have not had the opportunity to introduce corrections in it I deem necessary—corrections, frankly, that would involve rewriting the article. So let this note serve as an apology for my occasionally loose formulations on the one hand, or overassertiveness on the other, due above all to the needs of oral exposition and polemic. The date of the work, incidentally, explains the mention of certain events as immediate history. Bibliographical references have been added, and I have changed (amplifying and bringing the data up to date) the original statistical table presented. In the past three years I have had the opportunity to reexamine the article's theme. While I continue to think the article's central argument valid, I have tried to pose it in slightly altered terms —especially for the period following the 1930 depression: this was a period of the crisis in the hegemony of the oligarchies and of the difficulties the middle classes in these countries were having in constituting themselves as an authentic capitalist class ("bourgeoisie"). That is, elections should be seen only as an index of this more general dimension, from which the role of the armed forces as a stratum protecting those groups without the ability to rule by themselves ("sin vocación hegemónica") becomes intelligible. The interested reader may refer to "The Middle Class Military Coup Revisited," in Claudio Véliz, ed., *The Politics of Conformity in Latin America* (London: Oxford University Press, 1967).

Bibliographic References

Alba, Víctor: "La nouvelle classe moyenne latinoaméricaine," *La Revue Socialiste*, 133 (May 1960), pp. 466-74.
——: *El militarismo* (Mexico: U.N.A.M., 1959).

Althusser, Louis: *Contradiction et surdétermination* (La Pensée, 106, December 1962, pp. 3-22).

Álvarez, Juan: *Las guerras civiles argentinas* (Buenos Aires: Editorial Coyoacán, abridged version, 1960).

Andreski, Stanislav: "Conservatism and Radicalism of the Military," *European Journal of Sociology*, II, 1 (1961), pp. 53-61.

Bachrach, Peter and Baratz, Morton S.: "Two Faces of Power," *American Political Science Review*, LVI, 4 (December 1962), pp. 947-52.

Bendix, Reinhard: *Nation-building and Citizenship* (New York: Wiley, 1964).

Benjamín y Castro, D.: "Doctrinas pontificias sobre el desarrollo de la clase media como soporte de la estabilidad y del progreso social," *Semanas Sociales de España*, XI, Las clases medias (Barcelona: 1951), pp. 183-209.

Bidart Campos, Germán J.: *Grupos de presión y factores de poder* (Buenos Aires: Peña Lillo, 1961).

Blanksten, George I.: "In Quest of the Middle Sectors," *World Politics*, XII, 2 (January 1960), pp. 323-27.

Bouglé, C.: "Avant-propos," in R. Aron *et al.*, *Inventaires III—Classes moyennes* (Paris: Felix Alcan, 1939).

Boulding, Kenneth E.: *Conflict and Defense: A General Theory* (New York: Harper Torchbook, 1963).

Bourricaud, François: "Démocratie et polyarchie: une forme nouvelle de pouvoir," *Esprit* (May 1959), pp. 772-88.

Braibanti, Ralph: "The Relevance of Political Science to the Underdeveloped Areas," in Braibanti, Ralph and Spengle, Joseph J. (eds.), *Tradition, Values and Socio-economic Development* (Durham, N. C.: Duke University Press.)

Burdeau, Georges: *Traité de Science Politique, tomes IV* (1952), *VI* (1956) (Paris: Librairie Générale de Droit et de Jurisprudence).

Cardoso, Fernando H.: *O empresário industrial e o desenvolvimento económico do Brasil* (São Paulo: Tese, 1963 mimeographed version).

Castro, Josué de: "A revolução social brasileira," *Revista Brasileira de Ciencias Sociais*, II, 2 (July 1962), pp. 197-21.

Cazeneuve, Jean: "Societé industrielle et societé militaire," *Revue Française de Sociologie*, II, 2 (April-June 1961).

Cerroni, Umberto: "Aspetti teorici del rapporto democraziasocialismo," *Critica Marxista*, I, 1, Jan.-Feb. 1963, pp. 45-74.

Costre, Pinto, L. A.: *Estructura de clases y cambio social* (Buenos Aires: Paidós, trad. Jofre Barroso, 1964).

Dahl, Robert A.: *A Preface to Democratic Theory* (Chicago: Phoenix Books, 1963).

Dahl, Robert A. and Lindblom, Charles E.: *Politics, Economics and Welfare* (New York: Harper Torchbooks, 1963).

Dahrendorf, Ralf: *Class and Class Conflict in an Industrial Society* (London: Routledge and Kegan Paul, 1959).

Diaz, Antonio: "Los partidos políticos del Ecuador, *Política*, III, 28 (November 1963), pp. 105-14.

Di Tella, Torcuato S.: "Economía y estructura ocupacional en un país subdesarrollado," *Desarrollo Económico*, I, 3 (October-December 1961), 123-54.

——: *El sistema político argentino y la clase obrera* (Buenos Aires: EUDEBA, 1964).

Domenach, Jean-Marie: "L'armée en République," *Esprit*, November 1958, pp. 632-43.

Dorselaer, Jaime and Gregory, Alfonso: *La urbanización en América Latina, tome I* (Madrid: F.E.R.E.S., 1962).

E.C.L.A. (C.E.P.A.L.): *El desarrollo social de América Latina en la postguerra* (Buenos Aires: Solar/Hachette, 1963).

Ferrer, Aldo: (a) *La economía argentina* (Mexico, F.C.E., 1963).

——: (b) "Devaluación, redistribución de ingresos y el proceso de desarticulación industrial en la Argentina," *Desarrollo Económico*, II, 4 (January-March 1963), pp. 5-18.

Furtado, Celso: *Desenvolvimento e subdesenvolvimento* (Rio de Janeiro: Fundo de Cultura, 1961).

——: *Formación económica del Brasil* (Mexico: F.C.E., trad. Aguilera Mata, 1962).

——: *Obstáculos políticos do crescimento económico no Brasil* (Yale: mimeographed version, 1964).

García Lupo, Rogelio: (a) *La rebelión de los generales* (Buenos Aires: Proceso, 1962).

——: (b) "Los militares nasseristas en América Latina," in Nasser, G. A., *La revolución nasserista* (Buenos Aires: Proceso, 1962), pp. 9-29.

Germani, Gino: *Urbanización, secularización y desarrollo económico* (Buenos Aires: Instituto de Sociología, Publicación Interna n 65, s/f).

Granger, Gilles-Gaston: *Pensée formelle et sciences de l'homme* (Paris: Editions Montaigne, 1960).

Grayson, Henry: *The Crisis of the Middle Class* (New York: Rinehart & Co., 1955).

Helguera, J. León: "The Changing Role of the Military in Colombia," *Journal of Interamerican Studies* (July 1961), III, 3, pp. 351-58.

Hempel, Carl G.: "The Functions of General Laws in History," in Feigl, H. and Sellars, W. (eds.), *Readings in Philosophical Analysis* (New York: Appleton, 1949), pp. 459-71.

Hoselitz, Bert F.: "El desarrollo económico en América Latina," *Desarrollo Económico*, II, 3 (October-December 1962), pp. 49-66.

Huntington, Samuel P.: *The Soldier and the State* (New York: Vintage Books, 1964).

Imaz, José Luis de: "Los que mandan: las fuerzas armadas en Argentina," *América Latina*, VII, 4, October-December 1964, pp. 35-69.

Jaguaribe, Helio: "Las elecciones de 1962 en el Brasil, *Desarrollo Económico*, III, 4, January-March 1964, pp. 607-30.

Janowitz, Morris: *The Military in the Political Development of New Nations* (Chicago: Phoenix Books, 1964).

Johnson, John J.: *The Military and Society in Latin America* (Stanford: Stanford University Press, 1964).

——: *Political Change in Latin America: The Emergence of the Middle Sectors* (Stanford: Stanford University Press, 1958).

——: "Whither the Latin American Middle Sectors?" *The Virginia Quarterly Review*, 37, 4, Autumn, 1961, pp. 508-21.

Kaplan, Abraham: *The Conduct of Inquiry* (San Francisco: Chandler Co., 1964).

Kautsky, John H.: "The Military in Underdeveloped Countries," *Economic Development and Cultural Change*, XII, 4, July 1964, pp. 436-43.

————: "An Essay in the Politics of Development," in Kautsky, John H. (ed.), *Political Change in Underdeveloped Countries* (New York: Wiley, 1962), pp. 3-119.

Kling, Merle: "Toward a Theory of Power and Political Instability in Latin America," in John H. Kautsky (ed.), *Political Change in Underdeveloped Countries* (New York: Wiley, 1961), pp. 123-39.

Lambert, Jacques: *Amérique Latine—structures sociales et institutions politiques* (Paris: P.U.F., 1963).

Lane, Robert E.: *Political Life* (Glencoe: The Free Press).

Lieuwen, Edwin: *Arms and Politics in Latin America* (New York: Praeger, 1961).

Lipset, Seymour M.: *Political Man* (New York: Doubleday, 1960).

————: "Problemas de la investigación en el análisis comparado de la movilidad y el desarrollo," *América Latina*, VII, 1, January-March, 1964, pp. 21-38.

Marshall, T. H.: "Citizenship and Social Class," *Sociology at the Crossroads and Other Essays* (London: Heinemann, 1963), pp. 67-127.

McAlister, Lyle N.: "Civil-military Relations in Latin America," *Journal of Interamerican Studies*, III, 4.

————: "The Military," in Johnson, John J. (ed.), *Continuity and Change in Latin America* (Stanford: Stanford University Press, 1964), pp. 136-60.

Mills, C. Wright: *White Collar* (New York: Oxford University Press, 1956).

Mosca, Gaetano: *The Ruling Class*, A. Livingston (ed.) (New York: McGraw-Hill, 1939).

Monteforte Toledo, Mario: *Guatemala—monografía sociológica* (Mexico: U.N.A.M., 1959).

Oeconomo, Constantin: "La version américaine du métier des armes," *European Journal of Sociology*, II, 1, 1961, pp. 119-31.

Orwell, George: *Coming Up for Air*, quoted by C. Wright Mills in *White Collar* (New York: Galaxy Books, 1956), p. xi.

Ossowski, Stanislaw: *Class Structure in the Social Consciousness* (London: Routledge and Kegan Paul, trans. S. Patterson, 1963).

Perón, Juan: "Lo que yo ví de la preparación y realización de la revolución del 6 de septiembre de 1930" (January 1931), pp. 10-86; and "Una política para la clase media" (July 1944), pp. 115-32, both in Perón, Juan: *Tres revoluciones militares* (Buenos Aires: Escorpión, 1963).

Polit, Gustavo: "Rasgos biográficos de la famosa burguesía industrial argentina," *Fichas de investigación económica y social*, I, 1, (April 1964), pp. 60-80.

Potash, Robert A.: "The Changing Role of the Military in Argentina," *Journal of Interamerican Studies*, III, 4 (October 1961), pp. 571-78.

Pye, Lucian W.: "Armies in the Process of Political Modernization," *European Journal of Sociology*, II, 1 (1961), pp. 82-92.

Radway, Laurence I.: "On Civil and Military Bureaucracies," in Silvert, K. H. (ed.), *Discussion at Bellagio* (New York: American Universities Field Staff, 1964), pp. 82-92.

Ramos, Jorge A.: *Historia política del ejército argentina, Logia Lautaro a la industria pesada* (Buenos Aires: A. Lillo, 1960).

Ranulf, Svend: *Moral Indignation and Middle Class Psychology* (New York: Schocken Books, 1964).

Sartre, Jean-Paul: *Search for a Method* (New York: A. Knopf, trans. H. E. Barnes, 1963).

Seton-Watson, Hugh: *Neither War Nor Peace* (New York: Praeger, 1960).

Smith, T. V.: "American Democracy: Expendable and Exportable," *The Virginia Quarterly Review* (Spring 1947).

Soares, Glaucio A. D.: "El sistema electoral y la reforma en Brasil," *Ciencias Políticas y Sociales*, VIII, 29.

————: *Congruency and Incongruency among Indicators of Economic Development: an Exploratory Study* (Berkeley: Mimeographed version, 1964).

Touraine, Alain: "Sociologie du dévelopement," *Sociologie du travail*, V, 2 (April-June 1963), pp. 156-74.

————: "Industrialisation et conscience ouvrière à São Paulo, *Sociologie du travail*, special issue, 4/61, pp. 77-95.

Vogts, Alfred: *A History of Militarism* (New York: Meridian Books, 1959).

Wagley, Charles: "The Dilemma of the Latin American Middle Classes," pp. 2-10, in *Proceedings of the Academy of Political Science*, XXVII, 4 (May 1964).

Whitaker, Arthur: "Nationalism and Social Change in Latin America," in Maier, J. and Weatherhead, R. W. (eds.): *Politics of Change in Latin America* (New York: Praeger, 1964), pp. 85-100.

Willems, Emilio: "Brazil," in Rose, Arnold M. (ed.): *The Institutions of Advanced Societies* (Minneapolis: University of Minnesota Press, 1958), pp. 525-91.

The New Industrialization and the Brazilian Political System

GLAUCIO ARY DILLON SOARES

The growth of new middle classes, essentially dependent upon the growing importance of foreign-controlled, large-scale economic enterprises, as well as the governmental bureaucracy, is, in fact, as Soares demonstrates for Brazil, occurring in the early phase of industrialization. And this industrialization, the "new industrialization," is based on large corporations that dominate industrial production and achieve a high level of productivity, without considerable expansion of industrial employment. Able neither to absorb the growing urban populations in industrial production, nor employ them in the administrative sector, the economy becomes characterized by chronic underemployment and unemployment. If Brazil is the shape of the future for other countries going through capitalist industrialization in Latin America, they will be increasingly polarized between the growing new middle classes and the growing unemployed urban working classes; in such a situation the latter are likely to offer a growing potential base for a revolutionary movement, while the former opt for military rule.

Glaucio Ary Dillon Soares, a Brazilian sociologist, is Director of the Latin American Faculty of Social Sciences (FLACSO) in Santiago, Chile, and author of *Economic Development and Political Radicalism* (New York: Basic Books, forthcoming).

ONE OF THE basic postulates of political sociology is that politics has a definite relation to socioeconomic structure and that changes in socioeconomic structure do have a bearing upon the electoral strength of political parties.

One of the main components of the socioeconomic structure is, of course, the class structure and, other things being equal, historical changes in the class structure will broaden the political possibilities of some parties and lower the electoral ceiling of other parties.[1]

The class basis of politics is not at all a black and white question. Most parties recruit their followers from many classes and socioeconomic strata, but unevenly so, for political parties tend to appeal more strongly to some classes than to others. This essentially means that the socioeconomic composition of the supporters of a given party is seldom similar to the socioeconomic composition of society as a whole. This also means that the socioeconomic composition of a party is more often than not different from the socioeconomic composition of another party and, conversely, that the political composition of a given class is different from the political composition of another class. Of course, the degree to which a party is linked to a given class is not a constant.[2] Some parties are more likely to concentrate on any specific class than others; therefore, some parties collect the bulk of their voters from a single class, whereas other parties spread their voters more evenly among the various strata of the class structure.

The Brazilian political scene prior to April 1, 1964 was characterized by the existence of three major political parties.

[1] The first theorist who heavily emphasized the determining power of the socioeconomic structure on the political system was Karl Marx. However, Marx did so in a scattered manner, as he never wrote a systematic presentation of his theory of social classes. (Actually he died just after having started the fifty-second chapter of Book III of *Das Kapital*, which was entitled "The Classes.") Nowhere in Marx's writings does one find a systematic presentation and analysis of the relationships between the socioeconomic structure and the political system. However, many authors have attempted a systematic elaboration of Marx's theory of social classes. Perhaps the best attempt to systematize the Marxist theory of social classes and its relation to politics is that of Ralf Dahrendorf, *Class and the Class Conflict in Industrial Society* (Stanford, Calif.: Stanford University Press, 1959) Chapter 1. Contemporary sociologists have documented empirically this relationship between class and politics. For a compilation and a systematic analysis of comparative results, see Seymour Martin Lipset, *Political Man* (New York: Doubleday, 1960). In previously published works the present author has dealt with this relationship with regard to Brazil. See Glaucio Ary Dillon Soares and Amelia María Carvalho Noronha, "Urbanização e Dispersão Eleitoral" in *Revista de Direito Público e Ciéncia Política*, III, No. 2 (July-December 1960), pp. 258-270, and Glaucio Ary Dillon Soares, "Classes Sociais, Strata Sociais e as Eleições Presidenciais de 1960" in *Sociología*, XXIII (September 1961), pp. 217-238.

[2] For a comparative analysis of the varying relationships between class and politics, see Robert Alford, *Party & Society* (Chicago: Rand McNally, 1963) and Angus Campbell, Philip Converse, Warren Miller, and Donald Stokes, *The American Voter* (New York: John Wiley, 1960), Chapter 13.

The P.S.D.—*Partido Social Democrático* (Social Democratic Party)—a conservative party in spite of the name; the U.D.N. —*União Democrática Nacional* (National Democratic Union) —also a conservative party; and the P.T.B.—*Partido Trabalhista Brasileiro* (Brazilian Labor Party)—a working-class party. There were several other competing parties, and the number of Brazilian parties competing in any given election since 1945 was usually above 10. However, in terms of their numerical strength, the other parties were quite small. Jointly, the aforementioned three large Brazilian parties always accounted for at least three-fourths of the total number of elected federal congressmen from 1945 to 1962. Whereas the U.D.N. and, above all, the P.S.D. are rural-based parties, the P.T.B. has been essentially an urban working-class-based party. The P.S.D. is perhaps the one party that approaches the ideal type of a rural and small-town-based party, whereas the U.D.N., while competing with the P.S.D. for the rural vote, also has a strong appeal to the urban middle class. The P.T.B. approaches the ideal type of urban working-class party, although in small towns its leadership, composition, and behavior is often similar to that of the conservative parties.[3]

The theories that deal with the development of societies—economic, sociological, or otherwise—and assume that presently developing countries are now passing through a stage through which presently developed countries have passed in the past implicitly or explicitly make use of the assumption of unilinear evolution. Thus, most stage theories also fit this pattern and subscribe to the same assumption. From a methodological standpoint, theories that infer historical trends from the knowledge of comparative data also subscribe to the assumption of unilinear evolution.[4]

I am willing to admit that there are many similarities between some of the characteristics of the industrializing societies of today and those of the industrial societies of today when they were at a comparable level of economic development. However, there are many differences and these differ-

[3] For a description of rural politics in Brazil, see Luis Silva, "Implicações Políticas do Desenvolvimento Industrial em Barroso—M. G.," *Revista Brasileira de Estudos Políticos,* 9 (July 1960), and Silvio Gabriel Diniz, "Quatorze Anos de Eleições na Vila do Pará, M. G. (1861-1875)" *Revista Brasileira de Estudos Políticos,* 17 (July 1964), pp. 139-191. Victor Nunes Leal, *Coronelismo, Enxada e Voto—o Municipio e o Regime Representativo no Brasil* (Rio de Janeiro, 1948).
[4] For an interesting discussion of how most stage theories, and modernization theories as well, are disguised evolutionary theories, see the article by H. Hoetink, "El Nuevo Evolucionismo" in *América Latina, VIII* (October-December 1965), pp. 26-42.

ences are likely to outweigh the similarities.[5] For one thing, the international situation of today is quite different from the international situation of the nineteenth century, and these differences cannot be said to have no influence whatsoever on the development process and its characteristics. Secondly, the industrializing countries of today import technology from the industrial countries of today. Obviously, the same is true of the industrializing countries of yesterday. However, the difference lies not so much in the possibility of borrowing technology as in what *type* of technology could be borrowed.[6] In the last century the developing countries *could* import nineteenth-century technology, whereas today the developing countries import twentieth-century technology. The differences between these two types of technology are not solely quantitative in nature, for they have qualitative implications: thus, whereas nineteenth-century technology was labor-intensive, twentieth-century is capital intensive.[7] One of the many consequences of

[5] I want to emphasize here not so much the fact that each country's economic development has, from a historical viewpoint, a certain specificity of its own, but rather that the industrialization process itself has changed markedly from the last two centuries to the 20th century. Although most stage theorists acknowledge a certain degree of specificity in the economic development of each country, as does Rostow in the very introduction to his well-known *The Stages of Economic Growth* (Cambridge: Cambridge University Press, 1963), they fail to pay due attention to the very fact that besides the individual variations among countries, there is a fundamental difference in the characteristics of the industrialization process in the present century compared with similar processes in past centuries.

[6] The orthodox stage theorist, being addicted to unilinear evolution, would tend either to ignore or to underplay the diffusion process. We are concerned here with two specific aspects of the diffusion process—cultural or otherwise. The former is the possibility of borrowing capital, and the second, and perhaps more important, is the possibility of borrowing technology. Flexible stage theorists, of course, accept the fact that technology can be borrowed and has been borrowed for many centuries. Basically there is no difference between our views and the stage theorist's views of borrowing technology as a process. However, what we emphasize is that although the process in this century and in past centuries is perhaps similar, the *content* is fundamentally different. Technology borrowed in this century is qualitatively different from the technology borrowed in the nineteenth century.

[7] Of course, it could also be argued that industrial machinery is imported from industrialized countries, which at present cannot be produced by underdeveloped countries, and that developed countries produce industrial machinery that uses a minimum of manual labor. Obviously we agree that this is a fact; however, we cannot agree that this must *necessarily* be so. As a matter of fact, we have living examples of industrialization processes that have taken place with a *minimum* of imported machinery. Of course, the employment problems generated by the importation of technology would only look natural and necessary from the standpoint of an observer who is unable to reason outside of an international system based upon a capitalistic mode of production. I am not arguing against this system or in favor of another; I am simply arguing that there are alternative ways to industrialize with different benefits and with different social costs.

this industrializing under twentieth-century technology is the possibility of achieving a high level of productivity *without* a considerable expansion of industrial employment. Another consequence is that the patterns of industrial organization have changed, partly under the impact of the technological differences and partly under the impact of one hundred more years of industrial experience and competition. By comparison with the industrial enterprises of yesterday, some companies of today would look like mammoths. Therefore, the *size* of the industrial enterprises is also different. As a consequence of this growth in size, there is a growing need for bureaucratic organization, which essentially means a growth in nonmanual employment. Whereas in the case of the developed industrial societies this growth in nonmanual employment started only at the turn of the century, in the developing countries this phenomenon appeared "prematurely" (if we can judge by the advanced countries' standards).[8] Thus, "middleclassization" in the developing countries of today seems to be a concomitant of *early* industrialization rather than of mature industrialization.[9]

One further difference between the new industrialization and the old industrialization is the degree to which the industrialization process requires the employment of vast quantities of manual labor. By definition, if nineteenth-century technology was labor-intensive and not capital-intensive, it used large amounts of manual labor, whereas twentieth-century technology uses more capital and relatively little manual labor. Empirical data

[8] There have been attempts to explain this "premature" growth in the nonmanual employment by the increasing pressures derived from the growth in educational facilities. However, comparison of the new industrialization with the old industrialization reveals that the new industrialization goes hand in hand with a *lower* rate of literacy, by comparison with the literacy rates that characterized the old industrialization. Although I certainly would agree that a growth in educational facilities puts pressure on the social structure toward an increase in nonmanual occupations, the "premature" bureaucratization of the new industrialization cannot be satisfactorily explained, if one considers the later-date bureaucratization of the old industrialization by means of this pressure. If the educational level determined the occupational structure and were a sufficient condition to promote a considerable growth in nonmanual employment, the old industrialization should have been characterized by a much larger nonmanual sector than was actually observed. Furthermore, given the higher educational standards of the old industrialization, the new industrialization should have been *less* bureaucratized than the old one at a similar level of development. Hard data show that the opposite is true.

[9] For a theoretical statement of the relationships between Economic Development and the class structure, see Glaucio Ary Dillon Soares, "The Economic Development and the Class Structure" in Rinehart Bendix and Seymour Martin Lipset (eds.) *Class, Status and Power: Social Stratification in Comparative Perspective* (New York: The Free Press, 1966), pp. 190-199.

do not seem to warrant the conclusion that there is only *one* process of economic development that must be followed by all societies that aim at developing, regardless of historical circumstances. On the one hand, we have seen that some of the socioeconomic and technological differences are relevant and, on the other hand, we must also emphasize that the twentieth century provides alternative *political* models for development whose adoption may increase the pace of industrialization and shift part of its burden from one class to another. The present article will use Brazilian data, and attempt to prove that the new industrialization in Brazil has characteristics that are quite different from the old industrialization, which marked the past of the industrial societies of today.

Twentieth-century technology is not labor-intensive. Partly as a consequence of the outward orientation of engineers, business administrators, and industrial managers, the building of an industry is an operation isolated from any consideration of national problems as such. What matters is to build an industry that is efficient by the developed countries' standards. However, the developed countries' problems are different from the developing countries' problems in that they emphasize the need to cut down employment and increase productivity.

TABLE 1—EMPLOYMENT IN MANUFACTURING
AND IN THE SECONDARY SECTOR, 1900-1960

	Absolute numbers	Manufacturing as percentage of the total labor force	Absolute numbers	Secondary as percentage of the total labor force
1900	(229,000)[1]			(2.3%)[4]
1940	1,137,000 [2]	7.7%	1,791,000[3]	12.1% [5]
1950	1,608,000 [2]	9.4%	2,615,000[3]	15.6% [5]
1960	2,079,000 [2]	9.1%	3,428,000[3]	15.1% [5]

Sources: for 1900: João Camillo de Oliveira Tôrres, *Estratificação Social no Brasil* (São Paulo: Difusão Européia do Livro, 1965) for 1940, 1950 and 1960, IBGE, *Censo Demográfico: Resultados Prelimnares, Série Especial, Vol. II* (Rio de Janeiro: IBGE, 1965).

[1] Includes manufacturing and extractive industries (*indústrias extrativa e manufatureira*).
[2] Includes only manufacturing (*indústrias de transformação*).
[3] Includes manufacturing, extractive, and construction industries (*indústrias de transformação, extrativas, e de construção*).
[4] Excludes nonproductive occupations (*profissões unprodutivas*).
[5] Labor force defined as: Persons present 10 years and over minus nonactive persons (*condições inativas*).

As a result, Brazil has been industrializing by means of a strategy that probably is adequate for developed countries (with lower population growth rates and lower urbanization rates) but utterly unable to solve the main problems of a developing economy. This generates an unemployment problem. Looking at Table 1, we can see that manufacturing employment accounted for 7.7 percent of the labor force in 1940, experienced a considerable increase from 1940 to 1950, up to 9.4 percent, and from 1950 to 1960 *decreased* to 9.1 percent.

The same reasoning applies to the secondary sector as a whole, which includes construction and extractive industries, besides manufacturing. From an insignificant sector in 1900, it grew to a sizable 15.5 percent in 1950, suffering a small *decrease* from 1950 to 1960.

TABLE 2

SECTORAL COMPOSITION OF THE LABOR FORCE, BRAZIL 1940, COMPARED WITH SELECTED COUNTRIES IN DIFFERENT HISTORICAL PERIODS

Country	Year	Primary	Sector Secondary (in percentages)	Tertiary
Brazil	1940	64	12	24
Finland	a1920[1]	63	20	17
France	1845[2]	62	18	20
Italy	1861[3]	62	25	13
Sweden	b1890[4]	62	22	16
U.S.A.	1850[5]	65	18	17

a Excludes women in agriculture.
b Data cover total population, including dependents.

[1] Colin Clark, *Conditions of Economic Progress* (Macmillan, 1957, 3rd ed. rev.), p. 512.
[2] "La Croissance Économique Française," *Income and Wealth, Series III* (London: International Association for Research in Income and Wealth, 1953).
[3] F. Coppola d'Anna, *Popolazione, Reddito e Finanze* (Rome, 1946).
[4] Ingvar Svennilson, *Wages in Sweden*, 1860-1930 London, 1933.
[5] Colin Clark, *op. cit.*, p. 520.

Looking at Table 2, we can see that in 1940 Brazil had a level of economic development, as negatively measured by the percentage of labor force in the primary sector,[10] comparable to that of Finland in 1920, of France in 1845, of Italy in 1861, of the U.S.A. in 1850, and of Sweden in 1890. However, the employment composition outside of the primary sector is quite different. Whereas in all cases except one (that of 1845 France) the secondary sector percentage was always larger

[10] This indicator, as any other, has its advantages and its shortcomings. There are countries with a substantial percentage of the labor force in the primary sector that are developed. However, this is one of the few indicators for which adequate historical data are available. Furthermore, I'm not convinced that this indicator's shortcomings are substantially more damaging than those of other indicators.

than the tertiary sector percentage and, in some cases, the secondary sector was considerably larger than the tertiary sector, in Brazil the opposite pattern could be observed. Whereas secondary employment meant 12 percent of the labor force in 1940 Brazil, the tertiary sector meant no less than 24 percent, or exactly twice the secondary sector percentage.

TABLE 3

SECTORAL COMPOSITION OF THE LABOR FORCE, BRAZIL 1950, COMPARED WITH SELECTED COUNTRIES IN DIFFERENT HISTORICAL PERIODS

| Country | Year | | Sector | |
		Primary	Secondary (in percentages)	Tertiary
Brazil	1950	58	16	26
Finland	a1930[1]	57	23	20
Italy	1881[2]	57	28	15
Norway	1890[3]	55	22	23
U.S.A.	a1860[4]	60	20	20

a Excludes women in agriculture.

[1] Colin Clark, *Conditions of Economic Progress* (Macmillan, 1957, 3rd ed. rev.), p. 513.
[2] F. Coppola d'Anna, *op. cit.*
[3] Data from Simon Kuznets, "Quantitative Aspects of the Economic Growth of Nations, II—Industrial Distribution of National Product and Labor Force," in *Economic Development and Cultural Change*, Supplement to Vol. V, No. 4 (July 1957), p. 86.
[4] Colin Clark, *op. cit.*, p. 520.

Data for 1950 and 1960 yield similar results. Comparing 1950 Brazil with 1930 Finland, 1881 Italy, 1890 Norway, and 1860 U.S.A., we can see that whereas in Brazil the tertiary sector was considerably larger than the secondary sector, in the other countries they were similar in size, or the secondary actually was somewhat larger.

1960 data are even more striking. In many countries the secondary sector accounted for about the same percentage of the labor force as does the tertiary sector, and in a few it was considerably larger. However, in Brazil the secondary sector represented less than half the tertiary sector. By comparison with other countries with similar levels of development, as negatively measured by the percentage of the labor force in the primary sector, we see that the relative share of the secondary sector in Brazil is between ten and twenty percentage points smaller than those of countries that developed at an earlier date.

TABLE 4

SECTORAL COMPOSITION OF THE LABOR FORCE, BRAZIL 1960,
COMPARED WITH SELECTED COUNTRIES IN DIFFERENT
HISTORICAL PERIODS

Country	Year	Primary	Sector Secondary (in percentages)	Tertiary
Brazil	1960	52	15	33
Austria	a1880[1]	50	28	22
Canada	1881[2]	51	30	19
Denmark	a1880[3]	52	24	24
Finland	a1940[4]	47	28	25
France	1866[9]	52	29	20
Ireland	a1841[5]	51	34	15
Italy	a1871[6]	52	34	14
Sweden	b1910[7]	49	32	19
U.S.A.	1880[8]	50	25	25

a Excludes women in agriculture.
b Data cover total population, including dependents.

[1] Colin Clark, *Conditions of Economic Progress* (New York: Macmillan, 1957, 3rd ed. rev.).
[2] O. J. Firestone, "Canada's Economic Development, 1867-1953," to be published by the International Association for Research in Income and Wealth.
[3] Kjeld Bjerke, "The National Product of Denmark, 1870-1952," *Income and Wealth, Series V* (London: International Association for Research and Wealth).
[4] Colin Clark, *op. cit.*
[5] Colin Clark, *op. cit.*
[6] Colin Clark, *op. cit.*
[7] Data from Svennilson, *op. cit.*
[8] Simon Kuznets, "Long-Term Changes in the National Income of the United States of America," *Income and Wealth, Series II.*
[9] François Simiand, *Le Salaire, L'Évolution Sociale et la Monnaie* (Paris, 1932).

The analysis of changes in the sector composition of the Brazilian labor force reveals a continuous growth of the tertiary sector and a continuous decrease of the primary sector. The secondary, which had been growing continuously from the turn of the century up to 1950, actually decreased from 1950 to 1960. Obviously, one might attribute this decrease to conjunctural effects, and scientific prudence would caution against extrapolations or generalizations, as this might be an isolated trend unlikely to be found elsewhere. However, analysis of the situation in other developing countries reveals a similar pattern. Far from being a Brazilian peculiarity, the secondary employment stagnation is common to several developing countries. Comparing 1950 with 1960, we see that secondary employment often did not increase its share in the case of Argentina, Chile, Panama, and Venezuela, and when it did, it increased very slightly. It experienced small increases in El Salvador and Mexico and it experienced a sharp *decrease* in Ecuador. In Peru, between 1940 and 1961, the percentage of the labor force in the secondary remained stable at 19 percent, while the tertiary increased by more than 10 percent. Declared unemployment grew continuously in several countries, such as Panama and Venezuela, and in 1960 it reached frightening proportions, as in the case of Ecuador (17.2 percent), Venezuela (13.7 percent), and Panama (11.2 percent).[11] *These percentages do not include underemployment.* Therefore, the Brazilian case is part of a more general process that includes other Latin American developing countries. Furthermore, these same tendencies can also be observed in non-Latin countries, such as India, Thailand, the Philippines, and the like. This leaves us with the conclusion that twentieth-century industrialization—the new industrialization—has some essential differences from nineteenth-century industrialization—the old industrialization.

The accelerated population growth on the one hand, and the high migration rates on the other, account for unparalleled urbanization, which characterizes the industrialization process in many countries now developing. The very fact that technology can be imported and that this technology is twentieth-century technology means capital-intensive technology. This, coupled with the fact that decisions that affect policy regarding what type of industrial organization will be adopted are decentralized and dependent on decision-makers such as engineers, proprietors, and business administrators, who are concerned with high efficiency levels and with a market situation, help to account for the fact that industrializing countries of today have not been able to offer industrial jobs to this rapidly growing urban population.

One might argue that this, perhaps, is not necessarily a bad thing to happen and that the industrializing countries of today are going straight into a service society instead of going through the stage of a working-class society as did most of the countries that industrialized in the past. However, this reasoning fails to take into account the growing unemployment, both declared and concealed. The developing countries are *not* marching straight into a middle-class service society. Rather, their class structure indicates that they are becoming polarized societies

[11] These figures were taken from Unión Panamericana, *La Población Economicamente Activa en América Latina, Versión Preliminar* (Washington: Departmento de Asuntos Sociales, mimeographed, 1964).

with a growing middle class (as indicated by the growth in the percentage of nonmanual occupations over the total labor force) *and* a growing unemployment sector in the working class.[12] Brazil is perhaps a fair example of this tendency and, although the Brazilian statistics fail to report adequately the class structure and the extent of the unemployment, declared or disguised, both the agreement of many other aspects of the Brazilian economic development process with the process of other countries that exhibit this growth in unemployment and underemployment, and the indirect evidence of unemployment and underemployment, suggest that Brazil is also becoming a polarized society, with a growing urban middle class *and* a growing reserve army of unemployed workers. The question then arrives: what sort of political system can this socio-economic infrastructure engender?

Looking at the historical figures, we see that the employment situation has deteriorated considerably since 1950. From 1940 to 1950 the growth in the employment in the manufacturing sector was relatively greater than either the growth of the total population or the growth of the urban population. From 1940 to 1950 the growth in the secondary employment was 49 percent[13] of what it was in 1940, which is considerably larger than the 39 percent growth in the urban population and much larger than the 26 percent growth in the total population. Therefore, from 1940 to 1950 the Brazilian economy was able to increase

[12] The concept of class polarization here is used in a sense that differs somewhat from the original Marxist sense. By polarization I do not mean a small number of owners of the means of production and a large working class. This polarization is, of course, an ideal type that was perhaps best approximated by the old industrialization and not by the new industrialization. I am little concerned with the actual size of the upper class, if we define as upper class the capitalists and large land-owners. My concept of polarization emphasizes the simultaneous growth of a new middle class composed mainly of salaried employees, bureaucrats, and professionals, *and* the unemployed, *without a large enough employed working class between them.* As I see it, the future main political conflicts, if the trends I have analyzed are to continue, will not derive from the opposition between the interests of the owners of the means of production and the proletariat; rather the main sources of political conflict would be the conflicting interests of the growing middle class and the growing unemployed and underemployed sectors of the working class. I should note that this conceptualization of class polarization differs from my previous uses of the same expression. It is interesting to underline that if the theorists of the old industrialization saw the middle class as a cushioning element between the conflicting upper and working class, I see the steadily employed working class as a cushioning element between the middle class and the unemployed and underemployed sectors of the working class.

[13] This figure is considerably lower—41 percent—if we take manufacturing industries (indústrias de transformação) alone.

employment in the secondary sector at a higher rate than the urban population growth and a much higher rate than the total population growth.

TABLE 5

INCREASE IN THE TOTAL POPULATION, THE URBAN POPULATION, AND THE EMPLOYMENT IN MANUFACTURING AND IN THE TOTAL SECONDARY SECTOR, 1940-1960

	Total Population	Urban Population	Employment in Manufacturing Sector	Employment in the Total Secondary Sector
1950/1940	126	139	141	149
1960/1950	137	154	129	128

This meant that from 1940 to 1950 the Brazilian economy was able to offer industrial jobs to the rural migrants who account for a sizable portion of the exploding urban population. However, from 1950 to 1960 the situation was drastically reversed. The growth in employment in the secondary sector slowed down, whereas the growth rates both in the total population and especially in the urban population increased sharply. Secondary employment was only 28 percent higher in 1960 than in 1950,[14] but the urban population was 54 percent larger in 1960 than in 1950. This shows the inability of the Brazilian economy to keep the pace of industrialization at the same level as the pace of urbanization. This also means a growing mass of urban unemployed and underemployed. From 1950 to 1960 the growth in the secondary employment was even slower than the growth of the total population. This all leads us to a picture that is close to the ideal type of the underindustrialized city, which is perhaps best exemplified by Cairo and selected Indian cities. Thus, demonstratedly, the Brazilian industrialization has been unable to absorb the growing urban population. It is interesting to emphasize that these tendencies have gone hand in hand with a high rate of growth in industrial *production* and with an increase in productivity.

Part of this rapidly growing urban population that has not been absorbed by the manufacturing sector has gone into nonmanual occupations. Inside the manufacturing sector itself, there is a noticeable increase in the proportion of nonmanual occupations. Thus, Brazil is generating a new middle class,

[14] In the manufacturing sector alone (indústrias de transformação) the figure is only slightly altered—up one percentage point to 29 percent.

which is essentially a salaried class, *at the same time* that it is producing a reserve army of unemployed workers, to use the Marxist expression.

What is the outcome of the changes in the class structure? First of all, since urbanization seems to be a continuing and intense process, political parties based mainly upon rural and agricultural classes are likely to lose electorally. This is probably the most evident relationship, and rural-based parties must either change their class appeal or ultimately succumb. However, other socioeconomic changes are also relevant for political analysis. Thus, the growth of the nonmanual occupations obviously means that parties based on an urban middle class have an increasing social basis for electoral power. Nevertheless, in a developing society no party can win a majority election based solely on the urban middle class. Firstly, a large sector of the population still lives in rural areas; secondly, the urban working class and the urban unemployed are far more numerous than the urban middle class. Nevertheless, this growth in the middle class provides a substantial basis for urban middle-class parties. To a large extent this role of attracting politically the urban middle class has been played by the U.D.N. (União Democrática Nacional).[15] On the other hand, the growth in the urban working class and in the unemployed will favor leftist parties or labor-oriented parties. National electoral data confirm these hypotheses.

The analysis of the changes in the percentage over the total number of seats in the Federal Congress occupied by the major Brazilian political parties reveals a constant decrease of the P.S.D. (Partido Social Democrático), which is based on the local political domination of the rural upper and middle classes. From an overwhelming 53 percent in 1945, the P.S.D. decreased to 37 percent in 1950, to 35 percent in 1954 and 1958, and further on to 30 percent in 1962. The U.D.N. (União Democrática Nacional) had a slower decrease from 27 percent in 1945 and 1950, to 23 percent in 1954, and to 21 percent in 1958, recovering slightly to 23 percent in 1962. The U.D.N. is clearly a dual party. On the one hand, it is rural-based and, to this extent, its leadership and electorate have the same socioeconomic composition as the P.S.D.'s. On the other hand, the U.D.N. is also a party that appeals to the urban middle classes. It is therefore possible that the U.D.N. is partly compensating

[15] For supportive data, see Glaucio Ary Dillon Soares, "The Political Sociology of Uneven Development in Brazil" in Irving Horowitz (ed.) *Revolution in Brazil* (New York: Dutton, 1964), pp. 164-195.

TABLE 6

PERCENTAGE OF THE TOTAL NUMBER OF SEATS HELD BY
SELECTED BRAZILIAN PARTIES IN THE FEDERAL
CONGRESS, 1945-1962

	PSD	UDN	PTB	PCB	TOTAL NUMBER OF SEATS
1945	53%	27%	8%	(5%)	(286)
1950	37%	27%	17%		(304)
1954	35%	23%	17%		(326)
1958	35%	21%	20%		(326)
1962	30%	23%	27%		(409)

Sources: *Tribunal Superior Eleitoral, Dados Estatísticos, Eleições
Federal, Estadual e Municipal Realizadas no Brasil a partir de 1945*
(Rio de Janeiro: Departamento de Imprensa Nacional, 1950), p. 20;
Tribunal Superior Eleitoral, *Eleições Federais e Estaduais Realizadas
no Brasil em 1950* (Rio de Janeiro: Departamento de Imprensa Na-
cional, 1952), p. 37; Tribunal Superior Eleitoral, *Dados Estatísticos, 3°
volume (la parte), Eleições Federais, Estaduais e Municipais, Realizadas
no Brasil em 1952, 1954 e 1955, e em Confronto com as Anteriores*
(Rio de Janeiro: Serviço Gráfico IBGE, s/d), p. 99; Tribunal Superior
Eleitoral, *Dados Estatísticos, 4° volume Eleições Federais, Estaduais,
Realizadas no Brasil em 1958 e em Confronto com as Anteriores* (Rio
de Janeiro: Departamento de Imprensa Nacional, 1961), p. 30 e *Anuário
Estatístico do Brasil*, 1963 (Rio de Janeiro: IBGE, 1963).

for the electoral losses derived from the urbanization process
and from the relative decrease in the rural and agricultural
population, with gains derived from the growth in the urban
middle classes. On the other hand, the labor party, P.T.B.
(Partido Trabalhista Brasileiro) increased its share from 8
percent in 1945 to 17 percent in 1950 and 1954, to 20 percent
in 1958, and to an overall high of 27 percent in 1962. Even if
one adds the Communist Party vote in 1945, this would bring
the P.T.B. vote up to 13 percent in 1945, and therefore the
P.T.B. still would have been increasing its electoral strength
from 1945 to 1962. It is our understanding that this increase is
due mainly to changes in the Brazilian class structure. The
P.T.B. has been profiting from the creation of an urban working class and, in the absence of more extreme popular parties,
from the creation of an urban lumpenproletariat. What proportion of the 1962 vote would have been given to the Communist
Party, if the Communist Party were allowed to compete, is
hard to say. However, I would venture the hypothesis that the
higher the proportion of unemployed, the higher the proportion that would prefer the Brazilian Communist Party and not
the Brazilian Labor Party. Industrial employment may be

crucial in deciding whether the urban underprivileged will go labor or socialist, on the one hand, or communist, on the other.

In accordance with our theory, to the extent that the urban unemployed become employed and to the extent to which the country will be further industrialized, the Brazilian Labor Party would benefit. However, to the extent that the industrialization process is unable to absorb the growing urban population, social restlessness will grow. One possible outlet for this restlessness would be participation in radical political activities. On the other side of the coin, the growing middle class has entrenched interests and is extremely powerful. It largely controls the means of communication; its interests are very close to the interests of the military and, above all, the socioeconomic composition of the military leadership itself is largely middle class. This middle class is unlikely to surrender with no further ado to a socialist type of government. Therefore, as I see it, Brazil has no short-term, peaceful, bloodless, revolutionary solution. Brazil already has a large enough middle class that is politically and militarily powerful, and this middle class will oppose—using force if needed—any attempt to reduce considerably its privileges. This seems to be the socioeconomic origin of the April 1964 coup; this will also help to explain the overwhelming support given to the coup, however unconstitutional, by the middle class. With or without the present governmental orientation, the future of Brazilian politics looks bleak. On the one hand, the middle class is large and powerful enough to resist a revolutionary movement based on the working class, even if it received no outside help. On the other hand, the country's industrial expansion has not been able to cope with the magnitude of the structural changes that have been taking place in the past decades. It has not offered industrial employment opportunities to the growing urban population and, in all likelihood, a reserve army of unemployed is growing, in absolute numbers and possibly in relative figures as well.[16] How long repressive measures and a dictatorial militaristic government will keep these masses from rebelling is an empirical

[16] It is interesting to note that a slow rate of growth in industrial employment is not incompatible with a high growth rate in industrial production; thus, whereas industrial employment between 1950 and 1960 grew at a yearly rate that is smaller than 3 percent, industrial production grew at a 9-percent yearly rate. However, what concerns us here is that whereas industrial employment grew at less than 3 percent yearly, the urban population grew at almost 6 percent. See Celso Furtado, "Obstáculos Políticos para el Desarrollo del Brasil" en *Desarrollo Económico, XVI* (April-June 1965), p. 383.

question. On the other hand, obviously we cannot think of proletarizing the middle class without armed political resistance. On the other hand, this urban mass of discontented and unemployed individuals cannot grow forever without serious political turmoil of a revolutionary character.

The April 1st dictatorship may have closed one of the outlets for working class aggression, namely, the possibility of voting for a political party that represents the interests of the working class. However, political repression does not solve the socioeconomic situation. The problem is still there and growing. What will happen next is, of course, an empirical matter. The magnitude of socioeconomic problems may be decreased by means of a high industrial investment rate and by adopting labor-intensive policies in many sectors.[17] However, if the socioeconomic problems continue to grow, it is easy to believe that if an electoral outlet is provided for, this dissatisfaction may find a political outlet in the vote for leftist parties and, by means of this vote, attempt to change the socioeconomic structure. If no effective electoral outlet is provided for, in a closed, hydraulic model, the working class would search for an outlet elsewhere. On purely theoretical grounds, one might argue for an increase in the homicide rate; one could also argue that working-class parents would beat their children more often, etc. However, since I believe that the working class already perceives its socioeconomic problems as political in nature and as the "government" is seen as the institution that may solve these problems, I feel that it is only a matter of time until the working class starts offering a mass response to revolutionary appeals.

[17] Of course, such policies would create other types of problems, and whether these other types are "better" than the present problems is, above all, an ideological question.

Aspects of Class Relations in Chile, 1850-1960

FREDERICK B. PIKE

Military rule is not the only way the dominant economic classes of Latin America retain power. In Chile, as Pike shows, by the early twentieth century a hybrid ruling class of landowners, middle classes, and industrialists coalesced politically and socially at the expense of the working classes. The middle classes became integrated into the prevailing system of rule rather than offering it a challenge. The stability of the Chilean social structure and political order, based on tacit alliances and coalitions of social forces, may have contributed to economic stagnation.

Frederick B. Pike, Professor of History at the University of Notre Dame, is the author of *Chile and the United States, 1880-1962* (Notre Dame, Indiana: University of Notre Dame Press, 1963).

BETWEEN 1830 and the outbreak of the War of the Pacific in 1879 Chile made remarkable progress in establishing political stability and devising smoothly functioning politicoeconomic institutions. Still, many Chilean observers remained highly critical of their country's accomplishments. Of all the analysts

Reprinted from *The Hispanic American Historical Review*, Vol. XLIII, No. 1 (February 1963), pp. 14-33, by permission of the Duke University Press and the author. Notes have been considerably shortened.

of the contemporary scene, perhaps the most brilliant was Miguel Cruchaga Montt, economist of the laissez faire school and professor of economics at the University of Chile. A prolific author, Cruchaga published his major work in 1878, *Estudio sobre la organización económica y la hacienda pública de Chile,*[1] which contains one of the first criticisms of the Chilean middle class to appear in nonfiction writing.

Examining his country's past, Cruchaga concluded that colonial practices had bequeathed a legacy that impeded economic progress. Cruchaga felt that Chile's only hope for development and progress lay in giving the lower classes some share in society. Education might not only encourage the masses to lead better moral lives, but equip them to produce and therefore to earn enough to enjoy adequate material comfort. Education might also instill in the middle class respect for the virtues of work, efficiency, and frugality. Once these goals were achieved, Cruchaga hoped the Chilean upper classes would abandon their inordinate devotion to economic activity and leave the nation's material development to the middle class. The upper classes could then, by turning to pursuits of mind and soul, produce a Chilean culture.

Subsequent developments in the nineteenth century prevented realization of the division of labor between middle and upper classes urged by Cruchaga. Instead, the trend toward the creation of a middle-class, upper-class amalgam gained momentum. Actually, this trend, initiated in the 1830's, had become an important aspect of national life by the mid-nineteenth century. The Chañarcillo silver mine began operation in 1832[2]—a mine that yielded 450,000,000 of the 891,000,000 pesos worth of silver produced in Chile by the beginning of the twentieth century.[3] The mining boom had commenced, and the age of fabulous silver strikes continued until 1870, the date of the discovery of the northern Caracoles vein. By the time of the Caracoles find, Chilean nitrate produc-

[1] A second edition of the work, in two volumes, was published in Madrid in 1929. Cruchaga's son, the distinguished diplomat Miguel Cruchaga Tocornal was instrumental at this time in having his father's writings republished by a Spanish firm.

[2] See Roberto Hernández, *Juan Godoy, o el descubrimiento de Chañarcillo,* 2 vols. (Valparaíso, 1932). Hereafter, unless specifically indicated otherwise, the place of publication for all works cited is Santiago de Chile. Hernández, a resident of Valparaíso, has been one of Chile's more reliable historians of nineteenth-century events.

[3] Oscar Álvarez Andrews, *Historia del desarrollo industrial de Chile* (1936), p. 90. Written by a man of leftist leanings who held important governmental posts, this is one of the more valuable economic histories of Chile. For peso-to-dollar conversion rates, see note 18.

tion had begun, and the country was already saddled with a dependence on extractive industries that rendered unlikely a balanced economic growth. In 1864 approximately 70 percent of Chile's exports consisted of mine products, while by 1881 the figure had risen to 78.5 percent.[4]

By the 1850's a new class, its wealth based on commerce, industry, banking, and above all on mining, was coming to occupy positions of social and political importance formerly reserved to landowners who could trace their lineage back to colonial times. Augustín Edwards Ossandón, Gregorio Ossa, Tomás Gallo, and especially the coal and nitrate magnate Matías Cousiño, were the first outstanding representatives of the new class.[5] In 1857 the traditional landlord aristocracy suffered a rude blow with the abolition of *mayorazgos* (roughly equivalent to a combination of primogeniture and entail), which facilitated redistribution of landed estates. A depression from 1858 to 1860, moreover, caused a disastrous decline in agrarian land values, impoverished many members of the old order, and permitted the new rich to acquire land and, thereby, social prestige and acceptance.

Chile, by the mid-nineteenth century, was revealing a remarkable tolerance for allowing entry of new blood into the ranks of the social elite. Even more striking, by the latter part of the century the upper class was studded with the names of foreigners whose grandfathers had arrived in the country only around the time of independence. From the United Kingdom had come settlers with the names of Ross, Edwards, Lyon, Walker, MacClure, Garland, Mac-Iver, Jackson, Brown, Price, Phillips, Waddington, Blest, Simpson, Eastman, Budge, Page, and others; from France came the Cousiño, Subercaseaux, and Rogers families; while from Slavic and German areas had come the Piwonkas and the Königs. A survey of Chilean biographical encyclopedias, or membership lists for such elite organizations as the Club de la Unión, or of the roll of the stock market founders,[6] and a scanning of prominent

[4] *Ibid.*, p. 131.
[5] See the excellent study of Julio Heise González, *La constitución de 1925 y las nuevas tendencias político-sociales* (1951), pp. 126-130. The works of Heise González, a prominent university professor, are typical of those of most recent Chilean intellectuals in revealing a certain Marxian influence. Pagination for the cited work is based on its first publication in the *Anales de la Universidad de Chile*, No. 80 (4° trimestre, 1950).
[6] See Luis Escobar Cerda, *El mercado de valores* (1959). This fine work, by a Harvard-trained Chilean economist who in 1962 was serving as Minister of Economy, contains a good analysis of the rise of corporate finance after 1850, and reveals the prevalence of first-and-second-generation Chileans among the founders of the stock market.

names in diplomacy, politics, and the fine arts will reveal the prominence that these names have enjoyed from the mid-to-late nineteenth century to the present time. A conspicuous factor in this development was the "well-known preference" of Chilean ruling classes for marrying their children to financially successful immigrants and their descendants.[7]

The rapid transformation in Chilean society was noted by the leading Valparaíso daily, *El Mercurio,* in May 1882. Of the fifty-nine personal fortunes in Chile of over one million pesos (of forty-eight pence), twenty-four were of colonial origin, and the remainder belonged to coal, nitrate, copper, and silver interests, or to merchants, all of whom had begun their march toward prosperity only in the nineteenth century.[8]

Political developments strengthened the ties between new middle groups and traditional upper social elements. Many of the principles espoused by the essentially middle-class liberals or *Pipiolos,* who had been crushed in 1830 at the Battle of Lircay, gradually reemerged in the Chilean intellectual scene of the 1840's. Resurgent liberal forces attempted revolutions in 1849 and 1851 but were harshly suppressed on both occasions. In addition to urging political and social reform, the reviving but harassed liberals instituted a spirited anticlerical campaign. In fact, the staunchly conservative writer Alberto Edwards Vives is undoubtedly correct in asserting that the religious question, above all others, gave rise to party politics in Chile.[9]

The conservative aristocracy, dominant since 1830, was torn by dissension in 1856 because of a jurisdictional dispute between ecclesiastical and civil tribunals known as the "affair of the sacristan." The outcome was that the Chilean Supreme Court exiled the inflexible Archbishop of Santiago, Rafael Valentín Valdivieso y Zañartu, and was backed in its sentence by President Manuel Montt and his energetic cabinet leader, Antonio Varas. Some members of the ruling class assumed a pro-Church stand and came together to found the militantly Catholic, proclerical Conservative Party, membership in which, according to author-statesman Abdón Cifuentes, brought one closer to God.[10] Many other Chilean aristocrats approved the

[7] Heise González, p. 154.
[8] *Ibid.,* p. 132.
[9] Edwards, *La fronda aristocrática* (1959 edition), pp. 93-95.
[10] See Armando Donoso, *Recuerdos de cincuenta años* (1947), p. 143. This delightful collection of character sketches by one of Chile's most prominent journalists devotes a chapter to Abdón Cifuentes.

stand of the Supreme Court and the president. This second group formed the National or Montt-Varista Party, which, though anticlerical, was authoritarian and as aristocratic in its makeup as the rival Conservative Party.

The Conservative Party now had a common grievance with the forces that had been crushed by military action in 1849 and 1851 and that had banded together in the mid-1850's to form the Liberal Party. Both Conservatives and Liberals opposed the National Party. Dislike of a common foe served to mask the fundamental differences between Conservatives and Liberals, and the two groups united to form the so-called Fusion Party.

Unalloyed political considerations created the Fusion Party, driving together the aristocratic Conservatives and the Liberals, many of whom could only claim a social status considerably beneath the top level. In the search for political allies, class distinctions often melted. The continuing divisions among the Chilean ruling classes served throughout the nineteenth century to break down upper-class social barriers, as the traditional elite faced the necessity of winning recruits from a social class they might otherwise have preferred to ignore.

The social and political merging of middle and upper groups produced a cross-pollenization between apparently opposed political philosophies. Championed largely by middle groups, nineteenth-century liberalism in Chile taught that poverty was something of a disgrace, but that the humble man could and should rise and thereby gain honorable status and the power of self-protection. The upper groups, on the other hand, generally advanced the conservative belief that poverty was no disgrace but rather the estate richest in the means of salvation, and that lower groups should not aspire to political articulateness or to a status of comfort that they themselves could not safeguard and augment. To gain even the tolerance of the advocates of the liberal philosophy, the masses had to attain precisely what the conservatives were dedicated to prevent them from attaining: self-improvement, self-assertiveness, and a rise in social status. Through the years, beginning in the latter nineteenth century, the social and political contact between middle and upper groups led to a mingling of their philosophical principles. Liberals, at least those who became successful, were enticed by the practical convenience of the concept of a providentially ordained, stratified society. They came to question the perfectibility of the lower class, and thus grew increasingly indifferent to supplying its members with opportunities to advance. Conservatives, influenced by secular, material standards, questioned the feasibility of supplying paternalistic protection to groups that appeared to lack economic virtues and the capitalist mentality. Middle and upper groups tended therefore to join in a disparaging attitude toward the lower mass.

This disparaging attitude contributed significantly to the neglect shown by the ruling class to the social problem that began to manifest itself during the parliamentary period, 1892-1920. Other factors also contributed to the indifference with which urban middle and upper groups regarded a growing urban proletariat. Between 1892 and 1920 the Chilean population increased by only one-half million, rising from 3.3 to 3.8 million.[11] Yet, the demographic shift underway was startling. The urban population, only 27 percent of the total in 1875, had risen to over 43 percent in 1902.[12] From 1885 to 1895 the population of Santiago went up over 30 percent and by 1907 had increased an additional 22 percent. During the same two periods the population of Antofagasta rose 58 percent and 73 percent, of Iquique 76 percent and 16 percent, of Concepción 50 percent and 27 percent, and of Valparaíso 15 percent and 24 percent.[13]

In short, the period from 1885 to 1907 witnessed the most dramatic population shift in Chile's history. The inquilinos, or serfs, who had previously labored on the vast estates of southern Chile and the central valley flocked in unprecedented numbers to northern and central towns. In their migration the rural masses passed directly from a manorial situation— in which they had been cared for paternalistically, had never learned to protect themselves in a competitive society, and had almost never acquired education—into the modern conditions

[11] Oficina Central de Estadística, *Sinopsis estadística y geográfica de Chile en 1891* (1892), and Dirección General de Estadística, *X censo de la población efectuado el 27 de noviembre de 1930* (1935), III, xix.
[12] *Memoria presentada al Supremo Gobierno por la Comisión Central de Censo* (1910), p. 1262. This is the 1907 census. See also León Alterman P., *El movimiento demográfico en Chile* (1946. *Memoria de Prueba*); Alfredo Rodríguez, *Los movimientos de población* (1900); and Armando Vergara, *La población en Chile* (1900). Julio César Jobet, the prominent Marxian socialist, has written a valuable essay pertaining to this topic, "Movimiento social obrero," Universidad de Chile, *Desarrollo de Chile en la primera mitad del siglo XX* (1953), I, especially 66 ff. *Desarrollo de Chile* is a two-volume set consisting of unusually high quality essays by many of the top Chilean scholars.
[13] Dirección General de Estadística, *X censo*, II, 167. By 1930, fifty-three cities of more than five thousand each were inhabited by 1,684,957 persons, or 41.63 percent of the population.

of semiindustrial urban life. In the rural setting they had at least possessed sufficient skill to be useful to their patrones. In the cities they had no skills to offer. They comprised a vast pool of untrained, largely unproductive, brute labor. The rising industrial and commercial capitalists would have been more than human if they had not exploited the new urban masses. And even as the element of *noblesse oblige* disappeared from the employer-employee relationship when the rural masses crowded into the city, so also the bonds between the patrón and the inquilinos who remained on the agricultural estates were weakened as the landowners began to maintain their principal residences in Concepción, Santiago, or Paris.[14] Under these conditions human labor fell increasingly into disrepute.

The economy of Chile as well as its population was shifting to the cities. In 1889 mining products worth over fifty-five million pesos were exported. The value of agrarian exports that year was less than 7.5 million.[15] In the twentieth century the importance of agriculture to the national economy declined further as Chile began to import wheat and meat from Argentina.[16] By 1912, while Chile exported animal products worth 19.8 million, and wheat worth 7.1 million, the value of mineral exports had soared to 336 million.[17]

Chile's biggest money earner was nitrates, and contrary to the common assumption that exploitation of this natural resource was controlled by British and other foreign groups, domestic capital accounted for well over half of the total nitrate investments in the early twentieth century.[18] In addi-

[14] For an account of the growing Chilean colony in Paris in the late nineteenth century, see Eduardo Balmaceda Valdés, *De mi tierra y de Francia* (1932).

[15] Heise González, *La Constitución*, p. 133.

[16] *Ibid.*, p. 134.

[17] See *El Diario Ilustrado*, the conservative Santiago daily, October 5, 1914, and Julio César Jobet, *Ensayo crítico del desarrollo o económico-social de Chile* (1955), p. 139.

[18] Figures of the Oficina Central de Estadística quoted in Jorge González von Marées, *El problema obrera en Chile* (1923, *Memoria de Prueba*), p. 67. This work by the later leader of the Chilean Nazi movement is in many ways a careful and reliable study. Chilean nitrate capital at this time totalled 125,440,080 pesos, foreign capital only 116,-797,120. See also the very popular but somewhat chauvinistic work of prominent Radical Party politician Alberto Cabero, *Chile y los chilenos* (1926), pp. 310-311. The value of the Chilean peso fluctuated considerably in the nineteenth and twentieth centuries. In 1880, with the peso still relatively sound, it was worth on the London market 30⅞ pence, or roughly the equivalent of US$ 0.64. By 1905 it had sunk to approximately 17 pence, or about US$ 0.33, while by 1925 its value was 6 pence, or US$ 0.1217. For more complete conversion tables see Frank Fetter, *Monetary Inflation in Chile* (Princeton, N. J., 1931), pp. 13-14.

tion, Chilean capital to the extent of over thirty million pesos of eighteen pence was invested in the seventy-million peso copper industry, and comprised the total of the approximately 153 million invested in the coal industry.[19] Chileans also took advantage of the protectionist policies adopted by their government in the early 1900's. By 1920 more than half of the approximately 800 million pesos invested in nonextractive industry was native capital. Moreover, nonextractive industry by this time employed 30 percent of the entire active labor force and was creeping up on agriculture, which employed 40 percent.[20]

Socially, the important feature of Chile's move to the cities was the manner in which a landed aristocracy either became, or merged with, an urban upper or middle class earlier and more completely than elsewhere in Latin America. A strictly landowning aristocracy dwindled in importance as absentee owners, continuing the process initiated in the middle of the nineteenth century, invested in urban pursuits and married into the new-money classes of the mushrooming cities. In addition, the urban rich found continuing opportunities to gain the distinction of rural landownership, especially when many older families of social prominence lost their fortunes in the 1907 stock market crash and were forced to sell their lands.[21] By the turn-of-the-century period, then, urban and rural interests

[19] Jorge González von Marées, pp. 68-70. See also Dr. F. Landa Z., "Nuestro sistema educacional y la pasividad económica de la población de Chile," El Mercurio, January 1, 1922, who estimated that of the total of 465,849,765 pesos of 18 pence invested in mining and metallurgy in Chile, 243,732,765—or 52.32 percent—were in Chilean hands. This article was one in a valuable series published by Landa in El Mercurio, January 1-25. El Mercurio began publication of its Santiago editions in 1900, while also retaining the older Valparaíso editions. Unless specifically indicated, references are to the Santiago editions, considerably different in content from those published in Valparaíso. See also F. Javier Cotapos Aldunate, El aporte del capital extranjero en la industria minera de Chile (1947).

[20] Jorge González von Marées, pp. 70-72. See also note 13; El Mercurio, January 1, 1922, and June 6, 1926; Oscar Álvarez Andrews, Historia del desarrollo industrial de Chile, pp. 184-194; and Angel C. Vicuña Pérez, Proteccionismo aplicado a la industria chilena (1905, Memoria de Prueba).

[21] On acquisition of land by new classes see Humberto Fuenzalida Villegas, "La conquista del territorio y la utilización durante la primera mitad del siglo xx," Universidad de Chile, Desarrollo, I, 11-34, and Cámara de Senadores, Boletín de sesiones extraordinarias, Sesión 40°, January 8, 1895. Moreover, Carlos Keller in his excellent study La eterna crisis chilena (1931) estimates that between 1880 and 1930, 70 percent of Chilean territory was claimed and/or occupied for the first time. See also José Gómez Gazzano, La cuestión agraria en Magallanes (1938); Marcos Goycolea Cortés, Colonización de Magallanes y Aisén (1947); and Agustín Torrealba Z., La propiedad rural en la zona austral de Chile (1912).

were crossed and crisscrossed to such a degree that the distinction was often meaningless.[22]

From these conditions resulted a close union between new, urban-middle and old, rural-upper classes. A hybrid aristocracy, together with urban middle-class supporters, came into being, and neither aristocrats nor middle sectors were under pressure to minister to the needs of the lower classes. The urban *nouveaux riches*, both upper and middle class, found it totally unnecessary to enlist the aid of the city proletariat in a struggle with the old order, for they had already joined or were in the process of joining the old order. Nor were the landowners willing, as occasionally they have been in Peru and other countries, to support modest reforms of strictly urban application. In Chile urban and rural interests were becoming too intertwined to permit landowners to pursue this policy. Similarly, because of interlocking features, urban interests were unwilling to press for rural reforms. Thus, upper and middle classes, old and new or potential aristocrats, rural and urban sectors united in regarding the lower classes, wherever found, as fair prey.[23]

Contributing to this social pattern was the role of the immigrant in Chile. Although the limited immigration to the country did not have notable effects upon the population as a whole, it greatly affected the composition of the middle class.[24] In 1930, while foreigners accounted for only 2.46 percent of the population, they constituted about 17 percent

[22] Carlos Contreras Puebla, an aristocrat who wrote an interesting reply and rebuttal to *Sinceridad* by Alejandro Venegas which was highly critical of the established ruling class (see note 48), made this point tellingly. See Contreras (pseud. Juvenal Guerra), *Verdad: réplica a "Sinceridad" del doctor Julio Valdés Canje* (1911). See also the interesting plea of Juan Agustín Barriga in 1896 that Chile's upper classes continue to woo the rising middle class: *Del Partido y de los intereses Conservadores: carta que el diputado de Concepción dirige a sus colegas del dirección general.*

[23] For brief but effective confirmation of this see Jorge Ahumada, *En vez de la miseria* (1958), p. 53, and Alberto Edwards Vives and Eduardo Frei, *Historia de los partidos políticos chilenos* (1949), pp. 145-163. The portion of this excellent work that deals with political history after 1891 was written by the brilliant intellectual and leader of the Christian Democrat Party, Senator Eduardo Frei Montalva.

[24] The following works are among those providing some information on Chilean immigration, a topic that has not yet received adequate study. Pedro Pablo Figueroa, *Diccionario biográfico de extranjeros en Chile* (1900). Alberto Hoerll, *Los alemanes en Chile* (1910). Mark S. W. Jefferson, *Recent Colonization in Chile* (New York, 1921). Amadeo Pellegrini C., *El censo comercial industrial de la colonia italiana en Chile* (1926). Pellegrini and J. C. Aprile, *El progreso alemán en América*, Vol. I, *Chile: resumen general de las actividades que ha desarrollado en Chile la colonia alemana* (1934). The two works on Italian and German immigration are quite extensive, between them amounting

of the urban middle class.[25] Insecure in status because of foreign birth, it was only natural that these middle-class elements would try to assure acceptance by emulating the standards and value judgments of the established aristocracy.

The alliance of middle and upper groups in what came to assume characteristics of a class war against the lower mass has continued through the years. Chile's urban middle sectors have largely persisted in manifesting indifference to the social problem. At the same time, they have dedicated themselves to the defense of traditional, upper-class value judgments.[26] The readily observable traits of the middle class have led to the introduction into the Chilean vocabulary of the word *siútico*. Such a person is a middle-class individual who emulates the aristocracy and its usages and hopes to be taken for one of its members.[27] It is generally agreed that Chile's middle class abounds in siúticos.

Because of their desire to assume upper-class attitudes, middle groups have developed very little consciousness of themselves as members of a distinct class. It is extremely difficult to detect opinions, customs, and value judgments in Chile that are demonstrably middle class. Almost the only clear middle-class trait has been the tendency to shun the lower mass and to embrace the aristocracy.

A large number of Chilean writers have turned their attention to the middle class. In 1919 an editorial in *El Mercurio*

to over 1800 pages. Salvador Soto Rojas, *Los alemanes en Chile, 1541-1917: progreso y servicios que les deben la república* (Valparaíso, 1917), and "Los ingleses en Chile," a series of articles in *El Mercurio*, beginning January 21, 1918. Both of the Soto Rojas pieces are superficial.

[25] Some 45,000 of the active foreign-born population of 60,000 were registered in the 1930 census as above the *obrero* or laborer class (most of the foreign-born obreros were accounted for by Peruvians and Bolivians in the northern nitrate zone), and 85 percent of foreigners above the laborer level resided in cities. Therefore, some 38,250 foreigners were in Chile's urban middle sectors. Roughly 1,000,000 of the total national population were listed as active, and of these 450,000 were middle class or above. About 50 percent of those in this category resided in the cities, in short, some 225,000. The foreign-born, middle-class urban population therefore represented at least 17 percent of the total urban middle class in Chile. Computation is based on figures in Dirección General de Estadística, *X censo de la población . . . 1930*, II, 167, and III, v-xix.

[26] When aristocrat Luis Orrego Luco published his powerful novel *Casa grande* (1910), in which he attacked the vices of the oligarchy, it was primarily middle-class writers who rallied to the defense of their allegedly affronted brethren. See Domingo Melfi, "La novela *Casa grande* y la transformación de la sociedad chilena," *Anales de la Universidad de Chile*, CXI, Nos. 69-72 (1948).

[27] See Ricardo Valdés, "Sobre el siútico criollo," *Pacífico Magazine* (January, 1919).

asserted that the middle class had traditionally remained aloof from political and social agitation. The paper held that the middle class, concerned with protecting its dignity, had been content to support the position of the established ruling sectors.[28] Later in the same year *El Mercurio* editorials commented that because of the manner in which the upper class had opened its ranks to the middle, there were really only two classes in the country: the united upper and middle, and the lower.[29] It is also revealing that the first attempt to mold the middle class into a cohesive, articulate group, leading in 1919 to the formation of the *Federación de la Clase Media*, produced a platform that, although containing a mild warning to the oligarchy to refrain from some of its more notorious abuses, said absolutely nothing about aiding the lower classes.[30] A decade later Santiago Macchiavello speculated that Chile's main ills had stemmed from exploitation of the lower by the middle class, and from the attempt by members of the latter to pose as aristocrats and therefore to shun all useful and productive work.[31] In the early 1930's, when Chile was suffering from the effects of the depression, *El Mercurio* noted approvingly that in these times of crisis the Chilean middle class had once again demonstrated its customary responsibility by siding with the upper classes in the attempt to cope with economic disruption.[32]

Journalist Jorge Gustavo Silva observed in 1930 that "in whatever profession they enter, middle-class elements seek to obscure their humble origins and to convert themselves, even at the risk of appearing ridiculous, into aristocrats and oligarchs."[33] A much more scathing attack against the middle class was delivered by Gabriela Mistral. The great poetess charged it with having turned viciously upon the manual laborers and with having failed to contribute to balanced national development.[34] She noted also the revulsion felt by novelist Pedro Prado for the middle class because of the manner in which it had harassed the humble people.[35] Distinguished au-

---

[28] *El Mercurio* (January 14, 1919).
[29] *Ibid.* (January 14, 1919).
[30] *El Diario Ilustrado* (May 19, 1919).
[31] Macchiavello, *Política económica nacional* (1929).
[32] *El Mercurio* (April 1, 1932). See also the January 24, 1933 edition, noting the election of Rafael Maluenda as president of the *Unión de la Clase Media*. The Unión was dedicated to maintaining the established order, and its membership agreed that class conflict could not be tolerated in Chile.
[33] Silva, *Nuestra evolución político-social, 1900-1930* (1930), p. 100.
[34] Mistral, *Recados contando a Chile* (1957), pp. 92-93.
[35] *Ibid.*, p. 99.

thor Domingo Melfi suggested in 1948 that the plot situation which had most intrigued Chilean novelists in the twentieth century was the rise of a middle-class hero into the aristocracy, either by the acquisition of wealth or by a judicious marriage. To Melfi, this indicated the lack of middle-class consciousness.[36] Other journalists and critics, as Raúl Silva Castro, Manuel Rojas, and Hernán Díaz Arrieta (pseud., Alone), have agreed that middle-class and upper-class authors alike have tended to ignore in their fiction the theme of Chile's social problem and the plight of the masses.[37]

Raúl Alarcón Pino, author of the principal—but nonetheless superficial—university dissertation that has been written on the Chilean middle class, notes that the main vice of this social sector is its adoration of the aristocracy's way of life.[38] Alarcón Pino asserts that the Chilean middle class has remained steadfastly unconvinced that it has any common purpose with the lower classes.[39] Much the same message is conveyed by Francisco Pinto Salvatierra, who argues that the overriding cause of Chilean stagnation, which allegedly threatens to become retrogression, is the total indifference of the middle class to the mounting social and economic problems of the masses.[40]

As much as any single Chilean writer and intellectual, Julio Vega has studied the role of the middle class. Vega has concluded that in Chile there is no artisan tradition. The artisan's chief desire is that his son should enter one of the professions that is recognized as the province of the upper classes.[41] Members of the lower middle class, Vega observed, will spend most of their income on clothes and housing, trying to present an upper-class façade. The result is that not enough of the budget is allocated for food and consequently some middle-class members are actually more undernourished than the lower classes.[42]

An observer of the social scene in 1951, Julio Heise González, offered assurances that the middle class had begun finally to develop a class consciousness, to emancipate itself

[36] Melfi, "La novela *Casa grande.*"

[37] *La Nación* (Santiago daily and since 1927 the organ of the Government) (November 28, 1930).

[38] Alarcón Pino, *La clase media en Chile* (1947. *Memoria de Prueba*), p. 95.

[39] *Ibid.*, pp. 98-99.

[40] Pinto Salvatierra, *La clase media y socialismo* (1941), p. 9. A general thesis of the work is that middle-class political groups, such as the Democrat and Radical Parties, had by insincerely espousing socialism disgraced the socialist cause in Chile. See also the same author's *La lección tremenda* (1933).

[41] Vega, "La clase media en Chile," in *Materiales para el estudio de la clase media en la américa latina* (Washington, D. C., 1950), p. 80.

[42] *Ibid.*, p. 87.

from prejudice, to withdraw from the traditional aristocracy, and to approach the proletariat. Two pages later in the same work he seemed to contradict himself when he stated that members of the middle class were perpetuating their poverty by their conspicuous consumption, apparently in the desire to create the impression that they belonged to a higher social level than actually they did.[43]

The number of authors who have commented upon the middle-class betrayal and exploitation of the manual laborers is imposing.[44] Because of their number and their close agreement, their charges cannot be lightly dismissed. This writer's own observations and conversations in Chile have confirmed, moreover, that the country is still to a large degree characterized by a close association between upper and middle groups, which works to the disadvantage of the lower mass.

The agricultural situation in Chile tends to confirm some of the unfavorable appraisals of the middle sectors. During the 1950's Chile, with some of the finest land resources in Latin America, capable according to most authorities not only of feeding its own population but of providing food for sister republics as well, had to devote an annual average of approximately one-sixth of its foreign-currency expenditures to food imports.[45] What was the reason? According to one authority: "The basic reason underlying the failure of Chilean agriculture to keep up with growing needs may have to be sought in its semifeudal structure."[46] At first glance this appears to be an indictment of a traditional, landowning aristocracy. Actually, between 1925 and 1960 some 60 percent of the arable land in Chile's fertile central valley changed hands. The new landowners, primarily from the middle class, emulated the inefficient, absentee ownership patterns of the old landowning aris-

[43] Heise González, La constitución de 1925, pp. 159, 161.

[44] [A list of works on the middle class' support for the aristocracy that appears in the original note to this article has been omitted here. (Eds.)]

[45] Instituto de Economía de la Universidad de Chile, Desarrollo económico de Chile, 1940-1956 (1956), pp. 111, 115, 116. Radical Party economist Alberto Baltra "Los factores sociales y el desarrollo económico," Panorama Económico, No. 182 (December 1957), estimates that in the fifteen years previous to 1957 agricultural production increased 1.69 percent annually, while consumption of agricultural products went up 2.3 percent. See also Ministerio de Agricultura, La agricultura chilena en el quinquenio 1951-1955 (1957), p. 29.

[46] Ernest Feder, "Feudalism and Agricultural Development: the Role of Controlled Credit in Chile's Agriculture," Land Economics, Vol. XXXVI, No. 1 (February 1960), p. 92. Based in part on a research study entitled "Controlled Credit and Agricultural Development in Chile" to be published in Spanish by the Instituto de Economía de la Universidad de Chile, the Feder article is one of the best to be found on Chilean agriculture.

tocracy, and often productivity of the lands they acquired declined. Frequently, moreover, land acquisition by new urban middle sectors resulted in deteriorating conditions for agrarian laborers.[47]

Probably the attitudes of Chile's middle class have produced an important superficial advantage for the country. Because this group has in its political, social, and economic thinking so closely reflected the attitudes of the aristocracy, there has been almost no disruption as middle sectors have won increasing power in Chilean politics. This has contributed notably to Chilean stability. The role assumed by middle sectors may also have contributed to economic and social stagnation.

Obviously, not all middle-class members uphold aristocratic values. As of 1960 there were many signs that middle groups might be seeking an alliance with the lower classes and not, as in the past, simply trying to play the game of political opportunism. Stung by inflation and with their hopes for expanding opportunities frustrated by Chile's lack of real growth, some middle-class supporters of the Christian Democrat Party, of the activist wing of the Radical Party, and of the FRAP (an alliance of Socialists and Communists) seemed intent upon siding with the lower mass in a genuine attempt to alter the traditional sociopolitical structure. Some of the young members of the Conservative Party seemed also to fit into this category. This was a relatively new development in Chilean politics, one that could in the years ahead prove to be of great significance.

There are still many obstacles to middle group-lower mass cooperation. One of these is the educational structure. Since early in this century Chilean educators and intellectuals have pointed out the inadequacy and outmoded orientation of national education. In 1910 Alejandro Venegas in *Sinceridad*[48] charged that education in Chile produced stuffy sycophants of the aristocracy, utterly devoid of interest in the common good and unable to contribute to the vitally needed economic prog-

[47] See Gene Ellis Martin, *La división de la tierra en Chile central* (1960), esp. pp. 11, 133-136. Martin's excellent study was originally written as a doctoral dissertation at Syracuse University under the direction of Preston James, with research in Chile made possible in part by a Doherty Foundation grant. See also Thomas Frank Carroll, "Agricultural Development in Chile" (1951. Unpublished doctoral dissertation, Cornell University).

[48] The full title of the Venegas work is *Sinceridad: Chile íntimo en 1910*. This remarkable work, one of the first to expose the social problem in Chile, was written under the pseudonym of Dr. J. Valdés Canje. Venegas feared that if the authorship of the book became known, he would lose his job as a teacher in the public school system.

ress of their country. *El Mercurio* in 1916 observed: "We have among us thousands of university graduates who are true monuments of uselessness, and at the same time a living indictment of our national educational system."[49]

More recently, criticisms of a similar nature have been made. Many of these are well summarized in the writings of Amanda Labarca, who for longer than she might care to recall has been one of Chile's outstanding *pensadores*, feminists, and educators. Possessing faith in the ultimate role of the middle class in moving Chile ahead, Labarca feels that a superannuated educational system has unduly delayed this class in fulfilling its destiny.[50] Coming to the heart of the problem, another writer-educator urged in 1950 that education begin to emancipate itself from the social prejudices that led 99 percent of those entering the *liceo* to want to be professionals to gain access to the world of the aristocracy. Educators, it was further alleged, had passively permitted the continuing neglect of those studies that would be genuinely useful in developing the country.[51]

Chilean education has continued to be characterized by its lack of attention to technical training and by its emphasis on the philosophical approach. This has not only slowed the rate of economic progress, but has meant that the typical middle-class product of the national educational system—which is largely controlled by middle-class, Radical-Party bureaucrats—has been taught to think like an aristocrat of a past century and to disdain manual labor and those who perform it.

Contributing also to a gulf between middle and lower groups are racial considerations. The majority of Chile's lower classes display recognizable Indian features, often manifest in some degree of skin-darkness. On the other hand, the great majority of the middle and practically the entirety of the upper classes do not clearly exhibit physical characteristics attributable to Indian blood. This fact has exercised profound effects upon the nation's social structure.

Racist interpretations are commonplace in Chile. Early in

[49] *El Mercurio* (February 10, 1916).

[50] See Amanda Labarca, *Bases para una política educacional* (Buenos Aires, 1944); *Historia de la enseñanza en Chile* (1939); and *Realidades y problemas de nuestra enseñanza* (1953).

[51] See Vega, "La clase media en Chile" (note 41). There is a lengthy list of works suggesting that the educational structure in Chile foments class prejudice, leading the middle class to shun labor and the laboring classes while striving to emulate the upper class. [Some of these works were cited in the original note to this article. They have been omitted here. (Eds.)]

the twentieth century Nicolás Palacios, in a very popular book, *La raza chilena*,[52] suggested that Chilean superiority over other Latin American populations stemmed largely from the predominance of Basque, or actually Gothic, blood. In later times one of the most convinced of Chile's many racists has been the distinguished and prolific historian Francisco Antonio Encina, who basically repeats the Palacios assertions about the superiority of Gothic blood.[53] Marxian-socialist author Julio César Jobet appeared to be largely justified when he accused Encina in 1949 of believing in the racist theories of Joseph Arthur de Gobineau and Houston Stewart Chamberlain.[54] Similar charges could be leveled against such Chilean *pensadores* as the extremely active Carlos Keller,[55] the late Alberto Edwards Vives,[56] and a multitude of lesser writers, especially those active in neofascistic and *hispanista* movements.

If Chilean superiority is regarded as the consequence of Basque or Gothic blood, what place is left for the Indian and those who share his blood? It is not necessary to search far in Chilean literature for the answer, for anti-Indian writings are vast in number.[57] A random sampling illustrates the broad aspects of the prejudice that is an important national characteristic. One writer asserted that the reason for high infant mortality is the stupidity and proneness toward uncleanliness and drunkenness that Indian blood inevitably produced in the lower classes;[58] another stated that the mental inferiority of the Araucanians is recognized by almost all Chileans;[59] while from still a different source came the pronouncement that the racial superiority of the white upper classes made unavoidable the exploitation of the inferior, mixed-blood, lower classes.[60] A prom-

[52] The Palacios work was published first in 1911.
[53] The racist slant is particularly strong in Vol. III, chapters 3, 4, and 5 of Encina, *Historia de Chile desde la prehistoria hasta 1891* (1943). The twentieth and last volume of this work was published in 1952.
[54] Jobet, "Notas sobre la historiografía," in Ricardo Donoso, *et al.*, *Historiografía chilena* (1949), pp. 354-355.
[55] Keller contributed the principal intellectual force to the Nazi movement in Chile.
[56] Keller and Edwards were both strongly influenced by Oswald Spengler's *El hombre y el técnico*, which preached the supremacy of white over colored races. This book, the most widely read of Spengler's in Chile, appeared in its first Santiago edition in 1932. Three years later the third edition was already exhausted.
[57] [A partial list of works not referred to in the text that display or comment upon the prevailing anti-Indian bias in Chile was given in the original note to this article. It has been omitted here. (Eds.)].
[58] León Alterman P., *El movimiento demográfico en Chile* (1946), p. 60.
[59] Enrique L. Marshall, *Los araucanos ante el derecho penal* (1917. *Memoria de Prueba*), p. 41.
[60] E. Maguire Ibar, *Formación racial chilena* (1949), pp. 13, 64.

inent army general contended that Indians are lazy, dirty, irresponsible, and that southern Chile was doomed unless Indian
influence was eradicated by European immigration.[61] A noted
intellectual was even more pessimistic, observing that because
Chilean lower classes in general had a certain proportion of
Indian blood, national progress was unlikely unless a veritable
flood of white immigration descended upon the entire country.[62] Echoing this pessimistic tone, another writer suggested
that the Indian mentality, which could not advance beyond
concepts of subsistence production, was responsible for Chile's
problems.[63] On the other hand, there have been many writers
who, although defending the Indian, have sadly noted the prevailing tendency to hold aborigines and those sharing their
blood in contempt,[64] and to consider the Indians and mixed-
bloods as an impediment to national progress.[65]

The anti-Indian prejudice may explain why the visitor to
Chile is assured over and over again, "We have no Indians,
and therefore no Indian problem, here." The typical Chilean
attitude was expressed once by Deputy Ricasio Retamales,
who during congressional debates interjected: "What, are there
still Indians in Chile? I think not."[66] For a Chilean who is
proudly nationalistic and optimistic about the progress potential of his country, and who is at the same time convinced of
the inferiority of Indians and mestizos, it is convenient to forget the overwhelming evidence of Indian blood among the
lower classes and the fact that, as Benjamín Subercaseaux has
observed, the Chilean lower class is distinguished primarily
by its color.[67] It is possible that the cruel treatment of the
mixed-blood lower classes has stemmed from the fact that
upper and middle sectors would really be happier if somehow
the reminder of Indian inheritance in Chile could be stamped
out.

The factor of Indian blood has contributed in telling manner
to the traditional middle-class rejection of the lower mass.

[61] Arturo Ahumada, quoted in *El Mercurio* (March 4, 1928).
[62] Onofre Lindsay, *El problema fundamental: la repoblación de Chile y los estados unidos de Sudamérica* (1925), p. 38.
[63] Francisco Javier Díaz Salazar, *La influencia racial en la actividad económica de los indígenas chilenos* (1940. *Memoria de Prueba*), p. 13.
[64] Humberto Gacitúa Vergara, *Estudio social y consideraciones legales del problema indígena en Chile* (1916. *Memoria de Prueba*), p. 4.
[65] José Inalaf Navarro, *Rol económico, social, y político del indígena en Chile* (1945. *Memoria de Prueba*), p. 9.
[66] Cámara de Diputados, *Boletín de sesiones extraordinarias, 1929,* Sesión 15°, November 20.
[67] Subercaseaux, "La super gente bien," *Zig Zag* (March 27, 1954), p. 51.

Priding itself on its whiteness, the middle class to a large extent has believed in the inferiority of Indians and mixed bloods. Clinging to the aristocracy, it has erected a psychological barrier between itself and at least one-third of the population. To a subtler, but just as deep-rooted, extent as in Peru, Ecuador, Bolivia, and Guatemala, the Indian problem, or a variant of it, is involved in Chile's social and economic ills.

It is presumptuous for a United States writer to moralize on a Chilean problem that in part involves racial prejudice. Still, it does seem likely that if Chile's ruling class, made up of an amalgam of upper and middle sectors, does not accommodate itself to new forces, it may be swept away. Despite their many human shortcomings and failures, the ruling classes of Chile have demonstrated wisdom, talent, and responsibility in degree sufficient to compile a proud political tradition for their country. An established aristocracy learned in the nineteenth century how to accommodate to new forces. If this success is not repeated in the present century, then the ruling group instead of assimilating will likely be replaced by men who initially at least may possess less ability and whose exercise of power will not necessarily bring greater integrity or balance to national administration.

The Social Determinants of Political Democracy in Chile*

MAURICE ZEITLIN

The reasons why Chile historically has been a stable political democracy are sought by Zeitlin. His leading question is: "What struggles in Chile between what interest groups, in what phases of the country's development, led to a legitimation and institutionalization of formal political democracy?" He suggests seven working hypotheses taking into account (1) the early conflict between British and American political economic interests; (2) the confidence of the Chilean ruling classes, as the result of the early breadth and pace of Chilean economic development; (3) the characteristics of foreign investment; (4) the relationship between the pattern of early economic development and the rise of the industrial working class; (5) the mode of integration of new industrialists into the old ruling class; (6) the regional economic differentiation of sectors of the ruling class; (7) the relative timing of the social and economic integration of the ruling class and the emergence of the working class as an independent political force. The question is whether the stable political equilibrium established in Chile by the pattern of social conflicts and their resolution is still viable.

Maurice Zeitlin, Associate Professor of Sociology at the University of Wisconsin, is the author (with Robert Scheer) of *Cuba: Tragedy in Our Hemisphere* (New York: Grove Press, 1963), and of *Revolutionary Politics and the Cuban Working Class* (Princeton, New Jersey: Princeton University Press, 1967).

* Reprinted with some revisions from *Revista Latinoamericana de Sociologia*, Vol. II, No. 2 (July 1966), pp. 223-235.

FORMAL POLITICAL democracy, "that institutional arrangement for arriving at political decisions in which individuals acquire the power to decide by means of a competitive struggle for the people's vote,"[1] is always a precarious achievement, but especially so for underdeveloped countries. In fact, "political democracy has proved so vulnerable to changes in social structure that the better understanding of these processes has become one of the major tasks of social science."[2] In this paper I offer a number of brief, even schematic, hypotheses concerning the social determinants of political democracy in Chile, because I believe that the reasons why Chile historically has been a stable political democracy are of general theoretical relevance.[3]

Why has a stable multiparty system, whose political parties range along an ideological spectrum from left to right, endured in Chile for the last 100 years or so? This question is merely a particular and limited formulation of the general theoretical question: what are the social and historical conditions that are responsible for the development and institutionalization of stable political democracy? Focusing our study on Chile is of particular theoretical relevance because she is a "deviant case" in Latin America not only in the significant sense that her parliamentary democracy is unique

[1] Joseph Schumpeter, *Capitalism, Socialism, and Democracy* (New York: Harper and Row, 1962), p. 269. This definition, while hardly capturing the central symbolic meaning of democracy as a society of participating, aware citizens who control their own destiny, suffices to give us a fairly easy criterion to recognize *formal* political democracies.
[2] Seymour Martin Lipset, Martin Trow, and James S. Coleman, *Union Democracy* (Glencoe: The Free Press, 1956), introduction.
[3] Chile "has a record of stability unique in Latin America." The party system, based on groups of 'notables' in the Chilean aristocracy, has had a continuous existence in Chile since 1831; the country has "a record of representative government unsurpassed in Latin America," and a "tradition of respect for constitutionally established order and the decision of the ballot box." Hubert Herring, *A History of Latin America* (New York: Alfred Knopf, 1956), p. 573; John Johnson, *Political Change in Latin America: The Emergence of the Middle Sectors* (Stanford: Stanford University Press, 1958), pp. 72 and 92; Institute for the Comparative Study of Political Systems, *Chile: Election Factbook, 1964* (Washington, D. C.: Operations and Policy Research, Inc., 1964), p. 13.

in Latin America, but for another reason as well: Chile would seem to deviate from much prevalent (if not dominant) theory concerning the social requisites of stable political democracy.[4]

Contemporary Western students of political democracy and revolutionary (so-called "extremist") politics have more or less consistently linked what they consider to be the social requisites of political democracy—the conditions under which democracy arises and remains viable—to conditions opposite from those in which mass-based revolutionary movements (at least, ideologically speaking) subsist and grow. Thus, for instance, the existence of the Anglo-American democracies is often "explained" in the same terms (and by the same general variables) used to explain these countries' lack of major revolutionary (anticapitalist) working-class movements. Stable parliamentary democracy and a gradualist reformist (non-Marxist nonrevolutionary) working class are alleged to be different sides of the same coin, minted of the same materials and having their causes in the same social processes and relations. "The instability of the democratic process in general and the strength of the Communists in particular" are seen to be directly related.[5]

Such countries, for example, as France and Italy are alleged to be *un*stable democracies not only for the same reasons that caused the emergence and sustenance of their major working-class-based Communist parties, but even *because* of the presence of these parties. Thus, the political sociologist Sey-

[4] Chile presents an outstanding opportunity to test out the assumptions and hypotheses of some present "theories" of stable democracy developed primarily on the basis of the historical experience of European and Anglo-American countries. In so doing, we may acquire a more adequate understanding of the social determinants of political democracy. As in any other "deviant case analysis," our study may reveal additional variables that have to be incorporated into a theory of political democracy—variables that might otherwise be overlooked. Analysis of the "deviant case," Chile, may actually add further data to the general theory of political democracy by showing that there is an underlying explanation for both the deviant and the nondeviant. (Unhappily, we must leave this latter task for another time when we can do a systematic comparative analysis of Latin American political systems.) William J. Goode and Paul K. Hatt, *Methods in Social Research* (New York: McGraw-Hill, 1952), p. 89; Patricia L. Kendall and Katherine M. Wolf, "The Analysis of Deviant Cases in Communications Research," *Communications Research, 1948-49*, Paul F. Lazarsfeld and Frank M. Stanton, eds. (New York: Harper, 1949), pp. 152-179.
[5] Seymour Martin Lipset, *Political Man* (New York: Doubleday, 1959), p. 129.

mour Martin Lipset, in his important article on "Some Social Requisites of Democracy," has gone so far as to define stable democracies in Europe as those characterized by "uninterrupted continuation of political democracy since World War I *and the absence over the past twenty-five years of a major political movement [Fascist or Communist] opposed to the democratic 'rules of the game.'"*[6] By this approach, as if by conceptual prestidigitation, a major theoretical problem is obscured: namely, the circumstances that cause (allow) self-proclaimed revolutionary socialist working-class political parties to coexist with (and exist within) a stable political democracy.

Chile, of course, is precisely the case in point: it is a country characterized not only by stable political democracy, but also by the presence of a Socialist-Communist "proletarian front" (FRAP [Frente de Acción Popular]) that received 38.9 percent of the presidential vote in the 1964 election and 28.9 percent in 1958. The combined Communist-Socialist vote has not gone below 20 percent in any of the congressional elections of the past two decades. If not for the low women's vote for the FRAP candidate, Salvador Allende, in 1958, Chile would have been the seat of the first revolutionary socialist government to gain power through elections in a capitalist political democracy. Among all voters Allende lost by less than three percent; but among the men he actually won a majority by about the same margin by which he lost the election in the electorate as a whole!

Neither particular "explanations" of the stability of political democracy in Chile nor general theories of stable political democracy that are widely accepted seem to me to be adequate to the Chilean case. A number of simple "explanations" for Chilean political democracy found in the writings on Chile are not really explanations at all: the "genius of Diego Portales," the fact that the people respect the constitution, that Chileans are moderate, legalistic, and pragmatic, that the government is legitimate, that democracy is a "tradition," that the parties (although there are many of them) have been able to form coalitions easily, that the military has not inter-

---

[6] "The latter requirement," Lipset says, "means that no totalitarian movement, either Fascist or Communist, received 20 percent of the vote during this time." His "somewhat less stringent criterion for Latin America is whether a given country has had a history of more or less free elections for most of the post-World War I period." *Political Man*, p. 48.

fered (except for a brief interlude 1925-31) in politics, etc.[7] Most of these "explanations" are less explanations than low-level *descriptions* of some aspects of the Chilean political system that denote it as a stable political democracy. These confuse noting a syndrome with explanation, much like saying that the reason that someone feels inferior is because he has an inferiority complex. My focus in this article is on identifying the aspects or features of the social structure as a whole that underlie or determine the stability and democracy of the Chilean political system.

There are also some general theories of political democracy that, while explaining something, still explain far too little and assume too much. For example, the theory that political democracy is rooted in a high level of economic development tends to be *ahistorical*. First, when a country is "developed" is not specified, but rests on an eclectic selection of indices of development, shorn of their historical and class content. The emergence of political democracy in the essentially agrarian nation of postcolonial and frontier United States, for instance, is left completely unexplored and untouched by such a theory. Also Britain, for example, evolved most important democratic rights and liberties, such as habeas corpus, a good deal of freedom of expression, etc., long before she became a "developed nation." German Nazism, on the other

[7] Two quotes, one from a Chilean study written forty years ago, and another from a North American study just published, will have to suffice: "If a tyranny has not been able to sink roots in this country, it is not because our country has lacked governing individuals with the stature of caudillos. We have had men who, like the tyrants of other countries in South America, have been able in decisive moments of our history to solidify the efforts of the lower orders against the governing classes. What these individuals—these vigorous personalities—lacked in our country was an atmosphere (*ambiente*) propitious to the fulfillment of such ambitions. . . . *The strong habit of respect for the laws* of the land has withstood any sympathies there might be for an aspiring caudillo; the high *Chilean character* has rejected the unconditional submission of the courtier." Alberto Cabero, *Chile y los Chilenos*, 3rd edition. (Santiago: Editorial Lyceum, 1948), p. 73 (My italics). "The stability of the democratic regime in Chile is to be attributed, not to economic and sociological factors, but to something so completely intangible as mere tradition." Ernest Halperin, *Nationalism and Communism in Chile* (Cambridge: MIT Press, 1965), p. 27. Most Chilean historians simply "explain" the establishment of stable government in Chile by attributing it to the genius of Diego Portales, the major statesman behind presidents from 1831 to 1846. See, for example, the work by the major Chilean historian of the contemporary period, Francisco A. Encina, *Portales* (Santiago: Nascimento, 1964); Hugo Guerra Baeza, *Portales y Rosas: contrapunto de hombres y políticas* (Santiago: Editorial del Pacífico, 1958); and, though far superior from an analytical point of view, even Alberto Edwards Vives, *La Fronda Aristocrática* (Santiago: Editorial del Pacífico, 1927).

hand, came to power in a highly developed capitalist country —perhaps the most developed in Europe. Secondly, even a cursory look at the kinds of statistics adduced to "explain" stable democracy shows that Chile falls in different rank order depending on which indices are used. A theoretical rationale for given indices is usually lacking. More important, *on many strategic indices Chile falls well below some countries in which instability and dictatorship have been characteristic.* Thus, for example, while Chile's per capita income was $360 (U.S. dollars), two countries not noted either for stability or democracy in the past three decades, Argentina and Venezuela, were well above Chile, with per capita incomes, respectively, of $460 and $540. The only other country with a per capita income over $300 was Batista's Cuba, at $310.[8]

Using a variety of indices of economic development, we find that Chile's rank in Latin America is not consistent with the simple theory that economic development *ipso facto* allows a country to be a political democracy. A theory that fails to specify what interconnections there are supposed to be between economic development and democracy is no theory at all. Correlation is hardly explanation, especially when even many correlates are "wrong!"

Any theory of the relationship between economic development and political democracy must go beyond the mere demonstration of a close association between the level of development in a country and the probability that it will be a stable political democracy. Usually, once specification of

[8] In the ratio of doctors to inhabitant, Chile is outranked by Cuba and Argentina and is about the same as Venezuela. In the proportion of the population owning radios, Chile is outranked by such countries as Peru, Panama, Venezuela, Cuba, and Argentina. In newspaper copies per inhabitant, Cuba and Panama are essentially the same as Chile, while Argentina is well above Chile. Argentina's labor force has a smaller proportion in agricultural employment than Chile's. Venezuela is far higher in per capita energy consumed, while Argentina is but slightly lower. The rate of literacy is higher in Argentina than in Chile, while Cuba and Chile are essentially equal. Argentina and Paraguay [!] report a higher proportion of enrollment in primary education, while the Dominican Republic [!] reports about the same proportion as Chile. Panama and Argentina both report a higher postprimary enrollment than Chile. The proportion of the population with a university education is higher in Argentina than in Chile and about the same as in Cuba. Chile's infant mortality rate is reportedly the highest in all of Latin America. All of these types of figures have been used by one authority or another as crude indices of economic development. "Tipología Socio-económica de los países latinoamericanos," Roger Vekemans, ed., *Revista Interamericana de Ciencias Sociales*, Segunda Época, Vol. 2, número especial, 1963, p. 31; "Revolución en América Latina," *Mensaje*, No. 115, número especial, 1962, pp. 153ff.

the theory begins, a multiplicity of variables is introduced which have little to do with the level of economic development per se. Lipset, for example, explores the impact of religion, "key" historical events, the *rate* of development, the governmental structure itself as it feeds back into the larger political system, questions of legitimacy, and the reactions of the ruling or conservative classes, etc.

Beyond a certain level of economic development necessary to sustain any political structure, there is a vast realm of uncertainty about the type of political system that will emerge. *What is crucial about economic development, as far as its effects on politics is concerned, is its interrelationship with given types and patterns of social conflicts and their resolution.* Neither, in fact, can be understood without the other. "Democratic rights," as Lipset, Trow, and Coleman have put it, "have developed in societies largely through the struggles of various groups—class, religious, sectional, economic, professional, and so on—against one another and against the group that controls the state."[9] It is this general idea, sometimes referred to as the "conflict theory of politics," that has guided my research into the sources of Chilean political democracy. My leading question may therefore be put as follows:

What *struggles* in Chile between what *interest groups* (regional, class, intraclass, international), in what *phases* of the country's development, led to the *legitimization* and institutionalization of formal political democracy?

I suggest the following very schematic working hypotheses concerning the question:

1. The conflict between British and American political-economic interests in the first decades of national Chilean history was relatively two-sided.

(a) In the period after Chile won her independence, British alliances with one sector of the ruling classes and the United States with another sector split the ruling classes internally and created conflicting centers of power within it, each interested, therefore, in legitimizing the right to differ. (O'Higgins, for example, was more closely allied with England, Carrera with the U.S. O'Higgins won his conflict with Carrera. The division lingered on after their deaths as an important basis of political alliance and disalliance.) Contrast this to the situation in the Caribbean, especially the role of the U.S. in Cuba. Spain's incompetence, the U.S. intervention in the Cuban War of Independence, and its imposition of the

[9] *Union Democracy*, p. 16.

Platt Amendment transformed Cuba into a political protectorate. This happened, moreover, when the major leaders of Cuba's independence struggle had already died, and the leading colonial families, who had been pro-Spanish and not pro-independence, could easily *attach themselves* to the new foreign power in Cuba, rather than have to *secure their own base* in the country.

(b) In Chile the conflict between British and American interests, combined with Chile's own relatively developed economy and *independent* military strength (see below) prevented her from becoming either a direct colony or political protectorate of either power—the result of which would have been to prevent her democratic development, as is clear from the history of American intervention and occupation of the Caribbean. Toppling "incompetent," "insolvent," or "unfriendly" governments at will scarcely serves to implant either stability or respect for constitutional order (or one's own rulers).

(c) Chile's internally based ruling classes thus had sufficient *time* after achieving independence from Spain and the *economic basis* (see below) to demonstrate their own effectiveness and reinforce their legitimacy, a legitimacy they had never lost, since many of their representatives had played a leading role in the independence movement itself. Their legitimacy as rulers was never put in jeopardy, as was the legitimacy of "ruling classes" in the Caribbean—which classes often didn't rule and were in covert or open alliance with and dependent upon a foreign government and foreign-owned industries. The Chilean Constitution of 1828, the first after independence, may be said to have reflected the thought of the so-called Liberal "party" in the *Chilean* ruling classes; the Constitution of 1833, destined to last almost a century, reflected the so-called Conservative "party." The 1901 Constitution of Cuba was written during the first United States occupation and, therefore, reflected *United States* influence and could hardly be revered as a symbol of *national* order or the embodiment of the *national* will. In Chile the legal order was identified with a legitimate national government and could serve as a strong source of authority. In Cuba the legal order was identified with the interests of an imperialist exploiter.

2. The *early* breadth and *rapid pace* of Chilean economic development gave her ruling classes unbounded confidence in themselves and their country's "destiny in Latin America,"

and thus enhanced their ability to rule on a subjective and objective level (the nature of the resources they had available). They had the might to secure their rule and to define the rules of the political game, and their demonstrated "success" enhanced their prestige and secured their legitimacy among the citizenry. Their success also helped them develop an ideology of "freedom" and laissez faire not only in the market proper but also in the political arena.

(a) Chile's own imperialist policies were critical both in her early sustained economic development and in reinforcing her already relatively stable political institutions. The War of the Pacific (1879-83), in which Chile got Antofagasta from Bolivia and Tarapacá from Peru provided her ruling classes with secure control of the richest source of nitrates in the world, made possible significant public works in the 1880's, and provided seemingly inexhaustible funds for the national budget.

(b) The rulers of Chile *demonstrated their capacity to rule effectively* in the "nation's" behalf, maintaining order at home and competently directing a victorious and immediately enriching war against two nations double her population. By demonstrating their effectiveness, Chilean *civilian* rulers further enhanced their legitimacy, prevented the rise of an independent military elite within the country as a possible threat or even a competing center of prestige or power, and, in fact, reinforced the subordination of the military to the civilian authority.

(c) The mineral resources (nitrates and copper) acquired in the War also served to enlarge and strengthen the base of the newly developing banking-industrialist-mining stratum in the ruling classes, which joined its forces to those of the opposition parties, Liberal and Radical, in their competition for power with the Conservative Party based on the older landed aristocracy and mercantile elements centered in Santiago and Valparaíso.

(d) The imperialist war also furthered the development of a sense of national identity and national "destiny," and a renewed jealousy of her independence. Moreover, the United States now appeared as a concrete threat in its attempts to prevent Chile from securing her control over the newly won territories, and thus provided a negative stimulus to Chilean nationalism. The War also served to strengthen a national quasiracist sense of uniqueness and superiority in Latin America.

3. Foreign economic investment was never predominant in Chile's agricultural sector, so that the Chilean aristocracy was not weakened or displaced by a foreign absentee-ownership class, as was true, for instance, in Cuba, where any genuinely landed aristocracy was impossible because of American penetration of agriculture.

(a) The pattern of economic development in Chile was also such that the agrarian social structure and therefore the base of the *terratenientes* as a class was left largely intact. Traditionalist and paternalistic relations had been maintained in the countryside within the haciendas until recently with little change. Isolated, localized, and few in number within the haciendas, the peasants and inquilinos formed a secure base for the power of the landlord class. In Cuba, in contrast, the development of foreign-owned large-scale units of production in the sugar sector based on the employment of masses of wage laborers destroyed traditionalism and paternalism, while, in addition, displacing the native ruling class. Present in the midst of the agricultural laborers and peasants of Cuba also were the "factories in the field," the sugar mills, employing industrial workers proper, who became an early threat to the political and economic order in Cuba and an ever-present potential revolutionary force, whose influence radiated throughout the country. In Chile the mines early became important centers of working-class power (see below) and exerted influence on the development of militance among certain peasants, especially the communal peasantry of the North; but these were essentially isolated from the peasantry as a whole and posed no threat to stability of the social order.

(b) Despite the importance of early British economic investment in Chile, the copper and nitrate mines continued to provide a developed Chilean class of entrepreneur-industrialists with a secure economic base (more or less) of their own. This enhanced their early nationalist and "antiimperialist" ideology (with the additional impetus of the War of the Pacific and the ensuing diplomatic difficulties with the United States), and their loyalty to Chilean sovereignty and the Chilean political system. Their demonstrated nationalism, in turn, helped to sustain their rule and their legitimacy with the citizenry. Contrast Cuba, where when a certain level of "business nationalism" began to develop in the 1920's, it was under American tutelage and encouraged by the U.S. as a means of bolstering a cooperative businessman's government with a facade of self-assertive nationalism.

4. The pattern of early economic development in Chile was also such that within a short period after independence was gained a genuine industrial working class appeared that demanded and won the right to organize and whose leaders were the bearers of democratic ideology.

(a) The strength of industrial working class organization was in the South and the North of the country and centered in the copper mining, coal, and nitrate areas outside of the big cities and far from the capital. These were, then, major independent and autonomous centers of social power countering to some extent the power of the ruling classes and encouraging the legitimatization of the workers' right to organize.

(b) Dispersion of these centers of working-class strength served as sources of countervailing power without posing a real threat to the power of the ruling classes, because local and regional struggles tended to remain confined to (and be dissipated in) these areas rather than grow into national struggles between the classes as a whole. In Cuba, in contrast, the sugar *centrales* were scattered throughout the country and located in the midst of the countryside; there was regular contact between agricultural laborers and mill workers, and coordination of strikes in the nationwide industry inevitably became a national struggle. Moreover, the proportion of workers involved in and/or dependent on the sugar industry made them a national force, in contrast to the situation of the Chilean miners, who always constituted a numerically insignificant minority of the working class, even including those in associated processing plants.[10]

(c) In the struggle for influence between the new mining industrialists and the old landed aristocracy, the workers in the mining areas were initially courted by both electorally and they apparently played a significant role in support of the mid-nineteenth-century political movement of the mining industrialists (represented by such men as Pedro León Gallo, Urmaneta, Vicuña Mackenna, Matías Cousiño, Gregorio Ossa,

[10] The relative political isolation of the miners has been gradually broken down. Today the cohesive working-class communities of the miners act as centers of radical political influence that diffuses throughout the countryside 'educating' the peasantry and other workers in socialist politics. In the mining municipalities *and their "satellites,"* i.e., those municipalities bordering on one or more mining municipalities, a political culture has been established that cuts across the diverse strata of the rural exploited, making them areas of broad-based support for the Socialist-Communist coalition in the 1958 and 1964 presidential elections. See James Petras and Maurice Zeitlin, "Miners and Agrarian Radicalism," *American Sociological Review*, Vol. XXXII, No. 4 (August 1967), pp. 578-586. Reprinted in this volume, pp. 236-248. Also, see their "Miners and Urban Working Class Radicalism," forthcoming.

Agustín Edwards Ossandón). This helped to secure the latter's entry into the ruling classes while also enhancing the political organization and consciousness of the workers.

5. The combination of the apparent strength of the new labor movement, based on the miners, the rapidity of economic development and the attraction of the new fortunes to an aristocracy many of whose members had recently been impoverished by the depression of 1858-60, the fact that mining was rooted in the countryside, and the foreign origins of many of the new wealthy helped to integrate the new wealth into the old ruling classes by familial, social, and economic bonds.

(a) The legitimacy of the aristocracy (old "names") and the wealth of the new industrialists tended to lend themselves to each other and to stabilize the new hybrid ruling class.

(b) Introduction of so many new men with new ideas and talents also probably contributed to securing the *stability* of rule of the new ruling class amalgam, while the endurance of divisions and competing centers of power based on early conflicts tended to reinforce an ideology of political compromise and legitimize the right to organize and compete for political power.

(c) Since the old aristocracy had itself participated directly in party politics, entered government service, and elective office, so too did the newer elements in the ruling classes. Men of ability and energy, therefore, of whatever social origins, looked on politics as a respectable career and, often after serving an apprenticeship in private affairs that provided them with a fund of common experience and values, took to politics as a vocation. In Cuba respect for elective office was lacking, fundamentally because such office carried with it little real authority over the nation's destiny, controlled as it was by a foreign power. "Politics" was a dirty word; opportunism, corruption, and gangsterism were identified with public office; and men of quality either spurned politics as a career or were deformed in the process of becoming seasoned "politicians."

6. Regional economic differentiation between sectors of the ruling class also probably made it easier to live and let live politically and to believe in it, since within these zones of the country different sectors of the ruling class could hold sway; on the other hand, all would have to defer to each other on the national level in order to conciliate and form coalitions and alliances to accomplish their ends and protect their perceived interests.

(a) Zonal or regional loyalties, moreover, crisscrossed class lines and reinforced the bases of different political parties and factions within these parties.

7. Ruling class economic and social integration was accomplished to a great extent, its legitimacy secured and the party system established, before the working class became an independent political force having its own leaders who articulated, at least, a revolutionary *ideology*. Therefore, the political formula or ideology of the peaceful struggle for power, while severely tested in the period of social crisis, 1925-31, could survive and be reinvigorated in the following years. The institutional patterns for the resolution and *containment of social conflict* had been set, and the rule of the rulers was sufficiently secure to *allow* them to be flexible in dealing with working-class demands (though even here the Alessandri-Ibañez epoch [1925-1938] indicates the frailty even of the Chilean system).

(a) The ideology of the peaceful struggle for power was of such sufficient strength in Chile, in fact, that it impressed itself directly on even the early prebureaucratic phase of the so-called revolutionary Socialist and Communist movement. The Popular Front then inaugurated an epoch of the participation of the Left in *institutionalized social conflict*, and of parliamentary socialism as a method of containing conflict within acceptable channels, that has endured until the present.

(b) In fact, the Popular Front period served to implant an institutionalized working relationship between so-called revolutionary parties (Socialist and Communist) and the party representing the newer elements in the capitalist class (Radical Party), as a mode of trading the political support of the Left and its containment of working-class demands in exchange for "policies of national development" desired by both the Left and the capitalist-industrialists. Politically, a major consequence of this alliance was the stabilization of ruling-class rule and the reinforcement of parliamentary democracy during the critical period following the demonstration of the fragility of even the Chilean political structure in 1925-31. Moreover, this was also a period of sustained economic development, which saw the rapid growth of the working class.

(c) The essentially parliamentary nature of the Chilean Left has rested on a working class that is *organizationally* fragmented and, therefore, could form little else but an *electoral* base. So long as its leaders opted only for parliamentary and "peaceful" methods of struggle, and failed even to put its resources into a sustained drive to organize the unorganized, the working class, *as a class,* did not and could not really present a threat to Chilean stability. Apart from the copper, coal, and nitrate mines, and the steel and textile plants, in fact, Chilean unionism is even today essentially craft in nature, localized, isolated, and politically, even economically, impotent. (Of 296 municipalities in Chile, only 20 of them, or 6.7 percent, have as much as 25 percent of the labor force organized. Ten of these are in mining communities. All told, less than 15 percent of the entire labor force is organized.)[11] Thus, the paradox and the basic weakness of the Chilean Left is that while it has deep political roots in the working class—and this class is in many senses very politicized—the working class has been organizationally unable to act with sufficient cohesiveness to destabilize the system.

(d) Chilean political democracy has rested until the present, therefore, on an equilibrium of social forces more or less in stalemate, more or less willing to act toward each other in the political arena on the tacit assumption that each would respect the "rights" of the others concerning their fundamental interests as they define them. None has been willing or able to upset this equilibrium and risk the consequences. The result of this equilibrium, however, and of the Left's unwillingness to challenge it and risk a genuine confrontation of social interests outside the parliamentary arena, has been that, as Frederick Pike has recently put it so well: "What we have praised as democracy in Chile since 1920 has amounted to little more than a system in which a small, privileged class has been gentlemanly in determining, through very limited electoral processes, which of its members would rule the country."[12]

In turn, this equilibrium of interests has meant that "Chilean democracy and Chilean capitalism have gone hand in hand toward producing outrageous social injustice . . . and [the] political hierarchical control that characterizes Chilean politics."[13]

The Christian Democratic government, however, under the leadership of Eduardo Frei, seems to be breaking with this past and upsetting the equilibrium—an equilibrium that may, in fact, have already been upset or in jeopardy at least since the 1958 presidential elections. Many cadre of the Christian Democratic Party speak in a revolutionary idiom about chang-

---

[11] Calculated from figures provided by the Dirección de Estadística y Censos, Demografía, Año 1960; and Dirección del Trabajo, Depto. de Organizaciones Sociales, *Nómina de Sindicatos Industriales, Profesionales y Agrícolas de la República*, 1964, Santiago de Chile.

[12] Frederick B. Pike, *Chile and the United States, 1880-1962* (Notre Dame, Ind.: University of Notre Dame Press, 1963), p. XXV.

[13] *Ibid.*, p. 296.

ing the old structure of power, of making a fundamental agrarian reform, of the dignity of the *campesino,* and of the defense of Chilean independence. At the same time, their government has launched a severe attack on FRAP (the Socialist-Communist alliance) as the scapegoat of the nation's ills, is trying to establish a dual union movement under its tutelage and to break the power of organized labor, especially in the copper mines, and to outlaw the right to strike except under explicit government approval. The government is also trying to organize its own mass base in the working-class neighborhoods, especially among the most impoverished slum dwellers, where under its program of "Promoción Popular" it is establishing what it calls "nonpolitical" neighborhood associations, women's clubs, and so on. Unions of peasants are also being organized in the countryside under its tutelage. The middle strata have displayed increasing mass support for the government, including attendance at mass rallies supporting its repressive policies against the mining unions. The present slogan of the Frei Christian Democratic government is "la mano dura," but against whom is still the big question. At the moment it seems clear that it is not against the large landowners, the bankers, the industrialists, or American investment in the copper mines, and throughout the economy, but rather against the old and institutionalized Left that had essentially accommodated itself to the existing political system of bargaining and trading. The question is whether the system of political democracy in Chile will survive the Christian Democrats' refusal to play according to the established rules of the game.

Miners and Agrarian Radicalism*

JAMES PETRAS   MAURICE ZEITLIN

Chilean mining municipalities, Petras and Zeitlin show, are centers from which political radicalism is diffused into surrounding nonmining agricultural and nonagricultural areas. The greater the number of mining municipalities a "satellite" municipality adjoins, the more likely it is to have a "high" vote for the presidential candidate of the Socialist-Communist coalition (FRAP). Municipalities that are neither mining municipalities nor are adjoined to any, are least likely to have a "high" FRAP vote. In agricultural areas, political differences based on class position among the peasants tend to disappear in the mining and "satellite" municipalities. In the nonmining, nonsatellite municipalities, however, class structure does determine voting. Mining and adjoining municipalities develop a radical political culture that tends to eliminate the political importance of class differences among peasants, uniting them across class lines.

GENERALLY, EMPIRICAL analyses of class and politics focus on the relative chances for given types of political behavior in different classes but neglect *the interaction of these classes and the political consequences of such interaction.* Moreover, even when reference *is* made to the possible political relevance of such interaction, the emphasis has been on asymmetrical

* This is a joint work in the fullest sense; our names are in alphabetical order. We are indebted to Michael Parker for his helpful comments on an original draft of this article. Reprinted from *American Sociological Review*, 32 (August 1967), 4, pp. 578-586, by permission of the American Sociological Association.

influence, i.e., on how the privileged classes may moderate the politics of the unprivileged.[1] For instance, the possibility that the working class might modify the political behavior of the middle classes has scarcely been entertained, nor has the possible impact of the workers on the development of political consciousness in other exploited classes been explored. The latter is precisely what we focus on in this article: the impact of organized workers in Chile on the development of political consciousness in the peasantry.

In Chile agricultural relations have gradually become modernized, and traditional social controls have loosened considerably. In the central valley, where Chile's agricultural population is centered, the modernization favored by the Chilean propertied classes may be directly responsible for the growth of rural radicalism. As one writer has put it: "The principal impact of technological advance and farm rationalization has been to undermine the secure if impoverished position of the agricultural laborers, which has been an important feature of the traditional system of employment. Wage rates are barely keeping up with consumer price increases and [these rates] may have fallen recently. Thus while the attempts to increase output and productivity have not been very successful, these attempts have led to changes that adversely affect the landless laborer. These changes in Chilean agriculture may lead to demands for a more radical transformation in the future."[2] This breakdown of the traditional rural social structure, the growth of a "rural proletariat," and emergence of demands for radical reforms in the agrarian structure may allow other relatively oppressed groups who have similar demands and *are* highly organized to provide leadership for the peasantry as it enters the political struggle in Chile. The most highly organized and politically conscious working class centers in Chile are in the mining municipalities —centers from which the miners' political influence may be diffused into the surrounding countryside.

In Chile both the organized trade union movement and the emergence of insurgent political parties began in the northern areas of Tarapaca and Antofagasta, where 40 percent of the

[1] Cf. Seymour Martin Lipset, *Political Man*, (New York: Doubleday & Co., 1960), esp. pp. 231 and following.
[2] Marvin Sternberg, "Chilean Land Tenure and Land Reforms" (unpublished doctoral dissertation), University of California, Berkeley, 1962, pp. 132-133.

labor force was already employed in the mines by 1885. Soon after the middle of the last century, large-scale social conflict rivaling similar outbreaks in Europe were occurring with increasing frequency and intensity.[3] The northern nitrate city of Iquique and the southern coal mining area of Lota were frequently the scenes of struggles of civil war proportions in which hundreds if not thousands of workers were killed. The first general strike in 1890 originated in Iquique and spread throughout the country. Despite the violent reaction of the public authorities, the first labor organizations began to emerge —based predominantly in the nitrate mines of the north.[4] The Chilean Workers' Federation was founded in 1908 by Conservatives as a mutual aid society. By 1917 it had become a militant industrial trade union; two years later it called for the abolition of capitalism. Between 1911 and 1920 there were 293 strikes involving 150,000 workers. In 1919 the Chilean Workers' Federation (FOCH) became affiliated with the Red Trade Union Federation. The FOCH, the largest national union, contained an estimated 136,000 members, of which 10,000 were coal miners and 40,000 nitrate miners—miners accounting for almost 37 percent of all union members. Of all industries, it was only mining in which a majority of the workers were organized. In 1906 the first working-class Socialist leader, Emilio Recabarren, was elected from a mining area—but he was not allowed to take office.

The Socialist Party that grew out of the establishment of the so-called "Socialist Republic,"[5] (June 4-16, 1932) had its most cohesive working-class political base among the copper miners. Although the Socialist Party condemned both the Second and the Third Internationals, it claimed adherence to Marxism and the establishment of a government of organized

[3] Over one-third of all the strikes and popular demonstrations occurring in the period between 1851-1878 involved miners, according to Hernán Ramírez Necochea, *Historia de Movimiento Obrero en Chile: Antecedentes Siglo XIX,* Santiago: Editorial Austral, no date, pp. 133-134.

[4] One of the worst massacres in labor history occurred in Chile at that time, when ten thousand nitrate miners marching in Iquique were machine-gunned, and two thousand died. Julio César Jobet, *Ensayo Crítico del desarrollo económico-social de Chile,* Santiago: Editorial Universitaria, 1955, p. 138.

[5] Following the Ibáñez military regime, in the midst of a general economic crisis, the "Socialist Republic" consisted of a series of four military juntas beginning on June 14, 1932, and ending on the 30th of that month. The officers had no social program and their only achievement was the establishment of the Socialist Party under the leadership of one of them, Marmaduke Grove.

workers as its goal. The Communists also secured their major
base in the mining areas. In the municipal elections of 1947
the last relatively free election before the ten-year ban on the
Community Party (1948-1958), the Communists received
71 percent of the coal miners' vote, 63 percent of the nitrate
miners' vote, and 55 percent of the vote of the copper workers';
nationally, in contrast, they received only 18 percent of the
vote.

The eleven major mining municipalities accounted for 20
percent of the total national Communist vote.[6] Their history

Copper Zone	%
Chuquicamata	68
Potrerillos	47
Sewell	50
Total	55
Coal Mining Zone	%
Coronel	68
Lota	83
Curanilahue	63
Total	71
Nitrate Zone	%
Iquique	34
Pozo Almonte	70
Lagunas	64
Toco	79
Pedro de Valdivia	72
Total	63

of class conflict and organized political activity clearly established the miners as the most active revolutionary force in
Chilean society. Their political radicalism is in line with the
radicalism of miners all over the world,[7] in great part the
result of the structure of the "occupational community" of
the miners. The high degree of interaction among the miners
results in very close-knit social organization. Since they are
concentrated together, and in relative physical and social isolation from the influences of the dominant social classes in the
society, it is highly likely that a shared class outlook based on
the recognition of their common interests will develop. The
question we deal with here is the impact, if any, that these

[6] The Communist Vote in Mining Centers (1947)[a] (National Vote=
18 percent)

[a] Ricardo Cruz Coke, Geografía electoral le Chile (Santiago: Editorial
del Pacífico, 1952), pp. 81-82.

[7] Lipset, op. cit., pp. 242-246. See also Clark Kerr and Abraham Siegel,
"The Interindustry Propensity to Strike—An International Comparison,"
in Arthur Kornhauser, Robert Dubin, and Arthur Ross, (eds.) Industrial
Conflict (New York: McGraw-Hill, 1954), pp. 200-201.

highly organized, politically radical miners have on the traditionally conservative rural poor.

Sharp divisions have existed between the urban and rural sectors of the Chilean labor force. A fundamental factor in the stability, continuity, and power of the propertied classes was the social condition and attitudes of the rural labor force. The system of rural labor established in colonial times continued down through the twentieth century, little changed by the Revolution for Independence or by a century and a quarter of parliamentary and presidential democracy.

Formally free, the rural labor force was bound to the land by the fact that neighboring landowners would refuse to hire a tenant who had left a hacienda because he was discontented with his lot. The economic status of the *inquilino* (tenant worker) was the same throughout the nineteenth and most of the twentieth century: a few pennies a day in wages, a one-room or two-room house, a ration of food for each day he worked, and a tiny plot of land. Usually he was required to supply labor for some 240 days a year.[8] Debt servitude was widespread and opportunity for the inquilino to advance from that status and become an economically independent farmer was nonexistent. The social and religious life of the inquilino was restricted by the landowners (*hacendados*) who preferred that their employees have minimal contact with outsiders. The landowners organized the fiesta, the amusements and the "civil jurisdiction" within the hacienda (*"fundo"*). In the middle 1930's these fundos approximated the "ideal type" of an authoritarian system of social control and rigid social stratification.

Within the larger society, where some voluntary associations defending working-class interests were able to establish themselves, the rural poor lived in conditions in which the apparatus of violence and force was regulated by a single owner or family, alternative sources of information were prohibited, and voluntary associations were forbidden. Middle-class parliamentary parties such as the *Radicales* did not advocate a program of socioeconomic reform of the traditional landed system. They were unable to mobilize the peasantry and lower-class rural populace against the landowners' rule. In turn, this forced the middle-class parties to forego a meaningful and dynamic program for industrial and democratic development,

[8] George McBride, *Chile: Land and Society* (New York: American Geographical Society, 1936), pp. 148-155.

and allowed the Socialists and the Communists, and then the Christian Democrats, to become spokesmen for the rural poor and agrarian reform.

In his control of the inquilino, the landowner held an effective counterweight to any political program of social and economic development that negatively affected his interests. The alliance of foreign investors, large landowners, and those urban entrepreneurs integrated with them, rested on the control the landowners had of the inquilino; this was the condition *sine qua non* for their continuing political hegemony.

Apart from the inquilino, there was a sector of the rural labor force which was not attached to the land, and consequently was less directly under the dominance of the landowners. These "free laborers" have constituted about one-third of the rural work force; three decades ago they were already said to "have the reputation of provoking many difficulties in the relation between the inquilino and the farm owner."[9] The free laborers were reputed to be frequently more independent in their outlook and more likely to object to any excesses committed by the landowners against the workers. With the gradual mechanization of agriculture and the increased payment in wages in recent years, the rural population has become like wage laborers.

Only with industrial development, and especially mining, did the agricultural labor force in Chile begin to have even a hint of political consciousness, impelled largely by their contact with industrial workers. The landowners' strategy had been to isolate the inquilinos from the urban working class, prohibiting their independent organization. By restricting their experience to the fundo itself, the *patrón* had inhibited the development of their political awareness. With the rapid growth of the urban working class in the period after World War I, strikes spread to the rural districts for the first time in the history of the country. Uprisings took place on a number of fundos. The miners took the leadership in this early attempt at rural organization. In 1919 an abortive attempt was made to organize the inquilinos into a nationwide federation in the Cometa region in the Aconcagua Valley, "the intention being to federate the inquilinos with an organization of miners."[10] Again in the 1930's a broad militant movement

[9] *Ibid.*, p. 164.
[10] *El Agricultor*, May 1920, p. 113, cited in McBride, *op. cit.*, p. 166.

of peasant unionization developed, supported by sectors of the urban working class; it was violently repressed by the state and politically defused by the electoral strategy that the leftist parties adopted during the Popular Front.[11]

In recent years the closed system of the large fundos has begun to change under the impact of the growth of commercial-capitalistic economic and social relations and, more important, as political organization, trade unions, and outside communications networks have been able to undermine the information monopoly of the large landowners.

In the 1958 presidential election significant sectors of the Chilean peasantry shifted their traditional allegiance away from the Right. The Socialist-Communist coalition, Frente de Acción Popular (FRAP), and the Christian Democratic Party are competing for the allegiance of this important and newly emerging social force; they have formed their own peasant "unions" and advocated programs for agrarian reform. In both the 1958 and the 1964 presidential elections FRAP campaigned actively throughout the countryside. With old political alignments shifting and the balance of social forces changing, the political direction that the Chilean peasantry will take is seen by all major political parties as a major factor in determining the future of Chilean society. The decisive role that the miners can play in determining the direction taken by the peasantry will become clear from our findings.

Our analysis is based on the electoral returns of the presidential elections of 1958 and 1964, with primary emphasis on the 195 agricultural municipalities. An ecological analysis of these election results is meaningful; distortions of the results through vote-tampering and coercion are believed to have been minimal. In these elections competing political programs that included the socialist alternative were presented to the Chilean peasantry at a moment when it was emerging as a national political force. Our focus here is on the political impact of the organized mining centers on the peasantry, and on the differential political response of different types of peasantry.

FINDINGS

We define as agricultural municipalities those in which 50 percent or more of the economically active population are

[11] Luis Vitale, *Historia del movimiento obrero* (Santiago: Editorial POR, 1962), p. 88 *et passim*.

engaged in agriculture.[12] Mining municipalities are those in which at least 500 individuals *or* 50 percent or more of the economically active population are in the mining sector. Each of the 296 municipalities in the country was located on a map (in Mattelart, *Atlas Social de las Comunas de Chile*) and each municipality that directly adjoined any mining municipality was defined as a "satellite."

The vote for Salvadore Allende, presidential candidate of the Socialist-Communist coalition (FRAP), is taken as an index of radical political behavior. We define a "high" vote for Allende in 1958 as 30 percent (the national average) or more in the municipality, and a "low" vote as 20 percent or less; in 1964 a "high" vote is 40 percent (the national average) or more in the municipality, and "low" is 25 percent or less.[13]

If our assumption is correct that the mining municipalities are not only centers of political radicalism but also centers from which political radicalism is diffused into surrounding nonmining areas, then we should find that the greater the number of mining municipalities a "satellite" adjoins, the more likely it is to have a "high" vote for Allende, the FRAP presidential candidate. (The number of mining municipalities adjoining a satellite ranges from one to four.) The municipalities that are neither mining municipalities nor adjoin any should be least likely to give a "high" vote to Allende.

As Table 1 shows, this is precisely what we find in both agricultural and nonagricultural municipalities in 1958 and in 1964. The same relationship holds when we look at the tail end of the vote—the "low" Allende vote (Table 2): the greater the number of mining municipalities adjoining it, the greater the likelihood in a municipality that Allende received a "high" vote (and the less the likelihood of a "low" vote). The greatest political differences are between the mining municipalities and

---

[12] The data were compiled from several sources: *Censo Nacional Agrícola—Ganadero*, Vols. I-VI, (Santiago: Servicio nacional de estadísticas y censos, República de Chile, 1955); *Censo de Población* (Santiago: Dirección de Estadística y Censos de la República de Chile, 1960); Armand Mattelart, *Atlas Social de las Comunas de Chile* (Santiago: Editorial del Pacífico, 1966).

[13] We have used "high" and "low" ends of the voting spectrum as an *index* of radicalism because we are concerned with municipalities as social units, and relative radicalism as an *attribute* of the municipality. Thus, a municipality with a "high" FRAP vote is a "radical" municipality. This procedure differs from simply taking the mean or median FRAP vote in the municipalities and therefore focusing on simple *quantitative* differences, whatever the actual vote. Neither procedure is intrinsically "correct." One or the other is more useful depending on the focus of the analysis; when looking for the determinants of political radicalism, in ecological analysis, we think our procedure is more useful.

the municipalities that are neither satellites nor have mines in them.

In addition to this demonstration of the political impact of the mining centers on surrounding nonmining areas, the following should be noted: (1) The agricultural municipalities, whatever their proximity to mining centers, have proportionately fewer "high" Allende municipalities among them than the nonagricultural ones. Despite FRAP's appreciable growth in strength in the agricultural areas, the nonagricultural, industrial, and urban municipalities still provide the major electoral

TABLE 1. PERCENT "HIGH" VOTE FOR ALLENDE AMONG MALES IN MUNICIPALITIES CLASSIFIED BY PREVALENCE OF AGRICULTURE AND MINING, 1958 AND 1964

	Prevalence of Agriculture					
	Nonagricultural Municipalities		Agricultural Municipalities		Entire Country	
Prevalence of Mining	1958	1964(N)	1958	1964(N)	1958	1964(N)
Neither "satellites" nor mining municipalities	45	67 (58)	31	51 (162)	35	55 (220)
"Satellites" [a]	73	93 (15)	60	80 (30)	69	82 (45)
Mining municipalities	93	93 (28)	...	...[b](3)	93	93 (31)

[a] A further breakdown of "satellites" according to the number of mining municipalities they adjoin also yields a direct relationship between proximity to mining centers and political radicalism. There are too few cases to examine the relationship among nonagricultural municipalities, however. Among agricultural municipalities 58 percent of the "satellites" of one mining municipality ($N=19$) gave Allende a "high" vote in 1958, and 82 percent of the "satellites" of two to four mining municipalities ($N=11$) gave him a "high" vote. In 1964 the respective figures are 74 percent and 91 percent. In the entire country, in 1958, of the first "satellite" group ($N=25$), Allende got a "high" vote in 64 percent, and of the second group, 75 percent of the municipalities. The respective figures for 1964 in these groups are 76 percent and 90 percent.

[b] All three mining agricultural municipalities gave Allende a "high" vote in both elections, 1958 and 1964.

base of the Left. (2) Yet the strength of the Left grew throughout the agricultural municipalities from 1958 to 1964. This indicates that the *Frapistas* are penetrating and broadening their support in the peasantry as a whole, and not merely in particular peasant "segments" or strata, a point to which we shall return below. (3) It is beyond the scope of this article but it should be pointed out that the miners' political influence apparently radiates out to other workers, perhaps even others in the *"clase popular,"* made up of a variety of poor from peddlers to artisans and manual laborers. As a cohesive, organized, politically conscious community, the miners' political influence is critical not only in the peasantry but also among other lower

strata. The existence of a major mining population whose
political influence reaches other exploited strata may explain
why class-based and class-conscious politics have emerged so
much more clearly in Chile than in other countries in Latin
America which, while having large strata of urban and rural
poor, lack cohesive working-class centers.[14]

The high degree of radical political consciousness in the
mining areas of Chile was indicated by the results of Trade
Union elections held shortly after Government troops killed
7 and wounded 38 miners during a military occupation of
striking copper-mining areas in April 1966. *El Mercurio,* the

TABLE 2. PERCENT "LOW" VOTE FOR ALLENDE AMONG MALES IN MUNICI-
PALITIES CLASSIFIED BY PREVALENCE OF AGRICULTURE AND MINING, 1958
AND 1964

	Prevalence of Agriculture		
	Nonagricultural Municipalities	Agricultural Municipalities	Entire Country
Prevalence of Mining	1958 1964(N)	1958 1964(N)	1958 1964(N)
Neither "satellites" nor mining municipalities	21 10 (58)	49 20 (162)	41 17 (220)
"Satellites"	7 0 (15)	20 3 (30)	16 2 (45)
Mining municipalities	4 0 (28)	... ... (3)	3 0 (31)

anti-Communist conservative daily, editorialized before the
election: "The election of union officers that will take place
in El Salvador, Potrerillos, and Barquito will be realized in an
atmosphere of liberty adequate for the workers to express
their preferences without the shadow of government pressure
over the voters or candidates. These acts are of considerable
importance because they will demonstrate what the spontaneous will of the workers really is when they do not feel menaced
or intimidated by agitators. . . . Now the workers can take
advantage of the new climate in the mines in order to form
union committees that serve their interests rather than subordi-
nating themselves to partisan politics."[15] The "spontaneous
will" of the workers resulted in an overwhelming victory for
the FRAP candidates, even when the elections were govern-

[14] We deal extensively with this question in another article. The Agricultural Census makes it possible to gauge the impact of the miners on
given agricultural strata but a comparable census for the nonagricultural
areas of Chile does not exist. The regular census does not include occupational breakdowns on the municipal level. Such an analysis will require
indirect indicators of class structure [see "Miners and Urban Working
Class Radicalism, forthcoming].

[15] *El Mercurio,* April 15, 1966, p. 3.

ment supervised.[16] The point is that the way the miners voted in the presidential elections represents real support for the Left —a high level of political consciousness that can be and is effectively transmitted to the peasantry.

In Chile the organized mining workers' "isolated" communities have a high level of participation in activities, controversies, and organizations—features that are essential to a democratic society. The reason may be, as Lipset suggests, that the "frequent interaction of union members in all spheres of life . . . [makes] for a high level of interest in the affairs of their unions, which translates itself into high participation in local organization and a greater potential for democracy and membership influence."[17]

More important, these same miners consciously seek to influence the politics of others. El Siglo, the Communist daily, recently reported that "The two hundred delegates attending the Eighth National Congress of the Miners Federation . . . has adopted a resolution that, throughout the country, it will lend the most active class solidarity to the workers in the countryside in their struggles in defense of their rights and for the conquest of a true Agrarian Reform. A few days ago the powerful unions [nitrate miners] of María Elena, Pedro de Valdivia, and Mantos Blancos in the province of Antofagasta adopted a similar resolution."[18] The politicization of the peasantry by the miners is both a conscious effort and a "natural process."

The Left, conscious of the diffusion of radical ideas through informal communication between the working class and the peasantry, intervenes to maximize their advantages from this situation, accentuating and deepening the process of the diffusion of radical ideas. The importance that the Left attributes to this interaction between class-conscious workers and the peasantry is shown by the remarks of Luis Corvalan, Communist Party General Secretary:

"The political and cultural ties between the city and the country, between the proletariat and the campesinos, have developed in many ways. The children of campesinos who go to work in industry learn many things that they soon teach to their relatives and friends who have remained on the fundo or in the village and with whom they maintain contacts. Thousands of inquilinos . . .

[16] The FRAP candidates obtained 16,227 votes, the Radical Party 3,278, and the Christian Democrats 3,263. The FRAP elected seven of the ten new union officers, replacing three Christian Democrats. Última Hora, April 19, 1966, p. 2.

[17] Op. cit., p. 408.

[18] El Siglo, February 20, 1966, p. 10.

and small owners have become laborers in the construction of hydroelectric plants, roads, reservoirs, and canals, or have been incorporated into the infant industries of sugar or lumber and live alongside numerous members of the proletariat who come from the cities. Furthermore, the crises and the repressive measures employed against the urban working class have caused many of the workers in the mines and factories to return to the country. *Throughout Chile, on the fundos and in the villages, we have seen many laborers, including some who were union leaders in the nitrate coal and copper* [industries]. It follows that the political work of the popular parties, and especially of us Communists, should also figure among the principal elements that have influenced and are influencing the creation of a new social consciousness in the countryside." [19] (Our italics)

As urbanization and industrialization impinge on the peasantry and cause migrations of the labor force, so also is the political awareness of those individuals who have roots in both cultures heightened. These individuals bring the new ideas of struggle and of class solidarity to their friends and relatives still living in the rural areas and employed in agriculture. To the extent that the Left political parties are effective in organizing and politicizing these newly recruited industrial workers, they have an effective carrier of radicalism into the countryside.

We discussed elsewhere the relationship between the structure of the agrarian labor force—the class composition of the countryside—and the FRAP presidential vote.[20] We find an inverse relationship between the proportion of proprietors in a municipality's agricultural labor force and the likelihood that it would give Allende a "high" vote. The higher the proportion of agricultural proprietors in a municipality the less likely it was to have a "high" Allende vote. This was consistent with our finding regarding the relationship between the proportion of wage laborers in a municipality's agricultural labor force and the vote—the higher the proportion of wage laborers, the greater the likelihood that the municipality gave Allende a "high" vote. From this evidence, we concluded that class position is a major determinant of peasant political behavior and that the rural proletariat, as distinguished from peasant proprietors, is apparently the major social base of the FRAP in the Chilean countryside.

[19] Luis Corvalan. "The Communists' Tactics Relative to Agrarian Reform in Chile" in T. Lynn Smith (editor), *Agrarian Reform in Latin America* (New York: Knopf, 1965), p. 139. Our translation of the original differs slightly from the version in Smith's book.
[20] James Petras and Maurice Zeitlin, "Agrarian Radicalism in Chile," *British Journal of Sociology*.

TABLE 3. PERCENT "HIGH" VOTE FOR ALLENDE AMONG MALES IN AGRICULTURAL MUNICIPALITIES CLASSIFIED BY PREVALENCE OF MINING AND PROPRIETORS, 1964

Prevalence of Mining	70 plus		Percent Proprietors 50-69		30-49		under 30	
Neither "satellite" nor mining municipality	29	(35)	46	(24)	51	(37)	80	(54)
Mining "satellites"	83	(6)	100	(3)	87	(8)	90	(10)
Mining municipalities	100	(1)	100	(1)		(0)	100	(1)

The question now is what impact the organized political centers, the mining municipalities and their satellites, have on the class determination of voting in the countryside. We find that the political differences based on class position among the peasants tend to disappear in the mining and satellite municipàlities. In the nonmining, nonsatellite municipalities, however, class structure continues to determine voting patterns. The mining satellites are more likely, whatever the structure of the agricultural labor force (or class composition of the peasantry), to give Allende a "high" vote than the nonmining, nonsatellite municipalities (Table 3). The theoretical point is clear: the mining and adjoining areas develop a distinct political culture, radical and socialist in content, that tends to eliminate the importance of class differences in the peasantry and unite the peasants across class lines.

The fact is that the Chilean Left not only specifically directs its working class activists in the trade unions to unite with peasants in support of their demands but also emphasizes the role they can play in uniting different peasant strata: El Siglo, the Chilean Communist daily, writes: "All the workers in all the unions should unite with the peasants, wherever the unions are near agricultural properties in which the peasants are initiating struggles in defense of their interests. The miners' unions must be there to help the organization of the peasant unions. All our fellow miners must be there to bring all their moral and material support to the peasants who are struggling for possession of the land."[21] The Communist Party general secretary urges that "the forms of organization should be in accord with the wishes of the campesinos themselves; but we Communists believe that the best form of organization is that of the independent union with headquarters in the village, in which are grouped the workers from various fundos and all of the modest sectors of the rural population from the wage-hand to the small proprietor, including the sharecropper, the poor

[21] El Siglo, February 20, 1966, p. 10.

campesino, etc."[22] Communist organizing strategy, the formation of independent organizations that include all of the rural "modest sectors . . . from wage hands to the small proprietor," adds a conscious element to further the general process of social interaction and diffusion of political consciousness that unites laborers and small proprietors in the areas adjoining mining centers.

CONCLUSIONS

The miners' organizational skills and political competence, the proximity of the mines to the countryside, the sharing of an exploited position, and conscious political choice enable the miners to politicize and radicalize the Chilean countryside. The sense of citizenship and the necessity of having their own leaders that develops in the mining communities, where the miners themselves, rather than "other strata and agencies," run their affairs, also expresses itself in the political leadership and influence that their communities exert in adjoining rural areas. Further, the miners can supply legal, political, and economic resources to aid the peasants concretely, and thus demonstrate to them the power of organization and of struggle in defense of their common interests against landowners. Where the miners have a strong political organization, peasant proprietors and agricultural wage laborers are equally susceptible to radicalism. Political men, such as the Chilean miners, who make an effort to organize or influence peasant proprietors spread over the countryside, relatively isolated and atomized, can provide a link between them. The miners' leadership and ideology provide the peasants with a form of communication and sharing of experience that is necessary for them to recognize and be able to act upon their common interests.

[22] Corvalan, op. cit., p. 141.

Stalemate or Coexistence in Argentina

TORCUATO S. DI TELLA

A "stalemate" of social groups contending for power has characterized the political scene in Argentina. The large landowners, the industrialists, the Army, the Church, the workers, and the middle classes have been locked in each other's embrace, Di Tella argues, none powerful enough to effectively win the struggle to run the country as they would like, yet each strong enough to veto effective action by other contenders for power. Thus, Argentina, a developed country, stagnates.

Torcuato Di Tella, an Argentinian sociologist, professor at the University of Buenos Aires till 1966, was Visiting Professor of Sociology at the University of California, Berkeley, in 1966-67, and is the author of several studies of political and social change, among them *El Sistema Político Argentino y la Clase Obrera* (Buenos Aires, 1964); *Argentina, Sociedad de Masas* (with Gino Germani, Jorge Graciarena, and others) (Buenos Aires, 1965), and *Sindicato y comunidad* (with L. Brams, J. Reynaud and A. Touraine (Buenos Aires, 1967).

ARGENTINA, one of the more highly developed Latin American countries, has been stagnating for the last thirty years or so as a result of political stalemate. The various contenders for power—large landowners, industrialists, Army, Church, middle classes, intellectuals, labor unions, and the Peronista Party—simply can't liquidate each other, though they have been trying hard for the last three decades. At times one or the other of those groups seems on the verge of succeeding,

249

but somehow society resists strongly, and a "social draw" is
reestablished. Each group has just sufficient power to veto
the projects originated by the others, but none can muster
the strength to run the country as it would like. . . .

In the beginning the oligarchy was not only strong, but
unchallenged. It was never rigid; rather it adapted itself
swiftly to changing circumstances. Rather early, by about
1850, it managed to organize its rule under a liberal, low-
coercion, high-immigration political system. Foreign capital
responded quickly, railways covered the country, and there
was an influx of hardworking Spanish and Italian farmers
and mechanics. Though land was not extensively subdivided,
a sizable rural and urban middle class was formed. Immigrants
succeeded and became the commercial and industrial bourgeoisie of the country. By U.S. or European standards there
was not enough Homestead legislation and protection for the
small farmer, but by third-world standards a very large
middle class of propertied and tenant farmers was created.
. . . Colin Clark concluded, in the mid-thirties, that Argentina
was among the eight richest countries in the world, in terms
of per capita production.[1]

But the giant had feet of clay. Growth had been too quick,
owing mostly to the seizure of the rich pampas from the
Indians, and the bourgeoisie was, for practical purposes, a
disenfranchised class, almost wholly foreign. While foreigners
in the United States never constituted more than 14 percent
of the population, in Argentina they formed close to 30 percent of the total population for several decades between the
1880's and the 1920's. In some occupational groups they were
in the immense majority; among industrial entrepreneurs and
urban business owners they constituted about 70 or 80 percent
of the total during the important formative years.[2] The task
of building up the country through mass migration from
abroad was *too* successful. Foreigners did not become Argentine citizens because it was more valuable for them to remain
citizens of Spain and Italy and to retain the protection of
their consulates, rather than rely on the protection of a weak,
politically unstable country. In the settlers' colony that was
created, the prosperous urban groups—the bourgeoisie and the
burgeoning middle classes—despised the *criollo* native masses
and traditions. The bourgeoisie alienated itself from politics

[1] Colin Clark, *The conditions of economic progress.*
[2] For further details, see Gino Germani, *Política y sociedad en una
época de transición* (Buenos Aires: Paidos, 1962).

by its sheer foreign status, its preoccupation with business, and its disregard for the problems of the people. . . .

One of the results of mass migration was that no respectable business-oriented liberal party was organized to oppose the oligarchy. The prosperous bourgeoisie, the only possible support for such a party, was too estranged from the country to maintain such a party. Its place in politics was filled by a populist alternative—the Radical Party. This party was a mixture of declining members of the provincial branches of the oligarchy with populist support from the marginal city dwellers and some members of the native middle classes. The Radical Party, though not very radical, was too populistic, too unrespectable, to be a legitimate alternative. The enlightened leaders of the modernizing oligarchy were not able to import a legitimate two-party system. . . .

The contending conservatism and liberalism characteristic of Europe (and with different labels of North America) was therefore replaced in Argentina by Conservatism and Populism. . . . The Argentine intellectuals in the 1940's misinterpreted Peronismo as the local variety of the latest phenomenon in European history—Fascism.

With many of the strategic social groups opting out for a variety of reasons, the political system could be nothing but unstable. An effort to establish a two-party system was attempted by the oligarchy in 1912, with the establishment of universal male secret suffrage and orderly transmission of power to a Radical, popularly-elected president in 1916, Hipolito Yrigoyen. But this unstable arrangement could not withstand the impact of the world economic depression, and in 1930 an Army coup—the first successful one in almost seventy years—reverted direct power to the oligarchy.

Yrigoyen and his Radical Party could not resist the Army coup, because they were weak and lacked the support of any powerful social group in the community. Yrigoyen did not fall because his reforms were too mild and too unenthusiastically received by the masses. There were no demanding masses around, no popularly felt need for radical reform; urban workers were anarchists or socialists engaged in bread-and-butter unionism. The Radical Party fell because it had not allied itself strongly enough with the only class that could have been its support: the industrial and commercial bourgeoisie. To consolidate that alliance it would have needed, not a more radical policy, but rather a more business-minded one, to attract the traditionally nonparticipating foreign bourgeoisie. Though the bourgeoisie was inclined to favor the Radical Party, it didn't control it, didn't provide leadership, prestige symbols, or influence. The Radical Party, relying too much on populist elements, was tolerated by the oligarchy only as long as the economy was basically prosperous. Once the crisis came, the reins of the country were immediately taken back by the oligarchy; they could no longer rely on the administration of "untrustworthy" Radicals. The mass of the bourgeoisie, the intellectuals and the organized urban working class, were simply spectators of this process, rather amused to see the end of the Radical government, which they considered too moderate, too *criollo,* or too populist.

Soon after the coup the oligarchy tried to reestablish the liberal democratic system by calling elections in 1932. They staged elections in one province, lost, and decided to have another election; this time, to minimize risks, the Radicals were outlawed, and ballot-box stuffing took care of the remaining dangers. But this was not a stable solution. Changes in the Argentine economy brought about by the war undermined the oligarchy's attempt to reestablish its rule.

When the war broke out, Argentina was firmly controlled by an alliance between landed interests, exporting firms, and British imperialism, which controlled foreign-owned railways and other commercial enterprises. The Radicals, the Socialists, and the expanding Communist Party had accepted, for all practical purposes, their roles as loyal opposition to the Conservative government. Foreign migration was being absorbed to some extent, owing to the end of mass migration in the late twenties. The Radical Party, more an expression of the bourgeoisie than it was in the early part of the century, lost most of its populistic components. The assumption was that, provided good behavior lasted another decade, an orderly transfer of power to the Radicals could again be attempted.

But it was too late for this. New social forces had been growing. During the thirties the need to solve the crisis, and particularly the shortage of foreign exchange, led the Conservative government to control imports to some extent, despite its being basically against industrial protection. Protectionism was an unforeseen and unplanned consequence of the slump in exports. This gave impetus to some industrialization.

The real push, however, came with the war. Full protection was suddenly created, mostly in textiles and metallurgical products, which normally would have had to compete with American or European imports. A light industry of consumer goods

products was created and expanded, and many new entrepreneurs appeared. By 1949 industrial employment increased
68 percent from the 1925-29 level, to a large extent concentrated in Buenos Aires. Migration from the countryside to
Buenos Aires provided manpower; the traditional European
sources were no longer available. Net migration from the interior into the metropolitan Buenos Aires area had been at an
annual level of 8,000 people for many years before 1936.
Between that year and 1943 the annual average jumped to
72,000, and between 1943 and 1947 it reached 117,000
yearly.[3] The population of Buenos Aires, always a large city,
reached colossal proportions, including in its metropolitan
area 7,000,000 people by 1960—or a third of the country's
population.

This boom produced two new groups: the new industrial
working class, which nearly doubled its numbers in ten years,
and the new entrepreneurs. The latter, though less numerous
than the former, were at least as important as the new group
of workers in the political process of Argentina, if not more so.

The new recruits to the industrial labor force were traditionalistic with a rural outlook, and unaccustomed to class organization; they could therefore be easily incorporated into a populistic movement with leadership from *outside* the working class.
The old trade unions, with a long history of labor struggles,
had managed to organize the upper layers of the working class
and had about 300,000 members by the beginning of the war
boom. The influx of workers from the interior, plus the stirring
up of the lower sectors of the urban workers, set an insoluble
problem for the old leadership. The transition from elite unionism to mass unionism is always difficult and very often goes
hand in hand with a change in the established leadership. This
had happened in France during the Popular Front years, which
witnessed an increase in the CGT from about 300,000 members to over 2,000,000. A similar situation had evolved in the
United States with the growth of the CIO and the comparative
decline of the AFL during the 1930's. In Argentina the mass
unionization was pushed by the political forces around Perón,
who had come to power after the 1943 Army coup. The result
was the mass organization of the working class and the complete removal of the old union leadership. The new masses of
workers were easily managed from the top because of their lack
of organizational experience. But the workers were not com-

[3] See Gino Germani, *Estructura Social de la Argentina* (Buenos Aires:
Raigal, 1955).

pletely passive. The trade unions developed very quickly the characteristics of modern, bureaucratized, massive unionism.

To understand what led to the Army coup of 1943 and eventually to the rise to power of Juan Domingo Perón, we must refer to another, less conspicuous new social group produced by the war economy—the new industrialists.

The political structure evolved during the thirties by the Conservatives had no place for the new industrialists. Some of the traditional industrialists, especially those linked to the food-processing industries (wine, sugar, oil and flour mills, and meat packing) did adapt themselves to the Conservative system, mainly because they didn't need protection or at least didn't compete with products from the imperialist powers. But for the new industries catering to the domestic consumer goods market the situation was very different: it was a question of *Protección o Muerte*.

The existing system was not prepared to give them the strong tariff protection they needed. The large landowners didn't want to pay the costs of industrial protection. The middle classes and the upper sectors of the working class were not prepared, either, to pay the high costs of an inefficient local industry, which included higher prices, higher taxes, lower-quality goods, and antagonization of the traditional customers of Argentine wheat and beef, who wanted to sell their industrial products in exchange.

During the war, industry grew despite the lack of legal high tariffs because European and North American manufacturers could not export to Argentina. But the end of the war was a Damocles' sword hanging over the heads of the newly expanded industrialist sector. The intense war-induced expansion had taken effect and local industrialists were now preoccupied by the lack of legal tariff protection. An important group had arisen and had profited under the naturally protected war conditions. This new group was not represented in the traditional parties. The Conservatives were wedded to the ruling coalition of landed, exporting, and British imperial interests. The Radicals and the middle class, which supported them, were a loyal opposition to that system, opposing it on political and redistributive grounds, but they were not prepared to risk changing the basic economic structure. . . . The Unión Industrial Argentina, mouthpiece of the industrialist class, which was controlled by the older, established groups, was not prepared to support a risky program of out-and-out tariff protection. An added problem was that among the new industrialist groups there was an important component of ethnic minorities (Jewish and Arab), which, though not predominant, did evoke anti-Semitic sentiments among the traditional elite that weakened the strength of the entire group. And some expected a postwar pattern similar to that which followed the First World War. At that time, during Yrigoyen's first presidency, some industrial growth had taken place also, but the lack of tariff protection after the War had resulted in most of the industrialization of that period being wiped out. . . .

There was a difference between the two war periods, though. During the first war Argentinian industry had had only a very limited growth in terms both of people and capital involved, while during the second war a numerically stronger group of industrialists was created, who felt menaced by the end of the wartime economy.

The oligarchy had opted for British-American imperialism abroad, and for a limited version of constitutional democracy at home . . . with only minor adjustments of the electoral process by occasional and discreet ballot-box stuffing. The Radical, Socialist, and Communist opponents of the oligarchy were oriented toward an extension of democracy under the liberal constitutional system. The new disaffected group of industrialists wanted stronger medicine, without, of course, going too far to the Left.

The available ideology was a form of *Falangismo,* a Hispanic version of Fascism (at that time the main opponent of liberal capitalism), which favored a considerable amount of State intervention in the economy. Nationalism, an essential component of Falangister ideology, appealed particularly to the military, which always included an expansionist group dreaming of Argentinian predominance in Latin America. This ideology united the right-wing intelligentsia, traditionalistic Church interests, the restless Army generals, and the newly arisen marginal industrialists, who provided the realistic element in the coalition.

It was this *anti-status quo* elite, formed during the war years, that was finally successful in staging the Army coup in 1943, overthrowing the Conservative government. The formation of this political elite was not, of course, so simple or conscious as the foregoing description may make it seem. Social conditions made it possible for a prominent individual like Perón to play an important role at critical moments, but the main point is that the special conditions arising in Argentina as a result of the war made a sector of the upper and upper-middle classes (the new industrialists and related Army, Church, and rightist intelligentsia) available for political change. And this strongly disaffected group in the upper layers of the social hierarchy made possible the formation of an important *anti-status quo* elite, bent on social change, with considerable resources in terms of money, weapons, and—through the involvement of the Church—an ideology, a millennaristic set of beliefs to justify its actions.

The link between the leader and the masses was the other group of "new men" brought to the fore by the war, the new industrial workers. They and the Peronista elite complemented each other. Although they possessed very different social, ideological, and cultural backgrounds, their common aversion to the Conservative Establishment was for a time a solid basis for mutual understanding. Perón, one of the more intelligent of the Fascist-oriented Army colonels who had taken over power in 1943, found to his surprise that it was the urban masses, the working class, who were interested in what he had to say, not the middle classes. . . . Apart from the small elite drawn from marginal industrialists, Army officers, and traditionalistic, Hispanic sectors of the Church, Perón was opposed to a man by the oligarchy and the majority of the middle classes. Resenting his appeal to the working class, most industrialists were against him, as were the more traditional industrialists who controlled the Union Industrial Argentina. The middle class did not support the corporatist political solution; social conditions were absolutely different in Argentina from what they had been in Italy or Germany at the time of the Fascist takeover. The country was booming with wartime prosperity, mass unemployment did not exist, the middle classes were solidly liberal or liberal-conservative, and the same was true for the majority of the intellectuals and the students.

The original Peronista elite slowly found itself in a completely different position from the one it had thought it would occupy. Its allies were the mass of urban workers, and its enemies were the majority of the middle classes and bourgeoisie, as well as the landowners. Many of the original Fascist-inclined supporters of Perón were disillusioned and abandoned the movement, but others remained and changed their views (especially the industrialists and intellectuals). A considerable number of secondary-level leaders of the Socialist or Radical parties had second thoughts about Perón and flocked to his support. This had the effect of eliminating for all practical purposes the working-class support of the Socialists and the

Communists, which became more and more middle-class parties. Many Radical Party leaders, especially from the interior provinces, joined forces with Peronismo. By 1946, when rather free presidential elections were held, Perón was at the helm of a strong coalition, deriving support from various sources but mostly from three groups:

(1) The original elite, somewhat decimated, drawn from the marginal industrialists, Radical Right intellectuals, traditional Church groups, and armed forces with a Falangista inclination.

(2) The new masses, made up mostly of the recent arrivals from the countryside and those lower sectors of the urban working class that had never been organized before, but also comprising many old trade unionists who joined the coalition once its populist character was apparent.

(3) Some of the impoverished middle classes from the interior of the country, who had been excluded by the previous oligarchic system. Many of them were represented by old Radical Party leaders, and some Conservative caudillos who joined forces with Perón.

This is a typical populist coalition.[4] The charismatic appeal of a leader provides one of the main bonds of organization, and the various segments represent different and sometimes opposing economic interests. The success of this coalition was most emphatically *not* attributable to the charms of the leader but to social conditions that made the existence of at least two of the three constituent groups possible. This new creature, populism, which had not existed in Argentina for decades, was very different from one of its godparents, the pro-Fascist group that had ignited the coup against the Conservative regime in 1943. . . . Peronismo was not a Fascist movement but rather a popular nationalist expression similar to the nationalist parties that have led several African and Asian countries to independence and sometimes to radical reform (as in Guinea, Ghana, Egypt, and even India and Indonesia). The authoritarian features of the Peronista government were certainly present, but they were not necessarily characteristics of a Fascist regime. Rather, they seem to be highly necessary aspects of a developing coalition in a semicolonial country. . . .

Far from being Fascist, the Peronista movement staged what is up to this day the most revolutionary mass action in Argen-

[4] See Torcuato S. Di Tella, "Populism and Reform in Latin America," in Claudio Veliz (ed.), *Obstacles to Change in Latin America* (London: Oxford University Press, 1965).

tinian history, the famous 17th of October, 1945. On that day the masses of the working class poured into the downtown area in large numbers, defying possible military and police repression to defend their leader, who was threatened by a stillborn conservative Army coup. Whatever the incongruities of this political act, it was the main expression of working-class power to this day in Argentina. It was an expression of class power, and as such it has taken permanent roots in the collective subconscious of the Argentinian working class, becoming as important a symbol for future actions as for decades the General Strike was for European workers.

The Peronista government undertook, as one of its main policies, an out-and-out tariff protection for local industry. In this way the dismantling of existing enterprises that took effect after the First World War was not reproduced. The IAPI (Instituto Argentino de Promoción del Intercambio), a State monopoly for the export of farm produce, sold at international prices the agricultural products it had bought at half their price. The huge profits made in this way were used for the government programs of social security and protection of industry.

However, because of pressures from industrial groups and because of the lack of expert staffs, there was no efficient economic planning. Indeed, from the 1945-1949 period till the present time there has been an almost absolute stagnation of industrial output and employment.[5] The important feat of the Peronista postwar economic policy was the rescue of Argentinian industry from the catastrophe that would have befallen it if prewar economic practices had been resumed. This was possible only because of the efforts of the special coalition that brought Perón to power. To criticize the economic planning of Perón is to miss the point: at that time the essential thing was to protect local industry at any cost, and this could be done only through the combination of disparate social forces in a populist coalition. From the viewpoint of national economic development it was better to have protection with bad planning and even corruption than to have good technical planning without protection. . . .

Great prosperity existed in the immediate postwar years. A considerable egalitarian redistribution of income and power between social classes took place in this period. The regime could be called Bonapartist because it represented a sector of

[5] See Aldo Ferrer, *The Argentine Economy* (Berkeley: University of California Press, 1967), p. 167.

the upper classes allied to unorganized and lumpenproletariat sectors of the working classes. Though this was part of the picture, it was not the whole picture. The organized working-class element in the coalition was much too big for the Bonapartist model, and it grew more and more important as time passed. The Peronista Party *was* a multiclass coalition, but its working-class component was not so hamstrung as is sometimes supposed. On the other hand, it is true that the working class never really exercised power during Perón's regime, and that the trade unions were very much controlled from Government circles (though they were never as directly run from Government departments as their counterparts in Brazil or Mexico).

By 1949 prosperity was coming to an end. By 1955 the terms of trade had deteriorated by about 30 percent over the last decade or so, slashing a large chunk of the country's foreign earnings with the harmful results one could expect in a country strongly dependent on export earnings. Though by this time exports were no longer so important a part of the national product as they had been in the early part of the century (they had diminished from about 25 percent to less than 10 percent), they were still very strategic in determining the availability of foreign exchange for capital goods.

With the onset of the lean years, social tensions within the ruling coalition emerged. It was difficult to keep everybody content. The working-class was the least well treated. As a result, a cooling-off of popular enthusiasm, if not support, set in, and the attacks from the oligarchy had greater possibility of success. The Church was one of the first groups to realize this situation and to dissociate itself as far as possible from the regime, with which it had had a number of very intimate links from the first. A number of steps were taken, among them the training of some labor leaders in Church-run schools, independent of the official Peronista-controlled institutions. A serious conflict between the Peronista government and the Catholic Church finally led to a complete break. The Government abolished religious education (which it had enacted) in public schools and legislated divorce laws. . . .

The Church, as usual, played its hand with greater skill and operated mostly within its own privately run associations, while the Government had to mobilize the legal system, or take police measures, which got much publicity. The Church sensed that Perón's days were numbered. Economic decline and the loss of prestige, coupled with the greater likelihood of success for the Conservative coups that were being tried every other year or so, caused the turn in Church attitude. Perón, in view of this betrayal by his erstwhile supporter, was forced to strike back, especially after the final part of 1954. . . . The reaction was soon to come. Many more of the old members of the Peronista alliance went into opposition, particularly the military and Church sectors, and finally an Army coup in 1955 ended the Peronista regime.

In the last years of Perón's rule the industrial sector of his coalition had drifted. They had become an accepted, though junior, partner of the oligarchy. Overcoming their fears of the war period, they sought stability to safeguard their success. But though they still needed protection, they had consolidated their position in Argentinian society and in the upper-class circles. Their interests were safe, and they didn't need to rely on populist combinations to exert a countervailing power against the oligarchy. They perceived any "populist solution" as dangerous, because nobody could be sure that the worker wouldn't get out of hand at the least-expected moment.

A certain "self-fulfilling prophecy" set in. The very fact that the industrialists—together with their associated military and Church elements—were no longer enthusiastic about the regime prompted Perón to lean on the workers, particularly after the first blows had been exchanged with the Church, which in turn alienated the industrialists even more, and so on. . . .

With its bourgeois support reabsorbed into the rest of the upper and upper-middle classes, with conditions becoming more "normal," the Peronista coalition was finished, and it soon lost its other non-working-class sector, the provincial middle classes. In the 1957 trial elections the Peronista political party was prohibited. It showed its strength by turning out 30 percent of the vote (by blank vote), which was still very much the greatest single electoral vote, but it was no longer the absolute majority party. The reduction from the early high popularity to this new and more moderate level came about partly because the party lacked legal access to mass media and full use of propaganda devices. Subsequent elections have shown that the force of Peronismo hovers about the 35-percent mark. The decline can be partly attributed to the departure from the coalition of the bourgeois elements, which did not account directly for much of the vote but which provided the organizational capacity and the leadership to mobilize the rather passive masses in the more backward parts of the country. These unorganized groups relapsed into apathy or into supporting the local conservative or radical caudillos.

But the fact that the coalition broke up didn't mean that this was the end of Peronismo. The third leg of the stool was strong enough, by now, to stand on its own; the trade union sector had steadily grown during the later years of Perón's rule and a new generation of unionists had come to the fore. Though they enjoyed State support, their unions were modern mass-based organizations and showed this characteristic very clearly after the downfall of Perón. The Aramburu regime intervened in the unions, attempting to replace the old leadership by new "democratic" unionists, but the workers rejected these leaders and after a couple of years most unions were again in Peronista hands. The trade unions were led by the new generation, less familiar with the experience of State patronage and occasional corruption. Since then the Peronista leadership in the CGT (Confederación General de Trabajadores) has been firmly entrenched and has shown its capacity to withstand successfully strong Government pressures against its independence. The Peronista movement, far from disintegrating, has been concentrated around the union movement, which holds most of the funds and power. Very few industrialists, right-wing intellectuals, high Church dignitaries, or military men are now to be found among the Peronistas. Peronismo is more a labor- and trade-unionist-oriented party, with a very definitely reformist outlook and with strong organizational and emotional links to the mass of the working class. Peronismo maintains its traditions, its folklore, and when the law permits, its name, but it is an altogether different animal. The fact that it has become more working-class-based than before has not resulted in a revolutionary or radical tendency in the party. On the contrary, this working-class base rather makes the party more reformist than before. The violent sectors in Peronismo were not based in the working class but originated in the early non-working-class elite, which had largely abandoned the Peronista coalition and was full of authoritarian and semi-Falangist ideas. The workers followed their natural inclination, which, as Lenin diagnosed several decades ago, tends toward bread-and-butter trade unionism when there is no revolutionary party around to change their minds. In fact, the Peronista organization and the strength of emotional allegiances is one of the main impediments to that kind of revolution.

The old Peronista coalition, then, is dead, but Peronismo as a labor movement is very much alive. There are two major currents of opinion within this movement. The remains of the non-working-class components of the old coalition, generally designated as the "political wing" of the movement, include a motley combination of politicos of various persuasions, mostly centrist, with important Catholic components. Then there is the main trade-union leadership, highly bureaucratized with complex, very efficient, and well-financed organizations that spend billions of pesos a year in social services for the membership. The total affiliation with the CGT is at about the 3-million mark. Dues collection is efficient, in some cases through direct or State-sponsored union-shop agreements, though in all cases the funds are controlled by genuine trade unionists, with no State interference. The dominant group of union leaders, of whom the best-known is the metallurgical workers' Augusto Vandor, is moderate and reformist, representative of the present mood of the majority of the working class. Leftist elements in the Peronist union movement control some minor unions, or local branches, and have important cadres in the youth organization. The anti-Marxist elements of Peronismo are fast disappearing, owing to the loss of the traditional non-working-class component of the coalition (from which anti-Marxist ideas emanated), and the party is coming to resemble ever more a Labor party with right and left wings.

The division between the Peronista union leadership and the intellectuals persists. The intellectuals either retain too many of their liberal prejudices against the movement or else have gone over to an extreme leftist position, which, though in theory favorable to Peronismo, attacks the leadership, the middle-level leaders, and the ideology as too reformist. The long-run trend is toward unity between these groups, but the process is slow.

If the Peronista movement is becoming a Labor party, why, then, should there be such an amount of social tension in Argentina? What is the basis for the continuing fears of the military that the Peronistas would be a first step toward Communism or social revolution?

. . . Tensions are not strong enough to make the power struggle explosive. Pressure groups have sufficient strength to keep other groups out of complete power, but no single group can completely control the situation. Therefore, Argentina is stuck with pluralism—or poliarchy, if one prefers. Since the downfall of Peronismo we have alternated between civilian (Radical Party) governments and military interventions, the last led by General Ongañia in June 1966. But military efforts to liquidate the Peronista Party or the trade unions have been unsuccessful. The stalemate situation continues. . . . The only major group to suffer in recent events was the University, with which the Government interfered, and most of its modern and progressive professors had to resign and leave the country. . . . In the next years the main test will come in the confrontation between the oligarchy (which has an important say in the present Ongañia regime) and the Peronistas. The military by themselves have little strength. The most likely outcome is that the military-favored measures will not solve the country's economic problems, so the military will lose prestige and support and will be forced to give way to a civilian regime in a couple of years or so. A civilian regime, of course, is no panacea, but there is absolutely no panacea and no solution in the immediate future to Argentina's economic problems. . . .

Political Generations in the Cuban Working Class[1]

MAURICE ZEITLIN

Common struggles develop a sense of social solidarity and revolutionary consciousness in the exploited classes; and such struggles may have enduring political significance not always visible on the surface. In Cuba, Zeitlin shows that this happened in the working class. Political generations emerged as the result of the impact on them of distinct historical experiences; and the response of these working-class generations to the Cuban revolution is understandable in terms of these experiences. The oldest workers, the "generation of the thirties," who were young men during the mass working-class and student insurrection and its subsequent suppression by Batista, under United States aegis, were second in the likelihood of supporting the Revolutionary Government only to the workers of the "rebel generation" formed during the anti-Batista movement.

Reprinted from *The American Journal of Sociology*, Vol. LXXI, No. 5 (March 1966), pp. 493-508, by permission of The University of Chicago Press. This article also appears, with some revisions, as Chapter 9 in Maurice Zeitlin, *Revolutionary Politics and the Cuban Working Class* (Princeton, N. J.: Princeton University Press, 1967).

[1] A brief portion of this article appeared in "Political Attitudes of Cuban Workers," a paper delivered at the meetings of the American Sociological Association, August 1963. I am indebted to the Center of International Studies, Princeton University, for a grant that made my research for this study possible and to its director, Klaus Knorr, for his encouragement. I should also like to acknowledge the theoretical stimulation provided by Norman Ryder's unpublished paper, "The Cohort as a Concept in the Study of Social Change," delivered at the meetings of the American Sociological Association, August 1959, and the helpful suggestions of my colleagues, Michael T. Aiken, Jerald Hague, and Gerald Marwell.

THE CONCEPT of political generation focuses on the intersection of biography, history, and social structure. It thus compels us to pay attention to variables of explanatory value that we might otherwise overlook. However, despite the wide interpretive use to which some variant of the concept of generation has been put (whether, for example, in creative literature, literary criticism, or qualitative political analysis), its use has been infrequent in the sociological analysis of politics, and especially so in the analysis of data gathered through survey research methods.[2] The most significant lack in this area is of studies of the formation of political generations elsewhere than in the advanced industrial societies of the West.[3]

This paper is about the formation of political generations in the Cuban working class and the relevance of these generations for the recent social revolution. Its thesis is that (a) different political generations were formed among the Cuban workers as a result of the impact on them of distinct historical experiences and that (b) the differential response of the generations to the revolution is understandable in terms of these experiences.

My approach to the specific problem of generations in Cuba is based essentially on Karl Mannheim's general formulation of the problem. He suggested that common experiences during their youth might create a common world view or frame of reference from which individuals of the same age group would tend to view their subsequent political experiences. Sharing the same year of birth, they "are endowed, to that extent, with a common location in the historical dimension of the social process." Much like the effect of class on its members, the generation also limits its members "to a specific range of potential experience, predisposing them for a certain characteristic mode of thought and experience, and *a characteristic type of historically relevant action.*" (Italics mine.)[4]

[2] Seymour Martin Lipset, for instance, recently noted again that, "unfortunately, there has been no attempt to study systematically the effect of generation experiences with modern survey research techniques" (*Political Man* [Garden City, N.Y.: Doubleday & Co., 1960], p. 265). The statement also appeared much earlier in Lipset, Paul F. Lazarsfeld, Allen Barton, and Juan Linz, "The Psychology of Voting," in G. Lindsey (ed.), *Handbook of Social Psychology* (Cambridge, Mass.: Addison-Wesley Publishing Co., 1954), II, 1124-70.

[3] See, however, S. N. Eisenstadt, *From Generation to Generation* (Glencoe, Ill.: Free Press, 1956), and Alex Inkeles and Raymond Bauer, *The Soviet Citizen* (Cambridge, Mass.: Harvard University Press, 1961).

[4] "The Problem of Generations," in Mannheim's *Essays on the Sociology of Knowledge*, ed. Paul Kecksckemeti (New York: Oxford University Press, 1952), p. 286.

From the standpoint of our analysis, it is particularly significant that the Cubans themselves see their history to a great extent in generational terms, a fact that is not at all surprising, given the dramatic and profoundly traumatic nature of the events that formed several Cuban generations. Cuban literature —political, historical, fictional—is replete with references to the "generation of '68" or the "generation of '95" or the "generation of the thirties," generations formed during singularly significant historical epochs in Cuba: respectively, the Ten Years' War against Spain (1868-78), the War of Independence (1895-98), and the abortive revolution of the thirties (1933-35). It is especially significant that the movement led by Fidel Castro, in common with other revolutionary nationalist and anticolonial movements, placed special emphasis on its being a new generation, shorn of the cynicism and the betrayal of revolutionary ideals typical of its elders. The movement's cadre consisted predominantly of young people in their late teens and early twenties and, to this extent, shared with other revolutionary youth movements an identification of the general social movement with their particular generation.[5]

The very first lines of the manifesto of the 26th of July Movement, which stated its general aims in the anti-Batista struggle, were: "The 26th of July Movement is resolved to take up the unfulfilled ideals of the Cuban nation and to realize them, . . . [counting] on the contribution and the presence of the reserves of *youth* who are anxious for new horizons in the chronic frustration of the Republic. *That is its credential and its distinctive feature."* (Italics mine.) The manifesto condemned "the colonial mentality, foreign economic domination, [and] political corruption" of the republic, and the regime of exploitation and oppression installed by Batista, and implicitly repudiated the older generation, saying that only the youth of the country had resisted this "storm of horror and shame' without bowing. The movement traced its roots directly to the revolutionary students and workers of the "generation of the thirties," who also had fought against "the intact chains of the past" and who, "in the 'hundred days' that the revolutionary forces held power . . . did more in the defense of the interests of the nation and of the people than all of the governments of the preceding thirty years."[6]

[5] See Eisenstadt, *op. cit.*, p. 311.
[6] "Manifiesto-programa del Movimiento 26 de Julio," Appendix to Enrique González Pedrero, *La revolución cubana* (Mexico City: Universidad Nacional Autónoma de Mexico, 1959), pp. 89-91, 97-99, 103-5, and 125.

On the one hand, the young rebels of the 26th of July Movement identified with the generation of the thirties, its accomplishments and aspirations; on the other, they condemned that generation for its failure to fulfill the ideals of its youth and for its capitulation to reaction—a capitulation that led, they believed, to the need for the revolutionary movement of their own generation.

Not only did this generational animus characterize a good deal of the rebel movement before the conquest of power, but apparently it also has continued as one significant source of self-identification since the revolution. In one of his first public speeches (on January 8, 1959) after the fall of Batista's regime, Castro again identified the youth of his generation as one of the decisive social bases of the revolution:

"When the 26th of July Movement organized itself and initiated the war, it . . . was evident that the . . . Movement had the sympathy of the people, and . . . that it had *the nearly unanimous support of the youth of Cuba.*"[7] (Italics mine.)

The generation of '53, the generation of Castro and his fellow rebels, is held up as a model of sacrifice and heroism on the nation's behalf. Its special quality has been reiterated in many speeches by Castro. "Ours is the generation for which no one set a good example . . . but it drew upon itself for the idealism, virtue, and courage necessary to save the country . . . *It is the best generation that the nation has had.* It grew up in the midst of negation and bad examples. But the coming generation will be better than ours. It will be inspired not only by the generations of '68 and '95 but also by *the generation of 1953.*"[8] (Italics mine.)

Thus, as a result of having lived through a history of rather abrupt social and political transitions and clearly demarcated political intervals, Cubans apparently have developed a relatively high level of generational self-consciousness. Stated formally, the major hypothesis of this paper is that *the specific historical period in which succeeding generations of workers first became involved in the labor movement had significant consequences for the formation of their political outlooks.* Shaped by the early experiences of their youth in the labor movement—that movement's conflicts, organization, tactics

[7] *Guía del pensamiento político económico de Fidel* (Havana: Diario Libre, 1959), p. 44.
[8] *Ibid.*

and strategy, ideology, and leadership—working-class political generations emerged in Cuba with measurably different attitudes toward the Castro revolution.

For our purposes, the concept of political generation will be defined, as Rudolf Heberle has put it, as "those individuals of approximately the same age who have shared, at the same age, certain politically relevant experiences."[9] The concept leaves open to empirical investigation the decision as to (a) which age groups to isolate for analysis and (b) which experiences to delineate as of decisive political relevance for that age group.[10]

Thus, in our analysis of political generations in the Cuban working class and their contemporary relevance in the context of the revolution, two strategic methodological decisions were necessary: (1) which age category or categories to locate in time and (2) in which historical periods, depending on which experiences were hypothesized to be politically relevant.

1. Normative expectations of political involvement in Cuba were established and perpetuated by the political activities of students, whose agitation and action since the foundation of the republic were often decisively bound up with the politics of the working class—whether, for instance, in the anti-Spanish colonial struggle for independence or in the abortive revolution of the thirties. The late teens and early twenties have been viewed in Cuba as a period in life demanding political commitment and involvement—the period of coming to manhood politically. In two of Cuba's most significant political periods, the political cadre that predominated in the movement of young men and women, the short-lived government of Ramón Grau San Martín during the revolution of the thirties rested to a considerable extent on the support of the youth. Raúl Roa, a student leader at that time, and now foreign minister of Cuba, dubbed that regime "the ephebocracy," or teenage government.[11] And in the guerrilla struggle and urban *resistencia* against Batista, men and women in their late teens and early twenties apparently formed the majority of the movement's

---

[9] Rudolf Heberle, *Social Movements* (New York: Appleton-Century Crofts, 1951), pp. 119-20.

[10] This concept is essentially identical with the concept of "cohort" used in demographic analysis; see Ryder, *op. cit.*

[11] Teresa Casuso, *Cuba and Castro* (New York: Random House, 1961), p. 64. Miss Casuso's work emphasizes especially strongly the generational politics of Cuba (see esp. pp. 77 ff).

leaders and cadre, whatever their class of origin.[12] On these grounds I chose the age category of eighteen to twenty-five to locate the generations temporally.

In addition, I chose this age category on more general sociological grounds. First, the meaning of age varies in accordance with social norms governing specific activities and their relationship to age, and it is precisely at the age at which coming to manhood is normatively defined that the individual becomes more responsive to the impact of social change, since he is relatively less subject to parental influence in his new role. That is, it is likely that the individual who has come of age is more "responsive to the impact of social change" than the child who is still "insulated from it by his home environment."[13] It is, therefore, reasonable to assume that the experiences of workers in the period after they enter the labor force, assume their own support, and are no longer under parental supervision would be particularly significant to them, especially if this occurs in a period of social upheaval.

Second, it is a central assumption here that the social pressures arising out of the work situation are fundamental in determining the worker's political outlook. The work place is probably the most important source of the worker's political socialization, more so than for nonworkers. A recent study found, for example, that French workers were more likely than

[12] Exact information is difficult, if not impossible, to obtain about the ages even of top revolutionary leaders, let alone of typical rebel cadre members. Fidel Castro's biographies are not consistent; Spanish sources usually place his birth date at August 13, 1927, English at August 13, 1926. See Gerardo Rodríguez Morejon, *Fidel Castro: Biografia* (Havana: P. Fernández, 1959), and such American sources as Jules Dubois, *Fidel Castro: Rebel Liberator or Dictator* (Chicago: Bobbs-Merrill Co., 1959), and Robert Taber, *M-26: Biography of a Revolution* (New York: Lyle Stuart, Publisher, 1961). Nonetheless, from talking to individuals who "should know" in a variety of positions in Cuba, including *comandantes*, administrative personnel, and union officials, aside from the workers interviewed in our study who had fought in the hills, a consensus emerged that the typical age of the rebel youth was about 18-25 years in 1952, when Batista came to power. Relatively reliable ages of some of the more important leaders in 1962, when we did our research in Cuba, were: Fidel Castro, 35; Ernesto "Che" Guevara, 34; Raúl Castro, 30; Armando Hart, 31; Osmany Cienfuegos, 32; Augusto Martínez Sánchez, 36. Camilo Cienfuegos, one of Fidel's top *comandantes* during the guerrilla war, who died in a plane crash in 1959, was about 30 when he died; Enrique Oltuski, a leader of the urban *resistencia*, was 31 in 1962; Faustino Pérez, coordinator of the abortive 1958 general strike and head of the urban *resistencia*, 31; Vilma Espin, Raúl's wife and an active leader of the *resistencia*, known romantically as "Deborah" during the war, was 28; Haydee Santamaría, another rebel heroine, 32.

[13] Herbert Hyman, *Political Socialization* (Glencoe, Ill.: Free Press, 1959), p. 131.

other Frenchmen to discuss politics at work.[14] Much of the most significant political socialization of workers—insofar as that involves assimilation of the political orientations current in their class—occurs after the inception of their work career. This being so, crucial historical events impinging on the working class are more likely to affect a worker's personal politics if he has been working for a few years than if he has just begun. These are additional reasons why I chose to focus on historical events when workers were in their late teens and early twenties rather than when they were younger.

2. From the standpoint of our analysis of political generations, five critical periods in Cuban political history of the past several decades can be distinguished. Their general social conditions, political issues, and "concrete internal political and social struggles"[15] constitute the decisive politically relevant experiences of succeeding Cuban generations—that is, of those who were eighteen to twenty-five years old when each of these critical periods began. In Table 1, I have briefly indicated the decisive events of each political generation analyzed in this paper and the predicted political consequences of those events. These events deserve fuller descriptions, nonetheless, so that the reader can ponder their significance for himself.

Sugar speculation in the aftermath of World War I ended abruptly with Cuba's economic collapse in the early 1930's (partly as a consequence of the Great Depression in the United States), and a period of social upheaval began. Working-class and student political strikes throughout the country resulted not only in the overthrow of the repressive Machado regime but also in increasingly more militant political initiatives. These included the students' taking control of the University of Havana and demanding its "autonomy" from government interference and the workers' occupation of several railroad terminals, public utilities, ports, thirty-six sugar centrals, and a number of adjoining towns, in many of which they established "soviets" of workers, peasants, and soldiers. Students, young intellectuals, and workers, aside from taking independent political action, were in liaison with each other, with the former acting in many instances as workers' delegates to the short-lived radical nationalist Grau regime. The young Communist party was dominant in the leadership of the workers, and,

[14] Richard Hamilton, *Affluence and the French Worker in The Fourth Republic* (Princeton, N.J.: Princeton University Press), Chapter IV.
[15] Heberle, *op. cit.*, pp. 122-23.

TABLE 1

TEMPORAL LOCATION AND DECISIVE POLITICAL EVENTS OF POLITICAL
GENERATIONS, AND PREDICTED POLITICAL CONSEQUENCES

AGE CATEGORY AT TIME OF STUDY (1962)	PERIOD THAT BEGAN WHEN WORKERS WERE 18-25	DECISIVE POLITICALLY RELE-VANT EVENTS	PREDICTED RANK OF GENERATION'S SUPPORT FOR	
			COMMU-NISTS	REVOLU-TION
21-27	1959 on	Establishment of the revolutionary government and ensuing revolutionary changes, including nationalization of industry and declaration of "socialist" regime	*	4
28-35	1952/53-58	Batista's coup; guerrilla war and urban resistance led by Castro; agitation and organization in working class; rebirth of working-class economic struggle; abortive national general strike; fall of Batista	3	1
36-43	1944-51	Relative political democracy and economic stability; alliance of government and anti-Communist labor officials; purge of Communists from CTC† leadership	4	5
44-51	1936/37-43	Suppression of insurrection; reemergence of Communist leadership of labor movement; collaboration with Batista; achievement of tangible socioeconomic benefits for organized workers	2	2
52-59	1928-35	Mass working-class and student insurrection; "dual power" of "Soviets" under Communist leadership; establishment of radical nationalist regime	1	2

* The youngest generation's response to the Communists before the revolution is excluded here and in the following tables, since the question refers to an attitude held before they were adults.

† Confederación de Trabajadores de Cuba.

despite the equivocal role of the Communists in the final overthrow of the Machado regime, they maintained and increased their influence among the workers throughout the revolutionary period. Repression of the revolutionary movement by Fulgencio Batista, who had led a revolt of the enlisted men and the noncommissioned officers and gained leadership of the army, led to his consolidation of power in late 1936 and early 1937.

The suppression of the revolution, forceful dissolution of working-class organizations, and the advent on the international Communist scene of the Popular Front period resulted in the transformation of the radical and independent workers' movement into a reformist movement under Communist leadership, which inaugurated an era of government-labor collaboration. The relative stability and economic security in Cuba during World War II accentuated even further the reformism of the workers' movement, as well as its growing bureaucratization. Under Communist leadership the organized workers were able to gain certain tangible economic and social benefits.

Batista relinquished power in 1944, and a period of relative political democracy began—a period, however, that also included an alliance of the government and anti-Communist labor officials that increasingly used extralegal and violent methods to harass the Communist leadership of the labor movement. The Communists were thus finally ousted in 1947 from official leadership of the Confederación de Trabajadores de Cuba (CTC), the national labor organization the Communists themselves had formed in 1938 under Batista's aegis. The growing bureaucratization of the unions, their loss of contact with the mass of the workers, and their collaboration with the government was heightened during this period of comparative internal economic stability and "prosperity."

CTC officials, under the leadership of Eusebio Mujal (whence comes the derogatory term *mujalista*), did not resist Batista's *coup d'état* of March 1952, in which he regained power. In the years following, and throughout the guerrilla war and *resistencia,* the CTC was largely an appendage of the regime and was often used as a weapon against the workers themselves; and the already significant union corruption of prior years became increasingly supplemented by gangsterism and intimidation of the workers. The Communists, having lost the government's tutelage and having been outlawed by Batista, regained a measure of grassroots influence among the workers and led some important victorious strikes, especially in the sugar industry. But the regime fell not as the result of a working-class insurrection, which never materialized on a mass level, but as the result of conflict with the guerrilla forces and urban *resistencia* under the leadership of Castro's 26th of July Movement, whose cadre included predominantly young men and women. Until the final demise of the regime in 1959, their age peers, whether active in the anti-Batista movement or not, and whatever their class, were both more suspect to the police and the military and more likely than Cubans of other ages to suffer arbitrarily at the hands of the regime.[16]

The role of the workers in the anti-Batista struggle contrasts strikingly with their decisive insurrectionary role against the Machado regime. Nonetheless, the years of the Batista regime saw a reinvigoration of the Cuban tradition of independent working-class economic struggle—under the leadership of Communists and non-Communists alike. The apparent political quiescence of the workers should not be exaggerated. For instance, in the 1955 strike in the sugar industry there were several militant actions, the sugar workers were joined by other workers in cities such as Santa Clara and some sugar towns of Camaguey and Havana provinces, and their economic demands became coupled with such political slogans as "Down with the criminal government!"

In eastern Cuba and in Santiago, Cuba's second largest city, there were especially significant instances of working-class political support of the anti-Batista movement. A spontaneous political strike set off by the funeral of two young 26th of July leaders on August 1, 1957, spread from Santiago to other cities in Oriente Province and several towns throughout the country. The strike was complete in Santiago, shutting down the Nicaro nickel plant and shops in the city for five days. In subsequent months "strike committees" were organized in many plants by 26th of July organizers and other opposition elements in preparation for a general strike in 1958. The general strike, called for April 9, 1958, collapsed in several hours in Havana, with little mass support; but it completely paralyzed industry and commerce in Santiago, where the workers stayed out despite the regime's threats of arrest and its offers of immunity from prosecution to anyone killing an advocate of the strike. Despite their failure to overthrow the regime, then, the events mentioned here were certainly significant in the move-

[16] "The most barbaric methods of torture, not excluding castration, were daily incidents in the police stations, where *the groans of a whole generation of youths* were heard as they were tortured for information, or for having aided the revolutionary movement" (Casuso, *op. cit.,* p. 134; italics mine). Miss Casuso resigned her position as Cuban ambassador to the United Nations in 1960 and sought asylum in the United States. Similar descriptions of the Batista regime's arbitrary violence against young people during the guerrilla war appear in all accounts of this period, such as Dubois, *op. cit.;* Taber, *op. cit.;* and Ray Brennan, *Castro, Cuba, and Justice* (New York: Doubleday & Co., 1959).

ment against Batista's regime and must have affected the workers' political outlook.[17]

If it is correct that the struggle against Batista and the events flowing from it were of decisive significance in shaping the political outlook of the workers of this generation of '53, then clearly they should be far more likely than the members of other generations to support the revolution. How correct this inference is, and the evidence regarding it, will be seen below. First, however, we must briefly describe our methods.

The data for this study are drawn from interviews with industrial workers in Cuba in the summer of 1962. By that time the revolutionary government had clearly consolidated its power (the Bay of Pigs invasion being a year in the past); the original relatively undifferentiated popular euphoria had already been replaced by relatively clear lines of social cleavage generated in response to actions taken by the revolutionary government; it was two years since the nationalization of industry and more than a year since Castro had declared the revolution to be "socialist." A study of the differential appeals of the ideology and social content of the revolution to Cuban workers could now be meaningful and valuable.

Interviews were carried out with a randomly selected sample of 202 industrial workers employed in twenty-one plants widely scattered throughout the island's six provinces. Plants were chosen from a list of all those functioning under the direction of the Ministry of Industries.[18]

The plants were selected by means of a self-weighting random sample in which the probability that a plant would be chosen was directly proportional to the number of workers employed in it. This sampling method tended to exclude the smaller industrial establishments ("chinchales") that abound in Cuba. In each plant ten workers were selected by a method

[17] For a more detailed account of these events, see Maurice Zeitlin, "Working Class Politics in Cuba: A Study in Political Sociology" (Ph.D. dissertation, University of California, Berkeley, 1964), and the references therein.

[18] The Ministry of Industries facilitated the completion of this study by providing me with credentials to the administration of the plants I wanted to visit. There was no interference with the wording or content of any questions, nor was there any prearranged schedule for my arrival at the plants, nor, it was evident, had the administrators or union heads been informed of my impending arrival. On several occasions administrators or personnel chiefs phoned Havana to check my credentials and my insistence that I had permission (which was apparently unbelievable to administrators trying to raise production levels) to take ten workers from their work for as long as the interviews required.

designed to obtain a simple random sample. My wife and I each separately interviewed five workers per plant, in Spanish. All interviewing was done in complete privacy, in a location provided within the work center, such as a storage room, an office, or a classroom. We told each worker interviewed (as well as anyone else concerned) that I was a correspondent for *The Nation;* that we had permission from the Ministry of Industries, the plant administration, and the union delegate to interview workers in the plant; that the worker was chosen by a scientific method of randomization; that he would not be identified personally in any way; and that his answers would be entirely anonymous; we simply wanted to know his opinions about some things at work and in Cuba in general to be able to write an objective report about the condition of the Cuban working class.[19]

It might be objected, of course, that such survey research could not obtain meaningful results since Cuba was already a police state in the summer of 1962. This obviously pertinent question cannot be discussed at length here. The reader will have to be content with the elliptical assertion that this objection is without foundation and that in our observation Cubans could and did inquire and speak freely about whatever they wished—at that time. There were no formal safeguards of freedom of speech and association, and the potentialities for totalitarian rule were great, but that potential had yet to become a reality. We were able to carry out our interviewing without disturbance or interference of any kind and to obtain, I believe, data quite as valid as those obtained in any competent survey research.[20]

The interview schedule began with questions that were, on the surface, far removed from political issues of any kind. These questions pertained to length of residence in a particular place, length of time working in the work place, and so on.

[19] Eight of the 210 workers selected for the sample refused to be interviewed, were not replaced by others, and are not included in our tables. As a precaution, the 8 were included in parallel runs defined as "hostile" to the revolution, and every significant relationship was either the same or strengthened.

[20] Professor Dudley Seers, the well-known British economist, who was also doing research in Cuba at that time, has referred to some preliminary findings of my study as follows: "[Zeitlin's] findings are not inconsistent with the general impression we all [Seers and his coauthors] formed during our stay in Cuba, where we traveled the length of the island and conversed with hundreds of people. (In general there was clearly little hesitation on their part about speaking their minds.)" (Seers [ed.], *Cuba: The Economic and Social Revolution* [Chapel Hill: University of North Carolina Press, 1964], p. 394, n. 70, and p. 31.)

Questions of more or less obvious political content came somewhere in the middle of the interview. Five of these, which I think together adequately indicate how the workers view the revolution, were combined into an "index of attitude toward the revolution." Of these five questions, two were open-ended and three were forced-choice questions.

The open-ended questions were: (1) "Speaking generally, what are the things about this country that you are most proud of as a Cuban?"[21] and (2) "What sort [*clase*] of people govern this country now?"

One hundred and fifteen workers gave answers to the first question that were favorable to the revolution. A response was considered "favorable" only if it clearly indicated, or explicitly stated, support for the revolution.[22]

The workers could be especially blunt, as was a young worker at a paper-milling plant in Cardenas, whose answer was simply, "Of nothing, *chico* . . . I don't like Communism," or a West Indian cement worker (with two teenage daughters in the militia) in Mariel, who explained (in English): "I stay only because I have two daughters who will not leave—otherwise I'd go away. . . . No one bothers me, I just do not like it. Why? I can't say why. I guess I just prefer the old Cuba."

In contrast to these clearly hostile remarks were such noncommittal replies as a shoemaker's: "Of our movies and our athletes"; or a brewery worker's equivocal: "I am a peaceful worker. I have no passionate interest in anything. After my work I pass my time in my house in Manacas with my little one and my wife"; or a cigar-maker's witty but equally noncommittal: "Our women and our cigars."

Occasionally a revolutionary worker would wax poetic, as did a copper miner in Matahambre: "Cuba is a cup of gold to me. It is the only country in the world that is now moving forward." A sugar worker's simple statement was more typical, however: "'I earn good money now. I lack nothing. . . . All of the workers are with the revolution." A Havana brewery worker said: "I am content with the revolution in general. . . . For the first time one can do what one wants without fear."

[21] This question was borrowed from the study then in progress by Gabriel Almond and Sidney Verba, *Civic Culture* (Princeton, N.J.: Princeton University Press, 1963), and my use of it is hereby gratefully acknowledged.

[22] Mention of the revolution itself, of the "socialist government," of specific economic and social reforms of the revolutionary government, of increased work security since the revolution, etc., were counted as "favorable." All other responses, whether more or less "neutral" or "clearly hostile," were classified simply as "not clearly favorable."

One hundred and twenty-five workers replied to the second question in terms clearly favorable to the revolution. Given the double meaning in Spanish of the word "clase," which can mean "type," "sort," or "kind," as well as "class," the workers could, of course, choose to interpret the question's meaning in a number of ways. As with the preceding question, we counted as "favorable" replies only those that could be clearly regarded as such.[23]

A worker at the nationalized Texaco plant responded that those governing Cuba "are completely Communists. All of their accomplishments have been through the work of others—including how they think. I have a sister-in-law and a brother-in-law in prison for speaking against the government—[sentenced to] seven years." Another antirevolutionary worker said: "Socialists, they say. The kids say Communists. I don't know. Listen, if somebody comes and take that pen of yours, and you bought it, what are you going to think?"

"Well, I've never been 'political,'" a cigarette-machine operator said, "for me, they are all right." A brewery worker's reply was equally equivocal: "My experience so far is good. I don't worry about such things—neither before the revolution nor now." A skilled electrician in Santiago committed himself only so far as to say that the men in the government are "persons with socialist ideas, who though they have good intentions have committed many serious administrative errors."

"The truth is," a carpenter in a sugar central said, "that now those who govern here are Cubans. They are honest and hardworking men." A sixty-seven-year-old maintenance man at the Nicaro nickel plant who had been an agricultural worker until recently said: "Look, before I couldn't look a boss in the eye—I looked at my feet. Not now. Now we have liberty and walk where we wish, and nothing is prohibited to us. It is a great joy to be alive now. These men [who govern us] are 100 percent better than before. I have known governments from [Mario García] Menocal [Cuban president, 1913-21] until Batista left three years ago, and I have never seen any like this government." Equally articulate in his support of the revolution was a twenty-year-old bootmaker in a newly estab-

[23] E.g., "the people," "the humble," "hardworking," "good," "sincere," "moral," "honest," "defenders of the poor and humble," "the working class." Responses such as "socialists" or "revolutionaries" that did not clearly commit the worker were not counted as favorable; neither were such equivocal replies as "Cubans," "Fidel," "Communists," nor hostile ones such as "Russians," "Soviets," "shameless," or "traitors."

lished factory in Guanajay: *"We* are the government, *we* run things. Go to a factory or *consolidado* anywhere, *chico,* and see: those who work govern, those who govern work, not like the capitalists who lived without working before the revolution triumphed. Now the power of the workers and peasants has emerged."

The workers were also asked the following questions with fixed alternatives: (3) "Do you believe that the country ought to have elections soon?" (4) "Do you think that the workers now have more, the same, or less influence on [*en*] the government than they had before the revolution?" (5) "Do you belong to the militia?"[24]

The index of attitude toward the revolution was constructed by coding favorable responses as +1 and all others as 0:[25]

Index

Points	Definition	N
3-5.	Favorable	142
2.	Indecisive	24
0, 1.	Hostile	36
Total.		202

FINDINGS

Comparison of the generations confirms our expectation that members of the rebel generation of Castro, or the generation of '53 are most likely to support the revolution (Table 2). United by the common political frame of reference they developed during the anti-Batista struggle, the generation of '53 stands out as the decisive generational base of the revolution. Further, the two other generations that stand out are precisely those whose members experienced the revolutionary events of the thirties as young men. It is, of course, possible to argue that, having experienced an abortive rather than a successful revolution, they should be cynical and pessimistic rather than optimistic about the Castro revolution, and this argument does make a good deal of sense. Yet, while the

[24] Answers to these questions were distributed as follows: (3) "no," 136; "yes," 44; "no opinion," 22; (4) "more influence," 170; "the same," 17; "less," 8; "no opinion," 7; (5) "yes," 110; "no," 92.

[25] Item analysis of answers to the five questions indicates that the questions form an acceptable Guttman scale, 88 percent of the workers giving answers exactly (67 percent) or consistently (21 percent) in conformity with a Guttman model. The coefficient of reproductibility equals .95.

TABLE 2

POLITICAL GENERATION AND ATTITUDE TOWARD THE REVOLUTION
(Percent)

Age Category at Time of Study (1962)*	Favorable	Indecisive	Hostile	N
21-27	55	19	25	36
28-35	90	2	8	51
36-43	61	17	21	51
44-51	69	15	15	26
52-59	70	9	22	23

* This and the following tables do not include eight workers who were under twenty-one and seven who were over fifty-nine in 1962.

social revolution was crushed, the Machado regime *was* overthrown, and thus the political revolution in the narrow sense was a success. Moreover, seen in retrospect, the revolution also yielded significant gains for the workers in subsequent years—especially the legitimatization of their right to political and economic organization, a right that allowed them to win substantial economic benefits. It is also relevant that the repression of the revolution of the thirties, which in any case had significant "antiimperialist" overtones, was widely believed in Cuba to have been the result of United States political intervention.[26] The antiimperialism of the revolutionary government may, therefore, be another source of their support. Thus, it is understandable that these generations may view the present revolution as the renascence and continuation of the struggles of their own youth and may be more disposed to support it than the generation who came to manhood during the republican interregnum of relative stability or the present generation, for whom prerevolutionary struggles are mere "history."

The low proportion of the present generation who support the revolution is unexpected. My own prediction (see Table 1) was that this generation would be outranked by those of '53 and the thirties but would itself outrank the republican generation. The explanation may be that the workers of this generation knew little if anything through personal experience about the prerevolutionary situation of the working class.

[26] See Dana Gardner Munro, *The Latin American Republics: A History* (2d ed.; New York: Appleton-Century-Crofts, 1950), p. 501; Charles A. Thompson, "The Cuban Revolution: Reform and Reaction," *Foreign Policy Reports*, XI (January 1, 1936), 261-71; Casuso, *op. cit.*, pp. 68 ff.; Robert F. Smith, *The United States and Cuba: Business and Diplomacy, 1917-1960* (New York: Bookman Associates, 1959), pp. 148–56; and Zeitlin, *op. cit.*, pp. 30–46, and the references therein.

Many of them (55 percent) were not yet workers before the revolution and thus could hardly appreciate the positive changes in the situation of the working class wrought by the revolution.

The impact of the anti-Batista struggle on the workers of the generation of '53 has made it the generational base of the revolution. Moreover, in a significant sense it was their generation that brought the revolutionary government to power. The leaders of the revolution itself, it will be remembered, who led the *resistencia* and were the rebel cadres in the hills and in the cities, are members of the generation of '53. In accordance with the hypothesis of political generations, the fact that the members of this generation acquired their political frame of reference in the course of the anti-Batista struggle should have made them more likely than members of other generations to support the revolution now, *regardless of the generation to which the rebel leaders themselves belonged.* But the fact that the rebels *were* predominantly of their own generation may have been an additional source of their support for and identification with the rebels and their cause. It may be surmised that the rebels became, in a significant sense, collectively the reference group of that entire generation, and the chief rebel leaders its foremost culture heroes or "reference individuals."[27] That the rebel leaders couched so much of their program in generational terms also may have considerably increased the likelihood that the members of the generation of '53 would identify with them. In turn, this act of identification may itself have reinforced the attitudes this generation was developing in response to the set of stimuli created by the historical situation.

If our assumption is correct that identification with the members of their generation who were actively participating in and leading the rebel movement was one more element in the complex of elements comprising the distinct politically relevant experiences of the generation of '53, we should expect a similar identification in the present. Are members of the generation of '53 more likely than others to identify with the leaders of the revolution? Using the question "Aside from

[27] As Robert Merton conceptualizes it, "Emulation of a peer, a parent, or a public figure may be restricted to limited segments of their behavior and values and this can be usefully described as adoption of a role model. Or, emulation may be extended to a wider array of behavior and values of these persons who can then be described as reference individuals" (*Social Theory and Social Structure* [Glencoe, Ill.: Free Press, 1959], p. 303).

personal friends or relatives—of all the people you hear or read about—could you name three individuals whom you admire very much?" as a rough empirical indicator, we found that the generation of '53 is distinct in this regard.[28] Its members were more likely than those of other generations to name a revolutionary leader (Fidel Castro, Raúl Castro, Ernesto "Che" Guevara, Juan Almeida, etc.) as at least one of the three individuals whom they admire greatly (Table 3).

TABLE 3

POLITICAL GENERATION AND REFERENCE INDIVIDUALS
(Percent) *

| AGE CATEGORY AT TIME OF STUDY (1962) | PROPORTION NAMING AT LEAST ONE REFERENCE INDIVIDUAL WHO IS A | | | | | | N |
	Cuban Revolutionary Leader†	Communist Political Figure‡	Cuban Hero or Martyr§	Popular Celebrity¶	High Culture Figure‡	Anti-Castro Political Figure**	
21-27....	55	11	11	17	25	8	36
28-35....	78	18	12	14	18	2	51
36-43....	55	14	13	9	22	2	51
44-51....	54	19	4	23	13	4	26
52-59....	57	4	9	4	22	13	23

* Percentages do not total 100 because three responses were required. Categories in which no more than 10 percent of any generation named a reference individual are excluded from this table.

† Only fidelistas or so-called new Communists.

‡ Cuban Partido Socialista Popular leaders ("old Communists") or international Communist figures, e.g., Mao, Khrushchev, Lenin, Ho.

§ Historic heroes or martyrs such as José Martí, Máximo Gómez, Antonio Maceo, Antonio Guiteras, or martyrs of the anti-Batista struggle such as Frank Pais, José Antonio Echevarria.

¶ Athletes, movie stars, radio and TV entertainers, etc.

‡ Scientists, novelists, artists, philosophers, poets, etc.

** Counterrevolutionary leaders such as Carlos Prío Socarras, José Miro Cardona, Manuel Urrutia, or political figures such as President Kennedy, Eisenhower, Allen Dulles, etc.

That the political generations vary in their response to the revolution in accordance with their historical location in prerevolutionary Cuba suggests also that they should have varied in their prerevolutionary political orientations as well. The political strength of the Communists in the working class, for instance, was significantly different in the critical periods that formed the political generations. We might predict, therefore, that the workers varied in their attitudes toward the Communists before the revolution in accordance with the role of the Communists during the workers' common youthful ex-

[28] This question was also borrowed from the Almond-Verba study (op. cit.) and is acknowledged gratefully.

perience in the labor movement. If the Communists were then a significant independent political force, the workers of that generation should have been more likely to support the Communists before the revolution than workers whose youthful experience in the labor movement came during a period of Communist weakness or irrelevance.

As a rough guide to their prerevolutionary attitude toward the Communists, the workers in our sample were asked: "How would you describe your attitude toward the Communists before the revolution? Hostile, indifferent, friendly, or supporter?"[29]

As Table 4 indicates, the political generations did view the Communists in expectably different ways. The two generations with the highest proportion of workers sympathetic to the Communists before the revolution are those that were

TABLE 4

POLITICAL GENERATION AND PREREVOLUTIONARY ATTITUDE TOWARD
THE COMMUNISTS

(Percent)

Age Category at Time of Study (1962)*	Friendly and/or Supporter	Indifferent	Hostile	N
28-35	29	43	27	51
36-43	29	35	35	51
44-51	38	38	23	26
52-59	39	39	22	23

* The youngest generation of workers (twenty-one to twenty-seven in 1962) is excluded from this table since the question refers to an attitude held before they were adults.

formed, respectively, during the anti-Machado struggles and the abortive revolution of the thirties, in which the Communists played a leading political role, and during the period when the Communists were dominant in the leadership of the CTC. It is significant, moreover, that although the workers of the revolutionary generation of '53 might be expected to "recall" favorable attitudes toward the Communists in the prerevolu-

[29] According to this crude measure, 28 percent of the workers in our sample classified themselves as prerevolutionary friends or supporters of the Communists; and, according to a report written after the Communists had been officially purged from the labor movement, the Communists still had "a strong underground influence in some unions, and some authorities estimate that perhaps 25 percent of all Cuban workers are secretly sympathetic to them" (International Bank for Reconstruction and Development, *Report on Cuba* [Baltimore: Johns Hopkins Press, 1951], p. 365).

tionary period, their generation does not differ in this respect from the generation of republican stability, although the latter has a higher proportion of workers who were hostile to the Communists. It was during the republican interregnum that the Communists were at their weakest level in the working class. During this period they were purged from official leadership of the CTC, and the workers who entered the labor movement at this time would have been more likely than other workers to assimilate anti-Communist political orientations. As to the attitude of the generation of '53 toward the Communists before the revolution, there are good historical reasons why they should have been, at best, ambivalent about the Communists. Fidel's leadership of the assault on Moncada was denounced by the Communists as a bourgeois, romantic, and *putschist* adventure,[30] and throughout the guerrilla war against Batista—until it entered its last months—the Communists' official attitude was at best equivocal. As late as May, 1958, the Communists were still referring to the 26th of July Movement as "those who count on terroristic acts and conspiratorial coups as the chief means of ousting Batista," although they described the movement as the "most militant and progressive sector of the non-Communist opposition."[31] In the unsuccessful April 9, 1958, attempt at a general strike the Communist leadership—though not opposing it—declared that it did not have enough support to succeed, and this statement, circulated by Batista, was construed by the 26th of July Movement as detrimental to the strike effort. As late as June 28, 1958, when the guerrilla war had reached a high point, the Communists had not reconciled themselves fully to the necessity for armed struggle, and the party's National Committee called for "clean, democratic elections" to eliminate Batista.[32] The fact is that the Communists, despite the influence they still retained among the workers, were the tail end of the anti-Batista struggle, with the unquestioned leadership of the struggle residing with the 26th of July Movement. Thus, it is understandable that members of this generation of '53 were no more likely than the generation of the republic to view the Communists favorably.

So far, our analysis of the political generations has treated them in terms of their members' common location in the historical process. The common politically relevant experiences

[30] *Daily Worker*, August 10, 1953, p. 2.
[31] Quoted in *Daily Worker*, May 4, 1958, p. 6.
[32] See Zeitlin, *op. cit.*, pp. 83–104, and the references therein.

of their members have, taken as a whole, differentiated the political generations from each other. It is clear, however, that the generations are themselves internally differentiated by structural factors and that individuals of the same generation sharing different locations in the social structure will have experienced the politically relevant events of their youth differently. As Bennet Berger has put it: "The temporal location of a [generational] group must first be kept analytically distinct from its structural location; second, when considering them together, we should be aware that the impact of structural (e.g., occupational) factors on the nature of the temporal location may, under some conditions, be such as to fragment the cultural 'unity' of a generation beyond recognition."[33]

One of the most significant structural determinants of the Cuban workers' response to the revolution, as I have shown elsewhere,[34] was their prerevolutionary employment status. The workers who were unemployed and underemployed before the revolution were more likely to be pro-Communist before the revolution and are now more likely to support the revolutionary government than those who were employed regularly.

It is therefore important to consider the impact of their prerevolutionary employment status on the workers of different political generations (Table 5). As we might expect, within every political generation the workers who were unemployed and underemployed are more likely to support the revolution than those who were regularly employed before the revolution. Moreover, among both the unemployed and the regularly employed, the generation of '53 exceeds the other generations in the proportion of prorevolution workers; and among the employed workers the generation of the thirties comes second, as we should expect. Among the unemployed workers, however, the generation of the republican interregnum has as great a proportion of prorevolution workers as does the generation of the thirties.[35] Here is a particularly

[33] "How Long is a Generation," *British Journal of Sociology*, XI (March 1960), 16. Cf. also: "In the comparison of different age groups in the *aggregate*, or the same age groups at different historical periods in the *aggregate*, any differences that appear to be generational may simply be *artifacts* of the different social composition of the groups. . . . In principle, this can be solved by the introduction of certain controls or matchings, but it may often be neglected in practice" (Hyman, *op. cit.*, p. 130).

[34] Maurice Zeitlin, "Economic Insecurity and the Political Attitudes of Cuban Workers," *American Sociological Review*, February 1966.

[35] See Table 4.

TABLE 5

POLITICAL GENERATION, PREREVOLUTIONARY EMPLOYMENT
STATUS, AND POLITICAL ATTITUDES*

AGE CATEGORY AT TIME OF STUDY (1962)	UNDER- AND UNEMPLOYED† Percentage Supporting			REGULARLY EMPLOYED Percentage Supporting		
	Revolution	Communists	N	Revolution	Communists	N
21-27......	75	‡	8	42	‡	12
28-35......	100	31	22	85	35	20
36-43......	81	41	21	43	17	23
44 plus§...	82	64	11	68	39	31

* Those who were not workers before the revolution are excluded from this table.
† "Under- and unemployed" refers to workers who worked, on the average, nine months or less per year before the revolution, while "regularly employed" refers to those who worked ten months or more.
‡ See Table 4, footnote.
§ This category combines the generations of the second Machado regime and the first Batista regime and is referred to in this paper henceforth as the "generation of the thirties."

instructive instance of how generational peers, located differently in the social structure, are differently affected by historical events. The relative stability, prosperity, and political democracy of the republican interregnum, having left the problem of unemployment and underemployment untouched, proved from the perspective of the unemployed workers to be irrelevant to their situation and may indeed (as our evidence seems to indicate) have inclined them (even more than their unemployment may otherwise have done) toward radical solutions to their problems.

As Table 5 indicates, among unemployed workers those in the generation of the republican interregnum were second only to the generation of the thirties in prerevolutionary support of the Communists. Also consistent with our findings on aggregate generational differences in prerevolutionary attitudes toward the Communists is the fact that the generation of the thirties, both among the employed and unemployed, had the greatest proportion of prerevolutionary Communist sympathizers.

Looking at the relationships differently, it might be expected that the unemployed, since they were generally more likely to support the Communists before the revolution, would also do so in each political generation. In fact, this is true in every political generation *but one*. In the generation of '53 unemployed workers were *not* more likely than their employed peers to sympathize with the Communists. In view of the experiences of the different political generations with the Communists, as pointed out earlier, this finding makes more sense than if they had been more likely than the employed to support the Communists. The most significant radical movement on the contemporary scene for the generation of '53, which possessed the political initiative and clearly led the anti-Batista struggle of that period, was not the Communist but the 26th of July Movement. There is little reason, then, why the unemployed of *this* generation should have been more responsive to the Communists than were their employed peers. Not only were the *fidelistas* leading the anti-Batista struggle, but their agitation among the workers was also radical in social content, and perhaps even more radical than the agitation of the Communists, who continued to counsel moderation for so long. Indeed, we already know that the unemployed of the generation of '53 are more likely to support the revolution than the employed workers, though they were not more likely to support the Communists before the revolution.

Finally, it is important to note that it is among the regularly employed workers that the relationships between generations most closely approximate those found when the generations are viewed in the aggregate. This is especially worthy of emphasis, since it is where unemployment (which tended to override the effects of their historical experiences) is absent that the generational relationships we predicted from knowledge of Cuban history are strongest and clearest. Thus, for example, among the employed workers of the generation of the republican interregnum, whose historical experiences were not "contaminated" by unemployment (which provides one basis for radicalism), the ideology developed under the impact of the republican experience became operative. Our findings are consistent, therefore, with the view that participation in historical struggles will have the greatest effect on the ideological development of precisely those workers who objectively have the least to gain from revolutionary politics.

In conclusion, then, not only does comparison of the political generations in the aggregate reveal significant political differences in accord with hypotheses based on the concept of political generation, but comparison of *intra*generation subgroups are also in accord with those hypotheses.

The theoretical significance of our findings lies, first, in their demonstration of the analytic utility of formulating specific hypotheses in terms of the concept of political generations. It may indeed be correct, as Herbert Hyman has argued, that the "generic process of learning of politics" does not include generational influence and that "susceptibility to this influence may not be universal or may be constrained in many cases by other factors," but this hardly warrants relegation of the concept to the conceptual dustbin, as is implied in Hyman's otherwise incisive and valuable discussion.[36] In fact, of course, it is precisely one task of sociological inquiry to discover under what conditions a particular type of social determinant may or may not be operative and to modify theory appropriately. The fact that some nonliterate bands do not have social classes, for instance, and that, therefore, "susceptibility to this influence may not be universal" hardly warrants discarding the concept of social class. On the contrary, such empirical findings lead to further conceptual and theoretical development. Failure to use the generation concept because its empirical demonstration is difficult may be detrimental to the analysis of political behavior. It is especially important from a theoretical standpoint to analyze the effects of generations in societies characterized by comparatively greater social instability and internal conflict than the advanced industrial societies of the West in which the few empirical studies utilizing the concept (whether implicitly or explicitly) have been done. This is important not only because of the necessary comparative perspective on generational politics such studies could provide but also because generational politics seem to be most associated with differences in social stability during the periods in which the different generations came of age.[37] Thus, our findings, based as they are on interviews with workers now living through a social revolution in a country whose history has been marked by social and political instability, are of particular theoretical interest.

Second, these conclusions bear indirectly on the issue of the relevance of "history" to sociological analysis and theory. The very concept of political generation implies the hypothesis that social processes, relationships, norms, and values sometimes may be inexplicable without reference to the events of the past and that analyses that are limited to consideration only of contemporary relationships may be deficient in significant ways.

Third, to the extent to which the concept attempts to link up

[36] Hyman, op. cit., p. 124. Hyman repeatedly refers to the concept of generation as "doctrine."

[37] Cf. Lipset, op. cit., p. 267; Richard Centers, The Psychology of Social Classes (Princeton, N.J.: Princeton University Press, 1949), p. 168; Hamilton, op. cit., Chapter 6.

behavior and character with *non*institutionalized but historically significant forms of social interaction, our findings also
impinge on social psychological theory. Such decisively relevant experiences as may be included under the rubric of "historically significant events" (major political issues, concrete
internal struggles, general social conditions) may or may not
themselves have significant consequences for the social structure and, therefore, for the character, norms, and values of the
men formed within it. But these very events may have independent psychological effects on their participants, aside from
their institutional consequences. "If you wish to understand
persons—their development and their relations with significant
others—you must be prepared," as Anselm Strauss has put
it, "to view them as embedded in historical context. Psychological theory and psychiatric theory, at least of the American
variety, underplay this context; and those sociologists and
anthropologists who are interested in personal identity tend to
treat historical matters more as stage setting, or backdrops,
than as crucial to the study of persons."[38] That the historical
context in which they came to manhood played a significant
role in the formation of the political identities of succeeding
generations of Cuban workers—their political allegiances and
norms and their response to the revolution—has, of course,
been precisely the point of this paper.

[38] *Mirrors and Masks: The Search for Identity* (Glencoe, Ill.: Free
Press, 1959), p. 164. See also Hans Gerth and C. Wright Mills, *Character and Social Structure* (New York: Harcourt, Brace & World, 1953),
p. xix.

Tendencies in Peruvian Development and in the Class Structure

ANÍBAL QUIJANO OBREGÓN

In Peru, in Quijano's analysis, the congenital weakness
of the new economic structure that is taking shape, and
of its newly emerging dominant strata, particularly the
industrialists, is its great dependence on the foreign interests that control it. An underdeveloped capitalist country that combines elements of advanced development with
those of extreme backwardness and traditionalism, a class
structure that is very much in flux, a growing middle class,
rapid urbanization, especially along the Coast, industrialization which is capital intensive, growing unemployment and pauperization, all while the rate of economic
growth is "truly impressive," are elements in an explosive
situation which has already bred peasant "unions" and
spontaneous land seizures, as well as guerrilla organizations that have been violently repressed by the Peruvian
government.

Anibal Quíjano Obregón is on leave with the Economic
Commission for Latin America in Santiago, Chile, from his
professorship of Sociology at the University of San Marcos
in Lima, Peru. He is the author of numerous articles on
agrarian change and peasant movements, and on the
urbanization process in Latin America.

PEOPLE OF ALMOST all ideological persuasions, from technicians and politicians to members of rebel leftist groups, look
upon modern Peruvian society as deriving from a feudal
structure established by the Spanish colonization. This struc-

289

ture supposedly began to be modified in a capitalist direction through the influence of postcolonial economic developments stimulated by foreign investments. As a consequence, this society became divided into one sector characterized by capitalist relations, situated along the coast, and another with feudal characteristics, found mainly in the Sierra.[1]

Supposedly, then, there are two coexisting societies. Each has its own historical characteristics and structural laws; and they are integrated by a common political apparatus. The capitalist sector of this society is directly dependent on foreign capital, while the feudal one is only peripherally and precariously dependent upon the capitalist sector and thus, also, indirectly upon foreign capital. Each sector has its own pattern of social domination and socioeconomic conflicts, only partially coordinated by the political-administrative system.

I cannot take space here to correct this traditional view of the early historical development of Peruvian society originally put forward by the generation of politicians and intellectuals

[1] Observe the red thread connecting the following texts:

a) "According to neo-Marxism, 'Imperialism is the last stage of capitalism.' This view, however, cannot be applied to all regions of the world. True, imperialism is the last stage of capitalism, but only in the advanced industrial countries which have already passed through their previous stages of development. But for those countries which are still economically backward, and to which capitalism comes as imperialism, it is the first stage." Haya de la Torre, V. R. "El Antiimperialismo y el Apra" Santiago de Chile 1936, 2nd edition, ed. Ercilla, p. 21.

b) "Our thesis—the Aprista thesis—is that our economy has a dual nature—imperialism has split it into two different intensities, two rhythms, two modes of production—the national retarded economy, and the accelerated imperialist one. This is the fundamental difference between our 'first stage' of capitalism imported by imperialism, and the 'last stage' which the more advanced countries are facing." Ibid., p. 26.

c) "A capitalist economy that is rapidly expanding, based primarily in metropolitan Lima, is counterbalanced by a feudal economy that exists throughout the rest of the country." Instituto Nacional de Planificación. Plan de Desarrollo Económico y Social, 1967-1970, Vol. 2, Lima 1966, p. 13.

d) "On a foundation of collective agriculture, a feudal system was established as a result of the Conquista in the sixteenth century, and aspects of a slave system with the importation of Negroes during the eighteenth century [sic]. The feudal regime became consolidated with Peru's independence from Spain during the first half of the nineteenth century, after the colonial yoke of the Spanish Metropolis had been broken. An incipient capitalism began to develop at the beginning of the second half of the nineteenth century, and imperialist penetration began in the first decades of this century and continues up to the present day. Thus, Peru is made up of a number of hybrid systems that we can term a 'feudal bourgeoisie imperialist system,' without even counting that minority which is still completely savage and/or barbaric living in the Peruvian Amazon region." "Luis de la Puente Uceda: La Revolución en el Peru. Concepciones y Perspectiva," Comision de Prensa del MIR (February 1966), p. 25.

of about 1919, which was based upon ideas and knowledge long since obsolete. I believe that this early conception of the nature of colonial and postcolonial society, prior to the present, is completely untenable in its main outlines. . . .

In any case, whether this traditional study is true or false as a view of the historical development of Peruvian society, there can be no doubt that it is inadequate as a view of the present. . . . Contemporary Peruvian society is neither bistructural nor semifeudal. On the contrary, it displays all the traits of an underdeveloped, dependent capitalist society, with all the features resulting from its historical development.

In this essay I wish to point out and elucidate those traits. Peru is perhaps the most complex and the most contradictory of all the Latin American countries. It combines elements and problems arising from the most advanced stages of development with those of extreme backwardness and traditionalism. . . .

The official figures indicate an impressive rate of economic growth; the currency seems stable, industry is expanding, and if we can judge by the number of votes obtained, the present government can boast of organized popular support. Nevertheless, there is a growing movement by the peasants against the traditional landowners, which in some areas has acquired a surprising degree of revolutionary political organization, in view of the fact that most of them are indigenous and to a large extent illiterate. One year of guerrilla warfare has forced the Government, with the help of the Pentagon, to bring into effect all of its repressive potential. In the cities certain sectors of the working class have gone out on violent strikes, using semiinsurrectional methods, such as occupying the factories and keeping the bosses as hostages. In the face of terrible repression they publicly denounce the ruling class, the increasing impoverishment, and the steady fall in the standard of living in the cities. University and high-school students appear to be entering a period of universal radicalism.

It is difficult to present a valid and coherent analysis of the situation, since there are hardly any basic studies available, and data are inadequate. Yet the attempt is necessary.

The most determining factor in the history and the present situation of Latin American society, and in Peru in particular, is its position of dependence upon the international capitalist market. Thus, the whole history of the development of this society can be considered largely as the history of successive modifications of this relationship of dependency. Once its colonial dependence had broken down, Peru immediately became dependent upon capitalism. We will first have to specify the type and the form of these relationships as they existed during our postcolonial history. Throughout its colonial period Peru suffered from the effects on the world market of the expansion and consolidation of capitalism and the shifts and displacements of power among the European centers of this system. In the same way, each period of postcolonial Peruvian history can be regarded as being directly related to the changes and tendencies of international capitalism. Since the beginning of the nineteenth century there have been three forms of definite dependence: (1) financial and commercial interests during the nineteenth century, dominated by Britain; (2) agricultural, mining, and financial interests approximately since the First World War, dominated by the United States; (3) industrial and financial interests, relatively recent, also dominated by the United States.

We wish to show how the center of power in our present economic dependence is shifting from the traditional U.S.-owned mining and oil "enclaves," and the agricultural and cattle "enclaves," controlled largely by landowning capitalists, toward industrial production in the cities, controlled by international capitalism in association with the native urban capitalists. This is not to say that the traditionally powerful sector of society is robbed of that power, but that it is concentrated in finance and trade and can thus be effective in new ways. This, in effect, is a rather recent characteristic. It can be generalized, though at varying degrees of development, for

TABLE 1

NET AMOUNTS OF PRIVATE UNITED STATES INVESTMENTS IN LATIN AMERICA, ACCORDING TO PRINCIPLE SECTORS, 1951-1962
(in millions of dollars and percentages)

Industrial Sector	1951-55		1956-60		1961-62		1951-62	
	$	%	$	%	$	%.	$	%
Oil	$ 348	20	$1,571	46	$ 7	1	$1,912	33
Mining & Foundries	339	19	301	9	46	7	686	12
Mfg.	613	35	791	23	370	60	1,774	31
Commerce & Misc.	451	26	735	22	207	34	1,393	24
Total	1,751	100	3,398	100	616	100	5,765	100

Sources: U.S. Department of Commerce, *Balance of Payments, Statistical Supplement to Survey of Current Business* (1963), and *Survey of Current Business* (various numbers from 1963-1964), (taken from: *El Financiamiento Externo de América Latina* (U.N., 1965) Table 179).

the whole of Latin America, as is illustrated in the table below:

Most of the investments in oil production are destined for Venezuela. In Peru the popular pressure toward the nationalization of oil has caused a withdrawal of investments.[2] In all Latin American countries foreign capital is invested mainly in commerce and urban industrial production. Previously, foreign capital was invested mainly in mining, agriculture, and cattle production, localized in "enclaves" that could be considered to belong to the national economy only in a geographical sense. Nowadays it tends to penetrate and control urban manufacturing and business without, however, relinquishing its traditional control over the other sectors.

In this way our economic dependence assumes a new form, and foreign capital strengthens its control over the national economy. What this means to Peruvian society as a whole, in the form of changing and modifying its development, will be seen in the following analysis.

Within the framework of this new kind of dependence, a system of internal control and domination has emerged that, while essentially no different from that which has always existed, does differ in its mode of expression and development.

From the point of view of its economic structure, Peru could be characterized as in a state of transition from a predominantly agricultural and mining economy to an incipient urban-industrial economy. Its previous economic structure was agricultural and mining, with a small sector of society involved in light industry, finance, and trade. This was a relatively modernized sector along the coast, basically a plantation mono-cultural economy, with both national and American enterprises owning the land, and the extractive industries of oil and mining, almost exclusively under foreign control, in enclaves. In the rest of the country, especially in the Sierra, the economy was stagnating agrarian capitalism characterized by strong authoritarian work relationships; it was lacking important and direct links with the international market.

Economic hegemony is now shifting to the urban and industrial sectors, with manufacturing concerns growing up in the cities. These, in turn, are replacing the traditional activities

[2] The ex-Deputy, Carlos Malpica, stated in *El Comercio*, Lima, that between 1953 and 1964 the investment of International Petroleum Company was reduced by $42 million. *Oiga*, a weekly in Lima (July 1966), No. 184, p. 7.

by means of expanding commercial and other tertiary developments, and thus slowly, but irreversibly, are causing primary activities, agriculture in particular, to be of less importance.

* However, these urban sectors of the economy are concentrated largely on the coast and particularly in Lima-Callao. Thus the previous economic matrix tends to change only in an uneven way between both the regions and the sectors of economic activity.

TABLE 2

COMPOSITION OF THE GROSS NATIONAL PRODUCT IN PERU BY ECONOMIC SECTOR

Economic Sectors	1950-1964 GNP in millions of Soles (1960 prices)				Breakdown by Percentage			
	1950	1955	1960	1964	1950	1955	1960	1964
Agricultural & Cattle	8,865	9,786	11,317	13,998	25.7	22.2	20.4	19.6
Fishing	167	238	785	1,266	0.5	0.5	1.4	1.8
Mining & Oil	1,831	2,793	4,908	5,448	5.3	6.3	8.8	7.6
Industry	5,349	7,777	10,467	13,992	15.6	17.6	18.8	19.6
Construction	1,179	1,955	1,768	2,921	3.4	4.4	3.2	4.1
Power	a	a	214	314	a	a	0.4	0.4
Transport	1,586	2,393	3,009	3,816	4.6	5.4	5.4	5.3
Trade	5,512	7,452	9,280	12,528	16.0	16.9	16.7	17.6
Banking, Insurance	1,050	1,635	2,062	2,639	3.1	3.7	3.7	3.7
Housing	3,201	3,661	4,470	5,261	9.3	8.3	8.0	7.4
Government	3,489	3,767	4,291	5,227	10.1	8.5	7.7	7.8
Services	2,187[b]	2,704[b]	3,079	3,602	6.4[b]	6.2[b]	5.5	5.1
TOTAL	34,411	44,162	55,650	71,272	100.0	100.0	100.0	100.0

Souces: National Planning Institute.
  a) Is included in services.
  b) Includes power.

The above table shows the emergence of secondary and tertiary activities as dominant in the Peruvian structure of production, and the outstanding place within that structure occupied by manufacturing industries. This becomes even clearer when we take into account that within the primary sector the most mechanized industries, such as fishing (the production of powdered fish) and mining, are the only industries that have continued to grow, whereas the agricultural sector has steadily reduced its contribution to the gross national product. . . . Thus, in 1964, 70 percent of all agricultural products were destined primarily for export. Meanwhile, agricultural production for the domestic market, carried on mainly in the mountains, tended to stagnate and deteriorate more and more. As a result, importation of food products rose "explosively" from close to 40 million dollars' worth in 1960 to more than 134 million dollars' worth in 1965. In 1966 alone, imports of food increased by 27 percent.[3] Of all the economic sectors in the country, only those that are directly connected with and controlled by foreign capital continue to

[3] Instituto Nacional de Planificación del Perú (INP), *Plan de Desarrollo Económico y Social 1967-1970*, vol. 1, pp. 126-128.

develop, regardless of their degree of participation in overall production. The increase in urban manufacturing industries and their tendency to dominate the economic structure of the country can be shown to be directly related to their dependence on foreign investment. The following table makes this very clear:

TABLE 3

GROSS INTERNAL INVESTMENT BY SECTORS OF ORIGIN

Sectors	% of all Sectors		% of Investment that is Foreign
	1960	1963	
Agriculture & Cattle	1.8	3.0	0
Mining	0.2	0.1	0
Industry	33.6	32.5	80.3
Construction	40.4	37.3	0
Power	—	—	—
Trade	24.0	27.1	19.4
Total	100.0	100.0	

Source: National Planning Institute.

As Table 3 shows, (a) investments in the country are being directed heavily into industry and other urban sectors, and (b) most of the capital invested is foreign. The official statistics leave no doubts about the profound changes taking place in the pattern of foreign investment in Peru and her dependence upon it. Industry itself, a sector traditionally engaged in light consumer goods manufacturing (foodstuffs, clothing, beverages, etc.) is moving into new areas of manufacturing in the intermediate basic industries (metallurgy, chemicals, cement, paper, wood, etc.). Thus, the traditional sectors are tending to diminish their participation in manufacturing, and these new "intermediate basic" industries are expanding and beginning to dominate this area of national production. The participation of the traditional group in industrial production went from 69 percent in 1955 to 62 percent in 1960 and 59 percent in 1963, while that of the "dynamic" group of industries went from 31 percent to 37 percent to 40 percent during the same years.[4]

On the other hand, while in 1955 E.C.L.A. calculated that manufacturing contributed 3,397 million *soles,* and production by craftsmen and artisans amounted to 254 million *soles,* the

[4] José Palomino Roedel, *El desarrollo Industrial en el Perú* (Documento presentado por la Oficina Sectorial de Planificación de Industrias, del INP, al Primer Seminario de Población y Desarrollo, Perú 1965), p. 9.

1963 Economic Census showed manufacturing contributing 12,900 million *soles*, and products from craftsmen and artisans only 270 million. The percent of the labor force employed in manufacturing in 1955 was estimated at 17.7, which was later corrected by several analysts to 14.2, while the figure for 1963 was estimated at between 19.5 and 21.3 percent, indicating that Peru must be one of the most rapidly industrializing countries in Latin America,[5] considering the previous point of departure.

This process of modification in the structure of industrial production shows that the tendency toward concentrating industry in the cities is here to stay, insofar as producers of durable consumer goods necessarily settle in the most important urban localities. So, too, as the whole economy moves from the primary to the secondary and tertiary stages it comes to be an urban industrialized economy. The increase in the tertiary sectors of the economy, demonstrated by the tables, undoubtedly strengthens this tendency toward the urbanization of industrial production and of the economy in general. At the same time, it helps (on a much smaller scale which for lack of any figures we cannot specify) to carry the market for the products of urban light industry, as well as other tertiary activities such as small business and public service activities, into the rural areas. The expansion of the system of transport and communications over the last few years is closely related to this process. Thus the rural areas have ceased to be as isolated from the cities as they traditionally used to be. Other social and cultural elements from the city have reached even the remotest areas and have caused profound changes in the traditional social and economic structure of the country. What these changes are will be shown later.

These changes in the framework of production are necessarily reflected as changes in the occupational structure of the country, and in the modification of the political and social structure in general. The displacement of labor among the diverse economic sectors can be seen from Table 4.

The table points out two important facts. On the one hand, there is a displacement of the economically active sector into tertiary activities, with a corresponding reduction in the sector engaged in primary activities. On the other hand, while the previous tables clearly showed an expansion in industry and

[5] *El Desarrollo Industrial del Perú,* Cepal 1959, pp. 54-69; Palomino Roedel, *op cit.,* pp. 8-9.

TABLE 4

ECONOMICALLY ACTIVE POPULATIONS, BY ECONOMIC SECTOR: 1940-1961
(in thousands of inhabitants and percentages)

Economic sectors	1940	%	1961	%	% Difference
Primary	1,591	64.3	1,622	51.9	−12.4
Secondary	426	17.2	524	16.8	−0.4
Tertiary	417	16.8	825	27.3	10.5
Others not specified	41	1.6	126	4.0	2.4
Total	2,475	100.0	3,125	100.0	—

Sources: National Census of Population and Occupation, 1940, Vol. I, Sixth Population Census, 1961.
a) Agriculture, cattle raising, forestry, hunting, fishing, mining, and quarrying.
b) Manufacturing, construction, electricity, gas, water.
c) Trade, transportation, communications, services.
Note: We are dealing with approximate percentages, so that in some cases they do not sum to exactly 100 percent.

construction, both in investments and in their contribution to the economy as a whole, the increase in the number of people involved in these activities, though important in absolute terms, represented no increase in percentage.

The figures used in Table 4 have been corrected recently by estimating the errors in the 1940 census, and the new figures (Table 5) show an appreciable increase in the number of people engaged in secondary activities. Nevertheless, this increase is insignificant compared with the sector's expansion in investment and production.

TABLE 5

ECONOMICALLY ACTIVE POPULATION, BY TYPES OF ACTIVITY: 1940–1961

Types of activity	1940*		1961		%
	1000s	%	1000s	%	Difference
Agriculture, Forestry	1,231	61.2	1,613	49.6	−11.6
Fishing & Hunting	45	2.2	69	2.1	−0.1
Manufacturing	231	11.5	437	13.4	1.9
Construction	46	2.3	109	3.3	1.0
Trade	112	5.6	292	9.0	3.4
Transportation	51	2.5	97	3.0	0.5
Services	254	12.7	505	15.5	2.8
Unspecified	41	2.0	132	4.1	2.1
Total	2,010	100.0	3,254	100.0	—

* Corrected figures. Boletín de Análisis Demográfico, No. 2. The corrections correspond to the female EAP.

The figures reveal a steep drop in the amount of cattle raising and agriculture between 1940 and 1961. The relative increase in the number of people engaged in manufacturing was not so impressive, while trade and services absorbed the largest number of people. The figures also demonstrate a fact that has been shown in other Latin American countries: besides the normal increase in tertiary activities, which always accompanies the development of an urbanized economy and the rapid growth of the cities, industrial expansion tends not to absorb the active population to the same degree as investments in it expand and as its output increases.

The most common explanation of this phenomenon is that industrialization in Latin America is still very weak and limited, so that its ability to offer employment to all the people flocking into the most industrialized cities is far less than its capacity to stimulate urban growth would imply.

Nevertheless, if we take into account the increase in investment and manufacturing output, the real explanation must be sought elsewhere. The fact is that the recent tendencies toward expansion in industry do not follow the same patterns of development characterized by the highly industrialized countries of today. As is common among dependent developing nations, they make use mainly of the latest technological advances and innovations. Not only does this take place at the production level, but also the latest ideas are applied to the organization of enterprises and labor, and the distribution and marketing of raw materials and manufactured goods. This phenomenon becomes still more important in a situation in which industrial growth is not the result of rational planning under a sovereign government but is carried out in accordance with the new tendencies and orientations of foreign capital, thus only accentuating the country's state of dependence. The growth of investment and increase in production in Peru, as in all the Latin American countries, is taking place at a time when, as a result of the importation of technological innovations from the highly developed capitalist countries, an ever *smaller* but much *more skilled* labor force is required. Just the opposite of what happened previously when the semimechanized methods of production were much more compatible with the unskilled nature of the labor force.[6] At the same time, the transition from what one could term cottage industries, with their characteristic "paternalism" and inadequate organization of labor and production, to the modern type of enterprise, with a high degree of efficiency in its organization of labor and enterprises, was relatively sudden. This innovation in the system of entrepreneurial organization is primarily the result of the monopolistic structure of the most efficient

[6] Glaucio Ary Dillon Soares, *The New Industrialization and the Brazilian Political System*, reprinted in this volume, pp. 186-201.

and productive enterprises, which control most of the investments and belong to powerful international financial concerns.

In Latin America as a whole, the restructuring of the poorly developed and dependent capitalistic economy is part of a process in which small- and medium-sized businesses are being replaced by large monopolistic international enterprises, which are redistributing the Latin American market. The most important factors, then, in explaining the relative lack of growth in the number of people employed in manufacturing industries in Peru and in other Latin American countries[7] are the following: industrial production has become controlled by large international enterprises; the organization of the enterprise, and of labor and production has become rationalized; and further innovations have been required by this whole process.

Though the growth, in relative terms, in the number of people employed by manufacturing concerns is slow, highly significant and important changes have taken place within this sector in the sense of new social and economic conflicts and a new framework of social domination.

More than 50 percent of the people in manufacturing industries are still employed by traditional concerns of light industry. However, the economic and social importance of the sector engaged in intermediate basic industries is now much greater because of the differences in productive methods, and because the new industries are expanding. The highest productivity in the traditional industries was that of tobacco, with 282,000 million *soles* in 1963; among the new industries, those of electric and nonelectric machines added up to 1,330,000 million soles in 1963.[8] This implies that the movement from the unskilled sectors into the more skilled sectors is extremely intense in each occupational group. Thus, in the sector engaging in traditional industry, 1.15 percent were professional people; in the new industries, they reached 4.96 percent. Among production workers, 24 percent, 95.85 percent, and 57 percent were, respectively, skilled, semiskilled, and unskilled. In the new industries, skilled, semiskilled, and unskilled were, respectively, 21.17 percent, 90.58 percent, and 32.90 percent. All of these figures were taken from the 1961 census.

The expansion of the tertiary sector is due to the constant immigration into the cities. One should, however, use these figures with care, since they could lead one to believe that the

[7] Paul Baran and Paul Sweezey, *Notas sobre la Teoría del Imperialismo*, Monthly Review, eds. en espanol, No. 31, Santiago.

[8] Palomino Roedel, *op. cit.*, p. 23.

urban middle class has grown proportionately, because it is usually connected with the tertiary sector. What the figures do not show is that the greatest part of people shown to be involved in tertiary activities are people who have neither employment nor income of any sort, and these people make up the great "marginal" masses of the principal cities. The latest research on immigration into Lima[9] shows that 70 percent of women immigrants go into domestic service, and 48 percent of the men "were self-employed." That is, they were underemployed, as the editors of the report pointed out. Nevertheless, it is clear that the increase in tertiary activities in the most important cities as well as in the country (though there to a much smaller degree) forms the basis for the expansion of the middle social and economic sectors. This has been happening during recent years. So, too, the modifications in the structure of production caused by the new tendencies in foreign investment have brought about changes in labor relations, and the development of a new structure of control and of social and economic conflicts that are very different from the traditional image of Peruvian society.

In 1965 the population of the country was estimated at 11,649,000, which represents an increase of 74 percent from 1940, and an average annual rise of 2.2 percent. But this average rate of growth shows a change from 1.72 percent in 1940 to 3.06 percent in 1965.[10] Thus, Peru has one of the highest rates of population growth on the continent.

The ecological-demographical structure has changed drastically during the last few decades and is tending toward new lines of development. This is a result of the country's development from an agricultural to an urban economy and the deterioration in agricultural production for domestic consumption, which had been carried on mainly in the center of the country. This change is also associated with the expansion of transportation and communications; ideas and products have been carried from the cities into the rural communities with resultant changes in the ecology and demography of the countryside. Apart from the reduction in the mortality rate, the high birth rate, and the youth of the population (45 percent

[9] *Encuesta de Migración. Lima Metropolitana* (Dirección de Estadística del Ministerio de Hacienda, Lima, 1966), p. 58, Table 27.
[10] *Población del Perú* (Documento de Trabajo No. R.H. 2-1, del Servicio del Empleo y Recursos Humanos, Ministerio de Trabajo, Lima, 1965), p. 4.

are younger than 15), the influence of the new industrialization is most strongly revealed in the rapid urban expansion.

The rate of growth of the cities as a result of immigration, between 1940 and 1961 was 3.7 percent, while the rural population increased at the rate of only 1.2 percent during the same period, even though the birth rate in the country continues to be higher than that in the cities. Consequently, the urban population went from 35.4 percent to 47.4 percent between 1940 and 1961, giving an estimated 1966 urban population of 50.4 percent of the total population. This is reduced to 43.1 percent if we consider as "urban" only those towns with a population of 2,000 or more. This criterion yields an average annual rate of urban growth that is even higher—4.4 percent.[11]

. . . Still, today about half the population lives in the country. Many observers deduce from this fact that the traditional relationships between city and country and the social and economic structure of the rural areas have not changed appreciably. But the reality is that the economic and social structure of the rural areas has been moving in the same direction as the whole of Peruvian society, though at a much slower and more irregular pace, toward a complete change in the relationships between country and town, and between the cities themselves.

On the one hand, the figures on present developments in the economic structure show that economic growth is concentrated in the cities, giving them complete economic domination of the rural areas. At the same time, moreover, the deterioration of agricultural production makes these rural areas completely dependent upon the urban areas. Thus, the present demographic relations between town and country by no means imply that the traditional economic relations between them, which granted the rural areas relative social, economic, and cultural autonomy, persist. In fact, the rural areas used to dominate the towns and cities, since the center of the country's economy was in agriculture and cattle raising.

As in the rest of the underdeveloped world, urban growth proceeds at different rates, depending upon the region and the situation of the city. Out of 37 cities enumerated in 1961, 21 were situated on the coast, 13 in the Sierra, and 3 in the forest or jungle regions. Among the cities along the coast, the ones that are growing fastest are in the region of most rapid industrial expansion—Lima-Callao and Chimbote. While

[11] John Grauman, *Population Re-Distribution in Peru,* Centro Latinoamericano de Demografía, Santiago, 1961, pp. 20-25 (mimeographed).

the average rate of growth for all towns of 2,000 or more inhabitants is 4.4 percent, the rate of growth of Lima-Callao is 5.2 percent. The other coastal towns grow at a rate of 4.2 percent, while the average annual rate of increase of the Sierra cities is 2.8 percent. The discontinuity in the rhythm of expansion and the size of these cities is not a Peruvian phenomenon only, although in Peru it reaches an extreme. The metropolitan density index for the urban areas in Peru is considered by some experts to be the highest in Latin America,[12] and by others, the highest in the whole underdeveloped world.[13]

Since more than 60 percent of the GNP comes from the coast, the concentration of urban areas along the coast should not be too surprising. If we also consider that 67 percent of all investment and industrial production is concentrated in Lima, it is no wonder that 63 percent of the urban population are in Lima-Callao. But the concentration of economic development along the coast, and in Lima-Callao in particular, directly corresponds to the coast's dependence upon foreign capital. Thus, the greatest amount of foreign investment is concentrated in Lima-Callao. That is, urbanization in Peru and its tendency toward regionalism on the one hand, and metropolitan concentration on the other, can be explained by observing the forms in which the country is dependent upon foreign capital. This shows the high degree to which dependence upon foreign capital determines the basic changes in our society. . . .

We have already seen that agriculture, in general, was growing at the average annual rate of only 2.6 percent. This is far below the rate of economic growth of the country as a whole during the period 1950-1964. During this time its contribution to the GNP dropped from 25 to 17 percent. Of this total agricultural output, 70 percent came from cash crops for export, grown mainly along the coast. This means that the areas of greatest stagnation in agricultural production are those situated in the mountains and producing for the domestic market. As a result, according to the figures obtained by the National Planning Institute,[14] the import of food products shot up. From this it can be seen that the traditional economic structure of the rural areas is disintegrating everywhere except

[12] Bruce Herrick, *Urban Migration and Economic Development in Chile* (Cambridge, Mass.: The M. I. T. Press, 1965), p. 28.

[13] Bert Hoselitz, "Generative and Parasitic Cities," *Economic Development and Cultural Change*, 3 (April 1955).

[14] INP, pp. 125-128.

along the coast. The migration of the rural population into the cities has been shown in the above tables. The labor force in the cities comes mainly from the traditional sector of agriculture, which provided the country with food, and it is this sector that is most strongly affected by a reduction in the required labor force. . . .

In the face of this situation the rural population has only three alternatives within the system: (1) immigration into urban or semiurban areas; (2) partial employment or unemployment if the people do not migrate; (3) getting into different, nonagricultural types of activity. Migration to the cities continues to increase, and rural unemployment and only partial employment stands at about 40 percent.[15] Anyone who travels through the country can see that a great number of people are turning to nonagricultural types of occupations.

To the extent that transportation and communications are improved, the influx of imported foodstuffs into the rural areas also increases. Thus, the countryside is no longer isolated from the city but is becoming increasingly dependent upon it. This is why not only subsistence farming but food production for the domestic market is stagnating. New types of activities springing up in the countryside include small business and trading; and during the last few years a vast network of small rural markets has formed. These markets, though very small when looked at individually, form an important and gigantic system when regarded collectively.[16]

The main products carried into the country from the cities are things like clothes, beverages, foodstuffs, utensils, and portable radios. This necessarily implies changes in consumer patterns and in the aspirations and the motivations of the rural population, which explains at least in part why they are so strongly attracted to the cities. The traditional role of agriculture was not just food production; it included domestic manufacture of clothes, tools, etc. The importation of manufactured goods from the cities tends to narrow the role of agriculture to food production alone.

The food output has, however, gone down to a seriously low level. The "independent farmers," mainly small landholders, reduced their contribution to the GNP from 22 percent in 1950 to 12 percent in 1963, whereas the "self-em-

[15] *Diagnóstico de la Situación de los Recursos Humanos* (Servicio de Recursos Humanos y del Empleo, Ministerio de Trabajo, Lima, 1966), p. 39.
[16] W. Mangin, *Classification of Highland Communities in Latin America.* Cornell Latin American Year, March 1966.

ployed" not in agriculture increased their share to 18 percent during the same period.[17] For this reason we must regard these new occupations, which were previously regarded as secondary and relatively rare, or even nonexistent, as permanently established in these areas. Small business and small-scale manufacturing are probably the most important occupations in the growing urbanization of the countryside. Thus, the changes brought about in the economic structure of the country in general are also taking place in the noncoastal regions, though only slowly and with differences according to each region.

What is the place occupied by the "traditional haciendas" in this pattern of change? Even today they often are regarded as characteristic of the feudal structure of the noncoastal areas. Certainly there was a great deal of "seigneurialism" in the relations between labor and the landowners, which was made all the more acute by the vast ethnic and cultural differences between them. Nevertheless, these productive entities (developed mostly during the years between the emancipation and the first half of the nineteenth century when the economy of the whole country became agrarian as a result of the economic slump following the emancipation) were always capitalistic, however traditional or primitive they may have been. They not only produced enough for their own needs, but supplied the local and regional markets. The reason they have always been referred to as "feudalistic" is that those elements that characterize "feudalistic" labor relationships were isolated and looked at separately, while they were really agrarian capitalist productive units.

Next to the disintegration of these units of agrarian capitalism, the most important phenomena are the changes taking place in the organization of production in these haciendas. Not only are the owners of these large properties completely tied to the urban economy along the coast and to the finance and credit markets of Lima-Callao, but many of these farms are being converted into large production "enterprises," with all the characteristics of the coastal plantations, in regard to their organization of labor and production.

. . . Primarily in the more important cities, and above all in Lima-Callao, a new urban society is emerging. In the country, also, a new social and economic structure is emerging, though more slowly and erratically.

[17] Aníbal Quijano, *Diagnóstico de la Situación de los Recursos Humanos* (Servicio del Empleo y de Recursos Humanos, Ministerio de Trabajo, Lima), p. 39.

The disintegration of agriculture in the traditional areas means that the economic base of the traditional landowning class is also crumbling. This has in fact been going on for some time. However, in the last twenty years the process has accelerated considerably. The principal reasons for this decline are the deterioration of agriculture, the constant division of the large estates through inheritance, migration into the cities, and the taking up of other types of employment, and the displacement of the most traditional sectors by large commercial agricultural enterprise. In addition, especially during the last decade, the movements among the peasants to reclaim the land from the landowners, though they were always ruthlessly put down, managed to gain hold of some of this land. More recently, the Government has started to redistribute land in some of the areas of greatest tension, which all contributes to a reduction in the power of the landowners. This does not mean that this social stratum has disappeared, because precisely its most powerful groups still continue to flourish. These remaining groups of landholders do not do so by means of the traditional methods, but take an active part in the industry and finance, and in changing the production methods on their farms. They thus change as a social class and can no longer be looked upon as "traditional landowners" or "feudal lords."

TABLE 6

OCCUPATIONAL STRUCTURE OF ECONOMICALLY ACTIVE
AGRICULTURE POPULATION
(in percent)

Occupation	1940	1961
Employers ("Patronos")	39.5	2.2
Salaried Employees	0.3	1.1
Laborers[a]	26.3	30.0
Unpaid family labor	21.1	16.9
Self-employed	12.5	49.8
Unspecified	0.5	0.0
Total	100.0	100.0

Sources: 1940 & 1961 Censuses.
     a) The 1940 category included "workers and peasants."

One can see that the figures are not strictly comparable. For there to have been such a drastic reduction in the category "Employers," a veritable revolution would have to have occurred. Unfortunately, there was no such thing. The 1940 figures were obviously considerably inflated, and in the 1961 Census the content of categories has changed.

Despite the inaccuracy of the figures, it is likely that there has been a decline in the number of agricultural employers, or better, that the landowning class has shrunk. This decline did not take place along the coast. The traditional rural areas in the mountains have been most affected by the new trend. In other words, the traditional landowning stratum is declining.

At the same time as the large landowning class is disintegrating and its characteristics as a class are changing, a significant sector of petite bourgeoisie is emerging. The number of self-employed farming people increased during the period between the two censuses, and the latest figures of the Banco de Reservas demonstrate that this group grew by about 15 percent from 1950 to 1965. Undoubtedly these figures include a great number of smallholders, so small that their inclusion in the rural middle class is hardly legitimate. The smallholders, though in one way middle class, tend to make a living in non-agricultural occupations or hire themselves out as farmhands, and as such their real status and character is that of wage laborers.

However, as a result of the constant dividing up of the large landholdings by inheritance, and of the lands becoming available for purchase by businessmen, an important percentage of the so-called self-employed shown in the censuses can be correctly placed in the rural middle class, which is constantly expanding.

The influx of such a large number of semiurban and new economic activities into the countryside, among which small- and medium-sized businesses figure most importantly, has contributed more than anything to the expansion of the rural middle class sectors. This has led to the disintegration of the "indigenous communities" in the areas most strongly exposed to the influence of the urban economies. The petite bourgeoisie in these rural areas is made up of small and medium-sized landholders, businessmen, and craftsmen, and in the latter years has come to be based much less upon the size of land owned by the individual than upon his monetary wealth.

Parallel to the above tendencies there is a continuing process of proletarianization of the rural population. The small landholders have been part of this process for some time because of the domination of the large landholders and the subdivision of the land as agricultural production continued to deteriorate. However, previously wage labor was much rarer and much less important. As things stand now, people have been forced to seek wage work as a result of rising population and the virtual destruction of food production (for immediate private consumption) by droughts, which the smallholder cannot afford to counter with irrigation. He is thus forced to find employment in nonagricultural occupations in the semiurbanized rural areas, or to hire himself out to large and medium-sized landholders.

On the other hand, the peasant who has been incorporated into the "traditional hacienda" as a nonwage laborer is now forced to make a living often under even prefeudal conditions, as a result of the disintegration of the traditional economic system of large estates, the increase in cattle raising, and cultivation of fodder instead of growing food for local consumption, the reduced labor force required in this type of agriculture, and the redistribution of Goverment-controlled land in some areas. Other peasants seek wage labor in the country, or migrate into the cities to add to the mass of underemployed and unemployed already there.

The idea behind the "agrarian reform" was to eliminate some of the least productive and more old-fashioned sectors of the traditional society, to increase the relatively large number of smaller and medium-sized landholdings, and to transform the rest of the rural population into wage workers. That is to say, it was basically only a limited and clever method of moderating the sources of tension, and of accelerating an already rapid rate of change in society. . . .

We should not forget that all of these are tendencies and that the new social structure has not yet definitely crystallized. Certainly in the more isolated regions this change is far from being realized. Rural society vacillates between the old and the new structural patterns. This causes a very noticeable ambivalance and conflicts in standards and norms between the groups that are just emerging and the traditional groups that are on their way out.

. . . We already know that a large proportion of the rural population belonged to the old indigenous rural subculture. The many factors contributing to the process of change in Peruvian society as a whole have combined to accelerate the cultural assimilation of part of the indigenous population and have modified the subculture itself. There is a growing search for a new cultural identity that is different not only from the powerful Western Creole culture but also from the suppressed indigenous culture. This is particularly pronounced among part of the Indian and mestizo sectors,[18] who conform to the "cholo" cultural group.

[18] Aníbal Quijano, *La Emergencia del grupo "cholo" y sus implicaciones en la sociedad peruana*, Lima, 1964 (mimeographed).

Insofar as ethnic differentiation has, since colonial days, constituted one of the most important bases of social evaluation, the emergence of a new structure of social differentiation in the countryside cannot but penetrate and complicate social relations and conflicts in the country as a whole.

The concentration of foreign investment in the urban sectors of the economy, the rapid process of urbanization, and the direct relation existing between urban development and foreign investment have caused a much more rapid rate of urban than of rural change. This affects many more people. While in the rural areas and especially in the most backward areas a new system of social conflict and social differentiation is emerging, the equivalent process in the cities is already firmly consolidated and is tending to expand.

The most important elements that stand out are the following: (1) the consolidation of the tertiary and industrial sectors as the main core of the national capitalist class, implying the rapid elimination from this class of the still remaining social and psychological characteristics of the traditional Spanish and French aristocracy; (2) the numerical increase of the urban "new middle class" as the result of increased bureaucratization and professionalization, and a growing petite bourgeoisie, based upon the expanding commercial sector and small industries engaged in tertiary activities; (3) the increase, especially in the large cities, and most of all in the metropolitan area of Lima-Callao, in the number of factory and nonfactory workers; (4) and the growth of a huge mass of unemployed and underemployed people who have no definite place in the newly developing socioeconomic structure except as oppressed outsiders.

Not only is the economic life of the country as a whole dependent on foreign capital, but so also is the development of cultural, social, and economic institutions in the new urban society, thus modifying the elements that used to characterize the social psychology and the subculture of the inhabitants of the large cities. In this way, a dependent urban culture has developed that is the result of the introduction and the imitation of modes of living of the advanced capitalist countries, especially the United States. The patterns of consumption, and the orientations, the aspirations, and the goals of groups and individuals among the middle class in particular are affected.

At the same time, however, the successive waves of migrants

coming from the rural and semiurban subcultures of the country, having strong indigenous characteristics, have contributed to the development of an urban subculture among the people belonging to the oppressed social class in the cities, which is characterized by values and institutions of indigenous tradition. Dominated and suppressed, they clearly express the cultural conflicts caused by changes in the whole of Peruvian society, and its consequences in the formation of social classes in the cities are important. Later on we will show what some of these consequences are.

On the basis of what we have seen of the principal changes and tendencies in urban and rural society we will attempt to give a brief outline of the nature of the national power structure. In general, one could say that this structure of national domination and conflict corresponds closely to the type of changes taking place in the structure of production. However, the forms of expression of the system arise not only from the immediate economic basis of the country and as a result of its dependence on the advanced capitalistic countries, but also from the cultural conflicts inherited from our previous colonial domination. . . .

I. The Dependent Bourgeoisie

The dominant class of this society can be correctly defined as a "dependent bourgeoisie." Previously, with our productive structure based primarily upon mining and agriculture, and mining directly controlled by foreign capitalists, the Peruvian bourgeoisie was primarily a bourgeoisie of large landowners, a few merchant-financiers, and still fewer light-industrialists.

The nucleus of the Peruvian bourgeoisie used to be the large landowners. Agriculture, cattle raising, and mining have been relegated to a place of secondary importance in the present economic structure, and industrial manufacturing and tertiary activities have taken their place. This means the displacement of the landowning bourgeoisie, producing for regional or international markets, from their traditionally dominating position in the bourgeoisie, and the emergence of the industrial and mercantile bourgeoisie in the cities as the dominating sector of this social class.

For this reason, the present dominating class in our society, whose dependent position should be emphasized, appears to be made up of the following sectors:

(1) The industrial bourgeoisie.
(2) The mercantile and financial bourgeoisie.

(3) The bourgeoisie of landowners producing for the export market.
(4) The bourgeoisie of landowners producing for local and regional markets.

This sectorial division of the whole of the dependent bourgeoisie in the country is primarily of analytical value. There is diverse social intercourse between these sectors at many levels. Nonetheless, some of the groups in the industrial-mercantile bourgeoisie have only recently arrived via social climbing from the upper middle class, usually by way of politics and by using government resources to their own private advantage. These social groups are directly or indirectly connected with all the others, primarily through mercantile and industrial activities.

II. The Middle Classes

The expansion of the administrative apparatus of government, increasing professionalization and mechanization, the growth of tertiary activities in the cities and their diffusion into the rural areas, have permitted the development of an intermediate social and economic class, though with considerable differences between city and country.

The principal sectors of this intermediate population could be defined as:
(1) The new urban middle class.
(2) The semiurban and urban petite bourgeoisie.
(3) The rural agricultural petite bourgeoisie.
(4) The rural commercial petite bourgeoisie.

The new middle class is made up of groups involved in nonmanual salaried occupations, in private and public bureaucracies, and professionals and technicians. Previously these people were drawn from the provincial landowning sectors as these began to decline, and from diminishment in the core of urban middle class people that the economic recovery, particularly the rise in exports, brought about in the middle of the nineteenth century. Nowadays, as well as coming from these two sectors, the new urban middle class is recruited from the rural and semiurban bourgeoisie, the skilled working classes, and from the previously existing urban middle class itself, which probably contributes the largest number.

The tremendous pressures for the expansion of higher education, for construction of universities and their equivalents, has produced a surprising proliferation of these institutions; in less than five years, from only five universities, the number has risen to almost 40. This is partly because the bourgeoisie has established its own professional and technical training centers in order to escape the risk of exposing the student body to the "excessive" political activities in the official universities. Whatever the academic effects of this proliferation of universities may be, it reveals, better than any statistics, the strong desire and pressures within the popular classes to move up the social scale.

The urban and semiurban petite bourgeoisie was created primarily as a result of the expansion of commercial and public service activities and small industry during the last few years. Not even during the colonial and postcolonial periods before the beginning of this century did the Peruvian petite bourgeoisie, insofar as they were owners of small producing concerns, become established as a definite and important social class. The small colonial middle groups that emerged throughout the seventeenth and eighteenth centuries became stagnant and were reduced to insignificance as a result of the decline of exports and the complete agrarianization of the economy; they began to develop once more very slowly in the second half of the nineteenth century, when exports once again became important. During the years following the Second World War, the rapid growth of the cities, the new trends in the structure of production, and the influx of foreign capital have led to a relative expansion in small manufacturing industries, and above all in activities such as sales, service of all kinds, and commercial advertising activities.

The rural petite bourgeoisie is, in part, the result of the disintegration of large landholdings in some sectors and the increasing amount of commercial activities that have sprung up in the country. For this reason, the rural petite bourgeoisie could be divided into two groups, the agricultural and the commercial rural petite bourgeoisie. They are both very widespread.

III. The Laboring Population

This class includes all the manual laborers directly involved in the production of goods and services. The principal sectors that make up the present working class can be characterized as:

(1) Urban factory and nonfactory workers.
(2) Semiurban workers employed in mining and on the plantations along the coast.

(3) Rural agricultural and nonagricultural laborers.

Previously, as the result of the structure of production itself, the socially and economically most important sectors of the working class were involved in agriculture and mining. Today, however, the urban working class has come to be the most important socially and economically. Moreover, since the urban manufacturing industries are developing more rapidly in intermediate basic industries than in the traditional industries producing for local consumption, the workers in this branch of production are coming to be the most important class; despite their decreasing importance, however, more than 50 percent of the urban working class are still engaged in traditional industries using outdated methods of production.

TABLE 7

ECONOMICALLY ACTIVE POPULATION, 1961 (in thousands)

	(Number)	(Percent)
Employers	69.6	1.9
Self-employed	1,409.7	38.5
Clerical and Sales Employees	402.8	11.0
Laborers	1,153.4	31.5
Domestic help	205.0	5.6
Unpaid domestic labor	333.2	9.1
Unspecified	87.9	2.4
Total	3,661.6	100.0

Sources: 1961 population census.

The largest sector of the economically active population is "self-employed." This category includes all the "odds and ends," such as self-employed professional persons, small and intermediate farmers, small businessmen, and artisans. *It also includes those who do not have permanent or definite employment, either in the city or in the country,* and it is this group that makes up the immense sector on the periphery of Peruvian society.

The agricultural laborers employed on the huge plantations along the semiurbanized coast make up the largest stratum in the whole working class. After them come the miners, the factory workers, and others in the cities. The agricultural wage laborers in the Sierras are important because of their large numbers. However, in most cases their position as wage laborers is ill defined since subsistence farming still plays an important part in these areas.

IV. Peasants

The decline of the large estates with their internal "semi-feudal" relationships is occurring very slowly in most regions, and a relatively large number of tenant (non-wage) laborers, probably most of them Indians, still exists. This sector is popularly referred to as the "servile" class, since it is true that many seigneurialistic elements persist in the relations between owners and laborers, carrying into the present the ancient hacienda system.

Nevertheless, these haciendas no longer produce only for their own and local consumption; they supply regional and even international markets. This is especially true of the coffee and tea plantations in the valleys of La Convención and Lares. Thus, these large haciendas are, in effect, small capitalist enterprises that use feudal means in labor relations to produce for capitalist ends.

These practices characterize a stagnant agrarian capitalism, continuing with feudal and prefeudal labor relations. While from the point of view of the labor relations on these farms, the agricultural laborers can be regarded as serfs, from the point of view of their role in the productive process as a whole, this is no longer true. They are producers of merchandise for an extensive market, and an integral part of the capitalist system as a whole; the term "nonwage laborers" describes this class much more adequately than "serf." Historically, this sector of the population is a vestige of the stagnation of capitalism in these regions and is now disintegrating. Its members are seeking wage work or becoming small farmers, or both; or they are migrating to the cities to become part of the large "marginal" urban working class.

V. The "marginal" urban population

I have already pointed out how the modernization of urban industry and the introduction and application of the latest methods of production, of enterprise, and of labor utilization—rather than the lack of industrialization—explains the fact that only a relatively small amount of the available labor force in the cities is actually required. And this is occurring when migration into the cities is greater than ever before, and the labor force is growing at a rate disproportionate to the capacity of the dependent and underdeveloped capitalist market in the cities. Lack of jobs and capital has created a tendency for these immigrants to move to the periphery of society. This "marginalization" is made all the more acute because most of them are not qualified for the types of work carried on in the cities. Many are illiterate or very nearly so, and are hindered also by restrictive hiring practices.[19]

The existence of a large urban class of this kind reveals clearly the trends of development in the dependent capitalist system in Peru. At the same time as the urban economy, including urban industry and manufacturing, is expanding, there is a parallel rise in the number of people who are not, and never will be, able to become integrated into this new economic and social structure.[20] Migration and the increase of this "marginal" population create, on the one hand, a "reserve labor force" for industry to draw from, but also, on the other hand, a sector "available" and ready for mobilization by political movements. . . .

Not all the sectors of the population can be defined and organized in terms of class. For this reason, I shall put down a few impressions here, which are nothing more than impressions, but which can provide some food for thought and, perhaps, the point of departure for future research.

In the first place, the development of a multiclass social structure of modern classes corresponds to the underdeveloped and dependent state of the country. This is a relatively recent process impelled by an economy that is still rather unstable, though with relatively clearly defined trends of development. . . .

(1) The dominant bourgeoisie, dependent upon its integration with foreign capitalist interests, reveals at least two traits that are important in themselves and in relation to the other groups. On the one hand, it is true that the dominating social sector is the urban industrial bourgeoisie. This does not mean, however, that its position of dominance has become completely established, for the economic activities on which its social and political power is based have themselves not yet become established as the leading sector of national economic production. Foreign economic interests are still closely tied to the landowning class, though its emphasis is clearly in new areas of production. Secondly, and closely related to this, the dominating class is split culturally. The landowners behave according to the patterns of the traditional French and Spanish

[19] Fernando Henrique Cardozo y José Reyna, *Industrialización, Estructura Ocupacional y Estratificación Social en América Latina* (Santiago: Instituto Latinoamericano de Planificación Económica y Social, 1966, mimeographed).

[20] See Aníbal Quijano, *Notas sobre el concepto de marginalidad*, CEPAL, División de Asuntos Sociales, 1966.

aristocracy, whereas the new urban business and industrial classes predominantly imitate the United States. This influence of the U.S. is predominant and ascendant in the dominant classes all over Peru. Traditional behavior is found mainly in labor relations on the large plantations, and in the "clientele" relations—though to a lesser degree—in the "new urban middle classes." The bourgeoisie, dependent on foreign capitalist interests, is the only clearly defined class in Peru in all aspects: its consciousness of its general interests, its organization in political and juridical associations, and its use of the government to secure its rule.

People who view Peruvian society in the traditional way regard the large estate landowners on the one hand, and the industrial and the mercantile sectors on the other, as forming two distinct social classes with conflicting interests. Thus, the landholders appear as a bourgeois feudal oligarchy, closely linked with foreign economic interests, and the others as the "national bourgeoisie" who, because they have interests that conflict with those of the large landowners, assume a "progressive" role in society and a "nationalistic" attitude toward imperialism in all its forms. This view of Peruvian society is erroneous. The sectors of the bourgeoisie involved in agricultural production for export as well as for domestic markets, and those that are primarily involved in financial, mercantile, and industrial activities, share the same class interests. They are inseparably interconnected economically, and through close family and social ties. In fact, today the financial, commercial, and industrial sectors are much more dependent on foreign capitalist interests than the agricultural, mining, and cattle producing sectors, and are, therefore, in the lead in representing modern imperialist interests within the country.

They are not a "national" bourgeoisie except in a geographic sense. There are plenty of conflicts—how could there not be?—between the sectors that make up this class, especially between the recent industrial urban bourgeoisie and the landowners. But the conflicts are not really conflicts of class interests. The fact that they generally share the same interests becomes very clear when their dominating position is in any way jeopardized. They showed this in a very violent way when they were confronted by the peasant and guerrilla movements. On the economic level, the intersectorial conflicts result from the expansion in production with which a given sector is connected and its efforts to defend its individual interests and ideas about society as a whole by using the State.

(2) The Peruvian working class is divided into different sectors, depending on the type and rate of development in the various branches of production. This division into sectors is not merely analytical, since each sector within the working class is directly tied to one specific kind of production, whereas each member of every sector of the bourgeoisie generally shares in the other. Moreover, the working class contains a complete cultural and ethnic cross section of the country. This is not the case in the bourgeoisie.

The urban-industrial working class is concentrated mainly in traditional light industries, and fewer than 50 percent are employed in the new intermediate basic industries. Yet, what is much more important, is that the greater part of this class is made up of recent immigrants from the countryside who belong to a subculture that is still permeated by rural or semiurban elements. The agricultural laborers on the large plantations along the coast, as well as the miners, are also members of a semiurban subculture, though the miners have many more working-class characteristics. Both sectors are intimately tied to and motivated by rural-peasant values. The rest of the rural wage laboring class is still in the midst of developing, and its position within the productive structure is only slowly becoming defined. . . .

The lack of development of class consciousness in the working class expresses itself in two ways. First, there is the low level of development of the unions. Most workers in the country do not belong to any unions at all, and there is little interindustrial union organization even where industrial sectors are well organized; there is no effective centralized union organization and coordination on a national scale.

Despite fierce battles at the end of the First World War for an eight-hour day, for unionization, and for a centralized national union organization, the working class at present tends to act only in isolation, and no attempt to attain national unity has so far been successful. But in general the workers' struggles are isolated, localized, and occur only on the level of the individual factory. Central national and regional organizations are merely formal bureaucratic apparatuses almost completely out of touch with the working class as a whole.

One reason for this is that for a long time the urban and semiurban union movement has been directed and led by political and ideological reformist movements, and the development of a class consciousness in the workers reflected these influences. To the extent that these new political reformist movements were identifying themselves with the new system of social domination, the unions came to be the instruments of the immediate political interests of these parties. The growth of the class struggle became distorted and produced the situation existing today. Nor did the organized political Left have a nonreformist line. The national political parties of the Left who claim to support the workers' interests, in fact, in their alignment with the unions often frustrated the attempts made to revitalize the unions. Yet, when all this has been said, it is also true that the workers' circumstances have given some reason for such reformist tendencies.

The urban working class is far better placed within the system than the peasants and the "marginal" urban sectors. They are integrated into the system of internal colonialism in Peru, where a large mass of peasants still belongs to the traditional sector of production and bears the brunt of the uneven and regional development of Peruvian capitalism. It is as if within the country itself certain aspects of the divisions and differences that exist between the advanced capitalist countries and the exploited and underdeveloped countries are reproduced.

The second factor retarding the development of class consciousness in the working class is the persistence of "paternalism" in the relations between employers and workers and between the Government and labor. One of the most pronounced characteristics of union struggles in Peru is that they turn into political battles rather quickly. The unions pressure the Government to arbitrate the disputes out of fear of the political consequences of union agitation.[21]

In fact, much of the present social legislation in the country was more a result of the Government's initiative in using it as an instrument in its battle against "The APRA," as early as 1936-1939, than something achieved by direct pressure from labor. It is true, of course, that this legislation was passed in favor of the urban working population and that, given the repressive nature of the Government and the ruling class of that time, they would never have been able to win it otherwise. Yet, it is also true that it contributed to the development of a "paternalistic" relationship between the working class and the Government, as well as with the ruling bourgeoisie. It also caused the survival of the influence of the reformist outlook.

In spite of all of these circumstances and difficulties, during

[21] James L. Payne, *Labor and Politics in Peru* (New Haven: Yale University Press, 1965).

the past decade a new class consciousness has been developing among certain sectors of the working class in new industries (such as metal) while the more traditional sectors (textiles) have continued to support the reformist position. The new sectors have developed new forms of union struggle, such as occupying factories and keeping the managers as hostages. Moreover, in its agitation it has used political pressure to obtain the very opposite of "paternalism," denouncing the state as the instrument of the ruling class rather than demanding that it intervene as arbiter over all classes. Thus, there are emergent political and ideological orientations that are forming the basis for a developing class consciousness in the new urban working class. This indicates also the double edged nature of the weapon that social legislation and political reform have put into the hands of the national bourgeoisie and of the reformist movements that still control the working class.

Nevertheless, those sectors that already take part in and those that are beginning to participate in these new movements within the working class are still quite few. In general, slogans displayed on the picket signs and union demands are directed exclusively to the branch of industry in which the union is organized, and not to industry in general, or rather, the class in general. Thus, the few unionized sectors frequently manage to get pay raises and gain access to a greater share of the market, while the nonunionized sectors, and the sectors whose unions are completely dependent upon the manipulations of the reformist political parties, constantly see their wages reduced. This situation has frequently provided the ruling class with a slogan to emphasize the "privileged" position of this or that sector of the manual or nonmanual workers, in comparison to the rest of the population. This has allowed them to influence the urban working population against these sectors and to neutralize, at least, its alliance with the striking sector, while the Government disarms and paralyzes the union organizations of these groups.

Moreover, the system of hiring manual labor is full of "paternalism" and the exclusiveness deriving from it. The hiring system is tied to a network within which the "personal recommendations" of the members of the bourgeoisie or the worker's application for work, made out by his friends or relatives, establish a working "clientele" and a "market of services" between the union bureaucracy and the bosses, which only increases the "marginalization" of the greater part of the labor force and emphasizes the "privileged" status of the unionized sectors. All this relates very closely to the present process of industrialization and its tendency not to absorb the unskilled labor force.

For these reasons, the development of class consciousness in the urban working class is colored by elements of exclusiveness with regard to other working-class strata, and the desire to maintain their favorable position. Thus, they see an extension of these benefits to the rest of the suppressed population as jeopardizing their own survival. This makes difficult and postpones any movement toward centralizing and coordinating all the existing unions within the working class.

(3) These elements of "patrimonial paternalism" are very much characteristic of the formation and expansion of the "middle classes," especially of what we have here referred to as the "new urban middle class." To the extent that the middle class emerges through the bureaucratization of society, its expansion is related to the recruitment practices of the system.

In Peru, as in all countries whose economies are in a state of transition, the bureaucracy develops by following simultaneously the traditional patrimonial hiring patterns inherited from colonialism, and those implied in the vacillating conditions of "modernization" and "mechanization" of the public and private bureaucratic apparatuses. Even the recent moves to modernize the system of recruitment and organization of the bureaucracy have been steeped in "patrimonialism." Although an effort is being made in a very restricted number of sectors to hire technicians and professional people rather than untrained personnel, they still tend to be hired because of their political and/or social affiliations rather than for any specialized knowledge.

Thus, the bureaucracy is made up of the vast clientele of powerful interests and pressure groups, and functions as a "services market" for these groups and those that emerge in the bureaucracy itself. The professionals and technicians are thus almost entirely dependent upon the groups with political and economic power and for that reason vigorously defend the present power structure from the other groups of society. Further, the dependent urban culture that is developing simultaneously with the urban middle class is strongly influenced by United States capitalism, U.S. patterns of consumption, life styles, and general values. This is leading the members of this sector into a state of pragmatic corruption unparalleled in any other Latin American country with the possible exceptions of Mexico and Venezuela. Though the same thing is happening to a certain extent in other Latin American countries (Argentina, Chile, and Uruguay) one gets the impression that part of the Hispano-European tradition, with its "humanistic values," still persists somewhat in these other countries. Perhaps this is so because they developed under the predominant influence of the traditional bourgeoisie and the formal and aristocratic views and strong moral and intellectual influence of Europe. The Peruvian middle class, on the contrary, is relatively young, and its process of development and socialization is taking place with nothing but the crude "cash-nexus" to form the core of its value system, under the guidance of the new urban bourgeoisie and the characteristic moral and intellectual influence of United States capitalism.

Without a doubt the character that these social sectors have recently acquired, coupled with the growing expansion of the urban middle classes as people from the "popular" classes move up into it, strongly and noticeably affects the orientation of its members. The search for status becomes their prime goal in life and to move up the social scale is their only desire, so that the status seeker has become the social type par excellence.[22] Nevertheless, the members of these classes appear to be trapped between the most strident social pragmatism and their daily frustrations: on the one hand, the pressures put on them by the new consumer patterns of foreign capitalism, and on the other, their not being able to afford them.

The channels through which they merge into the middle class have considerably widened and will continue to do so for a while, and so will certain channels of ascent into the still higher bourgeoisie that have been opened as a result of the recent economic expansion and by the use of politics and State resources. But they can never be wide enough to take in all the status seekers if those that have already "arrived" are to be able to maintain their patterns of consumption.

Perhaps these factors can explain why the members of the urban middle class, and in particular the young people, seem constantly to vacillate between social pragmatism and political radicalism. The strongest proof of this is to be found in the universities, by comparing the actual behavior of the various ideological groups. Strange as it may seem, but of real significance, is the fact that, whereas many students used to belong

[22] In recent years, foreigners have become the cultural models for the middle-class style of life in Lima-Callao.

to the *aprista* movement, so did many professional people. At present, though there are many students with revolutionary ideas, there are very few professionals who subscribe to these revolutionary ideologies. The *aprista* students came from the middle class but their professionalization did not necessarily imply upward social mobility. Most of the revolutionary students come from the lowest sector of the middle class or are on their way into this class. Their professionalization constitutes a relatively important change in social status.

All of these circumstances together with the contradictory character of society as a whole will probably become more acute in the near future. The very factors that will create revolutionary elements in these sectors are those that also bring about the fluctuations between social pragmatism and political radicalism in the youth of the urban middle class. . . .

(4) The rural wage workers in the more traditional interior of the country do not appear to have become sufficiently differentiated yet. This is not only because economic development in these areas is relatively slow and recent, but primarily because they are not merely wage laborers, but in most cases are also small proprietors or tenant workers.

Agricultural laborers can more easily identify a common enemy than can other peasant strata. Thus the battle against the large landowners has been joined by wage laborers who own no land, small proprietors, tenant workers, small traders, and semiurban craftsmen, who, in the face of the common enemy, recognized a communality of interests. However, to the extent that a given sector of this heterogeneous population achieves its immediate goals, and as the different sectors become socially differentiated, they cease to participate in the common movement against the landowners.

It is important to note in this respect that generally after a period of fierce struggles of the movement, after massacres and repressions, and after the estates have been invaded and a limited redistribution of the land in some areas has taken place, the rural unions, under moderate leadership, have shifted their struggles to the courts, and by so doing have completely conformed to the system of bourgeois legality. Though part of the reason for this has been the moderate leadership of these movements, it could not have occurred but for the profound differences in the immediate interests of the groups in the unions. Of these, the incipient agricultural and non-agricultural wage labor class in these regions is undoubtedly the weakest and least defined sector and has not yet organized to defend its own interests.

Figures indicate that the Peruvian economy has been expanding at an impressive rate over the past fifteen years. With a few fluctuations prior to 1958, but continuously since then, the annual rate of growth for the period 1950-1965 has averaged 5.6 percent; between 1958 and 1965 it rose to above 8 percent. The average rate in Latin America is about 2 percent.[23] The Peruvian GNP per capita rose by 3 percent annually and private incomes went up 3.3 percent in the same period. The annual rate of population growth is estimated at between 2.5 percent and 2.9 percent.[24] Thus one could say that Peruvian society really is developing. Nevertheless, the data reveal also that beneath those figures, which for a Latin American country are significant, there exists another hard social and economic reality.

The reasons for these indications of growth are, primarily, increasing exports, increasing participation of the government in the national economy, and the growth of urban industry. Expansion of exports has occurred mainly in powdered-fish or fish-meal and mineral products. During the period 1950-1965 exports grew at an average annual rate of 8.5 percent, permitting the flow of foreign exchange to rise to an average rate of 8.9 percent per year.[25]

Almost all mining production is directly controlled by American enterprises; and with the present mining legislation, which was passed under the dictator General Odría, they enjoy exemption from taxes and a multitude of other benefits. These mining "enclaves," can be considered as belonging to Peru only geographically. The increased export of mining products, whose benefits are reaped by foreign investors, is due mainly to United States requirements for the war in Vietnam. Production of fish-meal, which was started with Peruvian capital and supplied the European market with fertilizers, has come under foreign control (U.S., German, Japanese). This occurred both through direct purchase shares and by means of financial and credit controls; the latter are shared with national capital and are much more closely related to the national economy. But as other countries begin to produce their own fish-meal, Peru is bound to suffer. All this reveals the contingent character of this economic expansion and

[23] INP, vol. II, pp. 12-14; *Cuentas Nacionales del Perú, 1950-1965,* Banco Central de Reservas, Lima, 1966, p. 7.
[24] *Ibid.*
[25] *Ibid,* p. 10.

its inherent weakness. The exports are rising not only because of the general development taking place in the country as a whole, but also because of the increasing dependence of the economy on foreign capital.

The State channels 13 percent of all investments in the country[26] and its share in goods and services has risen at an average annual rate of 9.8 percent between 1950 and 1965, and in 1964 reached 16.5 percent.[27] Some of the revenue comes from internal taxation but most of it derives from foreign loans and credit. Between 1951 and 1962 alone, the national debt went above 500 million dollars.[28] Increased government participation in the economy is a result of an increase in the national debt and of the new orientations of foreign capitalism.

During this same period (1950-1965) manufacturing as a share of the GNP rose at an average annual rate of 7.5 percent and at present amounts to 20 percent of the GNP. Eighty (80) percent of all manufactured goods has been destined for the domestic market.[29]

In May 1966, the Peruvian government claimed in a report submitted to the "*Seminario de Industrialización*," that the greatest part of industrial investment came from the reinvestment of national capital and from credits at the *Banco Industrial*. However, their own data show that 80 percent of industrial investment is that of foreign capital. Moreover, their data also reveal that the *Banco Industrial's* credit is very closely connected to foreign financial and credit organizations.[30]

In fact, economic growth in Peru over the past fifteen years is a result of the new trends in foreign capital investment—its shift from agricultural and mining to the industrial sector and government economic activities. In other words, the present economic growth reveals our growing dependence on foreign capital, and American capital in particular. This is the congenital weakness of the Peruvian economy, and of the new strata in the bourgeoisie—their dependence on foreign interests. . . .

Though dominated by the agricultural and mining sectors of the economy, the past dependence of the other regions of the country on the coast and the metropolitan area of Lima-

[26] *Ibid*, p. 11.
[27] INP, vol. II, p. 12.
[28] *El Financiamiento Externo en Latinoamerica*, United Nations, 1966.
[29] INP, vol. II, p. 12.
[30] CEPAL, *El Desarrollo Industrial del Perú*, Simposio Latinoamericano de Industrialización (Santiago, March 1966), pp. 36-39 (mimeographed).

Callao never reached its present degree. The coast employed cheap labor from the Sierra, and used its food products and natural resources in general for the expansion and "modernization" of the coastal economy. Nevertheless, the mountain regions, and above all the rural areas, maintained a considerable amount of autonomy, which permitted the stagnation of their agricultural capitalism, their slow rate of change, and the social and political predominance of their landowners.

At present, this autonomy is being brutally and completely destroyed by the disintegration of the traditional rural economy, the flood of products from the urban coast, and the expansion of roads and communications, which are all part of the process of urbanization and the general state of transition of the Peruvian economy. Thus the rural areas are nowadays completely dependent upon the cities along the coast, and the whole country is dependent on Lima-Callao.

According to the 1961 census, 21 out of the 36 cities with populations exceeding 10,000 were situated along the coast, and only thirteen in the Sierra and three in the forest areas (selva). Lima-Callao constitutes 41.6 percent of the country's urban population. More than 60 percent of the GNP comes from along the coast, holding 47 percent of the country's population. Lima-Callao contains 67 percent of the country's industry, of which in 1960 54.4 percent was specifically in manufacturing, 59.1 percent in 1965. Thus Lima-Callao gained 4.7 percent while the total production within the other regions since 1960 dropped by 10.3 percent.[31] Lima-Callao receives 42 percent of the national income.

These figures show the pattern of internal colonialism between the coast and the other geographical regions of the country, with Lima-Callao as a metropolis dominating the whole country. Lima-Callao owes its position only partly to the colonial tradition of centralized administrations and to its situation on the coast. Above all, it owes its position to its function as a spearhead of the dependent economic expansion of the country where the bulk of foreign investment is concentrated, and to its function as the center of all American social and cultural influences.

According to official figures, the per capita income grew at an annual rate of 3.3 percent during the period 1950-1965, while the population grew at a rate slightly below 3 percent. In 1965 the average income per person was 9,763 soles (346

31 Palomino Roedel, op. cit., p. 9.

dollars).[35] A look at Table 8 shows that in 1961, 64.8 percent of the economically active population earned below 10,000 *soles* and received 18.9 percent of the national income. On

TABLE 8

PERU: ESTIMATED DISTRIBUTION OF INCOME, 1961

Income Level	Average Income (000s of Soles)	Total Income (millions of Soles)	Employed Population (in 000s)	Portion of Total Income (in percent)	Portion of Employed Population	Income (cumulative percentages)	Population (cumulative percentages)
Less than 3,000	2.6	697.8	275.9	1.4	9.2	1.4	9.2
3,000 to 5,000	4.1	3,948.1	983.9	7.8	32.7	9.2	41.9
5,000 to 10,000	7.1	4,889.1	688.4	9.7	22.9	13.9	64.8
10,000 to 20,000	15.3	10,479.5	737.7	20.8	24.5	39.7	89.3
20,000 to 30,000	27.2	1,453.5	53.5	2.9	1.8	42.6	91.1
30,000 to 50,000	34.7	6,313.4	182.2	12.5	6.0	55.1	97.1
50,000 to 100,000	57.5	1,784.6	31.1	3.5	1.0	58.6	98.1
100,000 and more	339.0	20,910.0	57.4	41.4	1.9	100.0	100.0
Total		50,479.0[a]	3,010.1	100.0	100.0		

Sources: *Instituto Nacional de Planificación.*
a Excluding rents.
(Taken from: *Distribución del Ingreso en el Perú*, CEPAL, 1966.)

the other hand, 1.9 percent of the population received an income above 100,000 *soles* a year or 41.4 percent of the national income. The concentration of *wealth* is of course far higher since these figures refer only to earned *income*.

If we compare the distribution of income between the most important occupational sectors, the figures are just as revealing. In Table 9 we see that the wage workers and salaried em-

TABLE 9

PERU: NATIONAL INCOME, 1961, BY OCCUPATIONAL CATEGORIES

Sector	Employed Population (In thousands)	Percentages	Income (millions)	Percentages
1. Wages and salaries	2,487.8	82.7	25,395.1	47.2
Wage Workers				
Permanent	1,145.9	29.8	11,286.8	21.0
Casual	721.9	32.3	2,986.0	5.6
Salaried Employees	334.2	11.1	10,354.8	19.2
Nonpaid Domestic Help	285.8	9.5	767.5	1.4
2. Incomes received by family units, self-employed professionals, and other unincorporated enterprises	522.3	17.3	28,413.9	52.8
Entrepreneurial and property incomes	57.4	1.9	24,240.0	45.0
Self-employed	464.9	15.4	4,173.9	7.8
Total	3,010.1	100.0	53,809.0	100.0

Sources: *Instituto Nacional de Planificación.*
(Taken from: *Distribución del Ingreso en el Perú*, CEPAL, 1966.)

[35] Banco Central de Reservas, p. 8.

ployees, who make up 82.7 percent of the employed population, received 47.2 percent of the national income. The incomes of the entrepreneurs, businessmen, and property owners, who make up only 1.9 percent of the active population, receive 45 percent of the national income. Of even more significance is the process of "marginalization" and pauperization of the large mass of the active population that these figures reveal. In fact, they show that the "casual laborers," that is, the underemployed, making up 32.3 percent of the economically active population, receive only 5.6 per cent of the national income.

While the economy is expanding vigorously, the rich are becoming richer and the poor poorer. Worse still, the poor are constantly growing in number.

In Peru, in the less well-developed as well as the more highly developed sectors, it has been shown that the concentration of wealth is growing and that, as industrialization continues, there is a growing tendency toward the concentration of wealth in the hands of the few.[33]

Thus, the country's economic growth has served only to accentuate our dependence on foreign investment, our internal colonialism and metropolitan domination, and the increasing tendency toward the pauperization of the largest part of the population.

Contrary to what is happening in other countries whose monetary policies are controlled by the International Monetary Fund, inflation in Peru (before this writing) has been relatively slow. This has continued to intrigue both foreign and national experts. The reason usually given is that Peruvian exports are sufficiently diverse in kind to cancel the fluctuating demands of the international market, while most other countries are "monoexporters," exporting only one commodity on which the country depends. The problem is still more difficult because of the drastic reductions in agricultural production that have been taking place over the past fifteen years and that have led to an explosive increase in imports which has influenced the prices and the cost of living in Peru. In the period 1950-1965, prices never rose by less than 3.4 percent a year; yet in 1965 alone they went up by 15 percent, according to *official* statistics.[34]

[33] David Chaplin, *Industrialization and the Distribution of Wealth in Peru* (Madison: Land Tenure Center, University of Wisconsin, 1966, mimeographed).

[34] Banco Central de Reservas, p. 8.

Doubtless, the diversified export base, and especially the favorable increase in exports of fish-meal, explain part of the problem. However, the fact that the working masses in general have been unable to prevent the constant reduction of their real wages and standard of living—their organization being impotent in this respect—explains much more.

A recent investigation revealed that the working classes, especially those in the cities, have not increased their share of the food market during the last ten years. Their fragmentation and lack of organization, especially among the unemployed and underemployed, have prevented the Peruvian working classes from exercising pressures strong enough to give them a greater share in the consumer market and in the distribution of income. In this way, Peru differs from Argentina or Chile where the unionized working population can maintain a certain minimum income and share in the market in spite of the fluctuations within the economy of these countries (though of course this has generally been responded to by the governments' devaluating the currency and raising the prices and cost of living). Thus, in Peru there is a close relationship between the distribution of income and the slow rate of inflation. The general undernourishment of the great mass of the population, which is growing at the rate of 3 percent per annum, is the cost of economic growth in Peru.

Finally, we have to include in the weaknesses and contradictions of the system the tendency toward "marginalization." The reduction in the labor market and in sources of income is occurring simultaneously with an increase in prices, pressures toward greater consumption, and the expansion of industrial production. There can be no doubt that the estimates regarding the numbers of unemployed and partially employed persons are only rough and not too trustworthy. But they show some of the tendencies. The 1961 census estimated 1.6 percent of the total economically active population, and 3.7 percent of the wage workers and salaried employees, as unemployed. More recent estimates, however, reveal that about 40 percent of the agricultural, 21 percent of the commercial, and 30 percent of the population involved in services, were unemployed in 1966.[35] Whatever the real value of these statistics may be, there is no doubt about the high rate of unemployment and underemploy-

[35] Rosemarie Thorp, "La Inflación Monetaria en el Perú," 1966 (mimeographed).

ment in the country at the present time, a time when the rate of economic growth, and of industrial expansion in particular, is truly impressive.[36] Thus, the irrationalities of the system are clearly revealed. . . .   January 1967

[36] *Diagnóstico de la Situación de Recursos Humanos*, pp. 38-39.

Revolution and Guerrilla Movements in Latin America: Venezuela, Colombia, Guatemala, and Peru[1]

JAMES PETRAS

The repression of guerrilla movements and the possibilities for successful ones elsewhere in Latin America are analyzed by Petras. The growing polarization in Latin America, the breakdown of traditional institutions of authority, and the inability of new commercial and industrial strata to integrate the excluded masses and incorporate them into the political process are conditions in which opposition to the social order takes on revolutionary dimensions. The emergence of guerrilla movements, he argues, and the growth of U. S. involvement in all levels of Latin American government, are opposing responses to the same problem; the fragility of the structure of domination and the growing gap between rulers and ruled. James Petras, Assistant Professor of Political

[1] This paper does not discuss the mass revolutionary struggle in the Dominican Republic, a subject worthy of careful study. One should note that in the Dominican Republic the revolutionary movement has taken the form of a classical social revolution rather than "rural guerrilla warfare": an armed uprising emanating from the urban centers and based to a large degree on the trade unions, the urban unemployed, and the university and secondary students. In Santo Domingo the high urban unemployment rate, the cleavage in the traditional basis of elite power (the army), and the availability of a highly mobilizable urban population provided the opportunity for an urban-based mass insurrection. The presence of an external occupation force (U.S. Marines) exacerbates all the latent hostilities generated by externally supported national exploitation and provides a unifying theme: antiimperialism. In this sense the Dominican Revolution resembles the European resistance movement during the Nazi occupation.

Science and Public Administration, is the author of numerous articles on Latin American politics, and of a forthcoming study of the Politics of Development in Chile, University of California Press, 1968.

THE DECAY OF traditional Latin American society has reached the stage where in Colombia, stronghold of the Opus Dei and a kind of Medieval Inquisitorial Catholicism, a significant number of "revolutionary priests" recently have openly called for the overthrow of Colombia's social and economic establishment. In Tunja, eighty miles northeast of Bogotá, in Plaza Bolivar, Tunja's largest plaza, a thirty-six-year-old Rome-educated priest, the Reverend Martin Amaya Martínez, delivered his revolutionary message:

> I protest in the name of my people against the desecration of the message of our Lord Jesus Christ because his message is profoundly human, profoundly progressive, and for that reason has been mutilated and converted into an instrument of exploitation and enrichment of a handful.

For his forceful speeches and exposure of the complicity of the church hierarchy in the "enrichment of a handful," and above all because he has acted as he has spoken—by leading large popular demonstrations in the streets—the bishops have forbidden Father Martin Amaya Martínez to speak, write, or wear his cassock in public. The struggle inside the Catholic Church between reaction and revolution is a reflection of the basic struggles going on in Latin society as a whole.

In Colombia, Guatemala, and Venezuela guerrilla movements have begun the struggle for the "reconquest" of Latin America by the Latin Americans. In Peru centuries-long-oppressed Indians are organizing peasants unions and land invasions, and are beginning to rejuvenate the old collectivist ethic.

Despite the voluminous writings—Left, Right, and Center—about the "coming Revolution," nowhere in Latin America does it appear that *the* Revolution is about to happen. The defeat of the revolutionary upsurge of 1958-1960, the failure of the middle-class governments of 1960-63, and the emerging U.S.-organized-and-supported military dictatorships of the last period have stabilized U.S. tutelage and Latin oligarchical control while exacerbating the underlying social and economic problems of these diverse societies. Conflict between the present superficial stability and the underlying social discontent is most evident in the fractures developing in traditional Latin institutions (Church, Army, University), and in the emerging mass participation of previously unincluded groups of peasants and Indians. The breakdown of authority on different levels is typified by widespread banditry (Colombia has had 130 kidnappings in the last six months of 1965) and guerrilla warfare, and by development of "autonomous republics" within Colombia, and local self-government in Peru and Guatemala. In the overt challenge for power found in the guerrilla movements the "crisis in authority" manifests itself.

Similarity in methods of struggle disguises the fact that each guerrilla movement in Latin America has gone through its own particular historical experience, reflecting and shaping the specific character that the "crisis of authority" has taken.

In Guatemala a significant guerrilla movement (divided into two sectors at the moment) primarily began in 1960-61, led by U.S.-trained Guatemalan Army officers.

The revolutionary movement of November 13 (MR-13) is the name of one of the guerrilla movements in Guatemala. Its leader, Comandante Marco Antonio Yon Sosa, is a strong supporter of the Chinese Revolution and the armed struggle road to socialism. Proposing an alliance of workers, peasants, and students toward the formation of a "workers-peasants government," MR-13 and Yon Sosa differ from the Guatemalan Communist Party, (PGT) which calls for a coalition with the progressive bourgeoisie leading to a "national democratic government." In 1965 Luis Augusto Turcios defected from MR-13 and formed an armed group called the FAR (Rebel Armed Forces), which appears independent of and yet supports the position of the PGT. The FAR functions as a pressure group on the military to allow the election of the national democratic government that the PGT advocates.

Indicative of the subordination of the armed struggle to the electoral road, Turcios, in line with the position of the PGT, evaluated the March 1966 elections in the following manner: "In synthesis, the elections will develop under the climate of popular advance toward liberation."[3] Before the elections FAR called for a vote for Menendez Montenegro, whose party was characterized after the elections (by the FAR) as an "oli-

[3] *El Popular*, Uruguayan Communist Party Daily, March 5, 1966.

garchical and proimperialist clique . . . answering to the North American Embassy."[4]

By the summer of 1966 the FAR group appeared to have grown considerably larger than MR-13 and to have a more effective organization. This has probably been due to (1) the recognition and support that Turcios received as the recognized Guatemalan delegate at the Tri-Continental Congress in January 1966; (2) the expulsion from the MR-13 of several influential members, leaders of an ex-Trotskyist grouping (Posadista) who openly admitted using funds to finance their "international"; and (3) the more "activist" orientation of FAR, which has been highlighted by the dramatic kidnapping of high government officials.

In late 1966, rumors persisted that there was an informal pact between the two guerrilla groups that could eventually lead to their merger. The political basis of such a unification is not yet clear. The FAR, while not supporting the government, focuses on the military, which they distinguish as the major institution blocking peaceful democratic reforms. The MR-13 continues as far as is known to demand a "worker-peasant government"—something the Menendez government is not. The government launched its announced plans to wipe out the insurgents, pushing the FAR closer to the position of MR-13 and loosening its ties to the PGT. The effect of the death of Turcios and the cause of his death are not yet clear, and especially how they relate to the future course of the FAR.[5]

In the initial revolt the military officers-turned-guerrillas were mainly concerned with vaguely nationalistic goals. In the beginning the officers lacked much of the ideological sophistication of their Venezuelan counterparts. One guerrilla leader is quoted by a Latin journalist as saying, "with some of us their training backfired, and today in the guerrilla movement we are using what we learned from them." Unlike their guerrilla counterparts in other countries, the cadres that made up the Guatemalan MR-13 (the revolutionary movement of November 13) have the important advantage of being militarily well prepared. The activity of MR-13, though less publicized and less dramatic than that of the MIR, has had the virtue of being more sustained—Yon Sosa, unlike de La Puente and Lobatón, has avoided head-on collisions with the military

[4] *El Siglo*, Chilean Communist Party Daily, April 4, 1966.
[5] See "Guatemala: Rebel Course Clouded," James Goodsell, *Christian Science Monitor* (October 6, 1966), p. 2.

and has concentrated on slowly building support among the Indian villagers around La Sierra de las Minas. Between 1961 and 1965, MR-13 became more and more oriented toward a Marxist point of view. In the January issue of the journal *Revolución Socialista,* MR-13 went beyond the national anti-imperialist character of the other guerrilla movements and explicitly defined their program as Marxist-Leninist and their movement as socialist.

Between MR-13 and the Guatemalan Communist Party (PGT) exists a profound division. The latter lends its support to anti-Communist liberal electoral candidates, such as Mendez Montenegro, while denouncing MR-13 as "adventurism." The continued intervention of the military in the election has weakened the position of the PGT in relation to the MR-13. The only serious defection from MR-13 was ex-comandante Luis Augusto Turcios, who renounced the socialist program and later appeared at the Tri-Continental Congress as a spokesman for "armed struggle."

The curious amalgam of nationalistic ex-military officers projecting an armed struggle for a socialist program within a largely rural Indian milieu is in contrast to an urban-based Communist Party that declares the need for a liberal parliamentary government elected in spite of military opposition. The crucial factors explaining the unclassical situation and their interplay with international politics are to be found in the recent political history of Guatemala. The period after Arbenz's fall from power and the subsequent establishment by the CIA of a military dictatorship produced a strong nationalist sentiment (against U.S. intervention) and pointed to the supremacy of armed forces as a determining element in deciding the fate of a popular government; there has been little in recent Guatemalan history to recommend the electoral route to social change. Fusing with this national sentiment and linked to the necessity for armed struggle was the development in Cuba of a government that redefined itself from a nationalist to a socialist government. The leadership of MR-13 and the FAR as post-Cuban Revolutionary guerrilla movements are however, by social origin less a peasant movement and more a reflection of the crisis in the old traditional authority structure: the leaders as former military men are largely from the traditional middle class, which has provided many of the officers in the military. Underneath the differing programs of the MIR of Venezuela and Peru, the *Frente Unido* of Camilo Torres, and the FALN of Venezuela (and the Caamaño forces in the

Dominican Republic) one finds that the key leadership group is largely composed of defectors from traditional institutions and elites.[6] Marx noted this phenomenon quite perceptively when he wrote in the Communist Manifesto:

"Finally in times when the class struggle nears the decisive hour, the process of dissolution going on within the ruling class, in fact within the whole range of old society, assumes such a violent, glaring character that a small section of the ruling class cuts itself adrift and joins the revolutionary class, the class that holds the future in its hands. Just as, at an earlier period, a section of the nobility went over to the bourgeoisie, so now a portion of the bourgeoisie goes over to the proletariat, and in particular a portion of the bourgeoisie ideologists, who have raised themselves to the level of comprehending theoretically the historical movement as a whole."

In Colombia, on the other hand, guerrilla warfare, civil war, banditry, "independent republics," and "red republic" have all converged and have become fixed features of national life for decades and have at times extended over half of the country. The death toll from civil war, banditry, and government violence during the last fifteen years is conservatively estimated to exceed 300,000. Here old-fashioned peasant communists, together with idealistic students, uprooted peasants, and university alumni, form the backbone of the Colombian leadership. One of the more successful guerrilla raids was led by an ex-student leader, a young woman called Mariela Amaya o Paulina González, who, after graduating from the university, packed a rifle and led a group of guerrillas in an attack on a government outpost in Santander province. Unlike the relative

[6] Data on the Brazilian revolutionary leadership tends to substantiate this thesis. Two key leaders of the Brazilian revolutionary movement, Father Francisco Lage and Francisco Julião, both originated from traditional large landholding families. Father Lage, an avowed revolutionary socialist, was instrumental in organizing the "favelados" in Belo Horizonte, capital of Minas Gerais. Along with him were five Brazilian bishops led by José Tavora, Archbishop of Aracaju, who edited a manual to teach illiterates entitled "To live is to struggle" ("Vivir es luchar"). Father Lage supported the armed-struggle road to socialism, rejecting the position of the Brazilian Communist Party, which supported the theory that capitalism was the next stage and hence the Brazilian bourgeoisie had to be supported. The split in traditional institutions like the Catholic Church was never more evident than in Brazil after the U.S.-supported military coup of 1964. While Father Lage was jailed and tortured for eight months, the majority of the high ecclesiastics were giving their blessing to the new anti-Communist savior, the military dictator Castello Branco. See Michel Bosquet, "Con Julio y Franciso Lage, *Marcha* (March 18, 1966), Uruguay.

novelty of guerrilla warfare in Guatemala and Venezuela, the contemporary guerrilla movement has a long tradition in Colombia. As early as 1930-31 armed groups demanding agrarian reform were emerging. The Colombian Communist Party (CCP), under the sway of the heady doctrines of the "Third Period," decided to establish socialism in one province. The CCP established a peasant zone under their control in a remote area of Southern Colombia that became known as "Red Viota," or the "Red Republic." Surrounded by jungles and virtually inaccessible to Government forays, they had their own administration. "Red Viota" could not be defeated from outside, but the hardworking peasants and Communists became so successful in their farming that they virtually lost all interest in extending their "good thing" to other areas, thus defeating, in a sense, their own original goals seeking agrarian reform. Nevertheless, the independent self-governing tradition of Viota became a rallying cry in the more recent period when similar areas of Colombia were occupied by peasants fleeing from both social and governmental violence. The development in recent years of the "independent republics" of Marquetalia reflect both the earlier attempt of peasants to establish a stable society, uncorrupted and based on local control, and a new approach to counter the repressive central government by extending the movement to other areas. This independent republic was weakened in 1964 because of the drive by the U.S.-directed 16,000-man Colombian Army to destroy it.

Out of the conflicts in the Colombian Church came one of the most dynamic and gifted revolutionary leaders in recent Latin American history, Camilo Torres. Son of one of the oldest aristocratic families in Colombia, educated in Lovain, he found his calling in the armed revolutionary struggle. But like others before him, Camilo Torres came to this decision after trying many other channels. In early 1965 Camilo Torres developed what few other recent Latin revolutionary leaders have been able to do: build an enormous popular urban following that included significant sectors of the trade union movement in addition to student and peasant support. From May to September of 1965 where Torres spoke, the major plazas were crowded to overflowing. His message was profoundly revolutionary: expropriation of all landed estates *without indemnification,* nationalization of all natural resources, urban reform, egalitarian wage scales, and popular control of government. The sources cited by Camilo and the mode of expression were distinctly Christian. It was this combination of a modern revolutionary social message presented within the framework of a traditional doctrine by a dynamic, articulate, and prestigious figure breaking from the traditional system of authority, which presented the greatest single challenge to the Colombian elite. Because Camilo Torres' own defection symbolized the break between the authoritarian elitist past and the revolutionary future, the legal political roads were closed and he was finally shot and killed in guerrilla combat. Camilo Torres' highly successful initial efforts at rural and urban mass mobilization, his gaining of the support of the trade unions, his highly appealing call for unity of all the *revolutionary* forces from Catholic to Communist, sooner rather than later, meant a decisive political confrontation. *Frente Unido,* the weekly newspaper Torres directed, was avidly read, its graphic revolutionary message digested: the archbishop and his business and political friends confront a table overflowing with food alongside a picture of one of the millions of ragged, hungry Indio-Colombian children. What was decisive in the emergence of Camilo Torres' political evolution was his turn away from the elite centers of power (the university where he taught, the church where he preached) to the people, the street, and finally the countryside. Explicitly rejecting "permeationist" or traditional formulas of the Communist Party calling for coalition with the "progressive" wing of the Liberal Party, Camilo turned toward the task of revolutionary opposition, the task of rallying popular forces through direct contact with the masses. His commitment to revolutionary change dictated the necessity of a new political organization, "Frente Unido." Camilo Torres' decision to turn to guerrilla warfare was a practical decision based both on a realistic appraisal of Colombian politics and a profound commitment to his radical ideals.[7] The suppression of legal political meetings, the blocking of peaceful mass mobilization, the constitutional provision confining the electoral process to competition between the two major parties, in all, the existing

[7] Before his entry into politics Camilo was one of the leading sociologists in Colombia and was a visiting fellow at the University of Minnesota (1961). In an earlier monograph, "The Proletarianization of Bogotá," Camilo Torres presents substantial evidence on the differential calorie intake of the working class and the middle class of Bogotá, pointing to the tremendous gap between these social classes. In addition to being an outstanding example of a committed revolutionary, Camilo Torres showed how modern sociological research could be applied to examining politically relevant problems from a popular democratic standpoint.

political system posed the question: accommodation to the legal system and hence to the social system—or armed struggle. Father Camilo Torres chose to live by the revolution and he died arms in hand fighting for it. The history of Camilo Torres highlights the existing political process: armed struggle as the means to social change in Colombia is a result of the ability of the government to impose its repression on peaceful political movements in an urban environment, while the marginal changes of the government serve only to buttress a highly authoritarian elite-ridden society. In the final analysis it is authority based on the violence of the few over the many. The experience of Camilo Torres, who originally thought in terms of building an urban rural political mass party based on the trade unions and peasants associations, points most clearly to the insurmountable difficulties found in the application of classical European modes of struggles. Nonetheless, Camilo Torres continued to maintain that the guerrilla struggle was always subordinate to the need to develop *mass* urban and rural revolutionary organization. His constant references to his own personal insignificance not only were an expression of personal modesty but were dictated by his political vision: the guerrilla movement was not a substitute for, but an instrument of, the larger mass movement of opposition.

The growing cleavages in Colombian society preceding Camilo Torres' death continue after it. Father Arango Trujillo has disappeared and is said to be with the guerrillas. Forty priests held a high mass for Camilo Torres against the orders of the hierarchy.

The Venezuelan guerrilla movement, perhaps the most publicized movement of its kind in the world, is the one least understood, either by its detractors or by its friends. Until recently both the U.S. Government and the Left throughout the world were predicting either an imminent "communist takeover" or a "popular revolution" that would smash the old order. Obviously, neither has occurred, and it does not appear likely for some time; the guerrillas continue to exist and appear to be older, wiser, and perhaps more firmly established. The Venezuelan guerrilla movement has been subject to erratic shifts in personnel and strategy. This is partly the result of functioning in a country that has very substantial oil revenues, the largest U.S. military mission in Latin America, and a sophisticated political leadership. This leadership has perpetuated sufficient violence to prevent the revolutionaries from functioning legitimately in politics. At the same time, a sufficient number of doles, jobs, and promises were distributed to keep the discontented populace from supporting the rebels and continuing to channel their grievances either through the "loyal" opposition or through the governmental apparatus.

The Venezuelan guerrilla movement began in the last analysis as a response to excessive governmental violence and to the violation of the constitutional rights that the "Venezuelan Democratic Revolution" was ostensibly upholding. Though there were frequent incidents of violent conflict between students, unemployed workers, and police prior to October 1960, the turning point in Venezuelan political life and the emergence of a guerrilla movement date from that period. An authoritative account of the U.S. version appears in *Venezuela: U.S. Army Area Handbook for Venezuela,* prepared by the American University's Foreign Areas Studies Division SORO (Special Operations Research Office).[8] The critical issue that is used to rationalize the violent behavior of the "democrat" Betancourt is a complete fabrication that has no basis in reality. The Army Handbook's version of the Betancourt government's resort to violence is that it was a defensive measure, a means to defend democracy against Castroite terror: "the radical Left came out overtly for the overthrow of the Betancourt government . . . because of the government's anti-Castro stand. In an October 1960 issue, the MIR (Movement of the Revolutionary Left) weekly newspaper *Izquierda* published an editorial advocating the overthrow of the government

[8] SORO is only one among a number of agencies and activities conducted by the American University in connection with the Army. It also operates a Counter-Insurgency Information Analysis Center. The direct working relationship between the American University and the Military Establishment is spelled out clearly in the *Bibliography of Research Studies and Related Writings on the Political Influence of Latin American Students,* published by SORO. This is prefaced by the statement: "The Special Operations Research Office (SORO) of the American University, operating under contract with the Department of the Army, conducts research on the military problems in support of requirements stated by the Department of the Army. As an added service SORO operates the Counter-Insurgency Information Analysis Center (CINFAC) to provide rapid-response replies in its field of competence to queries from Department of Defense agencies, their contractors, and, as directed, to other governmental departments and agencies." The interlocking between a sector of the academic world, the American University, and the U.S. military in Latin America is only one manifestation of a more general phenomenon. A more recent example is the exposure of the involvement of U.S. professors in a Pentagon-financed "research" project in Chile, the Camelot Project, whose purpose was to discover the Chilean military's attitude toward a U.S. military invasion in case of Communist subversion.

by violent means. *When, as a result of this editorial, three MIR leaders were arrested, 2,000 students of the Central University rioted"* (my emphasis). Subsequently, and as a consequence of these events, there was triggered off "riots . . . throughout the country, and the national guard and police took severe measures to put down the disorders" (p. 529 of the Army Handbook). It was during this period that the cycle of violence and counterviolence began to develop in a serious fashion and resulted in the students' finally taking to the hills. The editorial in *Izquierda* of October 14, 1960, on which the Army Handbook bases its argument justifying Betancourt's violence, actually stated the opposite. Domingo Alberto Rangel, who wrote this editorial, in fact stated that a popular insurrection could not succeed and even argued that the Betancourt government itself might, if it took the proper actions, avoid a revolution. The "evidence" presented by the government was so obviously contrived that the Chamber of Deputies in July 1961 (then still controlled by the government coalition) turned down the Supreme Court's request to waive Congressman Rangel's immunity in order that he might be tried. On October 22, 1960, MIR spokesman Saez Merida made perfectly clear that the Left preferred the ballot to the bullet, and that they were preparing for the 1963 elections. He went so far as to reaffirm his group's nonsubversive nature and continued to make positive references to Betancourt's regime: ". . . the MIR does not pursue popular subversion against the constitutional regime."[9] Unfortunately for the Left, their professions of faith in the constitutional regime saved neither their persons nor their party from persecution. Following the arrest of the three MIR editors, the political secret police (Digepol) raided the buildings of all the left-wing parties, while on the day of the arrests National Guardsmen opened fire on students inside the Central University, thus violating the autonomy of the University, an action that was condemned even by Conservative Catholic (Copei Party) leader Rafael Caldera. On October 22, Minister of Education Rafael Pizani, a moderate liberal who, however, believed in civil liberties, obtained the release of the arrested students and resigned in protest over the wave of government repression.[10]

[9] *El Nacional* (October 22, 1960).
[10] Most of this material can be found in a mimeographed, well-documented study by James Cockcroft, *Venezuela's Fidelistas—Two Generations* (Stanford University Institute of Hispanic American and Luso-Brazilian Studies, 1963).

It must be recognized that under these circumstances the student protesting was not "rioting" or part of a communist plot to "violently overthrow the government," but an attempt to regain the constitutional rights of the MIR editors who were being framed. Given the fact that the editorial was constitutional and an exercise of democratic rights, the subsequent student demonstrations and guerrilla activity appear in a different light: as an attempt to regain precisely those democratic liberties being denied. Likewise the government's repressive action ("severe measures to put down the disorders") appears quite different from a "defense of democracy." By denying the Left its freedom of expression, by repressing legitimate opposition and forcing it to utilize "illegal means," and then retrospectively rewriting history in order to prove that the outlawed opposition was acting illegally all along, the Betancourt government's own authoritarian violence came to be the midwife of a counterviolence, the guerrilla movement.

The outright falsification of the events in justifying the use of force in violation of democratic rights is one of the functions of the new intellectual jet-set, the "Political Men," who work "under contract" for the Army or who, like Arthur Schlesinger, write White House White Papers on Cuba.

The Venezuelan guerrilla movement began as a predominantly student group. While there are only about 150 seminarians attending the eleven junior and four senior seminaries, the guerrilla movement has had no problem enrolling hundreds of idealistic students. Most of the latter were Venezuelans concerned with the poor, and not Spaniards, as are the majority of the Catholic clergy in Venezuela, who are concerned with attending to the superficial piety of their predominantly upper and middle class clientele. Estimates of the size of the guerrilla force tend to be unreliable, but my guess is that there are 200-300 in Venezuela, 200 in Colombia and 100-200 in Guatemala. This is a fairly stable figure, as the turnover is not so high as when the movement first began and young students had a romantic view of life in the hills.

The Venezuelan guerrilla movement went through essentially three phases:

(1) The "student vanguardist" period 1960-62.
(2) The period of intense urban warfare involving a variety of urban action ostensibly electrifying the masses and covering the 1962-64 period.
(3) The "agrarian reform" phase—1964 to the present.

During the student vanguardist period the students engaged in gun battles with the police, either from the Central University or from buildings in the city. The dramatic episode called "The Battle of Stalingrad" typifies both the character and the nature of the guerrilla movement in the early period. Several hundred students barricaded a school building and exchanged shots with the police, finally being surrounded and forced to surrender, with heavy casualties. In this period there was a strong current among these guerrillas that the students were the carriers of social revolution. These were the days when young nationalistic military officers conceived of "Left coups" and in 1962 at Carupano and Puerto Cabello unsuccessfully attempted to realize them. In the second phase from mid-1962 to the end of 1963 the still predominantly urban-based guerrillas attempted desperate measures and sensational acts to dramatize the struggle, hoping in this way to electrify the masses. Famous art works were stolen, soccer players were kidnapped, pipelines were blown up, and so on. The substitution of this type of individual action for mass mobilization proved as ineffective as the previous "stand-up-and-shoot-it-out" approach. However, concomitant with the failure of the urban guerrilla movement, there began to coalesce a number of guerrillas in the countryside. The rural guerrilla force included a heterogeneous mixture of army officers fleeing from the defeats at Puerto Cabello, students turned guerrilla-fighters, a small number of peasants, and a number of older political leaders who were being sought by the government. There was great fragmentation and little coordination of activity. On February 20, 1963, all the diverse groups met and formed the FALN (Armed Forces of National Liberation).

The third and latest phase came following the failure of the electoral boycott called by the urban guerrillas during the 1963 elections. The predominantly urban orientation was shifted. Henceforth the rural areas became the center of guerrilla activities; the urban movement continued as an auxiliary activity. More fundamental was the discussion ensuing over the basic question of continuing armed struggle vs. attempting to seek legal means. Following the electoral defeat, the "legalists" got the upper hand, and a six-month truce was declared. Between January and June 1964 the guerrillas waited to see if the legal channels would open as their moderate colleagues had argued. Instead, in May of that year the new President, Leoni, simultaneously inaugurated a full-scale antiguerrilla military campaign and in an interview with a French correspondent declared that the guerrillas were finished. He interpreted the truce as a sign of weakness, not as a period of goodwill in which democracy could be restored. The "legalists" were defeated and some of the older leaders of the MIR like Alberto Rangel split and formed a new group. The armed guerrilla struggle was on once more, this time in the countryside. Since the reemergence of guerrilla warfare the FALN claims to have established four major fronts and to be gaining support among the peasants in the areas they control and in the periphery of those areas. In the fall of 1965, while the FALN was once again involved in combat, the Venezuelan Communist Party issued a call for a "democratic peace." It stated the willingness of the VCP to renounce the armed struggle in exchange for assurances that it would be granted legal recognition, that political prisoners would be released, and that there would be no reprisals. Early in 1966 a serious division appeared within the ranks of the FALN between those who sought in some manner to reach an understanding with Leoni and those who wanted to continue the revolutionary struggle. The old-line leadership of the VCP, including the Machado brothers and Pompeyo Márquez, took the former position, while the left wing of the MIR became the center for continuing the struggle. Within the Leoni government two trends developed: one sought to exploit this division by coming to some understanding with the VCP, while the "hard line" interpreted the renunciation by certain VCP leaders as proof of the successful applications of their all-out-war tactics. Shifts in the position of the Communist Party and the temporary setbacks have had their effects, but it would be a mistake to believe, as Betancourt and Leoni have found out after announcing every "decisive" defeat, that the guerrillas will disappear or be rendered harmless.[11] While the Communists move

[11] A highly informative extended interview (with illustrations) of the Commander in Chief of the FALN, Douglas Bravo, indicates that the guerrillas may have surpassed the internal crises of 1964–66. According to Bravo, the social composition of the guerrillas today is made up of between 50 and 70 percent peasants, and they are entrenched in several areas. Most important, they appear to have developed a coherent organizational structure between guerrilla fronts and between their political arm, the National Liberation Front, and the military group, the FALN. (See *Sucesos*, December 10, December 17, and December 24, 1966, Mexico City.)

With a firm political and social basis in the countryside and a rational organizational structure that can serve both as a communication network and a military-political weapon, the FALN may be able to sustain and expand its activities in preparation for the long march ahead.

toward the Right, a growing sector of radicalized Social Christian students and workers are looking less to reactionary Christion Democratic Party leader Rafael Caldera and more to the ideas of social revolutionary Camilo Torres. In Venezuelan public life the dialectic of governmental repression and guerrilla violence lessens or grows in tempo, but it never ceases. The Venezuelan "national revolution," more than being a mystique behind the gunplay of a few students, stands as the foremost driving force behind the continual radicalization of student generation after student generation. Each in its turn has sought to break out of the political confines set by an economy totally subordinate to the U.S. and rigidly defended by one of the most modernly equipped and highly disciplined armed forces in Latin America.

In Peru the revolutionary struggle has been centered around two types of movements: mass rural organizations and, later, guerrilla units. At first, unlike the situation in other countries, there was massive peasant and Indian involvement in revolutionary unions and land invasions in some cases associated with urban revolutionary parties. In his monograph, *El Movimiento Campesino del Perú y sus Líderes*, Aníbal Quijano, a Peruvian sociologist, wrote: "In the last ten years the Peruvian peasantry has developed an attitude that completely rejects the traditional order . . . and (the peasantry) has become an active force for changing it in a rapid and if necessary violent way. Sectors of increasing breadth are incorporating this new attitude and conduct despite the repressions and massacres on the part of successful governments and landowners, and they are seeking to coordinate themselves on a national scale and to enlarge their capability and goals." Unlike traditional peasant agitation, which was always sporadic, ephemeral, and isolated in limited regions of the country, the present movement involves the greater part of the Peruvian Sierra and the greater part of the coast, and is not confined to regional or communal isolation. The strength of the present peasant movement can be gauged by its support over the last ten years. It has secured total control in numerous regions, especially the valleys of La Convención and de Lares in the Department of Cuzco, where nuclei of autonomous power based on the peasantry now exists. Peasant activity has developed through three principal channels: unionization, land invasions, and incorporations with militant urban political groups. Unlike the armed detachments—the "vanguard" strategy—of the guerrillas in Venezuela, Colombia, and Guatemala, the emphasis in Peru was on mass mobilization, large-scale participation around immediate demands—"those who till the land shall own it"—and the use of relatively nonviolent direct action, i.e., occupation of a hacienda. Where armed detachments existed, they were an integral but subordinate part of the larger movement, and their functions were primarily to defend the squatters. Unlike the guerrillas, who functioned on a hit-and-miss basis (exhorting peasants to revolt during a raid on the local military barracks and then leaving), the Peruvian peasant organizers lived in the areas, worked, spoke the language of the Indians (Quechua or one of the other dialects), and were integrated with and subject to the control of their constituents. This type of movement was less elitist in conception and more democratic in practice; it directly involved those whom the revolution ostensibly concerned rather than having an urban (almost "foreign" from the viewpoint of culture, language, etc.) elite substitute itself and make the revolution "for" the peasant. Significant within this new Indian uprising was the revitalization of the collectivist traditions that had been eroded by the commercialization of life and values in recent years. Quijano, observing this "rebirth of community," noted: ". . . one of the consequences of the land invasion is the revitalization of communal property that was in an advanced state of disintegration. . . . Instead of the present big land-holding-tiny plot complex, there is substituted collective and communal ownership." Interestingly the need for cooperation in carrying off "land invasions" has resulted in the lessening of violence among the disparate and often previously conflicting Indian communities. The new unions being organized as part of the present peasant movement, principally in the mountains, are made up of a heterogeneous population from both the socioeconomic and the cultural points of view. They bring together serfs from the traditional hacienda, semiserfs, tiny landowning peasants, landless agricultural laborers, and also diverse groups such as small traders, etc. From the cultural viewpoint the constituent population of a peasant union varies from the strictly Indian and the cholos to elements belonging totally to the western Creole culture. These peasant unions are revolutionary. They are not oriented toward improving themselves within the master-serf system, but are oriented toward transforming the whole order of traditional authority through their action in invading the haciendas and organizing a basis of power independent from that of the official and traditional power. It is the mountainous zones where the peasant unions' action has been widest and most intense, and these are the zones where there is the greatest density of Indian and cholo population. The land-invasion stage of the peasant movement was an outgrowth of the unionization of the peasants in the valleys of La Convención and of de Lares in Cuzco under the leadership of Hugo Blanco in 1960. There was a general strike of serfs and semiserfs in the zone near the northern coast in Convención and de Lares that lasted two months. With no "strike benefits," the families sent their children to neighboring towns to avoid starvation, and husband and wife tightened up their belts until they won. The successful outcome encouraged Blanco and the regional federation to begin, early in 1961, the land invasions, taking over land in over one hundred haciendas in the Convención valley and in de Lares in a relatively peaceful and gradual manner.

As a result of massive subsequent repression by army units and the arrest of Hugo Blanco (he was held in jail three years without a trial), the movement ceased to expand and recruit new leaders and started to decline. However, unlike the other more publicized revolutionary movements (the Venezuelan FALN, the Colombian ELN, and the Guatemalan MR-13), which tend to be predominantly urban in composition, the National Federation of Peruvian Peasants (FENCAP) represented and still represents a mass, popular, rural challenge for power.

Unremitting pressures of the Belaúnde government and the violent attacks by the APRA *búfalos* (professional gunmen) seriously weakened the mass movement and caused a rethinking of the direction of the Peruvian revolutionary movement. As the mass peasant movement could not defend itself and was an easy target, guerrilla forms of struggle emerged. The Movement of the Revolutionary Left (MIR), a national popular breakaway from the APRA, took the leadership in organizing a series of guerrilla fronts under the leadership of Luis de la Puénte and Guillarmo Lobatón. The Peruvian Movement of the Revolutionary Left (MIR) was originated by a group of militants expelled from APRA (former nationalist party in Peru), who in October 1959 founded the *Comité de Defensa de los Principios y de la Democracia Interna.* Opposed to the APRA line of collaboration with U.S. imperialism and traditional landowners, this group was composed primarily of students and young militants who had been summarily expelled from the monolithic Aprista Party. At the beginning of 1960 they took the name of APRA Rebelde and in October 1960 declared their revolutionary principles in Chiclayo.

Coinciding with the struggle of the young APRA militants for internal democracy and a principled position in 1959 was the development of the Cuban revolution. Both developments, in Peru and in Cuba, radicalized these young rebels. In contrast to the stagnation, corruption, and authoritarianism of the APRA stood the self-sacrificing struggle of the Cuban revolutionaries. The joining of the APRA Rebelde to Fidelismo definitely separated the old APRA and the new national popular revolutionaries. While the rebels moved in the direction of social revolution, the APRA joined forces with the ultra-Right Odria military-landowning group.

In 1961 the APRA Rebelde adopted the present name, MIR, and in March 1964 they approved a resolution that attempted to reorient their previously university-urban base: *"Todos al campo"* (All to the field). On June 7, 1965, under the leadership of their Secretary-General, Luis de la Puente and Guillermo Lobatón, the MIR carried out its first armed action. Contemporary MIR strategy, while not excluding other means of struggle, underlines the principle that "armed struggle is the principal element of Peruvian revolutionary process," (*Voz Rebelde,* organ of the Peruvian MIR). Luis de La Puente, a young lawyer from a provincial lower aristocratic family, first became active as a student leader in the APRA. Later he led the rebels toward the formation of the MIR. During the year 1964-65 he lived among the peasants of Cuzco, sharing their life and preparing for the armed struggle.[12] Along with de la Puente and others, Guillermo Lobatón was one of the signers of the leaflet announcing the initiation of the war of national liberation. Later Lobatón, who was the most active guerrilla leader, functioned mostly in the central part of Peru. Lobatón was one of several Peruvian students who had been studying abroad and who had returned to form the nucleus of the de la Puente's guerrillas.

[12] *El Guerrillero,* No. 10, October 25, 1965; clandestine mimeograph publication of the MIR.

The seven-part program of the MIR identifies the reforms considered necessary for the realization of the national popular revolution:

(1) Immediate dissolution of Parliament as an instrument of the oligarchy and imperialism.

(2) General amnesty for political prisoners and punishment for all Government and military officials responsible for popular massacres.

(3) Authentic agrarian reform involving complete liquidation of the latifundia and the free transference of the land to the peasants, excluding the expropriation of middle farmers who work their own land and who are efficient producers; preferential treatment by the State to all aspects of peasant life and work.

(4) Sliding scale of family wages for workers, public and private employees, professionals, and technicians.

(5) Urban Reform expropriating large real estate interests, making the present tenants owners of their dwellings, except middle and small property owners.

(6) Immediate recovery of Peruvian petroleum.

(7) Recovery of broad national sovereignty; elimination of treaties and agreements that compromise national independence and establishment of diplomatic and commercial relations with all countries.

The MIR identifies three main groups opposed to this "National-Popular Revolution": North American imperialism, the big bourgeoisie, and the big landowners. On the other hand, the MIR estimates that the "revolution" will be the work of the peasants, the workers, and the patriotic and progressive sectors of the petty bourgeoisie and the national bourgeoisie under the leadership of the Revolutionary Party, which will be constituted in the course of the struggle in which the MIR is considered a factor.[13]

While the official organ of the pro-Soviet Peruvian Communist Party, *Unidad,* presented a formal program that appeared similar, this program differs from that of the MIR in three vital aspects: (1) in practice, if not always in theory, it rejects guerrilla struggle; (2) it is almost exclusively an

[13] "Llamado de los Guerrilleros del MIR Peruano," reprinted in *Revolución,* publication of the University MIR of Chile.

urban grouping; (3) it does not reject coalitions directed by the traditional parties. The pro-Peking Communist official newspaper, *Bandera Roja,* which probably has a wider circulation than *Unidad,* has two tendencies. One, led by José Sotomayer, is considered similar in approach to that of *Unidad.* The other, led by Saturnino Paradez, supports the insurrectional line.[14]

De la Puente, like Camilo Torres and Che Guevara, came from the oldest and most respected families, as likewise did Lobatón. These guerrilla leaders expressed the discontent found among university-educated individuals from the elite who are totally disaffected with a society in which several thousands satisfy every whim while millions suffer from hunger. At the same time as members of the educated elite they developed a global vision of society and they perceived the futility of confining their activities to the university or to their professions. They perceived the limits of operating within the legal system to effect basic changes; hence they tended to regard the traditional Left (first the APRA and then the Communist Party) and legal political activity as useless at best, and as a deception of the masses at worst.[15]

It is significant to note that almost all the guerrilla leaders were in their thirties, which seems to be the poststudent revolutionary crisis age. At least two alternatives confront the exstudent revolutionary: to combine "leftist" politics with an accommodation to the necessities of daily urban living (working in an office during the day, issuing leaflets or weeklies at night or on weekends) or to become integrated into clandestine armed struggle, apart from routine life, recognizing the fate that awaits him. The Peruvian guerrilla movement was largely a reflection of desperation on both the personal and the political levels, in the sense that the personal commitments of the Peruvian revolutionary was perceived in relation to an understanding of the general stasis in Peruvian society and politics. The astronomical rise to public notice of the guerrilla leaders de la Puente and Lobatón was related to their tactical decisions to directly confront the Peruvian army. Lacking significant organized urban support and intending to base their movement on the peasantry, they seriously underestimated the capability

[14] "Reportaje al Perú: Guerrilla," by Edgardo Da Mommio, *El Mundo* (Buenos Aires, March 3, 1966).
[15] Héctor Bejar is one of the examples of a guerrilla leader, a former Communist student leader who left the Party to form the Army of National Liberation (ELN).

and mobility of the Peruvian army. Peruvian rangers,[16] trained and equipped by the U.S. specifically for dealing with guerrilla movements, aided by several thousand Peruvian soldiers and by napalm bombing of peasant areas sympathetic to the guerrillas, converged and succeeded in killing most of guerrillas under the command of de la Puente and Lobatón. The "new variables" in the Peruvian situation were the new antiguerrilla techniques (helicopters, Rangers, napalm, etc.) that the U.S. had introduced, and the intensity with which the U.S. is pursuing the counterrevolutionary offensive in Latin America.[17] As a result, the guerrillas (despite their sensational early victories, their courage, and their commitment) were confronted with an overwhelming opposition at a time when the mass rural movement was ebbing because of violence and repression. This set the stage for a military encounter in which the guerrillas could not count on the political movement in the cities or the countryside to come to their aid by opening up new points of confrontation and hence taking some of the pressure off the guerrillas. Edgardo Da Mommio, writing for *El Mundo* (Argentina, March 5), noted the possible larger

[16] During the uprising the MIR reported that seven U.S.-trained Peruvian Rangers defected and joined the guerrilla forces, indicating that even among the highly select the influence of the revolutionaries' program was being felt. This also indicates the fissures that continue to be exposed in the traditional authoritarian institution, even after U.S. "modernization." The U.S. and Peruvian High Military Command are aware of the possible complete dissolution of their authority when the mass of the soldiers of peasant stock confront their kinfolk seeking to implement values that the peasant-soldiers recognize as legitimate. Hence the government's reliance on the elite Assault Guards in the recent repression of the peasants in the guerrilla areas. In addition, soldiers are stationed in army posts outside the region where they were born to lessen their resistance when the orders are given to shoot.

An official pamphlet on the antiguerrilla campaign published by the Peruvian Armed Forces (June 1966) boasts of having used the most modern techniques of counterrevolutionary warfare: "The Armed Forces, the Army, Air Force, and Marines put into use complicated machinery that bombed, burned, and utilized resources of psychological warfare and 'softening up' against the guerrilla-led popular forces." (*Las Guerrillas en el Perú su Represión* Ministerio de Guerra, Lima, Peru, 1966.)

[17] On the extent of force, which effected the liquidation of key guerrilla units, Peruvians who visited areas that were under government attack reported that upward of a thousand peasants were killed. The U.S. Military Mission apparently felt that saturation bombing-napalm and firebombing, coming as it would, unexpectedly, would have maximum results, in terms of undermining the growing popularity of the agrarian reform-minded guerrilla movement. Prior to this, massacres of peasants by the Peruvian government were common but never on the scale and intensity that has occurred under U.S. military-political tutelage.

In addition to the revolutionaries who have been killed, there are an estimated 1,000 political prisoners in Peru.

significance of the early guerrilla struggles. The students at the University of San Marcos, Lima, have become more committed than ever to the revolutionary struggle, while "de la Puente" urban units are active and functioning in Lima. In addition, Da Mommio points to a profound psychological guilt that permeates the city: those thousands who believe that de la Puente was right but simply do not have the courage to act as he did. Along with Camilo Torres, de la Puente is viewed as a symbol of courage and commitment in the midst of general social decay and personal opportunism. Values that determine career choices and the collective consciousness that becomes the reservoir for seemingly "spontaneous" popular outbursts are shaped by the examples and myths that grow around the lives of men like de la Puente. In creating a sense of a new moral authority as a spring for action against the old society, the fallen guerrillas can be looked upon as providing an important element in sustaining a new generation of revolutionaries.

In response to the Cuban Revolution and the Latin American popular revolutionary movements, U.S. policy makers devised a dual strategy: an Alliance for Progress that was supposed to promote social reform, economic development and political democracy; and the building of Latin American military forces to insure that Castroism was defeated. Most of the Alliance funds were loans, and a good deal was spent on refinancing previous loans and balancing the budget. Only a small percentage was ever applied to concrete reform projects. More important, the funds were directed toward a social structure whose dominant elites were not interested in agrarian reforms and economic development that would conflict with their own property holdings; hence, the "aid" funds became a social cement for bracing the old social elites against the winds of change rather than a stimulant for accelerated reform. Simultaneously, U.S. military aid to Latin America during the 1960's jumped 50 percent per year over that granted during the 1950's. In addition, the rationale for the buildup of the Latin military was no longer the old bogeyman, a Russian invasion, but internal popular forces. In June 1963 Defense Secretary Robert McNamara pointed to this shift: "Until about 1960 military assistance programs for Latin America were oriented toward hemispheric defense. As it became clear that there was no threat of significant overt external aggression against Latin America, emphasis shifted to internal security. . . ." Hence the rapid growth and expansion of counterinsurgency schools, U.S. military missions, and overall increased involvement by the U.S. in Latin political life. Interspersed between, and the ostensible agent of the socioeconomic "reform" aid and the military buildup strategy of U.S. policy makers, were a series of middle-class democratic governments that became (each in its turn) the "showcase" of the State Department. The inability of these governments— in Brazil, Ecuador, El Salvador, Argentina, Colombia, Venezuela, Guatemala, etc.—to carry out basic reforms while the military existed as a safeguard to the existing conservative elite became evident. The popular expectations, however, that both U.S. propaganda and native middle-class demagoguery aroused were a source of instability. The decision to shift frontiers in U.S. policy in late 1962 became clear: rather than turn to popular revolutionary forces as the alternative to the politically democratic but socially impotent middle-class-led forces, U.S. policy makers opted for "stability" and the military—and, in Walt Whitman Rostow's terms, disguised it as the new, vital "modernizing force" oriented toward "civic action." In this context one finds that over two-thirds of Alliance for Progress funds now go to military dictators or to military-controlled civilian governments despite the earlier injunction about using funds only to promote democracy. The U.S. Army Handbook on Venezuela notes that "the influence of the military over political affairs has been overriding and almost continuous. Nearly all rulers have realized that they could not stay in office if the army were antagonistic. Hence it has been courted and favored by those in power." Venezuela's Betancourt, who looked toward the armed forces as the major instrument for keeping power, raised the salaries of the officer corps and supported a military budget bearing approximately the same proportion to the national budget as had occurred under his predecessor, the tyrant Pérez Jiménez.

With the middle-class democrats discarded as unstable (or "put in their proper context") and the military now installed as the agency of development and security, no other social group or force exists in Latin America to safeguard this last hope of the U.S.—except the military force of the U.S. With the defection of the military during a popular revolution, the U.S. must confront the revolution directly with its own forces and substitute itself as the mainstay of the social elites and U.S. investments. There have already been a number of important defections from the Venezuelan navy and marines and the Guatemalan and Colombian armies to revolutionary guerrillas, in addition to the nationalistic Dominican officers who led the pro-Bosch forces in Santo Domingo.

The stagnant societies in Latin America hence have generated opposite and conflicting responses: military hegemony and guerrilla-led revolts. The question remains as to what are the social and political forces guiding these two protagonists. U.S. influence over Latin American Armed Forces has increased enormously in the past five years. This process has led to increasing control by the Latin American military of political life and the downgrading of political freedoms and social justice, contrary to the assertions of some academicians that Latin armies would become less political with increased contact with the U.S. military. U.S. military missions' influence on their Latin counterparts is indicated by numerous factors: command and staff of each of the services is similar to those of the U.S.; in Venezuela, Colombia, and Guatemala all the services use U.S. military doctrine, most texts used in the schools are direct translations; in addition large numbers of officers of all services have attended service schools in the U.S. and others have received specialized counterinsurgent training in the Canal Zone. U.S. military assistance has consisted of training and advising, and in the three above-mentioned countries U.S. officers have actually engaged in directing the "national" fighting forces. In this regard Venezuelan armed forces are under the closest "advice": the U.S. military mission of several hundred is the largest in Latin America and is indispensable to even the procedural functioning of the Venezuelan navy. The U.S. Air Force mission has personnel stationed with each tactical unit, in all schools except the cadet school, and at Air Force Headquarters. Recent napalm bombings in the Venezuelan hinterland are said to be part of the U.S. "vietnamization" campaign. In part, President Kennedy attempted to give some positive coloration to the historically regressive role that the military played in Latin America. "Civic Action" became the watchword, and in his message to Congress on March 22, 1962, Kennedy stated: "Military assistance will in the future more actively emphasize internal security, civil works, and economic growth of the nations aided." The only growth Latin nations immediately experienced was in influx of more U.S. military advisors and their initialed names: The Military Assistance Advisory Group (MAAG), the Mobile Training Teams (MTT's), etc. In Latin

America thirteen countries now have U.S.-supported military civic action programs. Bolivia, the first to organize one on a large scale, was also the country where the U.S. reorganized the army, since the traditional army was literally destroyed by the 1952 revolution and replaced by popular militias. It was with A.I.D. funds that the new-U.S.-organized Bolivian army built a few schools and recently seized the power and opened a frontal assault on the tin miners. "Civic Action" is an all-purpose formula. A pamphlet for army commanders on "Civic Action" describes it in terms similar to a manual on sex-immunization. ". . . a new dimension has been added to military civic action today as a weapon against communist-inspired subversion. It is considered as both a preventive measure and as a technique of guerrilla warfare and counter-insurgency." U.S. military and police involvement in Latin America is both intense and complex.[18] It involves not only the military missions, which are responsible for the suppression of popular movements, but the ambassador and his team, who are held responsible for on-the-spot decisions and who determine how much to involve the "host government," i.e., the current Latin government. The tie between counterinsurgency and civic action is coordinated by A.I.D. and MAAG or the military mission. These interlocking forces, all composed of citizens of the United States, determine major policy decisions affecting the Latin countries in which they are present.

The intense military-imperialist operations of the U.S. in Latin America is openly acknowledged by Secretary of Defense McNamara:

"During the past year serious insurgency and terrorist attacks have been successfully countered in several Latin American countries. In others, political threats have been contained. Venezuela has been able to improve substantially its control of guerrilla and terrorist elements during recent months. U.S.-trained units of their armed forces and police have spearheaded a government campaign both in the cities and in the countryside. In Peru the government has already made good progress against guerrilla concentrations, and U.S.-trained-and-supported Peruvian army and air force units have played prominent roles in this counterguerrilla campaign. In Colombia, U.S. training, support, and equipment, including several medium helicopters, have

---

[18] Exiled Brazilian intellectuals in Chile have recently stated that they were arrested, interrogated, and tortured by the Brazilian secret police (IPM) in the presence and with the collaboration of the FBI.

materially aided the Colombian armed forces to establish government control in the rural insurgent areas.

"Violence in the mining areas and in the cities of Bolivia has continued to occur intermittently, and we are assisting this country to improve the training and equipping of its military force.

"Pressure on the government of Guatemala resulting from Communist terroristic tactics has increased markedly during the past year. We are supporting a small Guatemalan counter-insurgency force with weapons, vehicles, communications, equipment, and training.

"In Uruguay protracted economic stagnation has contributed to popular unrest, which recently culminated in a serious wave of strikes throughout the country. Our military assistance to Uruguay is oriented toward improving the small arms, ammunition, communications, and transportation equipment of its security forces." [19]

Expressed U.S. policy in Latin America is a mixture of euphemisms, evasions, and violence. McNamara's reference to the repression of popular movements ("control of guerrilla and terrorist elements") is matched by a discreet silence over the exploitative social systems in Latin America to which the U.S. is supplying "weapons, vehicles, communications, equipment and training." According to McNamara, the real strategy of the U.S. in dealing with the striking miners of Bolivia ("violence") and the public employees of Uruguay ("popular unrest") is not to recognize their social and economic demands presented by the unions but to "improve the training and equipping of its military forces." McNamara's admission that his policy is directed against *"popular* unrest" caused by "protracted economic stagnation" is perhaps the clearest indictment of U.S. policy. In this period of popular awakening and mass politics the defense of U.S. business interests and the Latin ruling class depends on the U.S. strengthening and increasing its control over the repressive apparatus. Once mass popular movements are decimated or "contained" and the policies and institutions acceptable to the U.S. are established, elections between candidates acceptable to the U.S. are held. This mode of *satellite building* was once referred to as the "salami tactics." In this context, competitive elections are the outcome of violence against emerging popular forces;

[19] *Inter-American Economic Affairs*, Vol. 19; No. 4 (Spring 1966). Government Documents, U.S. Department of Defense Estimate of the Latin American Situation, February 1966. (Statement of Secretary of Defense Robert S. McNamara before a joint session of the Senate Armed Services Committee and the Senate Subcommittee on Department of Defense Appropriations on the Fiscal Year, 1967-71 Defense Program and 1967 Defense Budget.)

the electoral results are predetermined by the institutions and policies created or perpetuated during the repressive period. "Free elections" ("free" in the sense that popular revolutionaries do not have access to their constituents) then became a propaganda weapon utilized by the U.S. and Latin elites for legitimizing their hegemony. One likely consequence of this mode of establishing pseudo-legitimate governments is that resentments are accumulated, awaiting conditions propitious for another explosion. The Latin political cycle of violence-instability-repression is prolonged by U.S. policy, which in turn becomes the decisive factor in postponing necessary structural changes.

The most serious effort to institutionalize U.S. hegemony in the hemisphere and to protect the Latin social systems is found in the proposed Inter-American Military Force. Secretary of Defense McNamara sets forth the rationale behind this strategy in the following fashion:

> "We think that all of the OAS countries have an obligation to encourage the development of democracy and to help keep internal situations from spilling over and disrupting the peace of the Hemisphere. We think that some kind of peace-keeping force might be useful; that the system should have some more effective and responsive arrangement for dealing collectively with a clear and present danger to the peace and security of the Hemisphere. Such an arrangement, supported by a peace-keeping force, would represent a real sharing of responsibility and would also give pause to those elements that might seek to disrupt the peace. We believe the problem is being increasingly better understood now, and we shall continue to search for a formula acceptable to our Alliance partners." [20]

McNamara's appeal is to the existing Latin ruling classes; his fears are directed explicitly against national-popular revolutionaries, not "international Communism" (". . . internal situations . . . disrupting the peace of the Hemisphere"). The Secretary of Defense's proposal is designed to legitimize U.S. imperialist interventions such as occurred in Santo Domingo, Peru, Colombia, etc., by openly involving the Latin ruling class on a permanent *de jure* and not merely *de facto* basis (". . . a formula acceptable to our . . . partners"). Both

[20] Inter-American Economic Affairs, Vol. 19, No. 4 (Spring 1966). Government Documents, U.S. Department of Defense Estimate of the Latin American Situation, February 1966. (Statement of Secretary of Defense Robert S. McNamara before a joint session of the Senate Armed Services Committee and the Senate Subcommittee on Department of Defense Appropriations on the Fiscal Year, 1967-71 Defense Program and 1967 Defense Budget.)

McNamara statements, the description of the direct and intense military intervention of the U.S. and the Inter-American Military Force proposal, recognize the growing dissolution of Latin society and the development of popular dissatisfaction. Both are perceived by the U.S. Government as a threat to its interests; both are to be countered by an intensive and extensive military-organizational buildup.

Notwithstanding the current U.S. policy makers' success in isolating the Cuban revolution, in establishing the primacy of friendly military or military-controlled governments in most of Latin America, and in confining the guerrillas to the hinterland, the social and economic problems underlying the revolutionary opposition have worsened considerably. The price of militarily secure government has been the total failure of the Alliance for Progress to achieve a more equitable distribution of wealth, balanced economic growth, political freedom, and above all agrarian reform for the tens of millions of dispossessed and impoverished Latins.

It is important that a large part of the revolutionary opposition, the major guerrilla movements, the Guatemalan MR-13 (The Revolutionary Movement of November 13), the Venezuelan F.A.L.N., and the Colombian E.L.N. (National Liberation Army) are independent of and critical of the local Communist Party, and not subject to manipulations emanating from summit deals.[21] The example of Guatemala is clearest on this country: the guerrillas openly declare their socialist program while the Guatemalan Communist Party propounds for-

[21] In contrast to the popular-revolutionary position of Camilo Torres, the Colombian Communist Party supported the middle class liberal candidate, López Michelson, in the March 1966 elections during which over 65 percent of the Colombian populace abstained from voting to manifest its repudiation of the closed two-party dictatorship. The most decisive *political* struggle waged by Camilo Torres was against the Liberal-Conservative two-party system. His call was to the great masses outside of this electoral fraud and to all revolutionaries, whether they be peasants who had previously voted Conservative, or Communist workers who had been instructed to vote Liberal, to join the Frente Unido, against the two-party system and the oligarchies who controlled it. The broad support that Camilo Torres received from all sectors of the popular classes was a direct repudiation of the Communist position of coalition behind the candidature of the left wing of the liberal bourgeoisie, who received about 10 percent of the vote.

There appears to be a significant division between rural-based Communists who have espoused the road of armed struggle and the urban-based Communists who have opted for the electoral road and support of progressive sectors of the Liberal Party. See Alan Young, "Revolutionary Parties in Contemporary Colombia," Institute of Hispanic American and Luso-Brazilian Studies, Stanford University, 1963 (mimeograph).

mulas leading to alliances with the middle class on the basis of the latter's program and leadership.

Social and economic conditions that shaped the mentality of the reformers-turned guerrillas still exist. Decisive experiences that pushed them over the brink from debate to armed struggle continue to occur. The nationalist spur continues to prick army officers in Guatemala who witness their high infant mortality rate against the background of 650,000 acres of United Fruit Company-owned lands. Likewise Venezuelan and Colombian students seeking to implement the promises of their respective elites continue to find "legal channels" blocked or clogged by law or practice of the dominant institutions. While specific conditions may vary greatly from movement to movement, the problems and the direction of the struggle appear similar: national and economic independence (from the U.S.), social ownership of resources, agrarian reform, and some kind of popular participation in the system usually referred to as "the government." Today the fact that the Latin American guerrillas are not about to take power is less important than the fact that they are prepared to carry on a prolonged and determined struggle. The FALN has put it tersely enough: "Hacer la Patria libre o morir por Venezuela" ("Free the country or die for Venezuela").

Meanwhile, as U.S. policy makers continue to believe their own myths about the military as nation builders, and as public life in Latin America continues to disintegrate, the "socialist villages" in the rural areas of Guatemala, the guerrilla fronts of Venezuela, the "independent republics" of Marquetalia, Colombia, and above all the Indian "nation within a nation" in Peru could eventually become the source for a revitalized Latin America.

The emergence of guerrilla movements in Latin America reflected to a degree the example of the successful guerrilla-led social revolution in Cuba, and a convergence of both internal and external political factors: the continued and developing involvement by the U.S. in Latin America, especially after 1960, and the integration of the old "national popular parties" into the system of exploitation. While the major external factor —the Cuban Revolution—influenced generally the formation of all guerrilla movements, the decisive consideration in their emergence was the internal political situation brewing in each of the countries under consideration.

Beginning immediately after the Second World War, but

accelerating in the middle 1950's, discontent among the younger generation of militants began to manifest itself in the established opposition groups that monopolized the "national-popular" movements. As the decade of the 1950's reached a close and these once-revolutionary parties became reconciled to bargaining and transacting with the dominant elites the internal party crises was exacerbated. As the older leaders of the once-"national-popular parties" introduced political changes toward adapting the party to the existing society they also tightened the organizational apparatus as a means of maintaining control.

Reconciliation of the once-insurgent APRA to the Peruvian political system was the result of the slow process of social change that broadened without changing the basis of Peruvian society, hence opening channels for urban middle-class social mobility and economic opportunity. Coinciding with the fusion of the new commercial and industrial groups and the old landowning oligarchy was the new economic relationship that U.S. investors developed for exploiting the nation: political-economic partnerships with the new middle classes. Limited and unequal modernization of Peruvian society was decisive in effecting political change in the strategic political elite that controlled the APRA, the urban middle class. The political leadership faithfully reflected these socioeconomic changes, becoming less intransigent to the oligarchy and U.S. investors, finally accommodating itself once granted political legality along with social recognition of the urban middle strata that it represented. The institutionalization of the ex-opposition was the signal that the once-insurgent urban middle class had developed to the point where it felt it had more to lose from an overall change than it could gain within existing society. The new national-popular revolutionaries represent new social strata: those exploited lower classes with which the middle class transacted its entry into society (the threat that broadened traditional society and allowed for limited modernization).

Authoritarian organizational devices became a substitute for authority once based on political warfare with dominant elites. Accommodation to the status quo was paralleled by authoritarian discipline and the bureaucratization of the party. To maintain the bases of the parties, the loss of enthusiasm occasioned by the decline of revolutionary *élan* in the leader-ership was replaced by marginal favors, expulsions, and in some cases violence. The critical groups emerging in the late

1950's that had affiliated with the national-popular parties as a means of challenging the *status quo* found themselves in the "mass party," but with no prospects for effecting change. The monopolization by the older parties of substantial sectors of the popular forces capable of carrying out changes, the fact that the older leaders had not yet completely discredited themselves but still had the "halo" effect from earlier struggles with the traditional oligarchy, and the acceptance by many militants of the revolutionary pronouncements of the established leaders at face value appeared to offer the new Left oppositionists little hope for sustaining activities outside the party. Conflicts that would later find expression in armed confrontation between the old national-popular leaders-turned-government-officials and the new-generation-turned-guerrilla-fighters were first carried out in party debates and struggles inside the opposition parties. They fought over party principles, direction of the party, and control of the party base. What was at stake was the ability of the older leaders to transform a party organized for revolutionizing the masses into a machine for controlling the masses and making them unavailable to revolutionaries. The long-term results of those early discussions over "internal party democracy" and "revolutionary principles" were decisive in shaping the nature of future revolutionary activity. The old leaders were able to maintain their hold over the masses and to consolidate the party bureaucracy by expelling the new militants and forcing them outside the party. The organization was impermeable from the inside as well as from outside. Exclusion of the militants from the potential sources of revolutionary following in the established bureaucratically controlled organizations forced them to seek new constituencies outside those already established. Sectors of the working class were rigidly controlled by the APRA or the AD (*Acción Democrática*), the Partido Revolucionario in Guatemala, the Liberal or Conservative Parties of Colombia. Thus the militants were forced to orient to other social groups and classes that were available to new forms of organization. The student movement, which by its nature could not be rigidly enclosed in bureaucratic fetters, was the original major arena for recruitment. The previously unorganized peasantry and Indian population was another source. In Venezuela political activity was among the unemployed urban workers, slum dwellers, and nonunionized workers of Caracas, where over 80 percent of the working class was anti-Betancourt. The turn to the countryside in Venezuela resulted partly from government repression and the subsequent difficulty of maintaining the organizations of the Left. The established parties, including the newly coöpted "ex-revolutionaries" monopolized "legal politics." In addition, they used authoritarian and restrictive measures to prevent the new national-popular leaders from organizing new constituencies, thus forcing the militants into extralegal activity.

Guerrilla warfare is *one* variant of extralegal political activity. But other forms of extralegal struggle exist that do not exclusively rely on guerrilla activity: unofficial strikes, mass organization of the peasantry, the occupation of lands, or the establishment of regions under revolutionary control. Legitimacy based on political monopoly generated its opposite revolutionary politics bent on destroying the old order. The common thread running through all of the new movements, guerrilla or mass peasant movement, was the recognition that violence (illegal politics) was the mainspring of political change.

In summary, the physical presence of the bureaucratized parties controlling the urban centers of opposition, the impossibility of competing inside the party, the difficulty and danger of competing outside the party, and monopolization of politics leading to repression of political activity among new potential constituencies forced the new national-popular revolutionaries in the university and in the countryside to extralegal methods of struggle.

The inability of the Communist parties to attract new national-popular militants flowed from its orientation. On a lesser scale, the Communist Party experienced a process of schism comparable to that in the larger former national-popular movements. In Peru, Guatemala, Colombia, and Venezuela the Communist parties oriented their urban trade unionists toward electoral politics. (Earlier the Cuban Communist Party, which opposed Castro and the Cuban national-popular revolutionaries throughout most of the revolutionary struggle, followed a similar course.) For the Communist parties, apart from the fact that they were smaller and somewhat more restricted in their ability to collaborate and carry on transactions with the older elites, their policy was similar in practice to the old ex-"national-populists": marginal changes for their organized constituents, coalitions with the legal parties, and authoritarian organization and discipline to maintain the bases intact. Neither their proposed program nor the methods they espoused were in tune with the structural changes envisioned by the militants.

Where Communist parties controlled an urban constituency they contributed to isolating the new national-popular revolutionaries from potential urban constituents. This made it highly unlikely that the new militants would be able in the short run to organize an urban-based mass revolutionary party. The growth of the rural orientation both in Cuba and in the other Latin countries was based on political reality: the unavailability of political space in the urban milieux for creating a revolutionary constituency.

The organization of the peasantry, the insistence on rural-based guerrilla movements in the program of the national-popular movements, the disproportionate representation of students and former members of the traditional elite (military officers, priests, intellectuals), and the virtual absence of urban trade union leaders in the leadership of the national popular movements are indicative of the problems posed by already existing organizations in the urban setting. The once-revolutionary movement turned into a bureaucratic organization is a major factor conditioning the growth of a guerrilla movement as a source of change. The closing of urban channels forced the revolutionaries to attempt to open the urban constituency from the outside—by a rural-based movement. Use of violence was a response to the closed political system, whose continuance was premised on the inclusion of only those groups already organized. The only demands of organized groups that were recognized or considered legitimate by the dominant elite were those that filtered through the politically socialized and "housebroken" existing leadership. Introduction of a new mass constituency whose demands would be filtered through a revolutionary leadership would completely alter the relationships of power, not to speak of the structural changes that would be necessary to meet those demands.

Outside of the city was considered "illegal territory." Illegal politics was an attempt to break out of the stagnation of the totally urban-based traditional leftist and ex-leftist opposition. To open up politics meant to open rural society. In the final analysis armed struggle, as a technique, was the logical extension of an attempt to extend the conception of citizenship and nationhood beyond the confines of organized interest groups, beyond the scope of the major cities. In the context of the semicolonial societies of Latin America, revolutionary guerrilla warfare can be seen as an instrument fostering the development of citizenship to the extent that it weakens existing authoritarian institutions and creates the conditions for self-mobilizing autonomous social organizations in the countryside. By focusing on the foreign dependence of the existing government and by creating a larger identity based on indigenous control of national resources, the guerrilla movement contributes to the formation of a collective consciousness that later could become a decisive element in the process of "nation building."

A significant sector of the revolutionary leadership of the guerrilla movement is made up of intellectuals who have received an education abroad. Because of this, they are probably among the best-educated of the intellectuals. Camilo Torres and many of the revolutionary Colombian priests were educated either in Rome, France, or Belgium. Key members of the central leadership of the Peruvian MIR studied in European universities. Yon Sosa was trained at a specialized professional military school under U.S. auspices, and the same is true of Caamaño, the Dominican revolutionary leader. The higher levels of education appear to have sensitized these intellectuals' perception of the existing injustices. (This is not to ignore those who were political critics of the regimes before they went abroad.) The ability to evaluate their society from abroad may have given them an added perspective with which to view the need to change the system as a whole. The modern professional education and secure financial status that the guerrilla leaders obtained from their membership in the upper levels of the traditional society gave them the time and the opportunity to reflect on the functioning of the system as a whole. At the same time, it should be kept in mind that we are speaking of a small number of intellectuals. Most Latin intellectuals from the upper class who study abroad return to fill important government posts or work for private interests.

The revolutionary commitment of Camilo Torres was based not only on his perception of the all-too-common misery that is visible in the Latin slums, but on sociological investigations that he conducted. Likewise, Yon Sosa realized the necessity for a revolutionary strategy partly because of the teachings of his professional U.S. instructors. The commitment of these intellectuals bears special attention given the situation in most Latin countries, where specialized organizations of the United Nations and the U.S. offer handsome salaries and research opportunities to the all-too-willing majority of Latin intellectuals.

Recruitment of guerrilla leaders seems to indicate that a significant number originate in the upper-income or status groups. Many combine careers in traditional institutions with modern education sometimes carried to the point of studying abroad. A combnation of these factors usually becomes the basis for an overall critique of society.

Two related questions of more than tangential interest to a study of revolutionary movements in Latin America are the following: Why did the Latin American Communist parties not initiate guerrilla struggles anywhere during and after the Cuban revolutionary period? And why have the Communist parties failed to attract the new generation of revolutionary leaders? There are certainly sufficient examples of military guerrilla warfare in Latin America, and some, such as Mexico, Bolivia, and Cuba, have been cases of maximum success. Ironically, the early Communist movement (or at least part of it) prior to the worldwide popular front supported guerrilla-military warfare in Brazil (the famous Prestes Column) and in Colombia. In Colombia the rural guerrilla movement of the early 1930's that occupied geographic areas (similar to the events in China) was discontinued in favor of supporting the "progressive" oligarch, Alfonso López. Unlike in China, the Communists did not continue working in the countryside, using it as a springboard for revolutionary struggle. Only when national-popular revolutionaries organized movements like the July 26th Movement of Cuba or the MIR of Peru or Venezuela have the guerrilla movements in Latin America succeeded, or the initiative for their organization taken place.

This striking lack of revolutionary initiative by the Latin American Communist parties was, of course, highlighted by the Cuban Revolution and the total unpreparedness and lack of response by the Party to the Batista coup. Likewise, in the recent Dominican revolt the Communist Party wrote in self-criticism four months later: "Our party was not prepared for the armed intervention." The failure of the Communist Party to meet the most urgent political needs was the key factor propelling the formation of the independent July 26th Movement in Cuba. The inability of the Latin Communist parties to cope with the political needs of this historical period has been decisive in orienting revolutionary leadership away from the Communist Party. At the same time, the nonrevolutionary image of the Communists tends to attract the less dynamic elements of the new generation. Thus, both program and recruitment based on pre-existing policies mutually reinforce the reformist character of the C. P. in Latin America.

Political analysis and program have kept the Communist Party from fashioning a revolutionary orientation. As perceived by the Communists, Latin America is in the throes of a "democratic revolution" led by the progressive bourgeoisie and its parties against U.S. imperialism and the "feudal" landowners. This revolution is the first of two stages. The first stage is the "national democratic" stage, to be followed at some undisclosed date by the second step, a "socialist" revolution. In operational terms the Communists, in seeking to promote the national-democratic revolution, support the electoral aspirations of middle-class parties. Both the electoral support of middle-class parties and the absence of revolutionary initiative relate to the immediate task seen by the Communist parties. Construction of middle-class-led popular-front governments characterizes the first stage of the "revolutionary process." The inadequacy of this Communist strategy is based on two empirically unsound premises: (1) that the urban bourgeoisie is in conflict with the landowners (frequently they have close commercial and family connections), and (2) that the major conflicts are between national capitalists and imperialists, and not between workers on the one hand and native and foreign capitalists on the other. The convergence of interests between these supposedly antagonistic groups is indicated by the fact that not one of the middle class-led governments in the postwar period has either carried out an agrarian reform or consistently resisted U.S. economic or military penetration. On the contrary, evidence is accumulating that middle-class governments have been singularly incapable of maintaining their power where they have not become agencies for repression of the popular movements (see for example, Belaúnde and Betancourt).

Committed to a strategy that requires an electoral orientation and hence a certain modicum of legality, the Communists eschew all actions that might alienate the indicated middle-class political leaders. Beyond that, they frequently denounce as "adventurers," *putschists*, etc., those revolutionaries seeking to radically restructure society through "illegal" nonelectoral means apart from alliances with traditional parties.

A range of revolutionary strategies is to be found outside of the official Communist parties. The Guatemalan MR-13 and the Trotskyists view Latin society as polarized between the workers, the peasants, and the students on the one hand, and the landowners, U.S. imperialism, and the native capitalists on the other. They perceive the antiimperialist struggle as an integral part of the class struggle, and hence the "two stages" of the revolution (bourgeois and socialist) are telescoped. The struggle for one set of demands necessarily leads directly into the other, the theory of "permanent revolution." This analysis, of course, allows the Trotskyists and groups sharing similar outlooks to participate in the armed struggle where they have the forces, or to offer a theoretical basis for the new revolutionary strategy of armed warfare.

In most Latin countries "Trotskyism" is quite small and fragmented. However, in the Guatemalan MR-13 their ideas are apparent as were a few of their militants.[22] In Peru the leader of the mass organization of the peasantry in the early 1960's, Hugo Blanco,[23] was a Trotskyist. In addition, the Peruvian guerrilla movement received some support from the Peruvian Trotskyists. Finally, the Bolivian miners' unions and militia are influenced by Trotskyist cadres. More significant than their physical presence is the Trotskyist critique of Communist strategy, which has been assimilated by diverse groups without their necessarily accepting the "permanent revolution" thesis or the sectarian attitudes of these isolated groups.

Probably the most important non-Communist revolutionaries are found in the new-national-popular movements like the MIR of Peru and Venezuela. They combine an analysis that appears similar to that of the Communists (identifying the

[22] The individuals who were expelled from MR-13 and called themselves "Trotskyists" were members of a group led by an Argentine named Posadas. This group had split from the European-based Trotskyist movement and has been denounced as "Left sectarians" for its activities in Latin America and more recently for its "fund lifting" activities in Guatemala. For a more detailed account, see the September 1966 issues of *World Outlook*, published in Paris, France.

[23] Hugo Blanco was arrested in the summer of 1963 and was not brought to trial until the fall of 1966. Reliable informants in Arequipa report that Blanco, who was down to 90 pounds, had been kept in a miserable dungeon and subjected to innumerable indignities. There seems to be little prospect of his release. If Blanco dies, as appears possible, he will not be the first guerrilla who has suffered this fate in the hands of the police. The Peruvian Armed Forces reported that another guerrilla leader, Máximo Velando, allegedly died from "injuries in an attempted suicide." (*Correo*, Huancaye, June 19, 1966.) Similarly, the Venezuelan guerrilla leader Fabricio Ojeda was reported by the political police to have committed suicide. The two most likely hypotheses are that: 1) they were killed by the police, or 2) they were tortured or subjected to indignities similar to those suffered by Blanco, which forced them to take their own lives. The complete absence of juridical rights and the assassination of political prisoners is, of course, a hallmark of totalitarian and authoritarian regimes.

prime targets of the revolution as the landowners and U.S. imperialism) while accepting the strategy of the Trotskyists: armed struggle. The MIR differs from both parties, however, in pinpointing the social force for change in the countryside, among the peasantry, instead of in the urban working class. Further, the MIR projects the formation of a revolutionary vanguard as part of the process in which the guerrilla movement, through armed struggle and the creation of revolutionary *focos,* brings about mass mobilization. The Revolutionary party is built in the course of the struggle for power rather than through the prior politicalization and organization of the masses—the ideas of Guevara, not Lenin.

The relationship between the Cuban revolution and the Latin American revolutionary struggle is complex and changing. Between 1959 and 1962 the Cuban leadership basically supported a broad spectrum of Latin political forces ranging from left-wing to moderate nationalist forces, including personages like Quadros of Brazil. Beginning about 1962 until 1966 the Cuban leadership shifted its support more and more toward the official Communist Parties, perhaps hoping they would take the revolutionary road (as some did temporarily) and the left-wing nationalists (MIR of Venezuela and Peru). During this period there was a continuous "ambiguity" in Cuban policy toward the Latin revolution: the Cubans called for armed revolution and supported the Communist Parties (who had no pretension in this direction); "Che" Guevara left Cuba, Yon Sosa was denounced, and the first Tri-Continental Conference contained a preponderance of "official" Communists, though by this time (1966) there was considerable opposition to their policies present at the conference, as evidenced by the declarations in favor of armed revolution. Beginning in the latter part of 1966 the Cuban revolutionary leadership definitely shifted its support away from the "official" Communists toward the active militants conducting armed guerrilla warfare, whether they were nationalists, Communists, or independent revolutionaries. Evidence of this new position is present in the Cuban publication of "Che" Guevara's call for revolution and Castro's speech of March 15 and 16 (1967), where he openly denounced the official Venezuelan Communist Party and the Soviet Union and defended the guerrillas in Venezuela and elsewhere.[24]

[24] See Fidel Castro's speech in *Granma Weekly Review* (Havana, July 30, 1967). See also Raúl Castro's speech in the same issue.

The revolutionary crisis in Latin America is manifest in the self-doubt and disbelief that exists even in the very institutions that are under attack. This crisis of "rulership" finds its expression also in the bifurcation of the opposition. This division takes the form of a schism between the urban and the rural orientations, and the differences between strategies of the political generations; those of the nineteen-thirties/forties, and those of the fifties/sixties.

The social and political struggles organized around these differing orientations and strategies determine the specific content of economic development, modernization, and industrialization. In this sense, at this particular historical period in the semicolonial countries of Latin America, the political variables, including the problems of revolutionary transition, become foremost. Resolution of the question of political power is the key factor determining whether economic and social development will take place or whether economic subordination and social stagnation will continue to characterize society. Current debates regarding industrialization and social change are significant for the mass of society not directly related to these processes only. If these discussions concern themselves with the nature of the social order directing society. The failure in political rulership by the new business and commercial groups and their inability to handle the problem of social change and to direct the process of overall economic development have created two sources of real and potential opposition: (1) significant sectors that have been cut loose from traditional authoritarian institutions by social dislocation; and (2) the great majority of the countryside and the mass of rural migrants in the urban slums, who have been totally bypassed by the uneven economic development.

Important in the revolutionary process in Latin America is the attempt by the former members of the elite—who have been cut adrift—to overcome the present social dislocation, and at the same time to create the basis for a new political authority: the exploited rural and urban populace. But the revolutionary process in Latin America is but one aspect of the disintegration of the old ruling order; repression is another.

The real weakness of the guerrilla movements is not that they are "premature" or that electoral alliances of a popular-front variety are a viable alternative. The degree of U.S. military and political involvement in Latin America and the closed nature of the political system based on the existing fragile social structure makes legal, nonviolent politics highly ineffective. Rather the political weakness of the guerrilla movements has been their *lack of a mass peasant political organization and an urban working-class-based political apparatus* that could serve as both a means of materially and politically supporting the guerrillas and a means of countering the repression of the state. The guerrillas have attempted to substitute *focos* of armed resistance as a means of mobilizing the masses instead of mass mobilization of the rural peasantry and urban workers and the development of the guerrillas as defensive armed detachments (putting themselves at the vanguard of a mass movement; defending it against the inevitable government repression). One of the reasons for the failure of the first MIR guerrillas was their lack of a mass peasant organization that would have permitted them to fuse with the population. The problem of "security," frequently occurring, resulted from *a lack of trained cadre and disciplined organization.*

The Latin American revolution and its direction is not being debated in terms of armed struggle vs. popular front, but among those who are reflecting on how to combine the armed struggle with the mass mobilization of the countryside and the organization of the advanced sectors of the working class.[25] This perspective excludes the popular front strategy of the old national-popular and Communist parties. It also means that the Fidelista movements are deepening their political thinking beyond the pragmatic-empirical level of resolving revolutionary strategy on the basis of armed struggle alone. The new revolutionary synthesis sometimes called the *brazo armado* appears to encompass the mass political organization that Hugo Blanco was so successful in organizing among the peasantry, with the audacity and armed detachments of de la Puente and Lobatón. Recent history appears to indicate that mass movements without armed detachments simply invite official terror and repression; guerrilla detachments without mass movements are isolated, easily surrounded, and overwhelmed by the Armed Forces. The new strategy seems to call for multiple fronts and

[25] The Peruvian Army's defeat of the first guerrilla detachments has had a sobering effect: the euphoria that dominated the University of San Marcos during the guerrilla *focos* period has faded away. There seems to be confidence in the rebirth of the guerrillas, however, on the basis of the *brazo armado* theory, especially among the pro-Peking leaders of the San Marcos Student Federation. *Brazo Armado,* or the "armed wing," becomes the military component of a mass political movement instead of the catalyst of the revolutionary process.

combined action: urban working class and student cadre organization capable of mobilization; mass rural organization organized around concrete and immediate issues, such as land occupation; and guerrilla movements mobile and adaptable to the needs of the urban-rural mass movements.

With the Guerrillas in Guatemala

EDUARDO GALEANO

Eduardo Galeano, a regular contributor to the weekly *Marcha* and other magazines, and former editor of the Uruguayan newspaper *Época*, is in charge of publications at the University of Montevideo. He has written five books: two novels and three works of nonfiction.

CÉSAR MONTES, the leader of one of the two principal guerrilla groups operating in the Guatemalan countryside, unfolded an Esso map of his country. He was standing in a jungle clearing. "See here?" he said. "This is where the guerrillas started, in the Sierra de las Minas. Later they spread to the north—to the Vera Paces, the Indian regions, and then into the lowlands—Rio Hondo, La Palma, San Cristóbal, Rosario, Gualán, San Agustín, and Teculután. For some time now we have also been operating in the western region, the most densely populated Indian areas. Half the people in Guatemala are Indians, and you can be sure they will play a decisive role in our revolution. But it is a slow and difficult job. We are faced with four centuries of distrust that the Indians have had for the whites and the mestizos." Montes proudly pointed out several Indian guerrillas in his encampment, and added that they were devoted Catholics.

It seemed fitting that Montes was using an Esso road map to explain the whereabouts of the Guatemalan guerrillas. Although he had personally learned the art of warfare by actual fighting, a number of other guerrilla leaders had been taught by U.S. Army officers. Luis Augusto Turcios, a former commander of Montes' FAR (Fuerzas Armadas Revolucionarias) who was recently killed in an automobile accident at the age of 24, had been trained at the Army Ranger school at Fort Benning, Georgia. Yon Sosa, the commander of the other guerrilla group, MR-13, which controls part of Izabal in

Reprinted by permission from *Ramparts* magazine, the September 1967 issue.
Translated by Bernardo Garcia-Pandavenes.

Northeastern Guatemala, learned guerrilla warfare from U.S. instructors at Fort Gulick in the Panama Canal Zone.

But, of course, what the American military is trying to do is not to train the guerrillas themselves, but the people trying to suppress them. Even more so than with other Latin American countries, the U.S. is quietly pouring arms, money, and "advisors" into the antiguerrilla effort in Guatemala. It is an involvement beginning to look ominously like the U.S. presence in South Vietnam in the years before American combat troops arrived there. The war is no longer just Guatemala's.

Just what the extent of American military involvement is, no one knows for sure. Many Guatemalan officers have been trained by the U.S. Army at bases in the Canal Zone and in the U.S. itself. But U.S. involvement is greater than this. The guerrillas themselves claimed at one time that 1,000 members of the U.S. Special Forces were aiding the Guatemalan Army. This figure seems high, but the U.S. Government has officially admitted the participation of men from the U.S. Eighth Special Forces group in the military training of Guatemalans.

A former Guatemalan Army sergeant told me about the courses in antiguerrilla warfare he took from Special Forces instructors: "The classes were held at the 'La Cajeta' farm in Zacapa. We were there from May to October of last year. They told us that Cubans were heading the Guatemalan guerrillas. They taught us camouflage techniques, how to survive in the mountains, how to undo booby traps. As for prisoners, we were advised to do away with them whenever we were not able to take them with us."

General Robert W. Porter, Jr., commander of the U.S. Southern Army Command in Panama, told the House Committee on Foreign Affairs in April 1966 that the U.S. Army engineers and rangers were working on "civic action" programs in the border zone where troops from Guatemala and Honduras have been fighting guerrillas. The "civic action" consists mostly of distributing powdered milk, medicines, and promises to villagers under guerrilla influence. "The guerrillas must first be close by before we even get water," a peasant from the Izabal region said to me. But from reports both by Guatemalans and American newspapermen, it appears that American military involvement in Guatemala consists of more than "civic action" and is roughly similar to what it was in South Vietnam during the years before U.S. combat troops arrived there: the U.S. supplies many arms to the Guatemalan Army, American "advisors" accompany Army units on missions, and high-level advisors dispense their advice at offices in the headquarters of the various armed forces, the Ministry of Defense, and even the national police department. And on some occasions the U.S. appears to have dispensed more than advice. In an interview, Guatemalan Vice President Don Clemente Marroquín Rojas told me that one time a squadron of U.S. planes flown by U.S. pilots took off from Panama, made a napalm bombing raid on a suspected guerrilla camp on a Guatemalan mountainside, and returned to Panama without even landing in Guatemala. It is obvious that the U.S. considers Guatemala a test case for the survival of guerrilla movements in Latin America, and that it is not willing to risk another Cuba.

The forces of Yon Sosa and César Montes have squabbled fiercely over doctrinal differences but now seem on their way to a united front. Besides their war against the Guatemalan Army, the two guerrilla movements have something else in common: many of their members and leaders are very young. Montes is 25. One of his deputies, nicknamed *Manzana* (which means apple in Spanish—he got the name for having a red face), is only 20 and has been with the guerrillas since he was 17; two older deputies are only 24.

The guerrillas have to be young to survive. Their life is grueling, and they have to keep walking to retain their advantage of surprise and to avoid the regular Army forces pursuing them. Often all they have to eat are boiled wild leaves with salt. They keep moving continuously, clearing their way through the wet jungle with machetes. "Our columns are extremely mobile," Montes says. "This is why the Army can never catch us, despite all the operations they have launched. We have several patrols operating in different parts of the country. They have not been able to capture any of our camps for a simple reason: we never set up fixed camps. Only a few of our food deposits have been discovered, but that is all. It is hard to walk so much, but you soon become used to it. Guerrillas have walked, for instance, from the Izabal Lake to San Agustín Acasaguastlán, which means you have to go across the highest peaks in Guatemala. We have been able to do that in twenty days, without stopping, going from six in the morning until sundown every day, just eating breakfast before leaving and supper before going to sleep." Most of his troops, Montes said, are farmers; a few are students.

César Montes himself is called *el chiris,* a Guatemalan word meaning small child. Slightly built, he has features that seem almost delicate. "Don't ask me to look mean in a photograph because no one would be taken in," he laughingly told me. At the age of 13 he was expelled from a Catholic school, owing to his fury over the CIA's coup against the leftist Arbenz regime. At 18 he led student demonstrations and saw his fellow students shot dead before his eyes. At 20 he went to the mountains. By 24 he was leader of one of the most important guerrilla movements in Latin America.

To bring the local peasants over to their side, both groups of Guatemalan guerrillas used the method known as *propaganda armada* ("armed propaganda"). This, incidentally, is a method the Cuban guerrillas never practiced: guerrillas go into villages, occupy them for a few hours, explain to the peasants the principles behind their fight, and leave cell-like committees behind them. The guerrillas feel they can succeed only with the support of the peasants. "The peasants are the eyes and ears of the guerrillas," says Yon Sosa of MR-13. "We are always kept informed about the enemy, and the enemy never finds out where we are. They would have to do away with the whole population to defeat us. But before that ever happens, we will have turned the enemy into dust." The guerrilla weapons I saw included .45 caliber Thomson machine guns, Belgian Brownings and other automatics of Swedish and German makes, Garand guns of World War II vintage, a few M-1's, and some Colt .45's. "The Army claims it takes weapons from us quite often," César Montes said, "but they have never been able to show any of our weapons to be Cuban, Czech, or Soviet. And they have never found any foreign soldiers in our ranks. Our weapons don't come from Cuba but from the Guatemalan Army itself. We buy them. If they are capable of selling their country, why wouldn't the soldiers sell their weapons? And everyone knows where our money comes from: we collect ransoms from kidnapping big capitalists who have been exploiting Guatemalan workers for years. We always choose exploiters who are widely hated by everyone."

Montes was deeply scornful of the American "advisors" who are helping the Guatemalan Army in its antiguerrilla operations. In a sophisticated way, he knows that they too have read Mao and Guevara: "They operate in a mechanical way. They have read in Mao's works that the guerrilla is to the people what the fish is to water, and they know that fish die when taken out of water. They really believe that they can do the same thing to us, that they can isolate us. And perhaps they can deceive part of the people part of the time but not the whole time. The peasants need land but they don't have any. They need housing, but the government builds homes for military officers. You cannot stop the peasants from helping us when you don't give them the things that they need." Montes was holding Pope Paul VI's encyclical *Popularum Progressio,* from which he read at random: ". . . Farmers become aware that they are undeserving of poverty . . . the scandal of painful disparities. . . ." He winked. "The Pope is more intelligent than the Guatemalan Right. Read this over and you will see how clearly he explains the causes of violence."

Montes described to me how an American named Ronald Hornberger had once come to the guerrillas claiming to be a newspaperman. "He acted very confident; we talked with him in the mountains for a few days. He dropped names and addresses from the capital, but we double-checked within a few days and found that none of the people he had mentioned had ever heard of him. He also lied about the place he had supposedly left his luggage. He seemed to be interested only in the military aspects of our struggle and not at all in our political motivations. All his questions were of a highly specialized military nature. He was an ace in the handling of any weapon. He brought some military equipment that he said was a gift to us. We tried him and executed him. On his waist under the shirt he wore a fine nylon cord, the kind used by Green Berets for strangling."

The U.S. has given napalm bombs and other arms to Guatemalan troops, and sometimes crops and fields are razed in an effort to deprive the guerrillas of their food supply. As in Vietnam, this kind of action often results in the killing of innocent peasants, and the turning of more and more people against the regime. A guerrilla described to me how on the Alexandria Mountain near Río Hondo, he and a band of other guerrillas discovered the bodies of five peasants lying in the middle of a field, charred by napalm beyond recognition.

If ever there was a country ripe for revolution, Guatemala is it. An article by Dan Kurzman in the *Washington Post* of March 13, 1966, refers to Guatemala as "a country that has made virtually no political, economic or social progress since the Communist-infiltrated government of President Jácobo Arbenz was overthrown in 1954." The article goes on to discuss the achievements of Castillo Armas, who was put into power in the place of Arbenz by a CIA coup in 1954: "Castillo Armas proved to be something less than a democratic crusader. Instead of pushing land reforms, he earned the indignation of many peasants by returning to the big landowners virtually all of the estimated 1.5 million acres expropriated by the Arbenz regime. . . . Guatemala has known little but stagnant dictatorship and corruption since 1954."

Take just one example of the tremendous gap between rich and poor in Guatemala: taxes. Any Economics 101 college student knows that progressive income taxes tend to reduce the gap between rich and poor because the rich have to pay a somewhat higher proportion of taxes. Taxes on consumers, such as sales taxes, don't reduce the gap because they hit everyone equally. But out of the $119 million the Guatemalan government collects annually in tax revenues, *only seven million comes from income or property taxes,* and that seven million includes all the taxes paid by U.S. firms in Guatemala, like the United Fruit Company.

By every standard, Guatemala's extreme poverty is appalling. Only 15 percent of the federal land is under cultivation. Only 750 tractors are in use in the entire country. The country is short one million housing units. In the province of Quiché there is only one doctor per 120,000 people. A shortage of clinics, hospital beds, and medicine extends throughout the entire country. But, ironically, Guatemala is one of the seven Latin American countries that is repeatedly praised by the State Department for having joined the U.S. in shipping medicine to South Vietnam. Out of every 10,000 children born alive, 1200 die before the age of four. Most of the remainder are condemned to a life without schools, shoes, milk, and toys. Seventy-five percent of the population is illiterate, and shoeless, and gets less than one third of the minimum daily food requirements. Three quarters of the population earn 20 cents a day or less. A quart of milk costs two days of labor for the peasant of Alta Verapaz; three days of labor will pay for a pound of meat.

Guatemala's Army is probably the only one in the world that has one colonel for every 30 men. In many other ways as well it is corrupt and inefficient, the officers more interested in their fat salaries and special vacations than in pursuing their duties. The morale of enlisted men—many of whom have been "shanghaied" while wandering drunkenly along a city street and enlisted against their will, like sailors in the old British navy—is appallingly low. When a private is killed in battle, his corpse is seldom returned to his relatives. Given these conditions, it is not surprising that the American military has taken such a strong interest in beefing up the Guatemalan Army's will and ability to resist the guerrillas.

Far from alleviating the misery and the poverty of Guatemala, American involvement in that country has done much to cause it. Before 1944 Guatemala was just another Central American "banana republic." It was ruled by the dictator Ubico, a pro-Nazi general, who looked out for the interests of North American corporations and the local oligarchy. But when he was overthrown by the 1944 popular revolution, a vigorous plan for widespread education was put into effect, and the Indians began to become politically conscious, farm workers and city workers started joining labor unions, and Guatemala seemed to be demonstrating that a Latin American country can, on its own accord, break away from backwardness and poverty. The Arbenz regime accelerated many of these reforms, and in the first months of 1954 more than 100,000 Guatemalan families had received new land under the agrarian reform law. Then Washington decided that the Arbenz regime was "Communist-infiltrated" and was setting a dangerous example, and the CIA started preparing an invasion against Guatemala, with the blessing of the OAS. Included among the indignant Latin American leaders who raised their hands to condemn the Arbenz regime at a special OAS conference were some of the bloodiest dictators in the history of the continent: Batista, Trujillo, Somoza, Pérez Jiménez, Odría, Rojas Pinilla and others.

Castillo Armas, a graduate of the U.S. Command and General Staff College at Ft. Leavenworth, Kansas, invaded Guatemala with troops trained and paid by the United States. His invasion was supported by C-47 bombers piloted by the CIA. When he had taken over the country, Castillo Armas returned all the expropriated uncultivated land to the big landlords and gave away millions of acres of the country to an international oil cartel. The Guatemalan Oil Act was written in English and sent to the Guatemalan Congress in that language to be passed. One congressman, who still had some sense of dignity left, requested that it be rendered into Spanish. Opposition newspapers that had operated freely under Arbenz were closed; democratic political leaders, students, and labor union officers were sentenced to death, prison, or exile. Finally Armas himself was assassinated. "It is a great loss to his own nation and for the whole free world," Eisenhower said. The forces of the Right and of the Guatemalan military have been in control of the country most of the time ever since.

One day early in 1967, in an office in downtown Manhattan, blood rushed to the face of Abraham Weber as he shouted, "I am never going to allow a small Central American country to impose its will on an American company! Do you understand?" The person he was addressing was a Guatemalan, Carlos Rafael López Estrada, who had just resigned as the lawyer for the IRCA (International Railways of Central America). The IRCA used to belong to the United Fruit Company until a New York court applied the antitrust law and forced United Fruit to get rid of it. The railway ended up in the hands of investors Abraham Weber and Louis Yaeger. Guatemala hasn't profited one centavo by the change. These foreign trains, the only ones the country has, look as if they were taken from a documentary on the Mexican revolution of 1910. Ancient and squeaky, practically useless, they render the poorest service imaginable. The IRCA doesn't pay taxes. Yet in Guatemala even Indians who use carts to carry their produce to market and even bicycle owners must pay taxes. The railways do not even pay their own mailing expenses. The state no longer has the right to check the company's records. The IRCA statement that it is losing money is accepted as the truth. Weber's rage against López Estrada came because the lawyer had suggested a few discreet changes in the arrangement between the railway and the Guatemalan Government "to give the Government the feeling that its sovereignty was recognized," as López Estrada put it to me.

.American involvement in Guatemala since 1954 has not been restricted to exploiting the country's economy. Recent revelations have shown that the U.S. exercised a decisive hand in Guatemalan internal politics even after the CIA's 1954 coup. An article in the Chicago *Daily News* last December revealed that "the U.S. instigated and supported the 1963 coup by the Guatemalan military to overthrow the constitutionally elected president, Miguel Idígoras Fuentes." The reason for American support of the coup, the newspaper said, was to forestall what was thought to be an imminent victory in the Guatemalan presidential election by Juan José Arévalo, who had been president from 1944 to 1950 and who, despite his non-Communist stance, was too far left for American comfort. The paper goes on to explain why the American-supported military coup led to some of Guatemala's problems today:

"This is because it [the Guatemalan coup] was followed by a military dictatorship whose unpopularity helped a Castroite guerrilla movement to flourish."

The military regime that came to power after the 1963 coup finally did permit elections to be held early last year. But the middle-of-the-road government that was elected clearly depends on the Army for its existence. And the Army's behind-the-scenes influence shows who musters the real power.

In a recent pastoral letter the Archbishop of Guatemala wrote about the "silence of cemeteries" being imposed upon his country. His reference was to the wave of right-wing terrorism that has swept through Guatemala unchecked for the past year. Newspapers provide their readers with daily accounts of corpses, mutilated or burned on the roadsides, or floating down the middle of the Motagua river, most of them forever unidentifiable. Fishing in the region of Gualán has stopped—far too many corpses have been found caught in the improvised dams the fishermen have built to catch fish. In Gualán itself, American military men frequently visit the home of Mariano Sánchez, the Guatemalan Army's local representative and the leader of the local terrorist gang that hunts down "Communists" with a fury reminiscent of the Indonesian massacres.

Under none of its former military dictatorships has Guatemala known a systematic terrorism like the one that has taken hold of the country under the present regime. Even members of the President's own party have been assassinated by right-wing armed gangs. These groups have close ties with the Army and enjoy its full protection.

A man I met in Guatemala City had received several warnings. He had been "advised" to leave the country. A friend of his had received a pathetic letter from the Mexican border: "They tortured me and I gave them your name. I know that you have nothing to do with it, but I had to tell them something, something . . . you can't begin to imagine. . . ." Another prisoner he knew had had his testicles crushed with a pair of pliers. The large majority of these so-called "communists" are university professors whose sole crime consists in having participated in the reform governments of Arévalo and Arbenz. Or sometimes they are relatives of government enemies. For instance, the brother of guerrilla commander César Montes, who lived a totally unpolitical life, was found dead, crushed by torture, three days after he was detained by the Army.

Mario Julio Ruano Pinzón, a former sergeant in the Guatemalan military police, told me his experience: he is the sole survivor of four soldiers who witnessed the machine-gun massacre of 28 political and labor leaders a year ago in an Army warehouse. Three colonels were in charge of this job; one of them is now Minister of Defense, Colonel Arriaga Bosque. The soldiers had carried the bodies in bags, dripping in blood, to vehicles that took them to an airplane, from which the bodies were then dumped into the Pacific. Three of the soldiers later died. One was found stabbed to death in a boarding house, another was shot to death in a bar in Zacapa, the third was riddled with bullets in a bar behind the central station in Guatemala City. Julio Pinzón deserted. His photograph appeared in every newspaper. The Army is still looking for him.

Although the right-wing terrorist gangs officially operate without anyone's sanction, it is fairly clear that they represent the will of the Army. A *New York Times* story of July 14, 1967, under the headline "Guatemalan Rightists outdo Reds in Terrorism" summed up the situation: "No amount of Army denial has been able to shake the conviction, widely held among most informed persons here, that most of the rightist, anti-communist groups are, in fact, a creation of the Army and that many of their members are junior officers . . . these armed irregulars have been criticized for being so indiscriminate in their attacks that a large number of innocent persons, guilty perhaps of no more than leftist and liberal leanings, have been tortured, killed, or terrorized."

The terror goes on. Even in the center of the capital, men have been dragged from their homes or gunned down on the streets. Newspapers report six, seven cases each day.

A new law implies that no member of the security forces may be held responsible for a crime of homicide. Certain of the big landowners have been legally raised to the level of local political authorities, with full rights to bear weapons and to form their own private police forces. Vice President Marroquín Rojas justifies this measure because, "The landowners constitute the vital source of production."

There could be no more helpful aid than a government like this in making César Montes and Yon Sosa the first successful revolutionaries on the mainland of Latin America. What gives the Guatemalan situation a significance beyond that small country is that the Pentagon, as in the cases of other revolutions lately, is backing the wrong side. And as long as that way of thinking prevails in Washington, there are likely to be as many Guatemalas in Latin America as there will be Vietnams in Asia.

DEVELOPMENT AND POLITICS

Revolution, Reform, Conservatism

OSCAR DELGADO

The significance of policies for rural change that have been tried under the aegis of the dominant classes, and the Church and the Armed Forces, is analyzed and contrasted, by Delgado, with the agrarian transformations in Mexico, Bolivia, and Cuba. The so-called "agrarian reforms" instituted in Latin America with the approval of the United States, as in Colombia, for instance, have in practice been nothing more than parcelation and "colonization" programs that leave the great estates and existing distribution of property untouched. In contrast, Delgado argues, real agrarian transformations, minimally, result in increased economic security and improved "life chances" for the rural populations, as well as acting, as in Cuba and Mexico, to spur long-run development.

Oscar Delgado, Professor of Sociology at the University of Bogotá in Colombia, and an official of the Inter-American Committee of Agricultural Development in Washington, D. C., is the editor of *Reformas Agrarias en la América Latina* (Mexico: Fondo de Cultura Económica, 1965).

Reprinted from *Dissent*, Vol. IX, No. 4 (Autumn 1962), pp. 350-363, by permission.

Three Types of Agrarian Structure

LATIN AMERICA had a population of 199 million in 1960, according to a United Nations estimate. Of this total, 108 million, or 54 percent, live in rural areas, and of these, 28½ million are economically active.

All rural dwellers who are economically active have family and social responsibilities, but almost all of them are underemployed and many are victims of seasonal unemployment. Their income is extremely low, and considerable numbers of them live only on the margin of money economy. Generally speaking, they work the soil in a primitive or almost primitive fashion. The average percentage of illiteracy in rural Latin America is around 80; but vast areas have no schools at all and an illiteracy rate of 100 percent.

Indians form some 15 percent of Latin America's rural population. The majority of them speak only an Indian language, though some of them are bilingual. The Indian policy of Latin American governments generally aims to keep them isolated from the white peasantry of their countries. Moreover, Indian communities benefit very little from government aid or not at all, and it is an open secret that such programs have been a complete failure because of inadequate funds and lack of any real interest on the part of the governments concerned.

In spite of these obstacles, some Indians have established contact with the white peasants. These have adopted the cultural patterns of that peasantry. Wherever such cultural contacts take place, the Indians suffer from exploitation not only by the white bourgeoisie but also by the white and *ladino* (mestizo) peasants.

These 28½ million have to produce food not only for themselves but also directly for their 70½ million dependents and, more indirectly, for the 91 million urban dwellers. Moreover, in terms of the national economy, they have to produce a surplus for economic development. And yet, 63 percent of them—18 million adult farmers—have no land at all. Some 5½ million have an insufficient amount of land; 1.9 million have enough land, and 100,000—mostly absentee landlords—have too much land.

One out of every 185,000 Latin Americans—or one out of every 100,000 rural Latin Americans—owns over 1,000 hectares.* For 107,955 landlords, or 1.5 percent of all landhold-

* A hectare = approx. 2½ acres.

ers, own 471 million hectares, or 65 percent of all land in private hands.[1] Each of them owns an average of 4,300 hectares; but many have more than 10,000, and some have hundreds of thousands—even millions.

So much for individuals. But properties belonging to several members of a family can be registered under the name of its head. There are Latin American families who own more land than is occupied by a number of sovereign nations. In fact, there are families or groups of interrelated families in Argentina, Brazil, Chile, and Venezuela, of which each has more land than several countries put together. This is a situation with no parallel elsewhere. Statistically speaking, Latin America has the highest index of concentrated accumulation of rural property in the world.

Latin America is now beginning to develop, however, slowly. Its indices of urbanization[2] and industrialization are progressively rising. However, this progress is generally unnoticeable because the population rapidly increases at one of the highest rates of growth in the world. Internal migration to the cities is constant and growing, but it does not absorb the rural population explosion caused by the rising birth rate and the falling death rate. This migration, a product of urbanization and industrialization, makes the rural population decrease relatively, in proportion to urban population; but it does not decrease it absolutely.

It is estimated that the percentage of rural population will fall from 54 to 46 in 1970. However, the rural population as a whole and hence also the number of actual and potential agricultural workers, will actually rise by that date from 108 million to 133 million. . . . There can be no question that the rural—and agricultural—population of Latin America is increasing today in a geometrical progression. Every year, every month, and every day there are new mouths to feed and

[1] Oscar Delgado, *Estructura y Reforma Agraria en Latino-américa* (Bogotá: Sociedad Económica de Amigos del País, 1960); Thomas F. Carroll, *The Land Reform Issue in Latin America*, pp. 161-201 in Albert O. Hirschmann, ed. *Latin American Issues* (New York: The Twentieth Century Fund, 1961); T. Pompeu Accioly Borges, *A Reforma Agraria na América Latina*, in Desenvolvimento e Conjuntura, Rio, V, 12:51-68; VI, I: 55-83, 1962; René Dumont, *Terres Vivantes* (Paris: Plon, 1961), pp. 1-123.

[2] Philip N. Hauser, ed., *Urbanization in Latin America* (Paris: UNESCO, 1961); Pedro C. M. Teichert, *Economic Policy, Revolution and Industrialization in Latin America* (University of Mississippi, 1959); Howard S. Ellis, with Henry C. Wallich, eds., *El Desarrollo Económico y América Latina* (Mexico: Fondo de Cultura Económica, 1960).

new hands to be provided with work, land, tools, and money. Given an annual rate of increase of 3 percent, this means about 6 million new mouths and new pair of hands every year in all Latin America, and 3.8 million in the rural sector.

How can this problem be solved? The answer is simple and can be reduced to four words: economic and social development.

We can deal here only with one aspect of this urgent problem: the different agrarian policies that can become stimulants or obstacles to the improvement of agricultural production and productivity, and to the white, mestizo, and indigenous rural population that participates—or is unable to participate—in growing crops and raising cattle.

In three countries of Latin America a political revolution produced an agrarian policy of redistributing the property and tenancy of land: Mexico (1915), Bolivia (1953), and Cuba (1959). In these countries new ruling groups[3] and new ideologies replaced the old and changed the traditional values. The old ruling groups had governed with the support of traditional ideas, and their rule was tolerated by the masses, who lived in utmost ignorance, submission, and political apathy.

In two other countries conservative governments, representing a bourgeois-landlord-military-clerical coalition, have introduced a land reform: Venezuela (1959) and Colombia (1961). This reform has meant a "parcelation" of cultivated land or a "colonization" of virgin soil.

"Parcelation," as used in this article, means:

(1) The acquisition by a government agency of land used for crops or cattle by purchase from its private owners paid in cash and at once and

(2) the subdivision of this land for resale as private property to landless or landpoor peasants by payment of an amount of money equal or similar to that laid out by the government agency on the installment system, with a fixed term and a low interest rate.

[3] Gino Germani believes that the dissolution of the old-style army of the *ancien régime,* generally a bulwark of rural conservatism, is a necessary condition of agrarian transformation: "It may be a coincidence but it is certainly very significant that no military regime ever seriously modified the concentration of landed property and that the only countries that managed to achieve a true land reform dissolved their army and either substituted for it a workers' militia (Cuba and Bolivia) or a new army (Mexico)." Germani, *La Démocratie Réprésentative et les Classes Populaires en Amérique Latine* in Sociologie du Travail (Paris, October-December 1961).

Similarly, "colonization" means here the opening or preparation of new agricultural, cattle-raising, or forest land owned by the government or of no definite ownership, and the settlement in it of rural population.

In all the remaining countries of Latin America there has been no serious program of redistribution or parcelation. The countries that tried colonization in the course of the present century were successful only for a few fortunate individuals; for the rest, colonization completely failed to solve their agrarian problem.[4]

Parcelation as a method of land reform leaves the large estates practically intact. The concentration of land in a few hands is not affected by it, and it leaves the problems of the rural population unsolved. This is why it is the favorite method of land reform in "rural conservative" countries.

This phrase also requires some explanation. At first sight it seems strange to apply the label of "rural conservative" to seventeen countries that differ so much economically, socially, and politically. They include two countries at the very extremes of economic and social development: Argentina and Haiti. This is also true of political development: they include, on the one hand, the Central American republics dominated by "strong executives" and custodians of foreign interests and, on the other, a country like Uruguay, with its markedly developed democracy. Nor is it easy to include in the same group countries that never had any significant colonization or foreign immigration with others that have intermittently tried out colonization since the beginning of the nineteenth century, though on a small scale in relation to their open spaces and settled population.

Still, it is convenient to group together the countries of recent parcelation (Venezuela and Colombia), those of colonization (Argentina, Brazil, Chile, and Uruguay), and those dominated by large estates (the rest of the seventeen). They

---

[4] "It is disillusioning, says the FAO, that the effective progress has been so scanty and inadequate as to create the impression that the distribution and colonization of land, even if carried out with efficiency, benefit only a very limited number of people and affect only a small fraction of the idle land and underdeveloped resources of these countries. . . . Considering that in most of them the population increases at a rate of 2.5 to 3 percent and that, generally speaking, a large part of the families own no land, it is obvious the programs now in operation are far from providing a solution." Thomas F. Carroll, ed., *La Creación de Nuevas Unidades Agrícolas*, Report of the Second Latin American Seminar on Problems of the Land (Santiago: FAO, 1961), pp. 15-16, 19.

have something in common—rural conservatism—that distinguishes them from the countries of revolutionary land reform, which we may call countries of "agricultural transformation."

A closer look at the three countries where a revolution occurred with a broad popular participation will reveal certain distinctions that will require separate categories.

In Cuba the large estates and ranches were not divided by the Castro Revolution; they continued in operation by either a government agency or a peasant cooperative. Both in Mexico and in Bolivia land reform marked a notable social progress, though it was limited to only a part of the rural population. The national economy of these two countries benefited somewhat from the land reform,[5] but the benefits were limited by an excessive fragmentation of the estates that were distributed. Also, neither country made a sufficient effort to foster government, collective, or cooperative operation of agriculture and cattle-breeding.[6]

[5] Edmundo Flores, *Tratado de Economia Agrícola* (Mexico: Fondo de Cultura Económica, 1961); Giuseppe Barbero, *Realizaciones y Problemas de la Reforma Agraria en Bolivia*, in El Trimestre Económico (Mexico, 112; 612-650, 1961).

[6] "It is necessary to create a firmer foundation for collective organization—here lies, one might say without exaggeration, the salvation of the *ejido*." R. Fernández y Fernández and Ricardo Acosta, *Política Agrícola: Ensayo sobre Normas para Mexico* (Mexico: Fondo de Cultura Económica, 1961). A FAO document says: "Mexico, which carried out its land reform years ago, faces today's new problems, which require new kinds of action." Carroll, ed., *op. cit.*, p. 16. The Mexican economist Jesús Silva Herzog asks for "a reform of the Mexican land reform"; i.e., the abrogation during the Aleman administration, which has acted as a brake. *El Agrarismo Mexicano y la Reforma Agraria* (Mexico: Fondo de Cultura Económica, 1959), Hernández y Hernández writes: "The numerical predominance of small peasant property, possession and usufruct will maintain the foundation of the present agrarian regime, with its exploitation of poor and medium peasants by the local merchants and bosses. The system of small-scale production for the market will not free the peasant masses from misery and oppression. . . . The preconditions of total collectivization are: integration of the trading setup that now favors the big operators; taking over of basic industries by the government; growth of agricultural cooperation; creation of big state farms; the struggle to hand all the land to the *peasants*." Jesús Silva Herzog, *El Movimiento Campesino*, in *Mexico: Cincuenta Años de Revolución*, Vol. II (Mexico: Fondo de Cultura Económica, 1961), pp. 235, 238-9.

On the other hand, the XI International Conference of Agricultural Economists held at Cuernavaca in 1961 criticized the land reform in Bolivia "because insufficient attention has been paid to the transformation of Indian communities into market-oriented cooperative societies." *Report on Tenant Farming*, p. 4. Giuseppe Barbero says that Bolivia today "is characterized by the absence of the large estate but is dominated by a primitive type of agriculture though she has large unexploited natural resources." *Op. cit.*, p. 650.

We can now classify the Latin American countries as follows:

I. *Agricultural Transformation:*
1. Agrarian revolution (Cuba)
2. Land reform (Mexico and Bolivia)

II. *Rural Conservatism:*
1. Parcelation (Venezuela and Colombia)
2. Colonization (Argentina, Brazil, Chile, and Uruguay)
3. Rural conservatism, in the narrower meaning of that phrase (the remaining countries).

The countries of agricultural transformation have a dynamic agrarian situation: their agricultural population—or at least a large part of it—has a genuine opportunity to raise its standard of living. The countries of rural conservatism have a static agrarian situation; such an opportunity is limited or non-existent in them. . . .

The reason Cuba falls into a different category from Mexico and Bolivia is that the transformation happened there with surprising efficiency and speed. This is no longer land reform; it must be called an "agrarian revolution." In Mexico and Bolivia the rhythm of change has been much slower than in Cuba, for all the positive achievements of their land policies. But it has been very fast by comparison with Venezuela and Colombia.

In Mexico today, 47 years after the Land Reform Law was signed, 106 million hectares remain in private hands, and 71 million (76 percent) belong to private individuals who own more than 1,000 hectares each. In Bolivia land reform has moved at a faster pace than in Mexico; but even here, 9 years after the law was passed, 28.5 million hectares—87 percent of all utilized land—are still in the hands of landlords who own more than 1,000 hectares each.[7]

The land reform laws of Cuba, Mexico, and Bolivia stipulate that the former owners of expropriated land be indemnified with long-term bonds. But in actual practice none of these countries has paid the compensation required by the law. The small payment was made in money, not in bonds. How else

[7] Pan-American Union, *La Estructura Agropecuaria de las Naciones Americanas* (Washington, 1960), and *América en Cifras:* 1960, nr. 2, 1961; *Bolivia*, in FAO, *Documentación del II Seminario de la FAO sobre Problemas de la Tierra* (Montevideo, 1959), Doc. IP-2; CEPAL. *Actividad Reciente en Materia de Reforma Agraria en América Latina*, pp. 123-57 in *Estudio Económico de América Latina 1959* (Santiago: CEPAL E/CN. 12/541, 1960).

would it have been possible to redistribute 61 million hectares (52 in Mexico, 5 in Cuba, 4 in Bolivia)?

The laws of Venezuela and Colombia, on the other hand, authorize the expropriation of land, with payment partly in cash and partly in medium-term bonds. Both, however, have actually preferred parcelation.

The Venezuelan government has bought about half a million hectares, at market prices, from landlords who sold their land voluntarily. They actually received payment, almost full and immediate. This land has not been given to the peasants, as happened in Cuba, Mexico, and Bolivia. It was sold to them at cost price, which included the value of improvements and the wages of the officials in charge of the transactions. The peasants pay in annual installments for a medium-term period.

In Cuba the large estates and ranches were taken from individual owners and national and foreign companies. They were not subdivided, but continue to be operated as wholes by the government or by peasant cooperatives.

In Mexico and Bolivia, on the contrary, they were subdivided into very small farms—an average of 4 hectares of unirrigated lands—and handed over to the peasants. But the beneficiaries of the land reform were, in both countries, abandoned to their fate. Because of financial stringency or for other reasons,[8] they have received hardly any credit, technical assistance, and other services needed for efficient farming.

Among the different types of rural conservatism, parcelation deserves special treatment. In most of the literature on the subject, "land reform" actually means parcelation. This is because for many people parcelation means an "agrarian transformation," so they associate what is happening in Venezuela and Colombia with what happened in Mexico, Bolivia, and Cuba.

Several Latin American countries are planning to start a parcelation program in 1963; but they are careful to call it "land reform." (This is also true of Venezuela and Colombia

---

[8] "The lack of sufficient and timely credit and the bad faith of the officials in charge made the *ejidatarios* fall once more into the hands of unscrupulous operators and moneylenders. . . . Another reason is the small operating capital of the Banco Nacional del Crédito Ejidal—only 72 million dollars per annum, while the actual credit needs are estimated at 400 million." Victor Manzanilla Schaffer, *La Reforma Agraria,* in *Mexico: Cincuenta Años de la Revolución,* Vol. III, pp. 254-5. See also the study by Charles Erasmus of the important cotton area of the Yaquí Valley, with its ample documentation of corruption in official agencies in charge of agricultural credit. *Then Land Reform (in Northeastern Mexico)* in *Man Takes Control* (Minneapolis: University of Minnesota Press, 1961), pp. 209-37.

with their "land reform" laws.) The Congresses of two "colonization" countries (Brazil and Chile) and of two "rural conservative" countries (Peru and Ecuador) are now studying several "land reform" projects. If they are approved in the form they were presented,[9] they will certainly not provide the legal basis for an agrarian transformation, but only for parcelation. And their practical efficiency will depend on the amount of public funds assigned to buy land from private owners.

We stated earlier that parcelation permits preservation of the traditional structure, based on large estates. The case of Venezuela will prove this. That country is now engaged in the most expensive "land reform" ever made in the world, even more expensive than those of Italy and Japan, with their special difficulties.

Venezuela has financial resources unmatched by any Latin American country. Its annual per capita income is, through the revenue derived from petroleum, the highest in Latin America—$500, as against $92 in Bolivia, and a general average of $292. Also, Venezuela has an unusually small number of agriculturally active population—only 705,000, as against 10,300,000 in Brazil and 28,500,000 in all of Latin America. No other Latin American country could afford to invest the equivalent of 750 million dollars in a program devoted exclusively to parcelation and its auxiliary agricultural services.[10]

The sum seems disproportionately high when compared with the cost of land reform in Japan and Italy. Japan spent 390

[9] Jorge Alessandri, *Proyecto de Ley sobre Expropriaciones Agrícolas* and *Mensaje Presidencial* in *Boletín de la Cámara de Disputados* (Santiago: nr. 165, 1962). In accordance with this project, all expropriations have to be paid for in cash and in advance except "abandoned or notoriously ill-worked estates" where the compensation can be paid on installments and according to the market value, as follows: down payment of no less than 20 percent . . . and the rest in equal six-monthly installments, in cash, for a maximum total of 10 years and with adequate interest." According to a cable just received from Santiago, the Chilean Congress has passed this draft, which is now a law. Chile thus joins Venezuela and Colombia as another country that accepts "parcelation." Here, too, this false kind of land reform is bound to fail.

On Ecuador, see R. Fernández y Fernández, *Reforma Agraria en el Ecuador*, in El Trimestre Económico (Mexico, 112, 569-94, and Ecuador: Junta Nacional de Planificación y Coordinación Económica, *Anteproyecto de una Ley Agraria*).

On Peru, *La Reforma Agraria en el Peru, Exposición de Motivos y Proyecto de Ley* (Lima: Comisión para la Reforma Agraria y la Vivienda, 1960).

[10] Rómulo Betancourt, *Discurso de Carabobo*, in *Reforma Agraria Integral en Venezuela* (Mexico, no date). Also, *Reforma Agraria*, 6 vols. (Caracas: Ministerio de Agricultura y Cria, 1959).

million dollars to distribute 2 million hectares among 4 million beneficiaries. Italy spent only 120 million to give to over half a million beneficiaries 750,000 hectares of redistributed land and 28½ million hectares of improved and colonized land.[11]

The Venezuelan Four-Year program proposes to settle 200,-000 peasants on the parceled land; but in its first three years (1960-1962) only 50,000—a quarter of the number planned—have been actually settled.[12] This means 7 percent of the active agricultural population, as opposed to 41 percent in Mexico and 32 percent in Cuba. The Venezuelan beneficiaries occupy 1.5 million hectares of land: one-third taken from public lands (colonization); one-third bought by the government from private owners (parcelation); and one-third confiscated from the friends of the deposed dictator Pérez Jiménez, who had obtained it illegally when in power.

Venezuela has 29.6 million hectares of land used to raise crops and breed cattle. Before parcelation was started, 22 million hectares were occupied by large estates over 1,000 hectares.[13] Three years later, when the four-year plan is coming to its close, this figure has fallen to only 21.5 million.

Another difference between parcelation and agrarian transformation is that the latter limits the amount of land a person may legally own, and the former doesn't. Thus, in Cuba the limit for a private person or a corporation is 403 hectares; in Mexico 100 hectares of irrigated and 200 of unirrigated land;

[11] On Japan, Pan-American Union, *Report on the Agrarian Reform Program of Certain Countries* (Washington, 1960), p. 5.
On Italy, Giuseppe Barbero, *La Reforma Agraria Italiana*, in Boletín de Estudios Especiales (Mexico, XVII, 202; 486-90, 1960).
[12] The Instituto Agrario Nacional, in a Statement to the Associated Press, July 1, 1962.
The reports of governments that speed up the redistribution of land are often distorted by exaggerating the area of the land and the number of beneficiaries. This happened in Cuba as well as in Venezuela. For the sake of curiosity we collected and examined the reports of various officials and commissions in charge of these programs. We found serious contradictions between them. . . . President Betancourt, in his last Message to Congress, said that in three years—December 1958 to December 1961—1.3 million hectares were granted to 42,000 beneficiaries. However, the National Peasant Confederation corrected these figures to 15,000 beneficiaries who received official title to the land and 10,000 peasants settled on land without official title in the period under review. It seems advisable not to trust official data too much.
Similarly, in Bolivia, one official report says that 4.2 million hectares were given to 47,585 beneficiaries in 1955-1960. But another such report gives 1.5 million hectares and 63,414 beneficiaries, and a third—1,065,-000 hectares and 32,608 beneficiaries. All three reports are official and refer to the same period.
[13] Carroll, *op. cit.*, p. 187.

in Bolivia the limit varies according to the geographical zone.[14] No other country has such restrictions.

The amount of money Venezuela spent on its "land reform" would seem fabulous if we didn't compare it with the cost of agrarian transformation, truly insignificant by comparison: 133,000 dollars in Bolivia for 4 million hectares;[15] 14.5 million dollars in Mexico for 52 million hectares;[16] and 8.9 million dollars in Cuba for 5 million hectares.[17] (In all three cases the land was expropriated.)

In Colombia the government assigns annually, from 1962, 12 million dollars for "land reform," some 3 percent of the national budget. (Venezuela makes an annual assignment of 187.5 million dollars; the Peruvian draft law foresees one of 11.5 million dollars or about 3 percent of the budget.) In the years since the Colombian law was passed (November 1961), the Colombian Institute of Land Reform has so far parceled out only 15 thousand hectares, which were handed over to 750 persons. The two-year plan of the Colombian Ministry of Agriculture for 1962-3 proposes an expenditure of 18 million dollars for the purchase of land to be distributed to tenant farmers and sharecroppers.

Colombia and Peru have an active agricultural population of 2,023,000 and 1,546,000 respectively, i.e. roughly three times and twice that of Venezuela. Colombia has 27.7 million hectares of agricultural land. Of this, 7.4 million is owned by landlords with over 1,000 hectares each.[18]

[14] Bolivia, Decreto-Ley de Agosto 2, 1953; Cuba, Decreto-Ley de Mayo 17, 1959; Mexico, Codigo Agrario, Diciembre 31, 1942, art. 104.

[15] The budget for 1959; expenditure for assignment of 270,000 hectares, in João Gonsalves de Souza and Manuel Diegues Júnior, *Resumen de las Respuestas al Cuestionario Enviado a los Paises Latinoamericanos* (Washington: Pan-American Union), p. 90. However, the government bonds to be used for compensation have not been issued to date, in spite of demands and reminders. Cf. Barbero, *op. cit.*, p. 648.

[16] Edmundo Flores, *op. cit.*, pp. 335-44. From 1915 to 1962, the Mexican Government has paid only 14.5 million dollars in indemnification. Two million dollars were paid to 170 Mexican ex-owners in bonds, which were later cashed by the Government at a depressed market value of 5 to 16 percent of the nominal. From 1938 to 1955, 12.5 million dollars were paid to American ex-owners for lands expropriated in 1927-1940.

[17] Cuba, Instituto Nacional de la Reforma Agraria, Report of the Director, Antonio Nuñez Jiménez, in *Bohemia* (La Havana, May 28, 1961).

[18] Carlos Lleras Restrepo and others, *Tierra*, Bogotá, Ediciones Tercer Mundo, 1962. Alberto Aguilera Camacho, *Derecho Agrario Colombiano* (Bogotá: Ediciones Tercer Mundo, 1962); Hernan Toro Agudelo, Minister of Agriculture, *Plan Bienal para la Reforma Agraria*, in *El Tiempo*, June 3, 1962.

For Peru, see note 9.

Some "colonization" and "rural conservative" countries are preparing a parcelation for 1963. In Brazil and Chile there is a hope, still vague and distant, that parcelation may be transcended and a genuine land reform achieved. This hope is based on changes in the composition of their Congresses (Brazil will have elections in October 1962) and on the election of a new president of Chile.

As things are now, Brazil and Chile cannot be expected to go beyond a modest parcelation. Any serious land reform there is blocked by juridical considerations—always the most conservative and change-resisting in Latin America. The constitutions of these two countries bar any expropriations without a cash payment in advance for the property to be expropriated, and at market prices. Large parts of the Brazilian and Chilean public believe that such constitutional provisions make land reform impossible and they are pushing for constitutional amendments that would permit a deferred payment of the indemnification. In the present preelection campaigns they are concentrating upon obtaining more representative Congresses to neutralize—to say the least—parliamentary domination by big landowners and their allies.

It is worth recalling that in the last 10 years 208 projects of land reform laws or relevant legislation have been presented to the Brazilian Congress.[19] Not one of them was able to pursue its normal course through the commissions appointed to "study" them. None of these laws was actually rejected; they were all simply buried in the commissions.

Much the same thing happened in Peru and Ecuador. And yet a conference of agricultural economists agreed that "the majority of the tenancy contracts now prevalent in Latin America are archaic, unequal, rigid, and unsuitable for the full utilization of human and natural resources."[20]

Generally speaking, in the countries of agrarian conservatism the big landowners have exercised a powerful political and economic influence ever since Independence. Conditions vary from country to country;[21] but except in one or two cases

[19] T. Pompeu Accioly Borges, in a private communication. References to 41 projects in Universidade do Brasil, Instituto de Ciências Sociais, Bibliografia sobre Reforma Agraria (Rio, 1962), pp. 4-7.

[20] XIth Conference of Agriculture Economists, op. cit., p. 2.

[21] On the political power of landlords see Merle Kling, Toward a Theory of Power and Political Instability in Latin America and John H. Kautsky, An Essay on the Politics of Development, both in John H. Kautsky, ed., Political Change in Underdeveloped Countries: Nationalism and Communism (New York: John Wiley, 1962); C. Wright Mills, Listen, Yankee! and The Marxists (New York: Dell, 1962). An

the landed interests have been completely successful in blocking any structural change.[22]

Their resistance is certainly not without a logic of its own. An agrarian transformation may well make the landlords feel "lost." Their lands would be confiscated outright or they would receive an indemnity that they consider too small for investment in business. Moreover, they would not receive it in cash but in long-term bonds. They would lose their political power and their social status, which they derive from the ownership of land. Not only would they lose their prestige, but they would fall into the depths of unpopularity and be blamed by society as a whole for having prolonged a fundamentally unjust situation. From the point of view of defending their interests, the resistance of landlords to the land reform is perfectly logical, even if it is irrational in the present historical situation.

But whether they resist or not, the landlords are doomed to lose the fight for the retention of their long-held privileges.[23] Since society asked them to give up their lands, they have won many skirmishes and even some technical battles. But they are losing strategically and the fortress of their privileges —inherited rather than acquired—is beginning to succumb.

The more intelligent among the landlords will adapt themselves to the new situation. They will try to forget a lost world that had seemed ideal to them but that was too unjust to resist the passage of time. That ideal world, in which they had

ECOSOC report issued in November 1961, says on p. 24: "The necessity of a land reform in Latin America and the Middle East has been accepted on the international plane, but little has been achieved on the national scale. In actual practice, the national development programs have tended to concentrate on the nonagricultural sectors of the economy, where it is easier to achieve visible progress and where the resistance of interests opposed to progress and reform is less entrenched."

[22] "The land reform progressed little against a decided resistance by the landlords. A partial success was registered only by a violent social cataclysm, as in Mexico and Bolivia. . . . The forms in which the *ancien régime* accommodated itself to the new order have varied greatly. The strongest resistance came from the big landlords. Though their political control had disappeared, their economic power had been destroyed and their social monopoly broken, they successfully resisted land reform everywhere except in Mexico and Bolivia." Edwin Lieuwen, *Armas y Política en América Latina,* Buenos Aires, Sur, 1960, pp. 73 and 79.

[23] Cf. A. J. Toynbee, *The Present Revolution in Latin America,* lecture given at the University of Puerto Rico in February, 1962: "There exists in Latin America an oligarchy of landlords, a dominant minority surely doomed to disappearance, but dying with difficulty and refusing to die before it puts its mark on the 'new rich' of industry and commerce. . . . The oligarchs are now fighting from their last bastions a battle that they are losing." (Retranslated from Spanish text.)

been the center of attention and power, is now colliding with industrial civilization.

The landlords will find a refuge in the big cities (or will remain in them if they are absentee owners). They will be shareholders in industrial, commercial, and service enterprises. Some of them will stick to their old values and would rather become the victims of the hurricane of social transformation than give up an inch of their land. This type of landlord will die with his boots on and with his gun cocked.

Meanwhile, the United States Government insists that the Latin American countries carry out a land reform. But it has not, so far, clearly stated what kind of land reform it wants. Its pronouncements are marked by vagueness, diversity, and even contradiction.

President Kennedy himself has said in a speech that there exists in the rural areas of Latin America "an immediate necessity of a better distribution of wealth and income and of a broader participation in the process of development"—and that "the unequal distribution of land is one of the gravest social problems in many Latin American countries. . . . It is evident that, when the ownership of land is so concentrated, the efforts to increase agricultural productivity will benefit only a very small percentage of the population." To help solve these difficulties, the President added, the Bank for International Development (BID) has allotted 309 million dollars for *colonization* and improved *utilization* of the soil.[24] (Emphasis mine.)

The nations of Latin America, gathered under the leadership of the United States and with the promise of its aid, have signed two documents that refer to the land question.

The Bogotá Act of September 12, 1960, mentions "the improvement of rural life and use of the soil" and "the revision of legal systems with regard to the holding of land with the view of insuring a broader and juster distribution." The Charter of Punta del Este of August 17, 1961, outlines a program for the decade of 1961-70. One of its aims is "to prompt, within the particular conditions of each country, programs of integral land reform oriented toward the effective transformation of structures and of unjust systems of tenancy and exploitation of land wherever it is required and with a view of

[24] John F. Kennedy, Message to the Congress of the United States on Latin America, March 14, 1961.

replacing the regime of *latifundia* and *minifundia* by a just system of property."

The Sub-Committee on Inter-American Economic Relationships of the United States Congress, headed by Senator Sparkman, has recently published an extensive volume, *Economic Policies and Programs in South America, 1962,* that formulates its basic criteria of land reform. A careful reading of it will justify our reservations on the efficacy of the Alliance for Progress as an instrument of agrarian transformation. The key passages are:

> *The concept of agrarian reforms.* It seems to us that an official clarification of the meaning and objectives of "agrarian reform" in the context of the Alliance for Progress, especially the role of U.S. Government as a participant is not only in order but imperative. . . . Land reform is not exclusively a tenure problem but a problem of improved farming practices generally (rural education, research, extension services, credit institutions). . . . Land reform would include real estate tax reform. . . . The objective of land tenure changes is not to be punitively directed against large landholdings or absentee landowners as such; on the contrary, existing property rights under law are to be respected. The programming and administration of agrarian reform is, and must remain, an internal matter for each of the several nations. Certainly the United States is not pressing for any preconceived patterns of land tenure or agrarian reform; least of all can it undertake unilaterally to assure individual croppers of its support of ultimate landownership, no matter how seemingly meritorious cases may be. . . . As a first step in land reform and possible redistribution, the respective participating countries should first look to public lands and lands not presently under appropriation. To this end (1) an accurate survey of acreage and usability of the public domain, (2) an appropriate adaptation of the U.S. provisions for land grants in aid of schools and colleges dating back to 1859, and (3) the so-called homestead acts dating from back to 1861 are recommended for consideration.[25]

[And:]

> [The Charter of Punta del Este] recognizes that conditions and needs will vary from country to country. Largely as the result of events in Castro Cuba, the specter of widespread and uncompensated expropriation has unfortunately been read into the Alliance program and one of the conditions of U.S. aid. . . . To what extent are we committing ourselves in such internal matters as land tenure reform? In view of the sorry history of international commodity stabilization agreements, to offer another example, we had best be quite wary that the United States is not

[25] Congress of the United States, *Economic Policies in South America* (Joint Economic Committee, Subcommittee on Inter-American Economic Relationships), (Washington: U.S. Government Printing Office, 1962), pp. 24-25.

put in position of going along at the risk of being charged with their possible, if not probable, failure.[26]

These documents need no comment; they speak for themselves. It is enough to say that if the Alliance for Progress is to be guided by such concepts, its failure is practically certain. It will be even more certain unless the Alliance quickly acquires what it presently lacks—a program of specific measures to deal with controversial issues, to be formulated, in the first place, by the American Government. The only such measure formulated so far is the fixing of restrictive limits on land reform by the various governments. This being so, it is not difficult to view the Alliance, paradoxically, as a subtle form of resistance to social and cultural change—including a true land reform.

The Charter of Punta del Este refers to the "effective transformation of structures and of unjust systems of tenancy and exploitation of land." It seems to do it on the naive assumption that the neotraditional oligarchies might be moved by an instinct that Durkheim called "altruist suicide."

Some of these oligarchies seem to have found a magic formula that would permit them to maintain the existing agricultural structure while proclaiming that they had transformed it. The formula is "parcelation," i.e., the subdivision of large properties and the fostering of homesteads. . . . What this formula means in practice, however, is the stimulation of the *minifundio* in a disguised and uneconomic form, within the framework of a subsistence, rather than market-oriented, agriculture. The rural population will remain poor, and the backward tenancy systems and the exploitation of agricultural labor will continue. The levels of rural income and buying power will not stimulate savings and consumption, so they will not benefit industrialization. There will be, in fact, no social or political change.

As the president of the University of California, Clark Kerr, puts it: "the successful perpetuation of the family homestead . . . serves to maintain contact with the old society."[27] In other words, the old elites will continue in power at the expense of representative democracy and the participation of the

[26] *Ibid.*, p. 79.
[27] Clark Kerr, *Changing Social Structures*, pp. 348-59 in W. E. Moore and A. S. Feldman, ed., *Labor Commitment and Social Change in Developing Areas* (New York: Social Science Research Council, 1960), p. 354.

mass of the population in national life. Other investigators also point out this danger.[28]

There exist alternative policies to parcelation, namely co-operative and/or communal exploitation of land. A number of Latin American experts favor cooperatism on a large scale[29] while the American experts are divided.[30] But the official U. S. policy, as embodied in the Alliance for Progress, does not take these alternatives into consideration.

Of the Latin American countries themselves, the laws of Venezuela and Colombia indulge in some rhetoric in favor of cooperatives, but the actual policies of these countries have restrained rather than favored the growth of different types of cooperatives. In Mexico and Bolivia official support of co-operatives has considerably fallen off as their governments gradually veered away from revolutionary agrarianism.[31]

To sum up: the Alliance for Progress will make only an insignificant contribution to Latin American industrialization and land reform as long as it lacks effective means of coercion and a clear formulation of the means required to realize its objectives. It offers Latin American countries money—in amounts insufficient for the needs of their development—but does nothing to resolve the grave problem of the "terms of trade," which is an essential precondition of any increase in the rates of capital formation.

Politically speaking, the Alliance stimulates an irrational and unconditional adherence of Latin American governments to the foreign policy of the United States without any serious discussion on an international level. It gives the United States

[28] The economist John F. Timmins writes: "The Homestead Acts gave millions of acres to the settlers; but, only a few years later, almost a third part of that land had fallen into the hands of speculators and absentee landowners who rented it to the farmers. Our error lay in not taking complementary measures to assure to the farmers the permanent ownership of their land." *Tenencia y uso de la Tierra en América Latina,* in Selected Studies of the Latin American Seminar on Land Problems, Campinas, Brazil, 1953, published in Problemas Agrícolas e Industriales de México, Vol. VI, No. 1, January-March 1954, p. 254.

[29] For example, the Mexican economist Victor L. Urquidi: "It is very probable that, unless a new effort, combined with cooperative or collective forms of agricultural production, is made, economic development will not receive from agriculture all the contribution it requires." *Viabilidad Económica de América Latina* (Mexico: Fondo de Cultura Económica, 1962), p. 87.

[30] Among the American officials and Congressmen who favor cooperatives are Chester Bowles, Hubert Humphrey, and Wayne Morse.

[31] Cf. Giuseppe Barbero, *op. cit.;* Fernando Chaves, *Las Cooperativas, Elemento de Cambio Social,* in Americas, Washington, 13, 9:7-11; Rosendo Rojas Coria, *Introdución al estudio del cooperativismo* (Mexico: Talleres Gráficos de la Nación, 1961).

nineteen unconditionally favorable votes at the United Nations. It favors the Western bloc in the cold war and prevents Latin American countries from becoming neutralist.

All this is, however, achieved upon a tacit condition, namely that of United States support for the established political and economic oligarchies of the various Latin American countries. Their power would be seriously jeopardized if that support were withdrawn. This means a limitation on the supposed American pressure in favor of replacing these oligarchies by political, agrarian, industrial, and financial democracy.

The Industrialists of Argentina*

GUSTAVO POLIT

Given the conditions under which the dominant economic classes exist and the particular circumstances in
which industrialization is taking place in Latin America,
Polit argues, they are unlikely to play a dynamic role in
their countries' development. Analyzing the situation in
Argentina, he finds that the assumption of a conflict of
interest between landlords and industrialists that might
lead the latter to play a developmentalist role is incorrect.
These sectors of the owning classes have been intertwined
with each other by financial, social, familial and political
ties since the inception of industrialization.

Gustavo Polit, Professor of Mathematics, and graduate
of the National University of La Plata in Argentina, is an
editor of the journal Fichas de Investigación Económica y
Social, and an employee of the World Health Organization.

* Reprinted, with abridgement, from Fichas, Vol. I, No. 1 (April
1964), pp. 60-80.

THE ARGENTINIAN industrial class did not start at the bottom,
developing independently from artisanship to great industry,
like the English, French, and American industrialists. The industrialists of Argentina started out linked to the land; this
has been the distinguishing characteristic of this class from the
beginning. Both sectors, industrialists and landowners, are intertwined; the vague boundaries that separate them are at-
tenuated through the investment of agrarian rent in industry

and the investment of industrial profit in agriculture, converting the landholders into industrialists and the industrialists into landholders.

Moreover, the Argentinian industrial class is growing and developing in the era of monopoly, concentration, and centralization of capital. Since its birth Argentinian industry has been centralized in a few hands, inextricably intertwined with the landholders and foreign capital. The industry established in the country—it is not wholly correct to call it national—is little more than fifty years old, but the degree of concentration and centralization is superior to that found in developed capitalist countries. By 1936 only 47 factories (0.1 percent of the total) employed 15 percent of all workers, the degree of concentration exceeding by more than 10 times that of American industry.[1] In 1954, 1126 establishments (0.7 percent of the total) employed 39 percent of the workers and accounted for 52 percent of the production. Only 69 establishments (0.05 percent of the total) were responsible for 20 percent of the value of production of all industry.

Strictly speaking, it is not so much the concentration of industry that is occurring as it is the expansion of enterprises. The concentration and centralization of capital consists, in brief, of the expropriation of some capitalists by others, and the aggregation of the properties of many small capitalists to form a few large capital units. This is not what is happening in our country; in Argentina the gigantic establishments are not the result of a long competitive struggle; *they have been gigantic from the start*. This is not very surprising, considering that Argentinian industry consists in considerable degree of subsidiaries of large foreign companies. The large establishments did not grow from modest origins, displacing and absorbing weaker competitors but, like Minerva from the head of Jupiter, emerged in the economic arena of Argentina as fully developed offspring of large foreign enterprises.[2]

The structure of property in Argentinian industry is more oligarchical and antidemocratic than the structure of landownership, which is "archioligarchical." Gino Germani demonstrates the oligarchical structure of the Argentine industrial class. Fifty percent of all cattle is owned by 2.4 percent of the proprietors, while 1 percent of the proprietors have control of 70 percent of the land. This is the classic landed oligarchy. But in industry the concentration is even greater: only 0.2

[1] Felix Weil, *The Argentine Riddle* (New York, 1944), p. 260.
[2] Weil, *op. cit.*, p. 261.

percent of the proprietors control 65 percent of production and employ 50 percent of the workers. (It may be said in passing that this tremendous concentration and centralization of property is the primary economic reason why Argentinian industrialists cannot collectively play any democratic, revolutionary, or nationalist role.)[3]

In Western Europe the development of industry took place through the growth and reinvestment of the profits obtained in industry itself, independently of the landholders. Industrial capital was accumulated through the exploitation of wage labor, without the help of the landholders, or even of commercial and banking capital.

In Argentina industry was born in the ·monopoly phase of capitalism and from the first it has been characterized by strong links with foreign monopolies that control the national economy. Moreover, as Argentinian industry has developed it has increased its relationship with landholders and foreign capital.

The most serious historian of Argentinian history came to the conclusion that "The Argentinian industrial class was not born free. Indeed, it scarcely *has* been born since the umbilical cord that unites it with the landholders is strong and powerful, as powerful as the prominence of the cattle interests within the national economy."[4]

Presently the "umbilical cord" links the industrialists' and landholders' economic interests within the principal enterprises and partnerships of the country. It may be recalled that 2.6 percent of the industrial establishments—which possess capital assets of over one million pesos—employ 49 percent of the workers and manufacture 65 percent of the production. Thus, in practically all the enterprises or financial groups that control this decisive handful of industrial establishments, the heart of Argentinian industry, there is a pronounced participation of capital with landholding origins.

Finally, whoever analyzes the list of founders and directors of the Union Industrial Argentina can establish the high proportion of significant industrialists that belong to the Sociedad

[3] On the other hand, it must be noted that of the 221,485 "Proprietors or Managing Directors" listed by the Censo Industrial, only 16,698 individuals, who control establishments with more than 10 workers, that is, only 7.4 percent of the industrial proprietors, can be considered part of the bourgeoisie. The remaining 92.6 percent belong to the small working bourgeoisie, and either have establishments without laborers (48 percent of the total) or employ fewer than 10 laborers in their establishments (42.8 percent of the total).

[4] Adolfo Dorfman, in his *Historia de la Industria Argentina.*

Rural Argentina, that is, to the landholding and ranching class.

In 1959, of a sample of 106 of the traditional "agricultural oligarchy" residing in the Federal Capital and selected according to "social standing," 32 were agricultural producers belonging to the Sociedad Rural and 31 possessed industrial interests. On the other hand, of the 15 respondents with enterprises employing more than 100 persons, 50 percent are industrialists or ranchers and industrialists at the same time. Moreover, among the "relatives and friends" of the respondents the industrialists constitute the biggest group (slightly more than the ranchers) devoted to productive activities.[5]

The authority of the landholding oligarchy is maintained in the large estate system—or Latifundi. Latifundi is the concentration of land ownership in the hands of a small number of proprietors. The landholders can cultivate the land or leave it uncultivated, or use it for profit in some other way. They can exploit it in large tracts or lease it out in small parcels. In any of these cases the latifundium exists; it is a social category determined by the concentration of property, and not an agronomic category depending on whether the land is cultivated or not.

The following figures give an idea of the magnitude of land concentration. In the province of Buenos Aires 272 persons control 50,000 square kilometers, that is, one-sixth of the provincial territory. More than a million hectares belong to only 5 families.[6]

One thousand two hundred persons are lords of one-fourth of the area of the richest province in the country.[7] One thousand eight hundred persons possess as much land as Italy, Belgium, Holland, and Denmark put together. Two companies have as much land as Belgium and Switzerland together. As a result, while 160,000 persons cultivate only 1,500,000 hectares, 2,100 landowners have 53,500,000 hectares. Therefore, only 36 out of every 100 agriculturalists own the land on which they work, the rest being tenants or subrenters. In addition, 2.4 percent of the cattle owners possess 50 percent of all cattle, and 5 percent of the sheep owners possess 64 percent of the total.

Not owning the land, the peasant has little interest in building a permanent house that will not belong to him either. For

[5] Imaz, La Clase Alta de Buenos Aires (Buenos Aires, 1962), pp. 20-21, 23, 40.
[6] Journal of the Sesiones de la Cámara de Diputados de la Pcia. (July 8, 1942).
[7] Oscar Alende, Governor of Buenos Aires, Declaración ante representantes de la prensa extranjera (Sept. 10, 1959).

this reason, the weakest element on the level of rural life in Argentina is the dwelling place, principally because of latifundium.[8] Likewise, latifundium is the source of the backwardness of peasant social life, which in turn reduces the national domestic market. In general, the Argentinian peasant has an adequate standard of living as measured by quantity and quality of food and clothing. But the dwelling-place has already become extremely deficient; and considering the cultural components of the standard of living—facilities for education and entertainment, and community life—the standard of living in the countryside is extremely low because of the lack of all these things.[9] The farmers live isolated from each other and from the city, including the small cities located in country areas. The circulation of newspapers is exceedingly low (the organ of the Federación Agraria Argentina has a circulation of scarcely 77,000 copies, a large part being in the cities), and the only regular channel of social communication between the farmers and the rest of the population is the radio—but this is a one-way channel. The rural population has few schools and few places to go. The social contacts among farmers are consequently infrequent, and even more sporadic are the contacts with inhabitants that have a higher standard of living. This isolation of the rural population of Argentina limits the domestic market of national industry.

However, the industrial capitalists approve of the existence of the *latifundia,* which reduces their potential market in the rural areas because of the continual flow toward the cities of displaced farmers and workers. At the turn of the century the immigrant masses, finding no access to land ownership, "surged into the cities, filling the towns and pulling down the cost of labor. It is as if the unsolved land problem has started to influence the development of industries that have found just what they needed: relatively cheap labor."[10] Since then the *latifundia* system has continued to supply industry with the cheap labor force consisting of ruined and impoverished farmers who had emigrated to Great Buenos Aires. During the Second World War, when his products could not be exported, the farmer lived almost in misery, depending only upon the government program of acquisition of crops, which had been set up to maintain the value of agrarian income. Cattle raising, the rural business par excellence, enriched its ranchers and

[8] Carl C. Taylor, *Rural Life in Argentina,* p. 202.
[9] Taylor, *op. cit.,* p. 267.
[10] Dorfman.

displaced the farmer, who did not have the large capital necessary for engaging in extensive cattle raising. As a result, throughout the period of the war the farmers spread out over Great Buenos Aires, furnishing industry with the cheap labor it needed to raise its profits. In 1943 Torcuato di Tella, the prototype of the Argentinian industrialist, bluntly stated that migration from the rural areas in our country lowers the level of salaries in manufacturing industry. "Much has been said about the idyllic life in the country. But what is actually seen of it in our wide territory does not agree with what is said about it; the farmer leaves the farm at the first opportunity and heads for the urban centers, in spite of the city's unhealthy housing conditions, promiscuity, and insecurity of daily work."[11] This symbiosis between industry and the latifundia system, between industrialists and landholders, has the effect of making the industrialists lose all interest in the liquidation of the latifundia—which is, however, one of the basic conditions for any significant industrial development.

The Argentinian industrial capitalists, linked to the landholders, are incapable of seeing far enough to prefer the future expansion of the rural market, through the expropriation of the latifundia, to the present possibility of collaborating with the landholders in the exploitation of the peasant.

In the underdeveloped countries, the general backwardness of the economy and the lack of significant industrial development means that all branches of production use a high ratio of labor to machinery. This results in a high rate of profits in all activities, especially in those that take direct advantage of the elements of backwardness: the buying and selling of land, mortgage loans, and foreign trade. This is what happens in Argentina. The profits on invested capital of a sample of 15 taken at random were: 13 percent in 1945, 15 percent in 1946, 16 percent in 1947, 15 percent in 1948, and 13 percent in 1949. From 1946 to 1952 the average annual profit of 264 corporations, which represent 68 percent of all corporations, was 16 percent of the capital invested. Recently, the *Asociacion de Industriales Metalurgicos* reported: "On the basis of a study undertaken by our organization, it was demonstrated that the average profits of the 679 enterprises that responded to an inquiry was 28.7 percent in the recent period report."[12] In contrast, the reported average annual profit of major cor-

[11] *Revista de Economía Argentina* (September 1943).
[12] *La Nación* (February 26, 1957).

porations in the United States is more or less 9 percent.[13] This usual high rate of profit produces a strong inclination on the part of the capitalists to use imported luxury items. This in turn gives rise to other parasitic activities in which the profit rate also becomes particularly high: the black market in foreign exchange, importation, etc. None of the capital invested in these activities fulfills a productive function; thus the country suffers from a dearth of capital and remains backward. In addition, because a high profit rate is available elsewhere, capital moves away from the basic investments that the country needs.

In Argentina the high profit rate on speculative investments and the mentality it engenders—the habit of making large profits in a short time—is reflected in industry. Industry has been converted into a speculative activity; no capitalist invests without the assurance of high profits within a definite period of time. Capital does not get invested in the industries that do not yield a very high rate of profit comparable to that yielded by speculative activities. Consequently, capital flows toward industries that produce consumer goods and are already overdeveloped. What worsens the situation is that these industries, being exceedingly profitable, attract the major part of their own reinvested profits. The textile industries tend to invest their profits in new textile factories, or in enlarging those already established; and these branches become even more overdeveloped.

The monopoly of the market accentuates this tendency to invest capital in the industries producing articles for consumption. This increases the disequilibrium of the industrial structure, since it is not accompanied by a parallel development of the production of means of production. Customs tariffs, exchange controls, etc., which benefit the industries producing consumer goods, from textiles to tourism, while presented as saving foreign exchange, actually only stimulate the national production of luxury articles, thus diverting the means of production and labor force toward industries that perpetuate the economic disequilibrium and the backwardness of the country. But the basic industries necessary for economic development—power, fuel, transportation—do not attract national capital. In contrast with light industry, these are industries that require large investments and yield profits only at the end of a long period of time. Why should millions be invested in such items as blast furnaces if a much smaller

[13] *Harvard Business Review* (July 1950).

capital investment will bring high and immediate profits when invested in land, elegant buildings, the stock market, or textile enterprises? Moreover, the establishment of a factory can be a good pretext for obtaining preferential exchange, or for importing a raw material or otherwise unobtainable equipment and selling these at a huge profit. "It will be argued as a convenient excuse—in certain quarters—that the impossibility of obtaining the necessary foreign exchange for new acquisitions is the cause of this technical backwardness of Argentinian industry; but it would also be necessary to add the influence, to a large extent, of the withdrawal of profits, which, instead of being reinvested for the improvement of equipment or of the enterprise's organization, has rather been placed in speculative investments with large and immediate profits, or to serve the special needs of the managers."[14]

The monopolistic privileges enjoyed by Argentinian industrialists explain the lack of incentive for lowering the costs of production through technical progress. Capitalism rarely adopts advanced techniques unless pressured by competition and/or the necessity to avoid overly expensive labor costs. Among us the monopoly of the market and the cheapness of labor allows industry to utilize to advantage, in the capitalist sense—that is, to extract a high profit rate—antiquated equipment and methods of production. Take the testimony—which cannot be suspected of ill will toward Argentinian industry—of *Economía y Finanzas,* the official journal of the Perón government: "In some economic activities real monopolies have been formed that, at their discretion, set the prices of their products with relation to costs, which are not likely to diminish, to earn an excessive margin of ever-increasing profits. The ease with which they can dispose of their products does not induce these privileged industries to rationalize their manufacturing processes. Thus, the customer is placed at a disadvantage in terms of the quantity, the quality, and the price of the monopoly's products . . . some enterprises have artificially raised their selling prices and use intermediaries, which they could easily abolish, for the distribution of their commodities. Meanwhile, their profits are able to double the capital within a single term, and their stocks reach extraordinary values in the stock exchange."[15]

The Centro de Productividad de la Argentina, in a study conducted on 22 cotton mills that operate under very similar

[14] *Veritas* (April 15, 1956).
[15] *Economía y Finanzas* (December 23, 1954).

labor conditions, found that productivity varied between 84.9 percent and 38.9 percent, depending on the enterprise.

Evidently, it would be useless to introduce new technological elements in an organization that does not know how to use those that it possesses; moreover, it would be not only useless but also uneconomical, since the lack of efficiency would be compounded by the greater cost of the investment.[16]

We have industrial establishments that constitute the latest in technological development. They represent imported "progress" and remain like small advanced islands in the midst of general backwardness. The prices at which the products of these factories are sold are determined—in a monopolistic market like ours—not by their cost of production, but by the cost of production of the majority of the enterprises, which are outdated and inefficient. This yields great profits for the capital invested in the model factory, but it does not benefit the national economy in any way.

Raúl Prebisch and the CEPAL warn: "Behind the protection of high tariffs and other restrictions or prohibitions on importation, practices have spread that limit competition, if not virtually promote monopoly. Alongside well-endowed establishments operate others with high costs, in a tacit balance of mutual advantages; thus the latter are assured of their marginal subsistence, and the former, of the rich profits coming from the difference in costs."[17] In effect, overprotection and other monopolistic advantages yield benefits so great as to outweigh possible benefits from a competitive struggle to displace the small enterprises. This is especially so for the bigger and more technically perfect factories.

The tariff and exchange protection it enjoys, and the concentration of production in a handful of enterprises, create a pronounced parasitism and an aversion to progress in the Argentinian industrial capitalist class. Industrialists have opposed the importation of machinery for the use of such industries as textiles and footwear, on the ground that their introduction would precipitate a crisis of overproduction.[18] The Cámara de Metal Estampado, for instance, has petitioned for the prohibition of the establishment of new factories [del ramo] for a period of 10 years.[19] Recently, metallurgical

[16] Gerardo Lasalle, "Productividad Como Responsabilidad del Ingeniero," in *La Ingeneria* (September 1962-February 1963, No. 984), p. 38.

[17] Prebisch, *Hacia Una Dinámica del Desarrollo* . . . (Mexico, 1963), p. 57.

[18] Adolfo Dorfman, *La Intervención del Estado en la Industria* (Buenos Aires, 1944), p. 167.

[19] *La Nación* (November 1, 1956).

industrialists have complained of "the zeal for industrial protectionism in our country, which makes importation impossible for any manufacturing venture. We do not believe that trade in foreign metallurgical items must be abolished, since there will always be a need for the high specialization and advanced techniques of other countries. We think that the Federation, as a responsible organization, cannot support industries that will always be marginal or unstable because of the lack of technical means, the scarcity of the market, or for any other reason. Such a position must be strictly enforced for industries that aspire to manufacture delicate or precision items that other industries need for their manufacturing machinery or equipment."[20] The Cámara Gremial de Fabricantes de Caños y Tubos de Acero—which is "nationalist" and protectionist as far as the local manufacture of metal pipes and tubes is concerned—aroused the indignation of the Centro de Industriales Siderúrgicos with its accusations against the poor quality and high cost of their iron straps, and with its demands for the free importation of this product.[21]

Tomás Fillol, in his book *Social Factors in Economic Development: The Argentine Case*, indicated that Argentinian entrepreneurs tend to rely on cartels, monopolies, and nepotism—and, in general, on the concentration of property to guarantee their profits. They prefer a great profit and little risk and will not venture into untapped markets that would not only be profitable but socially necessary. In fact, they tend to subordinate the search for profit to prestige considerations and family and friendship ties. They have little understanding of modern tools and methods of business administration.

All these statements are allegedly disproved in a study, undertaken by CEPAL and the Centro de Investigaciones Económicas of the Instituto Torcuato di Tella, and directed by the economist Dr. Eduardo Zalduendo.[22]

Although the study is entitled "El Empresario Industrial en la Argentina," 22 percent of the 27 executives interviewed belong to established foreign enterprises in Argentina, so their attitudes do not represent Argentinian enterprise but foreign enterprise with Argentinian investments (Ducilo, Duperial, General Motors, Kaiser, Pfizer, Fiat). Another 26 percent—

---

[20] Federación Argentina de Industrias Metalúrgicas, *Memoria 1955*.
[21] *La Nación* (April 30, 1957).
[22] See *Primera Plana* (Feb. 19, 1963), and *CGE 200 Millones* (June 1963).

which, with the first group, adds up to 48 percent—belong to enterprises closely connected to foreign capital (and to a great extent influenced by their foreign associates (Siam, Alpargatas, Acindar, Grafa, Sudamtex, Tamet, Textil Oeste). This is what the sample actually represents. Regarding the results, we see that only 8 executives had completed courses in the organization of enterprises, but all of them are frankly protectionist and fail to show any concern for efficiency, high costs, etc.

On the other hand, the verbal responses of these 27 executives, who are conscious that their attitudes are being evaluated, are not as significant as their actual management of their enterprises in the market. And what kind of management characterizes the Argentinian industrial manager? Is it massive production, at low prices, with permanent enlargement of the market, and all the other economic virtues of the capitalist studied by Marx? The answers come from other sources, from the proceedings of the Comisión Honoraria de Reactivación Industrial. In 1963—when the capacity utilized in industry varied between 30 percent in the sector of moving and lifting equipment, and 75 percent in machine equipment—the Commission considered it "of great importance to warn that the new increase in demand does not in any way constitute the desideratum that would definitely solve the problems of industry. This is so because of the justified fear that an increase in purchasing power would not be reflected in greater economic activity (more production, more employment, and more consumption), but simply in higher prices. The indiscriminate raising of prices and salaries alarms the Commission because executives of different businesses—considered marginal—have emphasized that their present selling prices are much lower than can be considered normal; therefore it hopes that before demand rises again, this situation will be corrected. . . . Prices, which had not completely stopped rising even when demand was low, have started to increase anew in the past weeks in anticipation of better general conditions."[23]

If Dr. Zalduendo sincerely believes, on the basis of his study, that the Argentinian industrialist "is willing to sell many products at low prices, even if the profits would be the same as when he does the opposite,"[24] one can only exclaim at his naïveté. The more realistic Comisión de Reactivación Indus-

[23] Poder Ej. Nacional, Minist. de Econ. de la Nación, Comisión Honoraria de Reactivación Industrial, *Informe Sobre la Industria Argentina* (Buenos Aires, September 1963), pp. 6, 12, 13.
[24] *Primera Plana*, February 19, 1963, p. 56.

trial comments that "it was hoped that when demand was reduced to levels suggested by the International Monetary Fund, sales and production would be temporarily reduced. The beneficial effects of this would be the disappearance of the least efficient producers and the reduction of actual costs, in the effort to survive in a restricted market.

"In practice, nevertheless, these expectations are not fulfilled. Generally, managers are not greatly concerned over costs, in the hope that a return of inflation would solve their principal problems, reducing their debts and providing markets for any product, even the most inefficient and expensive, at the expense of a decreasing utilization of productive factors."[25] And, in earlier pages, "Argentinian industrialists often seek to solve their problems by protecting themselves against competition from imports through a disproportionate increase in customs and exchange taxes."[26]

In truth, the whole economic and social structure of Argentina, as of other backward countries, tends to block, discourage, and frustrate the development of an industrial entrepreneurial class, with motives and values that impel it to produce massively and at low cost and in areas important for industrialization.

Prebisch has observed:

"In Latin American countries certain forms of privilege considerably weaken the desire for any technical progress and consequently discourage the utilization of the capable men with initiative that our technology needs. But this fact is not confined to the country. Even in industry the incentives to technical progress are weakened by overprotection. To be kept alert, industrial initiative requires continuous competition. And Latin American industry does not generally have much of this. The great fortunes of the past in these regions came largely from monopoly and land speculation. Later came the other privilege of protection." [27]

The ineptitude and lack of inclination of the Argentinian industrialist class to increase technical efficiency and rationalize their enterprises is all the more significant because full employment, the unionization of the working class, and the strong negotiating power of the unions between 1943 and 1955 should have given them more than enough reason to do so to increase productivity. Such was the reaction, for instance, of the Japanese industrialists to the unionization of the Japa-

[25] Comisión Honoraria . . . , *Informe* . . . , p. 23.
[26] P. 35.
[27] Prebisch, *op. cit.*, pp. 56-58.

nese workers after 1945.[28] Argentinian capitalists, on the contrary, have always preferred to counteract the rise in salaries through increased prices and inflation.

The result of this practice is the steady decrease in labor productivity in Argentinian industry since 1937.

Eduardo Astesano is one of the principal exponents of the theory that industrialists and landholders have always been, and will always be, mutually antagonistic. Nevertheless, he published the *Historia de la Independencia Económica,* which has on its cover a picture of Carlos Pellegrini, prototype of the defender of industry and founder of the Unión Industrial Argentina. What Astesano did not say was that Pelligrini was also the founder of the Jockey Club, the traditional sociopolitical center of the landholding oligarchy. This is no light matter, since it underscores the harmony between industrialists and landholders.[29]

However, despite this general unity of interests, friction has often arisen over the problem of protectionism, demanded invariably by the industrialists, and free trade, needed at times by the landholders. I say *at times,* because the Argentinian landholders have not always been in favor of free trade. When they suffered in the world market, through low sales or low prices, the landholders would insist on developing industry in order to save foreign exchange and be able to rely on a domestic market for their products. In 1871, for example, the *Anales* of the Sociedad Rural Argentina said that "the factories are our anchor of salvation," and rejoiced that national industry had broken "the tutelage and bondage to which we have subjected it in exchange for the products of foreign industry."[30] Twenty years later the spokesman for cattle ranches indicated that industry and cattle raising are "concurrent and related forces."[31] On their part, the industrialists said that, far from being opposed to the landholders, they "recognize and give weight to the undisputed importance of agricultural production

---

[28] See Masao Sakisaka, *Desarrollo de la Economía Japonesa Después de la Segunda Guerra Mundial* (Japan; Ministry of Foreign Affairs, 1963).

[29] It is worthwhile noting that the first "Marxist" writer who attempted to establish a radical antagonism between industrialists and landholders was Juan B. Justo. In his article entitled "Porque los Estancieros Deben Ser Librecambistas," he said, "Landholders and agriculturists that produce for exportation have interests completely opposed to those of the manufacturers who produce for consumption."

[30] *Anales* of the Sociedad Rural Argentina (1871), p. 128.

[31] *Anales* of the Sociedad Rural Argentina (1899), p. 157.

and cattle raising in the national economy," and indicated that "in all actions in favor of industry many landowners, certainly not the least representative or least aware, are in agreement with the industrialists."[32] In 1933, when the international economic crisis was being intensely felt in Argentina, causing irritations and open clashes among all the capitalist sectors in the struggle to secure the largest bit of profit possible and to let other capitalists take the loss—when both worker and farmer were exploited to the limit—industrialists insisted on the fundamental unity of interests between them and the land-owners. "The theorists, at all costs," the spokesman for the industrialists said then, "find antagonisms where there can be only harmony: between manufacturing and agricultural interests." He added: "In new countries like Argentina there are no antagonisms or conflicting interests between cattle raisers, agriculturists, and industrial manufacturers."[33] That same year the president of the Argentinian industrialists association, Unión Industrial Argentina, declared that "there is not and can never be any division between industrial and cattle raising or agrarian activities."[34]

Declarations in this vein were often repeated. In June 1945 there appeared in the newspapers of Buenos Aires a "Manifiesto del Comercio y la Industria," signed by all the employers' associations—Cámara de Comercio, Bolsa de Comercio, Sociedad Rural, etc.—except Unión Industrial. Commenting on this document, Col. Perón, then Vice-President of the country, remarked that it was "gratifying to see that the industrialists are not represented in the manifesto," although it had the signatures of the landholders, enemies of industry, who "have represented the eternal economic oligarchy in this country." Immediately the Unión Industrial refuted Perón, declaring that it had ratified its solidarity with the Sociedad Rural.[35] After the 1946 elections the Unión Industrial Argentina, active financial sponsor of the Unión Democrática, was stripped of juridical representation and was replaced by the Asociación Argentina de la Producción, Industria y Comercio (AAPIC), which was later changed to Confederación Económica Argentina (CEA) and later still became the CGE. For obvious reasons these organizations proclaimed a general political stand opposed to that of the UIA, but like the UIA,

[32] *Anales* of the Unión Industrial Argentina (January 1900), p. 1.
[33] *Idem* (1933), p. 29.
[34] *Tribuna Libre* (July 27, 1933).
[35] *La Prensa* (June 16, 19, and 23, 1945).

they lost no time emphasizing the unity between industrialists and landholders. In 1949, for instance, the CEA president, speaking on the Día de la Industria, said that "grain and cattle still represent the essentials of our wealth," and that "the descriptions frequently given of the opposition between cattle raisers and industrialists are inaccurate. On the contrary, the former are the basis of the latter's wealth."[36]

In spite of this general harmony of interests, some friction occurred before 1933, because the landholders, who were selling their products in the world market, did not hesitate to sacrifice Argentinian industry to foreign competition. The industrialists, in turn, demanded protection for industry by restricting imports of merchandise, and drawing to the country the foreign capital that would produce this merchandise here. This was about all there was to their nationalism. However, in the period 1930-33, with their position endangered by the world crisis, the landholders once more turned protectionist and supported industrial development.

It is misleading to say *in general* that to the landholders "the creation of a domestic market was a disinterested move."[37] Actually, when the world market bought little and at low prices, the creation of a domestic market was to the best interests of the landholding capitalists, who could thus decrease and repay their debts in the world market. "The isolation brought upon us by a displaced world"—according to a statement made in 1933 by the Minister of Agriculture, a big cattle raiser and former president of the Sociedad Rural Argentina—"forces us to manufacture goods that we can no longer purchase from the countries that do not buy from us."[38]

The president of the Sociedad Rural Argentina, when asked whether, in anticipation of "an even more difficult prospect for our agricultural and cattle exports," he agreed that there was "a need to increase the domestic market and to encourage the industrial organization of the country," replied: "I am completely in agreement with that general orientation of our economic policy and with the new spirit that inspires and guides it. I wish, first of all, to make this point clear: contrary to what has been said many times, and without the least justification, there is definitely no antagonism whatsoever between the interests and aspirations of the agrarian economy

[36] *Boletín* of the Confederación Económica Argentina (December 9, 1949).
[37] J. A. Ramos, Preface to *El Porvenir de América Latina*, by Manuel Ugarte (Buenos Aires, 1953).
[38] *La Nación* (October 14, 1933).

and those of the industrial class of our country. We agree completely on the necessity and usefulness of helping industrial organization. Anything that can be done to encourage our industrial production would surely help the country rise above its difficulties, which we foresee will be brought on by the impending closure of the European markets."[39]

Precisely because of the decision of the landholding capitalists, Uriburu and Justo-Pinedo initiated a policy of industrial promotion that greatly accelerated the development of industry. It has been said that this formidable industrial development was "neither foreseen nor desired by the oligarchy."[40] But this is false. The landholding capitalists both foresaw and wanted industrial development. In 1933 Pinedo declared: "The carrying out of a vast program of public works is reflected in the increased demand for a great quantity and variety of merchandise that Argentina produces or can produce. And here we come to an important point: the control of imports will prevent this demand from simply stimulating imports and will promote domestic economic activity."[41] In 1934 the Banco de la Nación said in its *Memoria,* "The decrease in imports will give a new stimulus to the development of national industries, which have shown surprising progress in recent years. The Bank is trying to support this to the extent its resources allow." On its part the Banco Central said in its *Memoria* for 1938 that the restriction of imports gave reasonable hope that "the purchasing power that importation can no longer stimulate disproportionately will be diverted largely toward industry." Finally, the industrialists themselves realized that the landholders supported industry. Through the UIA president they expressed their satisfaction that the government of Justo-Pinedo did not spare efforts "to assure the development of industries as a source of the economic improvement needed by the country."[42]

[39] *Noticias Gráficas* (July 2, 1933).

[40] J. A. Ramos, *América Latina, Un País,* p. 152.

[41] *Revista* of the Unión Industrial Argentina (December 1933).

[42] *Revista* of the Unión Industrial Argentina, June 1937. At the turn of the century, Hilferding, in his analysis of the development of capitalism in Germany and in Europe as a whole, indicated that the cessation of export of agricultural products caused landholders to support a protective tariff for industry; that industrial development benefited the landholders, opening for them the possibility of developing the distillery, brewery, and sugar manufacturing industries, etc.; that the excess income of the landholders had to be put to use in profitable industrial investments, transforming the latifundist class from one whose income came from real estate rentals to one whose income came in increasing proportions from industrial profits, etc.

The foregoing discussion has revealed that the industrial capitalists cannot be depended upon to favor the abolition of the landholding oligarchy's power. The ties that unite them socially and economically will not be worn away by friction that consists only of exchanges of petitions in favor of or against the importation of tractors.

But however close the connections are between the industrialists and the landholders, there is an equally strong attachment between the industrial class and foreign capital. Don Arturo Frondizi wrote in his book on petroleum that "our industry has developed in a struggle against foreign capital, since the latter would like to maintain an importing market for its manufactured products."[43] Actually, what Argentinian industry has been struggling with is foreign capital invested in *foreign* industry. It has always combined eagerly with international capital invested in *this* country, or has, in fact, been directly established by foreign capital. The alma mater of the most important enterprises in Argentinian heavy industry was Tornquist, well-known agent of international finance capital. In 1887 Tornquist founded the Refinería de Rosario, and later the Compañía Azucarera Tucumana. In 1891 it acquired the refrigerating plant Sansinena. In 1897 it participated in the founding of Cervecería Palermo. In 1902 it joined the metallurgical firms Rezzonico, Ottonello y Cia., which then became Tamet. In 1907 it established the Compañía de Productos Conen (stearine, glycerine, candles, soap, and sulfuric acid), and founded the metallurgical firm Ferrum. The other financial group that promoted industries in the first decade of the twentieth century was Leng Roberts, a British partnership that participated in Bodegas Tomba, Bagley, and other important enterprises.

A report from Casa Baring, dated August 1907, stated that "in the last two or three years the development of industrial enterprises has increased rapidly," and added: "Naturally, much foreign capital is used in these enterprises." In effect, the industrial firms that were not established by foreign capital became large enterprises only when they tightened their connections with international finance capital. This was the case with Tamet and Siam, two pillars of the metallurgical industry, and with Alpargatas. Tamet started as a small factory established in 1880. This was absorbed by Tornquist at the turn of the century, and later expanded, absorbing the Argen-

43 *Política y Petróleo*, p. 1v.

tinian firm Compañía Argentina de Hierros y Aceros de Pedro-Vasena. Siam underwent a similar process when the Argentinian firm Di Tella was converted in 1927 into the Sociedad Industrial Americana de Maquinarias Di Tella, becoming dependent on foreign capital, particularly on the American firm Westinghouse. The Fábrica "Argentina" de Alpargatas was started by an Argentine trader and manufacturer of hemp sandals. In 1880 it became a branch of the British canvas manufacturers Douglas Fraser and Sons.[44] Abundant documentary proof supports the statement of Schlej, who studied the sugar industry, that as the industry developed, "foreign capital, technically and financially competent, displaced a part of genuinely native capital and assumed control of the industry."

In recent times, as in the first stages of its development, native industry has been linked to foreign capital as soon as it reaches a certain stage of development. What has happened to the automobile manufacturing industry is well known. Similar events are taking place in all the industries. If a firm (Heinonen Sociedad Anónima, Comercial e Industrial) wishes to establish a paper and cardboard factory, it takes steps to obtain the aid of American capital.[45] If an Argentinian industrialist owns the only typewriter factory in the country and wishes to increase his profits, he turns it over to Remington Rand and retains a minority interest. This is what happened to the factory EMA.[46] This takes place ad infinitum in all the branches of industry. If the Fábrica Argentina de Lápices wishes to establish a new factory, it merges with the American firm Eberhard Faber Pencil Co., etc., etc.

The intimate ties that have linked Argentinian industrial capitalists since their birth as a class to foreign capital are also manifested in the composition of their organizations. Among the diverse groups that founded the Unión Industrial Argentina are well-known foreign capital groups like Otto Bemberg, Bagley, Campomar, Conen, Noel, Rigolleau, Shaw, Tornquist, and Urien. The presidents of the Unión have been men like Padilla (Standard Oil) or Luis Colombo, acknowledged agent of the Leng Roberts group, one of the bulwarks of British finance capital in Argentina.[47]

Thus when Rodolfo Puiggros states in his book on political

[44] Manuel Chueco, *Los Pioneros de la Industria Nacional* (Buenos Aires, 1896).
[45] U.S. Department of Commerce, *Commerce Reports* (October 1950).
[46] *Clarín* (November 13, 1950).
[47] Américo Guerrero, *La Industria Argentina* (Buenos Aires, 1944).

parties that "the truth is that native [Argentinian] industry developed in conflict with imperialism, and not as an appendage of imperialism,"[48] he is making an erroneous statement contradicted by the whole history of Argentinian industry.

The two greatest authorities on Argentinian industrial economy, Adolfo Dorfman and Felix Weil, agree concerning the decisive role of foreign capital in native industry.

Dorfman observes that the subsidiaries of foreign enterprises, easily recognized because they carry the name of the mother company, constitute only one of the forms in which international finance capital is invested, and then says, "Aside from these obvious financial relations with foreign capital, there are various intermediate forms, such as companies, part of whose shares have passed into the control of foreign commercial or financial organizations, industries established through loans from foreign banks, etc. A detailed study of the different forms in which foreign interests are represented in Argentinian industry would be a long and tedious process. Little can be said in concrete terms about this because of the extreme complexity of the financial relationships operating in the field of modern industry. But it cannot be doubted that this influence is great." Considering only the firms that are most outstanding and most obviously supported by foreign capital, directly or indirectly, Dorfman concludes that foreign capital constitutes *half of the total capital of Argentinian industry, although the information supplied is obviously incomplete.*"[49] To paraphrase Weil, the words "Argentina" or "national" in the name of a company are a sure sign that a foreign interest is trying to hide itself behind a national facade. Weil knows whereof he speaks. He was the director of public relations for Bunge and Born, edited the revenue law for Pinedo, and has inside information on the operations of Argentinian capitalism.[50]

Twenty years after Weil, the Minister of Education and Justice decreed: "The expressions 'Argentinian' or 'of Argentina' may be used only by groups that guarantee their actual economic or legal independence of foreign entities."[51]

We may add that among the industrial firms that quote their shares in the *Bolsa de Buenos Aires,* those that have no

[48] P. 182.
[49] Dorfman, *Evolución Industrial Argentina,* pp. 300-301.
[50] Weil, *op. cit.,* pp. 127, 131, 149.
[51] *Boletín Oficial* (March 30, 1963).

links with foreign capital can be counted on one's fingers. According to the declaration of enterprises (in *La Nación*, Dec. 17, 1955), 53 firms controlling different industries supply approximately 40 percent of the industrial products consumed. Of these, less than 15 have no *apparent* connection with international companies. Forty of these firms that carry great weight in national industry are closely connected with foreign capital. In the textile industry, where national capital is most abundant, the most powerful enterprises (Alpargatas, Masllorens, Fabril Financiera, Textil Oeste, Sudamtex, Sedalana, etc.) are linked to some degree with foreign capital. Thus, as Weil says, the list of the principal Argentinian industrial firms reads like a list of the large international companies attending the meetings of the International Chamber of Commerce.

In 1954 the journal of the Confederación General Económica selected a group of 100 enterprises considered as the most important in Argentina according to the profits they brought to the country. Of these 100 enterprises at least 89 belonged to or were closely connected with foreign capital.

Furthermore, eight firms, openly American, and listed as such in the *Guia de la Cámara de Comercio Norteamericana* in Argentina, possessed 22 percent of the total sales realized by the industrial corporations in the Vehicles and Machinery branch. In Electric Machinery and Equipment 7 American firms had 19.2 percent of the sales; in Chemicals 13 American firms had 15.6 percent of the sales; and in Food, Drink, and Tobacco 18.8 percent of the sales were attributed to 5 American firms.[52]

The most important metallurgical industries established recently are also connected with foreign capital. This is the case with SIAT (Siam-Westinghouse) and with ARTAC (Acevedo y Shaw, Garavaglio y Zorraquin, Tornquist, and Republic Steel Corp., one of the ten largest siderurgical enterprises in the United States). Other important companies, such as the one established a few years ago in Haedo for the production of spiral welded pipes, are connected with the American Rolling Mill Co.

No less significant is the origin of the most outstanding

[52] Data from an unpublished work by Victor Testa. The figures on the sales of industrial corporations were taken from *Estadística de Soc. Anon.*, published by the Dir. Nac. de Est. (January 1963). The information on the American enterprises were obtained from the journal *Comments*, publication of the American Chamber of Commerce in Argentina (April 1961).

pillars of the "Argentinian" chemical industry. According to a study conducted by the American Senate on international cartels, Dupont and ICI organized *Duperial Argentina* in 1934, with 50 percent participation of each, to prevent development of nationalist-sponsored industry, to avoid a conflict of interests, and to assure its market position. The same was true of their establishment of Electroclor, S. A., Argentina to compete with *La Celulosa,* Argentina's electrolitic plant—which had taken it 30 years to construct.[53]

The very young automobile industry is following the same course as the siderurgical and chemical industries. It is wholly in the hands of foreign capital. Three American firms that made 45.6 percent of the total sales in 1963 (I.K.A. [Kaiser], General Motors, and Ford, with sales of [Argen.] $8,319,252,-000, of a total of $18,279,903,000 sold by the whole industry), and six European firms that made 44.7 percent (Fiat, Peugeot, Di Tella-British Motors, Citroën, DKW, and Isard, with $8,-164,233,000).

The manufacture of automobile spare parts is largely controlled by foreign capital through concessions of patents and manufacturing licenses. The piston ring factory constructed some years ago in Rosario, which is the most modern factory of its kind, revolves around Borg Warner International Corporation and Burd Piston Ring Corporation.

The industrial firms that produce for the domestic Argentinian market and can be found to have present connections with international capital (without having access to the records of all enterprises) number around 500. This is an insignificant figure in numerical terms, compared with the tens of thousands of industrial establishments in the country.

The foreign capital that controls these firms does not control the majority of industrial firms *in general,* but it possesses most of the large enterprises that determine the movements of each industry, which employ *thousands of laborers,* and produce *the bulk of the industrial* production of the country.

To illustrate the significance of the concentration and centralization of capital, we observe, for instance, that one single international company (Fabril Financiera) employs as many laborers as 12,000 national establishments; and its capital amounts to three times the annual production of 28,000 national establishments. As a whole, Argentinian industry is in a situation much the same as that of the mining industry

[53] Stockings and Watkims, *Cartels in Action* (New York, 1947), pp. 460-463.

described recently by the Unión Minera Argentina. There are three types of enterprises: the large enterprise, in which foreign capital generally predominates, which is greatly developed technically, and is highly mechanized; the medium enterprise, comprising Argentinian capital, with some advanced technical developments; and the small enterprise, with precarious economic means and without any mechanization. The first type represents 77 percent of the total production; the second, 20 percent; and the third, a paltry 3 percent.[54]

Its concentration in large enterprises gives foreign capital special weight that presses on the whole industry. The classic work by Berle and Means on the concentration and centralization of capital concluded that the influence of a large corporation extends far beyond the investments under its direct control. Especially, those small businesses dependent for sales or purchases on a large corporation are controlled to a great extent by that corporation. Their prosperity is often dependent on their links to a given giant, and their interests tend to become true interests of that giant corporation.[55]

Wythe, in his well-known work on Latin American industry, states about Argentina: "The Censo Industrial de 1935 estimated the total industrial investments at 4,314 million pesos. The census does not indicate the value of foreign investments in industry, but it may be estimated at some 600 million pesos. Therefore, between 60 and 65 percent of the total industrial capital was Argentine."[56]

Wythe does not reveal that, because of the high concentration and centralization of Argentine industry, the small number of large enterprises controlled by foreign capital has a weight infinitely superior to that of the thousands of native enterprises. Analyzing the figures of the same census in 1935, Dorfman showed that a little more than one hundredth part of the industrial enterprises—those with foreign connections—employed almost one third of the total number of workers and produced half of the total value of production. On the other hand, the small establishments totaled one eighth of the total, employed one-twentieth of the workers, and produced, yes, a *hundredth* of the total value. The contrast cannot be sharper. In addition, 700 large enterprises that, according to the classification of the 1935 census, employed at least 100 workers

[54] *La Nación* (January 3, 1956).
[55] Berle and Means, *The Modern Corporation and Private Property* (New York, 1934), p. 33.
[56] Wythe, *La Industria Latinoamericana* (Mexico, 1946), p. 95.

each, earned the same amount of profits as 39,600 smaller factories.[57]

The new foreign investments tend to be concealed by the nationality of the country in which they are based, with the result that they enjoy the protection that is given to the "national" industries. In order to control the enterprises that it owns in other countries, and that appear to be independent, foreign capital resorts, in general, to the same methods that in the metropolises permit the large companies to control immense constellations of firms. The basic procedures through which one enterprise may control another are total ownership, minority participation, preferred shares, chains of enterprises, technical direction, and the concession of patents and manufacturing licenses, and all the many possible combinations of these methods.[58]

On the other hand, enterprises are sometimes linked by informal or indirect agreement more than by formal ownership of shares. Informal associations, friendships, or a community of interests based on family ties can establish common policies for corporations that nominally have no connections with each other.[59]

The discovery of these combinations becomes much more difficult because a dead silence is kept about such activities. We get an idea of this in a memorandum from the president of Rohm & Haas, which gives information on a conference with a director of du Pont de Nemours. In this memorandum it was stated that there was no possibility of Imperial Chemical entering the American market, but Dupont did not want to put it in writing for fear such an agreement would be used by the politicians to show that the world was divided between Imperial Chemical and Dupont.[60]

International capital hides behind the native capitalists of the backward countries and converts them into their puppets. As one adviser to foreign investors points out, direct investments alongside of national capital gives these investments the *look* of being national. This reduces friction usually generated by foreign capital and impedes the movement toward expropriation or any form of taxation or discrimination against foreign capital.[61] Many foreign investors recognize that local capital

[57] Evolución Industrial, pp. 245-271.

[58] Berle and Means, *op. cit.*, p. 70.

[59] U.S. Senate, *Economic and Political Aspects of International Cartels*, p. 8.

[60] *Ibid.*, p. 22.

[61] Hal B. Leary, *The U.S. in the World Economy* (Washington, 1943), p. 20.

investment in an enterprise controlled by foreign capital interests the government in its welfare. Thus, foreign investors are now doing their best to encourage local capital to invest in association with them.[62]

A study by *Business Week* on American capital in Latin America states that the American enterprises increasingly encourage national capital to participate with them.[63]

Weil says that there is reason to doubt the authenticity of even the so-called national capital in Argentinian industry. Since the predominant form of enterprise in Argentina is the corporation, the identities of the shareholders are easily concealed. The directors and officials may all be from distinguished native families, the name of the company may contain the words "national" or "Argentinian," yet the enterprise may be controlled by a foreign group. But the meaning of "foreign" enterprise must be made clear, Weil adds, since Argentina is a conspicuous example of the difficulties encountered in distinguishing between national and foreign capital, particularly capital invested in industry. For practical purposes of taxation, statistics on trade and property, etc., a company organized under Argentinian laws is considered national, although the whole or a major part of its capital is owned by foreign groups. In dealing with the sociological phenomenon of foreign control, however, it is necessary to consider other criteria besides purely formal ones. Some "inside" knowledge of the problem is necessary in order to recognize foreign capital under its native disguise.

Some very revealing incidents have thrown light on the question of "national" enterprises. Siam Di Tella, for example, is to all appearances an Argentinian enterprise, registered under Argentinian laws, quoting its shares in the *Bolsa de Buenos Aires,* etc. Yet its interdiction in 1955 provoked a reaction from Westinghouse, which appeared to have nothing to do with Siam. Actually, of course, Siam is under its control. Foreign capital continually assumes the disguise of "100 percent Argentinian enterprise." The following statement, for instance, was given by the Director of Public Relations for Esso, an affiliate of Standard Oil of New Jersey: "My first concern was to emphasize that Esso was and is an Argentinian enterprise[!], almost 90 percent of its employees being citizens of Argen-

[62] The President's Materials Policy Commission, *Resources for Freedom* (Washington, 1952), Vol. I, p. 65.
[63] *Business Week* (November 20, 1954).

tina, identifying itself with Argentinian ideals, and having no leanings toward the origin of its American capital."[64]

Fortunately there are documents to prove that figures of the Argentinian capitalist class serve as agents for foreign capital, sitting in the directorates of large "Argentinian" but foreign-controlled firms. The *Informe de la Comisión Investigadora de las Concesiones Eléctricas* (the famous report of the Rodríguez Conde Commission) states (from page 446 on, the figures in parentheses corresponding to the paragraph divisions of the report):

"(790) The composition of the board of directors of the Sociedad Anónima Compañía Argentina de Electricidad (CADE) is illegal. It violates Articles 336 and 339 of the Commercial Code.

"Dr. Oliver—Actually, although the local directors carry the name of directors, they do not direct anything; they have neither voice nor vote; and they receive their appointments and instructions from the CHADE in Europe. They are better agents than directors, because the power of direction obviously does not belong to them."

It is known that in 1945, under pressure from the United States, the Government of Argentina attached German property in the country. Leading "national" industrial firms formed a very important part of this capital: *Thyssen Lametal, Tubos Manessman, Inag, Sema, Siemens, AEG, Osram, GEOPE, Bayer, Schering,* etc. All these firms were merged into the *Dirección Nacional de Industrias del Estado* (DINIE). A message referring to the activities of this organization, directed to Congress by the Executive, reads in part: "All the firms over which the Argentinian government assumed control, in compliance with wartime international agreements, were enterprises dependent on enemy holdings and cartels. This is the reason for their being placed under state control. That is to say, enterprises organized and established on Argentinian territory under Argentinian laws were controlled absolutely in all of their policies—even the most minimal ones—as has been proved through concrete cases, by organizations dedicated to foreign interests and policies."[65]

These enterprises were not only "organized and established on Argentinian territory under Argentinian laws"; their direc-

[64] *Mensaje,* Journal of the Asoc. Agr. de Agencias de Publicidad, July 1954, p. 17.
[65] *Diario de Sesiones* of the Cámara de Diputados de la Nación (June 24 and 25, 1948).

torates also included some of the most outstanding members of the national capitalism: Alejandro Shaw, Basilio Pertine, Zorraquin, García Merou, Ernesto Aguirre, Carlos Agote, Eduardo Sánchez Terrero, Carlos Meyer Pellegrini, Joaquín S. de Anchorena, Rubirosa, Julio César Urien, Carlos Santamarina, Ramón S. Castillo, Jr., Antonio Méndez Delfino. All these men, the elite of Argentinian capitalists, were figureheads for international financing capital. It is self-evident that the national firms to whose directorates these men belong scarcely deserve the credit of being called "Argentinian."

Juan Carlos Esteban postulates the division of Argentinian industrial capitalists into two sectors. One of these is the "conciliatory industrialists," whose policy is "monopolistic development, and is centralized in some branches of industry under the leadership of American financing capital."[66] The other sector would be "the nonconciliatory industrialists" about whose policy Esteban, in fact, says nothing.[67]

In truth, all sectors of the industrial capitalists need and aspire to association with foreign capital; no objective basis exists to hinder native industrialists from forming connections with international capital. But there do exist countless conflicts and disagreements in connection with the terms and conditions involved in establishing the relationship. The only impediment to friendly relations between Argentinian industrialists and foreign capitalists would be a situation in which (a) foreign capitalists would take an oath not to invest a single dollar in Argentinian industry, or to invest solely in competition but never in association with Argentinian capitalists, whether directly or indirectly; and/or (b) Argentinian industrialists, their need for capital and customers completely satisfied, would take an oath not to associate with foreign capital and not to become agents for foreign firms in the country.

As long as such a situation does not exist—and it is enough to describe it aloud to realize that it does not—there will be objective bases for conciliation and agreement between native industrialists and foreign capitalists, whether or not the contrary is asserted by Juan Carlos Esteban and his Communist Labor Movement.

The history of Argentinian industry leaves relatively few doubts. Every national firm, large, medium, or small, as soon as it feels the need to expand or consolidate its operations,

[66] J. C. Esteban, *Imperialismo y Desarrollo Económico* (Buenos Aires, 1961), p. 174.
[67] *Ibid.*, p. 193.

goes in search of foreign capital, patents, or licenses. Not even the smallest firm is free of this tendency. In the metallurgical industry, the favorite field of all seekers and makers of nationalist industrialists, the path followed by such enterprises as Rosatti y Cristofaro, Cura, Protto Hnos., Fundición Mira, etc., is significant. The same may be said of the path followed by the numerous small enterprises that have merged with foreign capital to manufacture refrigerators, television sets, washing machines, air conditioners, automobile spare parts, etc.

It is not accurate to say that the industrial capitalists of Argentina "aspire for a national policy" or "find their reason for existence in the framework of national development" when they produce for the domestic market.[68]

Argentinian industry certainly produces for the domestic market, but it is controlled by foreign capital and is increasingly dependent on it. No inherently national policy results in any way from production for the domestic market, as numerous examples will prove. Throughout the history of an unquestionably national institution like the YPF, for instance, it has generally been *protected* by the *cattle raisers* of the coastal zone, the prototypes of capitalists that sell their products in the world market. At the same time, YPF is systematically attacked, with the aim of destroying it, by *industrialists* like Patrón Costas, prototype of the industrial capitalists who sell in the *domestic* market, but is allied to American capital through the petroleum investments of Standard Oil in northern Argentina.

Before the start of the Second World War Argentina was part of the British Empire as a quasicolony. But the war initiated one of the most important changes in Argentinian history: the strongest economic and political pressure from the United States, which was to displace British dominance in the country; the increasing American intervention in Argentinian affairs; and the division of all sectors of the dominant classes into pro-American and pro-British wings. The anti-Perón intervention by Ambassador Braden in the 1946 elections, though the most colorful, was neither the only, nor the most decisive one, of the incidents that characterized the American offensive.

"The other Latin American countries have lost even the freedom to enter into agreements," President Castillo said in 1942, "and have ceased being free countries. Before making any move, they have to consult the United States. We are

[68] Arturo Frondizi, *op. cit.*, p. 38; Ramos, *A. Latina . . . .*, p. 147.

actually the only free country in South America." However, he added, "It cannot be denied that the situation is becoming more critical every day, with American pressure increasing by the hour. I believe that they will continue applying the tourniquet to us; we will have to struggle with more difficulties each day.[69] In fact, the pressure had become so strong that in 1943, on the eve of the presidential elections, all the presidential candidates were pro-American, the conservatives Patrón Costas, Justo, and Roca, as well as the "radical" Alvear.

What has been the attitude of Argentinian industrialists toward this American offensive to include Argentina among the rest of its Latin American quasicolonies?

The industrialists, whom their apologists choose to call *nationalists,* not only are attached to foreign capital, but their greatest aim is to attach themselves even more securely. Recently an Argentinian industrialist, the president of the board of directors of Indasbest, S.A., made the following categorical statements in New York: "The timidity of the Argentinian investor, and his tendency to improvise industrially needs to be corrected by the financial stimulus and technical orientation characteristic of foreign capital investments."[70] That this opinion is not confined to one industrialist is shown by the equally "nationalistic" journal *Qué,* which continually insists on "our ambition to incorporate into the country as much foreign capital as the progress of the national economy requires."[71]

The consequences of this eagerness of the industrial capitalists for foreign capital to support and expand their enterprises is of tremendous significance. Their class has pinned its hopes on American capital, which is both able and willing to become increasingly part of Argentinian industry.

In its early days Argentinian industrialists shared the traditional hostility of the Buenos Aires cattle raisers, who were allied with England, toward American capital. "We view with misgivings," the Unión Industrial Argentina declared in 1912, "the possibility of an overly intimate connection with the United States. This would endanger the absolute economic independence that should come hand in hand with our political independence." It also protested "against North American absorption into Central America." At the same time, however, it was singing praises for the increased British investments in Latin America.[72] This attitude changed as British capital weak-

[69] Cited by Carlos Ibarguren in *La Historia que he vivido,* p. 494.
[70] *La Nación* (August 9, 1956).
[71] October 2 and 23, 1956.
[72] *Anales* of the Unión Industrial Argentina (January 1912).

ened and the United States emerged as the only possible source of large capital. The turning point came in 1940, when Federico Pinedo formulated the first plan for the industrialization of the country. Entitled *Reactivación Económica*, the plan received warm praise from the Unión Industrial Argentina. After the plan had been formulated, Pinedo realized that the old British mother country was exhausted and that it would be impossible to develop Argentinian capitalism without the help of American capital. Argentinian industry supported his position. In 1941 Pinedo went to the United States and spoke before the Banker's Club in New York: "We Argentinians realize that we have often committed the serious error of taking Europe as the principal and almost only model, without considering that the center of the world has shifted. We are obliged to make amends, as promptly as possible and as completely as we can, for the consequences of our relative isolation from this country. When world commerce consisted of the exchange of American raw materials and European industrial products, accompanied by intensive immigration to the American countries of European men and capital, any project to unify or simply bring together the nations on this continent, which might lead to a separation of a Latin American country from Europe, seemed logically unjustified, if not impossible to realize. But now that the manufacturing production of the United States has surpassed that of all other continents in the most important sectors, we can only look on the United States as the provider of the capital necessary for the utilization of the great sources of wealth that lie untapped in all our countries. Very little now remains of the economic conditions that, up to the beginning of this century, accounted for our determination to look with more interest toward the countries of Europe."[73]

Naturally, the American managing circles believed that "the United States had no better friend in Argentina than Pinedo."[74] But Pinedo's policy was not his alone; it was shared by the industrialists as a class and by politicians with industrial connections, such as Patrón Costas, who advocated active collaboration with the United States to obtain American economic aid for the industrialization of the country. If Patrón Costas had become president of the Republic—and only the coup of June 4 prevented this—he would have put Pinedo's pro-American

[73] Federico Pinedo, *La Argentina en la Vorágine* (Buenos Aires, 1943), pp. 45-48.
[74] John Gunther, *El Drama de América Latina*, p. 308.

policy into practice, as Pinedo himself admits.[75] This is precisely why Patrón Costas' candidacy was supported by the industrialists, whose most distinguished representatives signed a testimony to this effect in the June 3, 1943, issue of *El Mundo*.

Pinedo spoke for all those interests when he defended, in a letter to President Castillo, that Argentina enter the war because "If Argentina wishes to preserve its characteristics, if it wishes to maintain its civilized life, if it aspires to defend its social organization and to preserve it from violent upheavals, it urgently needs to preserve its relations with the United States. Those who tell you the contrary do not understand the economy of Argentina, nor its production, nor its industry, nor its sources of supply, nor its possible markets."[76] It did not take long for American interests to note that their great opportunity to displace British capital and weaken its traditional allies, the cattle raisers of Buenos Aires, consisted in promoting and supporting the industrial capitalists, whose influence was growing with the growth of industry. An executive of the Banco Schroder who visited this country on an American mission wrote that "to change Argentina's status as a British colony, U.S. cooperation in her industrialization was necessary."[77]

An American writer stated that the U.S. should make every effort to lift Argentina's dependence on Europe, one way being to aid her to establish new manufacturing industries.[78] Others have stated clearly that the continued predominance of agrarian interests in Argentina would mean reinforcement of her ties with Great Britain and greater restriction of her market to American products. An industrialized Argentina could, however, liberate herself from such dependence and offer a great market for American machinery. The bases for Argentinian antagonism to the U.S. would thus disappear.[79] Finally, the most competent American specialist on Argentinian matters, Pinedo's collaborator and admirer, Weil, considered industrial development "the Big Chance for the United States," because the U.S. could then replace Britain in the postwar period.[80]

[75] Pinedo, *En Tiempos de la República*, Vol. I, p. 193.
[76] Pinedo, *La Argentina . . .* , p. 99.
[77] National Research Council, *Tour of Industrial Exploration* (South America, 1941), p. 58.
[78] John W. White, *Argentina* (New York, 1942), p. 310.
[79] Fisk and Rennie, *Argentina in Crisis*, Foreign Policy Reports (May 1, 1944).
[80] Weil, *op. cit.*, pp. 195, 220.

Castillo's government, however, remained loyal to the old British mother country and to the tradition of Buenos Aires as allies of England and enemies of the United States. Its policy was neutrality, to keep Argentina away from "pan-Americanism." Its neutrality, therefore, definitely supported British and cattle-raising interests.[81] In January 1942 Argentina clashed violently with the United States at the Rio de Janeiro Conference when it refused to declare war against the Axis. In retaliation the United States, instead of granting an Argentinian request for capital to establish the siderurgical industry,[82] started an economic war against Argentina. In March 1942 the American Government prohibited the export of electrical equipment, chemical products, and other essential articles to Argentina.[83] This had little or no effect on the cattle raisers but did direct damage to industry. Industrialists dreamily contemplated the ample American aid that was going to Brazil and Chile for the establishment of new industries, and agitated for entrance into the war and for an agreement with the American Government.[84]

The foremost consequence of the enormous role of foreign capital in national industry is that as the industrialists grow in number they become comparatively weaker *as a class*. With industrial development the class is strengthened in *absolute* terms, multiplying its capital and its profits. But at the same time, foreign participation in the economy of the country is increasing, as are the numbers and the concentration of industrial workers. The industrial capitalist class is like a dwarf growing between two giants, and its only salvation from the working class giant lies in throwing itself into the arms of the foreign capitalist giant.

In short, Argentinian industrialists are united to international capital by a thousand ties of economic interest, and above all by the solidarity that unites all capitalists against the working class, whose movements threaten the private ownership of factories, whether national or foreign. However, unity does not mean identity of interests; and it is certain that there are irritations and clashes between the industrial capitalists and foreign capital. The source of these conflicts, however, is not

[81] Weil, p. 23, and Sir David Kelly, *The Ruling Few* (London, 1954), p. 287.
[82] Ruiz Guiñazú, *La Política Argentina y el Futuro de América* (Buenos Aires, 1944), p. 21.
[83] *New York Times*, March 28, 1942.
[84] See the statements of Torcuato di Tella in *La Nación* (May 6, 1943).

the desire of the industrialists to abolish foreign control over the Argentinian economy, but their determination to raise customs barriers against foreign competition. This is the response of the Argentinian industrialists, together with the foreign companies which have invested capital in the industry of Argentina, when confronted with foreign industrialists who insist on exporting, *not* capital, but *goods* that compete with the local industry. Their antiimperialist struggle has never gone beyond this.

What has been the industrialists' stand throughout the history of Argentina from 1890 to the present? Rodolfo Puiggros' reply: "The industrialists propose the increase of tariffs."[85] It is surprising that Puiggros himself speaks of the "revolutionary fire" of the Argentinian capitalists. The only thing such "fire" might burn would be the accounts of importers and of smugglers, who have always been the sworn enemies of local industry. But the assaults of the industrialists on the tariff law fully reveal their lack of revolutionary impulses. In a country overrun by *latifundias* and dominated by foreign capital, a class that limits itself to work in behalf of greater tariff protection shows that it is nothing but an associate of the *latifundistas* and foreign interests.

[85] P. 277.

Foreign Investment and the Large Enterprise in Latin America: The Brazilian Case

TEOTONIO DOS SANTOS

In Brazil the large basic industrial enterprises are not really national. They are controlled by foreign capital, primarily United States capital; and national capital is integrated into a dependent relationship with it. Such concentration and interconnection of interests, Dos Santos argues, not only makes a progressive nationalist role for the industrialists improbable, it has negative implications for development as well. For the increasing penetration of foreign capital into the industrial sectors opened up during the Second World War by national capital has meant growing economic concentration, increasing scale of the enterprise, and monopoly. Under conditions of monopoly by foreign advanced capitalist enterprises, available opportunities for investment in consumer goods industries, real estate, and other speculative financial activities are far more profitable and less risky than investments in basic industry in competition with foreign capital. Monopoly pricing and production methods, moreover, make the survival of marginal industries an adjunct to the maximization of profits by the monopolies, which set their prices in accordance with the prevailing socially unnecessary productivity of marginal firms. Intensive exploitation of existing markets rather than the creation of new ones is encouraged by monopoly control.

THE CASE OF Brazil exemplifies the fundamental changes in the structure of foreign investment going on in Latin America.

431

In the past decade Brazil has received the principal share of United States investment in Latin America (excluding Venezuela, where oil is the principal resource). Between 1951 and 1962 U.S. investment in Brazil amounted to $1,102 million, out of a total investment of $5,765 million in Latin America (Venezuela, $1,754 million; Argentina, $577 million; Mexico, $552 million; Panama, $490 million; Cuba, $371 million, until 1958; Peru, $293 million; Chile, $281 million). About 20 percent of U.S. investments in Latin America went into Brazil, mostly into the manufacturing sector.

Secondly, the greatest industrial integration has taken place in Brazil. The study by CEPAL on the production of basic equipment in Brazil[1] concludes that Brazilian industry is capable of producing 86 percent of the electrical equipment necessary for the period from 1961 to 1971, 90 percent of the equipment for paper and cellulose, 64 percent of the equipment for oil refinement, oil pipelines, and petrochemical industries, 77 percent of the equipment-needs predicted for 1966-70 for the steel industry, and 62 percent for cement (80 percent in the event that international enterprises agree to yield the right to use their patents). The study also predicts that by 1971 Brazil should be able to manufacture 70 percent of the machine equipment that it would need.

For these reasons, Brazil can be studied as a paradigm of the development of the forms of Latin American economic integration under the new conditions of international division of labor and foreign capital dominance in manufacturing. Everything indicates that we can observe these conditions in Brazil in their most advanced form. In this way we can understand the general tendencies of the developmental process in Latin America.

In the present study, I attempt to demonstrate, by the case of Brazil, general hypotheses for Latin America.

The basic hypotheses of this study may be summarized as follows: the changes in the international division of labor during the phase of monopoly capitalism submit the dominated countries to: (a) the predominance of the large enterprise; (b) economic concentration under the rule of large industries, especially international industry; (c) monopoly of the market; (d) the emergence of an administrative stratum representing the interests of big capital; (e) the syndical and political organ-

---

[1] United Nations, CEPAL. *La fabricación de maquinarias y equipos industriales en América Latina. I. Los equipos básicos en el Brasil*, 1962.

ization of the interests of big capital; and (f) the control of politics and of the state in its interests.

Our focus here is on hypotheses (a), (b), and (c) in the case of Brazil, which I take as representing the general tendencies of the new phase of development of international capitalism.

The large enterprise is of recent origin in Brazil. In the 1930's no industry was yet sufficiently developed to engender it. This phase began with the end of the Second World War. The data on basic industry, by size of plant in São Paulo (where the industrial growth of the country is concentrated, and which represents about 55 percent of the productive value of the industrial sector), are indicative of the process of industrial concentration (Table 1).

From 1949 to 1959 there was no change in the distribution of number of plants by size. However, the value of production of the enterprises employing more than 100 workers increased from 63.2 percent to 69 percent. At the same time the relative value of the production of enterprises employing more than 500 workers increased from 28.7 percent to 40.2 percent. Within 10 years enterprises with more than 500 workers rose from an inferior position to predominate in the production of the industrial sector.

TABLE 1

BASIC INDUSTRY IN THE STATE OF SÃO PAULO

Size of Plant	Number of plants					Value of production in millions of cruzeiros	
	1949		1959			1949	1959
					Increase from 1949 to 1959		
Number		%	Number	%	%	%	%
6-100	7,940	91.0	14,589	91.0	83.5	36.8	30.1
101-500	655	7.5	1,178	7.4	79.8	34.5	29.7
More than 500	128	1.5	260	1.6	103.1	28.7	48.2
Total	8,732	100	16,027	100	83.5	100	100

Source: *Censos Industriales*.

The importance of the large enterprise in the industrial center of the country is seen more clearly in the distribution of workers by size of plant. According to the Industrial Census of 1960, enterprises employing more than 100 workers in the state of São Paulo represented 60 percent of the workers, and those with more than 500 workers represented about 28 percent. This further reveals the predominance of the large enterprise. Table 2 further shows that the 195 plants with more than 500 workers represented 31.4 percent of the salaries, and 32.8 percent of the value of production. Taking all plants with more than 100 workers, we have 61.3 percent of the workers employed, 64.7 percent of the salaries, and 63.7 percent of the value of production.

TABLE 2

GENERAL ASPECTS OF INDUSTRIAL ACTIVITY IN SÃO PAULO BY NUMBER OF WORKERS EMPLOYED, 1960

Size of plant	Plants		Workers employed		Salaries	Value of production
	No.	%	No.	%	%	%
1 to 4	22,876	63.3	32,824	5.0	3.8	5.4
5 to 100	11,839	32.8	218,202	33.7	31.4	30.8
101 to 500	1,038	2.9	210,736	32.6	33.3	30.9
Over 500	195	0.5	185,477	28.7	31.4	32.8
Total*	36,129	99.5	647,244	99.8	99.9	99.9

* Includes enterprises that did not answer the questionnaire.
Source: IBGE. *Censo Industrial de 1960.*

The facts described above generally apply to the rest of the country also because of the influence of the economy of São Paulo upon the national economy.

The following are the figures on a national scale: in 1958 enterprises with 4 to 49 workers represented 87.41 percent of all plants in the country with 4 or more workers, and 27.41 percent of the value of production. Those with 50 to 249 workers represented 10.11 percent of the plants and 30.75 percent of the value of production. Those with 250 or more represented 2.48 percent of the plants and 41.84 percent of the value of production.[2]

But what is the role of the industrial sector in the whole economic activity of the country? Does the predominance of the large enterprise in the industrial sector have general economic significance? The figures show that the participation of the industrial sector not only has outstripped the other sectors in growth, but also has become fundamental to the national economy. From 1939 to 1963, in 1939 prices, the industrial sector rose from 17.9 percent of the national income

[2] Heítor Ferreira Lima, "Amparo a Pequena e Media Empresa," *Revista Brasiliense*, No. 32 (São Paulo), p. 23.

to 35.3 percent. In this same period the income from agriculture dropped from 33.3 percent to 21.0 percent of the total. The data on the composition of the labor force are less striking. This is because industrialization now uses modern technology to save labor. Thus, the percentage of the labor force in industrial manufacturing increased only from 7.70 percent in 1940 to 9.10 percent in 1960. Putting together the construction industries and the transportation, communication, and warehousing sectors, which complement the manufacturing sector, we note that these parallel sectors rose from 12.90 percent in 1940 to 17.30 percent in 1960. During this period the tertiary sector as a whole grew from 25.60 percent to 36.70 percent. The agricultural population decreased from 66.70 percent to 54.20 percent.[3]

These figures indicate that the industrial sector and the urban sectors are increasingly important in the whole economy, in spite of the still-existing importance of the agrarian sector. Agriculture has a very low rate of productivity. Although 54 percent of the laborers work in the countryside, agriculture represents only 21 percent of the national income. Thus it becomes less and less a determining factor in the national economy. Moreover, with the growth of industrialization, agriculture is being subordinated to industrial development and is becoming simply one of its branches, as is happening now in the more capitalistic areas of the country.

At this point another question may be raised. The basic sector is increasingly concentrated and occupies a strategic place in the economy. But is it, perhaps, a consumer goods industry, not integrated, and consequently not able to serve as the center of the industrial economy of the country? Computations based on census data indicate the development of the relationship between the sectors of production goods and of consumer goods. Production goods represented 28.9 percent, 38.1 percent, 41.5 percent, and 56.5 percent of the value produced by industry in 1920, 1940, 1950, and 1960.[4] The increase in the value of production from 1940 to 1960 was 508.0 percent for production goods and 248.8 percent for consumer goods.

Concentration is much greater in the basic industries established in the past years, especially from 1950 to 1960.

[3] Data from the Population Censuses of 1940, 1950, and 1960 in Brazil, taken from IBGE, *Anuario Estadistico de 1965*.
[4] Figures drawn from *Desenvolvimiento & Conjuntura* (February 1966), pp. 118-119.

A comparison between a traditional sector like the textile industry and a modern sector such as the chemical industry[5] may confirm our statement on the concentration of basic industry. The textile industry, in spite of its high concentration of labor, is of low productivity and is more or less stagnant. As a result of the changes previously described, it is losing its position of leadership in the economy. In 1960 this sector had 220 percent more enterprises and 420 percent more workers than the chemical industry. In spite of this, the value of its products was only 25 percent higher than that of the chemical industry. A decade earlier, in 1950, however, the value produced by the textile sector was 270 percent higher than that produced by the chemical industry. The mechanical industry, metallurgy, electrical equipment, communications, and chemicals produced 28 percent of the value of textile production of São Paulo in 1950. In 1960 they produced 200 percent of the productive value of this sector. These changes, in a span of 10 years, show the intense concentration that has taken place in basic industries.

Side by side with industrial concentration is the process of market monopolization. A recent study by the Institute of Social Sciences of the Federal University of Rio de Janeiro[6] lists 276 "economic groups" with capital assets of more than 900 million cruzeiros apiece. The multibillionaires, consisting of 55 groups, each with capital assets of over 4 billion cruzeiros, were studied separately. The multibillionaires are the indisputable leaders of the principal sectors in which they move, dominating "a substantial part of the production and circulation of goods." From among the "billionaires" (over 900 million and less than 4 billion) a sample was taken, consisting of 83 groups in an estimated universe of 221. Of these 83 groups, 10 foreign and 2 national groups were leaders (foremost or sole producers) in the principal activity in which they were engaged. A closer analysis of the foreign groups reveals that 14 of the 29 billionaire foreign groups operate in an oligopolistic market, four groups (all U.S.) work under con-

[5] In the study by José Carlos Pereira, "A estructura de sistema industrial en São Paulo," *Revista Brasileira de Ciências Sociais*, Vol. IV, No. 1 (June 1966), based on studies by the Centro Sociologica Industrial de São Paulo (CESIT), it is stated that the chemical industry is among the most modern sectors, and the textile industry, among the most backward.

[6] Mauricio Vinhas de Queiroz, "Os grupos multibillionarios"; Luciano Martins, "Os grupos bilionarios nacionais"; José Antonio Pessoa de Queiroz, "Os grupos bilionarios estrangeiros," *Revista de Instituto de Ciências Sociais* (Rio de Janeiro, 2 (1), 1965).

ditions—although very precarious—of monopoly, and nine groups work in a market with imperfect competition. The local billionaire groups have not been studied as closely; however, all indications are that they function in oligopolistic markets or in markets with imperfect competition, although they do not occupy the positions of leadership of the foreign groups. Aside from the data at the beginning of this chapter, which show that the large enterprises play a decisive role in the economy, the following data also indicate the oligopolistic nature of industrial markets (Table 3).

TABLE 3

OLIGOPOLY IN THE METALLURGICAL INDUSTRY OF SÃO PAULO

Branches of activity	Number of enterprises	Percent of production by 3 largest enterprises
Metal structures	8	76
Agricultural implements	9	97
Plows	17	76
Electric motors	9	86
Refrigerators	8	91
Washing machines	6	82
Scales	19	74
Elevators	6	99

Source: Industrial Directory for July 1963, taken from CEPAL, *Auge y declinación del proceso de substitución de importaciones en el Brasil.*

The monopolization of the market is not the only aspect of the general process of economic concentration. This process operates as well on the financial level. Financial concentration takes place through the process of integration between enterprises, or of the domination of several enterprises and different branches by a single group. The process of integration between enterprises takes place basically through "holding companies," or financial organizations that coordinate the operation of a certain group of enterprises. This system in Brazil has the general character of an interfamilial organization under the leadership of a family head. Of the 55 multibillionaire groups, 28 (50.9 percent) possess stock in the firms they integrate. The great majority are national groups of local origin (not immigrants). The foreign groups prefer direct control of their enterprises, which, as we shall see, are more integrated, especially in the more restricted sectors. This allows a greater monopoly of the market. In general, foreign companies own at least 90 percent of the stock in their Brazilian subsidiaries.

These groups are among the biggest international groups; and the degree of concentration in the industrial economy of the country is, therefore, even greater. The Brazilian economy is in the hands of increasingly more powerful groups, as shall be seen below.

Industrial concentration occurs alongside a great concentration of land ownership. The latifundium-minifundium system (which is based on production for the market by large estates, utilizing the labor of subsistence agriculturists) has grown in the past years. This has happened because capitalism has penetrated the agricultural sector without destroying the structure of land ownership and the traditional means of exploiting labor.

Figures taken from the Agricultural Censuses of 1950 and 1960 show that the number of large estates dropped from 2.38 percent to 0.98 percent of the total of agricultural units. Thus, although the area dominated by these estates also decreased from 50.98 percent to 47.29 percent, land-ownership concentration also increased slightly. On the other hand, the medium and large estates, from 10 to 1,000 "alqueires," retained more or less the same proportions. At the same time, there occurred an expansion of the small estates (less than 10 "alqueires") from 34.43 percent to 44.77 percent, the total area occupied rising from 1.30 percent in 1950 to 2.23 percent in 1960. This illustrates the conjunction of the two poles: latifundium-minifundium (Table 4).

TABLE 4

BRAZIL, LAND OWNERSHIP, 1950-1960
TOTAL AREA HELD BY SIZE OF ESTABLISHMENT, TOTAL AREA,
AND CULTIVATED AREA, IN PERCENTAGE

	1950					1960				
Size	Less than 10	10 to 100	100 to 1000	1000 to 10,000	10,000 and over	Less than 10	10 to 100	100 to 1000	1000 to 10,000	10,000 and over
Establishments	34.4	51.0	13.0	1.5	0.1	44.8	44.6	9.4	0.9	0.1
Total Area	1.3	15.3	32.5	31.5	19.4	2.2	18.0	32.5	27.4	20.0
Cultivated Area	8.9	45.4	33.3	10.8	1.6	13.3	44.7	30.5	10.0	1.5

Source: Agricultural Censuses of 1950 and 1960.

The control of land ownership is complemented by the control of agricultural commerce by financiers ("acaparadores") who dominate the purchase of agricultural products via their

control of credit. The study by the Institute of Social Sciences
has shown that the exporting-importing groups are given
financial support by the organization of banking enterprises.
The report by Heítor Ferreira Lima on Brazilian banks and
their connections[7] shows that a great part of the banking structure is connected with agricultural commerce; agriculture
itself, because of its technological backwardness, requires little
financing.

Analysis of the financing given to agriculture by the Bank
of Brazil shows that in 1964, 78 percent of the finances were
allotted to planting and marketing, and only 13 percent to
productive investments. To this must be added the loans from
the general credit funds for the marketing of agricultural
products, corresponding to about 30 percent of the value of
the agricultural budget.

Unfortunately, the figures from the Commercial Census of
1960 do not permit any conclusions on the tendency toward
concentration in this sector, where the existence of a large
number of small businessmen actually denotes concealed unemployment, side by side with the large groups that manipulate
its finances.

It is possible to make a general estimate of this process of
concentration in the banking sector by relating the number
of banks and banking agencies to the number of main offices.
From 1950 to 1964, according to the Statistical Annual of
Brazil, the number of banks and agencies increased from 2,596
to 6,878, while the number of main offices decreased from
413 to 328.

The study by Heítor Ferreira Lima[8] shows the connections
of the principal banking organizations with industry, commerce, and agriculture. Of the 29 foreign billionaire groups
in the sample, 14 engage in activities other than the principal
one; of the 55 foreign and local multibillionaire groups, 35
engage in other activities in addition to the principal one. Of
the 54 local billionaire groups, 31 are engaged in other activities. Among the local groups, a large number of other activities
not technologically related was noted. What this seems to indicate is a process of compensation for the losses in one sector
by benefits in another sector—a process that also leads to a
profound integration of the interests of big capital in the most
diverse sectors.

[7] Heítor Ferreira Lima, "Notas sobre a estrutura bancária brasileira,"
Revista Brasiliense, No. 8, pp. 147 *ff*.
   [8] *Op. cit.*

Finally, it should be emphasized that concentration proceeds from the productive sector (concentration of industrial enterprises, concentration of land ownership) to financial concentration (concentration of capital in holdings, banking concentration, etc.), to the concentration of the means of distribution (trade, utilities, etc.) and concentration of income. The income tax declarations of 1960, in spite of the great amount of cheating involved, gives a rough idea of the situation. While 92.8 percent of the juridical individuals declaring received an income of 18 billion cruzeiros, 0.03 percent got an income of 41.6 billion.

The state participates greatly in the productive activities of the country. It controls a great number of the large enterprises. According to a study by *Desenvolvimento & Conjuntura*, of the 34 local enterprises with capital assets each of over 1 billion cruzeiros in 1960, 19 were state-owned. Of these 19, 3 were among the 4 biggest enterprises in the country. In 1965 the enterprise occupying the second place on this list was nationalized, meaning that the biggest four of the 66 largest enterprises in the country are state enterprises.

The enterprise with the largest amount of capital assets (61.3 billion) in 1961 was the Rede Ferroviaria Nacional, which has the monopoly of railway transportation; the second was the Petrobras (40.0 billion), now one of the 500 largest enterprises in the Western World, which has the monopoly of petroleum production; the third was Brazilian Traction (23.5 billion), now nationalized, merging with Electrobras, which has control of the production and distribution of electricity. In the fourth place was the COSIPA, the great steel enterprise, of mixed but predominantly state capital. Fifth was Erminio de Morais, a private national group. In sixth place was the Vale do Rio Doce S.A. Company (7.8 billion), a state-owned iron mining and exporting company. Seventh, was the CEMIG (7.0 billion), producer and distributor of electricity, owned by the province of Minas Gerais. From there on are foreign and national private groups, more or less alternating with state enterprises. The process of monopoly, concentration, and rationalization aided by the state's role on the economy is still new: all the state enterprises mentioned were formed after 1950.

Consequently, the state bureaucracy has become important in the national economy, dominating basic sectors and gaining a certain independence of action vis-à-vis private groups. This permits greater economic concentration and monopoly and sets patterns of rational direction in sectors spread over the whole economy.

The role of the State in building large enterprises in the country and in organizing monopolistic markets and a concentrated and programmed economy merits a separate discussion, which we cannot enter here.

So far I have tried to show:

(1) that there is a growing tendency toward concentration in the industrial sector;

(2) that the industrial sector, particularly the basic sector, is becoming predominant in the country;

(3) that this process leads to a monopoly of the market;

(4) that concentration is occurring on the financial, commercial, and agrarian levels, as well as on the level of utilities; and

(5) that concentration is becoming even greater with the domination of the key sector of the economy (the large enterprise) by increasingly more concentrated international groups.

Because of the importance of the last item, the next part of this article is devoted to its discussion.

We have seen that the process of industrial concentration is closely followed by monopoly and financial concentration, and that foreign capital is its great beneficiary. It is important to get a picture of the general magnitude of foreign capital. This will assure us of the importance of the mechanisms for economic control that will be described later.

The entry of foreign capital during the postwar period in Brazil followed the same pattern described in the introduction for Latin America: it was intensified in the years 1956 to 1960, and dropped off from 1961 on. Through this increase in the entry of foreign capital, the balance between the entry and income of foreign capital became positive during the period between 1956 and 1963, resulting in a general positive balance for Brazil (but not for Latin America) in the years 1946 to 1963 (Table 5).

The balance of capital in the last years (although the data for 1964 still have to be confirmed) has started to show a deficit, indicating that the tendency toward an improvement of relations was due to the boom during the period from 1955 to 1961, when a large part of the earnings from foreign capital was reinvested in Brazil. On the other hand, it must be re-

TABLE 5

BRAZIL: COMPARISON BETWEEN NONCOMPENSATORY NET ENTRY
OF FOREIGN CAPITAL AND INCOME OF INVESTMENTS
(in millions of dollars)

Year	Total Entry (net)	Total Income	Difference
1946-50	5	398	−393
1951-55	478	717	−239
1956-60	1,469	758	711
1961	424	187	237
1962	458	202	256
1963	220	147	73
1964 (a)	−147	124	−271

Sources: *El Financiamiento Externo de América Latina*, Tables 150, 151, 152, and 153; and *Anuario Estadístico do Brasil*, for the years 1962 to 1964.
(a) Provisional data.

membered that the majority of investments in Brazil were made in accordance with "instrucción 113" of SUMOC, which permitted the duty-free entry of foreign machinery and equipment, resulting in subsidies and in excellent conditions for foreign investment in Brazil.

Further, the exit of foreign capital is not exhausted in the items taken account of by the CEPAL study. The payments for royalties and technical services are presented in the item "various services" of the balance of payments, which is always negative. Taking the figures for the years 1960 to 1964, we have the following: 1960, -159; 1961, -86; 1962, -61; 1963, -37; and 1964, -32. These examples show how the positive balances are significantly reduced if the cost of services (which includes royalties and technical services) is included. A computation based on these complete figures presents another result for the 1950's.

TABLE 6

BRAZIL: BALANCE BETWEEN THE ENTRY OF CAPITAL AND THE
REMITTANCES FOR ROYALTIES AND TECHNICAL SERVICES

YEAR	1948	1952	1954	1956	1958	1960
Balance (entry less remittances)	−70	−68	−128	−21	−9	−227

Source: SUMOC—Caio Prado Júnior—*Revista Brasiliense.*

In this instance, a deficit appears in all the years studied, thus showing the importance of indirect forms of remitting profits. This puts Brazil in the same position of decapitalization that characterizes the majority of the Latin American countries.

The data on the location of investments in the past years confirm the observation made in the introduction regarding their tendency to concentrate themselves in the industrial manufacturing sector. As may be seen in Table 7, about 50 percent of American investments are concentrated in industry. Within the industrial sector, according to the figures

TABLE 7

BRAZIL: VALUE OF UNITED STATES INVESTMENTS IN THE ECONOMIC
ACTIVITIES INDICATED (U.S. $1,000,000)

Year	Total	Mining & Smelting	Petroleum	Manufac- turing	Public Utilities	Others
1963	1,137	30	60	664	193	38
1964	994	34	51	673	41	42

Source: OEA, *América en Cifras.*

in the budget of the Comercio Externo del Banco do Brasil (CACEX), basic industry is the recipient of 80 to 90 percent of the investments, except in 1964. It must be considered, however, that the bulk ($5,051 million) of investment in light industries during this year went to the light mechanical and electrical industries (Table 8).

TABLE 8

BRAZIL: VALUE OF INVESTMENTS OF FOREIGN CAPITAL ACCORDING
TO INDUSTRIES (U.S. $1,000,000)

INDUSTRIES	1960	1961	1962	1963	1964
BASIC	70,987	24,975	10,611	7,240	3,092
LIGHT	14,461	7,365	3,713	1,179	7,278

Source: CACEX, with *Anuario Estadistico* of the IBGE.

The questions may be raised: what role do these investments play in the economy of the country? What percentage do they represent in the world economy? It is a question of knowing the significance of this external sector in the whole of the economy. The general estimate for the whole of Latin America, made by the CEPAL, is that the total of payments for the use of foreign capital in Latin America rose from 2.5 percent of the gross national product in 1951 to 3.4 percent in 1957, and then dropped to 3 percent in 1960. Relating the payment for services with the gross internal savings, in accordance with the same study, we have a growth from 16 percent in 1951 to 20.5 percent in 1959 for all Latin America.

Table 9 shows the relationship between the payments for the use of foreign capital and the income from the shares of the country. We can thus see the portion of the income obtained by the country through the export of goods and services that goes into the payment of the income of foreign capital. The figures show that this percentage has increased in the past decade because of the increase in this income, as well as the decrease in value of the exports. The percentage of services of foreign capital over the total income obtained through exports rose from 15.1 percent during the period from 1946 to 1950 to 39.4 percent in 1962, indicating that more than one-third of the shares of the country would be needed to pay for the services of foreign capital.

TABLE 9

BRAZIL: COMPARISON BETWEEN PAYMENTS FOR LONG-TERM
SERVICES OF FOREIGN CAPITAL AND INCOME OF SHARES
IN CURRENT ACCOUNT, 1946-1962 (%)

YEAR	Income from direct investments	Service of long-term foreign debt	Service of total long-term foreign capital
1946-50	5.0	10.1	15.1
1951-55	6.2	9.5	15.7
1956-60	4.0	26.5	30.5
1961	4.0	28.7	32.7
1962 (a)	6.3	33.1	39.4

Source: El Financiamiento Externo de América Latina, Tables 163-64.
a Provisional data.

Table 9 indicates the importance of the foreign debt of the country (and of all of Latin America, where similar tendencies are found); it increased relatively from 10.1 percent to 33.1 percent during this period. In Brazil the foreign debt increased from $423.7 million in 1945 to $2,224.6 million in 1962.[9] The relation between the service of public long-term foreign debt and the income in shares in current account grew from 17.1 percent in 1959-1961 to 20.3 percent in 1962-1965. This is to say that the country pays one-fourth of its shares for the service of its long-term foreign debt.

The result of this preliminary investigation is very clear: foreign capital has intensified its penetration in the past decade; this penetration is basically directed toward the manufacturing sector, particularly toward basic industry; and this

[9] Table 166 of Financiamiento Externo de América Latina.

penetration requires a high fee in the form of profits, interests, royalties, technical services, etc., and leads the economy into increasing indebtedness. We must now study the internal effects of this penetration. What type of relationship does it establish within the economy itself?

In the first place, we must determine the relative importance of foreign capital compared to national capital and the forms of penetration that it uses. The strategy used by foreign capital to gain internal control of the economy, whether by design or because of its own structural character, may be described in the following manner:

(a) The high degree of technological integration of foreign-owned enterprises permits them to confine themselves to specialized sectors of activity in which they control the market, together with national economic groups dispersed in various sectors of activity and without strong monopolistic conditions.

(b) Foreign capital seeks to penetrate sectors in which it can obtain control of the market, establishing conditions of monopolistic competition.

(c) It seeks to maintain financial independence for its enterprises, utilizing local financial sources for secondary purposes. This comes from the character of its investments, which are made largely in the form of transfer of machinery (often obsolete in the country of origin), which do not involve actual disbursements of fixed capital.

(d) External control over the policies of the enterprises is assured through the use of advanced administrative techniques, complemented by the employment of managers who are national citizens of high prestige. Advanced administrative techniques afford them superior conditions for competing against national enterprises based on the personal management of the proprietor.

We shall attempt to prove these hypotheses in the following section.

The principal source of our information for the proof of the foregoing hypotheses is the study, already cited, of the Instituto de Ciências Sociais da Universidade de Rio de Janeiro.

Of the 55 multibillionaire groups (more than 4 billion cruzeiros) in the country, 31 (56.4 percent) are foreign[10] and 24 (43.6 percent) are nationals. This means that foreign

[10] The report of the ICS of the U. R. S. separates two groups as mixed because it has not determined whether the control of capital lies in Brazil or outside the country. For purposes of simplification, these groups are considered as foreign in this study.

capital predominates among the most important groups of the Brazilian economy. Such predominance becomes even more impressive if we compare the amounts of capital held by these groups. Of the twenty-four national groups, 19 (79 percent of the total) have between 4 and 10 billion cruzeiros in capital; 18 foreign groups (58 percent of the total) are in this category. In the middle rank, between 10 and 20 billion cruzeiros, we have 3 national groups (14 percent), and 10 foreign groups (32 percent). In the highest rank of more than 20 billion, there are 2 national (10.8 percent) and 3 foreign groups (10 percent). This indicates a *tendency* toward a greater predominance of foreign groups in the ranks of higher capital assets.

Of the 24 national multibillionaire groups, only 9 (37.5 percent) have no stock-ownership by foreign groups or enterprises. It should be noted that 2 of these 9 groups have interlocking directorates with foreign groups. Another type of link is the appearance of prominent figures of a national group as directors of important foreign firms. Finally, there are other forms of connection through royalties or technical aid, which are not included in the study.

The conclusion is evident that the large national enterprises and the groups that control them are predominantly foreign, or they are either controlled by or interlocked with foreign groups.

The comparison in the billionaire sector (between 900 million and 4 billion) shows a lower degree of integration. (It will be remembered that the sample taken in this case consisted of 83 groups out of a total of 221.) Of the 83 groups in the sample, 54 (65 percent) are national and 29 (34 percent) are foreign.[11] (Of these foreign groups, as we shall see, 44.8 percent are American and 55.2 percent from other countries.) Of the 54 "national" groups, 25 (46 percent) have connections with foreign groups.[12]

The foreign groups of the whole universe (billionaires and multibillionaires) added to the national groups linked through share-ownership with foreign groups represent 68.4 percent of the economic groups with capital assets of more than 900 million cruzeiros, and therefore of the economic groups that

[11] Again we have 3 groups that are difficult to classify. In this case the authors of the investigation included these among the foreign groups.

[12] In the study made by the review *Desenvolvimento & Conjuntura* in 1960 on corporations with capital assets of more than 1 billion cruzeiros, of the 66 enterprises included, 32 were foreign and 34 were national. Of this last group, 19 were state-owned. This agrees with the findings of the study by the ICS.

control the national economy. This relation rises to 83.6 percent among the multibillionaires and is 64.7 percent among the billionaires.

In the case of the billionaire groups, the classification by value of capital does not reveal a predominance of foreign groups, since they are concentrated in the lower ranks. In the category from 900 million to $1.5 billion there are 19 foreign (65.5 percent) and 15 national groups (27.7 percent); between 1.5 billion and 3 billion, there are 10 foreign (34.5 percent) and 34 national groups (62.9 percent); and between 3 and 4 billion there are no foreign groups in the sample, but there are 5 national groups (9.2 percent). Other figures, however, contradict this appearance of superiority of the national sector among the billionaires. We shall see that to a lesser extent they have a similar status.

The comparison between the American groups and those of other countries shows the predominance of the former. Of the 31 foreign multibillionaire groups, 14 are American (2 are mixed American and national groups), 4 are German, 3 are British, and 2 are French. One group is Italian, 1 Swiss, 1 Dutch, 1 Argentine, 1 Canadian, 1 Anglo-Dutch, and 1 Anglo-Belgian-American. The American groups comprise 45 percent of the foreign multibillionaires, and 25 percent of the national and foreign multibillionaire groups taken together.

This predominance is also found among the billionaires, where the U.S. is represented by 13 groups (48 percent), and the other countries by 16 (52 percent) of the total foreign billionaire groups. Thus, American groups represent 48 percent of the foreign groups and 15.6 percent of the total of both national and foreign billionaire groups.

It is clear that foreign capital, particularly that from the U.S., prefers the industrial sector. In the 55 multibillionaire and 83 billionaire groups we see the following division by basic sectors (Table 10).

TABLE 10

ECONOMIC GROUPS BY SECTORS OF PRINCIPAL ACTIVITY

| Sectors | Billionaire Groups | | | | Multibillionaire Groups | | | |
| | Foreign | | National | | Foreign | | National | |
	No.	%	No.	%	No.	%	No.	%
Industrial	25	86.2	40	74.0	26	83.8	17	70.8
Commercial	2	6.8	10	18.5	4	12.9	3	12.5
Banking	2	6.8	4	7.4	1	3.2	4	16.6
Total	29	99.8	54	99.9	31	99.9	24	99.9

Source: ICS, Study on economic groups.

As was noted earlier, this preference for the industrial sector is of recent origin. The foreign groups generally were established in the country during the period following World War II, while the national groups, especially the multibillionaires, were formed during the First World War.

Another index of the integration of the foreign groups compared to the national groups is the relationship between the number of enterprises and the volume of capital. Among the multibillionaires the national groups have on the average 21 enterprises, and the foreign groups, 8. In total, the 24 national groups possess 506 enterprises; but their total capital represents 219 billion cruzeiros. On the other hand, the 31 foreign groups possess 234 enterprises and a total capital of 306 billion cruzeiros. The average capital by enterprise is, in the national category, 432 million, and in the foreign, 1,307 million.

Among the billionaire groups the number of enterprises in the national (on the average, 7.5 enterprises per group) and foreign groups (on the average, 7 enterprises per group) is about the same.

The multibillionaire groups generally have control of the market in their principal sectors of activity. Among the billionaires 10 foreign and 2 national groups are leaders in the sector of their principal activity.

The investigators sought to establish whether the groups controlling the market of important products are national or foreign. They established a scale that ranged from nonparticipation of other foreigners in the market in which they operated to complete control (over 90 percent) of this market by foreign groups. This may be summarized in this table:

TABLE 11

DEGREE OF CONTROL OF THE MARKET BY FOREIGN BILLIONAIRE GROUPS

Degree of control	Foreign Groups	%	U.S. Groups %		Non-U.S. Groups %	
Over 90% foreign	10	34	6	46	4	25
Great	9	31	6	46	3	19
Medium	4	14	1	8	3	19
Little	6	21	—	—	6	38
Total	29	100	13	100	16	100

Source: ICS, Study on economic groups.

It may be noted that about two-thirds of the foreign billionaire groups of the sample operate in fields under great or total (over 90 percent) control by foreign groups. Among the foreign groups the U.S. groups operate in sectors where they have complete or great control and do not operate in sectors under little foreign control.

Of great interest are the figures on the degree of monopoly of the market in which the foreign groups operate, and their position in the market. Four groups (all American) operate in a monopolized or almost monopolized market, and 14 groups in oligopolistic markets (defined as those in which a maximum of 30 groups operate). If we study these groups according to their position in the market, in relation to the national billionaires, we have a clear picture of the monopolistic positions occupied by the foreign groups, particularly the American groups.

TABLE 12

POSITION OF THE BILLIONAIRE GROUPS IN THE MARKET

Position in the market	Foreign Groups	%	American Groups	%	Non-American Groups	%	National Groups	%
Predominant core, or first producer, or only producer	17	59	11	85	6	37	8	15
Outside the predominant core	12	41	2	15	10	63	46[a]	85
Total	29	100	13	100	16	100	54	100

Source: ICS—Investigation of economic groups.
[a] Closer investigation may change this figure but not significantly.

We see that 59 percent of the foreign groups are in the predominant core of the market and only 41 percent are outside of it. The situation is different among the national billionaire groups, where only 15 percent hold controlling positions in the market in which they operate.

Foreign capital tends to be more specialized, operating in technologically integrated sectors; this enables it: (a) to obtain a high degree of enterprise and financial concentration; and (b) to control the market in which it operates, not only occupying important positions of leadership but also obtaining control of the whole sector of production.

The phase of monopoly capitalism is characterized by the dominance of the managers of the large enterprises over the other sectors of capitalism. Finance capital, particularly important at the beginning of the twentieth century, is losing its importance as the integrator of the system to the extent that the gigantic multinational enterprises have their own internal financial sources. The production of the modern great enterprise is becoming the strategic center of the economic system.

The high technological and monopolistic integration of foreign capital in Brazil seems to indicate that these economic mechanisms of monopoly capitalism are being introduced in the "developing countries."

This, however, occurs within a completely different socioeconomic framework, producing different results. In these countries a large part of the population is not integrated in the capitalist market, while a great displacement is also going on, of people from the rural areas going to the city in search of employment. In addition, the rate of population growth is very high.

The high degree of technological integration is an obstacle to the increase in employment; on the other hand, monopolistic control of the market limits the need for its expansion by enterprises that can obtain high profits by intensifying their exploitation of the available market instead.

Foreign capital seeks to maintain the financial independence of its enterprises, utilizing local financial sources for secondary purposes; this may be deduced from the nature of their investments, which occur largely in the form of transfer of machinery, which does not imply actual disbursements from fixed capital.

Among the foreign multibillionaire groups only 3 groups had minority control of stocks. In general, a control of 90 percent, and in some cases 80 percent, is found. In a union of associated foreign groups this pattern is maintained. Among the national groups the control of the enterprises is carried out through a minority of stocks, a method generally used by the corporations.

Among the foreign billionaire groups the same pattern occurs. From a classification into 5 groups (A—with almost 100 percent of the capital coming from outside the country; B—with some national capital; C—with a minor but substantial part of the capital belonging to nationals; D—with the majority of capital belonging to nationals but controlled from outside; E—with doubts about the location of the center of decisions) we have the following results: 12 groups (41 percent) are in class A; 7 (24 percent), in class B; and 6 (21 percent) are in class C. Thus, 86 percent of the foreign groups have capital largely from foreign sources. Only 14 percent are in classes D (3.5 percent) and E (10.5 percent).

What could be behind this pattern? It may be because of

the absence of a market of organized capital, which would allow foreign groups to associate with constituted groups; or it may be because of the reason proposed earlier—that foreign corporations are not interested in capitalizing in the country since they bring fixed capital in the form of obsolete machinery already paid for in the country of origin, and rely upon subsidies and state finances.

On the other hand, it must be emphasized that the sale of stocks in the national market would not change the situation. The foreign economic groups would have control of the enterprises in the same manner. The so-called "democratization" of capital only enables a smaller organized group to gain control of the capital of the millions of dispersed stockholders who remain unable to influence the policies of the enterprise.

Finally, foreign capital uses more advanced administrative techniques, in contrast with the structure of national capital, where ownership-control, exercised by family heads and their relatives, predominates. The foreign groups are directed by managers entrusted with the rational execution of policies in the interest of the group, which is the meeting point of their international and national interests.[13] The national groups are controlled by family groups among whom are distributed the stocks and the duties of management. Of the national multibillionaires only 3 do not proceed according to family structure. Among the national billionaire groups 40 follow family structure, 7 groups are formed through the meeting of isolated managers, and only 2 groups could be considered as administrators.

The study on billionaire groups classified the types of directors into: A—*Professionals* who participate as stockholders and directors of various enterprises of the group; B—*Trustees* of foreign stockholders; C—*Experts* entrusted with technical

[13] The "rationality" of this policy occurs without difficulty in administrative questions. However, it becomes more complex in the policy of investments and market acquisitions. In this case the interests of the "multinational corporation" can—and, in general, this actually occurs —clash with the interests of the "national" enterprises. This takes place when profits are remitted outside the country instead of being reinvested; and when, because of the desire for higher profits or for political motives, the expansion of sales of the enterprises of certain countries is preferred to the detriment of others. Finally, the high degree of decapitalization to which the enterprises of the underdeveloped countries submit, by paying rigged prices for products they buy from their own home sources, makes its policies hardly "rational" for the economics of the underdeveloped countries. These and other aspects of the problem are discussed by Paul Baran and Paul Sweezy, *Monopoly Capital* (New York: Monthly Review Press, 1966).

decisions in accordance with norms established by other directors in the country or outside the country. Directors of Type A were found in 17 groups of the sample (59 percent of the total). As to the recruitment of national directors (generally of Type C) by foreign groups, it was established that "almost 60 percent of the groups recruited their principal managers in the countries from which the capital controlled by the group originated;" the proportion of American groups that entrusted the administration of their interests in Brazil to local managers is greater. The study was not able to determine to what extent this is because of the less decisive power held by the managers of the American enterprises.

Conclusions

The presentation and discussion of the data have shown:

1. The dominance of foreign capital in our economies.

2. The intensified penetration of foreign capital in recent years.

3. The high profits obtained by foreign capital, intensified by other forms of remuneration (technical services, royalties, inflation of costs of imported goods, etc.).

4. Its increasing flow into the industrial sectors.

5. Its tendency to organize large enterprises in the developing countries, which are integrated with large "multinational enterprises."

6. The conditions of superior competition to which they give rise.

These conclusions suggest some more general considerations. The tendency of the underdeveloped economies toward integration with international monopoly capital cannot possibly be counteracted within the framework of a competitive economy in which foreign capital is palpably superior. Consequently, the national capitalist classes do not have the capacity to lead the struggle for national independence in our countries.

The process of integration has a profound internal contradiction: while it introduces highly advanced forms of production in economies where very backward forms and relationships of production remain on a large scale, it does not generate sufficient incentive to break away from these forms. Not only does it create an unsatisfactory employment rate in the face of increasing population, but it also fails to lead to the expansion of the market and consequently to agrarian reform on the same level as the economic impact that it produces.

Finally, it produces the decapitalization of economies with already impoverished capital sources, and tends to control the state and the economy in order to consecrate this paralyzing and exploiting socioeconomic form.

Uruguay: Promise and Betrayal

EDUARDO GALEANO

Uruguay, a widely touted example of welfare-state capitalism in Latin America, has now made clear the limits to such development for her neighbors. Early political and social reforms that left untouched the basic distribution of ownership and control of the economy, especially the agrarian sector, and the emergence of a large state bureaucracy and its dependent middle class, from spurs to development have now become major obstacles. The strategic economic and political position of the exporting "oligarchy," Galeano argues, has not been touched; as a result, the country's status as an agricultural export economy dependent on world market fluctuations, and the stagnation in agricultural productivity, are seriously shaking the "Switzerland of America."

THIS SICK COUNTRY, stricken by an economic crisis and increasing political instability, was previously the testing ground for exciting and audacious social experiments that served as an example for the rest of the Latin American countries. A weak bourgeoisie, which nevertheless started out with strong social reform tendencies, and which was gifted with a relatively high level of enlightenment, effected important reforms that even today are envisioned as prospective conquests by their neighbors. Secret balloting, the democratization of political life, the nationalization of the main public services and of the insurance companies, the protection of the worker through an ambitious system of social security and social assistance, the eight-hour workday, the divorce law, the separation of church and state, and the dissemination of free secular education were all characteristic parts of a whole array of proposed and attained objectives of the first years of the present century, brought about under the influence of the creative capacity and the long-range political vision of Don José Battle y Ordoñez. This urban caudillo with positivistic training—who found the country torn by the civil war—was able to carry forward a program similar to that effected by other contemporary or succeeding Latin American leaders, such as Irigoyen in Argentina, Vargas in Brazil, the first Alessandri in Chile, Calles and Cardenas in Mexico, etc. Because of the confluence of a series of favorable factors, Battle was able to precede in time his political counterparts in other countries, and in many aspects he went even further than they. Since those times the harmonious equilibrium of its institutions, the exceptional climate of freedom, and the relatively high educational level of most of the population gave Uruguay a certain aura of prestige that allowed it to play a "good" international role. In fact, it was unique to find in Latin America a country like Uruguay that did not exhibit such violent social contrasts—between the offensive wealth of a minority and the sordid misery of the vast majority—as characterized the region. And it was highly unusual, as it still is, to find that neither the church nor the army intervened in the affairs of the state.

Today many of the above-mentioned virtues belong to ancient history, and others that have proven to be none-too-virtuous have brought to light their negative side. The middle class, which is in the majority, constitutes a cushion for social frictions and in many aspects is a guarantor of stability *in times of progress*. But *in times of crisis* this middle class is also the source of the strongest resistances to effecting the needed changes. Its political conformity turns the middle class into the involuntary accomplice of an oligarchy that because of its egocentrism, its blindness, and its power is increasingly indistinguishable from the typical Latin American oligarchies. Two other examples could be cited to illustrate how, at the time when the myth of the "Switzerland of the Americas" collapses, its positive traits could precipitate rather than prevent the downfall. The social security system and the management of the nationalized enterprises furnish, in effect, sufficient material to pass judgment on this. In the last years, the country has suffered from an accelerated process of internal deterioration of its entire social security system. Political speculation at the expense of the pensions has converted the right of the elderly to a dignified retirement into a fountain of favors that the politicians in charge of the system have been exchanging for votes. The distortion of the principles themselves that serve as inspiration for the system brings forth an irrational growth of the inactive population. The retirement system "protects," with a cloak of misery, a great number of workers who are still young and whose prospects for working are limited as a result of the general economic crisis. After age 55 only two of every three men remain economically active. Comparative data for seventy other countries indicate that such a low "activity ratio" following that age is found only in Uruguay. In addition, the decline in this ratio starts as early as age 45. The life expectancy of the inactive Uruguayans is unusually high (40 percent) in relation to that of the inactive population of industrialized (33 percent) as well as underdeveloped countries (less than 25 percent). Concomitantly, an equally irrational swelling of the entire bureaucratic machinery has taken place; the public offices serve to absorb a substantial portion of the unemployment labor force from the cities and the countryside. Thus, to the 350 thousand retired workers must be added, in a sense, a considerable number of the 230 thousand Government employees. A large, though difficult to estimate, percentage of the latter constitutes a parasitic bureaucracy that is only nominally included in the economically *active population*. To get an idea of the enormous weight that these figures carry, it would be sufficient to bear in mind that the active population of Uruguay is only slightly above a million people, of which 170 thousand are unemployed because of the partial or total shutdown of many factories.

Both of the major parties, the Colorado Party and the National ("Blancos" or "white") Party, share the responsibility for the deterioration of the social security system and the public enterprises in general. For many years these two major political parties have been ruling jointly in Uruguay through a power-sharing system that has experienced slight formal modifications in the last two constitutions, ratified in 1951 and

1966. The framework of this political system is so complexly interwoven that the "minority" is inevitably rendered the accomplice of the "majority." The National or the Colorado opposition shares the benefits of the National or the Colorado government. Up until some time ago a sketchy analysis of the local political picture could uncover a basis for opposition between the two parties, with roots in the opposing interests represented by them. The Colorado Party was liberal and could be regarded until a few years ago as the representative of the weak industrial bourgeoisie and the urban middle class. Both these groups had their genesis in the port of Montevideo under the influence of the two world wars and the capitalistic crisis of 1929. The conservative National Party was regarded as the champion of the landlords and of the agrarian population, which was politically tied to the caudillos. The traditional opposition between the Colorados and the Blancos was born out of the civil wars of the past century. The port businessmen —who later became the pioneers of the crumbling national industrial system—had as their enemies the landowners, who resisted with arms the invasion of the wire fences and the railroads of the British Empire. Today both of the big political parties are essentially indistinguishable. In the twentieth century the interests of the bourgeoisie and of the landlords are already intermingled, and both groups accept obediently and enthusiastically the dependent functions to which imperialism relegates the enterprises that these political forces manage jointly.

Today the opposition between the two parties is not the result of two differing conceptions of the destiny of the country. There is no National Government program as opposed to that of the Colorado; both parties fall to the left when they talk and to the right when they act. They have both ceased to be political parties in the real sense of the term, and are nothing more than chaotic conglomerations that bring together men of the most diverse and contradictory personal ambitions and of every kind of political tendency and interest. To this unarticulated "ideological" identity—which could be regarded as an absence of any and all ideologies—can be added an identity of action. Both parties deal with certain formulas that allow them to take turns in power, in the manner of the liberals and the conservatives of Colombia but with the aggravating condition that in Uruguay both parties are in control of the reins of the Government together. The Uruguayan political machinery—which is a factory of favors for a "clientele" expanded by the economic crisis that ails the nation—has two bosses. It was no accident that the recently amended Constitution, which had been unanimously rejected by the trade unions, was born out of an agreement between both parties.

The atomization of the two big parties has not hurt them arithmetically. Thanks to the complex system of the "law of symbols" the different candidates of the various groups, subgroups, and sub-subgroups accumulate votes, which are assigned to the person who obtains a majority under each of the "symbols" of the two parties, *white* or *red*. This system assures the perpetuation of both parties in power, even if they are torn apart by internal conflicts and have lost all traces of ideological coherence. In 1958 the National Party won the elections, after 93 consecutive years of Colorado majorities. In 1966 the Colorado Party recovered its position. This is the phenomenon of party *rotation* in the sharing of power. The winning candidate in these elections, who is under the *red* symbol, gained the *presidency* of the country, since the Collegiate was condemned out of existence by the same parties that brought it to life 15 years ago. This *rotation* engenders, with every election, hopes for change. In this latest instance the Government has, in addition, the confidence that the majority of the people have in the presidential system. The two big political parties did not find it difficult to convert the Collegiate system into the scapegoat of the crisis for which both of them were responsible, through action or inaction. The trick consisted in making the people believe that it was not deep and irreversible structural factors but superficial institutional conditions that caused the problems. The key to the survival of the political monopoly exercised by these two parties lies precisely in their ability to maneuver. This also explains why an acute crisis in the socioeconomic arena and the discrediting of the professional politicians has not led Uruguay to a *coup d'état*. Uruguay is the only Latin American country that has not suffered a military takeover, even though conditions have been propitious for this. In Uruguay "institutional stability" has its genesis in the changes that the institutions undergo to survive. But a system that is compelled to change its constitution every 15 years is admitting, unintentionally, its basic *instability*.

The moderating and determinant presence of a middle-class majority allows Uruguay to "change without changing" quite often. Neither the sudden banking crisis of 1965 nor the succession of increasingly violent strikes, nor the mass layoffs of workers, nor the scandal of the sudden accumulation of fortunes with each devaluation of the peso prevented the moralizing tone of the proposed constitutional reform from being effective. The same politicians who had imported and dealt in cars without paying taxes wrote the constitutional proviso that prevents them from using the privilege that they had granted to themselves. Those responsible for corruption and chaos in politics and in public administration have promised honesty and order with the new constitution. The Blancos and the Colorados assert that the new Magna Carta will eliminate the "three and two" system, through which the division of the management of the government corporations between the majority and the minority had been institutionalized. However, in reality, the only thing changed is the *procedure* for choosing the directorates of these corporations; both parties will continue to participate jointly in the directorates.

With the end of the Korean conflict, when Uruguay could no longer benefit from high prices for its export products, the already latent crisis was not long in coming. From 1957 on, the country began to suffer the consequences of the deterioration of the terms of trade, which was common to all of those countries producing raw materials and foodstuffs. Uruguay had to sell an increasing amount of wool in order to purchase the same tractor. With 1951 as the base period, the value of imports was about the same in 1961 (the index was 100), but the value of exports had fallen to 58.2. To the price deterioration is added a decline in the volume of exports. Like all Latin American countries, Uruguay's trade is essentially concerned with nonmanufactured goods. Since the production of these agricultural goods is stagnant while domestic consumption goes up with the increase in the population of the country, the amount of goods available for export becomes increasingly smaller. The constant deficit in the balance of trade has devastating consequences because Uruguay is a monocultural economy that depends on what it sells and cannot develop without buying goods. Uruguay's balance of trade deficit originates from the drop in prices, which is due to the foreign monopoly of the international markets, and a decline in production, which is the result of the internal property system, which redounds to the benefit of the landholding hierarchy.

The prosperity previously enjoyed by the country was not firmly grounded and hence deteriorated because of various causes, leading rapidly toward crisis. The weak basis of the country's prosperity was crudely exposed. Per capita gross domestic product declined 14 percent between 1957 and 1964. Manufacturing suffered the consequences of the contraction of the domestic market: the semiparalyzed factories are using only 60 percent of their productive capacity; the School of Economic Sciences estimated that there were 177 thousand workers without permanent employment in 1966. There are no jobs in industry, whose precarious structure was hit hard by the crisis. There are even fewer jobs in agriculture, where an unproductive and voracious system of large estates reigns.

Six hundred families are the owners, directly or indirectly, of about half the total arable land. On their vast unpopulated plains the rams, the bulls, and the rains are in charge of the spontaneous creation of wealth. Wool, meat, and wheat, produced under rudimentary conditions without the modern techniques of intensive production, are the country's main, and practically its only, sources of income. The destiny of Uruguay is tied up to the fluctuations of the prices of these items.

In spite of his good intentions, Battle could not include the Agrarian Reform among his accomplishments at the beginning of the century. The economic frustration of Uruguay was born out of this fundamental omission. This systematic "forgetfulness" of the bourgeoisie makes possible its present harmonious alliance with the landholding power, at the expense of sacrificing the only possible basis for an independent and solid industrial development. Lacking an expanding domestic market and an increasing pool of resources, industry, which had emerged as a conditioned reflex of foreign crisis, lost its footing. Neither the Blancos nor the Colorados have proven to be able to break, when they have entered the Government, the backbone of the oligarchy, which is the ownership of land. In spite of the fertility of the soils and the optimal climatic conditions, production is stagnant and even regresses, if the population growth is taken into consideration. The following table is rather eloquent:

CHANGES IN THE NUMBER OF LIVESTOCK		
Census	*Cattle*	*Sheep*
1908	8,192,600	26,286,300
1961	8,792,400	21,724,600

In 1908 there were 8 head of cattle and 25 sheep for each inhabitant. In 1961 there were only 3 head of cattle and 8 of sheep per person. Thus, the decline in per capita production is vertical.

The productivity indexes are at least as eloquent. Productivity is necessarily low in a country where only 3.6 percent of the total area under cultivation consists of reclaimed prairies. The big landowners do not invest in adopting new technology and improving production, but rather they export very large fortunes to their anonymous accounts in Swiss banks or build luxurious chalets on the coasts of Punta del Este. A sheep in Uruguay yields less than 4 kilos of wool, compared to almost 5 kilos in Australia and slightly less than 6 in New Zealand. To produce a ton of beef, Uruguay must have a stock of twice as many animals as France or Germany. The disequilibrium in crop yields is at least the same. Uruguay produces 772 kilos of wheat per hectare, compared to 2,507 for France; its corn yields are 564 kilos, compared to 3,521 for the United States. Each hectare of potatoes brings forth 15,070 kilos to Canada and 20,954 to the United States, compared with only 4,688 for Uruguay; sugar beets yields are twice as high in the United States as in Uruguay.

The Uruguayan economy has the lowest demographic growth rate in Latin America. Between 1930 and 1965 the Latin American population increased by 131 percent, while the increase for Uruguay was only 52 percent. Concomitantly, Uruguay has the highest percentage of urban population in the region: more than 80 percent of its population live in the cities. The other side of the coin of the big rural estates (latifundia) is the disproportionate growth of the "tertiary" sector of the economically active urban population. The startling growth of the "service" sector is not the result of economic development, but rather an index of underdevelopment, with all the distortions it implies. In fact, the "tertiary sector" weighs proportionally the same in Uruguay as in the United States, although the per capita income of Uruguay is only a fifth of that of the United States. Even though Uruguay is an agricultural country, relying for its livelihood on the foodstuffs it exports, only 18.5 percent of its active population—less than a fifth of the total—can be included in the "primary" sector. The latifundium system does not replace labor with machinery; "nature" does all the work, with the results we have observed.

As in Orwell's famous formula, in this democracy we are all equal, but some are more equal than others. Poverty and wealth are separated from one another as the blades of a pair of scissors, the rich becoming richer and the poor, poorer. This is the bitter and predictable fruit of the bourgeois' inability to bring about the economic development of the country. The establishment of a welfare state does not prove that the Uruguayan bourgeoisie is any more capable of fulfilling this historic function than other Latin American bourgeoisies. Having ceased its wave of accomplishments 40 years ago, the Uruguayan bourgeoisie is today an integral part of the constellation of power of the landholding oligarchy. The frontiers of its own power as a differentiated class are blurred to such an extent that it is not surprising to find that the Blancos and the Colorados have erased their political differences also.

Four percent of the industrialists control 70 percent of the capital invested in industry. The crisis has not harmed the all-powerful businesses of the same families whose surnames can be found among the directorates of the banks and of the most important business firms, which are, in addition, the owners of the land. Where the tide rises, the first ones to drown are the shortest. Many former small industrial entrepreneurs prefer today the devaluated but secure salary of a public employee, rather than the risks that the crisis makes them face as small capitalists. The situation of the powerful industrial concerns is quite different. They are intimately linked to foreign capital, and most of them are also tied to the large domestic and foreign middlemen. Furthermore, as we indicated before, the power of these industrial concerns is also measured in hectares.

It is not an accident that the famous international resort of Punta del Este is worth more than the entire national industry; nor is it by accident that it is in the same country.

The national and international decline in prestige of the Government-run enterprises contributes effectively to implement those policies that are most advantageous to the big landowners, the bankers, and the rentiers. Neither banking nor foreign trade have ever been nationalized in Uruguay. By means of financial speculation and through the control of exports and imports, foreign capital is draining a large portion of the wealth that the country produces. "Free exchange" and "free competition" make this possible. A complex machinery has been assembled for the purposes of looting, which has turned Uruguay into a "country of middlemen." The suction

pump is set in operation when credit is granted at very high
interest rates and when very low prices are set for the products
of the medium and small farmers. This process continues at
the export and import ports by means of the very expensive
freight and insurance charges. The process of looting ends in
the so-called international markets—which are controlled by
the gigantic trusts of the developed countries—where
Uruguayan products, as that of the entire Third World, are
systematically underpriced. Equally as grave is the "denationalization" of a great deal of the industrial capital of Uruguay.
The association, or rather, the identification of the urban
bourgeoisie with the landholding oligarchy thus coincides with
the sellout to foreign capital. The process of transference of
national industry to foreign hands is not, to be sure, an exclusive Uruguayan characteristic. This phenomenon has increasingly occurred in Latin America in the last few years.
It is difficult to measure the real extent of the imperialist
penetration in this respect, since it is almost never *apparent*.
Some enterprises continue to operate as if they were "national," although they are really nationals of the United States.
Brazil constitutes a typical example of a more or less disguised
"denationalization" of industry. It is well to note that the
plunder takes place without an increase in direct foreign
investments, simply by the appropriation by the creditor of
the goods of the delinquent debtor, or by the near-gratis
acquisition of the bankrupt enterprises, which continue to be
Brazilian, Uruguayan, or Argentinian enterprises, but only
in name.

The exploitation by foreign capital is even worse as a
consequence of the application of the "prescriptions" developed by the International Monetary Fund in order to "solve"
the problem of inflation in Latin America, fighting its effects
but strengthening its causes. The freezing of wages, the contraction of domestic credit, the war against public enterprises,
and the "green light" given to foreign products and capital,
in addition to the privileges granted to the traditional exporters, are all guidelines prescribed by the IMF. These
policies were adopted by the National Party during its two
administrations. The Colorado Party, which won the 1966
elections, took power under circumstances that, according to
specialized observers, would force it to develop its program
within the confines of these preestablished coordinates.

The suffocating pressure of the external debt determines, to
a great extent, that this would take place. This is the old

chicken-and-the-egg problem. Since the country is in a crisis, it is becoming increasingly indebted; in attempting to pay its debts, the country acquires more debts, and the crisis worsens. In 1967 alone, the Government has to pay about a hundred million dollars. Since exports are stagnant or declining—except for an occasional "respite"—they cannot bring forth enough currency to meet these short-run obligations. Therefore, it is necessary to refinance the debt. And this refinancing depends on the will of the International Monetary Fund, upon whose decisions rely the foreign banks that are creditors of Uruguay. The policy imposed by the IMF implies—as noted by the economist Pedro Sere—*the stabilization of the demand in a country that is notably afflicted by an inflation on the supply side,* and where income is declining, production is lower; consequently less and less is sold and at lower prices. In this way an attack is launched against the symptoms of inflation, thus vainly pruning the leaves while leaving untouched the roots, which feed themselves on the "remedy" itself and continue fostering inflation at a fast-moving pace. The cost of living increases without respite while the internal and external purchasing power of money declines. In 1963 one could buy a dollar with eleven pesos. Today, at the moment this article is being written, the same dollar is worth eighty pesos.

Between 1955 and 1966 the cost of living increased nineteen times. In a single year, 1965, prices went up 80 percent, while real wages have been going down. With 1957 considered as the base period (purchasing power equaled 100), the industrial real wage dropped to 85 percent in 1966. Even the income of the Government employees went down from 100 percent to 63 percent between 1961 and 1966. Can one speak, in this case, of an "excess demand"? The deterioration of the wage level shows that a "cost inflation" cannot be ascribed to this.

To the producers and sellers of wool and meat—which provide the currency for the payment, even when late, of the foreign creditors—the crisis turns out to be an excellent business. An official estimate recently made public uncovered data from which it can be asserted that since 1960 the total income transferred to the agricultural sector amounted to at least 150 million dollars. This sum of money, which is the official reward of the big exporters, was channeled in its entirety toward nonproductive investments, such as tourism, monetary speculation, foreign investments, and purchases of real estate and luxury articles. In contrast, the wages of the agricultural labor force—the poverty-stricken *peonadas*—declines rather than increases. Inflation has also been favorable to the most important banks, which have gained more money than ever through the successive devaluations of the peso, through their abusive interest rates, which are incredibly high, and through loans they grant to their subsidiary firms (a procedure of dubious legality). The big rentiers and the foreign export firms have also benefited and have experienced a sudden growth of their fortunes. The lowering of the duties for export articles raised the amount of pesos received for the same dollar value of a kilo of wool, meat, or wheat.

The constitutional reform was not the result of whimsical circumstances. The forty-five amendments of the previous constitution, intended to strengthen the executive power, allows the present government to carry out a policy of "stabilization" in a more relaxed manner. In addition, the new Magna Carta will facilitate the suppression of the labor movement. It is no accident that while the trade unions rejected, without exception, the newly born constitution, the Rural Federation—an association of big landowners—joyfully applauded it.

The fact that the reform was accepted by the majority of the people in free elections offers clear evidence that in Uruguay there is an incongruency between trade union and political consciousness. The National Workers' Confederation, which contains the vast majority of the working-and middle-class unions, unleashed, on the eve of the elections, a violent and sustained campaign against the constitutional reform that both parties had worked out and agreed on. Nevertheless, the reform triumphed. The class consciousness exhibited by the workers in their arduous struggles in the trade unions was not projected into the sphere of political decisions. In the same manner, although the left does not get any more than 6 or 7 percent of the votes in the elections, the leftist militants are the ones who lead the organized labor movement; the masses follow them when a union mobilization is called, but not at the moment of casting their ballots. The Uruguayan trade union movement is among the best-structured and most clearly oriented in the whole of Latin America. However, the emotional adherence to the Blanco and the Colorado banners, passed on from generation to generation, and the fear of change characteristic of the middle-class majority are more powerful than the consciousness acquired in the course of continuous harsh confrontations between workers and management. The working class—laborers and public employees alike—does not yet know how to differentiate between nostalgia and hope; it votes to recuperate a certain lost stability, but it does not plunge into the adventure of a radical change capable of providing it with surprises.

Mexico: The Dynamics of an Agrarian and "Semicapitalist" Revolution*

PABLO GONZÁLEZ CASANOVA

Mexico had a revolution, González maintains, that broke the base of feudalism in the country, and made national development possible, and the emergence of new strata—industrialists, urban and rural middle classes, and skilled workers. However, it took only the "anti-colonial step," he believes, to development of a "semicapitalist" type. It was a revolution that—in the thirties, at least—had as one of its most important phases, an alliance between the industrialists and peasants against the large landowners and foreign capitalists. Yet even this instance of a "successful bourgeois revolution" in Latin America, González believes, has been "semicapitalist" and restricted in its evolution. The country has yet to develop its own heavy industry or attain economic, political or cultural independence from the United States, upon whom it remains dependent as a market for its raw materials and a source of supply for manufactured goods.

Pablo González Casanova, Professor of Sociology and Director of the Instituto de Investigaciones Sociales of the University of Mexico, is author of La Democracia en México (Mexico: Siglo XXI, 1965), a translation of which is forthcoming in English by Oxford University Press.

* Reprinted with extensive revisions from Studies on Developing Countries, Vol. I (Warsaw: Polish Scientific Publishers, 1964), pp. 171-198.

MEXICO IS no longer the example for the rest of Latin America. Many Latin Americans and many people from outside Latin America are asking what happened in Mexico. They want to know from the Mexicans themselves whether or not the Revolution has failed. They want to know why our Revolution has not been a socialist revolution. They want to know what is happening today. And they want to know whether or not another revolution is possible, or what is the road that must be followed. These are also more or less the same questions that we often hear among ourselves. . . .

When the economic and social conditions of Mexico are compared with those of some of the more advanced countries of Latin America, the conclusions reached are not flattering.[1]

Mexico has economic, social, and political indices much higher than those of Colombia, Bolivia, Peru, and even, sometimes, Brazil, not to mention the countries of Central America. The high figures for mortality, infant mortality, illiteracy, malnutrition, population engaged in agriculture, working population not organized, population not voting, the present state of

[1] *Statistical Abstract of Latin America for 1957*, Committee of Latin American Studies, University of California, Los Angeles. *Statistical Abstract of Latin America 1960*, Center of Latin American Studies, University of California, Los Angeles. *Second World Food Survey*, Food and Agricultural Organization of the United Nations, Rome, November 1952. Mexico has a gross mortality rate of 12.5 per thousand (1958), higher than that of Chile (12.1), Peru (10.3), and Argentina (8.1). Infant mortality in Mexico (80.8 per thousand live births in 1958) is higher than that of Argentina (66.3). The number of persons per practicing physician is in Mexico 2,200 (1955), while in Chile it is 1,900 (1954), and in Argentina 760. According to figures published by the FAO, the population suffers a calorie deficit of 24.4 percent, while that of Argentina enjoys a surplus of 22.7 percent (1950). The urban population in Mexico is 42.6 percent of the total (1950), while in Chile it is 59.9 percent (1950), and in Argentina it is 62.5 percent (1950). The percentage of illiterates is in Mexico 43.2 percent (1950), while in Chile it is 19.4 percent (1952), and in Argentina 13.3 percent (1947). In Mexico there are 48 newspapers per 1,000 inhabitants (1952), while in Argentina there are 159 (1956), and in Chile 74 (1952).

Economic and political indices show a similar situation: per capita income is 282 dollars in Mexico (1958), 484 dollars in Chile (1958), and 313 in Argentina (1958). The economically active population engaged in agriculture is 57.8 percent in Mexico (1957), 25.2 percent in Argentina (1947), and 19.6 percent in Chile (1952). The proportion of the population engaged in manufacture is 11.7 percent of the economically active in Mexico (1957), while in Argentina it was 22.1 percent since 1947, and in Chile 18.7 percent (1952). In Mexico only 51.2 percent of the wage-earning population is organized (1950), while in Argentina 92.91 percent was organized in 1947, and in Bolivia 77.64 percent (1950). In the last elections (July 6, 1958), only 23.1 percent of the population voted, while in Argentina 44.8 percent voted on February 22 of the same year, and in Bolivia 28.8 percent on June 17, 1956.

labor organizations and the peculiar significance of political elections lead many people to ask: Did not indeed the Mexican Revolution fail? Was it for this that a million people died?

There is an extremely unequal distribution of income and enormous differences in standards of living; one percent of the population gainfully employed receives 66 percent of the national income, while the remaining 99 percent, the workers, receive only 34 percent.[2] An average income per family for the whole country of 700 pesos per month (56 dollars) was barely enough to satisfy the minimal requirements for food, clothing, shelter, and entertainment in 1956, and according to this standard, 33 percent of the families in the Federal District and the Pacific North, 60 percent of Gulf Coast families and those living in North Central states, and 80 percent of those living in the center of the country and in states along the southern Pacific coast were lacking in economic means to care for their minimum needs; "approximately two of every three families were lacking in economic means in the sense of having a below-average income, which average itself was already low";[3] these data indicate slightly the reality of the misery that large segments of the population suffer, and again raise the question: . . . Is it not true that the Mexican Revolution has failed?

In any attempt to answer this question objectively . . . we must consider what Mexico has come out of, what the starting point was.

Mexico in 1910 [the year the revolution began] was a country of poverty, a country in which the vast majority of the people lived in near slavery; in which the standard of living of the wage-earning population was much lower than that of other countries, such as Argentina or Uruguay; a country in which eleven thousand plantation owners had 60 percent of the land; in which 88.4 percent of the agricultural population were *peons*—a condition similar to that of slaves—97 percent were heads of families but landless, and only 0.02 percent were owners of plantations; in which 13 percent of the population did not speak Spanish; in which 52 percent of the people lived in miserable huts; and in which infant mortality passed the figure of 304 per thousand live births.[4]

That is what we came out of. What is more, Mexican revolu-

[2] Parra, German, 1955.
[3] Navarrete, Ifigénia: *La distribución del ingreso y el desarrollo económico de México* (Mexico: Escuela Nacional de Economía, 1960), p. 75.
[4] *Estadísticas Sociales del Porfiriato, 1877-1910* (Mexico: Dirección General de Estadística, 1956).

tionary governments achieved rates of growth much higher than those of Argentina, Brazil, and Columbia, and one of the highest rates of capital accumulation in Latin America. The idea that the—until recently—spectacular development of Mexico could have been achieved without the Revolution is not only completely unfounded in historical fact, it is absurd. With the distribution of land a large domestic market was created that had not existed previously. The expropriations of U.S.-owned oil properties made possible economic independence . . . and opened the way to the possibility of a national economic policy. With the high rates of public investment (often more than 40 percent of the fixed national investment),[5] a national economic structure was created; a highway system that increased the domestic market was constructed, and investment by Mexicans themselves—spurred the growth of the middle class and of a market for industrial production. With all this came national integration and a national consciousness, in a country that until the Revolution had suffered internal isolation. Today Mexico has one of the best transportation and communication systems and is one of the most nationally conscious countries in all Latin America.

If for a moment we suppose the absurd—that Mexico had not had a Revolution, what would we have to conclude? What would we have been but a nation like those of Central America? As in the case of so many of our neighbors, our development would have been of a typically colonial and dependent character. If indeed our present condition leaves much to be desired, theirs is even sadder: far from having a national political life or development policy, they have a tiny middle class, an almost nonexistent working class, standards of living even lower than ours, and governments that are dictatorial and servile.

It is true that the Mexican Revolution has not benefited the population as a whole. It is true that in the development it sparked and in the liberties it created, only certain sections of the population have been able to participate—businessmen and industrialists, urban and rural middle classes, skilled workers—while large population groups are still to be found outside the course of economic, cultural, and political progress. In reality the Mexican Revolution managed only to take the step from a colonial pattern of development to national development of a semicapitalist type.

From a dependent system whose benefits were limited to a

[5] *Informes Anuales*, Nacional Financiera.

very small group of foreigners, government officials, military men, and plantation owners, the Revolution opened the door to a system that increases the benefits of development and facilitates the growth of the middle classes, both urban and rural, and the growth of a skilled working class. That these benefits do not reach the whole of the population is a fact; that the expansion of these benefits—economic, political, and cultural—has not reached its maximum even within the capitalist system is also undeniable.

Why has Mexico not achieved maximum social benefits within the capitalist system?

In the historical process taken as a whole that goes by the name of the Mexican Revolution, there are two principal tendencies, one predominantly linear—cumulative development in the fields of industry, technology, education, etc.—and another circular, which approximates the "eternal return," the return to the point of origin. The second tendency is more complicated; it has two principal starting points: on the one hand, *Porfirismo*,[6] the semicolonial society, and on the other, the revolution in the strict sense, the breaking of the semicolonial structure both internally and externally by means of popular, political, and military pressures. . . .

In both cases the return is not complete. The cumulative development of the forces of production, of technology, of culture, and of the social classes themselves prevents return to an identical situation, *porfirista* or revolutionary. . . . The Mexican bourgeoisie now dominates the situation, and the feudal structure of Mexican rural life has disappeared, the colonial economy has been broken, moreover, those who hope for a return to the renewed revolutionary impetus of the Cárdenas era will never again find a Mexico like that of the thirties. Concretely, the alliance between the bourgeoisie and the peasants against the landowners and foreign imperialists can never occur again in the same terms, inasmuch as the feudal property system has disappeared and the rural bourgeoisie—big and little—exercise today direct control over production relationships in agriculture.

The national income in terms of real purchasing power was slightly less than one and a half billion dollars in 1940 and over four and a half billion in 1959 (base year 1950), with a development rate for the period 1939-1950 of 2.9 percent. Electric

[6] *Porfirismo* is the period that precedes the Mexican Revolution and it extends from 1870 to 1910.

energy consumed in the country was 2.4 billion kilowatt hours in 1942 and 9.6 billion in 1959. Highway kilometers jumped from 695 in 1925-28 to 37,615 in 1959. The use of mechanical horsepower per unit of cultivated land increased 428.57 percent in the twenty-year period 1930-1950. Infant mortality was 304.46 per thousand in 1910 and 80.8 in 1957. Mortality figures in general were 33.25 per thousand in 1910 and 12.5 in 1958. The number of occupants per unit of housing was 8.2 in 1900 and 4.9 in 1950. In 1910, 13 percent of the population spoke only indigenous languages and dialects, while in 1950 only 3.64 percent did. In 1910, 80 percent of the population was illiterate, while in 1950, only 43.2 percent was.[7]

The case of the revolutionary-counterrevolutionary cycle, which repeats itself at different levels, is typical of capitalist revolutions. In the "semicapitalistic" Mexican Revolution the same cycle is also to be found but in quite different structural circumstances. The revolution has put an end to the semifeudal plantation system, given new impulse to the nation's business, begun industrialization, and thus changed an infinite number of economic, political, and cultural structures. But the revolution is semicapitalistic, the country has not created heavy industry nor attained economic, political, and cultural independence for Mexico. It depends to a great extent for the supply of its means of production on the United States. Its capacity for participating in world economic competition is menaced by the great powers, especially by United States capital. It imports principally manufactured products and exports raw materials. It has a single foreign market that is predominant: the United States. Its domestic market corresponds to the early phases prior to full capitalist development, and its culture is typically heterogenous.

To break out of this situation is difficult. The revolution created a structure with its own bottlenecks—economic, political, and cultural—in which the classical dynamics of capitalist development are smothered. The ruling classes cannot turn imperialist; they cannot even achieve the bargaining power of the smaller capitalist countries. Their dependence on the foreign market is a function of the domestic situation in which they find themselves. They have continued being nationalistic even in their most regressive moments, under the forms of

[7] *Anuario Estadístico de México, 1960;* Jorge Echanis and Emilio Mújica: *La Realidad Económica de México;* Luis Yáñez Pérez: *Mecanización de la Agricultura Mexicana,* México, D.F., Instituto Mexicano de Investigaciones Económicas, Population Census.

international capitalist competition. They have not returned to the status of semicolonial employees and officials, separated from economic production and trade in national products. They participate in and defend economic production. Their mentality is that of the entrepreneur; they understand fully the dynamics of world capitalism. But if their bargaining power is weak in the face of imperialism, their domestic situation . . . is the principal reason for their weakness. While desiring to maintain and strengthen their bargaining power and competitive position by means of an independent national policy, they have failed to strengthen their position through extensive alliances with popular elements or through the free play of these latter forces; this course would give rise to the expansion of the domestic market and to a homogenization of national culture. Rather, they make alliances with only selected popular groups, which they then turn on the impoverished population, which itself is unorganized, without political experience and without national culture, and thus perpetuate the structural weakness characteristic of semicolonial states.

In capitalist and semicapitalist revolutions, nationalism continues strong; but whereas in the former it becomes aggressive and even imperialistic, in the latter it maintains its defensive and semicolonial character. In the case of capitalist revolution, an expansion of the benefits of development takes place that reaches a much higher proportion of the population, precipitating the type of alliances and class conflicts that lead to expansion of the national and international market and of the national state itself. In semicapitalist revolutions, developmental expansion does not lead to the type of alliance and class conflict needed for the expansion of national and international markets, but rather encourages the expansion of a dominant domestic market and a dependent foreign market. Semicapitalist revolution does not destroy the internal structure of colonial society, in which there are suppressed nationalities and races, large marginal population nuclei, and a heterogeneous culture, nor does it bring to an end the weakness of semicolonial states. The increase of productive forces, industrialization, urbanization, the growth of communications and the means of transportation which are promoted by semicapitalist dynamics, are not sufficient to break completely through the internal and external structure of the old colonial and semicolonial society, which at a later stage becomes the principal obstacle to the expansion of national and international markets, to the formation of the nation-state, and to the full expansion of capitalism itself.

This general situation gives a special meaning to all the regressive movements that appear in the course of the history of the Revolution and which, briefly set forth, are the following:

(1) From the elimination of the latifundia system and the establishment of a system of small private property and of collective property and usufruct (*ejidos*), the revolutionary cycle has gone on to a new latifundia system: the accumulation of land and the formation of capitalist agricultural corporations.[8] From a form of exploitation close to slavery (peonage), the transition has been made to capitalist forms of exploitation (wage labor combined with the historical vestiges of peonage). The small property owners and the members of the collective farms are themselves exploited through high interest rates and through speculation in agricultural products and market control.

(2) From aggressive nationalism, which allied itself with the peasantry and the working classes to break the colonial monopoly, the transition has been made to an integration of a sector of the national capitalist class with that of the United States in a mixed relationship of alliance and commercial competition. The nature of the relationship itself, as well as the economic struggle, requires a minimal level of bargaining power in order to obtain maximum profit. This bargaining power has been achieved through a limited, competitive independence. Nationalist revolutionary elements have been reduced to playing a political game of secondary importance, in which the pressure they exercise, together with that of popular and nationalist elements, is useful to the State only in negotiating more favorable agreements. On the other hand, the comprador capitalists and the foreign monopolies constitute a much more powerful pressure group, although they still do not dominate the situation directly and totally. On a national level, imperialist and extreme rightist groups fight to change the

---

[8] The new, capitalist-type latifundia system "exceeds by far what Article 27 of the Constitution, as amended, establishes as exempt property; that is, more than 100, more than 130 and more than 300 hectares, according to the crop cultivated . . . "; less than 0.5 percent of individuals or families are owners of more than half the productive land "in some regions of the North such as Lower California South, Nayarit, Sonora"; and the situation is similar in Sinaloa, Chihuahua, and Tamaulipas. Cf. Jesús Silva Herzog: *El Agrarismo Mexicano y la Reforma Agraria* (Mexico: Fondo de Cultura Económica, 1959), p. 565.

equilibrium of forces through both economic and political counterrevolutionary action; the impoverished middle classes and certain sectors of the working class have sought to return to the developmental stage of the nationalist front and later, when they have become more radical, to form a common front with leftist forces, with a coherent program of national capitalist development.[9]

From revolutionary measures that destroyed the imperialist and feudal interests, a change has been made to measures for economic and social growth that do not basically affect vested interests, thus confusing the growth of certain productive forces and services with a development policy.

The "vested interests" are national and foreign capitalists. A national front like that of the thirties to struggle against these interests is impossible, even though such a struggle could mean, in fact, an improvement and a step toward a policy of *capitalist* development through measures for the redistribution of income, diversification of foreign markets, control of foreign investments, and the planning of public investments. . . .

(3) From national capitalization derived from the expropriation of foreign investments, which constitutes a real original accumulation of capital, there has been a turning to accumulation based on the depression of popular consumption through inflationary methods that especially affect the fixed income groups. From the increase of the domestic market through measures of a general and national character, such as redistribution of wealth and especially of land, and the raising of salaries and wages and increasing social allowances, an expansion of the domestic market by areas and sectors has come to be preferred. Industrialization, with consequent urbanization and division of labor, the expansion of the area covered by the money economy, the growth of the middle class, and the increase in the number of skilled and semiskilled workers together generate an intermediate-level demand, insufficient in and of itself to give full employment to all productive resources; combined with the demand generated by foreign investments, the motive power for economic growth is the proceeds from tourist business and from migratory workers returning from the United States.

While the quasimonopoly exercised over the national

[9] Cf. *Programa y Llamamiento del Movimiento de Liberación Nacional* (Mexico, 1961).

economy by the United States was broken in limited degree, in the course of the cycle, it has been increased. Direct United States investments, which in 1938 constituted 60 percent of the total direct foreign investment, in 1957 increased their share up to 80 percent of the total.[10] Whereas in 1935 the United States accounted for 65 percent of our imports and 63 percent of our exports, in 1959 the same country accounted for 72.93 percent of our imports and 60.72 percent of our exports; thus, our dependence on the U.S. market was increased, with the exception of a slight decrease in exports. This occurred despite partial measures taken to diversify our markets.

At the same time, Mexico has maintained its privileged position in comparison with other Latin American countries and in comparison with its own previous situation; it is the owner of its own transportation and communications systems and of almost all its sources of energy. The process of appropriation of these basic instruments has continued, although there has been a transition from the original forms of appropriation (expropriation) to the commercial forms of nationalization. Thus, Mexico has acquired the railroads, the oil, the highway transportation companies and some airlines, the steel industry, electricity, and, progressively, the mining industry.

These instruments and the fact that the country no longer suffers from a one-crop colonial economy but rather has achieved a diversification of its production give Mexico a competitive strength of semicapitalist type; they remove it from the category of the "apparent nations" and cause it to approach the character of a developed and independent country. Nevertheless, they are not sufficient to break through the dominant position held by the United States in the fields of investment and foreign commerce [a domination] . . . against which the Mexican Revolution originally fought.

The structure of the foreign market and the structure of foreign investments in and of themselves limit any measure of an economically independent character. The danger of devaluation, of a halt to foreign investment, of a setback in the tourist trade, of a suspension of opportunities for migratory workers and of a boycott on imports and exports, constitute, in the structural conditions of the present phase in the revolutionary cycle, real and effective dangers, which influence political decisions of the Government in the struggle for national liberation.

From the discouragement of foreign investments the revolu-

[10] Source: Banco de México, S.A.

tionary cycle has carried us to the encouragement of such investment. This does not imply a position of semicolonial surrender like that of *Porfirismo,* but rather a political weakness of a structural nature; it corresponds to an economic and power structure in which resistance to imperialism and the striving for national liberation continue, but considerable obstacles must be faced that determine the Government's political reasoning and decision: the risks it takes, its caution, and its strategy. At a higher level of economic and political independence a semicapitalist country finds itself, nevertheless, facing international structures similar to those of the prerevolutionary period.

(4) Within the process of capitalization, corruption has been one of the more common forms. The system itself, the lack of political career stability, and the insecurity of the man without money are some of the principal factors that determine this form of primitive accumulation, characteristic of public officials in certain stages of capitalist development. In this area no revolutionary-counterrevolutionary cycle is to be noted. Peculation is part of the history of prerevolutionary and postrevolutionary governments. Its incidence in certain stages, in which the loss of revolutionary consciousness reaches considerable proportions (such as the *Maximato* and *Alemanismo*[11]), is followed by others in which there is much greater honesty in the management of public funds (such as *Cardenismo* and *Ruizcortinismo*[12]) during which progress was made toward the creation and perfection of a modern governmental bureaucracy.

From a structural point of view there are contradictions between government and private business, between the roles of manager of a government corporation and of a private enterprise—roles that are frequently played by the same person —inasmuch as the upper echelons of government spread out in the majority of cases to become owners of private companies and entrepreneurs. The commercial management of a good number of government operations for personal benefit is typical, even when there is no peculation strictly speaking. In addition, there are operations and concessions, which are made for personal and political reasons or because of circumstantial political pressures. This structure prevents or hinders the reali-

---

[11] *Alemanismo* is the period of President Miguel Alemán (1946-1952).
[12] *Ruizcortinismo* is the period of President Adolfo Ruiz Cortines (1952-1958).

zation of overall plans for economic development. Nonetheless, the appearance of public and private corporations produces the dynamics of capitalist development within the country and these limitations do not lead to the policy of plunder and hoarding characteristic of countries where there has not been a "businessman's revolution." . . .

The development of state and private capitalism has made necessary, in Mexico and elsewhere, the formation of a corporation bureaucracy much more efficient and productive than the traditional bureaucracy. This bureaucracy has managed its corporations successfully and has come to hold the initiative in matters of development; private investment has become dependent on public investment, and the latter has been the principal motive force behind national development. Here in full play are the logic and the dynamics of state capitalist development. The limitations that exist are outside of the public and private enterprise, in the structure of the national and international market; and these are the limitations that cause peculation to seek safety and protection often in foreign bank deposits instead of finding an outlet in the formation of working capital.

(5) One of the characteristic problems of the vast majority of colonial and semicolonial countries, which in fact, is essential to colonialism itself, is the existence within colonies and countries with a semicolonial structure of two cultures, one identified with the rulers and the other with the ruled.

In semicolonial countries the existence of these two cultures reveals the lack of national integration and is one of the instruments of national subjection. The lack of cultural integration and the existence of groups with a different culture who are repressed and discriminated against weaken the country as a whole. In Mexico this problem dates from the Spanish period and continues down to our day. The Mexican Revolution has been able to solve it only to a very limited and partial extent. The agrarian reform did not reach the indigenous communities to the same extent that it reached the *mestizo* communities, nor have the former enjoyed the same rights and resources as the latter.

Today at least ten percent of the population, i.e., three and a half million inhabitants, are indigenous.

These three and a half million people, who are Mexican citizens *de jure,* lack good lands and are sometimes landless;

they receive neither the credit, the equipment, or the services that the rest of the population receives.[13] They pay more taxes than other Mexicans and receive fewer services and investments than other Mexicans. "Whereas the Federal Government invests 197 pesos per person in the country's nonindigenous municipalities for agricultural credit, education, irrigation, roads, hospitals, and medical attention, it invests only 39 pesos per person in the indigenous municipalities for the same purposes."[14] Mexico has no racial discrimination per se, but "colonial" discrimination against the indigenous communities still survives. This problem is not only an indigenous problem, it is a national problem to the extent that it leaves the country with an internal colonial structure that weakens Mexico both in domestic and international affairs.

The plural structure of society in reality goes far beyond the dichotomy of national and indigenous culture groups. The country's development itself is dual or plural in that, as is typical of all colonies, there is a group that participates in the benefits of development and one that does not. Today the proportion of participants is greater than in the case of colonies and includes groups that are diverse in nature and immensely numerous, in comparison with the favored few who participate in the benefits of colonial development; but Mexico still has, however, the structure typical of colonial development: an immense sector participates in development and another is left on the sidelines, while the relations between the one and the other continue being those of the colonizer and the colonized.

The magnitude of the problem has not been sufficiently studied. Ifigenia Navarrete has stated that "it may be said that

[13] "On the basis of partial data available it may be estimated . . . that around 28 percent of the indigenous population occupied in agriculture thus far have no land of their own; and those who own land face a deplorable situation on account of the poverty of their soil, lack of rainfall, lack of transport and communication, lack of technological development, and the exploitation of which they are victims by the rest of the population, in addition to the insecurity in which they live with respect to their lands"; Instituto Nacional Indigenista: *La Situación Agraria de las Comunidades Indígenas,* Publicación del Gobierno del Estado de México (1960), p. 5. Other data are worse yet: "as may be proved by reference to the census, only 55,861 monolingual indigenous heads of families have received land in accordance with the *ejido* program, and if we consider the typical family composed of five persons, there live on *ejido* lands 279,305 monolingual people, or what amounts to the same thing, there are 1,143,266 who have not received any lands at all." Cf. Alfonso Caso in *Demografía Indígena* (1950) in *Indigenismo,* Instituto Nacional Indigenista, 1958, p. 21.

[14] Alfonso Caso: *Memoria de las labores del INI presentada al Secretario de Hacienda y Crédito público en 1954.* Unpublished work.

due to the low level of national income in the case of Mexico, only that sector of the population has been incorporated into the benefits of economic development, which has an income equal to or greater than the mean, i.e., 30 percent of the population in 1950 and 35 percent in 1957."[15] If we accept this preliminary observation, of each 100 Mexicans we have only 35 participating in the benefits of development while 65 are left out, and of these latter, at least 10, the country's indigenous population, are left far out.

What is worse, not only between the ins and the outs, but within the former group, in economic, political, and cultural relations, in national elections, in labor disputes, etc., there are to be found colonialist attitudes. Mexico is not evolving at the same rate toward the type of social relations to which the dynamics of capitalism leads in noncolonial countries. . . . Mexico has continued throughout its history with ruler-ruled social relations, forced solutions of conflicts, and violent repressions characteristic of colonial countries.

Moreover, this dual structure lends itself to the political manipulations that are also characteristic of colonial society: an alliance of participants in development is sought to control the marginal groups, which in Mexico include the indigenous communities, the poor peasants, and unskilled workers, i.e., the vast majority of the labor force. Wages and social allowances for the "participant class" of workers, are much more generous than for marginal workers, thus creating a privileged caste extending from businessmen to skilled workers. . . . The skilled workers have the largest organizations and the most effective possibilities for struggle and become intermediate groups, a species of privileged colonial working class, with a middle-class mentality.

This general structure of society not only was not broken by the Revolution but also led to the accumulation of capital at the expense primarily of the marginal sectors. These marginal sectors do not participate in the benefits of development, and their misery is similar to that of workers in colonial countries. On the other hand, an alliance forms between the skilled work-

[15] An idea of the degree of social mobility may be deduced from the following data: "In 1930 agricultural day workers represented 54 percent of the economically active population, while in 1950 they represented only 20 percent. . . . Mexico is ceasing to be a nation of agricultural day workers and is becoming a land of small property-owners and usufructuaries." Yáñez Pérez Luis: op. cit., p. 16. According to Ifigenia Navarrete, while the lower class constituted 70 percent of the population in 1950, it amounted to only 65 percent in 1957; op. cit., p. 89.

ers and government employees whose protests and demands for wages and social allowances . . . and whose standards of living in comparison with the indigenous communities and unskilled workers, are similar. They are the counterpart of white workers in the colonial societies of Africa.

The cyclical impoverishment of the urban working class, since it participates to some extent in the benefits of development, does not lead to radical forms of struggle; it is granted raises in wages and social allowances, at the expense of the unorganized marginal workers, whose political and cultural level, etc., is also very low . . . , and whose resistance is quietly attacked with the maximum of violence known in our society; this violence never provokes the protest reactions heard from the participating sectors of the population when they are the ones affected.

In such conditions the "dual structure" of society is the worst impediment to the country's political and economic development toward a higher stage of capitalism, which would at least mean a homogeneous society in which differences of income, culture, political knowledge, etc., would not be so great as in the present colonial or semicolonial society.

(6) There are also certain regressive features of the present structure of power: although the military have not again occupied the preeminent place they had in Mexico until thirty years ago, the oscillating character of national politics and the Government's alternating acts of strength and weakness may lead to their return. Other organizations have more clearly followed the revolutionary cycle: the clergy, defeated in its political and military activities, and reduced to its proper religious function, has returned to the political arena, organizing demonstrations and exercising political pressure unprecedented since the period of the *Maximato*. Manipulating popular discontent, the Church is again having success with the promise of bread and glory. Legal provisions whose original purpose was the defense of workers are being applied against them. Opposition parties continue to be of little importance; Mexico is still in reality a one-party country. But that party, which yesterday was a powerful instrument of national defense, today is reduced to indecision and rhetoric, although its local leaders and organizations continue to do an efficient job of organizing, and of solving local problems—which explains its strength. The Government and the Party react weakly and vacillate before a U.S. imperialism—an imperialism that can manipu-

late, at one and the same time, the economic situation, the principal newspapers, the Clergy, and popular discontent.

The semicapitalist development of Mexico has, therefore, restricted its own evolution; it continues as *semi*capitalistic. . . . Attaining the maximum historical dynamics of capitalism is difficult. Labor unions do not function to increase the domestic market for the whole working population, but rather only for the "white" sector. The dominant political party obtains benefits for that sector, and suffers the same weaknesses as the Government: it views with caution any economic, political, or cultural steps toward national liberation. Other parties neither try to solve the problems of the masses nor have success among them. There is not even an institutionalization of social conflicts that might achieve, as happens in developed capitalist societies, increases in wages and social allowances, fiscal reforms, more positive allocation of Government investment, etc. In these conditions the political struggle for the redistribution of income and social welfare, so necessary for the development of capitalism, is successful only within the structure of the dual society, which it is not able to transcend. The struggle for Mexico's economic independence has been maintained within the limits of a semicapitalist state, its international relations have not attained economic and political equality with the great powers. These factors in turn are important political impediments to the full development of Mexican capitalism itself.

(7) Revolutionary ideologies . . . are becoming commonplace among the politically conscious population. . . . The classics of the Mexican Revolution have become sources of inspiration even for the reactionary parties, who "defend" revolutionary ideas and even laws in order to win over a people who really have a revolutionary consciousness.

There thus develops a paradoxical situation. Those *not* in power are very "revolutionary," even when actually reactionary. Those in power are very cautious. In the latter case the ideology of the Revolution encounters the most varied forms of evasion: some rhetorical, and others retrospective, historical, and abstract. The cold war has transformed certain ideas from the classics of the Mexican Revolution, that are concrete in nature and concretely applicable, into "exotic ideas." The *courtier*, that is, the professional politician, knows that the language of success is a rhetorical language with reactionary-revolutionary ambiguities. Thus, while rightist demagoguery employs aggressive and concrete revolutionary language, mixed with religious symbols, the political *courtiers* use a language that is empty and ambiguous.

The left, and especially the "Marxist" left, has been seesawing between opportunism and sectarianism throughout the whole cycle. In addition to the effective united action of the left in the national front and the antiimperialist struggle that the Government periodically renews, there is the frequent collaboration of the left in the development of capitalism. There thus arises a "structural opportunism." Any and all leftists may, at the most unexpected moment, because of the concrete political situation join forces with the Government's national struggle; and to be effective they must be opportunists. The alternative is sectarianism.

The preoccupation with doctrinal purity is probably of maximum intensity among leftists in Mexico [because] of their difficulty in understanding and acting in the unexpected revolution that the social dynamics of a semicolonial Mexico have released; the class struggle has semicolonial characteristics, and nationalism is never imperialist, nor does it disappear entirely or permanently from governmental acts. Frequently the different social classes are obliged to ally against imperialism.

Some leftist fears are well founded. Many Marxists of yesterday are big businessmen of today. If Protestantism was the ethic of European capitalism, Marxism fulfilled the same role in Mexico. There was a Marxism of the bourgeoisie and for the bourgeoisie. In Mexico it is not uncommon to find bankers who made their fortune applying the laws of *Das Kapital,* or conservative politicians who have a Marxist past and who rationalize their position by talking of the "contradictions of capitalism" and of "increasing, in the present stage, the forces of production until the moment comes when they enter into definitive contradiction with the relationships of production." (This evolution of Marxism among many of the ruling elite is, in one sense, a serious obstacle to the cold war. The idea that the Marxist of today may turn out to be a businessman tomorrow weakens suspiciousness of Marxism.) The young bourgeois individual is a Marxist; the old, an entrepreneur. . . .

In the urbanizing and industrializing Mexico of today, there is continuous upward social mobility. The peasants of yesterday are the laborers of today, and their children may well enter the professions. The consciousness of the people is influenced by this possibility of individual opportunity through emigration from the country to the city and rising from one class to another through education, work, or luck.

We do not know the present level of . . . social mobility, but [many believe] that personal salvation is within the realm of practical possibility. . . . Moreover, in the "two Mexicos," the participant and the marginal, when the former turns radical, it is accommodated by the political and economic instruments of the Government. . . . Without permitting them organizational independence, the radical elements are often granted benefits that are even beyond those demanded by the leaders of the democratic union opposition. . . . Thus, this radical participating sector . . . sees its best chance in loyalty to the Government. . . . As for the marginal elements, some have a minimum capacity for demanding and for struggling, as is the case with the immense majority of indigenous communities; and others entertain the hope of becoming part of the sector that participates in the benefits of development—a sector whose growth . . . several generations of Mexicans have observed. In these conditions to think of an immediate revolution is absurd. . . .

General Lázaro Cárdenas has pointed out what seems at present to be the right road. . . . Support the Government when, albeit weakly, it takes measures in defense of national sovereignty; and strengthen the popular, independent organizations that both lead to the democratic institutionalization of social conflicts and favor measures that will accelerate the dynamics of Mexico's capitalist development. Thus, the foundation will be laid for a genuine democratic force that will offer the political and social pillars for the eventual establishment of democratic socialism.

The unknowns are, however, great in a history without precedent. Can Mexico, at this historical crossroads in the revolutionary cycle, pass from a semicapitalist to a capitalist stage, to a society of homogeneous culture, to a *polis* in which the free play of labor unions is a fact, in which popular organizations serve to resolve conflicts institutionally, and in which tomorrow we shall arrive peacefully at socialism? Or will the organization of the people be repressed? Will the extreme right take over the Government? Will the palace revolutionaries, the military, and the Roman Catholic clergy return again to the forefront, to maintain by force the plural society, semicapitalist development, and augment—as would be necessary to control the people—the nation's dependence on the United States? In this case the road to socialism would be a violent road, and the socialism that would emerge would be a dictatorial socialism without democratic culture. On the organization of popular forces, independent and institutional, would seem to depend the recovery and the future of a revolution that has stopped.

On Cuban Political Economy*

JAMES O'CONNOR

In contrast to the Mexican revolution, the Cuban revolution occurred in a capitalist country, as O'Connor shows. The revolution destroyed the old order of foreign-controlled monopoly capitalism—a prerequisite for Cuba's further development. Nationalization and consolidation of industry, collectivization of the large-scale sector of the agricultural economy, reorganization of banking and commerce, and central planning were necessary to end stagnation. O'Connor's view is that the Cuban economy had failed to grow before the revolution as rapidly as existing technology, savings, and the supply of labor and land permitted because of the way in which it was socially organized. The lack of a sustained internally based counterrevolutionary movement demonstrates how "ready" for revolution Cuba was.

James O'Connor is Assistant Professor of Economics at San Jose State College. His forthcoming book, *The Origins of Cuban Socialism*, is a study of Cuban political economy before and after the revolution.

* Reprinted from *Political Science Quarterly*, Vol. LXXIX, No. 2 (June 1964), pp. 233-247, by permission.

THE THESIS of this paper is that the social revolution in Cuba (1959-61) was inevitable in the sense that it was necessary for the island's further economic and social development. The nationalization and consolidation of industry, the collectivization of more than one third of Cuba's farm land, the complete reorganization of the labor unions and the banking and commercial systems, and thoroughgoing economic planning rescued the island from permanent economic stagnation.[1] For this reason, Cuban socialism can be explained and understood in the context of the social structure of the old society—not as the sour fruit of some "abnormality" or "conspiracy."

A corollary of this thesis is that any ruling group that failed fundamentally to modify or replace Cuba's old economic institutions could not count on a long and stable tenure. It also follows that the political orientation of any political leader of "liberal" or conservative persuasion who wished to retain power would have to shift more or less rapidly to the Left to correspond with social reality.

The argument may be summarized as follows:

(1) From a very early date the Cuban economy developed along capitalist lines. Pre-industrial capitalist forms of economic organization—traditional, feudal, or mercantile (excepting the neomercantile trade relations between the United States and Cuba)—were in no way important features of the old society. During the twentieth century the island's economy acquired the significant characteristics of monopoly capitalism, chief among which was the cartelization of markets. Monopoly controls blanketed Cuba's social economy and blocked the fulfillment of the island's true economic potential by wasting land, labor, and capital, and other economic resources.

(2) Throughout the political revolution that triumphed in January 1959, a small group of men acquired and retained the initiative. These men were non-Communists and, while forming an alliance with the Cuban Communist Party in late 1958 or early 1959, consistently kept the initiative during the social revolution of 1959-61. What is more, this social revolution was rapid, relatively peaceful, and defended by the vast majority of the Cuban people. These observations suggest that a

[1] The shift of the great part of Cuba's trade from the United States to the socialist countries and the reorientation of Cuba's foreign policy do not directly concern us here. They are questions related to the transition from capitalist to socialist economy, but they seem to have had an independent character as well. For this reason they are more simple and, at the same time, more complex than the question of Cuban socialism itself. On one level of analysis, it is obvious that the United States' refusal to trade with Cuba drove the island to the Soviet Union. Looking deeper, one is compelled to inquire into the nature of the relationship between the United States and Cuba for clues to its deterioration. Clearly, the rapid socialization of the Cuban economy contributed to the severance of ties between the two governments.

social revolution of a specifically socialist character was not merely an ideological product, but a realistic and authentic response to social reality.

(3) The political revolution was not marked by sharp class conflicts, and revolutionary programs drawn up before 1959 had appeal for nearly every Cuban social and economic class. Class conflicts developed out of the economic and political measures of the Revolutionary government, that destroyed revolutionary unity by systematically discriminating against some classes and in favor of others and by polarizing political attitudes on the questions of elections, political parties, and relations with the United States. It is said that these measures provide prima facie evidence that Fidel Castro betrayed the original spirit and aims of the revolution (the betterment of the economic, social, and political condition of the Cuban people) when in fact they may have been the logical outcome of an attempt to realize these very aims.

From a very early date Cuba exhibited the main features of modern capitalist economy. Unlike most Latin American economies, Cuba lacked an important subsistence sector, and nearly all segments of the population were integrated into the market economy. As early as 1899 over two-thirds of the rural labor force were engaged in the cultivation of cash crops, while subsistence farming employed probably less than one quarter of the work force.

By midcentury the subsistence sector had been nearly totally submerged by specialized agricultural production for export and home consumption. Throughout the countryside the propertied rural middle class gave way to foreign capital, which exploited opportunities for large-scale production, and corporate and absentee ownership. Following the sugar crises of the nineteen twenties a fine web of relationships began to bind together agriculture and high finance; the bankers also had a finger in commerce and, to a lesser degree, manufacturing.

The great part of the island's agricultural production was organized along monopolistic lines. Output restrictions, pegged prices, and other forms of monopolistic control blanketed sugar, tobacco, rice, potato, and coffee farming. In the key sugar sector, mill owners, growers, and wage workers all had powerful organizations. Outputs, wages, prices, and the distribution of sugar earnings were determined by the mill owners or growers cartels, or by a three-cornered bargaining relationship on the level of national politics.

In industry there were 150 employers' associations of one kind or another, many of them with wide powers over their members. Compulsory "producers' associations" dominated sugar and tobacco manufacture, and the great public utilities each had clear monopolies in their fields. As for the labor movement, it was, compared with the island's labor force, one of the largest in the world, and the central federation enjoyed unusual power over its affiliates. There was, besides, an extremely well developed "labor aristocracy," which had sealed off a number of important labor markets from outside competition, and which was mainly responsible for the extraordinarily low relationship between labor productivity and wages.

In short, the economic institutions we are accustomed to associate with the high income capitalist nations overlaid the island's market system. It should be stressed that monopoly practices in Cuba's product and labor markets sprang up in the soil of a market economy. Restrictions in the rural economy were not of the type ordinarily associated with a system of traditional agriculture, and controls in the labor market were not those customary in mercantile or neomercantile systems. Cuba's economic institutions were capitalist institutions, historically specific to Cuba. These institutions had, by and large, a monopolistic character, as well. For this reason, they placed limits on the pace of Cuba's economic development by inhibiting the improvement of agricultural yields, wasting land, barring the wide introduction of a mixed, scientific agriculture, placing ceilings on labor productivity and, in general, on the ability of the economy to mobilize and utilize domestic and foreign capital efficiently.

In an economy that had been stagnating since World War II (except for temporary ups and downs in the sugar market), the implications of these limits on economic growth for the nature and scope of the Cuban Revolution were profound.

Against this background the character of the political and social revolutions in Cuba is more comprehensible. In the *political* struggle against President Fulgencio Batista the decisive influence was apparently the dedication of a small band of young men. From the attack by Fidel Castro on the Moncada Barracks in July 1953, throughout the guerrilla war of 1957-58, until late 1959, when the Castro group firmly consolidated political power, not a single peasant revolt ignited the Cuban countryside. Passive resistance, surreptitious aid to Castro's forces, there were, to be sure; unlike a dozen other political revolutions, however, the peasant classes failed to grasp the initiative at any point in the struggle. Early in 1959 Comandante Ernesto (Che) Guevara, Castro's closest associate, appropriately described the Cuban peasants as the revolution's "invisible collaborators." The labor movement, in which over one half of Cuba's labor force was enrolled, figured even less prominently in the rebellion. It was in January 1959, after the regular army had received Castro's final blows, that the working classes shut down Havana's industry and commerce. Earlier, a general strike in April 1959 had been a total failure. The new revolutionary government consistently retained the political initiative; the general strike in late January in the port city of Manzanillo protesting the leniency shown by the revolutionary tribunals toward war criminals was apparently the only major reversal of roles.

In the *social* revolution of 1959-61 the liquidation of Cuba's private property system was invariably initiated by the ruling group. The peasantry did not spontaneously seize and cultivate idle lands; with a handful of exceptions, they failed to claim even the small fields in which they labored until the new government formally turned these tracts over to them. To be sure, a decree published in February denied rights to land under the coming Agrarian Reform Law to any peasant who without authorization occupied properties belonging to someone else. More significant than the existence of the law is the fact that it did not have to be enforced. Nor did the urban workers and sugar mill laborers independently occupy the factories (this was a sharp departure from the abortive social revolution of 1933); rebel army or militia units at the direction of the central government took possession of Cuba's farm land and industry.

These two sets of events—the exclusive and individualistic flavor of the political revolution and the almost bloodless social revolution—are intimately connected. The social revolution was more or less orderly because the political revolution transferred power from one relatively small group of men to another, and because the masses of Cubans at the very least passively supported the social revolution.

In this context it is significant that Cuba's is the only specifically socialist social revolution in history that was not authored by local Communist parties with or without the backing of the Red Army. Not until 1959, when the actual fighting had ceased, did Castro's 26th of July Movement win the open backing of the Cuban party (the Partido Socialista Popular, or PSP), although this is not true of some individual Communists who sided with Castro somewhat earlier, and, as might be expected, survived the 1962 spring and summer purges of old-line Communists almost to a man. The political careers of many of the old-line Communists were painfully brief. Subject to bitter public and private attacks by the 26th of July Movement's organ, *Revolución*, during most of 1959, the party members gained footholds in the new revolutionary organizations in 1960 *after* the major expropriations (with a few exceptions, most notably the trade unions, in which they had always figured strongly, and in two or three important offices in the National Agrarian Reform Institute [INRA]), and helped shape the mass organizations and the new party, the ORI (Integrated Revolutionary Organizations), into their image of revolutionary associations in 1961 and early 1962, only to be deprived of many of their positions in the spring and summer of that year and replaced by non-Communist revolutionary personnel.[2]

In connection with the question of the source of political initiative, it is important to point out that in the history of modern revolutions the Cuban experience was unique in another respect, and departed especially sharply from the October Revolution. Irresistibly drawn to the peasantry in order to consolidate power, Lenin paved the way for the seizure of the estates. By this very measure, though, the central authority deprived itself of effective control of the land. Fifteen years passed before the rural economy was collectivized and integrated into the structure of the planned economy. The Cuban Revolution spared Fidel Castro an analogous problem, since the seeds of a planned rural economy were planted *simultane-*

[2] For the events in 1959, see the study by Maurice Zeitlin and Robert Scheer, *Cuba, Tragedy of the Hemisphere* (New York, 1963). The role of the party in 1960 and 1961 is described in Theodore Draper's *Castro's Revolution: Myths and Realities* (New York, 1962). In this collection of articles is also "L'Affaire Escalante," which tries to interpret the purges at the top to North Americans. Monitoring of Cuban radio broadcasts and perusal of Cuban periodicals reveal that the purge had reached into the lowest levels of the ORI by midsummer, 1962. This was confirmed by the author in August 1963, by another American, Maurice Zeitlin ("Castro and Cuba's Communists," *The Nation*, November 3, 1962), and by an anti-Castro writer in "Pero Sigue la Purga," *Cuba Nueva*, May 15, 1962). That the PSP never had absolute initiative is unwittingly suggested by the leading exponent of the "revolution betrayed" thesis when he wrote that "if all had been going well in Cuba for the past year, the PSP's control might well have gone unchallenged. . . ." Draper, *Castro's Revolution*, 209.

ously with the transformation of land ownership. The fact that the Cuban farm worker and peasant never had the political initiative made possible the immediate collectivization of the cattle, rice, and sugar sectors of the rural economy. The fact that the better part of these sectors was already organized into large-scale producing units that had long utilized land, labor, and capital inefficiently made collectivization practical, feasible, and rational.

This development not only distinguishes the Cuban Revolution from the Russian Revolution, but sets it apart from the Chinese, the Mexican, and even the Bolivian experiences, as well. In Mexico the peasants at times had absolute initiative; before 1952 the Chinese leadership by force of circumstances emphasized individual ownership of the land; so did the Bolivian revolutionary group, and so it does today. The antifeudal character of all these upheavals, though, was mirrored very faintly in Cuba, for reasons we have already discussed.

A summary of our argument to this point discloses that: non-Communist revolutionaries made a socialist revolution on an island where feudalism (or the neofeudalism of prerevolutionary Soviet Union, China, Mexico, and Bolivia) was largely absent, but where capitalistic, monopolistic controls were prominently featured. The PSP never had the political initiative either before or during the key stages of the social revolution; the party, in fact, at first even opposed those sections of the May 1959 Agrarian Reform Law, which encouraged collective production of agricultural commodities. The aim of the revolutionary leadership was to get the stagnating Cuban economy off dead center to improve the social and material conditions of the Cuban people. When they turned to socialist forms of economic organizations to realize this aim, they were supported by the majority of Cubans. From all of this evidence, one can clearly make a case that socialist economic planning in Cuba was less an ideological product than an expression of hard economic necessity.

Socialism—public ownership of the means of production—sometimes emerges from class conflict and is invariably accompanied by more or less severe political warfare between classes. Cuba was no exception. The political revolution had a distinct classless character (at least no single class had the initiative during this phase of the struggle), but sharp class conflicts developed in the course of the social revolution. The emergence of these conflicts was accompanied by dramatic changes in the Revolutionary government's political line.

Beginning in mid-1959, after the Agrarian Reform Law put Cuba and the world on notice that a thoroughgoing social revolution was in the making, the Revolutionary government began to mark off sharply the "revolution" from the "counter-revolution." Departing from his previous position, Castro was the first to insist on the black and white nature of the struggle, an attitude that was quickly adopted by other government officials. Divisions and differences of opinion over revolutionary policy existed within the governing group—the struggle between the Castro group and the "old" communists is one instance—but the main lines of both domestic and foreign policy were (and are) seldom questioned, or in doubt. The extreme polarization of Cuban politics after mid-1959 is well exemplified in speech after speech delivered by Cuban government leaders. In this theme the revolution and the Cuban nation are made one and the same, as indicated by Castro in early 1960: "To be a traitor to the Revolution is to be a traitor to the country. The destiny of our sovereignty is at stake. . . . We have decided that either we are or we are not a free country. And we are and want to be a free country."[3]

From mid-1959 to the present, however, *genuine* cleavages in Cuban politics have been sharp and opposing opinions have been fiercely held, defining a political mood that corresponds in many ways to social and economic reality. From January 1959 on, a series of profound economic and social changes accompanied these inimical attitudes, and to a large degree were responsible for them. There were no less than *fifteen hundred* decrees, laws, and resolutions during the first nine months of 1959.[4] Unquestionably, nearly every new measure—especially those affecting the property system—drew some Cubans closer to the Revolutionary government and repelled others, leaving few indifferent. At the very least, each major law (the rent reduction and price control laws, agrarian reform, and the "intervention" of the utilities are some examples) compelled the ordinary Cuban to question his own political orientation; the most sweeping of these occasioned cabinet crises, resignations, and flights abroad; and their

[3] Radio interview with Fidel Castro reported in Havana *Post*, January 19, 1960, 10.

[4] Author's estimate based on *Primer Indice Anual de la Legislación Revolucionaria, Iro. de Enero a 31 de Diciembre de 1959* (Havana, 1960).

cumulative effect led to the short war at Playa Girón in April 1961. The basis for the demand to choose sides—for or against the Revolutionary government—was therefore laid by the government's early economic and political measures. To make such a demand required some confidence that a sizable body of opinion would confirm the government's position. This suggests that the original revolutionary legislation might be likened to a whirlpool expelling odd debris, yet sucking in the hull of the ship. Be that as it may, it is certainly likely that the slogan itself, together with the heady spirit in which it was launched, contributed to a political atmosphere in which a middle position became increasingly unrealistic and untenable. Castro's personality, after all, confers on the revolution a very special flavor. When he told an audience in the summer of 1960, at the time the United States acted to bar Cuban sugar from the mainland market, "In each cooperative we are going to build a town . . . with or without the quota. Each little town will have a school for the children of the members of the cooperative, with or without the quota . . . ,"[5] he conveyed a sense of boundless optimism apparent as early as the famous "History Will Absolve Me" speech in 1953 and by which his associates were invariably impressed. Reading through his speeches and declarations, one is struck by the fact that the image of defeat, or even retreat, rarely, and then only reluctantly, appears. This nearly limitless confidence undoubtedly has affected Cuban politics and the island's economic development.

That the new government chose to polarize opinion around the fundamental issue of its own support cannot be fully explained by Castro's optimism, however. It had the alternative —in place of isolating, indeed outlawing, any opposition, the logical climax of the government's actual policy—that of allowing his opposition to form into functioning interest groups. From there, employing the tactics of divide and conquer, he might have thwarted any potential majority coalition. These groups or parties would probably have ranged from the "Left-opposition" of the small Cuban Trotskyite movement all the way to the moderate Right of the large sugar and commercial interests (supposing that they had purged their numbers of pro-Batista elements). The leadership of the revolution,

[5] *Trabajo Cuba* (published by the Cuban Ministry of Labor), No. 3 (July 1960), 3.

by playing one group against another, ceaselessly probing the weaknesses of each, might have retained power indefinitely.

Yet this policy seemed to have little relevance to the Cuban scene of 1959-60. Its usefulness is evident if in a crisis the ruling group cannot count on clear majority support; an example that springs to mind is British rule in India. Had the British rulers been foolish enough to imitate Castro's policy, they would have driven the opposition together, in the process probably creating a majority capable of threatening their own rule. Only a ruling group that anticipates majority support can for very long afford to alienate opposition elements so thoroughly that they are compelled to form strong working alliances. The Castro government appeared to be well along this path in the summer and fall of 1960 at the height of the first crisis with the United States.

Finally, the only dialogue between the "revolutionary party" and the "counterrevolutionary party" was literally at gunpoint. The social revolution had been consummated. Relations with the United States had totally deteriorated. And Castro, together with thousands of 26th of July Movement "liberals" and "reformers," had been radicalized and labeled "betrayers." Why did events follow this course?

Early in 1959 Castro was in every sense a popular hero whom many did not hesitate to compare with Martí. Among the island's nearly seven million people, few concealed their esteem, fewer still their respect. Even for the business community the future seemed promising. A leading business and financial organ reported that "American concerns with Cuban interests generally did not expect the change in Cuba's government to hamper their operations."[6] In Cuba itself the United States embassy took an optimistic view of the long-term investment possibilities. Some firms prepaid taxes to help Castro consolidate his new government and others planned to accelerate investment programs temporarily postponed during the fighting.[7] Business leaders in Cuba who "as recently as one month ago were gravely concerned about the revolution"

[6] In a seminar at Princeton University held on April 21, 1959, Castro himself attributed this near-unanimous support to his failure to carry out a specifically *class* war in 1957 and 1958, and to the universal fear and hatred among the Cuban people of Batista's police. Havana *Post*, April 22, 1959, 1.

[7] Textilera Ariguanabo and the Cuban Telephone Company, for example, made advance payments on their profits taxes totaling $640,000. Havana *Post*, January 22, 1959, 1.

apparently had undergone a radical shift in temper.[8] Their
doubts would soon return, however, for a rather elementary
reason.

On the one hand, a wide range of pressing social, economic,
and political problems, some of which had lingered on for
years and others of which were fresh, containing unknown
implications, confronted the triumphant rebels. In a hundred
arenas, the new government struggled to make, implement,
and enforce measures demanded by these problems. On the
other hand, before assuming power, the Castro group had
published or broadcast certain policy statements and decreed
certain laws, enforced in those territories seized and occupied
by the Rebel Army. Castro, the guerrilla leader, however, had
embraced policies of a vague and ambiguous character; ideas
were endorsed that Castro, the national politician, would later
discard. The original (October 10, 1958) decree taking up the
agrarian problem will do as an illustration.[9] Article 2 promised
all farm operators cultivating fewer than 27.2 hectares a plot
of land of at least that size free of charge. This provision was
directly incorporated into the major May 1959 Agrarian Reform Law.[10] Where contiguous land was available this policy
was carried out in practice. Article 6 of the October decree,
which provided expropriated landowners with compensation,
was also contained in the law of May 1959, although, with a
handful of exceptions, it was not complied with. However,
nowhere does the early law touch on the related problems of
foreign properties or the *latifundium,* obviously political questions of a profound character. The vague reference to these
problems in the introduction of the October decree could only
raise more questions than it could answer.[11] This is but one

[8] *Wall Street Journal,* January 2, 1959.
[9] *Ley No. 3 de 10 oct. 1958,* Departamento Legal, Sección Asesoría
de las Delegaciones de Zonas Reforma Agraria (Havana, 1959).
[10] Law of Agrarian Reform, Article 18 in *Gaceta Oficial de la República de Cuba,* Edición extraordinaria especial, June 3, 1959.
[11] *Ley No. 3,* Por Cuanto (No. 13): "It will be the task of the future
government of the Republic to dictate an additional law to fulfill Article
90 (treating the *latifundium*) of the 1940 Constitution." While the
Cuban Constitution of 1940 established a legal basis for limiting the
amount of land that an individual owned, Article 90 is similarly vague,
and consequently any reference to it would be devoid of any real content. Article 90 merely "permitted the fixing by law of the maximum
amount of land to be held by a person or entity," and stated that means
shall be taken to "restrictively limit the acquisition and possession of
land by foreign persons and companies and . . . to revert the land to
Cubans." "Agrarian Revolution in Cuba," *Foreign Agriculture,* Foreign
Agricultural Service, U.S. Department of Agriculture, XXIV (March
1960), 5.

instance of the vagueness that seems to have characterized Castro's early outlook, and not a very conspicuous one at that. One authority has compiled a whole catalogue of other of the revolutionary's "broken promises."[12]

A great many people were therefore understandably uncertain about the concrete steps the new government would take in the areas of economic development and domestic politics. The regime began to show its hand almost at once (by "intervening" the Cuban Electric Company, for instance), but the anti-Batista moderates whom Castro placed in the first cabinet made it a point to reassure the business community. President Urrutia himself proclaimed that Cuba needed and wanted foreign investments.

With the benefit of hindsight it is tempting to conclude that Castro's group deliberately concealed their true designs from the Cuban population and opinion abroad as a tactical move to win all the support they could possibly get. It is not intended definitively to defend or refute this view here. It will be useful, though, to suggest that this hypothesis fails to exhaust the possibilities. Castro, for example, might very well have been confused or uncertain over the concrete problems—the agrarian problem, the question of economic development, and pressing political problems such as widespread government corruption, the fragile Cuban party system, and elections—that for years had been prominent features of the Cuban scene. The rebel leader, after all, surrounded himself with as varied a group of advisers as any national politician in memory: centrist careerist politicians, Keynesian economists, ex-and-would-be-bureaucrats, sincere liberals, professional revolutionaries, and amateur Marxist tacticians—there was very little advice Castro could not get if he wanted it. No less important, his own knowledge of Cuban economic and social life was apparently confined to three or four major areas. About the large class of small tenants and squatters in Oriente Province, the sugar industry, and the condition of the very poor throughout the island, he certainly knew a great deal. He had never been, however, in close touch with the problems of the tobacco farmers and other more or less well-to-do Cuban rural workers (apart from the sugar growers). And on the subjects of urban industry and trade and the city working class, he had much—as it turned out—to learn. In this connection, it is

[12] Draper, *Castro's Revolution*, 15-20.

interesting to point out that in his first essay on the Cuban Revolution, Theodore Draper, who was later to develop the "revolution betrayed" thesis, wrote: "When Fidel Castro entered Havana . . . no one knew what he was going to do. It is doubtful whether he himself knew, except in the most general terms."[13] As a matter of fact, this actively squares with Castro's own self-evaluation, expressed on numerous occasions but never so frankly as in the famous "Marxist-Leninist" speech of December 1, 1961. Two months later he characterized the revolutionary leadership in these terms: "We were like a man with a vocation for music. But a man's vocation for music does not grant him a right to call himself a musician if he has not studied musical theory. When we started our revolutionary struggle, we already had some knowledge of Marxism-Leninism and we were in sympathy with it. But, by virtue of this, we could not call ourselves Marxists-Leninists. . . . We were apprentice revolutionaries."[14]

There is also the possibility that both opinions, the one favorable to Castro, the other, because he is made out to be a deliberate liar, very unflattering, are partially true. In this event the "conspirator" theory loses much of its bite; it is not hard to understand why a politician would hesitate to reveal plans that he knows may be unrealistic and never be put into action.

Whatever the case, the fact is that his early support was extremely heterogeneous, and, for this reason, any policy would be bound to appear as a kind of betrayal to someone. No policy, though, would likely be considered a betrayal by everyone. To put it differently, a few measures, and no really important ones, could possibly be universally popular; at the same time, every measure would heighten the loyalties of some of his followers. It was certain, therefore, that his universal popularity in January 1959 would be transitory. The struggle between the Association of Sugar Cane Planters and the Sugar Workers Federation over the issue of cane cutters' wages is a good example of the many class conflicts that would eventually spoil revolutionary harmony. (On April 15, 1959, the new government decreed a fifteen percent rise in the wage rates of the cane cutters. The cane planters (*colonos*) were ordered to pay the wage increases in full; they were to be

[13] Theodore Draper, "The Runaway Revolution," *The Reporter*, XXII, May 12, 1960, 14-20.
[14] Radio interview, Moscow Domestic Service, January 29, 1962.

reimbursed, however, by the mill owners, to the extent of one third of the extra wage costs.[15] The *colonos* quickly voted among themselves to repeal the decree, arguing that the wage advance would make their farms "nonoperational." Their protest was without effect. It goes without saying that the disputes that raged over the May Agrarian Reform Law and the Urban Reform Law a little later were argued strictly in class terms.) And over the issues of elections and reconstruction of the Cuban political party system, and relations with the United States, it was the professional and middle classes that turned against the Revolutionary government. In the ranks of the poorer rural and urban workers and the marginal peasants there was little or no agitation for the reintroduction of the political forms and institutions dominating the Cuban scene prior to Batista's coup in 1952, nor was there great fear of the island's powerful northern neighbor.

While the economic and social measures divided the island along class lines to produce a kind of "reactive" class conflict, there was no mass agitation for the reorganization of the Cuban economy. The interventions and expropriations of 1959-60 clearly had the *support* of the majority of Cubans (even the relatively conservative sugar growers supported the seizure of the estates); but the poorer, underprivileged classes failed to *initiate* these actions. For this reason, an explanation of Cuban socialism that runs along the lines of pure "class struggle" doctrine is obviously forced and overly abstract.

This admission, however, does not rule out the possibility that Castroism and Cuban socialism were built on economic —not ideological—foundations. First, one cannot characterize the Cuban Revolution as primarily antifeudal; quite the contrary, the Cuban economy exhibited all the main features of well-developed (one is tempted to say, overdeveloped) capitalism. What is more, Cuban capitalism was monopoly capitalism; *for this reason, the Cuban economy failed to grow as rapidly as existing technology, savings, and the supplies of labor and land permitted.* What inhibited the island's economic growth was not the absolute supplies of factors of production, but the way in which they were *organized*. Viewed in this context, it is highly suggestive that the "ideologists" apparently failed to have the political initiative at any time; we know that the

[15] Havana *Post*, April 17, 1959, 1, April 28, 1959, 1. In January the Association had asked the government for an advance to meet wage payments. They had not anticipated that the wage hike of the year before would be retained in 1959; Havana *Post*, January 28, 1959, 4, citing *Diario de la Marina*.

Cuban Communist Party did not make the revolution, and it remains to be proved that Fidel Castro was inevitably to term himself a "Marxist-Leninist." Finally, we know that it was possible more or less peacefully to forge socialism in Cuba, implying that most Cubans were ready (or at least willing) to accept a socialist economy, in marked contrast to the Russian experience.

INDEX

Other Titles
in the
Political Perspectives Series

BLACK PROTEST: HISTORY, DOCUMENTS AND
ANALYSES, 1619 TO THE PRESENT*
    edited by Joanne Grant   P397 $1.25

    "By far the fullest (as well as the least expensive) docu-
mentary history of three and one half centuries of Negro-
American protest and agitation available."
                                 —*The New York Times*

CHINA IN REVOLUTION: HISTORY, DOCUMENTS
AND ANALYSES*
    edited with commentary by Vera Simone
                                   M371 95¢

    China's past and present as revealed in documents and
analyses by John K. Fairbank, Mao Tse-tung, Franz Schur-
mann and others.

PEKING DIARY: 1948-1949, A YEAR OF REVOLUTION
    by Derk Bodde   M348 95¢

    An impartial and fascinating account of the year Peking
fell to the Communists.

VIETNAM: HISTORY, DOCUMENTS AND OPINIONS ON
A MAJOR WORLD CRISIS*
    edited by Marvin E. Gettleman   M912 95¢

    Selections from the writings of statesmen, analysts, poli-
ticians, journalists and a rich collection of basic documents.

FAWCETT CREST & PREMIER BOOKS

If your dealer is sold out, send only cover price plus 10¢ each for postage
and handling to Book Department, Fawcett Publications, Inc., Greenwich,
Connecticut 06830. Please order by number and title. If five or more books
are ordered, there is no postage or handling charge. * No Canadian orders.

A COMPLETE CATALOG OF FAWCETT PAPERBACKS AVAILABLE FREE,
ON REQUEST.